NON-CONTENTIOUS
PROBATE PRACTICE

NON-CONTENTIOUS PROBATE PRACTICE

in the

ENGLISH-SPEAKING CARIBBEAN

Karen Nunez-Tesheira

The Caribbean Law
PUBLISHING COMPANY LTD

Kingston

First published in Jamaica 1998

Revised and reprinted in 2004 by
The Caribbean Law Publishing Company Ltd
11 Cunningham Avenue
Kingston 6, Jamaica W.I.

© Karen Nunez-Tesheira

ISBN 976-8167-42-4 paper

All rights reserved. No part of this publication may be reproduced, stored in a retrieval system or transmitted in any form or by any means electronic, mechanical, photocopying, recording or otherwise without permission from the publisher.

A catalogue of this book is available from the National Library of Jamaica

Nunez-Tesheira, Karen
   Non-contentious probate practice in the English-speaking Caribbean/ Karen Nunez-Tesheira

Rev. ed.

   p.; cm

Includes index

ISBN 976-8167-42-4

1. Probate law and practice - Caribbean, English-speaking
I. Title

346.729052   dc21

Cover design by Shelly-Gail Cooper
Book design by Robert Harris
Set in Adobe Garamond
Printed and bound in the USA

For Russell, Christopher and Nicola

Contents

Preface / *ix*
Preface to the Second Edition / *x*
Table of Succession and Related Statutes / *xii*
Table of Abbreviations / *xx*
Table of Cases / *xxii*
Introduction /*1*
1 Wills /*20*
2 Wills Cont'd /*46*
3 Grants of Representation /*71*
4 Practice and Procedure with respect to Obtaining Grants of Representation /*85*
5 Grants of Probate /*99*
6 Grants of letters of Administration with Will Annexed /*126*
7 Grants of Letters of Administration Preliminary Considerations /*160*
8 Grants of Letters of Administration /*191*
9 Small Estates, Nil Estates, Unrepresented Estates /*226*
10 Stamp and Estate Duty /*254*
11 Administration Bond/ Surety Guarantee /*271*
12 Minority and Life Interest and Second Administrators /*283*
13 Deceased Dying Domiciled outside Jurisdiction /*291*
14 Grants to Trust Corporations, Non-Trust Corporations and the Public Trustee /*310*
15 Commorientes /*324*
16 Limited Grants /*329*
17 Limited Grants cont'd /*360*
18 Leave to Swear Death /*384*
19 Second or Subsequent Grants of Representation /*391*
20 Resealing of Grants /*398*
21 Renunciation and Retraction /*414*
22 Amendment and Notation of Grants /*427*
23 Revocation and Impounding of Grants /*431*
24 Caveats/ Cautions /*437*
25 Citation Proceedings /*450*

26   Family Provision /467
27   Cost and Fees /499
     Appendix 1:   Non-contentious Probate Business Rules
     Appendix 11:   Rules under the Probates
                     (Re-sealing) Law, 1936
     Index

Preface

It has been five years since the publication of the first edition of *Non-Contentious Probate Practice and Procedure in the English-Speaking Caribbean*. Since that date, several radical and fundamental changes have been made to the probate procedural and/or substantive probate laws of three of the territories considered in the text.

In the case of Jamaica, commencing January 1, 2003, new probate rules were passed, replacing rules which date back to the nineteenth century.

The Bahamas has also experienced nothing short of a revolution with regards — to its substantive probate laws — laws which in some instances were over four centuries old. Since 2000, the real and personal estate of an intestate has been assimilated for inheritance purposes, and the child born out of wedlock to an intestate father now has the same rights of inheritance as a child born out of wedlock.

In the case of Trinidad & Tobago, the classes of persons entitled to apply for family provisions have been expanded by the passage of Part VIII of the Succession Act, 1981 as amended by the Distribution of Estates Act 28/2000, to include *inter alia*, a child of the family and a co-habitant. The Administration of Estates Ordinance Ch. 8 No. 1 has also been amended so as to include new categories of beneficiaries, most, notable of which is the co-habitant.

Clearly the last five years has witnessed a number of far-reaching changes made to the succession law, both substantive and procedural, of the above-mentioned countries.

These changes in fact prompted, if not necessitated, the writing of a second edition, but they also provided an opportunity to rewrite the text and expand on areas when it was felt there was a further need for development and more in-depth treatment. In this regard, it is hoped that the second edition will prove to be of assistance, not only to students of the law, but more particularly to probate practictioners in the English-speaking Caribbean.

Preface to First Edition

When I first undertook the task of writing a book on non-contentious probate practice for the Caribbean practitioner, little did I appreciate the enormity of this undertaking.

However my desire to write remained unswayed, fuelled in large part by the unique position in which I felt I had been placed, that of being a Course Director at the Hugh Wooding Law School, St Augustine, and consequently having, to teach the law of succession, on a jurisdictional basis, to students from over ten Caribbean territories.

Indeed I felt that being so privileged I was almost duty-bound to attempt to make some enduring and hopefully meaningful contribution to legal education in the Caribbean.

My task, though daunting, was made immeasurably easier, largely because of the assistance which I received, from probate practitioners and registrars, current and past, throughout the Caribbean. Whether it was during my visits to undertake practical research or one of my countless telephone calls checking and rechecking information and material, everyone with whom I met and spoke was willing, even eager to assist me.

However it would be remiss of me to leave the impression that this undertaking was not without its frustrations and difficulties. I say this not by way of disclaimer or criticism. The inadequacies and in some instances, the lack of indigenous probate rules and practice directions, coupled with local practices, unsupported by any apparent authority, save and except *this is what is done*, often left me little choice but to adopt a less than scientific approach to my research.

Uncertainty as to the scope and extent of reception of English probate practice and, in some instances, probate law, in the various Caribbean territories, an uncertainty due mainly to the legislative vagueness of the so-called reception provisions of these territories, served only to compound these difficulties.

With respect to the contents of the book, readers will note that I have included a chapter entitled 'Family Provision', although the scope of this book is intended to be restricted to non-contentious probate practice. However after much consideration, I felt that Family Provision was such a critical area of practice, that it was worth running the risk of the title of the book being considered a misnomer.

I would also like to stress that this book is not intended to be academic or substantive in approach. However I took the liberty of expanding on the subject of wills in a more substantive manner than is generally applicable to a book on probate practice. Again I felt this was necessary, as to my knowledge, there is no text to date which considers the area of wills in the Caribbean on an inter-jurisdictional basis.

I now wish to turn to the pleasant task of thanking first and foremost my employer, the Council of Legal Education, without whose tangible support, this book would not have been a reality. In particular I wish to acknowledge and thank Austin Davis, the former Principal of the Hugh Wooding Law School, who, on behalf of the council made many facilities available to me, including visiting the various Caribbean territories, making overseas telephone calls and providing me with secretarial services.

I also wish to thank my secretary Cherry Ann Smart, who had the unenviable task of typing my handwritten manuscript.

On a professional level I wish to acknowledge and thank my colleague Wesley Gopaul, who has been, for the past ten years, an associate tutor at the Hugh Wooding Law School in the Law of Succession course and whose depth of knowledge and understanding of succession is truly invaluable. I thank him most sincerely for allowing me, time and time again, to avail myself of his wealth of knowledge and experience.

Last but by no means least, I wish to thank my family, in particular my husband, Russell, whose unwavering support and confidence in me and my 'mission' were a source of great encouragement and inspiration and my parents whose example of hard work and determination contributed, in no small measure, to my seeing this project to its end.

Karen Nunez-Tesheira
March 31, 1998

Table of Succession and Related Statutes

ANGUILLA

1. Administration of Estates by Consular Officers Act Cap. 136
2. Administration of Insolvent Estates Act Cap. 3
3. Adoption of Children Act Cap. 322
4. Consular Conventions Act Cap. 138
5. Courts of Justice Fees Act Cap. 247
6. Death Duties Abolition Ord. 6/1977
7. Eastern Caribbean Supreme Court (Anguilla) Ordinance 9/1982
8. Guardianship of Infants Act Cap. 323
9. Intestates Estates Act Cap. 36
10. Law Reform (Illegitimacy) Ordinance 15/1982
11. Law Reform (Miscellaneous Provisions) Ordinance Cap. 43
12. Probates (Resealing) Act Cap. 62
13. Real Representative Act Cap. 277
14. Registration and Records Act Cap. 69
15. Stamp Act Cap. 257
16. Trust Corporation (Probate and Administration) Act Cap. 80
17. Trusts Ordinance 8/1994
18. Unrepresented Estates Act Cap. 82
19. Wills Act Cap. 84

ANTIGUA & BARBUDA

1. Adoption of Children Act Cap. 9
2. Administration of Estates by Consular Officers Act Cap. 6
3. Administration of Insolvent Estates Act Cap. 7
4. Administration of Small Estates Act, Cap. 8
5. Age of Majority Act Cap. 11
6. Consular Convention Act Cap. 95
7. Courts of Justice Fees Act Cap. 115
8. Eastern Caribbean Supreme Court (Antigua) Act Cap. 143
9. Guardianship of Infants Act Cap. 323
10. Intestate Estates Act Cap. 225
11. Probates (Resealing) Act Cap. 344
12. Public Trustee Act 16/1995

13. Real Representative Act Cap. 291
14. Settled Estates Act Cap. 398
15. Stamp Act Cap. 270
16. Stamp Amendment Act 21/1969
17. Status of Children Act 414
18. Trust Corporation (Probate and Administration) Act Cap. 445
19. Trustee Act Cap. 446
20. Unrepresented Estates Act Cap. 459
21. Wills Act Cap. 473
22. Wills (Soldiers and Sailors Act) Cap. 474

BARBADOS

1. Administration of Estates (Jurisdiction and Procedure Act) Cap. 242
2. Adoption Act Cap. 212
3. Consular Conventions Act Cap. 17
4. Evidence Act 4/1994
6. Family Law Act Cap. 214
7. Mental Health Act Cap. 45
8. Minors Act Cap. 215
9. Probates and Letters of Administration (Resealing) Act, Cap. 247
10. Property Act Cap. 236
11. Public Trustee Act Cap. 248
12. Stamp Duty Act Cap. 91
13. Status of Children Reform Act Cap. 220
14. Succession Act Cap. 249
15. Supreme Court of Judicature Act Cap. 220
16. Trustee Act Cap. 250

DOMINICA

1. Administration of Estates by Consular Officers Act Chap. 9:08
2. Administration of Insolvent Estates Ordinance Act Chap. 9:07
3. Administration of Small Estates Act Chap. 9:06
4. Adoption of Infants Act Chap. 37:03
5. Age of Majority Act Chap. 37:01
6. Consular Conventions Act Chap. 17:51
7. Court of Justice Fees Act Chap. 4:31
8. Eastern Caribbean Supreme Court (Dominica) Act Chap. 4:02
9. Estate Duty (Amendment) Act 18/1985

10. Evidence Ordinance Cap. 64
11. Guardianship of Infants Act Chap. 37:04
12. Interpretation Act Chap. 3:01
13. Intestates' Estates Act Chap. 9:03
14. Legitimation Act Chap. 37:02
15. Mental Health Act Chap. 40:62
16. Probates (Resealing) Act Chap. 9:02
17. Real Estates Charges Act Chap. 54:08
18. Real Representative Act Chap. 9:05
19. Stamp Act Chap. 68:01
20. Trustees Act Chap. 9:50
21. Trustees and Mortgages Act Chap. 9:52
22. Unrepresented Estates Act Ch. 9:04
23. Wills Act Ch. 9:01

GRENADA

1. Adoption Act Cap. 3
2. Consular Convention Act Cap. 63
3. Deceased Americans Consular Representation Act Cap. 77
4. Deeds and Land Registry Act Cap. 79
5. Estate Duty Ordinance (Repeal) Act 21/1984
6. Estate Duty Ordinance Cap. 108 repealed by Estate Duty Ordinance (Repeal) Act 21/1984
7. Evidence (Amendment) Act 9/1995
8. Intestates Estates Act Cap. 154
9. Intestates Estates (Amendment) Act 19/1992
10. Law Reform (Misc. Torts) Act Cap. 167
11. Probate Act Cap. 255
12. Public Trustee Act Cap. 269
13. Real Estate Devolution Act Cap. 274
14. Status of Children Act 39/1991
15. Supreme Court Fees Act Cap. 315
16. The W.I. Supreme Court (Grenada) Act Cap. 336 renamed Eastern Caribbean Supreme Court of Judicature (Grenada) Act by Act 19/1991
17. Trustee Act Cap. 329
18. Wills Act Cap. 340

GUYANA

1. Adoption of Children Act Cap. 46:04
2. Children born out of Wedlock (Removal of Discrimination) Act 12/1983
3. Civil Law of Guyana Act Cap. 6:01
4. Consular Conventions Act Cap. 18:02
5. Deceased Persons Estates' Administration Act Cap. 12:01
6. Estate Duty Act Cap. 81:23 repealed by Taxation Laws (Relief) Act 6/199 1 (with savings)
7. Family and Dependants Provision Act 22/1990
8. High Court Act Cap. 3:02
9. Income Tax Act Cap. 81:01
10. Infancy Act Cap. 46:01
11. Intestates Estates Act 1890 (UK) adapted by Civil Law of Guyana Act Cap 6:01
12. Land Registry Act Cap. 5:02
13. Public Trustee Act Cap. 13:01
14. Representation of the People (Adaptation and Modifications of Laws) Act Ch. 1:09
15. Tax Act Cap. 80:01
16. Taxation Laws (Relief) Act 6/1991
17. Trustee Act 1893 (UK) incorporated 1917 by Civil Law of Guyana Act Cap. 6:01
18. Wills Act 1837 (UK) incorporated by s.7 of the Civil Law of Guyana Act Cap. 6:01
19. Wills Act Cap. 12:02

JAMAICA

1. Administrator General's Act 1973 Revised Laws
2. Children (Adoption of) Act 1973 Revised Laws
3. Children (Guardianship and Custody) Act 1973 Revised Laws
4. Consular Conventions Act 1973 Revised Laws
5. Deceased Persons (Payment of Salaries and Pensions) 1973 Revised Laws
6. Estate Duty Law 1954
7. Estate Duty (Amendment) Law 23/1963
8. Inheritance (Provisions for Family & Dependants) Act 14/1993
9. Intestates Estates and Property Charges Act 1973 Revised Laws

10. Judicature (Resident Magistrates) Act 1973 Revised Laws
11. Judicature (Resident Magistrates (Amendment) Act 32/1995
12. Judicature (Resident Magistrates (Amendment) Act 2000
13. Judicature (Rules of Court) Rules of the Supreme Court (Fees) Act 2002
14. Judicature (Rules of Court) Act 1973 Revised Laws
15. Judicature (Supreme Court) Additional Powers of Registrars Act 1973 Revised Laws
16. Judicature (Trust Corporation) Act 1973 Revised Laws
17. Law Reform (Age of Majority Act) 1/1979
18. Law Reform (Commorientes) Act 1973 Revised Laws
19. Probate of Deeds Act 1973 Revised Laws
20. Probates (Resealing) Act 1973 Revised Laws
21. Status of Children Act 36/1976
22. Transfer Tax Act 1973 Revised Laws
23. Trustee Act 1973 Revised Laws
24. Trustees, Attorneys and Executors (Accounts etc.) Act 1973 Revised Laws
25. Wills Act 1973 Revised Laws

MONTSERRAT

1. Administration of Estates by Consular Officers Act Cap. 127
2. Administration of Insolvent Estates Act Cap. 3
3. Administration of Small Estates Act Cap. 4
4. Administration of Small Estates (Amendment) Act 12/1972
5. Adoption of Childrens Act Cap. 296
6. Adoption of Childrens (Amendment) Act 24/1982
7. Consular Convention Act Cap. 12
8. Courts of Justice Fees Act Cap. 230
9. Guardianship of Infants Act Cap. 297
10. Intestates Estates Act Cap. 36
11. Probates Resealing Act Cap. 63/Probate Resealing (Amendment) Act 1/1968
12. Real Representative Act Cap 255
13. Registration and Records Act Cap. 69
14. Stamp Act Cap. 238
15. Stamp Act (Amendment) Ordinance 13/1966
16. Trust Act 1998
17. Trust Corporation (Probate and Administration) Act Cap. 80

18. Unrepresented Estates Act Cap. 82
20. Wills Act Cap. 84
21. Wills (Soldiers and Sailors) Act Cap. 85

ST CHRISTOPHER & NEVIS

1. Administration of Insolvent Estates Act Cap. 3
2. Administration of Small Estates Act Cap. 4
3. Adoption of Children Act Cap. 322
4. Age of Majority Act 15/1983
5. Consular Conventions Act Cap. 138
6. Intestates Estates Act Cap. 36
7. Probates (Resealing) Act Cap. 62
8. Real Representative Act Cap. 277
10. Registration and Records Act Cap. 69
11. Status of Children Act 19/1983
12. Stamp Act Cap. 257
13. Trust Corporation (Probate and Administration) Act Cap. 80
14. Trustee Act Cap. 355
15. Unrepresented Estates Act Cap. 82
16. W.I. Supreme Court of Judicature (St Kitts & Nevis) Act 17/1975 renamed Eastern Caribbean Supreme Court of Judicature (St Kitts & Nevis) Act by S.I. 881 of 1983
17. Wills Act Cap. 84
18. Wills (Soldiers and Sailors) Act, Cap. 85

ST LUCIA

1. Administration of Estates by Consular Officers Ordinance Cap. 22
2. Administration of Small Successions Ordinance Cap. 20
3. Administration of Small Successions (Amendment) Act 14/1972
4. Administration of Small Successions Act 5/1981
5. Adoption Ordinance Cap. 19
6. Civil Code (Amendment) Act 4/1988
7. Civil Code (Amendment) Act 13/1991
8. Civil Code Ch. 242 Part First, Part Third; Succession — Civil Code Ch. 242 Part Third Book First
9. Code of Civil Procedure Cap. 243, Part Sixth
10. Consular Conventions Ordinance Cap. 23
11. Deceased Persons Salary Ord. Cap. 171

12. Eastern Caribbean Supreme Court (St Lucia) Act 17/1969
13. Stamp Duty Ordinance Cap. 219
14. Succession Duty Ord. Cap. 220
15. Succession Duty Ordinance (Repeal) Act 10/1988
16. Trustees — Civil Code Cap. 242 Part Fourth
17. Trust Corporation (Probate and Administration) Ordinance Cap. 21
18. Wills (Formal Validity of) Ordinance 37/1965

ST VINCENT & THE GRENADINES

1. Administration of Estates Act Cap. 377
2. Administration of Estates by Consular Officers Act Cap. 378
3. Administration of Small Estates Act Cap. 379
4. Adoption of Children Act Cap. 163
5. Age of Majority Act Cap 164
6. Consular Convention Act Cap. 134
7. Eastern Caribbean Supreme Court (St Vincent & the Grenadines) Act Cap. 18
8. Estate Act Cap 307
9. Estate and Succession Duties Act Cap 380
10. Estate Duty and Succession Duties (Amendment) S.R.O. 24/1992
11. Estate and Succession Duties (Amendment) Act 25/1993
12. Evidence Act Cap. 158
13. Law of Minors Act Cap. 169
14. Mental Health Act Cap. 228
15. Powers of Attorney Act Cap. 91
16. Probates (Resealing) Act Cap. 381
17. Public Trustee Act Cap. 382
18. Registration of Births and Deaths Cap 179
19. Registration of Documents Act Cap. 93
20. Registration of Documents (Amendment) Act 11/1991
21. Trustees Act Cap. 383
22. Stamp Act Cap. 318
23. Status of Children Act Cap. 180
24. Wills Act Cap. 384

THE BAHAMAS

1. Administration of Estates Act 2002
2. Adoption of Children Act Ch. 117

3. Equal Status of Children Act Ch. 117
4. Guardianship and Custody of Infants Act Cap. 118
5. Inheritance Act 2002
9. Mental Health Act Ch. 215
7. Mental Health (Amendment) Act 9/1991
8. Minors Act Ch. 6
9. Powers of Attorney Act 12/1992
10. Registration of Records Act Ch. 175
11. Stamp Act Ch. 33
12. Wills Act 2002

TRINIDAD & TOBAGO

1. Administration of Estates Ordinance Ch. 8 No. 1
2. Adoption of Children Act Chap. 46:03
3. Age of Majority Act Chap. 46:06
4. Distribution of Estates Act 28/2000
5. Family Law (Guardianship of Minors Domicile and Maintenance) Act Chap. 46:08
6. Finance (Miscellaneous Provisions) Act 39/2000
7. Interpretation Act Chap. 3:01
8. Mental Health Act Chap. 28:02
9. Public Trustee Ordinance Chap. 8 No. 4
10. Registration of Deeds Act Chap. 19:06
11. Stamp Duty Act Chap. 76:01
12. Status of Children Act Cap. 46:07
13. Succession Act 27/1981 (Part VIII)
14. Supreme Court of Judicature Act Chap. 4:01
15. Trustee Ordinance Ch. 8 No. 3
16. Wills and Probate Ordinance Ch. 8 No. 2

ENGLAND

1. Administration of Estates Act, 1925
2. Law of Property Act, 1925
3. Supreme Court of Judicature Act, 1925
4. Supreme Court of Judicature Act, 1981
5. Wills Act, 1837
6. Wills Act, 1963

Table of Abbreviations

AC.	Appeal Case
Add	Adam's Ecclesiastical Reports
All E.R.	All England Law Reports
All E.R. Rep	All England Law Reports Reprint
Beav.	Beavan's Rolls Court
BRO CC	Brown's Chancery Reports
C.A.	Court of Appeal
C.D., Ch.D.	Law Reports, Chancery Division
Ch.	Chancery
CLY	Current Law Year
CPR	Civil Procedure Rules
Curt.	Curteis's Ecclesiastical Report
Dea. & Sw.	Deane and Swabey's Ecclesiastical Reports
Dick.	Dickenss Reports
ECC & Ad.	Ecclesiastical and Admirality
E.R.	English Reports
Eq. Cas.	Equity Cases
FLR	Family Law Reports
Hare	Hare's Chancery Reports
H.C.A.	High Court Action
HL	House of Lords
JLR	Jamaica Law Reports
K.B.	King's Bench
L.R.B.G.	Law Report of British Guiana
LJ	Law Journal Reports
L.R.P.D.	Law Reports, Probate and Divorce
L.T.	Law Times Reports
M. & W.	Meeson and Welsby Ex
Moo.	Moore's Privy Council Reports
N.C.B.R.	Non-Contentious Business Rules
N.C.P.R.	Non-Contentious Probate Rules
P.	Probate
P.C.	Privy Council Cases
P.C.C.	Prerogative Court of Canterbury
P.D.	Law Reports, Probate Division

P. & D.	Law Reports, Probate and Matrimonial
Phill.	Phillimore's Ecclesiastical Reports
Q.B.D.	Law Reports, Queen's Bench Division
Rob.	Roberisons Ecclesiastical Reports
R.S.C.	Rules of the Supreme Court
Sol. Jo.	Solicitors' Journal
Sw. & Tt.	Swabey and Tristram's Reports
TLR	Times Law Reports
Ves. Sen.	Vesey's Chancery Reports
W.I.R.	West Indian Reports
WLR	Weekly Law Reports

Table of Cases

Page No.

A

Adams (deceased) Re [1990] 2 All E.R. 97..50
Ainsworth, In the Goods of (1870) L.R. 2 P & D 151......................42
Ali *v* Zaman and Neisha (1969) Law Reports of Guyana 612..................44
Alvarez *v* Chandler (1962) 5 W.I.R 226...44
Appiah and Others *v* Hookumchand and Another
(1972) 12 W.I.R. 244...66
Arthur *v* Gomes (1967) 11 W.I.R. 25 453

B

Bankay et al *v* Sukhdeo (1973) 24 W.I.R. 9......................................44
Banks *v* Goodfellow (1870) L.R. 5 Q.B. 549............................34,35,44
Barnes, In the Goods of, Hodson *v* Barnes (1926) 96 LJP 26 136 LT 380..........41
Barry *v* Butlin (1838) 2 Moo. P.C.C 480; 1 Curt 637; 12 E.R. 1089.......44
Battan Singh *v* Amirchand [1948] A.C. 161; [1948] 1 All E.R 152......37
Bean, In the Estate of [1944] P.83; [1944] 2 All E.R. 348....................42
Beaumont (dec'd) Re [1980] 1 All E.R. 266, [1980] Ch 444..............486
Biggs, In the Estate of [1966] P.118 [1966] 1 All E.R. 358.............382,460
Bishop *v* Plumley [1991] 1 All E.R. 236..485
Blewitt, In the Goods of (1880) 5 P.D. 116; (1880) 42 L.T 329............69
Booth, Re, Booth *v* Booth [1926] P. 118, [1926] All E.R. Rep. 594..........49,66
Boughton *v* Knight (1873) L.R P & D 64, [1861-73] All E.R Rep 40.....35
Boyse *v* Rossborough [1857-60] All E.R. Rep. 610, ...39
Bradshaw *v* Bradshaw [1956] P 274..390
Braithwaite *v* Braithwaite (1945) L.R. B.G. 10.................................70
Brasier, In the Goods of [1899] P. 36; 79 L.T. 478...............................69
Brassington, In the Goods of [1902] P.1; 18 T.L.R. 15.........................49
Bravda, In the Estate of Bravda *v* Bravda [1968] 2 All E.R. 217;
 [1968] 1 W.L.R. 479..33
Brownbridge, Re, (1949) LT JO 185..480
Browne, Re, Robinson *v* Sandiford (1963) 5 W.I.R. 505....................44
Brown, In the Goods of [1942] 2 All E.R. 176....................................65
Brunt *v* Brunt (1873) L.R 3 P & D 37; 28 L.T. 368............................49

C

C, Re [1995] FLR 24..479
Cartwright *v* Cartwright (1793) 1 Phill 90; 161 E.R. 923...................44
Casson *v* Dade (1781) 1 Bro. CC. 99; 28 E.R. 1010..........................42
Chalcraft, In the Goods of [1948] P.222; [1948] 1 All E.R. 700..............41
Chamroo *v* Rookmin and Satnarine (1968) 13 W.I.R 470......482,483,493
Chambers, Yatman *v* Queen Proctor (1840) 2 Curt 415....................44
Champion, Re, Dudley *v* Champion [1893] 1 Ch. 101;
    67 L.T. 694 61,69
Cheese *v* Lovejoy (1877) 2 P & D 251; 37 L.T. 295............................66
Cholwill, In the Goods of (1866) L.R. 1 P & D 192; 14 L.T. 338..........382
Clarke, Re [1968] 1 All E.R. 451..496
Cleare *v* Cleare (1869) L.R. 1 P & D 655; 20 L.T. 497........................44
Coleman, Coleman *v* Coleman [1976] Ch. 1, [1975] 1 All E.R. 675........52
Cook's Estate, Re Munson *v* Cook [1960] 1 All E.R. 689;
    [1960] 1 W.L.R. 35..28
Cotton, Re (1965-1970) 2 L.R.B.G. 61..65
Coventry, re [1980] Ch 461, [1979] 3 All E.R. 815............................487

D

Dadds, In the Goods of (1857) Dea. & Sw. 290; 164 E.R. 529..........66
Davis, In the Goods of (1860) 4 Sw. 3Tr213....................................425
Davis, In the Estate of [1952] P.279..70
de Castro Re -C.A. 578/1964 Trinidad and Tobago(Unreported).............17
De Nobriga *v* De Nobriga [1967] 12 W.I.R. 342................................44
Dew *v* Clark (1826) 3 Add. 79; 162 E.R. 410..............................35,44
Dewell, In the Goods of (1953) 1 Ecc. & Ad. 103; 164 E.R. 60................69
Dixon *v* Treasury Solicitor [1905] P.42; 92 L.T. 427..........................67
Dowds, In the Goods of [1948] P 256..390
Drawmer, In the Estate of (1913) 108 L.T. 732..................................382
Dufour *v* Pereira (1769) Dick. 419..40
Dunn *v* Dunn (1866) L.R. 1 P& D 277..69

E

Escot, In the Goods of (1858) 4 Sw. & Tr. 186..................................382

F

Fereira *v* Cabral (1923-24) L.R.B.G. 17..40
Ffinch *v* Coombe [1894] P.191..69
Finn, In the Estate of [1935] 105 L.J.P. 36; 154 L.T. 242
    [1935] All E.R. Rep. 419...41

Franklyn v Biddy (1960) 2 W.I.R 346..493,496
Fredericks Re (1931-37) L.R.B.G. 211..42
Fullard (dec'd), Re [1981] 2 All E.R. 796...483
Freke v Lord Carbery (1873) L.R. 16 Eq. 461....................................308

G

Galbraith, In the Goods of [1951] P.422 [1951] 2 All E.R. 470.............382
Garthwaite v Garthwaite [1964] 2 All E.R. 233..................................10
Gibson, In the Estate of [1949] P. 434 [1949] 2 All E.R. 90.................43
Gilbert, In the Goods of [1893] P. 183...57
Giles v Warren (1872) L.R. 2 P & D 401..49
Goddard v Jack (1959-62) 1 W.I.R. 169...44
Goldie v Adams and Ors. [1938] P. 85...70
Goodchild (dec'd), Re [1996] 1 All E.R. 796....................................487
Greville v Tylee (1851) 7 Moo. PCC 320; 13 E.R.. 904.......................68
Griffith v Coward H.C.A. 478 of 1985 Barbados (Unreported)..........494
Griffith v Coward H.C.A 845/1985 Barbados (Unreported).................494
Guggenheim's, Re (1941) Times, 20 June 328
Gunstan, In the Goods of (1882) 7 P.D. 102; 46 L.T. 641.................42

H

Hagger Re, Freeman v Arscott [1930] 2 Ch. 190; 143 L.T. 610..............40
Hall, In the Goods of (1871) L.R. 2 P & D 256..................................69
Hall v Hall (1868) L.R. 1 P & D 481; 18 L.T. 152..............................45
Hardyman, Re, Teesdale v McClintock [1925] Ch. 287
    [1925] All E.R. Rep. 83 62
Harrinarine v R (1963) 6 W.I.R. 399..44
Haslip Re [1958] 2 All E.R. 275; [1958] 1 W.L.R. 583.......................290
Headlie v Arneaud Reports of Judgments of High Court
    of Justice and of the Court of Appeal of Trinidad and Tobago
    Vol. XIX [1966.69] Part 11 258...44
Heath, In the Goods of [1892] P. 253; 67 L.T. 356..........................69
Heath's Wills Trusts, Re, Hamilton v Lloyds Bank [1949] Ch. 170;
    [1949] 1 All E.R. 199..69
Hewson v Shelley [1914] 2 Ch 13..462
Heyliger v Burgess (1931-37) L.R.B.G. 507......................................44
Heys, In the Estate of [1914] P. 192..40
Hickman v Peacey [1945] AC 304, [1945] 2 All E.R. 215..................328
Hinds v Smith H.C.A 969/1984 Barbados (Unreported).....................494
Hobbs v Knight (1838) 1 Curt. 768...66

Hodgkinson, In the Goods of [1893] P. 339; 69 L.T. 540....................70
Hogton v Hogton (1933) 50 TLR...390
Hornby, In the Goods of [1946] P. 171; [1946] 2 All E.R. 150;
    175 L.T. 161...42

I
Israell v Rodon (1917-23) Vol. 2 Stephens Law Reports 2124
    (Supreme Court decision of Jamaica)..67
Itter, Re, Dodman v Godfrey [1950] P.130; [1950] 1 All E.R. 68............69

J
Jacob, In the Goods of (1842) 1 Notes on Cas. 401................................68
Jelley v Illife [1981] 2 W.L.R. 801...486
Jenner v Ffinch [1879] 5 PD. 106; 42 L.T. 327......................................42
Jennings (dec'd), Re [1994] 3 All E.R. 27...................................488, 497

K
Keigwin v Keigwin (1843) 3 Curt. 607...42
Kimpton, In the Goods of (1864) 3 Sw. & Tr. 427, 10 L.T. 137...............42
Kinneally v Zazula (1975) 26 W.I.R. 29...67
Kitkat v King [1930] P. 266; 143 L.T.408...69
Knight, In the Goods of [1939] 3 All E.R. 928...............................52, 382

L
Langston, In the Estate of [1953] 1 All E.R. 928; 1953 P.100................52
Last, In the Estate of [1958] P. 137, [1958] 1 All E.R. 316...................382
Lemage v Goodban (1865) L.R. 1 P & D 57; 13 L.T. 508.......................66
Lewis, In the Goods of (1858) 1 Sw & Tr...66
Lewis v Baker (1966) 10 W.I.R. 122.................467, 481, 482, 483, 496
Little, Re Foster v Cooper [1960] 1 All E.R. 387....................................42
Long-Sutton, In the Estate of [1912] P.97..390
Lowthorpe-Lutwidge v Lowthorpe-Lutwidge [1935] P. 151,
    [1935] All E.R. Rep. 338..65
Lucky v Tewari (1965) 8 W.I.R. 363...38
Lutchman, Ramcoomarsingh v Administrator General (2002)
    61 W.I.R. 525...44

M

Maharaj Chintaman: In the Estate of HCA 4315/1982
    Trinidad and Tobago (Unreported)..44
Mann, In the Goods of [1942] P. 146; [1942] 2 All E.R. 193............42
Mette *v* Mette (1859) 1 Sw & Tr. 416..51
Mohansingh *v* Simon HCA 5 14/1 982 Trinidad and Tobago
    (Unreported)..42
Mohammed *v* Mohammed (1968) 12 W.I.R. 125....................17,18,189
Moonan *v* Moonan (1963) 7 W.I.R 420..44
Morton, In the Goods of (1887) 12 P.D. 141..66

N

Nicome *v* Pacheco, Reports of Judgments of the High Court of
    Justice and of the Court of Appeal of Trinidad and Tobago
    Vol. (XIX) [1966-69] Part III 263..44

O

Oldham Re [1925] Ch. 75; [1924] All E.R. Rep. 288............................40
Owen *v* Bissoondath, Bernet and Ors. H.C.A 229/1979
    47 Trinidad and Tobago (Unreported)..44

P

P. *v* P. (1977) 30 W.I.R. 8..18
Panacom Int. *v* Sunset Investments (1994) 47 W.I.R. 139............7, 326
Parfitt *v* Lawless (1872) L.R. 2 P & D 462; 27 L.T. 215......................40
Parker *v* Felgate (1883) 8 P & D 171..36, 37
Parsons *v* Lanoe (1748) 1 Ves. Sen. 189..40
Pepin *v* Bruyere [1902] 1 Ch. 24..308
Pereira *v* Pereira (1925-26) L.R.B.G. 134..40
Piggott *v* Royal Bank Trust Co. (T'dad) H.C.A 1375/1983,
    Trinidad and Tobago (Unreported)..480
Pilot *v* Gainfort [1931] P. 103..67
Potticary, In the Estate of [1927] P.202....................................382, 460
Powell *v* Powell (1866) LR P & D 209..67

R

Ramdaram *v* Seusahai and Or. Reports of Judgments of the High
    Court of Justice and of the Court of Appeal of Trinidad and
    Tobago Vol. XIX 1966-69; Part II 284..495
Rapley, In the Estate of [1983] 3 All E.R. 248......................................41

Reade, In the Goods of [1902] P.75 70
Reeves, Re Reeves *v* Pawson [1928] Ch. 351;
    [1928] All E.R. Rep. 342..69
Reynolds, In the Goods of (1873) L.R. 3 P & D 35..........................70
Roberts, Re [1934] P. 102...42
Roby Re[1908] Ch.71..188
Rodriguez *v* Rodriguez [1882-1916] Judgments delivered
    in the Supreme Court of Trinidad and Tobago Vol. 11 299...............66

S
Sallis *v* Jones [1936] P. 43; 154 L.T. 112................................67
Salmon (dec'd) Re [1980] 3 All E.R. 248..................................480
Sargeant Re (1975) 18 W.I.R. 244..66
Sattar *v* Dass (1990) 44 W.I.R. 257......................................66
Schlesinger, In the Goods of [1950] CLY 1549.............................390
Schuler's Estate of Re (1985) 37 W.I.R. 371.................17, 189, 449
Shearn, In the Goods of (1880) 43 L.T. 736, 50 L.P.J. 15..................69
Shires *v* Glascock (1689) 2 Salk. 688; 91 E.R. 584.......................42
Sin Young Chin and Anr. *v* Kelly and Ors. (1968) 12 W.I.R. 429...........44
Sivyer, Re [1967] 1 W.L.R. 1482..487
Skeets Re, Thain *v* Gibbs [1936] Ch. 683................................188
Smith Re, Bilke *v* Roper [1890] 45 Ch. D. 652............................69
Spenceley, In the Goods of [1897] P. 28..................................390
Spratt, In the Goods [1897] P.28..40
Southerden, In the Estate of Adams *v* Southerden [1925] P.177............54
Stalman, Re (1931) 145 L.T. 339; [1931] All E.R. Rep. 193.................42
Steele, In the Goods of [1861-73] All E Rep 209, (1868) 1 P & D 575....69, 70
Stephens *v* Taprell (1840) 163 E.R. 475 (1840) 2 Curt 458................66
Stock v Brown [1994] 1 FLR 840...479
Stone *v* Hoskins [1905] P. 194 3...40
Straker *v* Luke (1974) L.R.B.G. 187......................................44
Sykes, In the Goods of (1873) L.R. 3 P & D 26.............................69

T
Taylor, Taylor *v* Philbert H.C.A 1345/1977 (Trinidad and Tobago)
    (Unreported)...478, 495, 496
Thomas *v* Thomas (1969) 20 W.I.R. 58.................................38, 44
Thompson, Re *v* Hoo Seung (1964) 6 W.I.R. 220............................65
Thompson *v* Roach and Roach (1968) 13 W.I.R 297..........482, 483, 496
Townsend *v* Moore [1905] P. 66.......................................47, 66

Trotter Re [1899] 1 Ch. 704..69
Truro (Lady) In the Goods of [1866]LRI P & D 201...............................69
Tyrell *v* Painton [1894] P. 151..38

W

Walcott *v* Alleyne HCA no. 192/1985
    (unreported) Trinidad and Tobago 462
Walker, In the Estate of (1912) 28 T.L.R. 466...44
Wallace, In the Estate of (1952) 2 T.L.R. 925..37
Walsh *v* Severin (1939) L.R.B.G. 240..44
Wayland's Estate Re [1951] 2 All E.R. 1041...65
Webb Re, Smith *v* Johnson [1964] 2 All E.R. 91....................................66
White Re, Barker *v* Gribble and Anr. [1991] Ch. 1,
    [1990] 3 All E.R. 1, [1990] 3 W.L.R. 187.................................69
Williams *v* Williams Judgments delivered in the Supreme Court of
    Trinidad and Tobago Vol. XIV- 1953-1954 1...............................67
Wingham Re, Andrews *v* Wingham [1948] 2 All E.R. 908;
    [1949] P. 187...24
Wingrove *v* Wingrove (1885) 11 P & D 81..45
Winstone, In the Goods of [1898] P. 143...390
Wintle *v* Nye [1959] 1 All E.R. 552...38

Z

Zuliani et al *v* Veira C.A. 5/1991 St Christopher & Nevis
    (Unreported)...10

Introduction

SCOPE OF WORK

This book proposes to examine the non-contentious probate practice and procedure in the following English-speaking Caribbean territories:

Anguilla	Montserrat
Antigua & Barbuda	St Christopher & Nevis
Barbados	St Lucia
Dominica	St Vincent & the Grenadines
Grenada	The Bahamas
Guyana	Trinidad & Tobago
Jamaica	

Meaning of Non-contentious business

Non-contentious, or common form probate business as it is otherwise called, is concerned with the business of obtaining probate and administration where there is no contention to the right thereto and includes the granting of probate and administration in contentious cases when the contest is terminated and all business of a non-contentious nature to be taken in court in matters of testacy and intestacy not being proceedings in any suit, and also the business of lodging caveats against the grant of probate or administration.[1]

Accordingly, this book will focus on the following areas of non-contentious or common form probate business, including the procedure and practice relevant to:

(a) obtaining a grant of representation, whether general, limited, special or subsequent;
(b) resealing a grant of representation;
(c) amending or revoking a grant;
(d) pursuing citation and caveat proceedings.
(e) family provision applications

RULES OF PRACTICE AND PROCEDURE

In so far as the rules which govern non-contentious probate practice and procedure are concerned, the aforementioned Caribbean territories may be divided into two categories:

(a) those with indigenous probate rules; and
(b) those which have no indigenous probate rules. -

Territories With Indigenous Probate Rules
Barbados, Guyana, Jamaica, St Lucia, The Bahamas and Trinidad & Tobago

Although the above territories have indigenous probate rules, these rules, with the limited exception of Jamaica as of January 1, 2003, are not comprehensive. More particularly, none of these territories, with the exception of Jamaica, has probate rules which provide for the practice and procedure to be adopted with respect to special, limited or second grants of representation.

However by virtue of the relevant reception provision of these territories, which effectively provides for the importation of English probate practice and procedure where no indigenous rules of law or special provision exist[2] the English procedure and practice with respect *inter alia* to special limited and second grants are received and applied in these jurisdictions, and adapted to the existing local probate practice and procedure. The result is a curious and somewhat unsettling blend of indigenous and English probate rules, with no clearly defined parameters with respect to the application and applicability of these English rules to the local probate practices which have developed.

Reception Provisions and Applicable Probate Rules

Barbados

Reception provision — The Supreme Court of Judicature Act Cap. 117A which replaced the Supreme Court Act Cap. 117 contains no reception provision. However s. 3 of the current Supreme Court Act provides that:

> The Supreme Court of Judicature consisting of the High Court and of the Court of Appeal... continue to have and exercise the jurisdiction, powers and authority *heretofore vested* (emphasis mine) in those courts and any other jurisdiction, powers and authority conferred respectively on those Courts by this Act or by any other Act.

Prior to the passage of this Act, the English non-contentious probate rules were deemed, by virtue of s. 15 of the repealed Supreme Court Act Cap. 117,[3] to extend and apply to Barbados, subject to existing indigenous probate rules and practices.

Accordingly, the provisions of s. 3 of the current Act effectively operate as a cut-off date for the reception of the English non-contentious probate practice and procedure, the cut off date being the date of repeal of the former Supreme Court Act, Cap. 117. However it is to be noted that, although s. 15 of the repealed Supreme Court Act contains the ambulatory phrase *for the time being in force* and this Act was not repealed until the 3rd November, 1991, it is the practice in Barbados to apply the Non-contentious Probate Rules 1954, England.

Indigenous Probate Rules	The Supreme Court (non-contentious) Probate Rules 1959 made under s 46 of the repealed Supreme Court of Judicature Act Cap. 117.
English Probate Rules	The Non-Contentious Probate Rules, 1954.

The Bahamas

As a consequence of the repeal of the Supreme Court Act Ch. 41, in particular s.20 thereof, The Bahamas no longer has express reception provision. According to s.20 of the repealed Supreme Court Act, the probate practice and procedure in force in England was deemed to extend to the Bahamas subject to any rules and laws in force in The Bahamas.[4]

Although s.20 was repealed without replacement, s.13 of the current Supreme Court Act 15/1996 which became law on 1st January, 1997, effectively saves the English probate practice and procedure which was deemed to extend to The Bahamas prior to the repeal of the Supreme Court Act Ch. 41. Section 13 of the current Act provides:

> Subject to the provisions of Part V, the Court shall have all such jurisdiction in relation to probates and letters of administration as it formerly had and in particular all such contentious and non-contentious jurisdiction in relation to-

(a) testamentary causes or matters;
(b) the grant, amendment or revocation of probate and letters of administration; and
(c) the real and personal estate of deceased persons.

Accordingly the English probate practice which extended to The Bahamas prior to the passage of the current Supreme Court Act still continues to be applicable to The Bahamas.[5]

Indigenous Probate Rules	The Probate Rules made under s.41 of the Supreme Court Act Ch. 35, 1965 Revised Laws of The Bahamas.
English Probate Rules	The Non-Contentious Probate Rules, 1987.

Guyana

Reception provision — s.17 of the High Court Act Cap. 3:02 provides:

The practice and procedure of the Court shall, subject to any other written law, he regulated by this Act and by rules of court, and in the absence of any provision shall correspond to the practice and procedure of the Supreme Court of British Guiana (including the Court when exercising its admiralty jurisdiction) immediately before 26th May, 1966.

Indigenous Probate Rules	Deceased Persons Estates' Administration Rules made under s.32 of the Deceased Persons Estates Administration Act Cap. 12:01.
English Probate Rules	The Non-Contentious Probate Rules, 1954.

Jamaica

Reception provision - s.686 of the Judicature (Civil Procedure Code) Law Cap. 177 provides:

Where no other provision is expressly made by law or by rules of Court the procedure and practice for the time being of the Supreme Court of Judicature in England, shall so far as applicable, be followed and the forms prescribed shall with such variations as circumstances may require, be used.

Indigenous Probate Rules	Rule 68 Supreme Court of Jamaica Civil Procedure Rules 2002 (CPR 2002) made under s.4 of the Judicature (Rules of Court) Act, repealing and replacing the General Rules and Orders of the Supreme Court. Part III Probate and Administration made under the Judicature Law 1879.
English Probate Rules	The Non-Contentious Probate Rules, 1987.

St Lucia

Reception provision[6] — 5.11(1) of The Supreme Court of Judicature (St Lucia) Act 1969 renamed Eastern Caribbean Supreme Court of Judicature (St Lucia) Act provides:

> The jurisdiction vested in the High Court in civil proceedings including matrimonial causes and probate causes shall be exercised in accordance with the provisions of this Act, the Civil Code, the Code of Civil Procedure, any other law in force in the State and rules of court, and, where no special provision is therein contained, such jurisdiction shall be exercised as nearly as may be administered for the time being in the High Court of Justice in England.

Indigenous Probate Rules	Arts 1012-1030 Code of Civil Procedure Ch. 243; Arts 794-796 Civil Code Ch. 242.
English Probate Rules	The Non-Contentious Probate Rules, 1987.

Trinidad & Tobago

Reception provision — s.4 of the Wills and Probate Ordinance Ch. 8 No.2 to be read in conjunction with s.21 of the Interpretation Act Ch. 3:01.

Section 4 of the Wills & Probate Ordinance provides:

> In so far as any Ordinance and rules and orders of court do not extend, the Court shall be guided in the exercise of its jurisdiction under this Ordinance by the jurisprudence and practice for the time being of the Probate Division of the High Court of Justice in England so far as the same may be applicable.[7]

Section 21 of the Interpretation Act provides *inter alia*:

> Where any written law passed before 31st August, 1962 applies the law of England or of the United Kingdom to Trinidad & Tobago and such application is qualified by words of an ambulatory nature including the words 'for the time being in force' the same shall be construed as applying the law in force in England on 30th August, 1962.

Indigenous Probate Rules	The Non-Contentious Business Rules First Schedule made pursuant to s.24 of the Wills & Probate Ordinance Ch. 8 No. 2. (See also the Second, Third and Fourth Schedules thereto).
English Probate Rules	The Non-Contentious Probate Rules 1954.

Territories with no Indigenous Rules

Eastern Caribbean territories (save St Lucia)

The non-contentious probate procedural law of the above territories is encapsulated in s.11 of the respective Eastern Caribbean Supreme Court of Judicature Acts/Ordinance of the above territories.[8] Section 11 contains a reception clause embracing both the law and procedure of the High Court of England, *inter alia*, in matters of probate where no special provision or rule of law is contained in the laws of these territories.

Section 11 provides *inter alia*:

> The jurisdiction vested in the High Court in civil proceedings and in probate shall be exercised in accordance with the provisions of the relevant Supreme Court Act and any other law in operation and rules of court in the respective territory and where no special provision is therein contained such jurisdiction shall be exercised as nearly as may be in conformity with the law and practice...in the High Court of Justice in England.

With the exception of Dominica and St Vincent & the Grenadines the respective s. 11 provision of the Eastern Caribbean Supreme Court Acts contains the ambulatory phrase *for the time being in force,* which in effect allows for the reception of English probate law and practice up to the present date.[9]

As a consequence, the N.C.P.R 1987, England and any subsequent amendments thereto are received in these territories.

Cut off Dates for reception

St Vincent & the Grenadines[10]

Although s.11 of the Supreme Court Act of St Vincent & the Grenadines contains a cut off date for reception, the cut off date is 27th December, 1989. As a consequence the N.C.P.R 1987, England are received in St Vincent & the Grenadines.

Dominica[11]

Pursuant to s.11 of the Supreme Court Act of Dominica, the 1st June, 1984 is the cut-off date for reception of English probate law and practice. Accordingly the N.C.P.R, 1954, England are received in Dominica, together with any amendments made thereto up to the cut off date of reception.

Reception of English Probate Law

Eastern Caribbean territories (save St Lucia)

According to the provisions of s.11 of the respective Supreme Court Acts of the Eastern Caribbean territories (save St Lucia), the jurisdiction vested in the respective High Courts of these territories with respect to probate causes shall be exercised as nearly as may be in conformity with the law and practice administered for the time being in the High Court of Justice of England, where no special provisions are contained in any local Acts and rules of court. This is of course subject to the cut-off dates for reception in the case of Dominica and St Vincent & The Grenadines.

There is, however, a divergence of opinion regarding whether this provision allows for the reception of English procedural probate law *and* English substantive probate law.

In this regard Sir Vincent Floissac, then Chief Justice of the Eastern Caribbean Supreme Court observed in *Panacom Int. v. Sunset Investments*:

> Section 11 of the Supreme Court Act relates solely to the manner of the exercise of the jurisdiction of the High Court. It is therefore an intrinsically procedural provision. The words 'provision', 'law' and 'law and practice' appearing in section 11 are evidently intended to be references to procedural (as distinct from substantive) law.[12]

Although the former Chief Justice was commenting on s.11 of the Eastern Caribbean Supreme Court Act of St Vincent & the Grenadines, his comments are equally relevant to the other Eastern Caribbean territories (save St Lucia), since these territories not only comprise one jurisdictional unit (including St Lucia) but also, with the exception of St Lucia, all have the identical reception provision.

Chief Justice Floissac continued:

> The English law intended to be imported by s.11 is the procedural law administered in the High Court of Justice in England. In enacting section 11, the legislature of St Vincent & the Grenadines could not have intended to import English substantive law nor English procedural law which is adjectival and purely ancillary to English substantive law.[13]

The former Chief Justice may have arrived at the conclusion that the English substantive probate law is not received in St Vincent & the Grenadines because of the enactment in this territory of the Administration of Estates Act Cap. 377, which Act came into operation on the 27th December,

1989. Part II of this Act in effect reproduces most of the English substantive probate law which is contained in Part IV of the Supreme Court Act 1981, England. The extent of this reproduction is highlighted by the inclusion in this Act of the equivalent of the English provisions with respect to sureties guarantees[14] and settled land grants.[15] These inclusions may have been as a result of a legislative oversight as in St Vincent & the Grenadines:

(a) administration bonds, not surety guarantees are still applicable according to the current laws of St Vincent & the Grenadines;[16] and
(b) settled land grants which were brought into existence in England as a result of the passage of the Law of Property Act 1925 and the Settled Land Act 1925 are not applicable to St Vincent & the Grenadines as the equivalent of these two English Property Acts have not been enacted to date in St Vincent & the Grenadines.

However it must be emphasised that before the enactment of the Administration of Estates Act, Cap. 377 the position in St Vincent insofar as non-contentious probate practice was concerned was the same as that which currently obtains. The essential difference between St Vincent & the Grenadines and the other Eastern Caribbean territories is that in St Vincent most of the English substantive probate law which was formerly received by virtue of s.11 of the Supreme Court (St Vincent) Act now forms part of the substantive probate law of this territory. Accordingly the extent of reception of English probate substantive law has been virtually eliminated.

An excellent example of the reception of English probate law in these territories is provided by the requirement in all the Eastern Caribbean territories, save St Lucia, that the oath to lead to a grant of letter of administration must include a recital with respect to minority and life interest.[17]

Furthermore, wherever a minority or life interest arises under a will or intestacy the grant of letters of administration is required to be made and is made to not less than two individuals, unless the proposed grantee is a trust corporation or otherwise where the Registrar so directs.[18]

With the exception of St Vincent & the Grenadines these procedural requirements are as a consequence of s.114(2) and (3) of the Supreme Court Act 1981, England[19] and in St Vincent & the Grenadines, as a consequence of s.14 of the Administration of Estates Act Cap. 377 which was enacted on the 27th December, 1989. However prior to the enactment of the Administration of Estate Act, the practice in St Vincent was to appoint a second administrator in such instances and to include a recital with respect to minority and life interest in the oath of the applicant.[20]

By way of comparison, in St Lucia, Jamaica, Trinidad & Tobago, Guyana and Barbados the oath to lead a grant of letters of administration does not include a recital with respect to minority or life interest nor is there any requirement for a second administrator to be nominated in such instances. It is submitted that this is so because the relevant reception provision of these territories provides for the reception of English procedural probate law, not English substantive probate law.[21] However, it is to be noted that with respect to Jamaica, with effect from January 1, 2003, although neither the substantive law nor the new probate rules so require, the forms prescribed in respect of the representative oaths to lead the various grants of representation, include a recital with respect to minority and/or life interests.

The Bahamas

As stated previously s.13 of the Supreme Court Act 15/1996 which became law on 1st January, 1997 effectively provides, subject to the provisions of Part V thereof,[22] for the saving of the English probate law practice and procedure which was deemed to extend to The Bahamas, prior to the passage of the current Supreme Court Act. Accordingly the English probate law which was received and applied by virtue of s.20 of the repealed Supreme Court Act Ch. 41 is still applicable to The Bahamas in so far as Part V of the current Act which is intituled Probate Causes and Matters does not so provide.[23]

It is to be noted that much of the substantive English probate law which was formerly received in The Bahamas has essentialy been incorporated, into the indigenous probate law of this territory, by the passage of the current Supreme Court Act, in particular Part V thereof, and in addition by the Administration of Estates Act 2002 and the Wills Act 2002.

St Lucia

It will be noted that s.11(1) of the Supreme Court of Judicature (St Lucia) Act 17/1969 is worded differently from that of the other Eastern Caribbean territories.

In this regard, s.11(1) provides:

> The jurisdiction vested in the High Court in civil proceedings including matrimonial causes and probate causes shall be exercised in accordance with the provisions of this Act, the Civil Code, the Code of Civil Procedure, any other law in force in the State and rules of court, and, *where no special provision is therein contained such jurisdiction shall be exercised as nearly as may be administered for the time being in the High Court of Justice in England.*

The words highlighted do not appear in the repealed Supreme Court Ord. Ch. 1 of the Revised Ord. of St Lucia Ch. 1.

Further Art 5 of the Civil Code Ch. 242 states that the law of the colony applies to the jurisdiction and procedure of the court. According to Diplock L. J. in *Garthwaite v. Garthwaite*,[24] the expression jurisdiction is capable of being used in a wide sense and a strict sense. He noted that:

> In its wider sense it embraces also the settled practice of the court as to the way in which it will exercise its power to hear and determine issues which fall within its "jurisdiction" (in the strict sense), or as to the circumstances in which it will grant a particular kind of relief which it has "jurisdiction" (in the strict sense) to grant, including its settled practice to refuse to exercise such powers or to grant such relief in particular circumstances.

Based partly on this 'wider sense' interpretation of the expression 'jurisdiction' and the notable absence of any reference to English probate law in this provision, the expression 'jurisdiction' as used in s.11(1) of the Supreme Court Act of St Lucia has been interpreted to extend to St Lucia the rules of probate practice and procedure *but not probate law* of the High Court of Justice in England where there exists no indigenous provision or rule of law with respect therto.[25]

General Observations

All Jurisdictions

The difficulties and challenges inherent in applying English probate law,[26] practice and procedure in the various Caribbean territories were summed up succinctly by Byron JA, of the Court of Appeal, St Christopher & Nevis, in his written judgment dated March 23, 1992, in the case of *Zuliani et. al. v. Veira.*[27]

Although he was addressing the issue of reception of English law and practice in so far as it related to solicitors' costs, his observations are equally pertinent to the general problems inherent in the reception in the Caribbean territories of English probate law and practice. Byron JA observed:

This highlights a serious drawback to the practice of importing wholesale the law and practice of another country *on any given subject* (emphasis supplied). England has institutions and laws which support the law and practice relating to solicitors which do not exist in St Christopher.[28]

He did, however, concede that:

> The court cannot blind itself to the real and practical situation that exists locally and must apply the law with common sense.

The difficulties of adopting the 'common sense approach' suggested by Byron JA are further seriously complicated by the failure or neglect of:

(a) the Eastern Caribbean territories (St Lucia excepted) to make any indigenous probate rules;
(b) the territories which have probate rules, with the exception of Jamaica, to update the existing rules and fill the many gaps which exist particularly with respect to the practice and procedure to be adopted with respect to special, limited and second grants of representation; This is in spite of the fact that the machinery exists in all the territories to make rules of Court[29]
(c) all the territories, with the limited exception of Jamaica, to issue practice directions with respect to probate matters, a practice which would be of immense assistance in determining the parameters with respect to reception of English probate practice and procedure in these territories particularly given the vagueness of the so-called reception provisions of these territories.

Powers of the Registrar

(1) Eastern Caribbean territories including St. Lucia

Position prior to passage of CPR 2000

Order 47 r.5, of the Eastern Caribbean Rules of the Supreme Court 1970 which came into operation on 17th April, 1971 and which provision was applicable to the Eastern Caribbean territories including St. Lucia, provided that:

(a) Grants of probate in common form or of letters of administration may be made by a registrar in the name and under the seal of the Court.
(b) No grant shall be made by a registrar in any case in which there is contention until the contention is disposed of, or in any case in which it appears to him that a grant ought not to be made without the direction of the Court.
(c) The registrar shall not allow probate or letters of administration to issue until all the inquiries which he may see fit to institute have been answered to his satisfaction. The registrar shall, notwithstanding, afford as great facility for obtaining grants of probate or administration as is consistent with due regard to the prevention of error or fraud.

Although R.S.C. O.47 r.5 applied to all these territories, the powers conferred under this rule were not applied in a consistent manner. By way of illustration, the registrar in Grenada, Antigua & Barbuda and Dominica, granted preliminary orders with respect to the issue of grants. However in St Lucia,[30] Anguilla, St Christopher & Nevis and St Vincent & the Grenadines, these applications were made to and granted by a judge in chambers. With respect to Montserrat, certain preliminary applications such as an application for an order for the assignment of a guardian were made to the registrar while applications to admit to proof a copy or draft of a will, were in all instances made to a judge in chambers.

As illustrated above, the powers of the registrar were not exercised in a uniform manner. In practice the determining factor regarding the exercise of these powers was to a large extent dependent upon the discretion of the individual Registrar.

Position on or after the passage of CPR 2000

The position with respect to the powers of the registrar in so far as non-contentious probate applications are concerned, remains unsettled primarily because of the non-inclusion in the CPR 2000, of a specific rule, addressing the powers of the registrar.[31]

However, it should be noted that in Anguilla s.7 of the Death Duties (Abolition) Ordinance no. 6 of 1977 also contains a similar provision as was provided for by the repealed R.S.C.O 47 r.5 with respect to the duties and powers of the Registrar in so far as grants of probate and letters of administration (with or without will annexed) are concerned and this provision has not been repealed or amended.

(2) Barbados and Trinidad & Tobago

In Barbados and Trinidad & Tobago the Registrars are empowered to:

(a) make and issue grants of representation;
(b) grant preliminary orders with respect thereto; and
(c) make orders with respect to all non-contentious probate applications including orders made pursuant to citation and caveat proceedings.

These powers are conferred on the Registrars in Barbados and Trinidad & Tobago by virtue of:

(a) the relevant statutory provisions of the Supreme Court of Judicature Acts;[32]
(b) the respective R.S.C. O.32 of the Order and Rules of the Supreme Court;[33] and
(c) the relevant non-contentious business/probate rules of these territories.

(3) The Bahamas and Guyana

The powers and duties of the Registrar in The Bahamas and Guyana are regulated by the relevant statutory provision contained in the Supreme/High Court Acts, the rules of the Supreme/High Court and the probate rules of these territories.

3(a) The Bahamas

Section 65(2) of the Supreme Court Act 15/1996 which came into operation on 1st January, 1997, provides that:

> The Registrar shall have the same jurisdiction, powers and duties as are by this Act or rules of court, conferred or imposed upon the Registrar.

According to the R.S.C. O.32 r.11, 1978 made under s.29 of the repealed Supreme Court Act Ch. 41, the Registrar shall have all powers and exercise all such authority and jurisdiction as may be exercised by a judge in chambers except *inter alia* in trials or other proceedings which are required to be heard solely by a judge. However with respect to applications for grants of representation and other non-contentious probate applications, these are required to be made to and granted by the Chief Justice pursuant to the provisions of The Probate Rules, Ch. 35, which have been in operation since 1917. According to these rules, applications for grants are required to be heard by a judge. Accordingly s.65(2) does not effect any change with respect to the powers and jurisdiction of the Registrar in so far as non-contentious probate matters are concerned as this section is subject to the existing rules of court. The current probate rules still require that applications for grants be heard by a judge.

3(b) Guyana

Although a grant of representation is issued by and under the hand of the Registrar in Guyana, the order for the grant to be issued is not made by the Registrar but by the Chief Justice or a judge in accordance with s.24(1) of the Deceased Persons Estates' Administration Act Cap. 12:01.[34]

Indeed, according to R.S.C. O.56, Guyana and ss.67 and 68 of the High Court Act Ch. 3:02 respectively, the Registrar is regulated to the role of chief executive of the court, a Marshall of the Court and an Administrator of Oaths.

It should, however, be noted that, by virtue of s.19 Deceased Persons Estates' Administration Act Cap. 12:01, small estate grants (estates the value of which is not in excess of $1,000) may be made by the Registrar without reference to the court.

(4) Jamaica

Section 2 of the Judicature (Supreme Court) Additional Powers of Registrar Act, provides that applications for grants of probate or of letters of administration or for the resealing thereof may be granted by the registrar where such applications are not opposed.

In spite of the provisions of the Judicature (Supreme Court) Additional Powers of the Registrar Act, preliminary applications with respect to the issue of grants and other non-contentious probate applications were made in practice to a judge in chambers or in open court. However, the position as of January 1, 2003, has now been clarified with respect to the powers of the registrar by the passage of the CPR 2002, in particular 68.48 thereof.

According to Rule 68.48 of the CPR 2002 all applications for probate and administration must be made in the first instance to the registrar in accordance with the form prescribed in Form P21, Appendix 2 Probate Forms. Further, Rule 68.48(3) and (4) respectively provide that the registrar may make an order where the application is unopposed and where opposed, the registrar may give directions and adjourn the application to a judge. It is therefore expected that preliminary applications will be made in the first instance to the registrar in accordance with Rule 68.48, CPR 2000.

Impact of New Civil Procedure Rules - Jamaica and the Eastern Caribbean Territories

Jamaica

(a) Role of the Administrator General

The passage of the new Civil Procedure Rules 2002, which came into effect January 1, 2003, is certainly welcomed, replacing as it does, archaic probate rules which date back to the nineteenth century. However, although these rules, in particular Rule 68 thereof, have to a large extent, simplified and clarified non-contentious probate rules by, *inter alia*, reducing the number of documents required for a grant, and establishing for the first time, an order of priority for grants in respect of the various classes of beneficiaries, the pivotal role of the Administrator General, in respect of probate applications, has essentially remained unchanged.

More specifically, the Administrator General is still entitled to apply for letters of administration with will annexed, in all instances, and for letters of administration in cases where there is a minor or where the value of the deceased's estate is under $1,000. And although the

Administrator General in practice gives his consent, pursuant to the specific provisions of Rule 68.19 CPR 2002, the consent must be obtained, as evidenced by the issuance of the Administrator General's Certificate, previously called the Formal Consent With the Will annexed of the Administrator General.

It is therefore submitted that the central role of the Administrator General has remained basically unchanged, in spite of the new Civil Procedure Rules primarily because of two pieces of legislation; the Administrator General's Act and the Intestates Estates and Property Charges Act. Accordingly, it is submitted that the backlog of probate applications will be reduced to a limited degree in spite of the new CPR rules.

b) Applications to Resident Magistrates

As discussed in chapter 9, with respect to applications for grants of probate and administration (with or without will annexed) made in the Resident Magistrates Court, pursuant to the Juridicature (Resident Magistrates) Act, such applications, in particular the forms used in respect thereof, are still those which were used in respect thereof, are still those which were used in respect of non-contentious probate applications made in the Supreme Court prior to the passage of Rule 68 of the CPR 2002. This anomaly has arisen primarily as a result of the failure to amend and/or repeal the relevant provisions of the Juridicature (Resident Magistrates) Act so as to bring the procedure, practice and forms used in the Resident Magistrates Court in conformity with the current probate procedure and forms used in Supreme Court of Jamaica.

Accordingly, the documents which were previously filed in respect of applications for grants including the inventory, declaration of counting of inventory, administration bond and will bond are still applicable to probate and administrations applications made in the Residents Magistrate Court.

Eastern Caribbean Territories

Mode of Application

The passage on December 31, 2000 of the Eastern Caribbean Supreme Court Civil Procedure Rules 2000 (CPR 2000), which rules repealed and replaced the Eastern Caribbean Rules of the Supreme Court (Revision) 1970, contains no provision with respect to non-contentious probate proceedings. Indeed Part 2.2 (3)(c) intituled Application of the Rules, specifically provides that the CPR 2000 does not apply to non-contentious probate proceedings.

As stated above, in the absence of indigenous probate rules s.11 of the Supreme Court Acts of the respective Eastern Caribbean territories provides in effect for the reception of the NCPR England 1954/1987 as the case may be, where no special provision is contained in the respective laws of the territories.

What this effectively means is that because of the non-inclusion of probate rules in the new CPR 2000, and the express provisions of Part 2.2 (3) (c), the practice and procedure in England in respect of the non-contentious probate proceedings should continue to apply. However, this would clearly create an incongruity with regard to preliminary applications to be made to a judge in chambers as the procedure and practice in relation to applications to the Court provides that such applications, whether made to the registrar or judge, should be made in accordance with the Part 11 procedure relevant to such applications and take the form as prescribed in respect thereto.

St. Lucia

St. Lucia is in an anomalous position, primarily because the Civil Code Ch 242, and the Code of Civil Procedure Ch 243, which form part of the substantive indigenous law of this territory, provides for non-contentious probate applications to be made by petition. Accordingly, in keeping with the indigenous laws of St. Lucia, non-contentious probate applications are, it is submitted, still required to be made by petition.

Notes

1 Grenada   - s.2 Probate Act Cap. 255
   Jamaica   - Rule 68.1, CPR 2002 repealing and replacing Rules
                         and Orders Part III Probate & Administration
   St Lucia   Art 585 Civil Code Ch. 242
   Trinidad & Tobago   - s.2 Wills & Probate Ordinance Ch. 8 No. 2.
2 It should be noted that the so called reception provision of the various territories speaks specifically of the jurisdiction of the High Court and more particularly, that the court should exercise its jurisdiction with respect to probate matters in the same manner as such jurisdiction is exercised by the High Court of England in so far as the same is applicable.
3 Section 15 of the repealed Supreme Court Act Cap. 117 provides that:
   Notwithstanding the provision of any other law, the jurisdiction vested in the High Court and Court of Appeal respectively shall, so far as regards procedure and practice, be exercised in the manner provided by this Act or by rules of court. With

reference thereto every such jurisdiction shall be exercised as nearly as maybe in accordance with the practice and procedure for the time being in force in the Supreme Court of Judicature in England.
See also s.2 of the Administration of Estates (Jurisdiction and Procedure) Act Cap. 242 which provides in effect for the High Court of Barbados to have the same powers as the Probate Division of the High Court in England.

4   Section 20 of the repealed Supreme Court Act ch. 41 provided that:
The Chief Justice and every Justice shall be a Judge Ordinary of the Probate Side and on the Divorce and Matrimonial Side of the Court; and, subject to any rules to be made under this Act and to the laws in force in The Bahamas, the jurisdiction of the Court of Probate, Divorce and Matrimonial causes and proceedings may be exercised in conformity with the law and practice, so far, as they are applicable, for the time being in force in England which shall be deemed to be hereby extended to The Bahamas.

5   See p.2 where the position in Barbados with respect to reception is similar.

6   See also Art 1017(2) Code of Civil Procedure Ch. 243 which provides that: "for the purpose of giving effect to subsection 4 of Art 586 of the Civil Code, the practice and procedure relating to limited grants in force in the principal registry of the Probate, Divorce and Admiralty Division of the High Court of Justice of England shall so far as the same is not inconsistent with the law of the colony and is applicable in local circumstances apply and have effect in the colony". Article 584(4) Civil Code Ch. 242 empowers the Court or a Judge *inter alia* to make limited grants.

7   See *Re Schuler's Estate* (1985) 37 W.I.R 371 at p.395 where Warner J observed that "section 4 requires the court to be guided in the exercise of its jurisdiction under that Ordinance by the jurisprudence and practice for the time being of the Probate Division of the High Court in England so far as the same may be applicable, and in so far as any Ordinance and rules and orders of the court do not extend." According to the learned judge "This will involve following the English practice on matters which our own laws including rules do not extend".
See also *Re de Castro Full Court of Trinidad & Tobago*, Appeal No. 578 of 1964 (unreported) and quoted with approval by Kelsick J. in *Mohammed v. Mohammed* (1968) 12 W.I.R. 125 at p.129 where the court observed that the expression in s.4 for the time being "includes the relevant rules that are in force in England from time to time and would therefore include the English Probate Non-Contentious Rules of 1954".

8

Anguilla	- Eastern Caribbean Supreme Court Anguilla Ordinance 1982
Antigua & Barbuda	- Eastern Caribbean Supreme Court (Antigua) Act Cap. 143
Dominica	- Eastern Caribbean Supreme Court (Dominica) Act Ch. 4:02
Grenada	- West Indies Supreme Court (Grenada) Act 17 of 1967 renamed Eastern Caribbean Supreme Court (Grenada) Act by Act 19 of 1991; See also ss. 3, 14 Probate Act Cap. 255
Montserrat	- Eastern Caribbean Supreme Court (Montserrat) Act (cited under S.I 1983 1108) as the Anguilla, Montserrat and the Virgin Islands (Supreme Court)

	Order 1983
St Christopher & Nevis	- West Indies Supreme Court (St Christopher & Nevis) Act 17/1975 renamed Eastern Caribbean Supreme Court (St Christopher & Nevis) Act
St Vincent & the Grenadines	- Eastern Caribbean Supreme Court (St Vincent & the Grenadines) Act Cap. 18. See also Application of English Law Cap. 8 in particular s.5 thereof

9   See *Mohammed v. Mohammed* (1968) 12 W.I.R. 125 at 127-128 where Kelsick J. noted with approval that the expression 'for the time being', had been defined in Stroud's Judicial Dictionary to mean the time present, according to the context or denote a single period of time, but its general sense is that of time indefinite and refers to an indefinite state of facts which will arise in the future, and which may (and probably will) vary from time to time.
10 Section 11 Eastern Caribbean Supreme Court (St Vincent & the Grenadines) Act Cap. 18.
11 Section 11 Eastern Caribbean Supreme Court (Dominica) Act Ch. 4:02.
12 (1994) 47 W.I.R 139 at p. 149.
13 *Ibid.*
14 See s.20 of the Administration of Estates Act Cap. 377.
15 See ss. 36-38 of the Administration of Estates Act Cap. 377.
16 See chapter 11 pp. 277-78.
17 See chapter 12 p. 283.
18 *Ibid.*
19 See *Tristram and Coote's Probate Practice* 27th ed. at London: Butterworths, 19 p.26l.
20 See chapter 12 pp. 209-210 seq.
21 See pp. 2-6. See also *P. v. P.* (1977) 30 W.I.R. 8, where it was held that the Law Reform (Miscellaneous Provisions) Act 1949 England, does not apply to Barbados and that s.15 of the repealed Supreme Court of Judicature Act Barbados, the provisions of which are similar in effect and intent to the current reception provisions of St Lucia, Jamaica, Trinidad & Tobago and Guyana, was inappropriate in the absence of special provisions, to incorporate a substantive amendment to the law of Barbados.
22 Part V of the Act contains substantive provision with respect to probate causes and matters, provisions which were previously received in The Bahamas by virtue of s.20 of the repealed Supreme Court Act Ch. 41.
23 Section 20 of the repealed Supreme Court Act Ch. 41 operated effectively as a provision for the reception of English probate law as it provided *inter alia* that subject to any laws and rules in force in The Bahamas, the probate law for the time being in force in England shall be deemed in so far as applicable to extend to The Bahamas.
24 [1964] 2 All E.R. 233 at 241.
25 See on this 'The Evolution of Land Law in St Lucia' by Winston F. Cenac pp. 49-51.
26 In the case of The Bahamas and the Eastern Caribbean territories (save St Lucia).
27 Civil Appeal 5 of 1991 [Unreported].
28 *Ibid.*
29

Barbados	- ss.81-84 Supreme Court of Judicature Act Cap. 117A
Eastern Caribbean	- s.17 of West Indies Associated States Supreme Court Order territories 1967 renamed Eastern Caribbean Supreme Court Order

Grenada	- See also s.14 Probate Act Cap. 232
Guyana	- ss. 67, 68 High Court Act Cap. 3:02
	- s.60 Deceased Persons Estates Administration Act Cap. 12:01
Jamaica	- The Judicature (Rules of Court) Act
St Lucia	- See also Art 610 Civil Code Ch. 242
The Bahamas	- s.76 Supreme Court Act 15/1996
Trinidad & Tobago	- ss.77-83 Supreme Court of Judicature Act Ch. 4:01
	- s 24 Wills & Probate Ordinance Ch. 8 No. 2.

30 St Lucia — This may be as a consequence of the provisions of Art 584(4) Civil Code Ch. 242 which empowers the court or a judge to make limited grants.

31 See also chapter 16.

32 Barbados — s.70 Supreme Court of Judicature Act Cap. 117A
    Trinidad & Tobago — s.67 Supreme Court of Judicature Act Ch. 4:01.

33 Barbados — Rules of the Supreme Court 1982 made under s.46 of the Supreme Court of Judicature Act Cap. 117A.

    Trinidad & Tobago — Order and Rules of the Supreme Court of Judicature of Trinidad & Tobago 1975 made under s.78 of the Supreme Court of Judicature Act Ch. 4:01.

34 Section 24(1) provides:
From and after the commencement of this Act the estates of all persons dying testate or intestate shall vest in the personal representative or representatives of the deceased and shall be administered and distributed according to law under a grant of probate or of letters of administration by the Registrar upon an order of the Court, in the manner and the form prescribed by this Act.

1

Wills

STANDARD WILLS

A will is a revocable declaration in a prescribed form, made in contemplation of death, expressing the intent of the person making it regarding the matters which he intends to take effect after his death.[1] In this regard, conditional wills, joint wills and mutual wills all prescribe to the requirements with respect thereto, but subject to the differences outlined below.

A   CONDITIONAL WILLS

A conditional will is a will made with the intention clearly expressed that it will take effect only on the happening or non-happening of a specified event or contingency. If the will is so expressed and the specified event or contingency occurs, or, in other words, if the condition is fulfilled, the will is valid and will be admitted to probate. If, on the other hand, the specified event or contingency does not occur, the will will be of no effect and will not be admitted to probate.[2] The deceased would therefore be deemed to have died intestate unless he had made an earlier will that the conditional will was expressed to revoke.

For a will to be refused probate on this ground, it must clearly appear from the language of the will that it was the testator's intention to limit the operation of the will, that is, for the will to be treated as conditional.

At times, because of the ambiguous nature of the language used, it is difficult to determine whether, in referring to a particular event, the testator meant to limit the operation of the will and so make it conditional or whether the possibility of that event's occurring was the reason or impetus for making the will. If the testator meant to limit the operation of the will, it will be deemed to be conditional. If it was the reason or impetus for making the will, it will be, that is, it will be valid whether or not the event happens. In such instances, the following two criteria are especially useful to the courts in determining whether or not a will is conditional:[3]

- whether the event or contingency specified in the will is associated with a period of danger to the testator. If it is, the Court takes the view that the danger was regarded by the testator only as a reason for making a will. On the other hand, if it is not co-incident with a period of danger, then according to the President of the Court in *The Goods of Spratt*[4] it is difficult to see the object of referring to a particular period unless it is to limit the operation of the will.
- whether the nature of the dispositions in the will bear some connection to the time or circumstances of the contingency specified. If it does, this is treated by the courts as evidence that the testator intended to limit the operation of the will to the contingency specified; in other words, to make his will conditional.

B JOINT WILLS

All Jurisdictions (save St Lucia)[5]

A joint will is a single instrument in which two or more persons (usually husband and wife) give effect to their testamentary dispositions.
Although written in one document, it is treated as the separate will of each person and as such it is:

- revocable at any time, by any of the testators, during their joint lives or by the survivor after the death of one of them; and
- it is proved separately following the death of each testator.

This type of will is cumbersome and inconvenient because, on the death of the first to die, when an application for probate is made, the original will is retained by the Probate Registry. On the death of the survivor, an office copy of the will must be obtained from the Registry. The copy must then be submitted with the application for the grant and reference made in the oath to the proceedings in which the original will is lodged.

C MUTUAL WILLS

A mutual will is one of two testamentary papers, made by two persons conferring reciprocal rights or interests on the other, for the purpose of giving effect to their respective intentions. By way of illustration, a husband and wife may make separate wills giving a life interest in his or her respective property to the other with the remainder to their child or children.[6]

Much of the advantage of such a will would be lost, however, if either testator remained free to unilaterally revoke his mutual will. In order to prevent such an occurrence, mutual wills are deemed to be made pursuant to an agreement between the two testators, first to make such wills and secondly not to revoke them without the consent of the other. This agreement can be oral or written, and the fact that a will is a mutual will should be stated in the body of the will itself. When wills are so made, a contractual relationship is thereby created, which seems to be at variance with a fundamental characteristic of a will, that is, that it is revocable.

The law resolves this apparent conflict by declaring that a mutual will may always be revoked but when it is done certain legal or equitable remedies may ensue depending on the circumstances.

In so far as the legal or common-law remedy is concerned, an action for damages for breach of contract will lie against the revoker or his personal representative; provided, however that the following two conditions are satisfied:

- there must be a unilateral revocation by one of the parties;
- the revocation must have taken place during the joint lives of the testators.

Effect of Notice Prior to Revocation

Although notice of revocation does not affect the revocability of the will or the aggrieved party's right to bring an action, it does affect the quantum of damages that may be recovered, since the court takes the view that notice gives the aggrieved party an opportunity to alter his position by revoking his mutual will.[7] And in this regard it is to be noted that notice of revocation is not limited to cases where the aggrieved party is fixed with actual written or verbal notice thereof. The aggrieved party to a mutual will is also deemed to be fixed with notice upon the death of the revoker, he being the first to die.[8]

Action for Breach of Trust

The far more effective remedy lies in equity in an action for breach of trust. An action for breach of trust will lie where certain conditions are met, that is,

- one of the parties must have died;
- this party must have kept his side of the bargain, that is, he must have died without revoking his mutual will; and
- the survivor must have revoked his mutual will without the knowledge of the first to die, usually after his death.

When these conditions are satisfied, the person entitled to benefit under the will of the first to die is entitled in equity to bring an action for breach of trust against the survivor or his personal representative, since such a person is deemed to be a trustee for its due performance.[9]

This right of action subsists whether or not the survivor or his estate derives a benefit and whether or not the would be beneficiary has predeceased the survivor.[10]

STATUTORY WILLS

Barbados, St Vincent & the Grenadines and Trinidad & Tobago[11]

According to the relevant statutory provisions of the respective Mental Health Acts of the above territories, the High Court may make an order authorising a person to execute a will for a mental patient.

Formalities

Such wills must be:

- signed by the authorised person with the name of the authorised person in the presence of two or more persons present at the same time;
- attested and subscribed by those witnesses in the presence of the authorised person; and
- sealed with the seal of the court.

Effect of will

A will executed in accordance with the formalities prescribed by the respective Mental Health Acts of these territories is deemed for all purposes to have and take force and effect as if:

- the patient were capable of making a valid will; and
- the will had been executed by the patient in the manner required by the relevant Wills Act of the above territories.

PRIVILEGED WILLS

Anguilla, Antigua & Barbuda, Barbados, Dominica, Guyana, St Christopher & Nevis, St Lucia, St Vincent & the Grenadines and The Bahamas[12]

The general rule is that a will must be in a prescribed form in that it must comply with certain formal requirements for it to be admitted to probate.

A privileged will is an exception to this general rule. Such a will may be made without complying with these formal requirements. It may be completely oral or completely in writing. If in writing it need not be signed or witnessed. It can be in the form of a letter or may merely be an oral indication by the testator of his wishes with regard to his estate after his death. Furthermore, such a will can be made by persons under the age of majority.

It is to be noted that:

- a testator may only exercise a privilege if it is allowed him by the law of his domicil, the relevant domicile being his domicil at the date of the will;
- a previous will of a testator whether privileged or not may be revoked by a later privileged will;
- for such a document to be treated as privileged there must be evidence that the document or declaration was intended by the testator to be of a testamentary character; and
- a gift by a privileged will to a subscribing witness thereto is valid.

Persons who may make privileged wills

This type of will is available to a limited class of testators. They are:

- soldiers in actual military service; and
- mariners and seamen at sea.

The law recognises that at times such persons may be faced with immediate and exceptional danger and may wish to make a will but because of the situation in which they are placed they may have little or no opportunity to seek legal advice.[13]

As a consequence, the law exempts these persons within certain specified circumstances from the usual formalities regarding the making and execution of testamentary documents.

Soldiers

For a soldier to claim this privilege he must be in actual military service. According to *Re Wingham, Andrews and Another v. Wingham*[14] a soldier is deemed to be in military service 'if he is actually serving in the armed forces in connection with military operations which are or have been taking place or are believed to be imminent[15]. The term 'soldier' is not confined to the people who are or will be actually fighting but includes noncombatant persons as well, serving with the armed forces such as doctors, nurses and chaplains.[16]

Mariners/Sailors

For a mariner or seaman to claim this privilege, he must be 'at sea', a term that has been held to mean 'on maritime service'.[17] Accordingly, persons not actually on the high seas but serving in vessels permanently engaged in harbour duties and in vessels engaged on services in a river are regarded to be 'at sea'. Additionally sailors in the course of a voyage are deemed to be 'at sea' even though at the time of execution of their will they may be on shore at a port of call. According to case law authority, the term 'mariner' or 'seamen' includes all members of the crew of a modern ship, such as doctors, nurses and typists.

HOLOGRAPH WILLS

Barbados and St Lucia[18]

A holograph will is a will written throughout in the proper handwriting of the testator and need not be signed by the testator nor witnesses. In Barbados it need not be signed by the testator nor witnesses. In St Lucia, however, such handwritten wills must be signed by the testator although they need not be witnessed.

NOTARIAL WILLS

St Lucia[19]

This type of will applies to St Lucia only. It is in the form of a notarial document. Such a will is received either before two notaries or one notary and two witnesses.

In accordance with the formal requirements governing the execution of notarial wills, the testator is required to sign the will in the presence of the witnesses or declare that he cannot do so after it has been read to him by one of the notaries in the presence of the other or by the notary in the presence of the witnesses.[20] The witnesses must then sign their names to the will in the presence of the testator and each other. Each witness must also be named and described in the will and the place and date of execution must also be stated.[21]

Persons who may be witnesses[22]

Any person who:
(a) is of full age;
(b) has not been convicted of a felony; and
(c) is not in the employment of the executing notaries.

Execution of Notarial Wills

A notarial will is retained by the notary who provides certified or ordinary copies of the will to the testator. By virtue of Art 783 Civil Code Ch. 242,[23] a will cannot be executed before notaries one of whom bears to one testator or to the other notary the relation of father, mother, son, daughter, brother, sister, uncle, aunt, nephew or niece.

In St Lucia all attorneys-at-law are notaries royal[24] with the result that once a will is witnessed by an attorney-at-law it, as a general rule, becomes a notarial will.[25] Indeed it is the most common form of will in St Lucia.

Probate Practice[26]

(a) A certified copy of the notarial will, not the original, is lodged with the papers to lead a grant of probate or letters of administration with will annexed.
(b) An affidavit of due execution is not required where the will admitted to probate is a notarial will.

INTERNATIONAL WILLS

Barbados[27]

An international will is a will that complies with the requirements of the Convention Providing for a Uniform Law on the Form of an International will.[28] This Convention provides for the recognition of such wills irrespective of the place made, location of assets and of the nationality, domicil, or residence of the testator. This is provided that the formalities as prescribed by the Annex to the Convention are adhered to.

So far as formalities are concerned, an international will must be in writing and must be read to the testator in the presence of two witnesses. In addition, such wills must be executed in the presence of an authorised person. This authorised person is appointed by the Minister of Legal Affairs to act in connection with international wills. He must be an attorney-at-law and in accordance with Art. 7 of the Convention he is required to prepare and sign a certificate of verification to the effect that the requirements regarding the formalities have been complied with.

Bahamas

With respect to the validity and recognition of wills and testamentary dispositions with a foreign element or executed on board a vessel or aircraft, s.56 of the Wills Act 2002 provides that the Minister may make regulations, which have regard to any conventions providing for a uniform law *inter alia* on the form of an international will.

VALIDITY OF WILLS

For a will to be valid and consequently to be admitted to probate, the following requirements must be met:

- It must be made by a person who has attained the age of majority (unless he is privileged);
- It must comply with certain formal requirements laid down by the statute.
- The testator or the person making the will must have testamentary capacity or what is referred to as the *animus testandi* to make such a will.

FORMAL REQUIREMENTS

For a will to be valid and consequently to be admitted to probate, the following requirements must be met:

- It must be made by a person who has attained the age of majority (unless he is privileged);
- It must comply with certain formal requirements laid down by statute.
- The testator or the person making the will must have the testamentary capacity or what is referred to as the *animus testandi* to make such will.

(i) *The will must be in writing*[29]

This does not mean that a will must be in the handwriting of the testator. As a result a will may be handwritten, typed, printed or be in any combination of these. It may be written in ink or with a pencil.

(ii) The will must be signed by the testator[30]

Another requirement of a valid will is that it must be signed by the testator, 'What constitutes a signature? This question has been interpreted quite liberally by the courts and what emanates from the cases is that the testator must put some mark on the will which he intends to be his signature.[31] An X mark, a thumb print, a rubber stamp and initials have all been held to constitute a valid signature. Furthermore, an incomplete name and an assumed name have also been held to be sufficient. Moreover, the testator need not sign any name at all. In the *Estate of Cook*,[32] for example, the words 'your loving mum' were held to be sufficient. The important fact is that whatever mark the testator puts on the will he must intend it to represent his signature.

(iii) Or by some other person in his presence and by his direction

The relevant statutory provision of each territory provides that the will can be signed for or on behalf of the testator by some other person in his presence and by his direction.[33] This is usually done if the testator is blind, illiterate or physically infirm. The person signing for the testator can either sign the testator's name or his own name.

(iv) Attestation Clause

Although statute does not require it, it is usual in such cases to include a special attestation clause which will state:

- that the will was signed on behalf of the testator in his presence and by his direction;
- the reason as to why the testator did not sign; and
- that the will was read over to the testator and he appeared to understand same.

It is advisable to include this clause in order to avoid problems of proof and possible litigation. The absence of such a clause may even raise suspicion in certain cases. Indeed, in instances where the testator is, for example, blind or illiterate the relevant non-contentious probate rule of the various territories[34] provides that the grant will not be issued unless the Registrar is satisfied that the will was read over to the deceased before its execution or that the deceased had at such time knowledge of its contents.

(v) Acknowledgement of signature[35]

Alternatively, the testator can also acknowledge to the witnesses a signature previously made by him. It is important to note that the acknowledgement refers to the signature and not the will itself and it is sufficient the testator merely ask the witness to sign the document which he produces once he can see his signature upon it or have the opportunity of seeing it. To constitute a valid acknowledgement, the following is required:

(a) The will must already have been signed before the acknowledgement.
(b) The testator must acknowledge his signature by words or conduct.
(c) At the time of the acknowledgement the witnesses must see the signature or have the opportunity of seeing it.[36]

(vi) Placement of testator's signature
1837 Wills Act Position- Trinidad & Tobago

According to s.42 of the Wills and Probate Ordinance Ch. 8 No. 2 the provisions of which are equivalent to s.9 of the 1837 Wills Act, England, the signature of the testator must be placed physically at the end or foot of the will.[37] Strict compliance with this provision is necessary, failing which the entire will is deemed to be invalid.

All other Jurisdictions (save St Vincent & the Grenadines)[38]

The wills legislation of the above territories contain the equivalent of the 1852 Wills (Amendment) Act England, which allows greater flexibility or latitude in the physical placement of the testator's signature. According to its provisions, if the signature of the testator appears at, after, following, under, beside or opposite to the end of the will, the entire will is regarded as valid once the court is satisfied that the testator intended to give effect by such signature to the writing signed as his will. The intention of the testator is paramount and emphasis is placed on when and not where the testator's signature was placed.[39]

As a result of this provision, the validity of a will is no longer affected by the fact that the testator's signature does not immediately follow the end of the will or that a blank space intervenes or that there was sufficient space in the preceding page to contain the signature.

Although the provisions of this amending Act give the testator some latitude with respect to the physical placement of his signature, there are certain restrictions. The Act provides that a signature cannot operate to give effect to any part of the will

- which is inserted later in time after the testator's signature was made; or
- which is underneath or which follows the signature in space unless it cart be proven that the lines appearing thereunder were written before the signature was made.[40]

It should be noted, however, that words that are beneath either wholly or partially or follow the signature may be regarded by reason of the use of asterisks or other signs of interpolation to be above it.[41]

St Vincent & the Grenadines

With effect from 27 December, 1989, a testator's signature need not appear at the end of his will for the entire will to be valid.[42] The only requirement is that it should appear that the testator intended by his signature to give effect to his will and that signature was placed there after the will was written.

Envelope Cases —All Jurisdictions (save Trinidad & Tobago)

Arising out of the 1852 amendment is what is referred to as "the envelope cases". Since these cases arise out of the 1852 amendment it is submitted that they are not applicable to Trinidad & Tobago. In these cases the testator's signature was written on an envelope enclosing the testator's will. In such situations the court takes the view that if the signature so appearing on the envelope was intended to be the signature to the will as opposed to merely a signature for identification purposes, that would be sufficient and the will would be admitted to probate.[43]

More than one page: With regard to the placement of the signature of the testator there are instances where the will is written on more than one page. In such instances a rule of thumb has been developed which requires that the various pages be connected in some way at the time of execution if all the pages are to be validated by the testator's signature.[44]

Non-Notarial wills only — St Lucia

In St Lucia when a will is written on more than one page each page must be numbered, signed and initialled by the testator.[45] This is a good practice to follow in the other jurisdictions where there is no corresponding provision.

(vii) Meaning of 'In the Presence of'

The testator must sign his will or it must be signed for him or his signature acknowledged by him in the presence of two witnesses who must both be present when the signature is so made or acknowledged. The meaning of the words 'in the presence of' is important here. It means that the witness must actually see or have the opportunity of seeing the testator sign or someone signing on his behalf or the testator acknowledging his signature.[46] The words opportunity to see means that the witness could have seen if he had chosen to look.[47]

As a general rule, in the absence of proof to the contrary, where there is a proper attestation clause or there is evidence available that the testator knew the law, the presumption is that the attesting witnesses either saw the testator sign or acknowledge his signature.

(viii) Attestation by Witnesses[48]

After the testator signs or acknowledges his signature in the presence of the witnesses, the witnesses must then sign or attest in the presence of the testator.

It must be noted that the witnesses can only attest after the testator has signed or acknowledged his signature in their joint presence. The witnesses must sign in the presence of the testator. However with the exception of St Lucia and Trinidad & Tobago[49] they need not sign in the presence of each other.

(ix) Attestation or Acknowledgement

In most jurisdictions, in accordance with the common law, a witness may sign by thumb print or initial. This is not the case in St Lucia and Trinidad & Tobago where the witnesses must sign their names.

In Trinidad & Tobago[50] if a witness puts an initial or thumb print he is an incompetent witness to due execution of the will, but the will itself remains valid.

In St Lucia, Art 789 Civil Code Ch. 242 states that the signature of a witness cannot be by a mark.

In The Bahamas, s.5 (4) of the Wills Act, 2002 provides that:

> No person is a competent witness to the execution of a will if he attests the will in any manner other than by signing his name in his handwriting.

However, in all jurisdictions save and except St Vincent & the Grenadines and The Bahamas,[51] a witness cannot acknowledge his signature.

(x) Position of Signature of Witnesses

There are no statutory provisions governing the position of a witness's signature. It can appear anywhere on the will but it must be made in point of time after the testator signed or acknowledged. Whether it is so made is a question of proof. Consequently if the signatures of the witnesses appear on a different sheet of paper, or are not physically underneath or are after the testator's signature, the affidavit of due execution must address this matter.

(xi) Competence of Witnesses

- Common law test of Competency

Although the general common-law rule is that no person under a disability should act as a witness, nevertheless, with the exception of St Lucia, a child who possesses the requisite competence to give evidence is not incompetent by reason of minority. It should be noted, however, that a blind man cannot be a competent witness.[52]

- Statutory Guidelines

Guyana

Section 6 of the Wills Act Cap. 12:01 provides in effect that persons above the age of fourteen years, competent to give evidence in any court of law, are competent and qualified to attest the execution of a will.[53]

St Lucia

According to Art 789 Civil Code Ch. 242 the two witnesses to an English will are required not only to be competent but one of them must also be a Justice of the Peace. According to Art 789 Ch. 242 the competency of witnesses is determined by the rules with respect to notarial wills.

(xii) Gifts to Witnesses[54]

Statute provides that a legacy to an attesting witness or the spouse of an attesting witness or anyone claiming under that witness and, in the case of St. Lucia, a gift to a relative in the first degree of the witness, will be null and void, although the person so attesting can be admitted as a witness to prove the execution of the will or its validity or invalidity, as the case may be.

(xiii) *Number of Witnesses*

All jurisdictions (save St Vincent & the Grenadines)

Statute also provides that a will must be witnessed by two or more witnesses[55]. Although no more than two witnesses are required, the presumption is that all persons who sign a will do so as attesting witnesses and consequently all legacies given to them or their spouses by the will are null and void.

Accordingly, if there are more than two witnesses, although two will suffice, all the names will be included in the application for probate, so that the question whether they did or did not sign as witnesses might be decided.

In the *Estate of Bravda*[56] the Court held that a daughter's signature at the back of her mother's will under the word 'witnesses' was that of a witness even though there were two independent witnesses to the will, and as a result, the gift to the daughter under the will failed.

St Vincent & the Grenadines and the Bahamas[57]

Section 17(2) of the Wills Act Cap. 384 provides that, for a testator dying on or after 27th December, 1989, and in the case of the Bahamas, S10(2) Wills Act 2002, provides in the case of a testator dying on or after February 2002, if more persons than are necessary sign their names to a will as witnesses, then, in applying the provisions relating to gifts to witnesses, the attestation by a person to whom or to whose spouse there is given or made any such disposition, such signature will be disregarded if the will is duly executed without his or her attestation.

(xiv) *Attesting Witness/Executor*

Guyana

According to s.8 of the Wills Act Cap. 12:02 a person who attests a will and is by the court also appointed or nominated executor, or guardian thereunder, such appointment or nomination will be thereby rendered null and void.

The Bahamas

Section 12 of the Wills Act 2002, expressly provides that no person is incompetent on account of his being an executor of a will, as a witness to prove the execution or validity or invalidity of a will.

(xv) Attesting Witness/Creditor

The Bahamas

Section 11 of the Wills Act 2002 provides in effect that a creditor of the deceased is competent as a witness to the execution of the will of the testator.

ANIMUS TESTANDI

In order to make a valid will, a testator must not only comply with the statutory formalities with respect to the execution of his will, he must also have what is referred to as *animus testandi* or testamentary capacity.
Animus testandi or, more correctly, the lack of it has been the basis on which the admissibility of many wills has been challenged in court and consequently has been the subject-matter of many contentious probate actions.

Animus testandi is a common law principle but it has been given statutory force in St Lucia[58] and Barbados[59], The Bahamas[60] and in Trinidad & Tobago when the yet-to-be enacted provision of the proclaimed Succession Act becomes law.[61]

In order to possess the necessary *animus testandi* to make a will, it must be established:

- that the testator had the mental capacity to make the will;
- that the testator knew and approved of the contents of his will; and
- that the will was that of a free and capable testator, that is, he must have exercised his genuine free choice in the making of his will and more particularly that he did not make it as a result of the undue influence or fraud of another.

A. Mental Capacity

The modern test of mental capacity was laid down in the case of *Banks v. Goodfellow*.[62] According to that case mental capacity means that the testator must be of "sound disposing mind and memory".

To constitute a sound, disposing mind:

- the testator must have an understanding of the nature of the business in which he is engaged;
- he must understand who are the persons who are to be the objects of his bounty; and
- he must understand the manner in which his property is to be distributed among them.

In order to be of sound disposing memory it must be shown that the testator is in a position or is capable of making a disposition of his estate with understanding and reason and therefore he must implicitly have a recollection of the property of which he means to dispose.

(i) Degree of Mental Capacity

But what is the degree of mental capacity required of the testator? It is not necessary that the testator possess these qualities in the highest degree. According to *Banks v. Goodfellow*[63] if that were so, very few persons would be able to make testamentary dispositions. Neither is it necessary that a testator possess these qualities in as great a degree as he may have formerly done, for even this may disable many in the decline of life. What must be determined is that the testator has sufficient intelligence to understand the testamentary act. Once this can be established this will be adequate even though the testator's mental powers are reduced below the ordinary standard.

(ii) Insane delusions

In relation to mental capacity there are instances where a testator may be in all other regards perfectly sane, in that he is able to handle his financial affairs, converse rationally, and so on but suffers from what is termed insane delusions.

In the case of *Dew v. Clark and Clark*[64] it was stated that a testator is said to suffer from a delusion if he holds a belief in any subject which no rational person could hold and which cannot be permanently eradicated from his mind by reasoning with him. In determining whether a person is suffering from an insane delusion S.J. Hannen in the case of *Boughton v. Knight*[65] told the jury:

> to put this question to themselves and answer it: Can I understand how any man in possession of his senses could believe such a thing? If the answer you give

is I cannot understand it, then it is of necessity that you should say that the man is not sane.

A will made by a testator who suffers from an insane delusion will nevertheless be upheld if it can be established that:

- the delusion remains latent at the time of the execution of the will[66];
- the testator is otherwise mentally competent to make a will; and
- the delusion has no direct bearing on the will or any connection with the provisions of the will.

In order to satisfy the court that the above has been established it is necessary to show either that the provisions of the will are lucid and reasonable or that the will was attested to by a medical doctor who is willing to testify as to the competence of the testator at the time of execution.[67]

(iii)   Lucid Intervals

There are instances when the testator is considered to be generally mentally incompetent but nevertheless experiences what is referred to as a lucid interval. He may be of unsound mind prior to the making of the will, but at the time the will is made he may either have recovered fully from that unsoundness or the will may be made during a temporary recovery, that is, a lucid interval.

To constitute a lucid interval[68] the following criteria must be satisfied:

- The act done by the testator must be a rational act.
- It must be rationally done.
- It must be the testator's own act without any assistance from another person.

The length of the lucid interval may be a day, an hour, a month.[69] The important factor is that the testator experiences a lucid interval at the time of execution of the will.

(iv)   Rule in Parker and Felgate

As a general rule the testator must have testamentary capacity at the time of execution of the will. In the case of *Parker v. Felgate*[70] this requirement was qualified or given a rather liberal interpretation. It was laid down in that case that if a testator has given instructions to a solicitor at a time when he was able to appreciate what he was doing and the solicitor prepares the will in accordance with these instructions, the will will stand although at the time of execution, the testator is only capable of understanding that he is executing a will for which he has given instructions but is no longer capable of understanding the instructions themselves or the clauses in the will giving effect to those instructions. To fall within the provisions of this rule, the following must be satisfied:

- The testator must have testamentary capacity at the time when he gives instructions for the preparation of his will;
- The will must be prepared in accordance with his instructions; and
- At the time of execution he must be capable of understanding that he is executing a will for which he has given instructions.

In the Privy Council Case of *Battan Singh v. Amirchand*[71] it was stated that the principle should be applied with the greatest caution when the testator gives those instructions through a lay intermediary who repeats them to the solicitor. The Privy Council observed that in such cases the court must be satisfied that the instructions given to the intermediary were unambiguous and clearly understood by the intermediary and faithfully reported by him and rightly apprehended by the solicitor.

B. Knowledge and Approval

A testator must not only have the mental capacity to make a will but he must also know and approve of its contents at the time of execution thereof, or, alternatively, as was stated in the case of in *The Estate of Wallace*,[72] it suffices if the testator knows and approves of the contents of the instructions that he gives to a solicitor for the preparation of a will provided that:

- the will is prepared in accordance with his instructions; and
- at the time of execution he is capable of understanding and understands that he is executing a will for which he has given instructions.

This case in effect adopts the principle laid down in *Parker v. Felgate* with respect to knowledge and approval.

(i) Classes of Persons

The presumption does not apply and the court would require affirmative proof of knowledge and approval with respect of certain classes of persons, for example, dumb, blind and illiterate persons.[73] When a person is unable to speak or read or write and gives instructions for his will by signs, the court would require evidence as to the signs used establishing that the testator understood and approved of the contents of his will. If the testator is blind or illiterate, the court usually requires evidence that the will was read over to him before he executed same and that he understood it. This is normally satisfied by an affidavit to that effect deposed to by one of the attesting witnesses.[74]

In cases in which persons are affected by mind-distorting substances such as drink and drugs there is a presumption of capacity.[75] If, however, there is opposition to the will or if testamentary capacity is challenged, the court would require affirmative evidence of the attesting witnesses or persons present at the time of execution that notwithstanding the inebriation the testator had the necessary capacity.

With physically infirm and elderly persons, if testamentary capacity is challenged, cogent proof is required that the testator knew and approved of what he was doing.[76]

(ii) Suspicious Circumstances

When a will is prepared and executed under circumstances which raise a well grounded suspicion that the will or some provision in it did not express the mind of the testator, the will or that provision will not be admitted to probate unless that suspicion is removed by affirmative proof of the testator's knowledge and approval. In the case of *Wintle v. Nye, Viscount Simonds*[77] noted that:

> [t]he degree of suspicion will vary with the circumstances of the case. It may be slight and easily dispelled. It may on the other hand be so grave that it can hardly be removed. As Cummings J. A., however, observed in his dissenting judgment in *Thomas v. Thomas*.[78] Each case must be determined upon the facts of that particular case.

One of the situations that will excite the suspicion of the court is when one of the beneficiaries under the will is also responsible for its preparation such as an attorney-at-law.[79]

But as Lindley LJ stated in *Tyrrell v. Painto*[80] suspicious circumstances are not confined to the single case in which a will is prepared by or on the instructions of a person taking large benefits under it, but extends to all cases in which exist circumstances that excite the suspicion of the court; a view which was echoed by Lord Wilberforce in the Privy Council decision of *LuckyTewari*.[81] And what are these circumstances?

- Marked departure from previous testamentary dispositions.[82]
- Absence of independent advice.[83]

- Secrecy surrounding the execution of a will.[84]
- Character of the attesting witnesses.[85]
- Signature of the testator shaky or materially different from previous signature.[86]
- Leaving property or making dispositions to strangers and disinheriting next of kin, for example, children in favour of others.[87]

It should be noted that these circumstances must attend or be present at the time of execution of the will and must not be extraneous and/or subsequent to it.

C. Undue Influence

The testator must not only be mentally competent and know and approve of the contents of the will but he must also exercise his free will, that is, the will must not be the result either of undue influence or of fraud of another.

Undue influence is pleaded interchangeably with suspicious circumstances by persons contesting wills. In probate matters there is no presumption of undue influence save and except for St Lucia where such a presumption arises in the following relationships; minister of religion/parishioner, medical doctor/patient, legal adviser/client.[88] As a result if one raises this plea, it must not only be specifically pleaded but it must also be affirmatively proved. It is difficult to succeed on this plea as distinct from want of knowledge and approval. This is reflected and confirmed by the case law in the area.[89]

What is Undue influence?

In the case of *Boyse v. Rossborough*[90] it was stated that undue influence must be an influence exercised in relation to the will itself. It must be of such a nature that the testator was not acting as a free agent but was acting under undue control. As Sir J.P. Wilde observed when summing up to the jury on the question of undue influence in the oft-quoted case of *Hall v. Hall*:[91]

> In a word a testator may be led not driven; and his will must be the offspring of his own volition and not the record of someone else's.

Undue influence may take different forms. At one extreme there may be force. At the other extreme the pressure exerted may simply be talking incessantly to a weak and feeble testator in the last days of his life so as to fatigue his brain and induce him, for quietness' sake to give way to pressure. But whatever form it rakes the testator must be coerced.[92]

Accordingly to constitute undue influence the testator must be coerced into making a will or part of a will which he does not want to make.[93] However persuasion, appeals to the affections or ties of kindred or to a sentiment of gratitude for past services are all legitimate and may be fairly pressed on a testator.[94] The case of *Parfitt v. Lawless*[95] is instructive on this point.

In that case a Roman Catholic priest had resided with the testatrix and her husband for many years as chaplain and for a part of the time as confessor. It was held that there was no evidence to go to a jury on an issue of undue influence and that natural influence exerted by one who possesses it to obtain a benefit for himself is undue *inter vivos*; but such natural influence may be lawfully exercised to obtain a will or legacy.

Notes

1 St Lucia — See Art 697 Civil Code Ch. 242 for a definition of a will. Further, it is to be noted that by virtue of Art 780 Civil Code Ch. 242 that a will other than a notarial or holograph will which is in accordance with the English form is called an English will.
2 *Parsons v. Lanoe* (1748) 1 Ves Sen 189.
3 See *Goods of Spratt* [1897] P. 28 at 30.
4 *Ibid.*
5 Joint wills are not applicable to St Lucia by virtue of Art 77 Civil Code 242 which provides that two or more persons cannot make their wills by one and the same instrument.
6 *Stone v. Hoskins* [1905] P. 194; *Re Oldham* [1925] Ch. 75; *In the Estate of Heys*, [1914] P.192 at 196-197 but see *Pereira v. Pereira* (1925-26) L.R.B.G. 134 where it was held that the fact that each of the spouses to a mutual will had dealt only with his other half of the property precluded the operation of consolidation into a mass and consequently the surviving spouse was entitled to accept the benefits conferred on him by the will without being deprived of his own half of the common property.
7 *Stone v. Hoskins* [1905] P.194.
8 *Ibid.*
9 *Dufour v. Pereira* (1769) 1 Dick 419, *Re Hagger, Freeman v. Arscott* [1930] 2 Ch. 190. Note the decision in *Fereira v. Cabral* [1923-24] LR.B.G. 17 where it was held that the children of the beneficiaries of the mutual will, having repudiated the earlier dispositions of the mutual will of their parents, and having received their legitimate portions of their father's estate, that the remainder of the joint estate became the absolute property of their mother who was therefore entitled to dispose of the same as she pleased and that accordingly there was no trust imposed on the remainder of the joint estate remaining in her hands.
10 *Re Hagger, Freeman v.Arscott* [1930] 2 Ch. 190.
11 Barbados - ss.39(1)(e), 20 Mental Health Act Cap. 45; St Vincent & the Grenadines - ss.22(1)(e), 23 Mental Health Act Ch. 228; Trinidad & Tobago - ss. 39(l)(e), 40 Mental Health Act Ch. 28:02.
12 Antigua & Barbuda - s.7 Wills Act Cap 473 and Wills (Soldiers and Sailors) Act Cap. 88 Barbados   - s.85 Succession Act, Cap. 249

Dominica	- s.12 Wills Act Ch. 9:01
Guyana	- s. 11 Wills Act 1837, England pursuant to s.7 Civil Law of Guyana Act Cap. 6:01 which provides in effect that where the Wills Act Cap. 12:02 and any other Act now or herein after dealing with wills and testaments is silent, the Wills Act 1837, England, shall be part of the law of Guyana
Montserrat	- s.5 Wills (Soldiers and Sailors) Act Ch. 85, s.11 Wills Act Cap. 88
St Christopher & Nevis, Anguilla	- s.11 Wills Act Cap. 84 - Wills (Soldiers and Sailors) Act, Cap. 85
St Lucia	- Art 787 Civil Code Ch. 242
St Vincent & the Grenadines	- s.13 Wills Act Cap. 384
The Bahamas	- Part V, Wills Act 2002

13 *In the Estate of Rapley* [1983] 3 All E.R 248; [1983] 1 W.L.R. 1069.
14 [1948] 2 All E.R. 908; [1949] P.187.
15 [1948] 2 All E.R. 908 at pp. 913-914.
16 *In the Goods of Hudson v. Barnes* [1926] 96 L.J.P 26; 22 L.T. 213.
17 *In the Estate of Rapley supra.*
18 Barbados - s.63 Succession Act Cap. 249; St Lucia - Art 788 Civil Code Ch. 242.
19 Arts 780-786) 792, 793 Civil Code Ch. 242; see also Civil Code (Amendment) Act 3/1991.
20 Art 781 Civil Code Ch. 242.
21 Arts 782, 792, Civil Code Ch. 242.
22 Art 782, Civil Code Ch. 242.
23 As repealed and replaced by virtue of the Civil Code Amendment (No. 3) Act 12/1991.
24 See The Legal Practitioners Ordinance Ch. 116.
25 Art 782 Civil Code Ch. 242. Note however Art 793 which provides that a will purporting to be made in one form which would be void if in that form alone, may yet be valid if fulfilling the conditions required for another form.
26 See Art 1015(1) (a), & (b) Civil Code of Procedure Ch. 243 and Art 795 Civil Code Ch. 242.
27 See ss.86-91 Succession Act Cap. 249, the Second Schedule thereto.
28 Washington, 26 October, 1973.

29
Anguilla	- s.7 Wills Ordinance Cap. 84
Antigua & Barbuda	- s.7 Wills Act Cap. 473
Barbados	- s.61 Succession Act Cap. 249
Dominica	- s.8 Wills Act Ch. 9:01
Grenada	- s.6 Wills Act Cap. 340
Guyana	- s.4 Wills Act Cap. 12:02
Jamaica	- s.6 Wills Act
St Christopher & Nevis, Montserrat	- s.7 Wills Act Cap. 84
St Lucia	- Civil Code Ch. 242 Art 789
St Vincent & the Grenadines	- s.12 Wills Act Ch. 384
The Bahamas	- s.51 Wills Act 2002
Trinidad & Tobago	- s.42 Wills & Probate Ordinance Ch. 8 No. 2.

30 *Ibid.*

31 *In the Estate of Finn* (1935) 105 L.J.P. 36; 154 L.T. 242; *In the Goods of Chalcraft* [1948] P.222.
32 [1960] 1 All E.R. 689; (1960) 1 W.I.R 353; See also *Mohansingh v. Simon* H.C.A 514/1982 Trinidad & Tobago [Unreported].
33 See note 29 above.
34 Barbados — r.15 Supreme Court (Non-Contentious Probate) Rule 1959
    Jamaica — Rule 68.35(3) CPR 2002 repealing and replacing r.40 General Rules and Orders of the Supreme Court Part III Probate and Administration
    Trinidad & Tobago — r.13 First Schedule N.C.B.R. Ch. 8 No. 2
    England Caribbean (save Dominica) The Bahamas, Eastern — r.13 N.C.P.R. 1987, Dominica, Guyana — r.11 N.C.P.R. 1954, England.
35 See note 29 above.
36 *Keigwin v. Keigwin* [1843] 3 Curt. 607; *In the Goods of Gunstan* [1882] 7 P.D 102.
37 Note however s.5 of the yet-to-be fully proclaimed Succession Act 27/1981 which contains the equivalent of the 1852 Wills (Amendment) Act, England.
38 Anguilla — s.9 Wills Ord. Cap. 84
    Antigua & Barbuda — s.9 Wills Act Cap. 473
    Barbados — s.61 Succession Act Cap. 249
    Dominica — s.10 Wills Act Ch. 9:01
    Grenada — s.6 Wills Act Cap. 340
    Guyana — s.5 Wills Act Cap. 12:02
    Jamaica — s.6 Wills Act
    Montserrat, — s.9 Wills Act Cap. 84
    St Christopher & Nevis
    The Bahamas — s.5(3) Wills Act 2002
39 *In the Goods of Hornby* [1946] P.171; *Re Roberts* [1934] P.102.
40 See *In the Goods of Ainsworth* [1870] L.R. 2 P & D 151; *Re Roberts supra.* Contrast with *Re Stalman* (1931) 145 L.T. 339; [1931] All E.R. Rep. 193.
41 *In the Goods of Kimpton* (1864) 3 Sw. & Tr. 427.
42 See ss.12(1) and (2) Wills Act Cap. 384.
43 *In the Goods of Mann* [1942] P.146. Contrast within the *Estate of Bean* [1944] P.83 where it was held that on the facts of the case that the envelope on which the signatures of the testator and the witnesses appeared that the signatures were inserted thereon for the sole purpose of identifying the contents of the will. It was therefore held that the document was not validly executed as a will. See also *Re Fredericks* (1931-37) L.R.B.G. 211
44 *Re Little Foster v. Cooper* [1960] 1 All E.R. 387.
45 Art 792 Civil Code Ch. 242.
46 *Casson v. Dade* (1781) 1 Bro cc 99 28 E.R. 1010; *Jenner v. Ffinch* [1879] 5 PD 106, *Shires v. Glascock* (1689) 2 Salk. 688; 91 E.R. 584.
47 *Ibid.*
48 Anguilla — s.7 Wills Act Cap. 84
    Antigua & Barbuda — s.7 Wills Act Cap. 473
    Barbados — s.61 Succession Act 1975 Cap. 249
    Dominica — s.8 Wills Act Ch. 9:01

Grenada	- s.6 Wills Act Cap. 340
Guyana	- s.4 Wills Act Cap. 12:02
Jamaica	- s.6 Wills Act
Montserrat	- s.7 Wills Act Ch. 84
St Christopher & Nevis	- s.7 Wills Act Cap. 84
St Lucia	- Arts 789, Civil Code Ch. 242
St Vincent & the Grenadines	- s.12 Wills Act Cap. 384
The Bahamas	- s. 5 (2) Wills Act, 2002
Trinidad & Tobago	- s. 42 Wills & Probate Ordinance Ch. 8 No. 2.

49
St Lucia	- Art 789 Civil Code Ch. 242
Trinidad & Tobago	- s.43 Wills and Probate Ordinance Ch. 8 No. 2.

50 According to s.42 Wills and Probate Ordinance Ch. 8 No. 2. No person shall be a competent witness to any will executed or purporting to be executed after the 16th of May 1921, who has attested such will by making a cross or mark or otherwise than by his signature in his own proper handwriting.
51 By virtue of s. 12(1)(d) of the Wills Act Cap. 384 St Vincent and the Grenadines and s.5(2)(c) Wills Act 2002, the Bahamas, each witness may either attest and sign the will or acknowledge his signature in the presence of the testator, but not necessarily in the presence of any other witness. Accordingly by virtue of this provision, a witness may now acknowledge a previous signature without having to resign his name.
52 *In the Estate of Gibson* [1949] P.434.
53 See Art 782 which provides that the witnesses to a notarial will must be of full age, not be convicted of a felony and not be in the employment of the executing notaries.

54
Anguilla	- s.14 Wills Ord. Cap. 84
Antigua & Barbuda	- s.14 Wills Act Cap. 473
Barbados	- s.66 Succession Act Cap. 249
Dominica	- s.15 Wills Act Ch. 9:01
Grenada	- s.10 Wills Act Cap. 340
Guyana	- s.7 Wills Act Cap. 12:02
Jamaica	- s.10 Wills Act
Montserrat,	- s.14 Wills Act Cap. 84
St Christopher & Nevis	
St Lucia	- Art 791 Civil Code Ch. 242 with respect to English wills Art 784 with respect to Notarial wills
St Vincent & the Grenadines	- s.17 Wills Act Ch. 384
The Bahamas	- s.10 Wills Act 2002
Trinidad & Tobago	- s.45 Wills & Probate Ordinance Ch. 8 No. 2

55 See note 29 above.
56 [1968] 2 All E.R. 217.
57 This provision is identical to s.1 of the Wills Act 1968, England.
58 Arts 770, 773, 775 Civil Code Ch. 242.
59 Section 60 Succession Act Cap. 249.
60 Section 4(b) Wills Act 2002.

61 See s.4 of the yet to be proclaimed Succession Act 27/1981 which provides that for a will to be valid it shall be made by a person who has attained the age of eighteen. . . and is of sound disposing mind.
62 (1870) L.R. 5 Q.B. 549.
63 *Ibid.* p.567.
64 (1826) 3 Add. 79; 162 E.R. 410 at 414.
65 (1873) L.R. 3 P & D 64 at 68.
66 *Banks v. Goodfellow supra.* Contrast with *Dew v. Clark and Clark* (1826) 3 Add. 79 at 90 where the court held that the will made by the testator, disinheriting his daughter was 'the direct unqualified offspring of that morbid delusion ... put into act and energy.'
67 *In the Estate of Walker* (1912) 28 T.L.R 466.
68 *Ibid.*
69 *Cartwright v. Cartwright* (1793) 1 Phill. 90; 161 E.R. 923; *Chambers-Yatman v. Queen's Proctor* (1840) 2 Curt. 415.
70 (1883) 8 P&D 171.
71 [1948] A.C. 16.
72 (1952) 2 T.L.R. 925. See also *Walsh v. Severin* (1939) L.R.B.G. 240.
73 See *Moonan v, Muonan* (1963) 7 W.I.R 420.
74 See chapter 5 pp. 110-11.
75 *Walsh v. Severin* (1939) L.R.B.G. 240
76 *Cleare v. Cleare* [1869] L.R. 1 P & D 655; *De Nobriga v. De Nobriga* (1967) 12 W.L.R. 342; *Alvarez v. Chandler* 1 (1962) 5 W.I.R. 226; *Headlie v. Mary Arneaud* Judgments of the High Court of Trinidad & Tobago and of the Court of Appeal Vol. XIX Part II. p. 258.
77 [1959] 1 All E.R. 552 at 557.
78 (1969) 20 W.I.R. 58 at 70.
79 See *Barry v. Butlin* [1838] 2 Moo PCC 480 where Parke B. laid down the so called rule in Barry and Butlin 'that if a party prepares a will under which he takes a benefit that is a circumstance which ought generally to excite the suspicion of the court and calls upon it to be vigilant and jealous in examining the instrument', Contrast with *Nicome v. Pacheco*, Reports of Judgments of the High Court of Justice of the Court of Appeal of Trinidad & Tobago Vol. 19 (1966-69) 263.
80 [1894] P.151 at 157.
81 (1965) 8 W.I.R. 363 at 367.
82 *Moonan v. Moonan* (1963) 7 W.I.R. 420; *Thomas v. Thomas* (1969) 20 W.I.R. 58.
83 *Thomas v. Thomas supra.*
84 *Ibid.*
85 *Sin Young Chin and Anr. v. Kelly and Others* (1968) 12 W.I.R. 429.
86 *Bankay et al v. Sukhdeo* (1973) 24 W.I.R 9; *Harrinarine v. R* (1963) 6 W.I.R. 399.
87 *Moonan v. Moonan* (1963) 7 W.I.R. 420.
88 Art 777, Civil Code Ch. 242. See on this *Lutchman Ramcoomarsingh v Administrator General* (2002) 61 W.I.R. 525
89 See *Moonan v. Moonan supra.* See also *Heyliger v. Burgess* [1931-37] L.R.B.G. 507
90 [1857-60] All E.R. 610.
91 (1868) L.R. 1 P & D 481 p.482.
92 *In the Estate of Chintaman Maharaj* H.C.A. No. 4315/1982 (Trinidad & Tobago); *Sin Young Chin and Anor. v. Catherine Kelly and Ors.* (1968) 12 W.I.R. 429; *Re Browne, Robinson v. Sandiford* (1963) 5 W.I.R. 505; *Owen v. Bissoondath, Bernet, Davis, Gafoor, Bissoondath*

H.C.A. 229/1979 (Trinidad & Tobago); *Goddard v. Jack* (1959-62) 1 W.I.R. 169; *Ali v. Zaman and Neisha* (1969) Law Rep. of Guyana 612.
93 *Straker v. Luke* (1974) L.R.B.G. 187.
94 *Hall v. Hall* (1868) L.R. I P & D 481.
95 [1872] L.R. 2 P & D 462 See also *Wingrove v. Wingrove* (1885) 11 P & D 81 at 83 where Sir James Hannen observed: To be undue influence in the eyes of the law, there must be, . . to sum it up in a word. . . coercion. The coercion may of course be of different kinds, it may be in the grossest form, such as actual confinement or violence, or a person in the last days or hours of life may have become so weak and feeble, that a very little pressure will he sufficient to bring about the desired result, and it may even be that the mere talking to him at that stage of illness and pressing something upon him may so fatigue the brain, that the sick person may be induced, for quietness' sake, to do anything.

2

Wills cont'd.
Revocation, Alteration, Rectification, Republication, Revival of Wills

REVOCATION OF WILLS

Statute prescribes the modes by which revocation of a will may be effected. These are as follows:

- by an attested document executed with the same formalities as are needed for the making of a will;
- by destruction;
- by subsequent marriage;
- by informal declaration;
- by divorce or annulment.

A.   Revocation by Attested Document[1]

All jurisdictions (save St Lucia)

According to the relevant statutory provisions of the various territories a will may be revoked by another will or codicil or by some writing declaring an intention to revoke the same and executed in the manner in which a will is required to be executed. Revocation of a will can therefore be effected not only by a later will or codicil but also by some writing which is neither a will nor a codicil but which is executed in the same manner as a will.

St Lucia

Art 828 (1) and (2) Civil Code Ch. 242 is of the same practical effect.[2] Art 828 provides that wills cannot be revoked by the testator except:

- by means of a subsequent will revoking them either expressly or by the nature of his disposition; or
- by means of a notarial or other written act, by which a change of intention is expressly stated.

Intention to Revoke

All Jurisdictions

However whether the will is revoked by another will, a codicil or some other document, there must be the intention to revoke — what is otherwise called *animus revocandi*. This intention may be expressed or implied:

(i) *Express Revocation:* An express revocation arises where a latter will contains a revocation clause—a clause which is usually inserted at the beginning of a will stating that the testator revokes all former will. It usually reads as follows:

> I hereby revoke all former wills and testamentary dispositions made by me and declare this to be my last will and testament.

Where there is a revocation clause in a will or codicil there is a presumption that the testator intended to revoke his earlier will or wills. This presumption is rebuttable by evidence of a contrary intention but the onus of proof which is required to displace this presumption is heavy.[3] Although strong, the presumption can nevertheless be rebutted in the following cases:

- where a contrary intention can be proved or shown;[4]
- where the revocation clause was inserted in the will by mistake.[5]
- where the doctrine of conditional revocation or dependent relative revocation applies.[6]

(ii) *Implied Revocation:*[7] Implied revocation arises where a later will or codicil contains no revocation clause but its provisions are inconsistent with an earlier will or codicil. In such cases, the earlier will or codicil is impliedly revoked by the later will or codicil, in so far as the latter contains provisions inconsistent with the former. An earlier will can be totally or partially revoked by implication. If the provisions of the later will are wholly inconsistent or repetitive, i.e. it deals with all the areas or matters dealt with in the earlier will, the earlier will is completely revoked, and only the later will will be admitted to probate. If on the other hand, some, but not all the provisions of the later will, are inconsistent with an earlier will, both or all of the testamentary documents will be admitted to probate, as together constituting the last will of the testator.[8] As was observed in *Townsend v. Moore*,[9] a person can die with only one will and in cases where there is partial revocation of an earlier will, all the

(iii) *Problem of Undated Wills.* Where two or more testamentary documents contain no revocation clause, have inconsistent provisions and one, both or all are undated, the court will endeavour as far as possible to construe the words of both or all the documents if more than two, so that they may stand together and be admitted to proof as expressing together the whole intention of the testator.[10] If however, one, both or all of the testamentary documents contain a revocation clause and the priority of the documents cannot be determined, none will be admitted to probate and the testator will be deemed to have died intestate.[11]

B. Revocation by Destruction[12]

All Jurisdictions (save St Lucia)

Statute provides that a will can be revoked by burning, tearing or otherwise destroying either by the testator or by someone in his presence and by his direction with the intention of revoking same.

St Lucia - Holograph and English wills

Pursuant to Art 828(3) Civil Code Ch. 242 wills and legacies may be revoked by means of the destruction, tearing or erasure of a holograph or English will, deliberately effected by the testator or by his order.

What constitutes Revocation by Destruction

To constitute an effective revocation by destruction:

(a) there must be a physical act of destruction;
(b) this act must be done by the testator or, by someone under his direction and with the exception of St Lucia, in his presence; and
(c) the act must be coupled with an intention by the testator to revoke.

(a) Physical Act of Destruction

There must be an actual and not merely a symbolic burning, tearing or otherwise destroying. Thus writing the words revoked or cancelled on the face of the will is not an act of destruction within the meaning of statute.[13] But while there must be some actual burning, tearing or otherwise destroying it is not necessary that the testator should tear up the will into pieces or completely burn it. What is required is that there must be a destruction of so much of it as to impair the entirety of the will. If a part of a will necessary for its validity is torn off or burnt such as the signature of the testator and or of the witnesses, this will be deemed to be a sufficient destruction within the meaning of the statute.[14]

(b) *Must be effected by the testator or by someone in his presence and by his direction*

The act of destruction must be effected by the testator or by someone acting under his directions and with the exception of St Lucia,[15] in his presence. The requirement that the act of physical destruction must be done in the presence of the testator and by his directions has been construed strictly.

Thus where a will was destroyed in the kitchen while the testatrix was in her bedroom, it was held that the statutory requirements were not complied with as the act of destroying the will was done at the testatrix's directions, but was not effected in her presence.[16]

It should also be noted as was stated *Re Booth, Booth v. Booth*[17] that if a destruction of the will is effected without the authority of the testator he cannot thereafter ratify it.

(c) *The testator must have the intention to revoke.*

The testator must have the intention to revoke and this intention must accompany the act of revocation. The following case law is instructive on this point — In *Brunt v. Brunt*[18] — where the testator who was suffering from an attack of delirium tremens tore up the will into small pieces; *In the Goods of Brassington*[19] — where the testator tore up his will in drunken stupor and In *Giles v. Warren*[20] - where the testator tore up will under the false impression that it was invalid — the wills were all admitted to probate. A common thread running through these cases, is that the testator picked up the pieces of the will and kept them and they were found after his death. Accordingly, in all these cases the statutory intention to revoke was held to be absent.

Meaning of Otherwise Destroying

All jurisdictions (save St Lucia)

The case of *Stephens v. Taprell*[1] is instructive on the statutory meaning of 'otherwise destroying'. In that case the testator struck through the body of his will with a pen. The attestation clause, names of the witnesses and name of the testator were also crossed out. The court was called upon to decide whether cancellation was equivalent to destroying within the meaning of s.20 of the Wills Act 1837. The court held that in common parlance it was, and that the will would have been so treated prior to the enactment of the 1837 Wills Act. However the court took the view that the term 'otherwise destroying' must have been inserted in the 1837 provision to mean a mode of destruction *ejusdem generis,* not an act which is not a destroying in the primary meaning of the word though it may have the sense metaphorically as being a destruction of the contents of the will. To further strengthen the court's interpretation of 'otherwise destroying' so as to exclude any form of cancellation, it was pointed out that the bill to the Wills Act 1837 as originally introduced, included the word cancelling, but this word was excluded when the bill was eventually passed and became law.

A modern case which illustrates the meaning of the term otherwise destroying is the case of *Re Adams (deceased)*[22] in which it was held that:

> Where a material part such as the signature of the testator and/or that of the attesting witnesses of a will or other testamentary documents is obliterated to an extent that that part of will is not apparent to experts using magnifying glasses, if necessary to decipher it but without physically interfering with the document, such a will is deemed to be revoked within the meaning 'otherwise destroying'.

St Lucia

According to Art 828(3) Civil Code Ch. 242, erasure constitutes a method of destruction. Although Art 828(3) does not specify the extent or manner of erasure it is submitted that:

(a) the erasure of some party of the deceased's will necessary for its validity such as erasure of the testator's signature and or those of the witnesses is sufficient, and that,
(b) the obliteration thereof as occurred in *Re Adams (deceased)*[23] would also constitute erasure which the meaning of Art 823(3).

Lost Wills

Where a will was last known to be in the possession of the testator but it cannot be found when he dies, there is a presumption that the testator destroyed it *animus revocandi*. This presumption can be rebutted by evidence to the contrary.[24]

Further a will which has been in the testator's possession but which is found to be mutilated at his death is presumed to be mutilated by the testator with the intention of revoking it in whole or in part. This presumption may also be rebutted by evidence to the contrary.[25]

St Lucia

By virtue of Art 797 Civil Code Ch. 242, where a will has been lost or accidentally destroyed, probate may be granted of the contents thereof upon proof of such contents and of the formalities required for execution and of the facts which render production of the will impossible. However if it appears that the testator knew of and acquiesced in the loss or destruction of the will, such will is deemed to have been revoked.[26]

C. Revocation by Marriage[27]

As a general rule marriage automatically revokes any will made by either party to the marriage, prior to the marriage.[28] This is an involuntary revocation and it is the only act which effects a revocation of the testator's will without the testator's intention and sometimes even contrary to his intention.

However for marriage to revoke a will, the marriage must be a valid marriage. This point was made in the case of *Mette v. Mette*[29] where it was held that a void marriage does not effect an involuntary revocation because it is treated in law as never having taken place. Avoidable marriage however revokes a will made prior to the marriage whether or not the marriage is subsequently annulled, because, the annulment of a voidable marriage is not retroactive in effect. There is therefore, until annulment, a valid marriage for the purpose of revoking any prior wills.

To this rule that marriage revokes an earlier will there are the following exceptions:

(i) *Wills expressed to be made in contemplation of marriage.*

Barbados and Trinidad & Tobago

In order to come within this exception, the will must be expressed to be made in contemplation of a particular marriage and must be followed by the solemnization of that marriage. So if a testator made a will in contemplation of his marriage to 'A', he must marry 'A' for the will to be valid. If he marries 'B' the will will be revoked. It is not sufficient to contemplate marriage in general. If for instance the testator says in his will that it is made in contemplation of marriage this is not sufficient.

The will must not only be made in contemplation of a particular marriage,[30] it must also be expressed to be so made. In *Re Langston*[31] the word 'fiancee' and in *Re Knight* unreported and mentioned in *Re Langston* the words 'my future wife' though not conclusive were held to be strong evidence that the will was expressed to be so made.[32] As was stated by Megarry J. in *Re Coleman, Coleman v. Coleman*,[33] the whole of the will must be expressed to be made in contemplation of the marriage and not merely a particular gift whether that gift is substantial or trivial. This decision has been criticised, and this decision is no longer good law in England with respect to wills made on or after 1st January, 1983.[34]

(ii) *Wills made in expectation of marriage*

St Vincent & the Grenadines

According to s.20(4) of the Wills Act Cap. 384[35] with respect to wills made on or after 27th December, 1989, if it appears from a will that at the time it was made, the testator was expecting to be married to a particular person and that he intended that a disposition in the will should not be revoked by his marriage to that person:

(i) the disposition shall take effect notwithstanding the marriage; and

(ii) any other disposition in the will shall take effect also, unless it appears from the will that the testator intended the disposition to be revoked by the marriage.

(iii) Wills made in exercise of a Power of Appointment
All jurisdictions (save St Lucia)

Marriage revokes a will made prior thereto unless the will was made in exercise of a power of appointment under which the wife, issue or other person entitled to benefit on an intestacy, would not be so entitled in default of such appointment.[36]

(iv) Marriage in Extremis
Anguilla Dominica, Montserrat, St Christopher & Nevis and Trinidad &Tobago[37]

In the above territories a will made prior to the solemnization of a death bed marriage or marriage in extremis is not revoked by such marriage.

D. Revocation by Divorce/Annulment

St Lucia[38] *and St Vincent & the Grenadines*[39] *and The Bahamas*[40]

According to the relevant provisions of the above territories where, after a testator has made a will, a decree of the court dissolves or annuls his marriage or declares it void:
  (a) the will takes effect notwithstanding the divorce or annulment; and
  (b) any other disposition in the will takes effect unless it appears from the will that the testator intended the disposition to be revoked by the divorce or annulment.

E. Revocation by Informal Declaration

All jurisdictions (save Grenada, Jamaica and Trinidad & Tobago)

A person who is entitled to make a privileged will[41] may informally revoke a will. This informal revocation can be either of a formal or informal procedure torn at the time of revocation the person is entitled to make a privileged will.

F. Other Revocation Instances

St. Lucia

Art 829 Civil Code Ch. 242 St Lucia provides other instances in which a will or legacy may be revoked.

These include:

(a) on the ground of conspiracy of the legatee in the death of the testator;
(b) by reason of grievous injury done to the testator's memory;
(c) instances where the legatee rendered the revocation or modification of the will.

Conditional Revocation

In order to revoke a will, the testator must have the intention to revoke or the *animus revocandi*. The intention may be absolute or conditional. If it is absolute the revocation will take effect immediately. If it is conditional the revocation will not take effect unless the condition is fulfilled.

For example a testator may revoke his will intending to make a new one but then it turns out that the new will is invalid or was never made at all.[42] Depending on the facts which come to light, the court will treat the revocation as dependant or conditional on the validity of the new will or the making of the new one and if this was not done, the original will remains unrevoked.

Another example of conditional revocation arises where a testator destroys his will under the mistaken belief that he is thereby reviving an earlier will. Depending on the circumstances the court may treat the revocation as conditional on the revival of the earlier will.

Still another example can be found in *Re Estate of Southerden's Estate Adam v. Southerden*[43] where the testator made a will giving all his property to his wife. He later burnt it intending to revoke it believing that his wife will be entitled to all his property on intestacy. The Court of Appeal held that the will was not revoked.

Whether the testator's intention to revoke his will was conditional or absolute is a question of fact, and in cases of revocation by destruction, evidence of the testator's declarations of intention at the time of revocation is admissible.

Where however the revocation is by will, codicil or duly executed writing, it is a question of construction and extrinsic evidence is only admissible in cases where it is allowed to assist in the interpretation of the document.

ALTERATIONS OF WILLS[44]

Meaning of alterations

Alterations are changes made in the original dispositions as contained in the testamentary instrument of the testator. Alterations can be in the nature of:

- an interlineation—words or figures written between lines and includes words or figures inserted on the lines or carried in by a cross or asterisk.
- an obliteration—where words of a will have been blotted out or by inking over or by covering with a strip of paper so as to make them no longer apparent within the meaning of statute.[45] There may be a total obliteration of a gift in a will or a partial obliteration and where there is an obliteration whether total or partial there may be other words or figures written over or substituted for the obliterated words.
- an erasure - erasures may be of such a nature that the words before the erasure are still apparent or they may be of such a nature that the words are no longer apparent within the meaning of statute.[46]

ALTERATIONS - WHEN MADE

Alterations made Prior to Execution

Where alterations are made in a testamentary instrument prior to its execution, execution of such alterations is not necessary and the will takes effect as altered. However, the difficulty which arises with respect to such alterations is this - how do you prove that an alteration was made prior to execution, as opposed to after execution, bearing in mind that there is a rebuttable presumption in law that unattested alterations appearing in a will are deemed to be made subsequent to its execution?

Unattested Alterations — **Rebuttal of Presumption**

The presumption that unattested alterations were made after execution can be rebutted from:

(i)   internal evidence, that is, from the will itself; or
(ii) by external evidence.
      (i)   Internal Evidence

      In so far as internal evidence is concerned, the presumption may be rebutted if it can be shown that without the alterations the will would not make sense e.g. if the will was originally written or printed with blanks and those blanks have been filled in they may be accepted as having been completed or filled in prior to execution.[47] The presumption can also be rebutted if it can be shown that the alterations were written in the same hand and with the same ink as the rest of the document.

(ii) External Evidence

As far as external evidence is concerned, the presumption maybe rebutted by direct proof from an attesting witness or someone present at the time of execution that the alteration had been made prior to execution or by evidence from the person who prepared the will that the will contained these alterations prior to execution. The presumption can also be rebutted by declarations made by the testator before or at the time of execution. Declarations made subsequent to execution are not however admissible.[48] The presumption may be further rebutted by showing that the testator knew the statutory requirements and would have therefore complied with same. This would be applicable where for example a lawyer prepares his own will.[49]

Affidavit as to Alterations

Where unattested alterations appear in a will an attesting witness or other person present at the time of execution is required to depose on affidavit that the alteration were made prior to the execution of the will in order for those alterations to be admitted to probate.[50]

It should be noted that the presumption that unattested alterations were made after execution does not apply to immaterial alterations or alterations of no practical importance, for example, where addresses of beneficiaries are filled in.

Alterations made after execution

Alterations made after execution are only admitted to proof if they are duly executed and statute provides for the way in which such alterations are to be executed. These are:

(a) by re-execution of the entire will or codicil in the same manner required by statute for the making of a will or codicil;[51] or
(b) by execution of the individual alterations in accordance with the relevant statutory provisions of the respective Caribbean territory.

Where the second method is adopted, the signature of the testator and the subscription of two witnesses must appear either in the margin or some part of the will opposite to or neat to such alteration or at the end of or opposite to a memorandum referring to such alteration and written at the foot or at the end of or some other part of the will.[52]

According to case law authority witnesses and the testator may initial the alteration rather than sign their names.[53] The witnesses and the testator must both either sign or initial their names to the alteration made after execution of a will.[54]

Where alterations are made after execution and those alterations are not duly executed, the will will be admitted to probate with those words omitted. However if the original words written are apparent, the will will be admitted to practice with those words included.

The meaning of apparent

Words are apparent within the meaning of the statute if they can be read from the face of the instrument by natural means, for example, by the assistance of a handwriting expert or by the use of a magnifying glass. However it is not permissible to ascertain the words by the use of extrinsic evidence, for example, the evidence of a draftsman is not admissible to prove what the obliterated words were. It is also not permissible to interfere with the will physically so as to render clear what may have been written, for example, by using chemicals to remove ink marks or removing a slip of paper pasted over it.[55] However it was held in *In the Goods of Gilbert*[56] that a slip of paper may be removed in order to ascertain whether it covers words of revocation which took effect before being covered. Finally, it is not permissible to ascertain the words by using infra red equipment.

Barbados

Although the word 'apparent' is not used in s.70 of the Succession Act Cap. 249 or The Supreme Court (Non Contentious) Probate Rules 1959, Barbados, r.20 thereof provides that only words or figures which are not entirely erased or obliterated may form part of the probate.

Conditional Revocation

Physical interference with the will is permitted where the doctrine of conditional revocation applies. According to this doctrine if the testator makes alterations which are invalid and these alterations render the original words no longer apparent within the meaning of stature and the court is satisfied that the ineffective alteration was referable solely to the testator's intention to substitute those other words of alteration for the original words only on condition that such substitution was effective, the courts may restore the original words in the application for probate by permitting physical interference with the document.[57]

However for the doctrine to apply the following is necessary:

(a) the alteration must be in the nature of an obliteration which renders the original words no longer apparent within the meaning of the statute;
(b) there must be only a partial obliteration, so that if the complete gift, that is, both the name of the beneficiary and the property devised or bequeathed are obliterated, the doctrine will not apply; and
(c) there must be words or a gift in substitution.

However, it is to be noted that even where these preconditions exist the court will nor give effect to the doctrine if it is satisfied that to do so will defeat the testator's intention. In the case of *In the Estate of Zimmer*[58] the words obliterated were no longer apparent and could only be deciphered by the use of infra red photographs. The court held that the doctrine was not applicable as the evidence available from the surrounding circumstances that is, the statement of intent made by the testatrix at the time of the alteration showed that it was not her intention that the original words were to be restored if the words substituted proved to be ineffectual.

RECTIFICATION OF WILLS

Eastern Caribbean (save St Lucia) and The Bahamas[59]

In circumstances where the court is satisfied that a will is so expressed that it fails to carry out the testator's intention, in consequence of a clerical error or of a failure to understand the testator's instructions, it may order that the will be rectified so as to carry out his intentions.

Except with leave of the court, an application for an order for rectification is requited to be made no later than six months, and in the case of The Bahamas, no later than 12 months, from the date on which representation of the estate of the deceased is first taken out.

Prior to the application for rectification a notice in writing must be given to all persons having an interest in the will whose interest might be thereby prejudiced:

- notifying such persons of the intended application; and
- calling upon such persons to submit their written comment, if any, to the application by a specified date including any grounds which such person may have for opposing the application for rectification.

Application for Rectification

A. Practice and Procedure

According to r.55 N.C.P.R. 1987, England, unless a probate action has commenced, an application for rectification may be made *ex parte* to a Registrar. However the practice in the Eastern Caribbean territories and The Bahamas in non-contentious probate matters, other than applications for general grants of representation, is to apply to a judge in chambers.

Contents of Affidavit

Pursuant to r.55(2) N.C.P.R 1987, England, the affidavit should set out:

(i) the grounds of the application;
(ii) the evidence, if any, as to the testator's intentions;
(iii) such evidence that can be adduced as to the nature of the alleged clerical error or otherwise in what respect the testator's intentions were not understood; and
(iv) that notice in writing of the application for rectification has been given to such persons having an interest under the will and whose interest might be prejudiced by the rectification applied for. (A copy of the notice in writing should be exhibited to the affidavit).

Comments in writing

In addition, the comments in writing of any such person mentioned above must be exhibited to the affidavit.

Order for Rectification

Once the Judge/Registrar is satisfied that requisite notice has been given and that the application is unopposed, the order for rectification will be granted. Otherwise an application for an order for rectification will have to be made on motion in open court.

B. Liability of Personal Representative(s)

It is to be noted that a personal representative will not be liable for having distributed any part of the deceased's estate after the end of the six month period from the date on which representation was first taken out, on the ground that such personal representative ought to have taken into account the possibility the court might have permitted an application for one side for rectification after the end of that period. However this in no way prejudices the power to recover any part of the estate so distributed.

Observations

Rectification of wills highlights once again the difficulty and uncertainty created by the so called reception provision of the various Eastern Caribbean territories. According to s.11 of the respective Supreme Court Acts of these territories, not only is English probate practice and procedure received in these territories, but more significantly English probate law, where no special provisions are contained in the indigenous legislation of these territories.[60]

In the absence of indigenous legislation, indigenous practice directions, and any comprehensive judicial or legislative interpretation of the scope and intent of s.11 and in particular the meaning, intent and scope of 'probate law' one is left to conclude that rectification of wills as provided for by s.20 of the Administration of Justice Act 1982, England extends to these territories. This submission is particularly troubling in the case of Dominica, which may be deemed to receive the Administration of Justice Act 1982, England, but not the N.C.P.R. 1987 which sets out the practice and procedure with respect to rectification of will.[61]

The Bahamas

It is to be noted, pursuant to s.31(6), Wills Act 2002 the rectification of wills is not applicable to the will of a testator dying before February 1, 2002, the commencement date of the Wills Act, 2002.

REPUBLICATION OF WILLS

Republication of a will operates to substitute the date of republication for the original date of the will so that the will with the alterations made thereto speaks and takes effect from the date of its confirmation rather than the date of its original execution.

In this regard, republication is effected either:

(a) by the re-execution of the original will; or
(b) by the making of a duly executed codicil to the will containing some reference to the will.

The following should be noted:

- whether the republication is effected by re-execution or by codicil the changes introduced will not be given effect if to do so would be contrary to the testator's intention.[62]
- the fact of re-execution of the original will raises a presumption that the testator intended to republish his will although that

presumption may be rebutted.[63]
- every codicil is *prima facie* a republication of the testator's will unless a contrary intention can be shown.[64]
- in order to republish a will it is not necessary to use express words of republication as in the case *Re Champion, Dudley v. Champion*,[65] where the testator wrote in his codicil 'I confirm my will in all other respects.'
- neither is it necessary for the codicil to contain any direct reference to the will which it republishes. However the codicil must at least impliedly bear some reference to the will it republishes even if not by date then by some other reference, for example, to the executors.[66]

Purpose of Republication

Prior to the 1837 Wills Act, England a will could not dispose of real property acquired between the date when the will was made and the time of the testator's death. As a consequence, the practice of republishing one's will became fairly common so as to ensure that real property acquired after execution formed part of one's estate at the time of death and would not pass by the common law doctrine of descent to the heir-at-law.

However with the passage of the Wills Act 1837, the main purpose of republication was no longer relevant as real property was now treated in the same manner as personal property in that both were now ambulatory in nature. However, the doctrine has retained some importance in the following circumstances:

- Republication validates a will which was not valid at the rime of execution due to want of formalities and/or because of the testator's unsoundness of mind. This is provided that the will or codicil is duly executed and the testator has recovered his testamentary capacity at the rime when the will is republished.
- Republication can also save a gift made to a witness or the spouse of that witness which would otherwise be void. Again this is provided the re-execution of the will or the codicil thereto is not attested to by that class of witness.[67]
- Republication of a will can validate unattested alterations but if the will is republished by a codicil, the codicil must refer to those unattested alterations otherwise the presumption is that they were made both after the will and the codicil which republishes it.[68]
- Republication of a will permits a document which is referred to

in the testator's will though nor in existence at the time of its original execution to be incorporated into and form part of the will and thus be admitted to probate.[69]
- Republication can also alter the construction of the testator's will so as to save a gift that would otherwise fail due to the operation of:

    (i) the doctrine of ademption; and
    (ii) the doctrine of lapse.

Doctrine of Ademption - According to the doctrine of ademption, a gift is treated as adeemed and fails if it is no longer the property of the testator or if he no longer has power to dispose of it, even if there is another gift answering that same description at the time of the testator's death. This doctrine relates only to specific gifts. So if T give to A his Toshka Roadking car and T subsequently sells it and acquires another Toshka Roadking car, T's gift to A will be adeemed. If however, the second Toshka Roadking was acquired prior to the republication of the will, A will get the second Toshka Roadking car.[70]

Doctrine of Lapse — Lapse arises where a beneficiary under a will predeceases the testator. Subject to certain statutory and common law exceptions, when this occurs, the gift to that beneficiary lapses and therefore fails. There again republication of the will can sufficiently alter the construction of the will so as to prevent the doctrine of lapse from operating. The case of *Re Hardyman Teesdale v. McClintock*[71] is instructive on this point. According to the facts of that case the testatrix left a gift to 'the wife of my first cousin'. The wife then died and the testatrix executed a codicil to her will. At the time of execution of the codicil the testatrix knew that the wife had died. The cousin subsequently remarried before the testatrix's death. It was held that the word 'wife' was used in the general sense and wife of the first cousin was deemed to refer to the wife in existence at the date of republication.

REVIVAL OF WILLS

Whereas republication brings forward in time a will which has remained valid throughout, revival on the other hand is the restoration to effect or 'the bringing back to life' as it were of a will or codicil which has been revoked. As with republication, a revived will takes effect as if it had been executed not on its original date but on the dare of its revival.

Statute prescribed the method by which a will may be revived. For a valid revival there must be:

(1) an act of revival; and
(2) the intention to revive.

Act of revival

Save and except for St Lucia, each territory has a statutory provision dealing with revival which prescribes the methods of revival. It is the same as for republication, that is, re-execution of the original will or the making of a properly executed codicil.[72]

Intention to revive

Whether the revival is by re-execution of the will or the execution of a codicil, statute requires that an intention to revive the will must be shown.[73] Where the revival is by codicil, the intention to revive must appear on the face of the codicil. This can be satisfied by the following:

- by express words referring to the will as having been revoked and expressing at the same time an intention to revive same.[74]
- by dispositions of the testator's property inconsistent with any other intention[75] — for example, testator makes a will in 1988 and leaves all his property to B. He revokes the will in 1989 because he has a quarrel with B. He then parches up things with B. In 1990 he makes a codicil referring to the 1988 will expressing an intention that B should have all his property. This will be treated by the court as a clear intention in 1990 to revive the 1988 will in which he in fact left all his property to B.
- by some other expression conveying to the mind of the court with reasonable certainty the existence of that intention.[76] *In the Goods of Davis*,[77] the deceased wrote on an envelope, in which he kept a will revoked by his marriage to the sole beneficiary, the following words: The herein named (executrix and sole beneficiary) is now my lawful wedded wife.

Those words were duly signed and attested. It was held that in view of the attendant circumstances the writing on the envelope constituted a codicil. The will was accordingly revived and both documents were admitted to probate.

Nature of Evidence: Evidence of intention is not limited to the face of the document but can be gathered from the surrounding circumstances. Save and except for St Vincent & the Grenadines and Barbados[78] the only form of evidence that is admissible is indirect evidence, that is, evidence of surrounding circumstances.[79] Direct evidence of the testator's intention — for example, things the testator actually said or wrote are inadmissible, except in Barbados and St Vincent & the Grenadines.

The court requires stronger evidence of revival as opposed to republication of a will. This makes sense because in a case of revival as opposed to republication what the testator is saying is that he wants to revive a revoked will—a will he previously did not want to take effect. As a result the court must be satisfied that this is in fact the testator's intention.

Existence of the document

Although this is not expressly provided by statute, it is a pre-condition to revival that the document to be revived—the revoked will—must be in existence at the time of revival. As a result if the testator physically destroys his will, for example, by burning it, the codicil irrespective of the clarity of its intention cannot effect a revival of the revoked will.[80]

St Lucia

In the absence of statutory provision governing the methods of effecting a revival of a will, it may be argued that the pre-statutory position is applicable, and accordingly it may be possible to revive a will by mere implication in St Lucia.[81]

Revocation of a Revoking Document does not Effect a Revival of an Earlier Will.[82]

With the exception of St Lucia, where a will has been revoked by a later will and that later will is subsequently revoked, the revocation of that later will does nor have the effect of reviving the earlier will. However according to the doctrine of conditional revocation, if the revocation of a later will is effected for the purpose of reviving an earlier will, then revocation of that later will may be treated as conditional, the condition not being fulfilled (the condition being the revival of the will) the second or later will, will be treated as not having been revoked. But there must be clear evidence that the testator intended the later will to be treated as not having been revoked. This is nor a question of construction but a question of fact. In such a case the court will admit direct, as well as indirect evidence of the testator's intention so that oral declarations and written statements of the testator are admissible in evidence.

St Lucia

Art. 832 of the Civil Code, Ch. 242 in St Lucia states that:

In the absence of express dispositions, the circumstances and the indications of the intention of the testator determine whether upon the revocation of a will which revokes another will, the former will revives.

Accordingly, a former will may be revived by revocation of a later will.

Importance of Revival

The importance of revival is basically the same as republication that is:

- revival can validate unattested alterations made before the date of execution.
- revival can incorporate a document coming into existence after the will was executed but before the date of revival.
- revival can also validate a gift otherwise void because a witness to the will or codicil is a beneficiary. This is provided the re-execution thereof is not attested to by the witness/beneficiary.

Notes

1. Anguilla,   - s.20 Wills Act Cap. 84
   St Christopher & Nevis
   Antigua & Barbuda - s.20 Wills Act Cap. 473
   Barbados   - s.69(2) Succession Act Cap. 249
   Dominica   - s.21 Wills Act Chap. 9:01
   Grenada   - s.15 Wills Act Cap. 340
   Guyana   - s.20 Wills Act 1837, England by virtue of s.7 Civil Law of Guyana Act Cap. 6:01
   Jamaica   - s.15 Wills Act
   Montserrat   - s.20 Wills Act Cap. 34
   St Lucia   - Art 828 (1) Art 828 (2) Art 830, 831 Civil Code Ch. 242
   St Vincent and
      The Grenadines - s.23 Wills Act Cap. 384
   The Bahamas   - s.16(b) and (c) Wills Act 2002
   Trinidad & Tobago - s.47 Wills & Probate Ordinance Ch. 8 No. 2.
2. See also Arts 830, 831 Civil Code Ch. 242.
3. *Re Wayland's Estate* [1951] 2 All E.R. 1041; *Re Cotton* (1965-1970) 2 L.R.B.G. 61 See by contrast *Re Thompson v. Hoo Seung* (1964) 6 W.I.R. 220 and *Lowthorpe-Lutwidge v. Lowthorpe-Lutwidge* [1935] P. 151, [1935] 3 All E.R. 338.
4. *Re Wayland's Estate* above.
5. *In the Goods of Brown* [1942] 2 All E.R. 176.
6. See pp. 53-54.
7. St Lucia - See Art 830 Civil Code Ch. 242 which provides that a subsequent will or notarial act which does not revoke the preceding one in an express manner, annuls only those dispositions which are at variance with it.

8   *Lemage v. Goodban* (1865) L.R. 1 P & D 57 P.66 at p.71.
9   [1905] P.66.
10 *Townsend v. Moore,* [1905] p.66 at 80 per Vaughn Williams L.J.
11 Ibid., 85.
12 Anguilla,   - s.20 Wills Act Cap. 84
    St Christopher & Nevis
    Antigua & Barbuda - s.20 Wills Acts Cap. 473
    Dominica   - s.21 Wills Act Chap. 9:01
    Grenada   - s.15 Wills Act Cap. 340
    Guyana   - s.20 Wills Act 1837, England (pursuant to s.7 Civil Law of Guyana
                           Act Cap. 6:01)
    Jamaica   - s.15 Wills Act
    Montserrat   - s.18 Wills Act Cap. 84
    St. Lucia   - Art 828(3) Ch. 242 See also Art 797 Ch. 242
    St Vincent & the   - s.23 Wills Act Cap. 384
      Grenadines
    The Bahamas   - s.16(d) Wills Act 2002
    Trinidad & Tobago - s.48 Wills & Probate Ordinance Ch. 8 No. 2.
13 *Stephens v. Taprell* (1840) 2 Curt 459 163 E.R. 475; *Cheese v. Lovejoy* (1877) 2 P & D 251.
14 *In the Goods of Morton* (1887) 12 P & D 141; *Hobbs v. Knight* (1838) 1 Curt. 769.
15 See p. 48.
16 *In the Goods of Dadds* (1857) Dea & Sw 290; 164 E.R. 579.
17 [1926] P.118 at 132.
18 (1873) L.R. 3 P&D 37.
19 [1902] P.1.
20 (1872) L.R. 2 P&D 401.
21 (1840) 2 Curt. 459.
22 [1990] 2 All E.R. 97.
23 *Ibid.*
24 *Rodriguez v. Rodriguez* (1882-1916), Judgments delivered in the Supreme Court of Trinidad
    & Tobago Vol. II 299; *Re Booth, Booth v. Booth* [1926] P.118; *Sattar v. Dass* (1990) 44
    W.I.R. 257; *Re Webb, Smith v. Johnson* [1964] 2 All E.R. 91; *Re Sargeant* (1975) 27 W.I.R.
    40; *Olga Appiah and Others v. Winifred Hookumchand and Another*(1972) 18 W.I.R. 244.
25 *Ibid.*; See also *In the Goods of Lewis* (1858) 1 Sw. & Tr. 31. See also chapter 5, p. 119-120,
    with respect to affidavit of plight, condition and appearance.
26 See also Art 828(3) Civil Code Ch. 242.
27 Anguilla   - s.18 Wills Act Cap. 87
    Antigua & Barbuda - s.18 Wills Act Cap. 473
    Barbados   - s.69 Succession Act Cap. 249
    Dominica   - s.19 Wills Act Ch. 901
    Grenada   - s.13 Wills Act Cap. 340
    Guyana   - s.18 Wills Act 1837 England pursuant to s.7 of the Civil Law of
                           Guyana Act Cap. 6:01
    Jamaica   - s.13 Wills Act
    Montserrat   - s.18 Wills Act Cap. 84
    St Christopher &   - Art 829 Civil Code Ch. 242
      Nevis, St Lucia

St Vincent & the   - s.20 Wills Act Cap. 384
Grenadines
The Bahamas   - s.13 WIlls Act, 2002
Trinidad & Tobago - s.48(1) Wills & Probate Ordinance Ch. 8 No. 2.
28 *Israell v. Rodan* (1774-1923) Vol. 2 Stephens Law Reports 2124 (Supreme Court decision of Jamaica).
29 (1859) 1 Sw & Tr 416.
30 *Sallis v. Jones* [1936] P.43.
31 [1953] 1 All E.R. 928.
32 See also *Williams v. Williams*(1953) Judgments delivered in the Supreme Court of Trinidad and Tobago, Vol. XIV 1953-1954 p.1; *Pilot v. Gainfort and Others* [1931] P.103.
33 [1976] Ch. 1. [1975]1 All E.R. 675.
34 See s.18 Administration of Justice Act 1982, England.
35 It is to be noted that the provisions of s.20 and s.13 respectively are identical to s.18 of the Administration of Justice Act 1982, England.
36 *All jurisdiction (save Trinidad & Tobago)* — According to the relevant provision of the various territories, this entitlement on an intestacy is based on the repealed English Statute of Distribution i.e. the pre 1926 — English intestacy rules. With respect to Trinidad & Tobago, s.48(2) is applicable to wills made on or after 1st January, 1928. As such the rules of distribution on an intestacy are in accordance with the rules of intestate distribution applicable to Trinidad & Tobago after that date.
37 Anguilla,   - s.18 Wills Act Cap. 84
St Christopher & Nevis
Antigua & Barbuda - s.18 Wills Act Cap. 473
Dominica   - s.19 Wills Act Ch. 9:01
St Lucia   - Art 829, Art 111 Civil Code Ch. 242
Trinidad & Tobago - s.48 The Wills & Probate Ordinance Ch. 8 No. 2.
38 See s.52 Divorce Act 1973 which amended Art 829 Civil Code Ch. 242 to include the word 'divorce'. See also *Kinneally v. Zazula* (1975) 26 W.I.R. 29.
39 Section 21 Wills Act Cap. 384.
40 Section 14 Wills Act, 2002.
41 Antigua & Barbuda - s.7 Wills Act Cap. 81
                      Wills (Soldiers and Sailors) Act Cap. 88
Barbados   - s.85 Succession Act Cap. 249
Dominica   - s.12Wills Act Ch. 9:01
Guyana   - s.11 Wills Act 1937, England pursuant to s.7 Civil Law of Guyana Act Cap. 6:01
St Christopher &   - Wills (Soldiers and Sailors) Act Cap. 85
Nevis, Anguilla
St Lucia   - Art 787 Civil Code Ch. 242
St Vincent &   - s.13 Wills Act Cap. 384
The Grenadines
The Bahamas   - s.39 Wills Act, 2002
42 *Powell v. Powell* [1866] L.R. 1 P & D 209; *Dixon v. Treasury Solicitor* [1905] P.42.
43 [1925] P. 177.
44   **Legislation**
Anguilla   - s.21 Wills Act Cap. 84

Antigua & Barbuda -	s.21 Wills Act Cap. 473
Barbados	- s.70 Succession Act 1975 Cap. 249
Dominica	- s.22 Wills Act Ch. 9:01
Grenada	- s.16 Wills Act Cap. 340
Guyana	- s.21 Wills Act 1837, England by virtue of s.7 Civil Code of Guyana Act Cap. 6:01
Montserrat	- s.21 Wills Act Cap. 84.
St Christopher & Nevis	- s.21 Wills Act Cap. 84
St Vincent & The Grenadines	- s.24 Wills Act Cap. 384
The Bahamas	- s.17 Wills 2002
Trinidad & Tobago -	s.51 Wills & Probate Ordinance Ch. 8 No. 2

Practice Directions

Jamaica	- Practice Directions of the Supreme Court, Jamaica dated 25th September, 1945, has been repealed and replaced by Rule 68.15 C.P.R. 2002

Rules

Barbados	- rr. 18, 19, 20. 21 The Supreme Court (Non-Contentious) Probate Rules 1959
Dominica, Guyana -	r.12 N.C.P.R 1954. England
Jamaica	- Rule 68.15 C.P.R., 2002 repealing and replacing rr. 9, 10, 11, 12 General Rules and Orders of the Supreme Court Part III Probate and Administration
St Lucia	- There are no statutory provisions or rules governing alteration of wills. However by virtue *inter alia* of s.11 of the Eastern Caribbean Supreme Court of Judicature (St Lucia) Act, r.14 N.C.P.R., 1987 England is received with respect to English and holograph wills
The Bahamas, Eastern Caribbean territories (save Dominica)	- r.14 N.C.P.R. 1987, England
Trinidad & Tobago -	rr. 16, 17. 18, 19 First Schedule N.C.B.R. Ch. 8 No.2.

45 See pp. 57-58.
46 *Ibid.*
47 *Greville v. Tylee* (1851) 7 Moo. P.C. 320.
48 *In the Goods of Syke* (1873) L.R. 3 P & D 26.
49 *In the Goods of Jacob* (1842) 1 Notes on Cases 401.

50 Barbados	- rr.19, 21 The Supreme Court (Non-Contentious) Probate Rules, 1959
Dominica, Guyana	- r.12(1) N.C.P.R., 1954, England
Eastern Caribbean/ (save Dominica) The Bahamas	- r.14(1) N.C.P.R., 1987, England

	Jamaica	- Rule 68.15 C.P.R., 2002 repealing and replacing rr. 10, 12 General Rules and Orders of the Supreme Court Part III Probate and Administration
	Trinidad & Tobago	- rr. 17, 19 First Schedule N.C.B.R. Ch. 8 No. 2.
51	Barbados	- rr. 18, 20 The Supreme Court (Non-Contentious) Probate Rules 1959
	Guyana/Dominica	- rr. 12(1) N.C.P.R., 1954 England
	Jamaica	- Rule 68.15 C.P.R., 2002 repealing and replacing rr. 9, 11 General Rules and Orders of the Supreme Court Part III Probate and Administration
	The Bahamas, Eastern Caribbean (save Dominica)	- r. 14(1) N.C.P.R., 1987 England
	Trinidad & Tobago	- rr. 16, 18 First Schedule N.C.B.R Ch. 8 No.2.

52 See note 44 above.
53 *In the the Goods of Blewitt* (1880) 5 P.D. 116.
54 *In the Goods of Dewell* (1853) 1 Ecc. & Ad. 103; *In the Goods of Shearn* (1880) 43 L.T. 736, 50 L.P.J. 15; *Re White, Barker v. Gribble and Another* Ch. 1, [1990] W.L.R. 187 [1990] 3 All E.R. 1; *In the Goods of Shearn* was applied and *In the Goods of Dewell* doubted.
55 *Ffinch v. Coombe* [1894] P. 191; *In the Goods of Brasier* [1899] P.35.
56 [1893] P. 183.
57 *Re Itter, Dedman v. Godfrey* [1950] P.130.
58 (1924) 40 T.L.R. 502.
59 Eastern Caribbean territories (save St. Lucia and St. Vincent and the Grenadines);- s.20 Administration of Justice Act 1982, England St Vincent & the Grenadines- s.37 Wills Act Cap. 384 (applicable to estates of persons dying on or after 27 December, 1989) Eastern Caribbean territories save St. Lucia -r.55. N.C.P.R. 1987, England, The Bahamas - Part III, Wills Act 2002
60 See Introduction p. 11.
61 See Introduction p. 11-12.
62 *Re Heath Will's Trust* [1949] 1 Ch. 170.
63 *Dunn v. Dunn* (1866) L.R. 1 P & D 277.
64 See *In the Goods of Steele* (1868) 1 P & D 575 where Sir J.P. Wilde, President of the Court observed at pp. 577-578 that 'The theory of the law is, and always was, that a codicil forms part of a will and consequently that to make a codicil to your will is first to affirm the existence of that will and secondly to republish or reaffirm its validity'.
65 [1893] 1 Ch. 101.
66 *Re Smith, Bilke v. Roper* [1890] 45 Ch.D. 632.
67 *Kitkat v. King* [1930] P. 266; *Re Trotter* [1899] 1 Ch. 764.
68 *In the Goods of Heath* (1892) P.253; *In the Goods of Hall* (1871) L.R. 2 P.D. 256; *In the Goods of Sykes* [1873] L.R. 3 P.D. 26.
69 *In the Goods of Lady Truro* (1866) L.R. 1 P.D. 201.
70 *Re Reeves, Reeves v. Pawson* [1928] Ch. 351; *Re Champion, Dudley v. Champion* [1893] 1 Ch. 101.
71 [1925] Ch. 287.

72	Anguilla, St Christopher & Nevis	- s.22 Wills Act Cap 84
	Antigua & Barbuda	- s.22 Wills Act Cap 473

Barbados	- s.71 Succession Act Cap 249
Dominica	- s.23 Wills Act Ch 9:01
Grenada	- s.17 Wills Act Cap 340
Guyana	- s.22 Wills Act 1837, England pursuant to s.7 of the Civil Law of Guyana Act Cap. 6:01
Jamaica	- s.17 Wills Act
Montserrat	- s.12 Wills Act Cap. 84
St Vincent & The Grenadines	- s.25 Wills Act Gap 384
The Bahamas	- s.18, Wills Act 2002
Trinidad & Tobago	- s.52 Wills and Probate Ordinance Ch 8 No. 2.

73 *Goldie v. Adam & Others* [1938] P.85. Prior to s.22 of the Wills Act 1837 England, (the equivalent of which is contained in the relevant wills legislation of the various territories), it was possible to revive a will by mere implication.
74 *Goldie v. Adam* [1938] P.85 at 89-90.
75 *Ibid.*
76 *Ibid.*
77 [1952] P. 279.
78 Barbados   - s.74 Succession Act Cap. 249
    St Vincent &   - s.38 Wills Act Cap. 384.
    the Grenadines
78 *In the Estate of Davis* [1952] P.279.
79 *In the Goods of Steele* (1868) L.R. 1 P & D 575; *In the Goods of Reade* [1902] P.75.
80 See *Goldie v. Adam and Others* [1938] P.85.
81 *Braithwaite v. Braithwaite* (1945) L.R.B.G. 10; *In the Goods of Hodgkinson* [1893] P.339; *In the Goods of Reynolds* (1873) 3 P & D 35.

3

Grants of Representation

INTRODUCTION

There are certain preliminary matters which must be attended to before the relevant grant of representation may be applied for. One such matter is whether the deceased died testate or intestate.

If he has died testate, the will must be obtained from the intended grantee unless the grant being sought is:

(a) a second or subsequent grant, in which event the will would have already been proved; or
(b) a special type of limited grant such as a *pendente lite* or an *ad colligenda bona* grant, in either of which instance the will is neither proved nor lodged with the papers to lead the grant.

Once the will is required, however, as is usually the case, it may be discovered that the will is not in the possession or custody of the proposed grantee, but may have been lodged with another firm of attorneys-at-law, in which event a letter will have to be written to the firm on behalf of the proposed grantee, requesting same. Alternatively, it may be discovered that the will is deposited in a safety deposit box with the deceased's bankers. In such instances the bank may not allow the executor access to the box so a letter will have to be written requesting that the proposed grantee (usually the executor) be permitted to take delivery of the will. Or, as in some territories, it may be deposited in the Registry of the High/Supreme Court for custody and safe-keeping.

PRELIMINARY MATTERS

1. Deposit and Extraction of Wills of Living Persons

Barbados, Dominica, Grenada, Guyana, Montserrat and Trinidad & Tobago[1]

In the above-mentioned territories, a testator may deposit his will in the Registry for safekeeping and custody.

Practice and Procedure

Barbados and Dominica

The testator or executor or other authorised person attends the Registry with the will in a sealed envelope. The will is duly indexed in the Register of Wills and a notation made on the envelope of the date of deposit. The executor/testator is then issued a receipt as proof of deposit. On the death of the testator, the executor is required to attend the Registry and bring in the death certificate of the deceased and, if possible, the receipt.

In *Dominica,* the will is delivered to the executor. In *Barbados* however, the original will is not delivered out. Instead the executor is required to attend the Registry and mark the will before a legal assistant either before or at the time of lodging the other papers to lead the application for the grant. In addition, he may obtain a certified copy of the will, on payment of the requisite fees.

Grenada

The testator or authorised person is required to complete and sign a deposit form in the presence of a witness containing the following information:

(a) the date of the will;
(b) the name and address of the executor and testator respectively; and
(c) an undertaking by the testator to notify the executor of the deposit of the will and his appointment as executor. Where the will is brought in by an authorised person, such person in required to bring in a letter of authority signed by the testator.

The deposit of the will is recorded in the Register of Deposits and the deposit form together with the will sealed in an envelope, duly indexed, is filed in the Registry vault. A certificate of deposit is also prepared in duplicate and signed by the Registrar. The original is retained in the Registry and the duplicate copy given to the testator. No deposit fees are payable.

On the death of the testator, the executor is required to bring into the Registry the death certificate of the testator and where possible the duplicate copy of the certificate of deposit, in order to secure the release of the will to him, if he so wishes. Upon receipt thereof, the executor is required to sign the Register of Deposits. Alternatively, the will may be retained in the Registry in which case the executor is required to attend the Registry and mark the will before the Chief Clerk.

Guyana

Pursuant to s.5 of the Deceased Persons Estates' Administration Act Cap. 12:01[2] anyone may lodge for safe custody with the Registrar a will made by him.

The testator or authorised person is required to bring into the Registry the will either opened or under a sealed cover. A memorandum of deposit is then completed in duplicate by the clerk. The memorandum in effect states that the testator or authorised person appeared before a sworn clerk and presented the will for deposit for safe keeping on the date stated therein.

If it is some person authorised by the testator, a letter of authorisation signed by the testator must also be lodged. Thereafter a $10.00 fee for deposit of the will is paid to the cashier in the Registry, and a notation to that effect made on the receipt. The memorandum and receipt are assigned a filing number and the memorandum is then executed in the presence of 'a sworn clerk' and two witnesses from the Registry. Alternatively the testator may bring in his witnesses. The memorandum and the receipt are then given to the testator or authorised person.

The will is put in an envelope together with a copy of the memorandum. The envelope is sealed in the presence of the testator/authorised person and two red seals are affixed thereto. The testator/authorised person then writes his signature across the sealed envelope and the sealed packet is filed in the Registry.

On the death of the testator, the executor/intended grantee is required to bring in:

(1) the death certificate of the testator;
(2) the memorandum of deposit and the receipt, if in his possession; and
(3) if the contents are nor known to the intended grantee, an affidavit is required to be sworn by him requesting that the will be opened.

A probate clerk then opens the will and reads it out in the presence of the executor/intended grantee. A copy of the will is given to the applicant, for the original will remains in the Registry. When the applicant is ready to apply for the grant he attends the Registry and marks the will before a sworn clerk.

Montserrat

The testator or executor attends the Registry and brings in the will in a sealed envelope. He is issued:

74 / Probate Practice and Procedure

(1) a receipt upon payment of the requisite deposit fee; and
(2) a certificate signed by the Registrar to the effect that the will sealed in an envelope was lodged by the executor/testator or other authorised person on the date stated therein.

On the death of the testator, the executor attends the Registry and brings in the death certificate and the Registrar's certificate in order to extract the will. Upon receipt of the will the executor signs the Register of Deposit as proof of receipt.

Trinidad & Tobago[3]

The testator or the person authorised to deposit the will is required to attend the Registry and bring in the will in a sealed envelope for deposit. An endorsement is duly recorded on the envelope to the effect that:

(i) the sealed packet contains the will of the testator bearing the date specified therein;
(ii) the person(s) specified therein is/are appointed executor(s); and
(iii) the will was brought into the Registry for safe custody.

The testator is required to sign his name or acknowledge his signature to the endorsement before the Registrar/Deputy Registrar.[4]

If the will is brought in by an authorised person, the testator is required to subscribe his name in the presence of a witness to an endorsement on the envelope in which the will is enclosed to the effect that the envelope contains the will of the testator and that the person depositing the will has been duly authorised to do so by the testator.[5]

In addition the authorised person is required to bring in -

(1) an affidavit of a witness to the effect that the signature of the testator to the endorsement is in the proper handwriting of the testator and was signed by him in the presence of the witness on the date stated therein;[6]
(2) an affidavit of the testator to the effect that the person bringing in the will for deposit was duly authorised by the testator;[7] and
(3) an affidavit of the person authorised, sworn to before the Registrar/Deputy Registrar to the effect that the packer produced for the purpose of being deposited for safekeeping and custody is at the time of making the affidavit in precisely the same condition as when received into the deponent's hand.[8]

Upon deposit of the will by the testator or authorised person, and payment of a deposit fee of $(3).00 in the form of postage stamps, a minute is drawn up in duplicate, setting forth the production of the packet containing the will and the affidavits, if any, and when and by whom the same were produced, and the declaration of the testator or his agent that he deposited the same in the Registry for safekeeping. The minute is then signed by the Registrar or Deputy Registrar[9] and a copy thereof is delivered to the testator.[10]

On the death of the testator, the executor is required to bring in the death certificate and where possible the copy of the Registrar's minute sheet. The executor will then be required to attend and acknowledge before the Registrar/Deputy Registrar that he is the executor named in the will.[11] In practice, the Registrar signs an order for the will to be opened. The Registrar then opens the will and reads it out in the presence of the executor and a court clerk. The executor is then asked if he recognises the testator's signature. Once the Registrar is satisfied that all is in order, the applicant is given a copy of the minute containing the Registrar's order to open the will and a photocopy of the will. (The original will is kept in the Registry). The executor marks the photocopy of the will before a Commissioner of Oaths and lodges the marked photocopy of the will together with the other papers to lead the grant of probate or letters of administration with will annexed as the case may be. Upon issue of the grant the original will is filed together with the papers to lead the grant.

2. *Proof of Death*

The original or a certified copy of the death/burial certificate of the deceased must also be obtained, since this, with the exception of Jamaica, is one of the documents required to be lodged in an application for a grant.[12] In Jamaica, prior to the passage of the CPR 2002, an affidavit of a witness to the deceased's internment was required to be lodged with the papers to lead the relevant grant. A death certificate was required in Jamaica only when the deceased died abroad.

However, with the effect from January 1, 2003, pursuant to Rule 68.10, CPR 2002, a certified copy of the deceased's death certificate is now required to be filed with the oath with respect to applications for grants made in the Supreme Court. An affidavit of a witness present at the deceased's funeral is now only filed where a death certificate is unavailable. In instances where neither is available, the applicant, pursuant to Rule 68.10(c) must apply to the registrar for directions as to the form which evidence of death must take.

The furnishing of proof of death, whether by way of a certificate or an affidavit, may seem quite simple and straightforward. Nevertheless, it may happen that the applicant is unable to obtain proof of death, for example, because the deceased has perished in an aircraft or boat accident and his body has not been recovered. In such circumstances a preliminary order must be obtained, granting the applicant leave to swear death. This is considered in chapter 18.

3. *Types of Grants of Representation*

Another matter to be considered is the type of grant to be applied for, since the type of grant is dependent in large measure on whether the deceased died with or without having made a valid will.

In this regard, grants of representation may be divided into four major categories. These are:

- Grants of Probate
- Grants of Letters of Administration with the Will Annexed
- Grants of Letters of Administration
- Second or Subsequent Grants

(a) *Grants of Probate*: These are general grants of representation and are issued either to the executor(s) expressly appointed by the testator in his will or codicil thereto or to the executor according to the tenor of the will or codicil.

(b) *Grants of Letters of Administration with Will Annexed*: These grants are issued in circumstances where a testator has died leaving a perfectly valid will but has either failed to appoint an executor of any kind or the executor so appointed is unwilling or unable to act. Depending on the circumstances such grants may be either general or limited in scope and they are issued in the following circumstances:

- when no executor is appointed.
- when the appointed executor has died in the lifetime of the testator or has survived the testator and died without proving the will.
- when the executor has renounced probate or has been cited to accept or refuse probate and has not appeared.
- when the appointment of an executor is void by reason of uncertainty as to his identity.
- in certain circumstances when the court exercises its discretion and passes over an executor.
- when the executor is unable to take out probate through some disability, for example, because he is a minor or may be incapable of managing his affairs;
- Where the executor appointed is out of the jurisdiction and a grant is to be made to his attorney.

- When the appointment of an executor in the will is nor in the English language and there is no person named who by the terms of the will could be regarded as an executor according to the tenor.

(c) *Grants of Letters of Administration*: Again depending on the circumstances, these grants may be either limited or general in scope.

- They are general in scope where it is shown that the deceased died wholly intestate in respect of his property and left no valid will;
- In the following special circumstances limited grants of administration are issued where the deceased left a will; and
    (i) it is necessary to obtain a grant of letters of administration *ad colligenda bona*; or
    (ii) it is necessary to obtain a grant of letters of administration *pendente lite*; or
    (iii) if no response is made to a citation calling upon the persons interested thereunder to propound a purported testamentary document.
- Finally a grant of letters of administration may also be issued when the persons entitled to a grant of letters of administration, whether general or limited, have either died or renounced their rights and entitlement or have been cited and have failed to enter an appearance with respect thereto.

(d) *Second or Subsequent Grants of Representation:* There are three types:

- Cessate Grants
- Grants De Bonis Non Administratus
- Grants of Double Probate

These will be considered in chapter 19.

4. Preliminary Applications

Depending on the facts that come to light, it may be necessary to consider whether any application has to be made to the court prior to the application for the grant itself. The most common instances of this arise in cases of limited or special grants of administration such as grants for the use and benefit of a minor or a lost will.

5. Persons Entitled to the Grant

Having determined the type of grant to be applied for, the next step involves ascertaining the person(s) entitled to apply for and obtain the relevant grant. In most circumstances, this is a fairly simple exercise: for example, with grants of probate, the executors are clearly the persons entitled to apply. But with grants of administration (with or without will annexed), general, second or limited, the entitlement and priorities are determined in accordance with the rules of priority relevant to the respective territory. This may pose a challenge mainly because of the lack or inadequacy of indigenous non-contentious probate rules in the respective territories. In any event, in most jurisdictions the relevant proof of entitlement, such as birth certificates, marriage certificates or paternity orders should be obtained as soon as possible.

6. Ascertaining the Assets of the Deceased

The extent and value of the deceased's estate must also be ascertained, since this is necessary for the purposes, amongst others, of:

(a) calculating the estate and succession duties payable in respect of the deceased's estate. This applies to territories in which estate and succession duties are still payable or otherwise in jurisdictions in which death occurred prior to the abolition thereof.
(b) ascertaining the probate fees, stamp and other duties that are payable in respect of the estate, since these duties are calculated on the basis of the value of the deceased's estate.
(c) ascertaining the attorney-at-law's fees, which, again, are calculated on the value of the deceased's estate.
(d) preparing the affidavit of value/statement of assets and liabilities, declaration and account of the estate or its equivalent in the various jurisdictions. In preparing the affidavit of value, inventory, statement of asset and liabilities, or its equivalent in the various jurisdictions, it is first necessary to ascertain the extent and value of the deceased's assets. Consequently, letters will have to be written to insurance companies, banks, credit unions, the deceased's employers, unit trust corporations, and others. If the deceased owned land, the certificate of title, certified copy of the deed of conveyance/transport as the case may be, should also be obtained. A valuation certificate of the real property should also be obtained.

7. Declaration/Affidavit and Accounts of Estate

Eastern Caribbean territories

It is to be noted that the declaration/affidavit and accounts of the estate are required not only for the purposes of obtaining the relevant Estate/Stamp Duty certificate from the Estate Duty/Stamp Duty Division (where required) but also as one of the documents which was (and in some of the territories still is) required to be lodged with the other papers to lead the grant, irrespective of whether or nor stamp/estate duty is still payable.

8. Stamp/Estate Duty, Certificate, etc.

In territories where stamp/estate and/or succession duties or its equivalent are still payable or where death occurred, prior to or, in St Christopher & Nevis, even after the abolition of these duties, an estate/stamp duty certificate (or its equivalent) must be lodged with the other papers to lead the grant. In such instances an application will have to be made to the Estate Duty/Stamp Duty Division, for the issue of an estate duty certificate or its equivalent in the respective territories.

This certificate, where required, is generally obtained prior to the application for the grant and lodged with the papers to lead the grant. However, in St Vincent & the Grenadines with respect to the estate of persons dying before the abolition of estate and succession duties, a certificate is not issued and the duties are paid after the application for the grant of representation is lodged but prior to the issue of the grant.

9. Stamp Duty on 'Probate' Documents

In Dominica, Antigua & Barbuda, Montserrat and Trinidad & Tobago, stamp duty is payable on the administration bond.[13] In Anguilla, Grenada, St Lucia, Guyana, Barbados, St Vincent & the Grenadines, The Bahamas and St Christopher & Nevis, stamp duty is not payable on any of the 'probate' documents. With respect to St Christopher & Nevis, although stamp duty is no longer payable on the administration bond and the Declaration and Account of the Estate[14] the applicant is still required to appear at the Stamp Duty section, Inland Revenue department for these documents no be stamped 'Exempt'. In Jamaica, with effect from 2002, stamp duty is payable on one probate document, the oath pursuant to the Judicature (Rules of Court) Rules of the Supreme Court (Fees) Act 2002.

The Bahamas

Although stamp duty is not payable on any 'probate' document, a stamp duty in the fixed amount of three dollars is payable to the cashier at the Supreme Court Registry prior to the filing of the application for the relevant grant. It is paid at the same time as the court and recording fees. The amount paid by way of court and recording fees is entered into the Court Account while the amount paid by way of stamp duty is entered into a separate Treasury Account.

Trinidad & Tobago — Filing Fees[15]

Prior to the filing of the 'probate' documents in the Supreme Court Registry, filing fees which are calculated on a graduated scale and based on the value of the deceased's estate are required to be paid to the Registrar General.

10. Consents of /Notices to Persons Equally Entitled

As a general rule if there are two or more persons equally entitled to letters of administration (with or without will annexed), the consent of the other persons who are *sui juris* and equally entitled to the grant should be obtained or a notice in writing informing them of the intention to apply for the grant should be sent to them. This consent in writing or notice in writing, as the case may be, should be lodged with the other papers to lead the grant.

11. Clearing Off of Prior Rights

In regard to letters of administration (with or without will annexed), when there are persons with a prior entitlement to the grant who refuse or neglect to take out the relevant grant, the clearing off of their prior entitlement, whether *inter alia*, by way of renunciation or citation, is necessary. This must be done before the papers to lead the grant are filed.

12. Administration/Will Bonds

Depending on the type of grant and jurisdiction concerned, the personal representative (and surety/ies) is/are required to enter into a bond with the Registrar. With the exception of Barbados, the bond is entered into prior to the lodging of the papers to lead the grant. It is to be noted that with respect to Jamaica, applications made in the Supreme Court subsequent to the passage of the new CPR 2002, in particular Rule 68 thereof, do not need to include administration bonds and will bonds as these are no longer required in that they no longer constitute probate documents.

PRELIMINARY REQUIREMENTS - BY JURISDICTION

1. Trinidad & Tobago, Barbados and Jamaica

Searches

In Trinidad & Tobago and Barbados, the applicant for the grant must lodge a certificate/affidavit of search respectively, with the other papers to lead the grant. As such, an application will have to be made for the requisite searches to be conducted prior no the making of the application, in order to ascertain whether any other will has been deposited and whether any other application for a grant of the deceased's estate has been made. In the case of Jamaica, pursuant to Rule 68.13(3), where a will is undated, the Registrar may require a search to be made for subsequent wills and evidence to be supplied in accordance with the form prescribed by form P9 Appendix 2, CPR 2002. Form P.9 in effect sets out essentially the same particulars required in respect of the affidavit of search, Barbados.

2. Jamaica

(a) Order of the Court

In certain specified circumstances the beneficiaries of a deceased's estate are required to obtain an order from the court, granting them leave to apply for a grant of letters of administration (with or without will annexed) as the case maybe.

(b) Administrator General's Certificate

With respect to letters of administration and with will annexed, when the applicant(s) for the grant is/are the beneficiaries, the consent of the Administrator General, as evidenced by the Administrator General's Certificate, must be obtained from the Administrator General and filed with the application for the grant. It is to be noted that prior to the passage of the CPR 2002, where the beneficiaries were the applicants, the Formal Consent of the Administrator General (as the document was formerly referred to) was required only in cases of letters of administration with will annexed, although it was the practice for the beneficiary applicants to obtain the Administrator General's consent by way of a go ahead letter, in respect of applications for letters of administration.

(c) Declaration of Particulars

Prior to the passage of the CPR 2002, as a matter of practice in all instances of letters of administration with will annexed and of letters of administration where the Administrator General is entitled to take out the grant, a Form of Particulars (obtainable from the Administrator General's department, Kingston Mall) was completed and submitted to the Administrator General prior to the making of the application for the relevant grant.

The Form of Particulars listed the relevant information about the deceased, including his place and date of death, his/her surviving relatives and particulars of the real and personal assets of the deceased. The form was signed by the declarant in the presence of a Justice of Peace and was subsequently referred to as a Declaration of Particulars.

With the passage of the CPR 2002, in particular Rule 68.19 thereof, this former practice has been effectively codified and accordingly an applicant for grant letters of administration or letters of administration with will annexed is required to file with the Administrator General, a declaration setting out details of the estate of the deceased, details of all persons who are or who would have been, had they not died before the deceased, entitled to a grant and in case of those persons who would have been entitled to apply in priority to the applicant, the reasons those persons cannot apply. This Declaration of Particulars is essentially the same document that was previously filed.

It is to be noted that, prior to the passage of Rule 68 CPR 2002, when the next-of-kin was first entitled by law to take out letters of administration, the Declaration of Particulars was not required to be made or submitted to the Administrator General. In practice, however, some attorneys-at-law, out of an abundance of caution, submitted the Declaration to the Administrator General. When this was done, a *go-ahead* letter signed by or on behalf of the Administrator General was issued to the intended grantee, informing him or her that the Administrator General had no objection to the application for the grant being made. Unlike the Formal Consent of the Administrator General, this letter was not necessary and it was not lodged with the application for the grant.

3. Montserrat

Advertisement for Grant

In Montserrat the notice of application for the grant is advertised by the proposed grantee prior to the lodging of the papers to lead the grant. The notice is signed by the applicant or his attorney-at-law and is advertised once a week for two consecutive weeks in one of the weekly newspapers. The two newspaper clippings of the notice must be lodged with the papers to lead the grant.

MISCELLANEOUS MATTERS

All Jurisdictions

Estate Accounts

Since the assets of the deceased are frozen at the time of his death, it may be necessary to write to the deceased's bank and request than an estate account be opened in order to pay for the burial of the deceased, if necessary, but also to prevent any cheque that may have been issued to but not cashed by the deceased prior to his death from becoming stale-dated. These cheques may include salary cheques, income tax rebates, and so on.

The Bahamas

Pursuant to s.50 of the Supreme Court Act 15/1996 the manager or assistant manager of a bank may, without the production of probate or letters of administration, pay any sum standing to the credit of a deceased person to any person who produces satisfactory proof of death and sufficient evidence that he or she is entitled by law to the said sum standing to the credit of such deceased person. This payment is subject to certain statutory conditions.[16]

Conclusion

Once these preliminary matters have been settled, some of which necessitate the obtaining of papers necessary to lead the relevant grant of representation, the next step involves preparing the other 'probate' documents. This procedure, of course, may be undertaken while the other preliminary steps are being pursued.

Notes

1. Grenada — See The Wills (Deposit for Safe Custody) Regulations 1978
   Dominica — made under s. 172 of The Supreme Court of Judicature Montserrat (Consolidation) Act 1925
   Guyana — s.5 Deceased Persons Estates' Administration Act Cap. 12:0 1

| Trinidad & Tobago - | s.83 Wills and Probate Ordinance Ch. 8 No. 2 |
| St Vincent & the Grenadines | - s.26 Administration of Estates Act Cap. 377 |

With respect to St Vincent & the Grenadines. It is to be noted that although s.26 of the Administration of Estates Act Cap. 377 makes provision for a safe and convenient depository for the custody of the wills of living persons, in practice wills are not deposited for safe custody with the Court.

2 See also ss.6 and 8 of the Deceased Persons Estates' Administration Act Cap. 12:01.
3 See s.83 Wills and Probate Ordinance Ch. 8 No.2. See also Fourth Schedule, Depository for Wills of Living Persons, Wills & Probate Ordinance, Ch. 8 No. 2.
4 *Ibid.* r.3.
5 *Ibid.* r.4.
6 *Ibid.*
7 *Ibid.*
8 *Ibid.*
9 *Ibid.* r. 6.
10 *Ibid.*
11 *Ibid.* r.8.
12 St Vincent and the Grenadines, see r.2 Application for Probate Rules (1936) preserved under s.97 of the Eastern Caribbean Supreme Court (St Vincent & the Grenadines) Act Cap. 18 which requires that a copy of the entry of the deceased in the Register of Deaths, duly certified as correct by the Registrar, be exhibited to and filed with the applicant's affidavit; in practice a certified copy of the deceased's death certificate is filed.
13 Antigua & Barbuda - $10.00 see Schedule to Stamp Act Ch. 410
    Dominica - $7.50 see Schedule to Stamp Act Chap. 68:01
    Montserrat - $2.00 see Schedule to Stamp Act Cap. 238
    Trinidad & Tobago - $2.50 see Schedule to Stamp Duty Act Ch. 76:01.
14 Stamp duty was abolished with respect to the above documents by virtue of Fees (Miscellaneous Provisions) Act 14/1985.
15 With respect to the filing fees payable, see the Provisional Collection of Taxes Order made pursuant to s.3 of the Provisional Collection of Taxes Act Ch. 74:01 (L.N. 10/1992). See also s.80 Wills & Probate Ordinance Ch. 8 No. 2 and ch. 27 Pp. 380-381 post.
16 See s.50(1) which provides that:
    (a) the claimant deliver to the bank a statutory declaration in the form prescribed by s.8 of the Oath's Act Ch. 48 to the effect that the deceased person has no real estate in The Bahamas and his total personal estate does not exceed the amount standing to his credit at the bank.
    (b) the claimant deliver to the bank, evidence that at least three months notice has been given by the claimant by advertisement in three issues of the gazette and in three issues of a daily newspaper in The Bahamas calling upon all persons having any claim to the estate of the deceased person to notify the bank in writing of such claims; and
    (c) no other claims to the estate of the deceased person have been received by the bank.

4

Practice and Procedure with Respect to Obtaining Grants of Representation

INTRODUCTION

Although there are some variations with respect to the documents required; the practice and procedure with respect to common form applications for grants of representation; whether general, limited, second or subsequent are essentially the same in the various territories.

PRACTICE AND PROCEDURE

All Jurisdictions (save Jamaica and St Vincent & the Grenadines)[1]

1. How Made

Applications for common form grants are made *ex parte* by lodging the requisite documents in the Probate Section of the Registry of the Supreme/High Court.[2]

Trinidad & Tobago

The application may also be made at either the Sub-Registry in San Fernando or Tobago provided that, at the time of death, the deceased had a fixed place of abode within the district in which the application is made.[3] In practice, however, only applications for small estate grants are filed in San Fernando.

2. To Whom Made

All Jurisdictions (save Guyana, Montserrat and The Bahamas)

The application for the grant of representation is addressed to and made by the registrar of the Supreme Court. In Tobago it is addressed to the deputy registrar of the Sub-Registry in Tobago.

Guyana

In Guyana the application for the grant is addressed to the High Court and granted by the registrar pursuant to an order of the Chief Justice[4] or, in the absence of the Chief Justice, by an order of a judge assigned for that purpose, by the Chancellor or the Chief Justice.

The Bahamas

The application for a grant of representation is addressed to the Registrar of the High Court. The grant itself is, however, signed by the Chief Justice and issued by the registrar.[5]

Montserrat

The application for the grant is addressed to the Supreme Court of Justice. The grant is, however, signed and issued by the registrar.

Post-Script

Although the application for the grant should properly be addressed to the registrar of the Supreme Court,[6] the practice still obtains in some of the Eastern Caribbean territories to address the application to a judge in chambers.

3. *Who May Apply*

With the exception of Trinidad & Tobago all large estate applications may be made either in person or by an attorney-at-law on behalf of the applicant.[7] The practice, however, in the other Caribbean territories is for the applicant to apply through an attorney-at-law. In the Eastern Caribbean territories where the legal profession is not fused, the application is made through a solicitor.[8]

Trinidad & Tobago

By virtue of r.2 First Schedule N.C.B.R. Ch. 8 No. 2 all large estate applications, that is, applications regarding estates valued at $4,800 and over[9] must be made through an attorney-at-law.

Procedure after Documents Lodged

After the documents are lodged in the Registry and where applicable the appropriate court fees or stamp duties paid, a file is opened and the papers are checked to ensure that they are correct and in order. All queries are noted on the fly-sheet to the file in which the papers are lodged. The applicant/applicant's attorney-at-law is then notified of the queries. Any additional information, whether *inter alia* in the nature of exhibits or supplemental affidavits, must be submitted until the registrar is satisfied that all the enquiries he may see fit to institute have been answered to his satisfaction.

The usual searches are conducted in order to ascertain whether any other application for the relevant grant has been filed or whether any caveat has been lodged in relation to the estate of the deceased.

4. Advertisement/Publication of Application for Grant

Barbados, Guyana, The Bahamas and Trinidad & Tobago

Barbados

Upon the lodging of the documents for the grant in the Registry, the notice of the application for the grant is prepared on behalf of the registrar. The notice is then published in the Gazette and a daily newspaper in accordance with r.7 of The Supreme Court (Non-Contentious) Probate Rules 1959. The application for probate is published once, while the application for letters of administration are done so twice. No fees are payable by the applicant.

Trinidad & Tobago

Pursuant to r.40 First Schedule N.C.B.R. Ch. 8 No. 2, the advertisement for the application for probate or administration is required to be advertised once a week for not less than two weeks in one of the local daily newspapers and once in the Gazette. The application for the grant is advertised by the Registrar and no fees are payable. The advertisement takes the form prescribed by Form No. 1 First Schedule N.C.B.R. Ch. 8 No. 2.

Guyana

According to r.4 of the Deceased Persons Estates' Administration Rules notice of the application for the grant is required to be advertised in the

Gazette. The notice is prepared in the Registry and signed by the Registrar.[10] The registrar then sends the notice of application to the official Gazette for publication. Recently, however, applications for the grant have not been published.

The Bahamas

Applications for grants of probate are not advertised. But applications for grants of administration must be advertised in accordance with r.11 of The Probate Rules. The Notice of Application, which takes a prescribed form, is inserted in three successive issues of the Gazette and a daily newspaper. The notice is prepared in the Registry and signed by the registrar.[11] An advertising fee of 14¢ is payable.[12]

Family Islands of The Bahamas

In accordance with r.11(3) of The Probate Rules, the Notice is screened on the Notice Board of Family Island Commissioner for a period of at least six days. The Commissioner is then required to forward by the next return post a notification of the receipt of such notice and of its publication. An advertising fee of 14¢ is also payable.[13]

Eastern Caribbean territories

There is no requirement for an application for a grant to be advertised and it is not the practice to do so except in Montserrat[14] and in Anguilla. In Anguilla the application for the grant is published in the Anguilla Gazette in three consecutive publications unless the registrar waives this requirement.

Post-Advertisement Procedure

Once the prescribed period of advertisement has elapsed (with respect to the territories where the application for the grant is advertised and or published), the necessary searches have been conducted and the probate papers examined and found to be in order, the next step is dependent on the jurisdiction concerned.

Grenada

In Grenada, prior to the signing of an order for the issue of the grant, a certificate to the effect that no caveat has been lodged is signed by the registrar.

Barbados

In Barbados, prior to an order for issue of the grant, a Registrar's Certificate of Advertisement is signed by the deputy registrar to the effect that the Notice of Application has been advertised for the prescribed period in compliance with r.7 of the Supreme Court (Non-Contentious) Probate Rules 1959 and that no cause has been shown nor any caveat has been lodged with the registrar.

5. Order/Direction

All jurisdictions (save Guyana, The Bahamas and Trinidad & Tobago)

An order/direction for the issue of grant is drawn up and it is signed by the registrar. It should be noted that in some of the Eastern Caribbean territories the order for signature by the registrar is prepared by the applicant/solicitor and it is lodged with the other papers to lead the grant. The grant is signed by the registrar, and sealed with the seal of the Supreme Court.

Anguilla and St Christopher & Nevis

In addition, it is the practice for the applicant's solicitor to prepare the grant for signature and lodge these with the other papers to lead the grant.

Guyana

The registrar checks the papers to lead the relevant grant of representation and, once he is satisfied, he makes a note on the flysheet of the relevant 'probate' file to the effect that the papers 'are correct and in order'. The order for the grant to issue is then prepared for signature by the Chief Justice in accordance with s.24 of the Deceased Persons Estates' Administration of Estates Act Cap. 12:01.[15] The file is then forwarded to the Chief Justice who, once he is satisfied, signs the order. The file is then returned to the registrar and the appropriate grant is accordingly prepared, signed by the registrar and sealed with the seal of the court.

The Bahamas

After the documents are checked to ensure that they are correct and in order, a certificate to that effect is signed by the registrar/deputy registrar and the grant is prepared. The certificate with the 'probate' papers and the grant are submitted to the Chief Justice for his approval. Once all is in order the grant is signed by the Chief Justice and the registrar issues the grant to the applicant.[16]

Trinidad & Tobago

After the documents are checked by the registrar and found to be in order, a note to that effect is made on the flysheet together with written directions for the relevant grant to be drawn up. Thereafter the grant is prepared in duplicate, signed by the registrar and issued.

6. Minimum Period for Issue of Grant

Trinidad & Tobago

From the date of the first advertisement, the minimum period for issue of the relevant grant of representation is three weeks.[17]

The Bahamas

According to r.10 of The Probate Rules, no probate can issue until after the lapse of 14 days of the death of the testator except in events of urgency. With regard to letters of administration the minimum period for issue of the grants is 14 days from the filing of the application for the grant.[18]

Barbados

From the date of the notice in the Official Gazette and from the date of the second notice in a daily newspaper no less than 14 days may elapse.[19]

Eastern Caribbean (save St Lucia)

The minimum period for issue of a grant of probate is seven days from the date of death of the deceased and 14 days in the case of a grant of administration (with or without will annexed) unless otherwise ordered by the registrar.[20]

St Lucia

Although no time limit is specifically prescribed for probate grants, Art 1024 of the Code of Civil Procedure Ch. 243 provides that no letters of administration can issue until after the lapse of 14 days from the death of the deceased unless under the direction of a judge.

7. Issue of Grant

In all the territories except Antigua & Barbuda, the grant which is signed by the registrar/Chief Justice in The Bahamas is prepared in duplicate. In Antigua & Barbuda only an original is prepared for signature and sealing. The sealed grant is delivered to the applicant and the order for the issue of the grant is filed in the Registry.

Furthermore, with the exception of St Lucia, with respect to probate grants only, and Trinidad & Tobago, with respect to all types of grants,[21] the original grant is delivered to the applicant and the duplicate is filed in the Registry.

Trinidad & Tobago

The sealed original grant and will, if any, remain in the Registry in accordance with s.76 of the Wills & Probate Ordinance Ch. 8 No. 2 and an office copy of the grant is delivered to the grantee. A certified and sealed copy of the grant and a certified copy of the will, if any, are transmitted to the Registrar General for registration in the Protocol of Wills in the office of the Registrar General. Registration fees are also required to be paid upon filing of the documents.[22]

The Bahamas

Pursuant to r.21 The Probate Rules Ch. 35, a duplicate or office copy of the grant signed by the judge (Chief Justice in practice) with the will attached must be transmitted by the registrar to the registrar of Records for recording purposes and thereafter returned to the registrar for filing.[23]

POSITION IN JAMAICA

As stated previously,[24] the practice relating to applications for grants of representation is unique to Jamaica. This is primarily because two sets of stamp duty are required to be paid before the relevant grant will be issued to the applicant.

Practice and Procedure

Once the relevant papers to lead the grant have been prepared, stamp duty on the 'probate' documents must be paid. The duty on the probate documents was previously calculated in accordance with the formula set out in the Fees (Supreme Court) Rules 1941 as amended by the Fees

(Supreme Court) (Amendment) Rules 1974. However, pursuant to the Judicature (Rules of Court) Rules of the Supreme Court (Fees) Act 2002, which repealed and replaced the 1974 Rules, Stamp Duty of $2,000 is payable on the oath only, on applications for grants of representation. The duty is payable at the Stamp Duty and Transfer Department, otherwise referred to as the Stamp Office.

Upon payment of the stamp duty on the documents, the papers to lead the grant are lodged at the Probate window of the Civil Registry. The documents are then indexed and filed. When the application is for a grant of letters of administration (with or without will annexed) the next step involves advertising the application. (It is to be noted that applications for grants of probate are not advertised).

Advertisement for Applications for Letters of Administration – With or Without Will Annexed

A notice of publication of the application for the grant is prepared in duplicate by an authorised clerk in the Probate Registry and signed by the deputy registrar. A sealed copy of the notice is then issued to the applicant, who collects the notice from a designated box at the Probate window.

In accordance with the directions in the notice, the notice is inserted once a week for two successive weeks in a daily newspaper of mass circulation. It is to be noted that Rule 68.35(1) CPR 2002, which repealed and replaced r.25 General Rules and Orders of the Supreme Court Part III Probate and Administration provides for the notice of publication to be advertised in the Gazette, unless the registrar otherwise directs. However as was previously the case, the application is, in practice, published in a daily newspaper; in part because of the backlog of publications in the Gazette. The newspaper clippings of the advertisement must thereafter be filed as the grant will not be issued until this is done. In some instances the attorney-at-law may, if he wishes, file an affidavit of advertisement.

Post-advertisement

After the application for the grant of letters of administration (with or without will annexed) is advertised, and with respect to applications for grants of probate (which, as stated above, are not advertised) the file is next submitted to the deputy registrar.

Once the application for the grant is in order, the deputy registrar recommends the grant by making the following notation on the oath and file jacket: Probate/Letters of Administration (as the case may be) Granted as Prayed.

The file is then submitted to the registrar who, if satisfied therewith, dates and signs the notation made by the deputy registrar. (It should be noted that at this stage the grant is deemed to be made although it is not issued. Consequently it will be necessary to apply to revoke the grant if for some reason the application for the grant is sought to be withdrawn).

The file is then returned to the Probate Section of the Registry, where an authorised clerk calculates the stamp duty payable on the grant. The Stamp Duty payable on the grant is based on the net market value of the deceased's real and personal estate at the date of death, particulars of which are contained in Oath, unlike the former position, where it was contained in an Affidavit of Value. In this regard it is to be noted that pursuant to the CPR 2002, in particular Rule 68, an Affidavit of Value is no longer required in applications for grants made in the Supreme Court.

A notice is then sent to the attorney-at-law for the applicant, stating the amount of stamp duty payable on the grant. The attorney then collects the original grant from the Probate Section of the Registry and then attends at the Stamp Duty and Transfer Tax Department (the Stamp Office) where the assessed duty is paid to a cashier in that department. Alternatively, the attorney-at-law for the applicant may himself calculate the duty payable on the grant, based on the prescribed formula and pay both the duty on the oath and the duty on the grant at the Stamp Office prior to the lodging of the documents in the Registry.[25]

In either event, a receipt of payment is issued to the applicant and the grant is impressed with a stamp/stamps reflecting the stamp duty paid. The stamped original grant is then lodged in the Registry.

The papers to lead the grant are then checked by an authorised clerk to ensure that all is in order. The original grant is then submitted to the registrar who, once satisfied therewith, signs the grant, which is then sealed and issued to the applicant. If the papers for the grant were lodged after payment of the stamp duty on the probate documents, but before payment of the stamp duty on the grant, the date of issue of the grant bears the date of the notation on the oath and file jacket, since that date is deemed to be the date on which the grant was made.

Issue of Grant

Pursuant to Rule 68.35(1), CPR 2002, which rule repealed and replaced r.24 General Rules and Orders of the Supreme Court Part III Probate and Administration, no probate shall be issued until after the lapse of seven days from the death of the deceased. It is to be noted that the current and former rule in respect of the time period for issuance of a grant of probate is the same save in one material particular, that is the registrar has no discretion under the current rule to abridge the time for granting probate, unlike the former position under the repealed r.24, which allowed for the period of seven days to be abridged in special circumstances.

With regard to letters of administration (with or without will annexed), Rule 68.35(1) (b) CPR 2002 which rule repealed and replaced r.25 General Rules and Orders of the Supreme Court Part III Probate and Administration provides that no letters of administration whether with the will annexed or not shall issue until the application for the grant shall have been published for two successive weeks unless the registrar otherwise directs. With respect to abridging the time for issuance of grants and letters of administration with or without will annexed, the current and former rules are effectively the same as both the former and current rule allows for the abridgement of the time for the issuance of such grants.

As stated above, upon the issue of the grant, the original grant is delivered to the applicant. The kalamazoo copy is stamped, dated and signed by an authorised clerk of the Registry on behalf of the registrar and is thereafter filed in the Registry for record purposes.

When there is a will, a notation is made on the original will to the effect that it is the last original will of the testator. If there is a codicil, the codicil is similarly notated. The notation on the original will/codicil is then dated and signed by the registrar. Thereafter, pursuant Rule 68.36 CPR 2002, which rule repealed and replaced r.42 General Rules and Orders of the Supreme Court Part III Probate and Administration, the original will/codicil is transmitted by the registrar to the Records Office for deposit and preservation. A copy of the will/codicil, duly notated and signed by an authorised clerk of the Registry on behalf of the registrar, is also kept for record purposes at the Registry.

POSITION IN ST VINCENT & THE GRENADINES

The procedure and practice governing the obtaining of grants of representation in St Vincent & the Grenadines are also unique to this territory. The documents for the grant of representation are submitted in the first instance to the Estates Duty Office, Inland Revenue Department, Ministry of Finance, where the papers are checked by an authorised clerk.[26]

When the estate includes land, a valuation certificate is included with the documents to lead the grant. The valuation is examined so as to verify that all the required information, in particular, the assessed value of the land, has been stated. The attending clerk then completes a Memorandum and Check of Valuation Form in accordance with the information contained in the valuation certificate. This form is then submitted to the Valuation Department of the Ministry of Finance, Department of Inland Revenue, Land and House Tax Division, where the value of the land is assessed to determine whether the valuation as stated on the certificate is fair and accurate. Once the valuation is accepted, the memorandum is signed by a valuation officer and the Chief Surveyor.

It is then dated and stamped with the Valuation Department stamp and returned to the Estate Duty Division. At this stage the attending clerk calculates the probate fees, and estate duties if any, that are payable.[27] A fee slip, containing the name of the deceased together with an itemised list of the fees and duties payable, including any interest with respect thereto, is sent to the applicant's solicitor, who, upon receipt thereof, pays on behalf of his client, the requisite fees and duties at the Registry of the Supreme Court. Upon payment, a receipt is issued containing a list of the fees, duties and the charges that have been paid. The receipt is then submitted to the Estate Duty Division where the receipt number and particulars of the fees and duties paid are recorded in the Fees Register.

A fiat for issue of the grant to the applicant is then prepared by the attending clerk for signature by the registrar. This is usually written by hand on the formal application for the grant. It is then sent to the registrar who sees the file for the first time. The registrar then examines the papers to ensure that they are in order.

Once the registrar is satisfied with the papers, he signs the fiat. The grant is prepared in duplicate and submitted to the registrar for signature and issue. Thereafter the file containing the probate papers is returned to the Estates Duty Division for indexing and filing.[28] The applicant's solicitor is then notified in writing that the grant is ready for collection.

IMMEDIATE GRANTS

Jamaica

Although the new CPR 2002 contain no express provision for an immediate grant in circumstanced where a grant is urgently required, the practice still obtains to apply to the registrar for an immediate grant. An immediate grant is a general grant of representation and is the preferred alternative to an *ad colligenda bona* grant[29] which is a grant also made in urgent circumstances but, unlike an immediate grant, is limited in scope, and in addition requires a preliminary order to be made before the grant can be applied for.

The practice, procedure and the papers to lead an immediate grant are the same as those required for general grants of representation, save that:
(a) the grant of probate may not be issued under seven days pursuant to Rule 68.35 (1)(a) CPR 2002.
(b) in the case of grants of letters in administration with or without will annexed, pursuant to Rule 68.35(1)(b) (which as previously stated is essentially the same rule as the former r.25 General Rules and Orders of the Supreme Court Part III Probate and Administration), the registrar has the discretion to effectively abridge the time for issuance of such grants.
(c) the requirement that a grant of letters of administration (with or without will annexed) be advertised is also waived, pursuant to the discretionary powers conferred on the registrar by Rule 68.35(1)(b) CPR 2002.

Notes

1 The probate practice and procedure with respect to Jamaica and St Vincent & the Grenadines, although essentially the same as the other jurisdictions are nevertheless sufficiently unique to warrant separate consideration. For the relevant practice and procedure with respect to these two territories, see pp. 91-95.

2 Barbados — r.5 Supreme Court (Non-Contentious) Probate Rules 1959
Dominica — rr. 3, 4 N.C.P.R. 1954, England
Guyana — r.2 Deceased Persons Estates' Administration Rules Gap. 1:0 1
Eastern Caribbean — rr. 4, 5, N.C.P.R. 1987,
(save Dominica,
St Vincent & the Grenadines,
St Lucia)
St Lucia — Art 1015 Code of Civil Procedure Cli. 243
The Bahamas — rr. 2, 3 The Probate Rules Ch. 35; See also s.32 of the Supreme Court Act 15/1996
Trinidad & Tobago — r, I First Schedule N.C.B.R. Ch. 8 No. 2.

3 Rule 1 First Schedule N.C.B.R. Ch. 8 No. 2.

4 Section 24 Deceased Persons Estates' Administration Act Cap. 12:01. See p. 19 note 34 with respect to the provisions of s.24.

5 See Introduction p 13.

7 Barbados — r.4 The Supreme Court (Non-Contentious) Probate Rules 1959
Dominica — rr.3, 4 N.C.P.R. 1954, England
Guyana — r.2 Deceased Persons Estates' Administration Rules Cap, 12:01
Eastern Caribbean (save — rr.4, 5 N,C.P.R. 1987, England, Dominica)
The Bahamas — rr. 2, 6 The Probate Rules Ch. 35.

8 It should be noted that pursuant to the respective Supreme Court Acts of the Eastern

Caribbean territories (with the exception of St Lucia) and with respect to St Lucia, The Legal Practitioners Act Cap. 116, barristers are entitled to practice as solicitors but solicitors are not entitled to practice as barristers. As a consequence, common form probate applications are invariably made by barristets as most legal practitioners in the Eastern Caribbean are admitted to practice as barristers not solicitors.

9   The value of large estates was increased from $480 to $4,800. by the Non-Contentious Business (Amendment) Rules 1983 made by the Rules Committee under s.24 of the Wills & Probate Ordinance Ch. 8 No. 2 and s.78 of Supreme Court of Judicature Act Chap. 4:01 (published in L.N. 16/1984).
10   See Schedule to Deceased Persons Estates' Administration Rules Cap. 12:02 with respect to the form of advertisement.
11   See Form 1A, The Probate Rules Ch. 35.
12   See chapter 27, p. 512.
13   *Ibid.*
14   See chapter 3, p. 82.
15   See Introduction p. 13.
16   See r.21 The Probate Rules Ch. 35.
17   Rule 40 First Schedule N.C.B.R Ch. 8 No.2.
18   Rule 11(2) The Probate Rules, Ch. 35.
19   Rule 7 The Supreme Court (Non-Contentious) Probate Rules 1959.
20   Eastern Caribbean   - r. 6(2) N.C.P.R. 1987, England territories
     Dominica   - r.5 (3) N.C.P.R, 1954, England.
21   St Lucia   - See Art 796 Civil Code Ch. 242; Art 102 1(2) Code of Civil Procedure Ch. 243
     Trinidad & Tobago   - s.76 Wills & Probate Ord. Ch. 8 No. 2.
22   See chapter 27, p. 505 with respect to the registration fees payable to the Registrar General.
23   Pursuant to s.33(l) of the Supreme Court Act 15/1996 records of all grants which are made by the court are to be continued to be kept in the Probate Registry.
24   See p. 85.
25   It should be noted that:
    (a)   in practice as a matter of expediency stamp duty on the 'probate' documents and stamp duty on the grant are usually paid at the same time i.e. prior to the flling of the application for the relevant grant;
    (b)   where the amount paid by way of stamp duty on the grant is subsequently increased, the grant will be 'up-stamped', that is, the grant will be further stamped to reflect the revised and increased duty payable. The stamp duty on the grant may be so increased as a consequence of the revaluation of the deceased's real estate by the 'Stamp Office' when calculating the transfer tax payable with respect to the deceased's estate. In calculating the transfer tax, which is payable after the grant is obtained, the value of the deceased's real estate as set out in the Affidavit of Value and the valuation certificate is subject to review and increase by the valuation officer attached to the 'Stamp Office'. Should the value of the teal estate be increased, the amount of stamp duty which was paid on the grant would have to he accordingly increased and the grant 'up-stamped'.
    (c)   partly to avoid paying interest for late payment of transfer tax and partly to avoid having the grant 'up-stamped', many practitioners have adopted the practice of paying transfer tax at the same time as the stamp duty on the grant is paid. Indeed

in practice many practitioners pay the stamp duty on the documents, the stamp duty on the grant and the transfer tax before filing the application for the relevant grant.

26 But see s.6 of the Administration of Estates Act Cap. 377 which provides that applications for grants of probate or administration and for revocation of grants maybe made to the Registry of the court, Kingston.

27 By virtue of the Estate and Succession Duties (Amendment) Act 25 1993, estate and succession duties are no longer payable with respect to the estates of persons dying on or after lst August, 1993. See also chapter 10, 266-267.

28 See s.24 of the Administration of Estates Act Cap. 377 which provides that all original wills and other documents which are under the control of the court shall be deposited and preserved in such place as a judge may direct; and any wills or other documenti so deposited shall, subject to the control of the court and to the probate rules, be open to inspection.

29 See chapter 17, p. 372-75.

5

Grants of Probate

PRACTICE AND PROCEDURE

As stated in chapter 4, applications for grants of probate are made *ex parte* by lodging the requisite documents in the Probate Section of the Supreme Court/High Court Registry and in addition in the case of Trinidad and Tobago, the sub-registry of the Supreme Court. The application for the grant of probate is made by the executor(s). It is to be noted that although the testator may appoint as many executors as he wishes, no more than four will be permitted to prove the will at any one time.[1]

DOCUMENTS REQUIRED

Listed below are the papers necessary to lead a grant of probate for the respective territories. As with other grants of representation, the documents required vary somewhat from jurisdiction to jurisdiction.

Barbados[2]

1. Application for grant made through an attorney-at-law or by the applicant in person.
2. Affidavit of executor.
3. Certified copy of death/burial certificate or a statement writing to the satisfaction of the registrar for the non-production thereof.
4. Original will marked by the signatures of the executor and the person before whom sworn (a legal assistant).
5. Affidavit of due execution.
6. Estate and Successions Duty Certificate (with respect to the estates of persons dying on or before 30th March, 1981).[3]
7. Affidavit of search.
8. Affidavit of Value/Property with Schedule thereto with respect to the estates of persons dying on or after 31st March, 1981.[4]

Guyana[5]

1. Application for grant — setting out a list of the documents lodged and signed by the attorney-at-law or by applicant if applying in person.
2. Oath of executor.
3. Affidavit of due execution.
4. Statement of assets and liabilities.
5. Certificate of proper officer.
6. Original will marked by the executor and the person before whom sworn (a Commissioner for Oaths to Affidavit/Sworn Clerk).
7. Certified copy of death certificate.

Jamaica[6]

Prior to January 1, 2002

1. Covering letter (addressed to registrar discretionary).
2. Oath of executor.
3. Affidavit of due execution.
4. Inventory.
5. Kalamazoo copy of inventory.
6. Declaration of counting of inventory.
7. Will bond.
8. Affidavit of value (not required where the applicant is the Administrator General).
9. Probate and copy will.
10. Kalamazoo copy of probate and will.
11. Declaration of counting of probate and copy will.
12. Affidavit in proof of death.
13. Will marked by the signature of the executor, an attesting witness and the person before whom sworn (a Commissioner for Oaths).
14. Stamp Commissioner's Certificate (with respect to the estates of persons dying on or prior to 20th July, 1963).[7]

On or after January 1, 2003

1. Covering letter addressed to registrar (discretionary).
2. Oath of Executor.
3. The original will duly marked.
4. Death certificate exhibited to oath or where not available, affidavit

in proof of death.
5. Draft grant with Kalamazoo copy.
6. Affidavit of due execution, if required by registrar.

The Bahamas[8]

1. Application in the form of a petition made in person or through counsel.
2. Oath of executor.
3. Original will or a photostatic copy thereof marked by the executor and person before whom sworn.
4. Affidavit of due execution.
5. Schedule of the personal estate of the deceased with the estimated value thereof (exhibited to Oath).
6. Schedule of the real property owned by the deceased (exhibited to Oath).
7. Death certificate or certified copy of the death certificate.
8. Bond for making return into registry and paying dues.
9. Return of the value of the personal estate and effects of the deceased.
10. Nomination/appointment of co-executor (where applicable).

Trinidad & Tobago[9]

1. Application for grant — made through an attorney-at-law.
2. Affidavit of executor.
3. Certified copy of death/burial certificate.
4. Original will marked by the signature of the executor and the person before whom sworn (a Commissioner of Oaths).
5. Affidavit of due execution.
6. Inventory.
7. Certificate of search.
8. Filing fee receipt.

Eastern Caribbean Territories[10]

Anguilla:

1. Application for grant made through a solicitor or by applicant in person.
2. Oath of executor.
3. Declaration on oath of the value of the estate.
4. Certified copy of death certificate.

5. Affidavit of due execution.
6. Original will marked by the signatures of the executor and the person before whom sworn (Commissioner for Oaths/Justice of the Peace).
7. Land Registry Valuation Certificate (where the application for the grant is made through the registrar).
8. Order for issue of grant for signature by registrar.
9. Two original copies of grant (with copies of will glued on inner leaf).

Antigua & Barbuda:

1. Application made through a solicitor or by applicant in person.
2. Oath of executor.
3. Affidavit of due execution.
4. Declaration and account of estate (with respect to estates of persons dying on or prior to 31st December, 1969).[11]
5. Certified copy of death certificate.
6. Original will marked by the signature of the executor and the person before whom sworn (a Commissioner for Oaths).
7. Certificate of Stamp Duty (with respect to estates of persons dying on or prior to 31st December, 1969).[12]
8. Order for grant to issue for signature by registrar.
9. Notice to executor with power reserved.

Dominica

1. Application for grant - made through a solicitor or by applicant in person.
2. Oath of executor.
3. Affidavit of due execution.
4. Declaration and account of the estate referred to as 'Probate'.
5. Certified copy of death certificate.
6. Original will marked by the signatures of the executor and the person before whom sworn (a Commissioner for Oaths).
7. Estate Duty Certificate (with respect to estates of persons dying prior to 1st July, 1985).[13]
8. Order for grant to issue for signature by Registrar.

Grenada

1. Application for grant made through a solicitor or by applicant in person.
2. Oath of executor.
3. Original or certified copy of death certificate.

4. Original will marked by the signatures of the executor and the person before whom sworn (chief clerk of the Registry/deputy registrar).
5. Affidavit of due execution (discretionary).
6. Estate & Succession Duty Certificate (with respect to the estates of persons dying prior to 1st October, 1983).[14]
7. Order for grant to issue for signature by registrar.
8. Notice to executor with power reserved.

Montserrat

1. Application for grant made through a solicitor or by applicant in person.
2. Oath of executor.
3. Original will marked by the signatures of the executor and the person before whom sworn (a Commissioner for Oaths).
4. Certified copy of death certificate.
5. Declaration and account of the estate.
6. Newspaper clippings of advertisement for application for grant of probate.
7. Affidavit of due execution.
8. Certificate of Stamp Duty (with respect to the estates of persons dying prior to 19 November, 1966).[15]
9. Two original copies of grant (with copies of will glued on inner leaf).
10. Notice to executor with power reserved.

St Christopher & Nevis

1. Application for the Grant made through a solicitor or by applicant in person.
2. Oath of executor.
3. Declaration and account of the estate sworn to before a Commissioner for Oaths.
4. Certificate of payment of stamp duty.
5. Original will marked by the signature of executor and the person before whom sworn (a Commissioner for Oaths).
6. Certified copy of death certificate.
7. Affidavit of due execution usually required in practice.
8. Order for grant to issue for signature by the Registrar.
9. Two original copies of grant (with copies of will glued on inner leaf).
10. Notice to executor with power reserved.

St Lucia

1. Application in form of petition.
2. Affidavit of executor in support of petition.
3. Affidavit of due execution (non-notarial wills only).
4. Certified copy of death certificate.
5. (i) Original English/holograph will marked by the signatures of the executor and the person before whom sworn (the Registrar). (English/holograph wills are required to be deposited and retained in the Registry. Notarial wills are retained by the Notary).[16]
   (ii) Notarial will — certified copy
6. Affidavit of assets and liabilities sworn to before a Justice of the Peace
7. Certificate of Non-Objection to Grant with respect to the estates of persons dying before 1st January, 1988.[17]
8. List of exhibits such as wills, marriage and birth certificates, death certificates, etc.

St Vincent & the Grenadines

1. Application for grant made through a solicitor or by applicant in person.
2. Petition.
3. Warrant to act (signed by the executor(s)).
4. Oath of executor.
5. Certified copy of death certificate.
6. Original will marked by the signature of the executor and the person before whom sworn (a Commissioner for Oaths).
7. Affidavit of due execution only when requested by registrar.
8. Affidavit and account of the estate.
9. A valuation certificate of real property listed in the Declaration and account.
10. Notice to executor with power reserved.

DESCRIPTION OF DOCUMENTS

1. Application for Grant of Probate

All jurisdictions (except Jamaica, St Lucia and The Bahamas)[18]

The application is intituled *inter alia* In the Matter of the Estate of the Deceased named therein. It is signed by the applicant if made in person or otherwise by his solicitor or attorney-at-law as the case may be, but in

Trinidad & Tobago large estate applications (estates value at $4,800 and over)[19] must be made through an attorney-at-law. The covering application also includes particulars of the date of the will and the date of death of the deceased named therein. In addition, in Guyana a list of the documents filed in the application is also included.

Jamaica

Although it is not required by Rule 68 CPR 2002, a covering letter is usually lodged with the papers to lead the relevant grant of representation. The letter, which is signed by the attorney-at-law on behalf of the applicant, is addressed to the registrar. The letter simply notifies the registrar that the applicant is applying for a grant of probate in the estate of the deceased named therein. The letter also operates as a receipt of the lodging of the documents for the grant, in that it sets out, in a list, the papers filed with the application for probate.

Petition

The Bahamas[20]

The application takes the form of a simple petition signed by the executor, and addressed to the registrar, in which the executor prays for the issue of a grant of probate of the estate of the deceased named therein to be made to him.

St Lucia[21]

The application for the grant takes the form of a petition. The petition is fairly comprehensive and includes most of the recitals contained in the affidavit of the executor, except the oath to administer the estate of the deceased.

Recitals in the Petition

Although there is no prescribed form, the petition includes the following recitals:

(i) The name of the deceased, his occupation and the date and place of his death.
(ii) Particulars of execution of the will.
(iii) The appointment of the petitioner as executor of the estate.

(iv) With respect to the estates of persons dying on or before 1st January, 1988,[22] notice that the requirements of the Succession Duty Ordinance have been complied with in so far as the estate and succession of the deceased are concerned and the Accountant General does not object to the grant of probate of the will.
(v) Statement to the effect that the petitioner will voluntarily accept the office of executor.
(vi) A prayer that probate of the will of the deceased will be granted to the petitioner.

St Vincent & the Grenadines

The petition contains the same recitals as are set out in the oath of the applicant. It should be noted that although a petition is required by law in The Bahamas in accordance with r.3 of The Probate Rules, Ch. 35 and in St Lucia in accordance with the Art 1015(1) of Code of Civil Procedure Ch. 243, there is no such equivalent legal requirement in St Vincent. The practice of filing a petition appears to be based on pre-1954 non-contentious English probate practice rules. Indeed, in most of the current applications for grants, the petition that attracts a stamp duty of $20.00 is not one of the documents filed with the papers to lead the grant.

2. *Executor's Oath/Affidavit*[23]

This is the principal document and, although there are some jurisdictional differences regarding the contents of the oath, it should nevertheless contain the following information:

(i) The name and identity of the executor.
(ii) The address and occupation, or description, of the executor.
(iii) The place and date of death of the testator and, with the exception of Antigua & Barbuda and St Lucia his domicil at the time of death.[24]

St Lucia: Recitals (iv) and (v) following are included in applications for probate of 'English' wills only:[25]

(iv) A statement covering the producing of the testamentary papers and marking thereof by the executors.
(v) A description of all testamentary papers to be proved. Accordingly the oath should state that the paper writing contains the true and original will and testament, of the testator if that is the case.
   The following points should, however, be noted:

(a) If the will is a copy or draft, the words 'as contained in a copy thereof' or 'draft thereof, as the case may be, should be added immediately thereafter.
(b) When a codicil is proved with the will the words 'together with a codicil thereto' should be added after the words 'last will and testament'.

(vi) The appointment of the applicant(s) as executor(s) of the deceased's estate.

(vii) The oath of the executor, that is, to administer according to law all the estate which devolves to and vests in the personal representative of the deceased named therein and to exhibit a true and perfect inventory of the said estate and render a just and true account:

In Barbados, Jamaica and Trinidad & Tobago within 12 months from the date of the grant;
In the other jurisdictions whenever required by law. (The actual wording varies somewhat among the territories, but it is substantially the same.)

All jurisdictions (save St Lucia and Barbados)[26]

(vii) A statement as to the gross value of the estate.

Barbados, Dominica and Trinidad & Tobago

(viii) A confirmation that diligent searches have been made among the papers and effects of the deceased and a statement to the effect that no application for probate or administration has been made previous to this application, and, when applicable, that no other will of the deceased other than that for which probate is now sought is deposited in Trinidad & Tobago and Dominica; in the Depository of Wills for Living Persons, and in Barbados; filed at the Registration Office.

Recital with respect to settled land

Eastern Caribbean (save St Lucia) and Jamaica

(ix) In practice the oath to lead the various grants of representation of the above territories includes a statement as to whether there is land vested in the deceased which was or was not settled previously to his death and remained settled notwithstanding his death.

There is no legal basis, however, for including this recital in the oath to lead the grant in the case of Eastern Caribbean territories, since such a recital became necessary in England only when settled land grants came into existence as a consequence of the passage of the Law of Property Act, 1925 and the Settled Land Act, 1925.

None of the Eastern Caribbean territories has enacted the equivalent of either of these two Property Acts. On this point, it is interesting to note that ss.36-38 of the Administration of Estates Act Cap. 377 of St Vincent & the Grenadines contains the equivalent provisions of the Administration of Estates Act 1925, England with respect to settled land grants. However, neither of the Property Acts which brought the settled land grants into existence, has been enacted in St Vincent & the Grenadines.

Jamaica

Pursuant to Form P1 Appendix 2, CPR 2002, Oath of the Executors, the oath to lead the grant includes a recital as to whether there is land vested in the testator which was or was not settled previously to his death.

Recital with respect to minority and life interest

The Bahamas and Jamaica

(x) With effect from 1st January, 1997, in the case of Bahamas, the date of coming into operation of the Supreme Court Act 15/1996, the oath to lead the grant of probate should include a recital with respect to whether a minority or life interest does or does not arise under the will of the testator. In the case of Jamaica, although the substantive succession law in Jamaica has not been amended to include a provision with respect to minority and life interest, Form P1 Appendix 2, CPR 2002 includes a recital with respect thereto.

Guyana

(xi) A statement as to whether the deceased was married, how many times and whether he or she was married after 20th August, 1904.[27]

3. Wills

The will and any other testamentary papers must be marked by the executor and by the person before whom the affidavit is sworn.[28] This simply means that the executor and the person authorised to administer oaths in the respective territories are required to mark the will by signing it.

Jamaica

Pursuant to Rule 68.16(1) CPR 2002 which has repealed and replaced r. 28 General Rules and Orders of the Supreme Court Part III Probate and Administration, in respect of applications for grants made in the Supreme Court, the will is required to be marked by the executor, an attesting witness and the person before whom sworn.

4. *Affidavit of Due Execution*

Barbados, Guyana, Jamaica, The Bahamas and Trinidad & Tobago[29]

In these territories, an affidavit of due execution, deposed to by one of the subscribing witnesses, is required to be lodged with the papers to lead the grant. When such an affidavit is not available, an affidavit deposed to by a person present or, with the exception of Guyana,[30] by some person who can identify the signature of the deceased and, if applicable, that of the witnesses, must be lodged instead.

Jamaica

Prior to the passage of the CPR 2002, an affidavit of due execution was required to be filed pursuant to rr 5 to 8 of the General Rules and Orders of the Supreme Court, Part III Probate and Administration. However, pursuant to Rule 68.13(1) CPR 2002, an affidavit of due execution is required in instances where:

(a) a will contains no attestation clause;
(b) the attestation clause is not sufficient;
(c) it appears to the registrar that there is doubt about the due execution of the will

With respect to (c), Rule 68.35(6) provides in cases where:-

(a) the will appears to have been executed;
    (i)   by a blind or illiterate person;
    (ii) by another person at direction and in the presence of the testator; or
(b) there is any reason to raise doubt as to the testator having had knowledge of the contents of the will,

the registrar must satisfy himself or herself that the testator had such knowledge.

Accordingly in practice, an affidavit of due execution should be filed as a matter of course in circumstances outlined in Rule 68.35(6) and Rule 68.13(1) CPR 2002.

In the first instance, the affidavit of due execution, as in the other territories, should be made by one of the attesting witnesses in the form prescribed by Form P7 Appendix 2, CPR 2002 and where no attesting witness is conveniently available, by any person who was present when the will was made.

If no such affidavit can be obtained, Rule 68.13(2)(b) provides that an affidavit of handwriting in the form prescribed by Form P8 Appendix 2, CPR 2002 may be accepted by the registrar.

Finally, if no such affidavit is available, evidence of any matter which may raise a presumption in favour of due execution may be accepted and in such instances, the registrar may require that notice of application for probate be given to any person who may be prejudiced by the will.

Eastern Caribbean[31]

In Anguilla, Montserrat, Antigua & Barbuda, Dominica, St Christopher & Nevis, St Vincent & the Grenadines and St Lucia,[32] an affidavit of due execution is in practice required. In Grenada an affidavit of due execution is not generally filed unless the circumstances so warrant. Examples of such circumstances include:

(a) when the testator is blind, disabled or illiterate;
(b) where the will is signed twice by the testator;
(c) where the will is signed by some person other than the testator;
(d) where the testator signs by making a mark; and
(e) any circumstances which may raise a presumption that the will was not duly executed.

St Lucia

By virtue of Art 795 Civil Code Ch. 242 and Art. 1015(1)(b) Code of Civil Procedure Ch. 243 an affidavit of due execution is required only where the will to be probated is a non-notarial will.

Probate is granted as a matter of course in the case of a certified copy of a notarial will.

A. *Affidavit of Attesting Witness*[33]

This is an affidavit deposed to by one of the subscribing witnesses to the effect that the statutory formalities governing the execution of the testator's will were complied with.

Accordingly it states, *inter alia*, that:

(i) the witness was present at the time of the execution of the will;
(ii) he saw the testator sign his will or acknowledge his signature in his presence and the presence of the other subscribing witness, both being present at the same time; and
(iii) both witnesses thereafter subscribed the will in the presence of the testator; and, in St Lucia and Trinidad & Tobago[34] in the presence of each other.

(a) Signature by mark
In circumstances in which the testator is blind, illiterate or otherwise physically disabled, he may sign the will by making a mark or directing some other person to sign on his behalf. The facts relevant thereto must be recited in the affidavit.

(b) Signature by direction of testator
Where the will was signed by some person other than the testator, the recitals in the affidavit should depose to the fact that the will was signed by the direction and in the presence of the testator.

(c) Acknowledgement of signature
In circumstances where the testator acknowledges his signature rather than signs in the presence of the witnesses, this fact must be deposed to in the affidavit.

(d) Irregularity in placement of signature
When the testator's signature appears in any other place other than at the end of the will, or above the witnesses' signature, or in the attestation clause, the witness must depose to these facts in his affidavit.

Trinidad & Tobago

With respect to (d) above it should be noted that, should the testator sign other than at the foot or end of the will, the entire will is defective for want of due formalities and, as such, will not be admitted to probate.[35]

B. Affidavit of person present

All jurisdictions[36]

If the attesting witnesses cannot be found or are dead, an affidavit setting out the facts regarding their unavailability or death of both witnesses may be deposed to by someone who was present at the time when the will was executed.

C. *Affidavit of handwriting*

All jurisdictions save Guyana[37]

If neither an affidavit of a subscribing witness nor that of a person present at the time of execution is obtainable, an affidavit setting out the circumstances that may raise the presumption of due execution, and deposed to by someone who can identify the signature and or handwriting of the testator, may be filed in lieu thereof.

Barbados, The Bahamas and Trinidad Tobago[38]

In addition, in these jurisdictions an affidavit sworn to by some person who can identify the handwriting of the subscribing witness is also required. Such an affidavit is discretionary in the other territories and is necessary only when the registrar so requests.

No Evidence as to Due Execution

All Jurisdictions (save Barbados, The Bahamas and Trinidad & Tobago)

When no evidence as to the due execution of the testator's will is obtainable, the consent of those persons whose interests are prejudiced by the admissibility of the will to probate should be filed. And in such circumstances, provided the registrar is satisfied that the will was duly executed, the probate application will be granted. Otherwise, probate will be refused and the will marked accordingly.[39]

Should the registrar have doubts, the application will be referred to a judge on motion.

Barbados, Jamaica, The Bahamas and Trinidad & Tobago

Based on the wording of the relevant non-contentious probate rules of the above territories, the registrar has a discretion whether or not to grant probate only in circumstances in which evidence of due execution is available,[40] whether by an affidavit of an attesting witness, a person present or handwriting.

Guyana

When an affidavit of a subscribing witness or of a person present is unobtainable, it is the practice in Guyana for the executor to apply by summons to a judge in chambers for an order that the last will and testament of the deceased named therein be admitted to probate without the affidavit of the attesting witnesses.

Prior to the application, the attorney-at-law is required to publish a notice in a daily newspaper calling upon the witnesses to attend at his chambers within the time prescribed, usually seven days. Once the prescribed period has elapsed the attorney-at-law files a summons for an order that the grant of probate be issued. The summons is supported by what is referred to as an affidavit of publication. The affidavit should set out, amongst other things, the following:

(i) notice that the applicant is the executor of the will of the deceased named therein.
(ii) the place and date of death of the deceased.
(iii) the act that enquiries have been made as to the whereabouts of the witnesses; more particularly that a notice was published in a daily newspaper requesting their attendance to the will at the chambers of the attorney-at-law named therein within seven days of the appearance of the said notice.
(iv) that the seven days have expired and the said witnesses have not attended.
(v) that the witnesses cannot be traced or are dead, as the case may be.

D. *Affidavit of Execution of Holograph Wills*

Barbados and St Lucia[41]

An affidavit by a person or persons who was or were well acquainted with the deceased and the character of his handwriting is required to be filed when the will in respect of which probate is being sought is a holograph will.

5. *Certificate of Search*

Trinidad & Tobago[42]

The applicant is required to lodge in the Registry a certificate signed by the registrar to the effect that a search was made in the Registry and that no other application for probate or administration in the estate of the deceased named therein has been made and that no will other than that for which probate is sought is deposited in the Registry.

The request for the search and the certificate for the search are both included in one document. The request for the required searches to be made is signed by the applicant's attorney-at-law and deposited in the Registry of the Supreme Court prior to the application for the grant.

Upon the required searches being made the certificate is then signed on behalf of the registrar. This is of course provided no will has been deposited and no other application for a grant has been made. Upon being signed and stamped it is returned to the applicant's attorney-at-law for filing with the other papers to lead the grant.

6. *Affidavit of Search*

Barbados

The applicant is required to swear an affidavit that a search has been made in the Registry to the above effect.[43]

7. *Certificate of Proper Officer/ Estate Duty Certificate/ Inland Revenue Certificate/ Certificate of Non-Objection/Stamp Duty Certificate*[44]

An Estate Duty/Stamp Duty Certificate or its equivalent must be lodged with the other probate papers with respect to jurisdictions in which estate or stamp duty has not been abolished. In countries where estate/stamp duty has been abolished, a certificate is still required in cases where death occurred prior to the passage of the respective legislation abolishing estate and succession duty.

St Christopher & Nevis

A Certificate of Payment of Stamp Duty is still required to be lodged, irrespective of whether or not the deceased died before the abolition of stamp duty.

8. *Inventory, Declaration and Account of the Estate, Statement/Affidavit of Assets and Liabilities, Affidavit of Value, Schedule of Real and Personal Estate*

With the exception of Grenada and Antigua & Barbuda and Jamaica[45] a document[46] in the form of either a declaration or an affidavit sworn to by the applicant is lodged with the papers to lead the grant of probate. The declaration or affidavit contains particulars of the estate of the deceased, showing the several items of property, the nature and extent of their estimated value at the date of death of the deceased, including particulars of the estate, if any, of the deceased situate abroad and in respect of which no grant is required. In all the other territories except Trinidad & Tobago and The Bahamas, particulars of the liabilities of the estate including the deceased's funeral expenses are included therein.

ADDITIONAL DOCUMENTS

9. Notice of Intended Application

Jamaica, The Bahamas, Eastern Caribbean (save Dominica and St Lucia)

With respect to the above-mentioned territories, when there is an executor to whom power is reserved, the proving executor is required to serve notice of the intended application for probate on the executor to whom power is reserved, unless otherwise directed by the Registrar. [47]

10. Affidavit of Undated Wills

With respect to Jamaica, pursuant to Rule 68.13(3) CPR 2002 where a will is undated, the registrar may require a search be made for subsequent will, and evidence thereof to be supplied in the form prescribed by Form P9, Appendix 2, CPR 2002. The search contains essentially the same facts as contained in the affidavit of search, Barbados. With respect to The Bahamas, Guyana, Trinidad and Tobago and to the Eastern Caribbean territories, the relevant NCPR 1954/1987, England[48] provides that where there is a doubt as to the date on which a will was executed, the registrar may require such evidence as he thinks necessary to establish the date.

OTHER PROBATE DOCUMENTS- BY JURISDICTION

1. Anguilla

Land Registry Valuation Certificate

When the deceased left land in addition to the Declaration on Oath, a Land Registry Valuation certificate, which is issued by the Land Registry Department, is also lodged with the papers to lead the grant.[49]

2. Jamaica

Prior to January 1, 2003

Prior to the coming into effect on January 1, 2003 of the CPR 2002, the following documents were required to be filed in respect of applications for grants made to the Supreme Court.

A. Declaration of Counting of Probate and Copy Will

This was a simple declaration filed on behalf of the executor, in which the words and figures in the probate and the copy of the will of the deceased named therein were accounted for and stated therein for the purpose of assessing and paying stamp duties an the rate of 3 cents per folio of 72 words.[50]

B. Declaration of Counting of Inventory

This was also a declaration filed on behalf of the executor, in which the words and figures in the inventory were counted for the purpose of paying stamp duty at the rate of 3 cents per folio of 72 words.[51]

C. Inventory, Kalamazoo Copy of Inventory[52]

The kalamazoo copy of the inventory (as is the case with other kalamazoo copies of documents) was prepared on bond paper and kept in a special binder in the Registry.

D. Affidavit of Value[53]

Apart from the inventory an affidavit of value was filed with the papers to lead the grant. The affidavit set out the liabilities and assets of the deceased's estate at the date of death in order to arrive at the net value of the estate, and it was used for the purpose of calculating the stamp duty payable on the grant.[54]

E. Affidavit in Proof of Death

An affidavit in proof of death was previously lodged instead of a death certificate.[55] It set out various information, including the following:

   (i) The fact that the deponent was well acquainted with the deceased named therein.

(ii) The date, place and death of the deceased.
(iii) The fact that the deponent attended the funeral of the said deceased and saw his body interned in the grave at the place and address stated therein.

It should be noted that, if the deceased had died abroad, a certified copy of his death certificate was required to be lodged instead.

F. Will Bond [56]

In accordance with the former r.5 General Rules and Orders of the Supreme Court Part III Probate and Administration, every executor was required to give a bond in the prescribed form. However pursuant to s.18 of the Administrator General's Act, the Administrator General was not required to give a bond. The bond was a penalty in the amount of the alleged value of personalty of the deceased and double the gross annual value of the real estate of the deceased which was required to be verified by affidavit or declaration. It should be noted that when the executor was resident abroad, a surety was required for the will bond.[57]

G. Probate and Copy Will, Kalamazoo Copy of Probate Will [58]

The probate grant and kalamazoo copy were (and still) are prepared by the executor's attorney-at-law, and lodged in the Registry. The kalmazoo copy, which was so named after the bond paper on which it was traditionally written, is kept in a special binder in the Registry.

On or after December 31, 2002

Draft Grant and Kalamazoo Copy

Pursuant to the provisions of Rule 68 CPR 2002, all the above documents are no longer required to be lodged with the application for the grant of probate save and except a draft grant and Kalamazoo Copy. The Kalamazoo copy is named after the bond paper on which it is written and is kept in a special binder in the Registry.

3. St Vincent & the Grenadines

In practice, a Warrant to Act signed by the executor and authorising the solicitor to apply for the grant on his behalf must also be lodged with the papers to lead the grant.

4. The Bahamas

A. Bond for Making Return into Registry and Paying Duties

According to s.2 of the Probate Act Ch. 55, the executor or administrator of the estate and effects of any deceased person is required to enter into a bond with two or more good and sufficient sureties in the sum of $400.00, with the condition that within six months after the date of such bond he or they will return to the Office of the Registrar a true and correct account of the deceased's estate.[59]

B. Return

The Return as it is called takes the form prescribed by the Schedule to the Probate Act Ch. 35. It sets out the value of the personal estates and effects of the deceased. In practice the applicant for the grant, whether executor or administrator, and two bondsmen attend the registry and swear the bond. In addition, in practice the bond that is entered into to ensure that the executor/administrator brings in the Return and the petition are usually lodged at the same time with the other documents to lead the grant.

It must be noted that, pursuant to s.41 of the Supreme Court Act 15/1996 an executor or administrator who mistakenly omits out of the Return any part of the testator's personal estate or effects will be permitted at any time within three months after the discovery of such omission to amend his return and to pay the additional fees due on the estate without being liable to any penalty or forfeiture.

C. Nomination/Order of Appointment of co-executor

According to s.42(2) of the Supreme Court Act 15/1996, where under a will a beneficiary is a minor, or a life interest arises, a grant of probate is required to be made to no less than two individuals except where the grantee is a trust corporation or the Court otherwise deems fit. Accordingly where there is only one proving executor, a co-grantee is required to be nominated or appointed, as the case may be. The nomination/order of appointment, where applicable, is required to be filed with the papers to lead the grant.

5. Trinidad & Tobago [60]

Filing Fee Receipt

This is a document addressed to the Registrar General, requesting him to accept the registration fees in respect of the filing of the application for the grant. Once accepted and the requisite filing fees are paid, a filing fee receipt is issued to the applicant.

OTHER DOCUMENTS REQUIRED- DEPENDING ON FACTS

Depending on the particular facts circumstances and the jurisdiction concerned, the following documents will be required to be filed:

1. Affidavit/Certificate of Delay [61]

Barbados, Guyana, Jamaica and Trinidad & Tobago

When probate or administration is for the first time applied for after a lapse of three years from the death of the deceased the reason for the delay in making the application must be certified to the Registrar. The reasons for the delay are usually included either in the body of oath/affidavit of the executor or in a separate affidavit or certificate sworn to by the executor.

2. Affidavit of Alias [62]

All jurisdictions

When the deceased is known by some name other than his true name, and such other name(s) appears in his will, for example, or property owned by him, an affidavit of alias must be deposed to by the applicant for the grant. The affidavit should set out the other name(s) by which the deceased was known, specifying the true name of the deceased. In addition, the deceased's true name and alternative names should be included in the application. The applicant is also required to state in the oath the true name of the deceased and to depose:

(i) that some part of the estate, specifying it, was held in the other name; or
(ii) as to any other reason there may be for the inclusion of the other name in the grant of probate.

Affidavit of Plight and Condition and Appearance [63]

An affidavit of plight, condition and appearance must be filed in every instance in which:

(a) erasures, interlineations or obliterations appear in a will or other testamentary paper;
(b) there is the appearance of an attempted cancellation of a testamentary paper by burning, tearing, obliterating or otherwise;
(c) there are any vestiges of sealing wax or other marks upon the testamentary papers leading to the inference that a paper memorandum or other document has been annexed to same.

Notes

1. Antigua & Barbuda, St Christopher & Nevis, Anguilla, Montserrat, Dominica, Grenada — s.114 Supreme Court of Judicature Act 1981, England
    Barbados — s.18 Succession Act Cap. 249
    St Lucia — Art 841 Civil Code Ch. 242
    St Vincent & the Grenadines — s.14 Administration of Estates Act cap. 377
    The Bahamas — s.42 of the Supreme Court Act 15/1996
    Trinidad & Tobago — s.16 Wills and Probate Ordinance Ch. 8 No.2.
2. Rules 5, 12-15 Supreme Court (Non-Contentious) Probate Rules, 1959.
3. See The Estate and Succession Duties (Repeal) Act 41/1981 which abolished estates and succession duty with respect to estates of persons dying on or after 31st March, 1981. As a consequence an estate and succession duty certificate is no longer required on or after 31st March, 1981. An affidavit of value is lodged instead.
4. *Ibid.*
5. See rr. 2-11 of the Deceased Persons Estates' Administration Rules Cap. 12:01.
6. See Rule 68.7 C.P.R. 2002 which repealed and replaced rr. 5-16, 23, 24, 26-28 General Rules and Orders of the Supreme Court Part III Probate and Administration.
7. See Estate Duty (Amendment) Law 23/1963.
8. Rules 4, 8 The Probate Rules Ch. 35.
9. Rules 3-14 First Schedule N.C.B.R. Ch. 8 No.2.
10. Eastern Caribbean — rr. 8-16, 18 N.C.P.R. 1987, England territories (save Dominica and St Lucia)
    Dominica — rr. 6-17 N.C.P.R. 1954, England
    St Lucia — Art 794-796 Civil Code Ch. 242; see also Arts. 1012-1015 Code of Civil Procedure Ch. 243.
11. Stamp Duty Probate abolished with respect to the estates of persons dying after 31st December, 1969, by virtue of the Stamp (Amendment) Act 21/1969.
12. Pursuant to Stamp (Amendment) Act 21/1969.
13. Estate duties abolished by virtue of Estate Duty (Amendment) Act 18/1985 with respect to the estates of persons dying on or after 1st July, 1985.
14. Estate duties abolished with respect to the estates of persons dying on or after 1st October, 1983, by virtue of the Estate Duty (Repeal) Ordinance Act 21/1984.
15. Stamp Duty Probate abolished with respect to the estates of persons dying on or after 19th

November, 1966 by virtue of The Stamp Act (Amendment) Ordinance 13/1966.
16 See Art 1015(1)(6) Code of Civil Procedure Ch. 243.
17 Civil Code (Amendment) Act 4/1988. See also chapter 6 p.153.
18 Barbados — Form No. 1 Appendix (Forms and Fees) Supreme Court (Non-Contentious) Probate Rules 1959
    Trinidad & Tobago — Form No. 9 First Schedule N.C.B.R. Ch. 8 No. 2.
19 Pursuant to r.2 First Schedule N,C.B.R Ch. 8 No. 2.
20 See r.3 The Probate Rules Ch. 35. See also Form 1 The Probate Rules Ch. 35.
21 See Art 1015(l)(b) Code of Civil Procedure Ch. 243.
22 The date of the abolition of succession duty. See The Civil Code (Amendment) Act 4/1988 with respect thereto. See also Art 1015(2) Code of Civil Procedure Ch, 243.
23 Barbados — r.5 Supreme Court (Non-Contentious) Probate Rules 1959
    Dominica — r.6 N.C.P.R. 1954, England
    Eastern Caribbean — r.8 N.C.P.R. 1987, England (save Dominica)
    Guyana — r.3 Deceased Persons' Estates Administration Rules Cap. 12:01
    Jamaica — Rule 68.7 CPR 2002, repealing and replacing r.27 General Rules and Orders of the Supreme Court Part III Probate and Administration.
    St Lucia — Although there is no requirement that an affidavit in support of the petition is required with respect to grants of probate, in practice an affidavit of the executor is lodged with the papers to lead the grant
    The Bahamas — r.4 The Probate Rules Ch. 35
    Trinidad & Tobago — r. 3(1)(a) First Schedule N.C.B.R. Ch. 8 No. 2.

Forms

Barbados — Form No. 2 Appendix (Forms & Fees) Supreme Court (Non-Contentious) Probate Rules 1959
Guyana — Schedule to Deceased Persons Estates' Administration

Rules

Jamaica — Form P1 Appendix 2, CPR 2002 repealing and replacing Form No. 2 General Rules and Orders of the Supreme Court Part III Schedule of Forms.
The Bahamas — Form III The Probate Rules Ch. 35
Trinidad & Tobago — Form No. 3 First Schedule N.C.B.R. Ch. 8 No. 2.

N.B. The Forms prescribed above are to be used with such modifications as are necessary to reflect the existing probate practices in the various territories.

24 The place of domicile of the testator is not requested to be recited in the affidavit to lead the grant of probate although it maybe recited if so desired.
25 Recitals (iv) and (v) are included in English wills only. (See Art 1015(l)(b) Code of Civil Procedure Ch. 243). In the case of notarial wills the oath should include a recital to the

effect that the will was executed in notarial form before AB & CD. Notaries Royal, on the date stated therein.

26 In The Bahamas only the gross value of the personal estate and effects is stated in the oath. With respect to Barbados and St Lucia, the gross value of the deceased's estate is stated in an affidavit of value/affidavit of assets and liabilities respectively; See p. 114-115.

27 This recital which is really an anachronism, came into effect *inter alia* as a consequence of the passage of the Matrimonial Persons (Property) Act Ch. 45:51. This Act in effect preserved certain proprietary rights which were acquired by a husband and wife in each other's movable and immovable estate such as community of goods provided these persons were married to each other prior to the 20th August, 1904, the commencement date of this legislation. See also r.5(1) of the Deeds Registry Rules made under the Deeds Registry Act Cap. 5:01 which provides *inter alia* that deeds executed after these Rules come into force by or in favour of women must state whether she was married with or without community of property or subsequent to the 20th August, 1904. The provisions of these rules have been applied in practice to recitals in the oath to lead the relevant grant irrespective of whether the deceased is male or female.

28 Barbados — r.8 Supreme Court (Non-Contentious Probate) Rules 1959
   Dominica/Guyana — r.8 N.C.P.R. 1954, England
   Eastern Caribbean — r.10 N.C.P.R. 1987, England (save Dominica)
   The Bahamas — r.8 The Probate Rules Ch. 35
   Trinidad & Tobago — r.6 First Schedule N.C.B.R. Ch. 8 No. 2.

29 Barbados — rr. 5(1)(b), 12-15, Supreme Court (Non-Contentious) Probate Rules 1959
   Guyana — s.7 Deceased Persons Estates' Administration Act Cap. 12:01
   The Bahamas — r.4(b) The Probate Rules Ch. 35
   Trinidad & Tobago — rr.3, 10-14, N.C.B.R. Ch. 8 No.2.

30 See p. 113.

31 Pursuant to rr.10-14 N.C.P.R. 1954, England and rr.12-16 N.C.P.R. 1987, England an affidavit of due execution is not required in England unless it appears to the Registrar that there is some doubt about the 'execution of the will'. Although these rules are applicable to the Eastern Caribbean territories, in practice an affidavit of due execution is required by the Registrar in every application for a grant of probate in Montserrat, Antigua & Barbuda, Dominica and St Christopher & Nevis. In the case of Anguilla s.6 of the Death Duties Abolition Ordinance 6/1977 provides in effect that an affidavit of execution must be lodged with the papers to lead a grant of probate.

32 St Lucia with respect to non-notarial wills only; See Art 1015(1)(b) Code of Civil Procedure Ch. 243.

33 Barbados — rr.5. 12(1)(b) Supreme Court (Non-Contentious) Probate Rules 1959
   Dominica — r.10 N.C.P.R. 1954, England
   Eastern Caribbean (save Dominica) — r.10 N.C.P.R. 1987, England
   Guyana — s.7 Deceased Persons' Administration Rules Cap. 12:01
   Jamaica — Rule 68.13 CPR 2002, repealing and replacing rr.5-7 General Rules and Orders of the Supreme Court Part III Probate and Administration
   The Bahamas — r.4(b) The Probate Rules Ch. 35

Trinidad & Tobago	- rr.3(1)(b), 10 First Schedule N.C.B.R. Ch. 8 No. 2.

Forms

Barbados	- Form No. 3 Appendix (Forms & Fees) Supreme Court (Non-Contentious) Probate Rules 1959
Jamaica	- Form P.11, CPR 2002 repealing and replacing Form No. 1 General Rules and Orders of the Supreme Court Part III Schedule of Forms
Trinidad & Tobago	- Form No. 4 First Schedule N.C.B.R. Ch. 8 No. 2.

34 See chapter 1 p. 31.
35 Pursuant to s.42 of the Wills and Probate Ordinance Ch. 8 No. 2. See also *Smee v. Bryer* (1848) 1 Rob. Ecc. 616 where a will was held to be invalid because the signature of the testatrix was not placed in eight-tenths of an inch left blank at the bottom of a page but on the next page.

36	Barbados	- r.13 Supreme Court (Non-Contentious) Probate Rules 1959
	Dominica, Guyana	- r.10(1) N.C.P.R. 1954, England
	Eastern Caribbean (save Dominica)	- r.12(1) N.C.P.R. 1987, England
	Jamaica	- Rule 68.13(2) CPR 2002, repealing and replacing r.8 General Rules and Orders of the Supreme Court Part III Probate and Administration
	The Bahamas	- r.4(b) The Probate Rules, Ch. 35
	Trinidad & Tobago	- r.11 First Schedule N.C.B.R. Ch, 8 No. 2.
37	Barbados	- r.13 Supreme Court (Non-Contentious) Probate Rules 1959
	Dominica, Guyana	- r.10(2) N.C.P.R. 1954, England
	Eastern Caribbean (save Dominica)	- r.12(2) N.C.P.R. 1987, England
	Guyana	- See p. 78 post
	Jamaica	- Rule 68.13(2) CPR 2002, repealing and replacing r.8 General Rules and Orders of the Supreme Court Part III Probate and Administration.
	The Bahamas	- r.4(b) The Probate Rules, Ch. 35
	Trinidad & Tobago	- r.11 First Schedule N.C.B.R. Ch. 8 No. 2.

Forms

	Jamaica	- Form P8 Appendix 2 CPR 2002 repealing and replacing Form No. 19 General Rules and Orders of the Supreme Court Part III Schedule of Forms.
38	Barbados	- r.13 Supreme Court (Non-Contentious) Probate Rule 1959
	The Bahamas	- r.4 The Probate Rules, Ch. 35
	Trinidad & Tobago	- r.11 First Schedule N.C.B.R. Ch. 8 No. 2.
39	Dominica, Guyana	- rr.12(2), 10(3) N.C.P.R. 1954, England
	Eastern Caribbean (save Dominica)	- r.10(2),(3) N.C.P.R. 1987, England.
40	Barbados	- r.13, 14 Supreme Court (Non-Contentious) Probate Rule 1959

	The Bahamas	- r.4(b) The Probate Rules, Ch. 35
	Trinidad & Tobago	- r.11, 12 First Schedule N.C.B.R. Ch. 8 No. 2.
41	Barbados	- r.5(1)(b) Supreme Court (Non-Contentious) Probate Rules 1959
	St Lucia	- Art 788 Civil Code Ch. 242.
42	Trinidad & Tobago	- r.3(1)(e) First Schedule N.C.B.R. Ch. 8 No. 2.
43	Barbados	- r.5(1)(d) Supreme Court (Non-Contentious) Probate Rules 1959.

44 See chapter 10.

45	Grenada, Antigua & Barbuda	- Affidavit/Declaration and Account of the deceased estate are not lodged with respect to the estate of persons dying on or after the date of abolition of estate/stamp duties.
	Jamaica	- Pursuant to the passage of the CPR 2002, an inventory is no longer required with respect to applications for the grants made in the Supreme Court.
46	Barbados	- Affidavit of Value/Property together with Schedules thereto
	Eastern Caribbean	- Declaration/Affidavit and Account
	Guyana	- Statement of Assets & Liabilities
	St Lucia	- Affidavit of Assets and Liabilities
	The Bahamas	- Schedule of Real Estate
		Schedule of Personal Estate
	Trinidad & Tobago	- Inventory.

47 Pursuant to r.27(1) N.C.P.R. 1987, England.

	Jamaica	- Rule 68.7 CPR 2002
48	The Bahamas, Eastern Caribbean territories (save Dominica)	- r. 14(4) NCPR 1987, England
	Barbados, Guyana, Trinidad & Tobago, Dominica	- r. 12(3) NCPR 1954, England

49 See chapter 10 p. 268.
50 See on this Practice Note of the Supreme Court, Jamaica, dated 3rd March, 1955 intituled Recording Fees, Inventories, Probates and Letters of Administration.
51 *Ibid.*
52 See the former Practice Note of the Supreme Court, Jamaica, dated 18th April, 1953 which provides *inter alia* for a copy of the inventory ' type written on special paper' to be filed with each application for Probate Letters of Administration with or without will annexed as the case may be.
53 See the former Practice Direction of the Supreme Court, Jamaica, dated 30th September, 1955 which provided that where an application for a grant of probate or administration is not accompanied by the Stamp Commissioner's Certificate of the filing of a Revenue Affidavit under the Estate Duty Law 1954, there must be filed with the papers, an affidavit by the applicant in duplicate in the form prescribed in the Schedule to the Practice Direction, showing the value of the assets of the estate, the debts payable thereout and the net value of the estate. Although this direction was made when estate duty was payable, it was still used for the purposes of assessing the stamp duty payable on the relevant grant of representation.

54 See chapter 3 p. 78.
55 The requirement that death must be proved by an Affidavit in Proof of Death was as a consequence of the former Practice Direction of the Supreme Court, Jamaica, dated 4th October, 1971. Although this direction was limited to applications for grants made by a trust company, the former practice was for an Affidavit in Proof of Death to be lodged in all applications for grants where the deceased has died in Jamaica.
56 See Form No. 5 of the former General Rules and Orders of the Supreme Court Part III Schedule of Forms.
57 Pursuant to the former Practice Direction of the Supreme Court, Jamaica, dated 25th April, 1946.
58 See Practice Note of the Supreme Court, Jamaica, dated 18th April, 1953 which requires that *inter alia* that with each application for probate a type-written copy of the Probate must be filed. See also Form No. 6 General Rules and Orders of the Supreme Court Part 111 Schedule of Forms.
59 Rules 16, 17 The Probate Rules Ch. 35. See also Form IX, The Probate Rules Ch. 35.
60 Section 81 Wills & Probate Ordinance Chapter 8 No. 2 and rr. 33-35 First Schedule N.C.B.R. Chapter 8 No. 2. See also chapter 3 p. 80.

61	Barbados	- r.9 Supreme Court (Non-Contentious) Probate Rules 1959
	Guyana	- r.9 Deceased Persons Estates' Administration Rules, Cap. 12:01
	Jamaica	- Rule 68.22 CPR 2002 repealing and replacing r.26 General Rules and Orders of the Supreme Court Part III Probate and Administration.
	Trinidad & Tobago	- r.7 First Schedule N.C.B.R. Ch. 8 No. 2.
62	Eastern Caribbean (save Dominica), The Bahamas, Jamaica, Barbados, Dominica, Guyana, Trinidad & Tobago	- r.9 N.C.P.R. 1987, England - r.7 N.C.P.R. 1954, England.
	Jamaica	- Rule 68.24 CPR 2002, repealing and replacing
63	Barbados	- rr. 18-21, 24, 25 Supreme Court (Non-Contentious) Probate Rules 1959
	Dominica	- rr. 12-14, N.C.P.R. 1954, England
	Eastern Caribbean (save Dominica), The Bahamas	- rr 14-16 N.C.P.R. 1987, England
	Jamaica	- Rule 68.15 (1 CPR 2002, repealing and replacing rr.9-13 General Rules and Orders of the Supreme Court Part III Probate and Administration. See also Rule 68.35(8) CPR 2002
	Trinidad & Tobago	- rr.16-19, 22, 23 First Schedule N.C.B.R. Ch. 8 No.2

6

Grants of Letters of Administration with Will Annexed

INTRODUCTION

Grants of letters of administration with will annexed, as is the case with other grants of representation, are issued to a maximum of four persons[1] in circumstances:

(a) where no executor is appointed;
(b) where the executor appointed has died in the lifetime of the testator or has survived the testator but has died without proving the will;
(c) where the executor has renounced probate or has been cited to accept or refuse probate and has not appeared;
(d) when the appointment of an executor is void by reason of uncertainty as to his identity;
(e) when the appointment of an executor in the will is not in the English language and there is no person named who by the terms of the will could be regarded as an executor according to tenor.

Limited special or second grants of letters of administration with will annexed may also be granted *inter alia*:

(a) in certain circumstances where the court exercises its discretion and passes over an executor;
(b) when the executor is unable to take out probate through some disability, for example because he is a minor or because he may be incapable of managing his affairs; or
(c) where the executor appointed is out of the jurisdiction and a grant is to be made to his attorney.

This chapter will focus on general grants of letters of administration with will annexed and the relevant procedure and practice. The various types of special, second, or limited grants of letters of administration with or without will annexed will be considered in chapters 16, 17, 18 and 19.

ORDER OF PRIORITY OF RIGHT TO GRANT LETTERS OF ADMINISTRATION WITH WILL ANNEXED.

Unlike probate grants, the personal representatives of a testator's estate in cases of letters of administration with will annexed are appointed by the court, not the testator. In making this appointment, the courts of the various Caribbean territories apply the relevant non-contentious probate rules and/or statutory provisions for the purposes of determining entitlement to the grant, and the order of priority with respect thereto.

Barbados and Guyana

Although,

(a) s.16 of the Deceased Persons Estates' Administration Act Cap. 12:01, Guyana, and
(b) s.19 of the Succession Act Cap. 249, Barbados give the courts of these territories, the discretion as to whom administration is granted, the practice in these territories, is to observe the order of priority with respect to entitlement to a grant of letters of administration with will annexed as set out in r.19 of the Non-contentious Probate Rules 1954, England, with necessary modifications to local probate law and practice.

By way of illustration, in determining priorities with respect to entitlement to grant of letters of administration with will annexed, the registrar may take into account the size and nature of the benefit conferred on the individual beneficiary. As such, beneficiaries enjoying a substantially large share of the deceased's estate may be permitted in the appropriate case to apply in priority, irrespective of his other classification under r. 19 of N.C.P.R. 1954, England.

In this regard rule 19 contains the following order of priority, *inter alia*:

(a) the executor;
(b) any residuary legatee or devisee holding in trust for any other person;
(c) any residuary legatee or devisee for life;
(d) the ultimate residuary legatee or devisee or, where the residue is not wholly disposed of by the will, any person entitled to share in the residue not so disposed or, subject to paragraph (3) or rule 25, the personal representative of any such persons.

Jamaica

According to s.12 of the Intestates' Estates and Property Charges Act[2] unless the court is satisfied that it would be for the benefit of the estate that the grant should be made to some other person, it is the duty of the Administrator General to take out letters of administration with will annexed. This is irrespective of whether the beneficiaries are all adults and are in agreement, or whether one or some of the beneficiaries is/are minor(s).

On or before December 31, 2002

(a) *Formal Consent of the Administrator General*

Prior to the passage of the Supreme Court of Jamaica CPR 2002, in particular Rule 68 thereof, the Administrator General in the appropriate case, issued a Formal Consent With The Will Annexed to the beneficiaries under the testator's will indicating that he would not oppose the grant in their favour even where one or some of the beneficiaries was/were minor(s).

The Formal Consent in effect provided the intended grantee(s) with the requisite authority to apply for the grant. Accordingly it had to be obtained prior to the filing of the papers to lead the grant.

To obtain the Formal Consent of the Administrator General, the following documents were required to be submitted to the Administrator General:

(1) the Declaration of Particulars[3]
(2) the original oath of the intended grantee, duly executed;
(3) the original will/codicil of the testator;
(4) the written consent(s) of the adults beneficiaries who were in agreement to one or more of them applying for the grant[4] and
(5) where applicable, copies of the notices[5] of the intended application served on the beneficiaries who have not given their consent to the application being made by the applicant.

Once the Administrator General was satisfied therewith, he issued the Formal Consent With The Will Annexed which had to be filed with the papers to lead the grant.

It should be pointed out at the outset that the issuance of the Formal Consent by the Administrator General was a matter of discretion. However, as a general rule, the Administrator General issued the Formal Consent to the beneficiaries where all the adult beneficiaries were in agreement and had given their written consent to one or more of them applying for the grant. However where the beneficiaries were not in agreement, the prior entitlement to the grant of those in agreement, was taken into account by the Administrator General for the purposes of determining whether or not to issue the Formal Consent.

In this regard, the residuary beneficiaries, as in the case in the other territories, were deemed to have a prior entitlement to a grant of letters of administration with will annexed. Accordingly, in the appropriate case, where the residuary beneficiaries were in agreement, the Administrator General usually issued the Formal Consent to them even if the other beneficiaries, i.e., the legatees and devisees who were deemed to all fall within the same lower classification, were not so agreed.

In such instances, the consents of the adult residuary beneficiaries had to be submitted to the Administrator General together with the notices of the intended application for the grant which was required to be served on the other beneficiaries who had not so consented.

It is to be noted that according to the repealed r.18 General Rules and Orders of the Supreme Court, Part III, Probate and Administration, notice of the intended application was required to be served only on those who were *equally entitled* to take out letters of administration. However in practice where one, some or all of the beneficiaries, not being residuary beneficiaries, had not consented to the application being made, notice of the intended application was nevertheless required to be served on them.

It must be re-emphasised that the issuing of the Formal Consent by the Administrator General, was purely discretionary and accordingly, where the residuary estate was comparatively small, the Administrator General may not have given his consent to the residuary beneficiaries making the application for the grant if the beneficiaries who were opposed to the application being made were entitled to a substantially greater share of the testator's estate.

Where all the adult beneficiaries belonged to the same class but they were all not in agreement, the Administrator General usually issued the Formal Consent provided the beneficiaries in agreement had given their written consent to the application being made by one or some of them and notice thereof had been served on those who were opposed to the application being made.

Again, where the size of the interest of the beneficiaries who were not in agreement was substantially greater than those who had given their written consent, the Administrator General might in such circumstances refuse to issue his Formal Consent.

On or after January 1, 2003

Administrator General Certificate

Rule 68, CPR 2002, has essentially codified the practice with respect to the procedure and practice relevant to obtaining the consent of the Administrator General in cases of applications for letters of administration with will annexed.

In this regard, Rule 68.19(1) and Rule 68.19(3) effectively provide that applications for letters of administration with will annexed are subject to the substantive provision of s.12 of the Intestates' Estates and Property Charges Act. According to s.12, the Administrator General is the person entitled to apply for letters of administration with will annexed, save and except where he otherwise consents or an order of the court is obtained.

The significant change introduced by the CPR 2002, though not of a substantive law nature, is the introduction of an order of priority for grants where the deceased left a will. Rule 68.11 provides for the following order of priority, *inter alia*:

(a) the executor;
(b) any residuary legatee or devisee holding in trust for any other person;
(c) any other residuary legatee or devisee; or
(d) where the residue is not wholly disposed of by will, any person entitled to share in the undisposed residue (including the Administrator General when claiming *bona vacantia* on behalf of the Crown), provide that:
   (i) unless the registrar otherwise directs, a residuary legatee or devisee who has a vested interest is to be preferred to one entitled on the happening of a contingency;
   (ii) where the residue is not in terms wholly disposed of, the registrar may, if he is satisfied that the testator has nevertheless disposed of the whole or substantially the whole of the known estate, allow a grant to be made to any legatee or devisee entitled to, or to share in, the estate so disposed of by the will
(e) the personal representative of any residuary legatee or devisee (but not one for life, or one holding in trust for any other person) entitled to share in any residue not disposed of by the will;
(f) any other legatee or devisee (including one for life or one holding in trust for any other person) or any creditor or the deceased, provided that, unless the registrar otherwise directs a legatee or devisee whose interest in a legacy or devise is vested is to be preferred to one entitled contingently;

(g) the personal representatives of any other legatee or devisee (but not one for life or one holding in trust for any other person) or of any creditor of the deceased.

Significantly, Rule 68.11(d)(ii) has effectively codified the practice of allowing the registrar to issue a grant to a legatee or devisee, where the value of the residuary estate is relatively small compared to the legatee or devisee's share thereof.

What this simply means is that the Administrator General is now subject to these express rules of priority, although he retains, by implication an overriding discretion under Rule 68.11(d)(ii) to issue the Administrator General's Certificate to a legatee instead of a residuary beneficiary.

Other changes of significance have been introduced or codified by Rule 68.

The Formal Consent of the Administrator General has been replaced, pursuant to Rule 68.19 CPR 2002, by the Administrator General's Certificate. This change is more formal than substantive. As was previously the case, the Administrator General's consent had to be obtained and filed with the application for the grant, unless an order of the court was otherwise obtained, pursuant to s.12 of the Intestates' Estates and Property Charges Act.

Pursuant to Rule 68.21(1) and (2) and Rule 68.19(2)(iii) where there are persons equally entitled to the grant, although the grant may be obtained without the consent of the persons entitled in the same degree, a notice of not less than 14 days must be served on such persons unless the registrar dispenses with the need for such notice. Further, Rule 68.21(3) provides that the registrar may require the applicant to file an affidavit of service of the notice or notices.

Pursuant to Rule 68.19(2)(ii), where there are persons with a prior entitlement to the grant, such persons must be accounted for.

In this regard, the renunciation, death certificate, or order of citation as the case may be must be filed together with the oath to lead the grant in accordance with Rule 68.19(2).

The oath takes a prescribed form (P3 Appendix 2 CPR 2002) and must recite the clearing off of persons with a prior entitlement together with the proof thereof, such as the renunciation or certified copy of the death certificate of the person, as the case may be.

As was previously the case, the declaration filed with the Administrator General is required, in accordance with Rule 68.19(2)(a) to contain details of the estate of the deceased including, as was stated above, details of all persons with a prior entitlement to the grant.

Once all is in order, and the Administrator General is satisfied that the provisions of Rule 68.19 CPR 2002, have been complied with, the Certificate of the Administrator General consenting to the grant being made to the applicant(s) is issued.

The oath together with all supporting documents, (for example, renunciation, death certificate) are thereafter returned to the applicant. In addition, the Administrator General's certificate is also handed to the applicant for filing with the registrar of the court at King Street, Kingston, pursuant to Rule 68.5 CPR 2002.

(b) Order of the Court

Alternatively, the beneficiaries may apply to the court for an order granting leave to them to apply for letters of administration with will annexed.[6] In practice an order of the court is sought where one or some of the beneficiaries is/are minor(s). Although the Formal Consent of the Administrator General/ Administrator General Certificate with effect from January 1, 2002, may be and is given where one or some of the beneficiaries is/are minor(s), some attorneys-at-law nevertheless apply to the court for an order pursuant to s.12 of the Intestates' Estates and Property Charges Act which permits the grant to be made to some person other than the Administrator General where the court is of the opinion that it would be for the benefit of the estate to do so.

(c) Application by Administrator General

In instances where the Administrator General will not give his Formal Consent and an order of the court is not obtained by the beneficiaries, the application for the grant of letters of administration with will annexed is made by the Administrator General pursuant to the provisions of s.12 of the Intestates' Estates and Property Charges Act.

The Bahamas

Position Prior to February 2002

By virtue of:

(a) s.13 of the Supreme Court Act 15/1996 which allows for the reception of English probate practice and procedure so far as it is applicable; and
(b) the succession laws of The Bahamas which were in effect English pre-1926 succession laws,

grants of letters of administration with will annexed were made in accordance with r.23 of the N.C.P.R. 1987, England.

Rule 23 provides as follows:

> Where the deceased died before 1 January 1926, the person or persons entitled to a grant shall, subject to the provisions of any enactment, be determined in accordance with the principles and rules under which the court would have acted at the date of death.

As a general rule, under the pre-1926 Probate Rules, the order of priority with respect to entitlement to a grant of letters of administration with will annexed is similar to the order of entitlement under the current N.C.P.R. 1987, England.

The order of entitlement is as follows:

(1) residuary legatees or devisees in trust;
(2) residuary legatees or devisees for life;
(3) residuary legatees and devisees;
(4) personal Representatives of a deceased residuary legatee or devisee;
(5) the surviving husband or widow, or if none survives the next of kin or heir-at-law;
(6) legatees, devisees or creditors;
(7) the Crown.

Position on or after February 1, 2002

With the passage of several pieces of succession legislation, in particular the Inheritance Act 2002, the Wills Act 2002, the Administration of Estates Act 2002 and the Equal Status of Children's Act 2002, the succession laws of the Bahamas have undergone radical and fundamental changes. Effectively, the succession laws of the Bahamas are now based on the post 1926 English succession laws and as a consequence heirship, dower, curtesy and the Statute of Distribution have all been abolished. Accordingly, with respect to the estate of persons dying on or after February 1, 2002, the order of priority for grants of letters of administration with will annexed is now based on Rule 20 CPR England 1987, in the absence of indigenous probate rules and or substantive provisions to the contrary.

Trinidad & Tobago

According to s.30(b) of the Wills and Probate Ordinance Ch. 8 No. 2, where no executor is appointed or is unable or unwilling to act the order of priority with respect to entitlement to a grant of letters of administration with will annexed is as follows:

(a) the residuary devisee or residuary legatee;
(b) the devisee or legatee;
(c) the next of kin;[7]
(d) the Administrator General

Eastern Caribbean territories (save Dominica and St Lucia)

Pursuant to s.11 of the respective Eastern Caribbean Supreme Court of Judicature Acts of the various Eastern Caribbean territories grants of letters of administration with will annexed are issued in accordance with the order of priority as set out in r.20 of the N.C.P.R. 1987, England.

This order of priority is essentially the same as that which is contained in r.19 of the N.C.P.R. 1954, England. Again the nature to size of the benefit conferred on the individual beneficiaries may also be taken into account by the Registrar in determining entitlement to the grant.

Anguilla

It is to be noted that although s.7(2) of the Death Duties (Abolition) Ordinance 6/1977 in effect provides that the Registrar may appoint as administrator with will annexed any person in cases where it shall appear to him proper and necessary to do so, the practice again is to apply the order of priority set out in r.20, N.C.P.R 1987, England as modified to local practice.

Dominica

By virtue of the cut off date[8] for reception of English probate law, practice and procedure as contained in s.11 of the Eastern Caribbean Supreme Court (Dominica) Act Cap. 18, r.19 of the N.C.P.R. 1954, England is applicable to Dominica, subject to the registrar's discretion to vary the order in the appropriate case.

St Lucia

According to Art 590 of the Civil Code Ch. 242, administration with the will annexed is granted in very much the same circumstances as in the other territories in particular in cases where:

(a) the testator has failed to appoint an executor; or
(b) the executor or executors have all died or become incapable of fulfilling the duties of their office; or
(c) the executor or executors have all refused or neglected to accept office; or
(d) the executor or executors have all been removed by the court; or
(e) the testamentary succession is left without a representative for any other cause.

Art 586(6) of the Civil Code Ch. 242 provides that:

> in granting letters of administration the court shall have regard to the right of all persons interested in the succession or the proceeds thereof and to any prescribed provision.

(a) Art 1016 of the Code of Civil Procedure Ch. 243 sets out the priority with respect to entitlement to applications for letters of administration; and
(b) Article 1015 (based on the documents mentioned therein) clearly uses the term *letters of administration* to include and apply to letters of administration (with or without will annexed).[9]

It is submitted that Art 1016 is referable only to persons entitled to grants of letters of administration simpliciter as the persons entitled thereto are the surviving spouse and next of kin (persons who would usually be entitled on an intestacy to take out grants of letters of administration).

Indeed in practice letters of administration with will annexed are granted in accordance with the order of priority set out in r.20 N.C.P.R. 1987, England subject to the discretion of the Registrar to vary the order of priority in the appropriate case.

PRACTICE, PROCEDURE AND DOCUMENTS REQUIRED

In all the territories, the application for letters of administration with will annexed is made *ex parte* by lodging the requisite documents in the Probate Section of the Registry or alternatively the Sub-Registry in the case of Tobago. For the practice and procedure with respect to applications for grants of representation see chapter 4.

The documents lodged with respect to grants of administration with will annexed are in effect a combination of those used in applications for grants of probate and letters of administration simpliciter. However it should be noted that the applicant is called an administrator and the grant referred to in the relevant documents is a grant of letters of administration with will annexed.

Listed below are the documents filed in each of the jurisdictions. Documents to be lodged at Registry:

Barbados [10]

1. Application for grant made through an attorney-at-law or by applicant in person.
2. Affidavit of administrator.
3. Certified copy of death/burial certificate.
4. Certified copies of marriage, birth certificate, affidavit of kin, paternity order, adoption order, affidavit as to duration of union (where applicable).
5. Original will marked by signatures of the administrator and person before whom sworn (a Legal Assistant).
6. Affidavit of due execution.
7. Estate and Succession Duty Certificate (required with respect to the estates of persons dying on or before 30th March, 1981).[11]
8. Affidavit of Search.
9. Affidavit of Value/Property with Schedule thereto (required with respect to the estates of persons dying on or after 31st March, 1981).[12]
10. Justification of Sureties.
11. Consent(s)/Notice(s) (where applicable).

Guyana [13]

1. Application for grant made through an attorney at law or by applicant in person.
2. Oath of administrator.
3. Affidavit of due execution.
4. Statement of Assets and Liabilities sworn to before Commissioner for Oaths/Sworn Clerk.
5. Certificate of Proper Officer.
6. Original will marked by signatures of administrator and person before whom sworn (a Commissioner for Oaths).
7. Certified copy of death certificate.
8. Certified copy of marriage, birth certificate, adoption order, affidavit of kin, affiliation order (where applicable).
9. Administration bond with will annexed.
10. Justification of Sureties (when requested by the Registrar).
11. Consent(s)/Notice(s) (where applicable).

Jamaica [14]

On or before December 31, 2002

1. Covering letter addressed to registrar (discretionary).
2. Oath of administrator.
3. Affidavit of due execution.
4. Administration bond with will annexed (not required where the applicant is Administrator General).
5. Original will marked by the signatures of the administrator, an attesting witness and person before whom sworn (a Commissioner of Oaths).
6. Consent(s)/Notice(s) to adult beneficiaries (where applicable).
7. Formal Consent of the Administrator General With the Will Annexed.
8. Inventory.
9. Kalamazoo copy of Inventory.
10. Declaration of Counting of Inventory.
11. Affidavit in Proof of Death.
12. Affidavit of Value (not required where the Administrator General is the applicant).
13. Letters of administration with will annexed.
14. Kalamazoo copy of letters of administration with will annexed.
15. Declaration of Counting of letters of administration with will annexed and copy will.
16. Justification of Sureties (not required where the applicant is the Administrator General; in all other cases only when requested by the registrar).

On or after January 1, 2003

1. Covering letter to registrar (discretionary).
2. Oath of administration.
3. Death certificate exhibited to oath.
4. Original will duly marked.
5. Draft grant and kalamazoo copy.
6. Administrator General's Certificate.
7. Copy of advertisements.
8. Affidavit of due execution, where required.

The Bahamas[15]

1. Application in the form of a Petition made in person or by counsel and addressed to the Registrar of the Supreme Court.
2. Oath of administrator.
3. Original will or a photostatic copy thereof marked by the administrator and sworn to before a Commissioner of oaths/Justice of the Peace.
4. Affidavit of due execution.
5. Schedule of the Personal Estate of the deceased with the estimated value thereof (exhibited to oath).
6. Schedule of the Real Property owned by the deceased (exhibited to oath).
7. Certified copy of the death certificate.
8. Certified copy of birth, marriage certificate, adoption order, affidavit of kin, affidavit of heirship (where applicable).
9. Bond for making Return into Registry and Paying Dues.
10. Administration bond with will annexed.
11. Justification of Sureties (when requested by the Registrar).
12. Consent(s)/Notice(s) (where applicable).
13. Nomination /order of appointment of co-administrator (where applicable).

Trinidad & Tobago[16]

1. Application for grant made through an attorney-at-law.
2. Affidavit of administrator.
3. Certified copy of death/burial certificate.
4. Certified copies of marriage, birth certificate, paternity order, adoption order (where applicable).
5. Original will marked by the signatures of the administrator and the person before whom sworn (a Commissioner of Oaths).
6. Affidavit of due execution.
7. Inventory.
8. Certificate of Search.
9. Filing Fee Receipt.
10. Administration bond with will annexed.
11. Justification of Sureties (when requested by the Registrar).
12. Consent(s)/Notice(s) (where applicable).

Eastern Caribbean Territories[17]

Anguilla:

1. Application for grant made through a solicitor or by applicant in person.
2. Oath of administrator.
3. Certified copy of death certificate.
4. Certified copy of marriage, birth certificate, paternity order, adoption order, affidavit of kin, affiliation order (where applicable).
5. Affidavit of due execution.
6. Original will marked by signature of administrator and person before whom sworn (a Commissioner for Oaths/Justice of the Peace).
7. Administration bond with will annexed.
8. Justification of Sureties (when requested by the Registrar).
9. Declaration on Oath of value of the estate.
10. Land Registry Valuation certificate (where the application for the grant is made through the Registrar).
11. Order for issue of grant for signature by registrar.
12. Two original copies of grant (with copies of will glued on inner leaf).
13. Consent(s)/Notice(s) (where applicable).
14. Nomination/order of appointment of co-administrator (where applicable).

Antigua & Barbuda:

1. Application made through a solicitor or by applicant in person.
2. Oath of administrator.
3. Affidavit of due execution.
4. Certified copy of death certificate.
5. Certified copy of marriage, birth certificate, paternity order, affiliation order (where applicable).
6. Original will marked by signatures of administrator and person before whom sworn (a Commissioner for Oaths).
7. Estate and Succession Duties Certificate (required with respect to the estates of persons dying prior to 16th December, 1969).[18]
8. Declaration and Account of Estate (required with respect to the estates of persons dying prior to 16th December, 1969).[19]
9. Administration bond with will annexed.
10. Justification of Sureties (when requested by the registrar).

11. Consent(s)/Notice(s) (where applicable).
12. Nomination /order of appointment of co-administrator (where applicable).

Dominica:

1. Application for grant made through a solicitor or by applicant in person.
2. Oath of administrator.
3. Affidavit of due execution (discretionary but in practice usually submitted).
4. Declaration and Account of the Estate (in practice referred to as "Probate").
5. Certified copy of death certificate.
6. Certified copy of marriage, birth certificate, adoption order, (where applicable).
7. Original will marked the signatures of the administrator and person before whom sworn (a Commissioner for Oaths).
8. Estate and Succession Duty Certificate (with respect to the estate of persons dying prior to July 1, 1985).[20]
9. Administration bond with will annexed.
10. Justification of Sureties (when requested by the registrar).
11. Consent(s)/Notice(s) (where applicable).
12. Nomination /order of appointment of co-administrator (where applicable).

Grenada:

1. Application for grant in practice is made through a solicitor or by applicant in person.
2. Oath of administrator.
3. Original death certificate.
4. Paternity order, adoption order (where applicable).[21]
5. Original will marked by the signatures of the administrator and person before whom sworn (the Chief Clerk of the Registry/Deputy Registrar).
6. Affidavit of due execution- when requested by the registrar.
7. Administration bond with will annexed.
8. Justification of Sureties (when requested by the registrar).
9. Consent(s)/Notice(s) (where applicable).
10. Estate Duty Certificate (with respect to the estates of persons dying on or prior to 1st October, 1983).[22]

11. Declaration and Account of Estate (with respect to the estates of persons dying on or prior to 1st October, 1983).
12. Nomination /order of appointment of co-administrator (where applicable).

Montserrat:

1. Application for grant made through a solicitor or by applicants in person.
2. Oath of administrator.
3. Original will marked by signatures of the administrator and person before whom sworn (a Commissioner of Oaths).
4. Affidavit of due execution.
5. Certified copy of death certificate.
6. Certified copy of marriage, birth certificate (where applicable).
7. Declaration and Account of Estate.
8. Newspaper clippings of advertisement for application for grant.
9. Administration bond with will annexed.
10. Justification of Sureties (when requested by the registrar).
11. Consent(s)/Notice(s) (where applicable).
12. Nomination /order of appointment of co-administrator (where applicable).

St Christopher & Nevis:

1. Application for the grant made through a solicitor or by applicant in person.
2. Oath of administrator.
3. Declaration and Account of the Estate sworn to before a Commissioner for Oaths.
4. Certificate of Payment of Stamp Duty.
5. Original will marked by signatures of the administrator and person before whom sworn (a Commissioner for Oaths).
6. Certified copy of death certificate.
7. Certified copy of marriage, birth certificate, paternity order, affidavit of kin, affiliation order (where applicable).
8. Affidavit of due execution (discretionary).
9. Administration bond with will annexed.
10. Justification of Sureties (when requested by the registrar).
11. Consent(s)/Notice(s) (where applicable).
12. Nomination /order of appointment of co-administrator (where applicable).

St Lucia:

1. Application in form of petition.
2. Affidavit of administrator in support of petition.
3. Affidavit of due execution (non-notarial wills only).
4. Death Certificate.
5. Marriage, birth certificate, adoption order, affidavit of kin, affiliation order (where applicable).
6. Original English/Holograph Will marked by the administrator and person before whom sworn (Registry/Deputy Registrar). (English wills are required to be deposited and retained in Registry, Notarial Wills retained by Notary); or
A certified copy of notarial will.
7. Affidavit of Assets and Liabilities sworn to before a Justice of the Peace.
8. Certificate of Non-Objection to Grant.
9. Consent(s)/Notice(s) (where applicable).
10. Nomination /order of appointment of co-administrator (where applicable).

St Vincent & the Grenadines:

1. Application for grant in practice is made through a solicitor or by applicant in person.
2. Warrant to Act signed by the administrator(s).
3. Oath of administrator.
4. Petition for the Grant sworn to before a Commissioner for Oaths.
5. Certified copy of death certificate.
6. Certified copy of marriage, birth certificate, baptismal certificate, paternity order, affidavit of kin, adoption order, affiliation order (where applicable).
7. Original will marked by signatures of the administrator and person before whom sworn (a Commissioner for Oaths).
8. Affidavit of due execution (when requested by the registrar).
9. Affidavit and Accounts of the Estate.
10. Consent(s)/Notice(s) (where applicable).
11. Administration bond with will annexed.
12. Justification of Sureties (when requested by the registrar).
13. Valuation certificate of such property listed in the Declaration and Account.
14. Nomination /order of appointment of co-administrator (where applicable).

DESCRIPTION OF DOCUMENTS

1. *The Covering Letter/Application for the Grant* [23]

All jurisdictions (save St Lucia and The Bahamas)

The covering letter (with respect to Jamaica) and the formal application for a grant of letters of administration with will annexed (with respect to the other jurisdictions)[24] is basically the same as that which is required for a grant of probate application in the various territories except that the application specified therein is a grant of letters of administration with will annexed and the applicant is referred to as an administrator not an executor.

Petition

The Bahamas

The application for the grant takes the form of a simple petition.[25]

St Lucia

The application takes the form of a petition, which though not prescribed, includes the following recitals:

(i) the name, address and description of the applicant referred to as 'Your Petitioner';
(ii) the place and date of death of the deceased;
(iii) in cases where the deceased was a married woman/man survived by her/his spouse, a recital stating *inter alia* that the deceased was married, in community of property (if that is in fact the case);
(iv) a brief description of the property owned by the deceased. Where the deceased was married in community of property,[26] the description of the property is limited to the testator's share of the property held in community.
(v) that an affidavit in support of the petition as required by Art 1015(b) of Code of Civil Procedure Ch. 243 is herewith filed.
(vi) that the assets and liabilities of the succession of the deceased are as set out in the affidavit of assets and liabilities of the Petitioner.
(v) the names and addresses of the persons entitled to the grant
(vi) a recital that the Accountant General does not object to the grant of letters of administration with will annexed to the petitioner

(vii) any necessary clearings off; and
(viii) consents

Unlike the other Eastern Caribbean territories recitals with respect to minority and life interest are not included.

2. *Administrator's Oath/Affidavit*[27]

The recitals in the oath/affidavit, are similar to those contained in the oath/affidavit of an executor for the respective jurisdictions. However the following should be noted:

(i)   the oath must include a description of the administrator;

and in all the jurisdictions save Jamaica, the class of beneficiary applying for the grant—whether as residuary devisee or legatee as the case may be—so as to establish his entitlement thereto.

Jamaica

Prior to the passage of CPR 2002, it was not necessary to describe the class of beneficiary making the application only that he/she was a beneficiary and that the other beneficiaries, where applicable, had consented in writing to him or her making the application for the grant. However in accordance with Rule 68.19 CPR 2002, the class of beneficiary, whether residuary or specific, as the case may be, is required to be recited in the oath and all consents or notices, as the case may be, exhibited to the oath. In addition, any beneficiaries with a prior entitlement to the grant must be expressly accounted for in the oath in accordance with Rule 68.19, CPR 2002.

(ii)   Clearing off[28]

Where there are persons with a prior entitlement to the grant, these persons must be cleared off and the oath must set out how such persons have been cleared off by stating, as the case may be:

(a) that there is no person in that particular class;
(b) that such persons with a prior right have predeceased the testator. In such cases it is advisable to exhibit a certified copy of the death certificate;
(c) that such persons have renounced their right to probate and/or

letters of administration with will annexed. A copy of the filed renunciation should be exhibited.
(d) that such persons have been cited to accept or refuse the grant of probate and/or letters of administration with will annexed but have not appeared to the citation. An office copy of the order granting leave to the citor or other interested person as the case may be, to apply for the grant of letters of administration with will annexed should be exhibited; or alternatively,
(e) as in Barbados, that such persons have given their written consent to a beneficiary with an inferior title, applying for the grant. In such cases, the written consent should be filed. It is to be noted that subject to the registrar's discretion, consents are not only used in cases of equal entitlement but also for the purpose of permitting a beneficiary with an inferior title, to apply for the grant. (See note on consent below).

Jamaica

As was previously the case in practice, prior to the passage of Rule 68 CPR 2002, which codified the practice, the beneficiaries to the deceased's estate are permitted to take out letters of administration with will annexed where they have obtained the Administrator General's Certificate, or as it was previously called, the Formal Consent With Will Annexed of the Administrator General or alternatively an order of the court.

In accordance with the former position, recitals with respect to clearing off of persons with a prior entitlement to a grant of letters of administration with will annexed did not arise except insofar as where the executor, renounced his right to probate and was thereby cleared off. In such cases, the renunciation of the executor was required to be recited in the oath. However, with the passage of CPR 2002, and in particular Rule 68.19, applicants for grant of letters of administration with will annexed, are now expressly required to account for all persons with a prior entitlement to the grant and all such persons must be specifically cleared off in the oath.

(iii)   In cases of Equal entitlement Consent(s)

In cases where the application for the grant is made by one or some of the persons entitled thereto, the oath should recite that the others equally entitled have consented to the applicant applying for the grant on their behalf

Barbados

As stated above, in the appropriate case and subject to the registrar's discretion, written consents are also used for the purpose of permitting a person with an inferior right, to apply for the grant. Accordingly, where applicable, the oath should recite that the beneficiary with the prior entitlement to the grant has consented in writing to the applicant applying for the grant.

Jamaica

In instances where the beneficiaries are the applicants for the grant, although the Formal Consent With The Will Annexed of the Administrator General, and with effect from January 1, 2003, the Administrator General's Certificate, is required in addition to the written consent of the beneficiaries, the consent of the Administrator General is not recited in the oath. However the Formal Consent With Will Annexed of the Administrator General, and with effect from January 1, 2003, the Administrator General's Certificate, must be lodged with the papers to lead the grant.

Notice(s)

All jurisdictions (save Jamaica)

Alternatively if such persons should refuse and/or neglect to give their consent, the oath should recite that a notice in writing of the intended application was sent to such persons inviting or calling upon them either to join in the application and to indicate their willingness to do so by the date specified therein or otherwise that the proposed administrator shall proceed with the application for the grant; the oath should further recite that such persons have failed or neglected to join in the application for the grant. A copy of the notice which usually takes the form of a letter written by the attorney-at-law for the applicant, should be exhibited to the oath/affidavit.

Jamaica

Although in the appropriate circumstances, as outlined previously, a notice was required to be given by the intended applicant, in order to obtain the Formal Consent of the Administrator General, the giving of the notice was not recited in the oath nor was a copy of the notice filed with the papers to lead the grant.

However, with effect from January 1, 2003 a recital with respect to the giving of the notice must be included in the oath and the notice(s) must now be filed.

Barbados

It is to be noted that in Barbados a notice may also be served, in the appropriate case, on a beneficiary with a prior entitlement to the grant. (See note on Notice of Intended Application below). The notice in such instances calls upon the beneficiary with the prior entitlement, to give his written consent within a specified time to the intended grantee applying for the grant. If the beneficiary with the prior entitlement will not give his consent, the oath should recite that the notice was given and that the beneficiary with the prior right to the grant has failed or refused to give his written consent.

(iv) Recitals with respect to Minority and Life Interest

Jamaica, The Bahamas and the Eastern Caribbean Territories (save St. Lucia)

In the above-mentioned territories the oath must recite whether or not a minority or life interest arises, and with the exception of Jamaica, administration must be granted to not less than two individuals or a trust corporation with or without an individual.

(v) Recitals with respect to Settled Land

As stated previously, with the exception of Jamaica, the recital with respect to settled land grants should not be included in the affidavit of the applicant/ oath of the applicant.

Guyana

In Guyana the oath must state that the number of times that the deceased was married and whether he/she was married after the 20th August, 1904.

3. *Consents of/Notices to Beneficiaries*

Consents

Although the written consent of the other persons equally entitled to letters of administration with will annexed is not required in order to permit those other persons equally entitled thereto, to make the application, their consent nevertheless should be obtained.

However it is to be noted that the consent of a minor, mentally or physically disabled beneficiary is not required, nor is it strictly necessary to serve notice on a beneficiary resident abroad. However notice of the application should be given to the beneficiary equally entitled and who is resident abroad if his mailing address is known. Additionally, in Trinidad & Tobago, it is the practice to obtain the written consent of a minor who is 14 years and over.

Barbados

As stated previously, consents are also used for the purpose of permitting a beneficiary with an inferior right, to apply for the grant. By way of illustration, a residuary beneficiary, may without renouncing, give his written consent to a devisee applying for the grant where the devisee is entitled to a larger share of the testator's estate. This written consent, subject to the registrar's discretion, is sufficient to permit the devisee to apply for the grant.

Further in the appropriate case the registrar may waive the requirement for the written consent where the beneficiary with the prior entitlement will not consent, having been called upon to do so by the attorney at law for the beneficiary with an inferior right to the grant.

It is submitted that the registrar may permit a beneficiary with an inferior right to take out the grant, with or without the consent of the beneficiary with the prior entitlement because:

(a) there is no indigenous probate rule which requires that the registrar observe a prescribed order of priority for purposes of determining priorities with respect to entitlement to letters of administration with will annexed; and
(b) although r.21 N.C.P.R. 1954, England, is applied for the purposes of determining the order of priority to letters of administration with will annexed, s.19(3) of the Succession Act Cap. 249 effectively confers on the Registrar the discretion as to whom administration may be granted.

However it is to be noted that depending on the fact circumstances, the registrar may require that beneficiaries who are deemed to have a prior entitlement to the grant, that their rights with respect thereto, be cleared off by 'passing over' or citation proceedings.

Form of Consent

All jurisdictions

The consent does not take a prescribed form, but it should nevertheless:

(i) state the name, place and date of death of the deceased;
(ii) include a brief description of the applicant and his entitlement to the grant;
(iii) include a brief description of the consenting beneficiaries and their entitlement to a grant of the deceased's estate, that is, as (residuary) beneficiaries under the deceased's will; and
(iv) that they have consented to the application for letters of administration with will annexed being made to the court by the applicant named therein.

Notice of Intended Application

There is no express requirement in any of the jurisdictions save and except Jamaica, with effect from January 1, 2003, that notice of intended application for letters of administration with will annexed should be given by the proposed grantee to those beneficiaries who are as equally entitled as the proposed grantee to apply for the grant. However it is a good practice, and in the case of Jamaica, a requirement of Rule 68.19 CPR 2002, is to give notice thereof, to those beneficiaries who have not joined in the application and who have refused and/or neglected to give their written consent to the proposed grantee applying for the grant.

It is to be noted that although notice of the application for the grant of administration with will annexed is not required to be served on a minor or on a mentally or physically incapable beneficiary or the guardian of such persons, the oath/affidavit to lead the grant, must nevertheless account for all persons equally entitled to the grant. Accordingly the oath should recite, where applicable, that the person equally entitled to the grant is a minor or is mentally or physically incapable as the case may be. However where an adult beneficiary who is equally entitled to the grant is resident abroad and the mailing address of the beneficiary is known, notice of the application should be sent to him/her and the oath should recite that notice of the application for the grant has been served on him/her.

Form of Notice

The notice which usually takes the form of a letter signed by the attorney-at-law for and on behalf of the proposed grantee, calls upon or invites the beneficiaries equally entitled to letters of administration with will annexed (who have not given their written consent) to indicate their willingness to join the proposed grantee in the application for the grant, by a date stipulated therein, or otherwise the proposed grantee shall proceed with the application for the grant.

Barbados

Additionally it is to be noted that in Barbados, it is the practice to serve notice of the intended application on beneficiaries who fall into a lower category with respect to entitlement to the grant, particularly where such beneficiary is entitled to a larger share of the testator's estate. This precaution is taken because as was stated previously the registrar has the discretion, pursuant to s. 19(3) of the Succession Act Cap. 249 as to whom administration may be granted. Accordingly, in the appropriate case, the registrar may permit a beneficiary who has an inferior right to the grant but who is entitled to a substantially larger share of the testator's estate, to apply for the grant, with, or in some cases without the written consent of the beneficiary with the prior entitlement to the grant.

Dispute Between Persons Equally Entitled

All jurisdictions (save Jamaica)

Obtaining the written consent of the other beneficiaries equally entitled, or giving notice to them of the intended application, where they will not consent, is advisable in the event that a dispute should arise between the persons entitled to the grant in the same degree.

In such instances, the dispute must be brought by summons supported by affidavit before the registrar/judge in chambers. Once the summons is issued, it operates in the same manner as a caveat and accordingly no grant may be sealed with respect to the estate of the deceased named therein, until the matter is determined by the registrar/judge in chambers.

The affidavit in support of the summons should set out the interest of each party, and the grounds of objection such as the bad character or insolvency of the intended administrator. It should also recite that where applicable, that the consent was given by/notice of the intended application given to those persons opposed to the application being made by the proposed grantee, factors which would be taken into account by the court in making the order with respect to entitlement to the grant.

Jamaica

Although the CPR 2002 introduced significant changes in respect of the procedure and practice relevant to non-contentious probate matters, the sole person entitled to letters of administration with will annexed is the Administrator General by virtue of s.12 of the Intestates' Estates and Property Charges Act. and s.12 of the Administrator General's Act respectively. As such obtaining the consent of the beneficiaries or giving notice of the intended application was and still is necessary for the purpose of obtaining the Formal Consent with Will Annexed of the Administrator General and with effect from January 1, 2003, the Administrator General's Certificate.

In addition, the Administrator General's Certificate is also necessary (as was not previously the case prior to the passage of the new CPR 2002) for the purposes of avoiding disputes between beneficiaries who are equally entitled to the grant of administration with will annexed. Indeed Rule 68.21(4)CPR 2002, expressly provides that any person challenging the right of a person in the same degree to a grant of administration may apply to the registrar for directions. Further, Rule 68.21(5) provides that no grant may be issued until the application is fully disposed of.

4. Administration Bond with Will Annexed

With the exception of St Lucia and Barbados, and with effect from January 1, 2003, in respect of Jamaica, an administration bond with will annexed (with or without surety/sureties) is also lodged by the applicant, with the other papers to lead the grant. In St Lucia, an administration bond with will annexed is not required in practice in the case of Jamaica pursuant to Rule 68 CPR 2002, and with respect to Barbados, although required, it is not lodged by the applicant. As was previously stated, the administration bond is no longer applicable in Jamaica with respect to applications for grants made in the Supreme Court.

5. Justification of Sureties

This affidavit is lodged subject to the discretion of the registrar and the practice and procedure relevant to the respective territory.

6. Marriage, Death, Birth Certificate, Paternity Order, Affidavit of Heirship, Affidavit of kin, Affidavit as to Duration of Union

All jurisdictions (save Jamaica)

In the very rare circumstances where a person had died leaving a valid will but no executor willing or able to act *and* there are no beneficiaries under the will, letters of administration with will annexed is required to be obtained by the persons entitled to the deceased's estate on an intestacy. In such instances the persons entitled to the grant are as a general rule the spouse and thereafter the children as next-of-kin of the deceased. Accordingly, the marriage certificate, birth certificate, adoption order, paternity order, affidavit of kin, affidavit of heirship where applicable, should also be exhibited as proof of entitlement thereto.

In cases where the spouse is the applicant, a certified copy of the marriage certificate should be lodged and where the applicant is the child of the testator, a certified copy of the birth certificate. However where the applicant is a child born out of wedlock and the father's name is not on the child's birth certificate it may be necessary to obtain a paternity order from the High Court to establish the relationship.

However in Anguilla, Barbados, Guyana, St Lucia, St Christopher & Nevis and St Vincent & the Grenadines, an affidavit sworn to by a person who can depose to the relationship of paternity between the applicant and the deceased may be accepted. Where the applicant is the adopted child of the deceased and entitled to apply, a copy of the adoption order should be filed.

Barbados

Affidavit as to Duration of Union

Where the applicant for the grant is a statutory spouse[29] separate affidavits from two persons respectively, who knew the deceased and the statutory spouse, and who can depose to the duration of their union must be lodged with the papers to lead the grant.

Jamaica

Where there is a valid will but no executor(s) and there has been a complete failure of beneficiaries under the will, it is submitted that the Administrator General may apply for a grant of letters of administration with will annexed or alternatively the next of kin will be permitted to apply for the grant provided they have obtained the Administrator General's Certificate. In such instances proof of the applicant's entitlement as next of kin whether by way of a marriage or birth certificate is not required to be filed with the application. It is submitted that the oath should merely recite that the beneficiaries under the will have predeceased the testator; that the applicant(s) is/are the spouse or child(ren) of the testator as the case may be and is/are a beneficiary(ies) of his estate; that where applicable, the other beneficiaries are all *sui juris* and have given their consent to the intended grantee making the application.

However it is to be noted that where the applicant is:

(a) the statutory spouse, an affidavit of facts sworn to by him/her deposing to the duration of the union is required to be lodged with the papers to lead the grant;
(b) a child born out of wedlock, a paternity order or affidavit evidence of paternity is required in cases where the father's name does not appear on the child's birth certificate.

ADDITIONAL DOCUMENTS – BY JURISDICTION

1. St Lucia

A. *Certificate of Non-Objection*

In St Lucia a Certificate of Non-Objection must be produced in cases of administration whether or not death occurred prior to or after 1st October, 1988 - the date of the abolition of succession duties. The certificate is still required because the Succession Repeal Ordinance Act 4/1988 which abolished succession duties with respect to the estate of persons dying on or after 1st January, 1988 did not repeal Art 1015(2) of the Code of Civil Procedure. Art 1015(2) in effect provides that letters of administration shall not be handed out until a Certificate of Non-Objection has been produced. As such a Certificate of Non-Objection is lodged with respect to all applications for grants of representation save and except probate grants.

2. Jamaica

A. *Order of the Court*

An application for an order of the court granting leaving to the beneficiaries to apply for letters of administration with will annexed is made in practice in circumstances where one or some of the beneficiaries is/are minor(s), although as was pointed out,[30] the Formal Consent of the Administrator General and with effect from January 1, 2003, the Administrator General's Certificate may be obtained in instances where one or some of the beneficiaries is/are minors.

The application is made in accordance with Part 11, CPR 2002 to a judge in chambers. The affidavit in support of the application should set out the facts necessary particulars to satisfy the court that it would be for the benefit of the estate that the grant be made to the applicant, rather than the Administrator General.

Accordingly the affidavit should recite *inter alia*:

(i) that the deceased died leaving a will but no executor (a brief explanation as to reason why there is no executor should be included, for example, that the executor renounced his right to probate, in which case a copy of the deed of renunciation should be filed with the application);

(ii) the belief of the applicants that there would be a substantial saving to the estate, in that, they would make no charges for their services, being the beneficiaries of the estate, whereas the Administrator General would be entitled to a commission as prescribed by law.

The consent of or notices of the adult beneficiaries who are not joining in the application should also be filed with the application. Upon filing the application in the Supreme Court Registry, a sealed copy of the summons and filed copies of the affidavit and consent(s) of/notices to the adult beneficiaries are required to be served on the Administrator General, who admits service thereof on the copy.

At the hearing of the application for the order, a representative from the Administrator General's department attends the court; so as to indicate to the court that the Administrator General has no objection, if that is the case, to the granting of the order. A copy of the order, where granted, must thereafter be lodged with the papers to lead the grant.

B. *Administrator General's Certificate*

In the appropriate case, where the beneficiaries are the applicants for the grant of administration with will annexed, the Administrator General's Certificate which has replaced the Formal Consent of the Administrator General with effect from Janaury 1, 2003 must be obtained and filed with the application for the grant. The Administrator General's Certificate is essentially the same document as the former Formal Consent. As such it includes the following information:

- the basis upon which the Administrator General is entitled to take out the grant of letters of administration with will annexed, for example, that the testator appointed no executor in his will, as the case may be;
- that the Administrator General will not oppose the grant of administration with will annexed to the beneficiaries as the beneficiaries under the will are adults, if that is the case, and have all given their consent to the application for the grant being made by the applicant, and;
- that payment of the commission of 6 per centum in the value of the estate to the Government of Jamaica by way of administration fee, would be obviated if the beneficiaries were permitted to apply thus resulting in an increase in the amount received by them.

It is to be noted that the recitals in the Formal Consent and with effect from January 1, 2003 the Administrator General's Certificate, would vary depending on the circumstances and facts of each case.

C. Letters of Administration With Will Annexed and Copy Will and Kalamazoo Copy [31]

As is the case with respect to probate applications the grant of letters of administration with will annexed and copy thereof are required to be prepared by the attorney-at-law for the applicant and lodged with the papers to lead the grant.

On or After January 1, 2003

It is to be noted that with effect from January 1, 2003, the following documents which were specific to letters of administration with will annexed are no longer required in respect of applications for such grants made in the Supreme Court:

- Declaration of Counting of Letters of Administration With Will Annexed[32]
- Inventory
- Kalamazoo Copy of Inventory[33]
- Declaration of Counting of Inventory
- Administration bond and With Will Annexed
- Justification of Surities

- Affidavit of Value
- Declaration of Counting of Letters of Administration with Will Annexed

3. The Bahamas

Affidavit of Heirship [34]

Prior to the passage of the Inheritance Act 2002, the common law doctrine of descent was applicable to thse Bahamas. As a consequence, where the deceased died prior to February 1, 2002, the date of the coming into operation of the Inheritance Act 2002, and the person entitled to administration with will annexed was the heir-at-law an affidavit of heirship was also required to be lodged with the documents to lead the grant.

4. Barbados, Guyana, Jamaica and Trinidad & Tobago [35]

Affidavit of Delay

An affidavit of delay may be necessary depending on the circumstances.

5. Eastern Caribbean territories (save St Lucia) and The Bahamas

Nomination/Order of Appointment of Co-Administrator

Wherever a minority or life interest arises under the will of a deceased and there is only one administrator, not being a trust corporation, a second administrator must be nominated or appointed subject to the registrar's discretion to waive this requirement. Accordingly the nomination or order of appointment of the second administrator must be filed with the papers to lead the grant. However it is to be noted that with respect to The Bahamas that this procedural requirement has not yet been implemented.

Documents Required Depending on Facts

All territories

It should be noted that the following documents should be included where applicable:

(1) an affidavit of plight and condition;[36] and
(2) affidavit of alias;[37]

Notes

1. Antigua & Barbuda,   - s.114 Supreme Court of Judicature Act 1981, England
    St Christopher & Nevis,
    Anguilla, Montserrat,
    Dominica, Grenada
    Barbados   - s.18 Succession Act Cap. 249
    St Lucia   - Art. 841 Civil Code Ch. 242
    St Vincent &   - s.14 Administration of Estates Act Cap. 377
      the Grenadines
    The Bahamas   - See s.42 of the Supreme Court Act 15/1996
    Trinidad & Tobago   - s.16 Wills and Probate Ordinance Ch. 8 No.2.
2. s.12 of Intestates Estates' and Property Charges Act provides that:
    Notwithstanding anything contained in the Administrator-General's Act, or any enactment amending or substituted for the same, where the residuary estate of the intestate does not exceed one thousand dollars, or where it exceeds that sum and a minor is entitled to a share thereof or where a testator does not appoint an executor or where the executor has died before the testator or renounces, it shall be the duty of the Administrator-General to apply for letters of administration to the estate and, unless the court is satisfied that it would be for the benefit of the estate that letters of administration ought to be granted to some other person, letters of administration to such estate shall be granted to the Administrator-General. See also s.12 of the Administrator General's Act. See chapter 9 p.184 post.
3. See chapter 3 p. 82.
4. See p. 149.
5. See pp. 141-151.
6. See pp. 153-154.
7. With respect to the persons who qualify as next-of-kin see chapter 8 p. 196.
8. 1st June, 1984. See also Introduction p. 6.
9. Art 1015 *inter alia* provides that:
    (1) The application for letters of administration shall be made in the Registry by petition and shall be accompanied by the following documents:-
        (a) a certified copy of the will of the deceased, if it is a notarial will, or the original will, if it is not a notarial will, (where the grant is to he annexed to a will),
        (b) the affidavit or affidavits of proof of due execution in the case of a non-notarial will (where the grant is to be annexed to a will).
10. Rules 5, 6, 8, 30, 31, Supreme Court (Non-Contentious) Probate Rules 1959.
11. Estate Duties repealed by Estate and Succession Duties (Repeal) Act 41/1981.
12. *Ibid.*
13. Rules 3, 5 Deceased Persons Estates' Administration Rules Cap. 12:01.
14. Rules 6-15, 20-29, General Rules and Orders of the Supreme Court Part III Probate and Administration.
15. Rules 4,5,7,8, 16-19 The Probate Rules Ch. 35.
16. Rules 1, 3, 10-14, 35 First Schedule N.C.B.R. Ch. 8 No.2.
17. Dominica   - rr. 6-14 N.C.P.R 1954, England
    Eastern Caribbean   - rr. 8-16 N.C.P.R. 1987, England
      territories

	(save Dominica and St Lucia)	
	St Lucia	- Art 1015-1025 Code of Civil Procedure Ch. 243.
18	Stamp Duty Probate abolished by virtue of Stamp Duty (Amendment) Act 21/1969.	
19	*Ibid.*	
20	Estate Duty abolished by virtue of Estate Duty (Amendment) Act 14/1985.	
21	In practice, marriage/birth certificate are not usually lodged unless the Registrar so requests.	
22	Estate duties abolished with respect to the estates of persons dying on or after 1st October, 1983 by virtue of Estate Duty (Repeal) Ordinance Act 21/1983.	
23	Barbados	- Form No. 4 Appendix (Forms & Fees) Supreme Court (Non-Contentious) Probate Rules 1959.
	Trinidad & Tobago	- Form No, 8 First Schedule N.C.B.R. Ch. 8 No. 2.
24	For Jamaica and other jurisdictions, see chapter 5, p.104.	
25	See Form No. 1 Probate Rules Ch. 35.	
26	See chapter 7 p. 180.	
27		**Rules**
	Barbados	- r.6 Supreme Court (Non-Contentious) Probate Rules 1959
	Dominica	- r.6 N.C.P.R. 1954, England
	Guyana	- r.3 Deceased Persons Estates' Administration Rules Cap. 12:01
	Eastern Caribbean (save St Lucia and Dominica)	- r.8 N.C.P.R. 1987, England
	Jamaica	- Rule 68.9 CPR 2002, repealing and replacing r.27 General Rules and Orders of the Supreme Court Part III Probate and Administration
	St Lucia	- Art 1015(1)(c) Code of Civil Procedure Ch. 243
	The Bahamas	- r.4 The Probate Rules Ch, 35
	Trinidad & Tobago	- rr. 4, 32 First Schedule N.C.B.R. Ch. 8 No.2
		Forms
	Barbados	- Form No. 5 Appendix (Forms & Fees) Supreme Court (Non-Contentious) Probate Rules 1959
	Guyana	- Schedule 2 The Deceased Persons Estates Administration Rules Cap. 12:01
	Jamaica	- Form P.5 CPR 2002 repealing and replacing Form No. 3 General Rules and Orders of the Supreme Court Part III Schedule of Forms
	The Bahamas	- Form No. IV The Probate Rules Ch. 35
	Trinidad & Tobago	- Form No. 2 First Schedule N.C.B.R. Ch. 8 No. 2.

N.B. The Forms prescribed above are to be used with such modifications as are necessary so as to reflect the existing probate practices of the various territories

28	Barbados	- r.6 Supreme Court (Non-Contentious) Probate Rules 1959
	Dominica, Guyana	- r.6(2) N.C.P.R. 1954, England
	The Bahamas, Eastern Caribbean (save Dominica and St Lucia)	- r.8(4) N.C.P.R. 1987, England

St Lucia	- Art 1022(1) Code of Civil Procedure Ch. 243
Jamaica	- Rule 68.11 CPR 2002
Trinidad & Tobago	- r.32 First Schedule N.C.B.R. Ch. 8 No. 2.

29 Pursuant to s.2(3) of the Succession Act Cap. 249 a spouse includes a single woman who was living together with a single man as his wife for a period of not less than five years immediately preceding the date of death (and vice versa). Note that single includes a reference to a widow or widower or to a man or a woman who is divorced.
30 Pursuant to s.12 of the Intestates' Estates and Property Charges Act; See note 2 with respect to the provisions of s.12.
31 See Form No. 7 of the former General Rules and Orders of the Supreme Court Part III Schedule of Forms. See also Practice Note of the Supreme Court, Jamaica dated 18th April, 1953 which provides for a copy of the grant 'type written on special paper' to be filed with the papers for the grant.
32 See Practice Note of the Supreme Court, Jamaica dated 3rd March, 1955 with respect thereto; see also chapter 3 for the contents and purpose of the Declaration.
33 See Practice Note of the Supreme Court, Jamaica dated 18th April, 1953 which provides for a copy of the inventory 'type written on special paper' to be filed with each application for letters of administration with will annexed.
34 See chapter 8 p. 218-219.
35 See chapter 5 p. 119.
36 Ibid.
37. Ibid.

7

Grants of Letters of Administration Preliminary Considerations

INTRODUCTION

Grants of letters of administration are issued in circumstances in which:

(a) The deceased died wholly intestate. This eventuality may arise because the deceased never made a will or any will made is invalid owing, amongst other causes, to a want of formalities or testamentary capacity or because all wills made have been revoked without effective replacement.[1]

(b) The deceased made a will appointing no executor and disposing only of foreign property, but leaving some estate within the jurisdiction where he died domiciled.

HISTORY OF INTESTATE SUCCESSION IN THE CARIBBEAN — AN OVERVIEW

Succession to personalty
All jurisdictions (save St Lucia and Guyana)

Historically, succession to the personal estate of an intestate was governed by the Statute of Distributions 1670, England. This statute was eventually repealed and replaced in England with effect from 1st January 1926 by the Administration of Estates Act 1925, the provisions of which not only created new rules of distribution with respect to an intestate's residuary estate but most significantly assimilated the residuary real and personal estate of an intestate for the purposes of such distribution.

Between the late 1930s to the early 1950s, the Eastern Caribbean territories[2] (with the exception of St Lucia) and more recently, with effect from February 1, 2002 the Bahamas,[3] followed suit and enacted similar intestate legislation which:

- declared that the Statute of Distributions would cease to have effect;
- assimilated the residuary real and personal estate of an intestate for the purposes of such distribution; and
- created new rules of distribution with respect to an intestate's residuary estate.

Jamaica also enacted similar provisions with the passage on 1st June, 1937 of the Intestates' Estates and Property Charges Ordinance Cap. 166. In Barbados, however, as late as November 1975, the distribution of the residuary personal estate of an intestate was governed by indigenous legislation the Administration of Estates Ordinance 1891, s. 19 of which was in fact a replica of the provisions contained in the Statute of Distributions 1670, albeit expressed in modern English, while s.20 thereof was a replica of the 1809 Intestate Children's Act, England.

Although this Ordinance has not been repealed in its entirety, all the provisions relating to the distribution of an intestate's personal estate were repealed and replaced in 1975 by the new provisions contained in the Succession Act Cap. 249. Part VI of this Act not only created new rules of distribution but also assimilated the personalty and realty of an intestate for the purposes of such distribution.

The history of intestate succession in Trinidad & Tobago is somewhat more convoluted. This is primarily as a consequence of a series of Ordinances which were enacted in 1902 (and which became law on 1st January, 1903), most notable of which were the Wills and Probate Ordinance No. 99; The Property Devolution Ordinance No. 101; The Distributions Ordinance No. 102 and the Administrator General's Ordinance No. 103.

Most significantly ss.2 and 5 of the Distributions Ordinance assimilated both the residuary personal and real estate of an intestate for the purposes of distribution on an intestacy. Thus in a sense, Trinidad & Tobago was a forerunner to England, which did not assimilate the real and personal estate of an intestate until 1st January, 1926 (with the passage of the Administration of Estates Act 1925).

However according to s.5 of the Distribution Ordinance this residuary estate was to be distributed in the same manner and in the same proportions as the personal estate of such person dying domiciled in England and intestate would be distributed by the law of England. The law of England at that time, in so far as the personal estate of an intestate was concerned, was governed by a piece of legislation dating back to 1670 - The Statute of Distribution.

The Distribution Ordinance (which was amended in 1912) together with The Property Devolution Ordinance No. 101, and the Administrator

General's Ordinance No. 103 were repealed and replaced by the Administration of Property Ordinance No. 35 of 1913, the provisions of which *inter alia*:

(a) consolidated and amended these disparate pieces of legislation;
(b) re-enacted the provisions of s.5 of the Distributions Ordinance; and for the first time made provision for the surviving spouse and issue in the following manner and proportions:
 (i) if there was no lawful issue, the surviving spouse took the entire estate;
 (ii) if there was lawful issue, even if only one, one third to the surviving spouse, the remainder to the lawful issue in equal shares;
 (iii) if there was no surviving spouse, the lawful issue took the entire estate.

The Administration of Property Ordinance was subsequently repealed and replaced by the current Administration of Estates Ordinance Ch. 8 No. 1. This Ordinance essentially re-enacted the provisions of the repealed Ordinance in so far as the distribution of an intestate's estate was concerned. In particular, s.24 provided in effect that subject only to the express provision contained in s.24, which governed the entitlement of a surviving spouse and issue to the estate of the deceased intestate, the residuary real and personal estate of an intestate in Trinidad & Tobago was to be distributed in accordance with the provisions contained in the Statute of Distribution 1670, England.[4]

The Wills and Probate Ordinance No. 99 was in turn repealed and replaced on the 21st May, 1937 by the present Wills and Probate Ordinance Ch. 8 No. 2, which re-enacted many of the provisions contained in the former Ordinance, most notably those dealing with entitlement to a grant of administration in cases of intestacy.

Although these two pieces of legislation; the Wills and Probate Ordinance Ch. 8 No. 2 and the Administration of Estates Ordinance Ch. 8 No. 1 still comprise the current succession legislation of Trinidad & Tobago, significant amendments have been made to the intestate provisions of the Administration of Estates Ordinance by virtue of the passage of the Distribution of Estates Act 28/2000. The amendments introduced to the Administration of Estates Ordinance, which apply to the estates of persons dying on or after September 25, 2000, have not only introduced new classes of persons beneficially entitled as an intestacy, but in addition have significantly altered the proportions by which beneficiaries are entitled to benefit from the intestate's estate.

Succession to Real Estate of an Intestate

Eastern Caribbean, (save St Lucia) Jamaica, Barbados and the Bahamas

Until the passage of the various intestate estates legislation in the Eastern Caribbean, the enactment of the Intestates' Estates and Property Charges Act in Jamaica; and as late as 13th November, 1975 in Barbados with the passage of the Succession Act Cap. 249, and even more recently, in the Bahamas with the passage on February 1, 2002 of the Inheritance Act 2002, realty, which was not disposed of by will, passed to the heir at law by the common law doctrine of descent.

The main concern of this common law doctrine was the identification of the heir-at-law, the lineal descendant. This was accomplished by the application of a number of rules partly derived by custom and partly by the decisions of the Courts of England during the thirteenth and fourteenth centuries. These rules of practice were codified and rationalised with the passage of the Inheritance Act 1833, England. The equivalent of this Act, also called the Inheritance Act, was also enacted in Barbados and the various Eastern Caribbean territories, save St Lucia.

In addition, the rules of inheritance to realty at that time hardly considered the position of the widow whose slight inheritance was embodied in the doctrine of dower and was limited to a life interest in one-third share of her intestate husband's freehold estate which could easily be alienated by him during his lifetime or by his will. The husband, on the other hand, had rather more extensive rights to his intestate's wife's real estate. These rights were embodied in the doctrine of curtesy which entitled the surviving husband to a life interest in the whole of the property of his deceased's wife.

Escheat to the Crown, a doctrine embodied in the provisions of the Escheat Act, England, and based on the principle that all ownerless lands within the realm belonged to the Crown, also formed part of the succession laws of many of the Caribbean territories. In England, however, with the passage on the 1st January, 1926 of the Administration of Estates Act 1925, descent to the heir, curtesy, dower and escheat were abolished. The residuary, real and personal estate of an intestate was also assimilated for the purposes of distribution and was subject to new rules of distribution.

Following suit:

- The Eastern Caribbean territories with the passage of their respective Intestates Estates Acts, during the 1930s to 1950s.

- Jamaica with the enactment of the Intestates Estate' and Property Charges Act on 1 June 1937; and
- Barbados with the enactment on 13th November, 1975 of the Succession Act Cap. 249 and
- The Bahamas with the passage on Febraury 1, 2002 of the Inheritance Act, 2002, abolished heirship, curtesy, dower, and escheat to the Crown.

In their place new rules of distribution were enacted which assimilated the residuary real and personal estate of an intestate for the purpose of intestate succession, with the exception of the Bahamas, escheat to the Crown[5] was replaced by the Crown's or State's rights to ownerless property as *bona vacantia,* a common law right which had previously applied only to ownerless personal goods of an intestate.

St Vincent & the Grenadines

Although escheat has been abolished and replaced by the Crown's right to ownerless property as *bona vacantia,* the Escheat Act Cap. 306 which was enacted on 29th October, 1921 is still law in St Vincent & the Grenadines. Presumably the intention in not repealing this Act is to give effect *inter alia* to the Crown's statutory discretion to waive its rights to an intestate's estate in favour of some person upon legal moral and equitable grounds established to the satisfaction of the Governor General.[6]

Indeed s.62(e) of the Administrator of Estates Act Cap. 377, which sets out the rules of distribution of the residuary estate of an intestate, provides that:

> In default of any person taking the estate of the intestate under the foregoing provisions, the same shall belong to the Crown as *bona vacantia,* in lieu of any right to escheat and shall form part of the Consolidated Fund and be appropriated in the manner provided for by the Escheat Act in that behalf.

Trinidad & Tobago

In Trinidad & Tobago, as stated above, the residuary real and personal estate of an intestate was assimilated since 1st January. 1903.

Since 1903 in Trinidad with the passage of the Distributions Ordinance escheat was also abolished 'by necessary implication', if not expressly according to Wooding CJ in the case of the *A. G. of Trinidad & Tobago v. Maharaj and Maharaj.*[7]

The doctrine of dower, which was modified by s.6 of the Distribution Ordinance, was eventually repealed with the passage in 1916 of the Administration of Estates Ordinance Ch. 8 No. 1 while the doctrine of curtesy, although not *de jure,* was *de facto* repealed, since it applies only to cases where the intestate was married to the surviving spouse before 1903.

St Lucia [8]

Until the passage of the Civil Code Ordinance 1876, the laws governing intestate succession in St Lucia were the ancient French laws as they existed prior to the promulgation of the Code Napoleon. These ancient laws were a combination of the *Coutume de Paris* and the *Code de la Martinique.*

According to these ancient laws of intestate succession, the intestate estate passed in order of priority to:

(a) lawful heirs;
(b) lawful consort;
(c) the Crown.

The lawful heirs include all descendants, ascendants and collaterals of the intestate up to the twelfth degree so that the lawful spouse was at the bottom of the hierarchy in the order of entitlement. If the spouses were married in community of property, however, it was only the deceased's share of the property that would be distributed on intestacy.

Furthermore, prior to 1879 the testamentary freedom of the husband was restricted by the laws relating to dower. According to these laws the wife was entitled to a life interest in her husband's estate. The wife forfeited her rights to dower by committing adultery or desertion or if she abused her enjoyment of the property.

With the passage of the Civil Code Ordinance in 1876 many aspects of English law were introduced. By and large, however, the present Civil Code Ordinance is an adaptation of the Civil Code of Lower Canada, which is in fact a modern form of Roman Civil law with the mere alteration of the local terms.

Minor amendments were also made to the Code in 1907 and 1913. In 1916 and more significantly 1956, in so far as the succession laws are concerned, many of the provisions of English trust and succession law were introduced, thus assimilating the provisions of the Civil Code with those of the English law. Dower too was abolished.

Guyana

Guyana, as with other Caribbean territories, has no indigenous legal system. Indeed, prior to the passage of the Civil Law Act Cap. 6:01 in 1917, succession to the residuary real and personal estate of an intestate in Guyana was governed by Roman-Dutch law. More specifically, in Demerara and Essequibo, succession was regulated by the Law of North Holland, while in Berbice one had a choice between North and South Holland laws.

Although the Civil Law Act preserved certain aspects of the Roman-Dutch law (in particular it excluded the English common law of property with respect to immovable property and preserved existing rights acquired before 1st January, 1917), Roman-Dutch law as at that date ceased to apply to Guyana and was replaced with, amongst other laws, the English law of wills and English common law.

CLASSES OF PERSONS ENTITLED TO INHERIT ON AN INTESTACY

The persons entitled to inherit the residuary estate of an intestate vary somewhat from jurisdiction to jurisdiction. But as a general rule, the surviving spouse and issue of the intestate qualify as the primary beneficiaries of the intestate's estate. However, because of the sheer volume of the material, it is impossible in a text of this nature and scope to examine the rules of distribution on an intestacy exhaustively.

Trinidad & Tobago

Prior to September 25, 2000

With respect to the estates of persons dying prior to September 25, 2000, according to the former provisions of s.24 of the Administration of Estates Ordinance Ch. 8 No. 1, the persons beneficially entitled to the intestate's estate in order of priority were:

(a)   if there was no lawful issue, the surviving spouse;
(b)   if there was lawful issue, one third thereof to the surviving spouse and the remainder to the lawful issue of the deceased (even if only one);

According to the repealed s. 24 of the Ordinance the surviving spouse was entitled to:

- the entire estate of his or her intestate spouse if there was no lawful issue; and
- one third thereof, if there was lawful issue of the intestate.

Apart from the case of the surviving spouse, the Ordinance prior to its amendment, made no specific provision for any other class of beneficiary and most notably the Ordinance made no express provision with respect to the beneficial entitlement of the issue of the intestate.

In this regard, beneficial entitlement to an intestate's estate, for any other class of beneficiary, other than a surviving spouse, was governed by the former provisions of s.23 of The Administration of Estates Ordinance, Ch. 8. No. 1.

According s. 23 thereof, if there were no surviving spouse:

> the undisposed of residuary estate of such person, whether real or personal in its nature, shall be distributed amongst the same persons, being of kin within the meaning of section 3 in the same manner and in the same proportions as the personal estate of such person dying domiciled in England and itestate would be distributed by the law of England.

The law of England according s.2 of the Wills and Probate Ordinance Ch. 8 No. 2, (which Ordinance according to s.1 of the Administration of Estates Ordinance Ch. 8 No. 1 is to be read as one with the Administration of Estates Ordinance) means the law in England as in force on the 16th of May 1921. On 16th May 1921, the Statute of Distribution 1685 was the law in force in England in respect of beneficial entitlement to an intestate's personal estate.

Accordingly, with the noticeable exception of the surviving spouse, the Statute of Distribution 1685, England, in essence governed the devolution of an intestate's personal and real estate in Trinidad and Tobago, prior to September 25, 2000 in so far as determining the proportions to which persons who qualified as being 'of kin' under the former provisions of s. 3 of the Administration of Estates Ordinance were concerned. In essence, , the persons beneficially entitled to an intestate's estate were to be determined in accordance with the indigenous provisions of s. 3 of the Administration of Estates Ordinance but the proportions to which they were entitled was to be determined in accordance with the Statute of Distribution of England.

- **Who qualified as being 'of kin'**

According to s.3(1) of the Ordinance, 'of kin' were the following:

lawful issue of the deceased or his father or mother or a grandfather or grandmother or great great grandfather or great grandmother of the deceased or the lawful issue of any such person.

In addition s. 3(2) provided that:

> 'next of kin' of a deceased are meant the person or persons nearest in degree in relationship, among those of kin within the meaning of the last preceding subsection, each step to or from the common ancestor reckoning as a degree of kinship; the half-blood reckoning together immediately after the whole blood of the same degree.

In this regard, based *inter alia*, on the provisions of s. 23 of the Administration of Estates Ordinance, it is clear that the terms 'next of kin' as used in s. 3 of the Administration of Estates Ordinance was to be given the same meaning for the purposes of determining the order of priority to beneficial entitlement to an intestate's estate. This view is fortified by the fact that s. 1 of the Administration of Estates Ordinance Ch. 8 No. 1 as previously stated is to be read as one with the Wills and Probate Ordinance Ch. 8 No. 2 and according to s. 2 of the Wills and Probate Ordinance next of kin mean the person or persons entitled under an intestacy according to the provisions of the Administration of Estates Ordinance. In this regard, s. 3 of the Administration of Estates Ordinance provided not only for the persons entitled under an intestacy but also the order of priority to which they were entitled.

- **Rights of Grandchild to take Per Stirpes**

For purposes of beneficial entitlement, where a child of an intestate (there being other surviving children of the intestate) predeceased his parent but left a child surviving at the date of death of the parent, the grandchild, i.e. the issue of the pre-deceasing child of the intestate was not entitled per stirpes to his pre-deceasing parent's share of the intestate's estate. In such circumstances, the intesate's estate is divided between or among the surviving children of the intestate and the surviving spouse, if any.

In order for a grandchild to take in such circumstance the common law rule of the law of succession which requires a beneficiary to survive a deceased in order to inherit, would by necessity have to be displaced by a statutory provision as for example in the case of a will where the common law doctrine of lapse is displaced by s. 63 of the Wills and Probate Ordinance Ch. 8 No. 2. Section 63 of the Wills and Probate Ordinance in effect provides that a gift by will of real or personal estate left to a pre-deceasing child shall not lapse provided the pre-deceasing child leaves issue living at the date of death of the testator. However, with respect to an intestacy, it is significant to note that although s. 3 of the Administration of Estates Ordinance, set out who qualifies as next of kin, the statutory provision did not provide for grandchildren to take per stirpes their parent's share of an intestate's estate.

By contrast, in the case of England, the Statute of Distribution makes clear provision for grandchildren to take per stirpes a share of the intestate's estate so that where a child pre-deceases his or her parent whether survived by other children or not, the child/children of the pre-deceasing child is/are entitled to a share per stirpes of the intestate's estate along with the surviving child or children of the intestate.

- **On or after September 25, 2000**

The passage of the Distribution of Estates Act 28/2000 introduced the following significant amendments to the Administration of Estates Ordinance Ch. 8 No. 1:

A co-habitant

By virtue of the new provisions of ss. 24 and 25 of the Administration of Estates Ordinance, a co-habitant has been included as a new class of beneficiary. According to s. 2 of the Ordinance, a co-habitant is defined as:

> a person of the opposite sex who, while not married to the intestate, continuously cohabitated in a *bona fide* domestic relationship with the intestate, for a period of not less than five years immediately preceding the death of the intestate.

It is to be noted that no clarification of what is meant by *bona fide* domestic relationship is provided for in the Act, nor is there currently any case law which can shed light on the meaning and purport of this phrase.

What is clear however is that for the purposes of beneficial entitlement to an intestate's estate, neither co-habitant need be a single person, that is unmarried or widowed or divorced to be deemed to be in a *bona fide* domestic relationship. An intestate can therefore be survived by a lawful spouse and also by a co-habitant who may himself or herself be married.

By way of jurisdictional contrast the succession legislation of both Jamaica and Barbados provide for a 'common law' spouse as defined by the respective succession legislation of these territories to inherit on an intestacy. However in both instances the definition of spouse is limited to a single man and single woman co-habiting for the requisite statutory period. The definition of single is limited to a single widowed or divorced man or woman.

In the case of Guyana, although a 'common law spouse' has no rights of inheritance on an intestacy, he or she may apply for family provision under the Family and Dependents Provision Act 1990. However for purposes of entitlement to family provision, the definition of spouse is limited to a single man and single woman. And according to the statutory definition single means unmarried, widowed or divorced.

In the case of Trinidad and Tobago, the rather expansive and vague definition of a co-habitant, particularly with regard to the requirement that the parties co-habit in a *bona fide* domestic relationship, when combined with the beneficial entitlement accorded to a co-habitant under ss.24 and 25 of the Ordinance, can, it is submitted, lead to unintended consequences.

In this regard, according to the new s. 25 (1) of the Administration of Estates Ordinance, where a deceased dies intestate without leaving a lawful spouse, the co-habitant is treated as if he or she were a surviving spouse of the intestate. And according to s.24 of the ordinance, as amended, the surviving spouse is entitled to one-half share of the intestate's estate, where the intestate leaves issue surviving and to the entire estate if there are no issue.

Based on the above provisions, the following fact circumstances can arise:

(a) A man and woman can be legally married, say for 20 years. During this period, as often occurs, particularly with respect to a person employed in the oil sector, the husband's job may require him to work and live at another location during the working week and reside at the matrimonial home on weekends only. He may during the weekday period enter into a co-habitational relationship with a married woman who is not judicially separated from her spouse, but who for all intents and purposes is regarded as his reputed wife. He can therefore be effectively in two *bona fide* co-habitational relationships at the same time.

In the above fact situation, if the lawful spouse who may be of independent and substantial means were to predecease her husband, dying intestate, her husband would, as her surviving spouse, be entitled to a minimum of one half share of her estate. If the husband should then die intestate leaving the co-habitant surviving him, the co-habitant would be entitled to one half share of the husband's estate, which would also include a minimum of one half of his pre-deceasing lawful wife's estate. As a married woman, who is not judicially separated from her spouse, she would also be automatically entitled to a minimum one half share of her lawful husband's estate should he predecease her and die intestate without himself entering into a co-habitational relationship.

(b) A lawfully married wife leaves her husband to live with an unmarried childless man in a co-habitational relationship. The unmarried man predeceases her after a period of six years, leaving a substantial estate. In such circumstances, she may be deemed to be in a *bona fide* co-habitational relationship and would therefore qualify as the surviving spouse for purposes of beneficial entitlement on an intestacy. She would accordingly be entitled to the intestate's entire estate to the exclusion of the parents of the intestate. In addition, if the lawful spouse is not judicially separated from her husband, she would be entitled to a minimum of one half of her lawful husband's estate should he predecease her dying intestate with issue and to the lawful husband's entire estate should he die without issue.

Clearly, the vague and imprecise definition of a co-habitant as illustrated in the above examples allows for a co-habitant to enjoy a double benefit arising from both relationships, a benefit not accorded to any other beneficiary under an intestacy.

Another negative consequence of the inclusion of a co-habitant as defined by the Distribution of Estates Act 28/2000 is the potential for tying up of estates in litigation in circumstances where an intestate dies leaving a spouse and a co-habitant and the spouse and intestate were living apart from one another at the time of his death. According to s. 25(2) of the Distribution of Estates Act, the co-habitant is entitled to such part of the estate of the intestate as was acquired during the period of co-habitation.

However, the rights of the co-habitant according to the sub-section is subject to the rights of a surviving spouse and issue of the intestate. What is meant by subject to the rights of the spouse and issue? No clarification is given in the legislation nor are any guidelines or parameters set. And how are these rights to be established, if not by litigation, where there is no agreement among the interested parties?

Additionally, according to s. 25(3) a surviving co-habitant claiming a share of the estate of an intestate must make an application within 28 days of the death of the intestate for an order from the court affirming the co-habitational relationship. The difficulty which arises in this regard is in establishing that there was a *bona fide* domestic relationship, particularly while the existence of the co-habitational relationship is challenged by the surviving spouse and issue of the intestate. The lack of clarity and precision in the definition of a co-habitant, only serves to complicate the issue. It is to be noted that again no rules or regulations have to date been enacted setting out procedural guidelines to be followed.

Posthumous Births

Section 26A of the Administration of Estates Ordinance as amended by the Distribution of Estates Act expressly provides that descendents and relatives of an intestate conceived before the intestate's death but born afterward inherit as if they had been born in his lifetime and survived. It is to be noted that the category of next of kin who is included under this provision is not limited to issue of the intestate but extends to all categories of relatives of the intestate for the purposes of beneficial entitlement under an intestacy.

- **Rights of Parents**

Prior to the passage of the Distribution of Estates Act 28/2000 there was uncertainty as to whether the mother of an intestate was equally entitled as the father to a pre-deceasing child's estate in circumstances where the child died intestate without surviving spouse or issue.

In this regard, many practitioners were of the view that the Statute of Distribution 1685 England applied carte blanche to all classes of beneficiaries of the deceased other than the surviving spouse or issue of the intestate so that where a person died intestate without a surviving spouse or issue, the provisions of the Statute of Distribution would be deemed to apply both in respect of the persons entitled and the proportions to which they were entitled to the intestate's estate. Therefore, in accordance with the provisions of the Statute of Distribution, a father was entitled to the entire estate of an intestate child, when that child died without spouse or issue. The mother would only be entitled in the event that the father had pre-deceased the intestate child and even then she would be entitled to only part of the estate, having in such circumstances, to share the estate with the intestate's child's surviving brothers and sisters.

With the passage of the Distribution of Estates Act 28/2000 all doubt and uncertainty have been removed as according to the new provisions of s.26 of the Administration of Estates Ordinance, where an intestate dies leaving no spouse, no co-habitant or no issue, the estate goes to the parents in equal shares or the survivor of them.

- **Rights of Grandchildren**

As stated above, under the repealed provisions of the Administration of Estates Ordinance Ch. 8 No. 1, grandchildren were only entitled to a share of the estate of their grandparents where the grandparent died intestate, leaving no child surviving him. Once a child survived the intestate parent, grandchildren whether issue of the surviving child or issue of a pre-deceasing child, were excluded from so benefiting.

It appears that, based on the new provisions of s.24 of the Administration of Estates Ordinance, children of a predeceasing child of an intestate are entitled to share in the intestate's estate along with the intestate's surviving child/children only in circumstances where there is no surviving spouse.

- **Meaning of Issue**

According to s.24(1) of the Administration of Estates Ordinances, as amended by the Distribution of Estates Act 28/2000, where an intestate dies leaving a surviving spouse but no issue, the spouse is entitled to the entire estate.

Section 24(2) further provides that where an intestate dies leaving issue, but no spouse, his estate shall be distributed per stirpes among the issue.

According to s.24(3) and s.24(4) respectively, if there is a surviving spouse and child or more than one child, the surviving spouse is entitled to one half of the intestate's estate, and the child/children to the other half as the case may be.

One of the difficulties with the above provisions lies in the definition of issue as provided for in s.3 of the Administration of Estates Ordinance as amended.

According to s.3 'issue' includes all lineal descendants of an ancestor, whether born within or outside of marriage. This definition is somewhat troubling as the definition of issue specifically states that the term 'issue includes' therefore contemplating that others apart from the lineal descendants of an ancestor, could satisfy the definition of issue. Additionally, s.24(1) seems to contemplate that, had the deceased died survived by a spouse and issue, the issue would be entitled to a share of the intestate's estate. However, s.24(3) and (4) restrict the persons entitled to benefit in cases where there is a surviving spouse, to a child/ children of the intestate.

Accordingly, based on the above provisions, with regards to the rights of a grandchild/ grand children, the following is to be noted:

(i) where an intestate is survived by a spouse, the grandchildren (issue) would not be entitled to a share of the intestate's estate; and
(ii) where an intestate is not survived by a spouse, and one or more of his children predecease him, leaving children alive at the intestate's death, the children of the predeceasing child (i.e. grandchildren of the intestate) would be treated for the purpose of s.24 as issue and would not be entitled to a share of the intestate's estate in place of their pre-deceasing parent.

Share of the Estate

The Distribution of Estates Act 28/2000 introduced significant amendments to the Administration of Estates Ordinance Ch. 8 No. 1 with respect to the actual proportions in which an intestate's estate is to be distributed. Under the current legislation a surviving spouse (which now includes a co-habitant as defined by the amending Act) is entitled to one-half share of the intestate's estate where there are issue and to the entire estate when there are no issue (issue of course including grandchildren and great-grandchildren)as the case may be.

Guyana

The rules governing the distribution of an intestate's estate in Guyana are contained in the Civil Law of Guyana Act Cap. 6:01. According to s.5 of this Act, the surviving spouse is entitled to one-third of the intestate's residuary estate and the rest in equal parts to the children of the intestate; if any of the children are dead, to their descendants per stirpes. In the event that the intestate leaves no children or descendants, one-half goes to the surviving spouse, the remainder to those persons being next of kin of the intestate. Such persons include in order of priority, the mother, father, the great-grandmother and great-grandfather of the intestate.

Barbados

The rules governing distribution of an intestate's residuary personal and real estate are set out in Part VI and Part VIII of the Succession Act Cap. 249. This Act provides that if an intestate dies, leaving:

- a spouse and no issue or next of kin, the spouse will take the whole estate;
- a spouse and no issue but next of kin, the spouse will take two-thirds of the estate, the remainder to be distributed in equal

shares among the next-of-kin;
- a spouse and one child, the spouse two-thirds and the remainder to the child;
- a spouse and children, the spouse will take one-third and the remainder to the children.

Eastern Caribbean (with the exception of St Vincent & the Grenadines, Grenada and St Lucia)

By virtue of the respective Intestates Estates' Acts of the above mentioned Eastern Caribbean territories,[9] the residuary personal and real estate of an intestate is distributed or held on trust *inter alia* in the following manner:

- If the intestate leaves a husband or wife, the surviving spouse will take personal chattels absolutely.
- The residuary estate (other than the personal chattels) shall be held. If the intestate leaves no issue, upon trust for the surviving spouse for life;
- If the intestate leaves issue, upon trust as to one-half for the surviving spouse for life and subject to such life interest, on the statutory trusts for the issue of the intestate and the other half on the statutory trusts for the issue of the intestate,

Grenada

The Intestates Estates (Amendment) Act No. 48 of 1991 provides *inter alia* that:

- if the intestate leaves a surviving spouse but no issue, the surviving spouse is entitled to one half of the intestate's estate and the remainder devolves in order of priority to the persons being of next of kin of the intestate;
- if the intestate leaves a surviving spouse and issue, the surviving spouse is entitled to one half absolutely and the issue to the remaining half in equal shares;
- if the intestate leaves issue but no surviving spouse the issue is entitled to the whole estate in equal shares;
- if the intestate leaves no surviving spouse and issue, then the father and mother are entitled to the whole estate in equal shares.

Variation Order

It is to be noted that by virtue of s.4(2) of this amending Act, a surviving spouse of an intestate may apply to the court for a variation order so as to increase the share of the intestate's estate, to which he or she is entitled. The variation order will be granted by the court provided that the spouse can prove on a balance of probabilities that he or she contributed, whether directly or indirectly, to the building up of the estate of the intestate to such a degree that he or she should be entitled to more than his or her statutory share of the intestate's estate. On making the application for the variation order s.4(2) further provides that any person who may be affected by the order is entitled to appear and be heard on the hearing of application for such variation order.

St Vincent & the Grenadines

According to Part V of the Administration of Estates Act Cap. 377 if the intestate leaves:

- a surviving spouse but no issue, one-half to the surviving spouse, the remainder to the next-of-kin of the intestate being in order of priority, the mother and father of the intestate, the brothers and sisters of the whole blood;
- a surviving spouse and issue, one third to the surviving spouse and the remaining two-thirds to the issue of the intestate;
- issue but no surviving spouse, the issue is entitled to the whole estate in equal shares.

Jamaica

Distribution prior to 25th March, 1988

Section 4 of the Intestates' Estates and Property Charges Act enacted on 1st January, 1937 provided:

- That if the intestate leaves a husband or wife with or without issue, he or she takes the personal chattels[10] absolutely as defined by s.2 plus a charge on the residuary estate of $100, or a sum equal to 10% of the net value of the estate, whichever is the greater free of death duties and costs with interest at 5% from date of death.
- Subject to the above provision, the residuary estate (other than the personal chattels) is held

(i) for the surviving wife or husband during his or her life if the intestate leaves no issue;
(ii) if the intestate leaves issue, upon trust as to one-half for the surviving husband/wife during his/her life and subject to such life interest, on the statutory trusts for the issue;
(iii) if those statutory trusts fail, or come to an end during the lifetime of the surviving husband or wife, on trust for the surviving husband/wife during the remainder of his/her life.

Distribution Post-24 March, 1988

The Intestates' Estates and Property Charges (Amendment) Act 1988 introduced significant amendments to the principal Act, including the following:

- The definition of personal chattels was expanded specifically to include furniture and personal effects, motor vehicles and bicycles but does not include money or securities for money, nor does it include furniture, motor vehicles or other effects used at the time of the death of the intestate exclusively or principally for business purposes.
- The definition of the spouse now includes a single man or woman living together within the prescribed statutory period.
- The distribution of the residuary estate was also adjusted so that the surviving spouse takes:

(i) the personal chattels absolutely;
(ii) $10,000 or a sum equal to 10% of the net value of the estate;
(iii) two-thirds of the residuary estate absolutely if there is only one issue;
(iv) one-half if more than one issue;
(v) if no child or other issue, but parent or parents two-thirds of the residue absolutely.

The Bahamas

Position prior to February 1, 2002

With respect to the estates of persons dying prior to February 1, 2002, the personal estate of an intestate in The Bahamas was distributed essentially in accordance with three pieces of legislation: the Statute of Distribution Ch. 97, the Intestate Children's Act Ch. 93 and the Widows of Intestates

Act Ch. 94, which are all in fact verbatim replicas of English pre-1926 intestate succession laws.

According to the provisions of these Acts, the surviving husband was as a general rule entitled to the entire personal estate while the surviving widow was entitled only to one-third share with the remainder to the issue or next of kin. If there was no surviving spouse, the children were entitled in equal shares or grand children or great-grand children sharing per stirpes.

On the other hand, the residuary real estate of the intestate passed to the heir-at-law by virtue of the common law doctrine of descent, The rules governing the identification of the sole heir-at-law were contained in the Inheritance Act Ch. 99, which is a replica of the Inheritance Act 1833, England. Where there was no heir-at-law, the property of the intestate devolved to the Crown, pursuant to the Escheat Act Ch. 141.

Current Position

With the passage of the Inheritance Act 2002, where an intestate dies on or after February 1, 2002, the devolution of his estate is governed essentially by ss.4 to 6 of the Inheritance Act 2002.

In this regard, s.4 essentially provides that the estate shall be distributed as follows:

- where there is a surviving spouse and no children, the entire estate to the surviving spouse.
- where there is a surviving spouse and child/children, one-half to the spouse, the other half to the child or children
- where there is no surviving spouse, and child/children, the entire estate to the child/children
- where there is no surviving spouse or child/children, the grandchildren, if any
- where no surviving spouse, child(ren) or grand child(ren) to the mother and father in equal shares if both survive and if only one survives, the survivor takes the entire estate.

In addition, it is to be noted:

- that pursuant to s.5 of the Act, the child of a predeceasing child of the intestate, is entitled to take his predeceasing parent's share of the intestate's estate; and
- that s.6 of the Act provides that the surviving spouse of a person dying testate or intestate shall have preferential rights in respect of acquiring the matrimonial home in which the spouse was

residing, and the household chattels. Where the share of the surviving spouse is insufficient to enable such appropriation, the right thereto may be executed in relation to any minor for whom the surviving spouse is a trustee.

In such instances, the personal representative is under a duty pursuant to s.6(3) of the Inheritance Act, to notify the surviving spouse of his or her rights of appropriation.

In such cases, the surviving spouse may apply to the Court under s.7 of the Act, for an order of appropriation on the spouse's behalf and on behalf of any minor of which the surviving spouse is a trustee.

St Lucia

In St Lucia the persons entitled to the intestate's residuary estate are the spouse capable of inheriting, children and descendants and collateral relations within the stipulated order of priority.[11]

In general, if the deceased leaves:

- a spouse capable of inheriting and issue, the surviving spouse takes one third and the child or children take the remainder in equal shares;
- no issue but leaves a spouse capable of inheriting and a father and mother or either of them and collateral relations up to nieces or nephews in the first degree inclusive of the surviving spouse takes one-third; the father and mother or the one of them surviving take one-third, and the collateral relations mentioned above one-third.[12]

Spouse Capable of Inheriting

In order for a wife to qualify as a spouse capable of inheriting she must abandon all her rights to community of property which may have existed between the deceased and herself, as well as all rights of survivorship accruing to her under her marriage contract or by law. Similarly, for the husband to succeed to his wife's estate he must first pay into the mass his share in any community of property which may have existed between his wife and him, and any rights conferred on him by any marriage contract which may have existed between them.

Community of Property [13]

In the absence of a pre-nuptial agreement all property acquired after marriage is deemed to be community property unless the contrary is shown. This property is placed under the exclusive management of the husband, and on the death of either spouse the survivor is entitled to a vested interest in one-half of the assets comprising the property held in community. The remainder is distributed in equal shares amongst the children, if any, of the intestate as next-of-kin.

Separate community comprises:

- the property, movable and immovable, that the spouse possesses on the day when the marriage was solemnised;
- property, movable and immovable, acquired by succession, or by donation or legacy made to either spouse particularly;
- the income and earnings of either spouse, investments in the name of one spouse, and insurance policies taken out on the life and in the name of one spouse;
- property acquired by one of the spouses while they were living separate and apart from each other by virtue of a separation deed unless the contrary is shown.

Clearly, from the above examples a substantial portion of an intestate's estate may not be held in community. In this regard the surviving spouse may renounce within the time stipulated his or her right to community property and thus qualify as a spouse capable of inheriting. In such cases the surviving spouse is entitled to, amongst other things:

(a) one-third and a child or children to the remaining two-thirds in equal shares; and
(b) one-half if the deceased dies leaving no issue.

It should be noted that when a surviving spouse elects to retain the property held in community the heirs of the deceased spouse are entitled to share in all profits made and income earned from such property.

Specific Classes of Beneficiaries

As the above examples illustrate, the persons entitled in order of priority to an intestate's estate, in the various Caribbean territories are usually the intestate's surviving spouse and children. Accordingly, a more detailed examination of these specific classes of persons will be considered.

Common Law Spouse

Barbados, Jamaica and Trinidad and Tobago

In all the jurisdictions except Barbados and Jamaica, and with effect from September 25, 2000, Trinidad and Tobago, a common-law spouse has no rights of inheritance on an intestacy.

Barbados and Jamaica

By virtue of s.2 of the Succession Act Cap. 249 Barbados and s.2 of the Intestates' Estates and Property Charges Act, Jamaica, reference to a spouse for the purpose of the respective Acts of these territories include:

- a single man living together with a single woman as her husband for a period of not less than five years immediately preceding the date of his death;
- a single woman who was living together with a single man as his wife for the same period.

Reference to a single man or woman includes a widow, or widower or a man or woman who is divorced.

Trinidad and Tobago

As previously stated, with respect to the estates of persons dying intestate on or after September 25, 2000, a co-habitant as defined by the Distribution of Estates Act 28/2000 is entitled to a share of the estate of an intestate co-habitant. In this regard, a co-habitant is defined by s.2 of the Distribution of Estates Act 28/2000, which Act has amended the Administration of Ch. 8 no. 1 Estate Ordinance as:

> a person of the opposite sex who, while not married to the intestate, continuously cohabited in a *bona fide* domestic relationship with the intestate for a period of not less than five years immediately preceding the death of the intestate.

Spouses excluded from Succession

Barbados

Section 102 of the Succession Act Cap. 249 lists the spouses who are excluded from taking any share in the estate of the deceased as a legal right on an intestacy.

Included in this category are:

- a spouse against whom the deceased obtained a judicial separation;
- a spouse who fails to comply with a decree of restitution of conjugal rights obtained by the deceased;
- a spouse guilty of desertion, which desertion has continued up to the death for three years or more; and
- spouses who have separated from each other for a period of five years or more preceeding the death of the intestate.

Trinidad & Tobago

By virtue of s.10 of the Administration of Estates Ordinance, Ch.8 no.1 as amended by Schedule 1 of the Matrimonial Proceedings and Property Act No. 2/1972, judicially separated spouses are not entitled to claims in intestacy with respect to the estate of each other.

St Lucia

Spouses married in community who do not renounce their rights with respect thereto obtain a vested interest in half-share of the property held in community of property and are by such election excluded from succeeding to the intestate's estate.

St Vincent & the Grenadines and Grenada

By virtue of:
- s.26 of the Matrimonial Causes Act Cap. 176 St Vincent & the Grenadines; and
- s.40 of the Matrimonial Proceedings Property Act 1970, England, the provisions of which are received and form part of the matrimonial law of Grenada[14] for the purpose of devolution on intestacy the surviving spouse is deemed to have predeceased the intestate while a decree of separation is in force and the separation continues.

Children of the Intestate

Illegitimate Child

With the exception of the Bahamas and Montserrat a child born out of wedlock to an intestate father has the same rights of inheritance on an intestacy as a child born in wedlock with effect from the date of commencement of the relevant status of children legislation or its equivalent in each of these territories.

This is provided that the child can establish that the intestate is his father within the guidelines laid down in the respective status of children acts or its equivalent in the various territories.

PROOF OF PATERNITY

Statutory Guidelines[15]

Anguilla, Antigua & Barbuda, Barbados, Grenada, Jamaica, St Christopher & Nevis, St Vincent & the Grenadines, The Bahamas and Trinidad & Tobago

According to the provisions of the respective status of children legislation of the above territories, paternity may be established *inter alia* by:

- a certified copy of the entry made of the father's name on the Register Book of Births;
- an instrument signed by the child's mother and any person acknowledging he is the father of the child;
- an affiliation order or other paternity order made pursuant to proceedings brought in the Magistrate's Court;
- a declaration of paternity made pursuant to proceedings instituted in the High Court.

Barbados

Section 7 of the Status of Children Reform Act Cap. 220 sets out the several circumstances, including those mentioned above in which a presumption of paternity may be raised. In practice, where a child born out of wedlock applies for a grant of letters of administration of his/her intestate father's estate, proof of paternity may be furnished by:

- affidavit evidence i.e. by an affidavit of the child's mother deposing to the relationship between herself and the intestate in accordance with the relevant statutory presumptions outlined in s.7 or alternatively an affidavit of the child if he/she is old enough, deposing to the relationship between himself and the intestate. Where there is opposition to the application an affidavit of a disinterested person such as a sister of the deceased, who

can swear to the relationship between the deceased and the mother in accordance with one or more of the presumptions set out in s.7 may be lodged or as is usually required;
- the child's birth certificate with the father's name entered therein or where this cannot be furnished;
- a declaration of paternity obtained from the High Court,

In this regard it should be noted that according to s.9 of the Status of Children Reform Act, the application for a declaration of paternity may be made after the death of the father provided the court finds that a presumption of paternity exists under s.7. However, where there is no person recognised under s.7 to be the father of the child, then pursuant to s.10(1)(2) of the Act, the application for paternity, may not be made unless both persons with respect to whom the relationship is sought to be established, are living.

Grenada

Section 5(2) of the Status of Children Act 39/1991, outlines the circumstances in which a presumption of paternity may be raised, including those listed under the general statutory guidelines above. However in instances where an application for declaration of paternity is made either where a presumption of paternity exists or in cases where no presumption exists, paternity must be proved beyond a reasonable doubt, if at the date of the application, the alleged father is dead. It is to be noted that for the purposes of proving entitlement to a grant of letters of administration as a child of the intestate, a declaration of paternity is required or alternatively the child's birth certificate with the father's name entered therein.

Antigua & Barbuda, Jamaica and Trinidad & Tobago[16]

In these territories an application for a declaration of paternity may be made whether or not the father or child or both of them are living or dead at the date of the application. With respect to Antigua & Barbuda and Trinidad & Tobago, for the purposes of entitlement to letters of administration, proof of paternity must be established either by the father's name entered on the child's birth certificate or otherwise by a declaration of paternity. In Jamaica proof of paternity may additionally be satisfied by affidavit evidence of a disinterested person deposing to the relationship of paternity between the child and the intestate father.

St Christopher & Nevis [17] *and St Vincent & the Grenadines*

It is to be noted that in St Vincent & the Grenadines where paternity is sought to be established for any purpose related to succession to property and in St Christopher & Nevis in any instance where paternity is sought to be established, such paternity must be established during the lifetime of the alleged father. Additionally with respect to St Vincent, where paternity is sought to be established for the benefit of the father, such paternity is required to be established during the lifetime of the child or during the period when the child was conceived. In both territories an affidavit of kin subject to the registrar's discretion, may be filed in instances where more formal proof of paternity is not furnished or is unavailable. Additionally in St Vincent & the Grenadines less formal proof of paternity including the child's baptismal certificate with the father's name appearing thereon may also be accepted, subject to the registrar's discretion.

Anguilla

The Law Reform (Illegitimacy) Ord. 15/1982 contains minimal provisions with respect to establishing or proving paternity. Apart from providing:

(a) for the use of blood tests in any civil proceedings in which the paternity of any person falls to be determined; and
(b) for the amendment of the registration of births of an illegitimate child by the addition of the relevant particulars in respect of the father, the Act is silent as to whether paternity must be established prior to the death of the alleged father and as to the evidence necessary to prove paternity. In practice the child's birth certificate with the father's name entered therein or affidavit evidence sworn to by a disinterested person, deposing to the relationship of paternity between the child and the intestate or alternatively an affiliation order of the court is accepted by the Registrar as proof of paternity for purposes of entitlement to the grant.

The Bahamas

With effect from February 1 2002, the date of passage of the Equal Status of Children's Act 2002, the presumption of paternity arises not only in the circumstances outlined above, but in addition pursuant to s.7 *inter alia*, where the alleged father, has by his conduct implicitly and consistently acknowledged that he is the father.

However, it is to be noted that for the purposes of establishing proof of paternity an application for a declaration of paternity when no presumption of paternity arises, may not be made after the death of the alleged father in accordance with s.10(2).

Where a presumption of paternity arises under the s.7, statutory guidelines an application may be made not only after the death of the presumed father, but also after the death of the child, pursuant to the provisions of s.9 of the Act.

- **Other Considerations**

Dominica

There is no status of children legislation per se in Dominica. However, according to s.2 of the Intestates Estates Act Ch. 9:03 a child or issue includes *inter alia* an illegitimate child who has been accepted as his child by the intestate and an illegitimate person who lived with or was maintained by the intestate.

It is to be noted that the Act does not provide or stipulate the mechanism for establishing paternity particularly in instances in which it may be challenged. In practice, for purposes of entitlement to a grant of administration, the only proof of paternity which is accepted by the Registrar, in the case of an illegitimate child, is the child's birth certificate with the father's name appearing thereon.

St Lucia

The position in St Lucia is similar to that which obtains in Dominica in that in St Lucia there is also no status of children act per se and no statutory mechanism for proving paternity. It is to be noted that for the purpose of succession to property, a child born out of wedlock may inherit on the intestacy of his mother or father where the mother is a single woman and the father a single man. In this regard, according to Art 579 Ch. 242 as amended by Act No.4 of 1988 the definition of a single woman includes a widow, a married woman living apart and separated from her husband and a divorced woman. The definition of a single man, on the other hand, is limited to a man who has never been married. The Civil Code (Amendment) (No. 3) Act No. 12 of 1991 (which came into operation on 4th January, 1992) has further amended Act 579(1) by providing that a person shall be regarded as a child of a deceased in cases where:

- he was at any time a member of the deceased's household as his child;
- there is or was in relation to him a maintenance order against the deceased as his putative father under the Affiliation Ordinance;
- the name of the deceased appears as his father on his Birth Certificate;
- the deceased in his lifetime contributed to his maintenance as his father;
- the deceased has been adjudged by a court of competent jurisdiction to be his father;
- the deceased in his lifetime consented to that person assuming the surname of the deceased as his father.
- the person at the instance of the deceased assumed the surname of the deceased as his father evidenced by a deed poll pertaining to a notice of change of name.

In practice, where the father's name is not entered on the child's birth certificate or where no other more formal proof of paternity is available such as an affiliation order, paternity may be established by an affidavit of kin. However the registrar in the appropriate circumstances may require that the applicant publish on two occasions a Notice of Intention to apply for the grant, either in the weekend newspaper or the Gazette which is published bi-monthly. In such instances the newspaper clippings or gazette pages must be lodged with the papers to lead the grant.

Guyana

Pursuant to The Children Born Out Of Wedlock (Removal of Discrimination) Act 12/1983, s.5 of the Civil Law Act of Guyana Cap. 6:01 was amended by the insertion of a subsection 7. According to the subsection:

> In determining relationships for the purposes of this section no regard shall be had to whether any person is born in wedlock or out of wedlock and a person born out of wedlock shall be entitled to the same rights under this section as a person born in wedlock.

It is to be noted that where the child born out of wedlock claims a beneficial interest in the estate of his intestate father, no guidelines have been laid down with respect to the factors to be taken into account for establishing paternity. In practice an affidavit of kin, sworn to by some disinterested but credible person such as a relative of the intestate or a parish priest, may subject to the discretion of the Chief Justice, be accepted as *prima facie* proof of paternity, in cases where *inter alia* the father's name is not entered on the child's birth certificate or where an affiliation or other similar court order has not been made.

Adopted Child

Barbados, Dominica, Grenada, Guyana, Jamaica, St Lucia, St Vincent & the Grenadines, The Bahamas and Trinidad & Tobago[18]

For the purposes of inheritance on an intestacy, at or after the making of an adoption order on the death intestate of the adoptee, the estate of an intestate devolves in all respects on the adopted child as if that child were born of the adoptee and not the child of his or her natural parents. This rule applies to the estate of an intestate dying after the commencement date of the respective legislation of each jurisdiction.

Anguilla, Antigua & Barbuda, Montserrat and St Christopher & Nevis[19]

For the purpose of inheritance on an intestacy, an adopted child is entitled to share in the estate of his/her natural parents only, and not the adoptee parents, whether or not the adoptee parent dies before or after the making of the adoption order.

Notes

1   It is to be noted that where there is a total intestacy with respect to dispositions of property but the testator has left a valid will, that from a procedural point of view, a grant of probate/ letters of administration with will annexed is required to be obtained and the executors or administrators with will annexed, as the case may he, will be deemed to be the trustees of the testator's undisposed of estate and the estate of the deceased will be distributed in accordance with the rules governing distribution on intestacy in the various territories. See *Re Skeets, Thain v. Gibbs* [1936] Ch. 683; *Re Roby* [1908] Ch. 71 at 81.

2   Anguilla, Montserrat   - ss. 3, 9 Intestates Estates Act Cap. 36
    Antigua & Barbuda   - ss. 3, 9 Intestates Estates Act Cap. 225
    Dominica   - ss. 3, 9 Intestates Estates Act Ch. 9:03
    Grenada   - ss. 3, 9 Intestates Estates Act Cap. 154
    St Christopher   - ss- 3, 9 Intestates Estates Act Cap. 36
    & Nevis
    St Vincent &   - ss. 3,9 Intestates Estates Act (repealed and replaced
                                   as of 27 the Grenadines December, 1989 by the
                                   Administration of Estates Act Cap. 377

3   The Bahamas   - The Inheritance Act 2002

4   Section 23 of the Administration of Estates Ordinance provides in effect that the undisposed of residuary estate of a person dying intestate in Trinidad & Tobago is to be distributed in the same manner and in the same proportions as the personal estate of such person dying domiciled in England and intestate would be distributed by the law of England. On this see *Re Schuler's Estate* (1985) 37 W.I.R. 371 at pp. 388-389 where Warner J.A. observed that 'The Administration of Estates Ordinance and the Wills and Probate Ordinance are to be read, as one and, by section 2 of the latter law of England means the law of England as in force on 16th May, 1921. On 16th May, 1921 in England on an intestacy personalty was distributed among those entitled under the Statute of Distribution 1670 . . .'. See also *Mohammed v. Mohammed* (1968) 12 W.I.R. 125 at p.128 where Kelsick J remarked that Section 23 of the Administration of Estates Ordinance Ch. 8 No. 1 provides an excellent example of where the law or practice in England is applied simpliciter or at a specific date. For a further discussion on the above see K. Tesheira, "A Case for Reform in the Law of Succession". (1996) *International and Comparative Law Quarterly*, July 1996.
5   See chapter 9, p. 240.
6   See ss. 4 and 16 Escheat Act Cap. 306.
7   (1966) 11 W.I.R 53 at 56.
8   See Article on the History and Development of the St Lucia Civil Code by N.J.O. Liverpool, Essays on the Civil Codes of Quebec and St Lucia, University of Ottawa Press.
9
Anguilla	- s.4 Intestates Estates Act Cap. 36
Antigua & Barbuda	- s.4 Intestates Estates Act Cap. 225
Dominica	- s.4 Intestates Estates Act Ch. 9:03
Grenada	- s.4 Intestates Estates Act Cap. 154
Montserrat	- s.4 Intestates Estates Act Cap. 36
St Christopher & Nevis	- s.4 Intestates Estates Art Cap. 36.

10 Pursuant to s.2(l)(c) of the Intestates Estates' and Property Charges Act 'personal chattels' means furniture and effects, including, where relevant:
    (i)   articles of household or personal use or ornament, plate, plated articles, linen, china, glass, books, pictures, prints, jewellery, musical and scientific instruments and apparatus, wines, liquors and consumable stores;
    (ii) bicycles, stables, horses and domestic animals; and
    (iii) motor vehicles and accessories therefor;
    but not including-
    (iv) furniture, motor vehicles or other effects, used at the time of the death of the intestate exclusively or principally for business purposes; or
    (v)   money or securities for money.
11 Art 567B Civil Code Ch. 242.
12 Art 567C Civil Code Ch. 242.
13 Art 1188-1307 Civil Code Ch, 242.
14 The Matrimonial Proceedings and Property Act 1970 England is received and forms part of the matrimonial law of Grenada by virtue of s,11 Eastern Caribbean Supreme Court of Judicature (Grenada) Act.
15
Anguilla	- ss. 1,8 The Law Reform (Illegitimacy) Ord. 15/1982
Antigua & Barbuda	- s.6 Status of Children Act Cap. 414
Barbados	- s.7 Status of Children (Reform) Act Cap. 220
Grenada	- s.5 Status of Children Act No. 39/1991

	Jamaica	- s.8 Status of Children Act 36/1976
	St Christopher & Nevis	- s.6 Status of Children Act 19/1983
	St Vincent & the Grenadines	- s.8 Status of Children Act Cap. 180
	Trinidad & Tobago	- s.8 Status of Children Act Ch. 46:07.
16	Antigua & Barbuda	- s.10 Status of Children Act Cap. 414
	Jamaica	- s.10 Status of Children Act 36/1976
	Trinidad & Tobago	- s.10 Status of Children Act 46:07.
17	St Christopher &Nevis	- s.5(1) Status of Children Act 19/1983
	St Vincent & the Grenadines	- s.7(1) Status of Children Act Cap. 180.
18	Barbados	- s.24 Law of Minors Act Cap. 215
	Dominica	- s.6 Adoption of Infants Act Ch. 37:03
	Grenada	- s.14 Adoption Act Cap. 3
	Guyana	- s.20 Adoption of Children Act Cap. 46:04
	Jamaica	- s.17 Children (Adoption of) Act 1973
	St Lucia	- ss.13, 14 Adoption Ord. Cap. 19
	St Vincent & the Grenadines	- s.19 Adoption of Children Act Cap. 163
	The Bahamas	- s.12 Adoption of Children Act Ch. 117
	Trinidad & Tobago	- s.15 Adoption of Children Act Ch. 46:03.
19	Anguilla	- s.6 Adoption of Child Ord. Cap. 322
	Antigua & Barbuda	- s.6 Adoption of Children Act Cap. 9
	Montserrat	- s.6 Adoption of Children Act Cap. 296
	St Christopher & Nevis	- s.6 Adoption of Child Act Cap. 322.

8

Grants of Letters of Administration

INTRODUCTION

PERSONS ENTITLED TO GRANT

The persons entitled in priority to take out a grant of letters of administration of an intestate's estate are generally those entitled to benefit on an intestacy. With the exception of Jamaica, St Lucia, The Bahamas and Trinidad & Tobago, none of the other territories has statutory provisions and/or rules which stipulate the order of priority with respect to entitlement to grants of letters of administration. In the other territories, pursuant to the respective reception provision contained *inter alia* in the Supreme/High Court Acts of these territories the English Non-Contentious Probate Rules 1954/1987;[1] (depending on the cut off date for reception thereof) are received and applied, for the purposes of determining the order of priority with respect to entitlement to grants of letters of administration.

Order of Entitlement to Grant of Letters of Administration

Barbados

According to s.19 of the Succession Act Cap. 249, the court has a discretion as to the person to whom administration is to be granted. However the practice in Barbados is to follow the order of priority with respect to entitlement to grants of letters of administration as set out in r.21 N.C.P.R. 1954, England, subject to the overriding discretion of the registrar to determine the ultimate order of priority with respect thereto.

Guyana

According to s.16 of the Deceased Persons' Estates Administration Act Cap. 12:01 the Court may where it appears expedient to do so, appoint any person or persons to be an administrator to administer the estate of a deceased person where the person dies intestate.

Although s.60 of the Deceased Persons' Estates Administration Act provides for probate rules to be made under s.67 of the High Court Act Cap. 3:01, no rules have to date been made which set out the order of priority with respect to entitlement to grants of administration. However, pursuant to s.17 of the High Court, which allows in effect for the reception of the N.C.P.R. 1954, England, where no local rules of probate practice and procedure exist, it is the practice, when applying for grants of administration, to adopt the order of priority with respect to entitlement to grants as set out in r.21 N.C.P.R. 1954 England subject to the overriding statutory discretion conferred on the court, under s.16 of the Deceased Persons Estate Administration Act cap. 12:01.

Jamaica

The position with respect to entitlement to grants of letters of administration is regulated by s.5 and s.12 of the Intestates' Estates and Property Charges Act, (which in general terms, sets out the order of priority with respect to beneficial entitlement to an intestate's estate) and with effect from January 1, 2003, by Rule 68 CPR 2002 which has replaced the former practice which had developed.

Position prior to January 1, 2003

According to the provisions of the above Act and the former practice, the following persons were entitled to take our letters of administration:

- the beneficiaries of the intestate's estate; where the value of the residuary estate exceeded one thousand dollars and the beneficiaries were all adults and were in agreement and had been given their written consent to one or more of them, if more than one, applying for the grant;
- where the adult beneficiaries were not in agreement; one or some of those persons who in accordance with s.5 of the Intestates' Estates and Property Charges Act, were beneficially entitled to the intestate's estate provided they had obtained the consent of those in agreement and had given notice of the intended application to those so opposed. By way of illustration, according to s.15 of the Intestates' Estates and Property Charges Act where the intestate dies leaving a spouse and child/children surviving him, the surviving spouse *and* child/children were exclusively entitled to the intestate's estate, albeit, in varying proportions. As such the surviving spouse would be permitted to take our

letters of administration although the children or one or some of them had not so consented.

However the surviving spouse was required to serve on those children who had not consented, notice of the intended application for the grant of administration in accordance with r.18 of the General Rules and Orders of the Supreme Court Part III Probate and Administration as the children were deemed to be equally entitled to take out letters of administration. Conversely, where the children were all adults and were in agreement but the surviving spouse had not consented, the children might be permitted to apply for the grant of letters of administration provided they had given the surviving spouse notice of the intended application.[2]

However it is to be noted that where the adult beneficiaries were not in agreement that although the practice had decreased (primarily in an effort by the Administrator General to reduce the number of applications for letters of administration which were made by the Administrator General), applications for grants of letters of administration were nevertheless often made by the Administrator General where the adult beneficiaries so requested.

- the Administrator General where the value of the residuary estate exceeds one thousand dollars and a minor is a beneficiary.

Position on or after January 1, 2003

The entitlement to a grant of letters of administration is still regulated by the substantive provisions of s.12 and s.5 of the Intestates' Estates and Property Charges Act. However Rule 68.18 CPR 2002 has replaced the former practice and introduced an order of priority with respect to letters of administration. The conjunctive effect of the substantive law and Rule 68:18 is as follows:

- the beneficiaries of the estate are still entitled to apply for letters of administration where the value of the intestate's estate exceeds one thousand dollars in accordance with the provisions of the Intestates Estates and Property Charges Act;
- where the value of the estate exceeds one thousand dollars, and a minor/minors is/are beneficiaries, the Administrator General is required to apply for letters of administration, unless the court otherwise orders. This position has been codified by Rule 68.18, CPR 2002;
- Unlike the former practice of putting all beneficiaries into one

class, Rule 68.18 has introduced an order of priority in respect of entitlement to the grant. In this regard, Rule 68.18(1) provides, inter alia, for the following order of priority:

a) the surviving spouse of the deceased;
b) the children of the deceased and the issue of any child who died before the deceased;
c) the father and mother of the deceased; and
d) brothers and sisters of the whole blood and the issue of any deceased brother or sister of the whole blood who died before the deceased.

Pursuant to Rule 68.18(2)(b) in particular, persons falling into a higher category are no longer required to obtain the consent of any person in the same or any lower degree of priority. However where persons are entitled in the same degree, and one or some of them will not give their consent, pursuant to Rule 68.21, the applicant for the grant is required to serve notice on those persons entitled in the same degree, not less than 14 days before applying for the grant unless the registrar dispenses with the need for such notice.

Order of the Court

It is to be noted that with respect to instances where the estate is valued over one thousand dollars and a minor is a beneficiary the Administrator General is the person entitled to take out letters of administration, but s.12 of the Intestates' Estates and Property Charges Act provides that the court may grant administration to some person other than the Administrator General where it is satisfied that it would be for the benefit of the estate.

Accordingly, in practice, the application for the grant is usually made by the adult beneficiaries or a trust corporation on their behalf pursuant to an order of the court.

The Bahamas

Position Prior to February 1, 2002

According to the effect of s.3(1) and s.4(4) respectively of the Real Estate Devolution Act Ch. 91:

(a) where the deceased leaves real estate only, the heir-at-law, or if the heir-at-law is dead, the personal representative of the heir-at-law has a right to the grant;

(b) where the estate comprises real and personal estate, the heir-at-law's right to the grant is inferior to that of the surviving widow or husband but superior to that of the next of kin if the husband or widow renounces. Apart from this exception the heir-at-law's right is equal to that of the next-of-kin, superior to that of the personal representative of the next-of-kin.

However where the real estate is greater than the personal estate, the grant will be given to the heir-at-law in priority to the next of kin and only to the next-of-kin if the heir-at-law consents or there is evidence that notice of the application has been given to the heir-at-law. The opposite holds true where the estate consists mainly of personal estate.

Where the estate of the intestate comprises realty only, and the heir-at-law has died since the intestate's death, a grant will be made to the personal representative of the heir-at-law. However where the estate comprises of both real and personal property and both the next of kin and heir-at-law have died since the intestate's death a grant will not be made to the personal representative of the heir-at-law without clearing off the next of kin.

Position on or after February 1, 2002

With the passage of several pieces of succession legislation, in particular the Inheritance Act, 2002, the distribution of an intestate's estate is now governed by new statutory rules. In particular, as was previously stated, heirship, curtesy and the Statute of Distribution have all been abolished and the real and personal estate of an intestate have been assimilated for the purpose of such distribution.

Accordingly, the entitlement to a grant of letters of administration is now subject to the new provisions of the Inheritance Act read in conjunction with s.44 of the Supreme Court Act 1996.

In this regard, s.44 confers a wide discretion on the Court as to whom administration is to be granted, and provides that in granting letters of administration, the Court is required to take into account the rights of all persons interested in the estate of the deceased persons or the proceeds of sale thereof. The effect of s.44 which effectively provides that the right to the grant shall follow the right to property, read in conjunction with the new rules of beneficial entitlement on an intestacy as provided for by the Inheritance Act 2002, and the respective provision contained in the Supreme Court Act 15/1996 is that, in the absence of specific rules to the contrary, Rule 21 NCPR 1987, England is applicable to the Bahamas, for purposes of determining the order of priority in respect of entitlement to a grant of administration, subject to the overriding discretion conferred on the Court by the provisions of s.44 of the Supreme Court Act.

It is to be noted that s.44 of the Supreme Court Act 15/1996 provides that in granting letters of administration the court is required to take into account the rights of all persons interested in the estate of the deceased person or the proceeds of sale thereof.

Trinidad & Tobago

According to s.30(a) of the Wills and Probate Ordinance Ch. 8 No. 2, the following persons are entitled in order of priority to a grant of letters of administration:

- the surviving widow or husband of the intestate;
- the next of kin;
- the Administrator General.

Prior to the passage of the Distribution of Estates Act 2002, the Administration of Estates Ordinance Ch. 8 No. 1 which is still to be read as one with the Wills and Probate Ordinance Ch. 8 No. 2 defined next-of-kin as:

> The person or persons nearest in degree of relationship among those of kin within the meaning of the last preceding subsection each step to or from the common ancestor reckoning as a degree of kinship; the half-blood reckoning immediately after the whole blood of the same degree.

Section 3(1) defined 'of kin' in a negative, rather than positive manner. It provided that:

> No person shall be deemed of kin to a deceased intestate for the purpose of beneficial succession to his estate who is not either lawful issue of the deceased or his father or mother or a grandfather or grandmother or great grandfather or great grandmother of the deceased or the lawful issue of any such person.

Based on the provisions of s.30(a) of the Wills & Probate Ordinance Ch. 8 No. 2 and the former provision of ss.3(1) and 3(2) of the Administration of Estates Ordinance Ch. 8 No. 1, the following persons were entitled in order of priority to a grant of letters of administration *inter alia*:

- the surviving husband or widow of the intestate.
- the child or children (as next-of-kin) of the intestate;
- the grandchild or grandchildren (as next-of-kin) of the intestate;
- the great-grandchildren or great grand-children or other lineal

descendants (as next-of-kin) of the intestate;
- the father or mother (as next-of-kin) of the intestate;

Position on or after September 25, 2002

While the persons who qualify in order of priority to a grant of administration of an intestate's estate remain unchanged, there have been significant statutory changes in respect of the persons beneficially entitled to the estate of an intestate, by virtue of amendments made to the Administration of Estates Ordinance Ch.8 No.1, by the Distribution of Estates Act 28/2000

In this regard the failure to bring the provisions of the Wills and Probate Ordinance in line with the changes made to the Administration of Estates Ordinance has had unintended consequences in so far as the persons who are now qualified to apply for a grant of the intestates estate. This legislative oversight is particularly apparent in the case of the following classes of beneficiaries:

(1) The Surviving Spouse:

The definition of surviving spouse has not been amended under the Wills and Probate Ordinance. Accordingly for the purpose of entitlement to the grant, a co-habitant is not entitled to apply for the grant, although he or she may qualify as a spouse for the purpose of beneficial entitlement to an intestate's estate.

In addition, a judicially separated spouse in accordance with s. 10A of the Administration of Estates Ordinance is not entitled to share in the estate of his or her intestate spouse. However, a judicially separated spouse still qualifies as a surviving spouse for purposes of entitlement to the grant of administration.

As a consequence of the above, where a deceased dies intestate, leaving a co-habitant surviving him, although the co-habitant may be entitled to the entire estate of the intestate, he or she is not entitled to take the grant and in the case of the judicially separated spouse, although he/she is not entitled to a share of the intestates estate, he or she, as the surviving spouse, is first entitled to the grant.

(2) The Children of the Intestate:

According to s. 2 of the Wills and Probate Ordinance, next of kin means persons entitled under an intestacy pursuant to the provisions of the Administration of Estates Ordinance. Section 3 (2) of the Ordinance which has been repealed clearly set out the order of priority in respect of persons who qualify as next-of-kin, the first being the issue of the intestate.

However the definition of next-of-kin as amended by the Distribution of Estates Act does not now include issue of the intestate but includes, inter alia, the brothers and sisters of the deceased and the issue of the grand parents of the deceased. In fact, issue of the deceased is separately defined under the Act. And as previously stated, the Wills and Probate Ordinance, according to s.1 of the Administration of Estates Ordinance, is to be read as one with the Administration of Estates Ordinance. The situation which now arises by the failure to amend s.30 (a) of the Wills and Probate Ordinance is that for the purposes of entitlement to the grant of letters of administration of an intestate, the issue of the intestate do not qualify as next-of-kin and are not entitled to the grant. Instead the brothers and sisters, who, in such circumstances, are not beneficially entitled to a share of the intestate's estate, are the persons first entitled to grant of administration according to the current definition of next-of-kin.

(3)   Duplication in Meaning

Section 2 of the Administration of Estates Ordinance Ch.8 No.1 as amended by s.2 of the Distribution of Estates Act 28/2000 provides that next-of-kin means in relation to a deceased person, *inter alia*:

(a)   the issue of the grand parents of the deceased;
(b)   the brothers and sisters of a parent of the deceased

In this regard, both (b) and (c) refer to the same classification of next-of-kin; the uncles and aunts of the deceased.

Eastern Caribbean territories (save Dominica and St Lucia)

Pursuant to s.11 of the respective Supreme Court Act of the above territories r.22 of the N.C.P.R. 1987, England is received and applied with respect to entitlement to grants of letters of administration.

Anguilla

According to s.7(1) of the Death Duties (Abolition) Ordinance 6/1977, where a person dies intestate an application for a grant of letters of administration may be made to the registrar by the husband, wife, issue, father, mother, or issue of the father or mother of the deceased person. However the order of priority with respect thereto is not stipulated. Accordingly, r.22 N.C.P.R. 1987, England is applied in practice for the purposes of determining entitlement to grants of letters of administration.

Dominica

In accordance with the cut-off date for reception of English probate law and practice as contained in s.11 of the Supreme Court Act of Dominica, r.21 N.C.P.R. 1954, England is received and applied for the purposes of determining the order of priority with respect to entitlement to grants of letters of administration.

St Lucia

According to Art 1016 of the Code of Civil Procedure Ch. 243 letters of administration shall be granted to the persons entitled in the following order of priority:

(a) to the persons within the heritable degree in order of their right to succeed to the deceased;[2] or
(b) failing such persons, to the surviving wife or husband as the case may be, or
(c) failing such surviving wife or husband, to the person nominated by the Crown to apply for administration.

Powers and Duties of the Administrator-General

Trinidad & Tobago, St Lucia and Jamaica

In Trinidad & Tobago, St Lucia and Jamaica, statute has conferred quite extensive powers on the Administrator General most notably in Jamaica, to administer the estate of an intestate in certain circumstances.

Trinidad & Tobago

Pursuant to the provisions of the Administration of Estate Ordinance Ch. 8 No. 1, the Administrator General:

(a) may administer small estates under $960 in the absence of the executor or person entitled to administration;[3]
(b) shall apply to the court for letters of administration to the estate of a deceased dying intestate leaving no next of kin and the estate is valued over $960.[4]
(c) may also be constituted by the committee or joint committee of the estate and effects of persons of unsound mind.[5]

(d) may, subject to the Wills and Probate Ordinance Ch. 8 No. 2 apply for letters of administration to the estate of any person whether domiciled in Trinidad & Tobago or not who has died either intestate or testate leaving no person entitled to the grant who has either renounced, cited to apply and failed to appear or otherwise has failed or refused to act.[6]

In practice the Administrator General, rarely applies for grants of administration except on behalf of the State in cases where the deceased died intestate without next of kin. In such instances the State is entitled to claim the estate as *bona vacantia*.

St Lucia

Pursuant to the Eastern Caribbean Supreme Court (St Lucia) Act 17/1969, the Administrator General is empowered:

(a) to administer the estate of bankrupts as may be prescribed by the Commercial Code or any other enactment.[7]
(b) to order the payment, transfer or delivery of the estate to any person who has died out of the State and whose estate has come into the possession of the Government, to any person who the Government considers is lawfully or equitably entitled to the same provided:
 (i) three months have elapsed since the estate came into possession of the Government; and
 (ii) it is proved to the satisfaction of the Administrator General that no will has been admitted to probate and no administration has been taken out to the estate to such deceased person.[8]
(c) to administer and to take possession of the estate of a person who is absent from the State, and is not represented therein by any duly constituted attorney or agent.[9]
(d) *ex officio* to take possession of and administer the estate and effects of any person judicially declared to be an idiot, a person of unsound mind, or otherwise insane, and whose next-of-kin is unwilling, or is declared by the High Court incompetent to administer such estate and effects.[10]

Jamaica

The powers, duties and responsibilities of the Administrator General in Jamaica is without parallel in any of the Caribbean jurisdictions. It is therefore worthy of special mention and consideration as the statutory powers conferred on the Administrator General with respect to the administration of estates affect all facets of non-contentious probate practice and procedure, making the practice thereof unique to this territory.

As was stated previously, the Administrator General is under a legal duty to take out letters of administration (with or without will annexed) in a number of instances, unless the Court is satisfied that it would be for the benefit of the estate that the grant be made to some other person. By contrast, in St Lucia and Trinidad & Tobago (the only other Caribbean territories in which statute provides for this office), the Administrator General's role with respect to administration of estates is quite limited and in practice the Administrator General usually takes out letters of administration in instances where the deceased died without next of kin or where there are no next of kin willing or able to take out the relevant grant. The opposite is true for the Administrator General in Jamaica.

In this regard, the powers and duties of the Administrator General with respect to applications for letters of administration (with or without will annexed) are codified essentially by two pieces of legislation:

- The Administrator General's Act, enacted on 26th August, 1873; and
- The Intestates' Estates and Property Charges Act enacted on 1st June, 1937.

According to s. 12 of the Administrator General Act:

> The Administrator-General shall be entitled to, and it shall be his duty to apply for, letters of administration to the estates of all persons who shall die intestate without leaving a widower, widow, brother, sister, or any lineal ancestor or descendant, or leaving any such relative if no such relative shall take out letters of administration within three months, or within such longer or shorter time as the Court to which application for administration is made, or the Judge thereof may direct; and also to the estates of all persons who shall die leaving a will but leaving no executor, or no executor who will act, if no such relative as aforesaid of such deceased shall, within the time aforesaid, take out letters of administration to his estate. The Administrator-General shall be entitled to such letters of administration in all cases in which, if this Act had not been passed, letters of administration to the estates of such persons might have been granted to any administrator.

Although the Administrator General's Act appears to qualify or limit the circumstances in which the Administrator General is required to take out letters of administration (with or without will annexed), by providing *inter alia* that applications for letters of administration shall be made in cases where no 'relatives shall take out letters within three months', the provisions of this Act are expressly subject to the far more expansive provisions of s.12 of the Intestates' Estates and Property Charges Act. Section 12 of this Act provides:

> Notwithstanding, anything contained in the Administrator-General's Act, or any enactment amending or substituted for the same, where the residuary estate of the intestate does not exceed one thousand dollars, or where it exceeds that sum and a minor is entitled to a share thereof, or where a testator does not appoint an executor or where the executor has died before the testator or renounces, it shall be the duty of the Administrator-General to apply for letters of administrator to the estate and, unless the Court is satisfied that it would be for the benefit of the estate that letters of administration ought to be granted to some other person, letters of administration to such estate shall be granted to the Administrator-General.

The cumulative effect of these two Acts and in particular the overriding provisions of s.12 of the Intestates' Estates and Property Charges Act is that the Administrator General and by extension the Administrator General's Department are simply unable to cope, with any degree of expedition, with the sheer volume of applications for letters of administration (with or without will annexed) which the Administrator General according to the provisions of the above Act, is required to take out.

This problem is further exacerbated by the administrative requirement that all estates which are to be administered by the Administrator General must be investigated before the application for the relevant grant can be made. The sheer number of these estates coupled with this administrative requirement have only added to an already unwieldy situation resulting in literally thousands of estates remaining unadministered years after the death of the deceased.

In an effort to minimise, if not completely solve these difficulties, the following are some of the measures which have been implemented over the years and in more recent times:

(a) with respect to those estates which are actually administered by the Administrator General, private practitioners have been and are routinely retained to prepare and file on behalf of the Administrator General the papers to lead the relevant grant of representation.
(b) as of 1st July, 1996, with a view to reducing, if not completely phasing out this practice, a legal department staffed with attorneys-at-law, has been established.

However it is submitted that a more cost effective, and long term solution may be for the Government to undertake the rationalisation and modernisation of the succession laws with a view to enacting legislation which would:

(a) reduce or limit the role and function of the Administrator General in so far as the administration of estates is concerned, and place this responsibility in the hands of the persons beneficially entitled to the deceased's estate, as is the case in the other jurisdictions;

It is to be noted that since the writing of the first edition of this text, the non-contentious probate rules which came into effect into 1879 have been replaced by Rule 68 of the CPR 2002 which *inter alia* now include an order of priority with respect to letters of administration (with or without will annexed).

- *Bona Vacantia*

All jurisdictions (save The Bahamas)

The Crown's/State's right to succeed to the personal estate of an intestate dying without next-of-kin *bona vacantia* replaced escheat to the Crown with the passage of intestate estates legislation in the various Caribbean territories. This common law right, based on the Royal Prerogative is now a statutory right in these jurisdictions and applies both to ownerless personal estate and ownerless real estate of an intestate.[11]

The application for the grant of administration of an intestate's estates is made by and issued to the person nominated on behalf of the State/Crown such as the Administrator General/Registrar of the Supreme Court in his capacity as *ex officio* Administrator of Estates. However in accordance with the relevant statutory provisions of the respective Caribbean territories, the State/Crown with the exception of Grenada[12] invariably waives its right to this ownerless property in favour of persons whether kindred or not who *inter alia* have established a legal, equitable or moral claim to the intestate's estate or otherwise have established a level of reasonable expectation that they would be provided for out of the intestate's estate.

In recent years these applications have significantly decreased, primarily because of:
(a) the impact of the Status of Children legislation; and
(b) with respect to Jamaica and Barbados the statutory recognition of the common law spouse,

both of which have effectively created new classes of lawful applicants for grants of administration.

The Bahamas

The State's right to ownerless real property of an intestate was until the passage of the Inheritance Act 2002 governed by the Escheat Act Ch. 141. According to the provisions of this repealed Act, whenever a landowner died without leaving heirs, his land escheated to the Crown as the ultimate owner under the feudal system of land tenure. However in such instances, the Crown usually waived its rights to the intestate's estate in favour of persons who the intestate might reasonably have been expected to make provision.[13]

It is to be noted that the Inheritance Act expressly repealed The Escheat Act and there is no provision contained in the Inheritance Act with respect to devolution of ownerless property of an intestate. Accordingly, in the absence of express statutory provision to the contrary, and the repeal of the Escheat Act, it is submitted that the position in respect of ownerless property is now subject to the common law principles governing, escheat to the Crown, which is essentially the same as that which is contained in the repealed Escheat Act.

APPLICATION FOR GRANTS OF LETTERS OF ADMINISTRATION

Procedure and Documents

Applications for a grant of letters of administration are made in accordance with the practice and procedure with respect to general grants of representation outlined in chapter 5.

The documents as with other grants of representation vary on a jurisdictional basis and are lodged as follows:

Barbados [14]

1. Application for grant made through an attorney-at-law or by applicant in person.
2. Affidavit of administrator.
3. Certified copy of death/burial certificate.
4. Certified copies of birth certificate, adoption order, marriage certificate, affidavit of kin, paternity order, affidavit as to duration of union (where applicable).
5. Estate and Succession Duty Certificate (with respect to the estates of persons dying on or prior to 30th March, 1981).[15]
6. Affidavit of Search.
7. Consent(s)/Notice(s) (where applicable).

8. Justification of Sureties.
9. Affidavit of Value/Property with Schedule thereto (with respect to the estates of persons dying on or after 31 March, 1981).[16]

Guyana [17]

1. Application for Grant made though an attorney-at-law or by applicant in person.
2. Oath of administrator.
3. Statement of Assets and Liabilities.
4. Certificate of Proper Officer.
5. Certified copy of death certificate.
6. Administrator's bond.
7. Justification of Sureties (when required by the registrar).
8. Marriage/birth certificate, adoption order, affiliation order, affidavit of kin (where applicable).
9. Consent(s)/Notice(s) (where applicable).

Jamaica[18]

Position prior to January 1, 2003

1. Covering letter addressed to the registrar, Supreme Court (discretionary).
2. Oath of administrator.
3. Administration bond (not required where the Administrator General is the applicant).
4. Inventory.
5. Kalamazoo copy of Inventory.
6. Declaration of Counting of Inventory.
7. Affidavit in Proof of Death.
8. Declaration of paternity, affidavit of kin, order of recognition of statutory spouse (where applicable).
9. Justification of Sureties (not applicable where the Administrator General is the applicant; with respect to the beneficiaries, where required by the registrar).
10. Affidavit of Value (not required where the Administrator General is the applicant).
11. Letters of Administration.
12. Kalamazoo copy of Letters of Administration.
13. Stamp Commissioner's Certificate (with respect to the estates of persons dying prior to 21st July, 1963).
14. Consent(s)/Notice(s) (where applicable).

15. Copy of Order granting leave to beneficiaries to apply (where applicable).
16. Declaration of Counting of Letters of Administration.

Position on or after January 1, 2003

1. Covering letter addressed to the registrar (discretionary)
2. Oath of administrator
3. Death certificate exhibited to oath
4. Draft letters of administration with Kalamazoo copy
5. Consents/Notices, where applicable
6. Copy of Court Order, where applicable
7. Administrator General's Certificate
8. Declaration of paternity affidavit of kin, where applicable

The Bahamas[19]

1. Petition sworn to by the Petitioner.
2. Oath of the administrator.
3. Administration bond.
4. Justification of Sureties (where required by the registrar).
5. Bond for making return into Registry and Paying Duties.
6. Return.
7. Affidavit of heirship, affidavit of kin with respect to estates of persons dying prior to February 1, 2002.
8. Birth, marriage certificate, adoption order, birth certificate, with respect to the estate of persons dying on or after February 1, 2002 (where applicable).
9. Schedule of the Personal Estate of the Deceased.
10. Schedule of the Real Property owned by the deceased.
11. Consent(s)/Notice(s) (where applicable).
12. Nomination/order of appointment of co-administrator, (where applicable).

Trinidad & Tobago [20]

1. Application for grant of letters of administration made through an attorney-at-law.
2. Affidavit of administrator.
3. Certified copy of death/burial certificate.
4. Certified copies of marriage, birth certificate, paternity order, adoption order (where applicable).

Grants of Letters of Administration / **207**

5. Inventory.
6. Administrator bond.
7. Justification of Sureties (where required by the registrar).
8. Certificate of Search.
9. Estate Duty Certificate (with respect to the estates of persons dying prior to 1st January, 1981.
10. Filing fee receipt.
11. Consent(s)/Notice(s) (where applicable).

EASTERN CARIBBEAN TERRITORIES [23]

Anguilla:

1. Application for grant made through a solicitor or by applicant in person.
2. Oath of administrator.
3. Declaration on Oath of the Value of the Estate.
4. Certified copy of death certificate.
5. Certified copy of marriage certificate, birth certificate, paternity order, affiliation order (where applicable).
6. Administration bond.
7. Justification of Sureties (where required by the registrar).
8. Affidavit of kin.
9. Land Registry Valuation Certificate (where application for the grant is made through the Registrar).
10. Order for issue of grant (for signature by the registrar).
11. Two original copies of grant of letters of administration.
12. Consent(s)/Notice(s) (where applicable).
13. Nomination/order of appointment of co-administrator, (where applicable).

Antigua & Barbuda:

1. Application for grant made through a solicitor or by applicant in person.
2. Oath of administrator.
3. Certified copy of death certificate.
4. Administration bond.
5. Justification of Sureties (where required by the registrar).
6. Certificate of Stamp Duty (with respect to the estates of persons dying on or prior to 31st December, 1969).[22]
7. Declaration and Account of the Estate (with respect to the estates of persons dying on or prior to 31st December, 1969).[23]

8. Certified copy of marriage, birth certificate, paternity order, affiliation order (where applicable).
9. Consent(s)/Notice(s) (where applicable).
10. Order for grant to issue (for signature by registrar).
11. Nomination/order of appointment of co-administrator, (where applicable).

Dominica:

1. Application for grant made through a solicitor or by applicant in person.
2. Oath of administrator.
3. Estate Duty Certificate (with respect to the estates of persons dying on or prior to 30th June, 1985).[24]
4. Declaration and Account of Estate (otherwise called 'Probate').
5. Certified copy of death certificate.
6. Administration bond.
7. Justification of Sureties (where required by the registrar).
8. Certified copy of marriage, birth certificate and adoption order (where applicable).
9. Consent(s)/Notice(s) (where applicable).
10. Order for issue of grant (for signature by registrar).
11. Nomination/order of appointment of co-administrator, (where applicable).

Grenada:

1. Application for grant made through a solicitor or by applicant in person.
2. Oath of administrator.
3. Original death certificate.
4. Administrator's bond.
5. Justification of Sureties (where required by the registrar).
6. Paternity order, adoption order (where applicable).[25]
7. Declaration and Account of the Estate (with respect to the estates of persons dying on or prior to 30th September, 1983).[26]
8. Estate Duty Certificate (with respect to deaths occurring on or prior to 30th September, 1983).[27]
9. Consent(s)/Notice(s) (where applicable).
10. Order for grant to issue (for signature by registrar).
11. Nomination/order of appointment of co-administrator, (where applicable).

Montserrat:

1. Application for grant made through a solicitor or by applicant in person.
2. Oath of administrator.
3. Declaration and Account of the Estate.
4. Certified copy of death certificate.
5. Marriage/birth certificate (where applicable).
6. Advertisement clippings from newspaper in which application for grant was advertised.
7. Administration bond.
8. Justification of Sureties (where required by the registrar).
9. Consent(s)/Notice(s) (where applicable).
10. Stamp Duty Certificate (with respect to the estate of persons dying before 19th November, 1966).[28]
11. Nomination/order of appointment of co-administrator, (where applicable).

St Christopher & Nevis:

1. Application for grant made through a solicitor or by applicant in person.
2. Oath of administrator.
3. Declaration and Account of the Estate.
4. A certified copy of original death certificate.
5. Administration bond.
6. Justification of Sureties (where required by the registrar).
7. Certified copy of marriage, birth certificates, paternity order affiliation order, affidavit of kin (where applicable).
8. Certificate of Payment of Stamp Duty.
9. Order for issue of grant (for signature by the registrar).
10. Two original copies of grant of letters of administration.
11. Consent(s)/Notice(s) (where applicable).
12. Nomination/order of appointment of co-administrator, (where applicable).

St Lucia [29]

1. Application in form of Petition sworn to by Petitioner.
2. Affidavit of administrator in support of Petition.
3. Affidavit of Assets and Liabilities.
4. Certificate of Non-objection.
5. Death certificate.

6. Marriage/birth certificate, adoption order, affiliation order, affidavit of kin (where applicable).
7. Administrator's bond (when required by the registrar).
8. Affidavit of the Administrator General (where applicable).
9. Consent(s)/Notice(s) (where applicable).

St Vincent & the Grenadines:

1. Application for grant made through a solicitor or by applicant in person.
2. Warrant to Act.
3. Petition.
4. Oath of administrator in support of Petition.
5. Certified copy of death certificate.
6. Certified copy of marriage, birth certificate, baptism certificate, paternity order, affiliation order, affidavit of kin, adoption order (where applicable).
7. Administration bond.
8. Justification of Sureties (where required by the registrar).
9. Declaration and Account of the Estate.
10. Consent(s)/Notice(s) (where applicable).
11. A valuation certificate with respect to land.
12. Nomination/order of appointment of co-administrator, (where applicable).

Description of Documents

Many of the documents necessary for letters of administration are similar to those required for probate grant applications and grants of letters of administration with will annexed. Accordingly this chapter will focus on the documents, peculiar to grants of letters of administration.

A. *Covering Letter/Formal Application for the Grant*

All jurisdictions (save St Lucia)

The covering letter (with respect to Jamaica) and the formal application for the grant (with respect to the other territories)[30] is the same in form as an application for other non-contentious applications for grants of representation save that the grant specified therein is a grant of letter of administration.

Petition

The Bahamas

The petition takes the simple form of a prayer for letters of administration to be granted in the estate of the deceased named therein.[31]

St Lucia

The Petition is quite comprehensive and although it does not take a prescribed form it should include the following:

(i) the name, place and date of death of the deceased intestate.
(ii) the names, addresses of the heirs-at-law of the deceased and their relationship to the deceased.
(iii) in cases where the intestate was a married woman/man survived by her/his spouse, a recital stating *inter alia* that the deceased was married in community of property (if that is in fact the case).
(iv) that an affidavit in support of the petition as required by Art 1015(b) of Code of Civil Procedure Ch. 243 is herewith filed.
(v) that the assets and liabilities of the succession of the deceased are as set out in the affidavit (of assets and liabilities) of the petitioner.
(vi) a brief description of the property owned by the deceased. (Where the deceased was married in community of property, the description of the property is limited to the intestate's share of the property held in community.)
(vii) a statement to the effect that the Accountant General does not object to the grant of letters of administration to the petitioner.
(viii) that the surviving heirs have no objection to the petitioner being appointed administrator.
(ix) where the application for letters of administration is made after the expiration of one year since the death of the deceased, the petition should include a recital that the Administrator General has not intermeddled in the deceased's estate.

Affidavit of the Administrator General

It is to be noted that an affidavit of the Administrator General to the above effect must be filed or alternatively the petitioner may depose to this fact in the affidavit/oath in support of the petition.[32]

St Vincent & the Grenadines

The petition, where filed, contains essentially the same information as the oath/affidavit of the applicant.

B. Administrator's Oath/Affidavit[33]

All Jurisdictions

The oath/affidavit which is sworn to by the administrator is quite similar in content to that of the oath/affidavit to lead the grant of letters of administration with will annexed. It should contain *inter alia* the following recitals:

(i) the name, address and a description of the intended administrator; his relationship, if any, to the deceased and the capacity in which he is applying;
(ii) the name, address and description of the deceased;
(iii) the date and place of death and with the exception of St Lucia and Antigua & Barbuda, the domicil of the deceased;
(iv) an undertaking by the applicant to get in and administer the estate of the deceased, and to distribute the residue according to the law;
(v) in all the jurisdictions save Barbados and St Lucia, the gross value of the estate of the intestate to be administered by the applicant.
(vi) in the Eastern Caribbean territories (save St Lucia) Jamaica and The Bahamas:[34]
   (a) *Recital with respect to Life and Minority Interest*
   that a life or no life interest arises and that a minority or no minority interest arises as the case may be under the said intestacy;
   (b) *Recital with respect to settled land*
   Although a statement as to whether there was land vested in the deceased which was settled previously to his death and which remained settled land notwithstanding his death is included in the oath, this practice it is submitted, with the exception of Jamaica is incorrect as it is without legal basis.
(vii) *Jamaica*
where the applicant is the next of kin, than the applicant beneficiaries are all *sui juris* and pursuant to Rule 68.21 CPR 2002 that, where applicable, they have given their written consent to the proposed grantee making the application, or alternatively that notice of the application has been given to those persons equally entitled to the grant.

(viii) *Guyana*
that the deceased was married only once (if that is the case) and that he/she was married prior to the 20th August, 1904.[35]
(ix) *Barbados, Dominica and Trinidad & Tobago*
that the intended administrator has caused a search to be made among the deceased's personal papers and in the Depository of Wills of Living Person/Registration of Deeds (Barbados) and that no documents of a testamentary character was found;
(x) *The Bahamas, Guyana and Eastern Caribbean territories (save St Lucia),*
that the applicant *when required* by law, will exhibit a true inventory of the said estate.
(xi) *Trinidad & Tobago and Barbados*
that the applicant will file in the Registry within 12 calendar months from the date of the grant a Statement and Account verified by affidavit of his administration of the deceased estate. In practice this is hardly ever done unless an application is made by some person interested in the estate, calling upon the administrator to file an account of his administration.

Additional Recitals

Clearing off Prior Rights
All Jurisdictions (save Jamaica)

Where the application for letters of administration is made by a person with an inferior title thereto, the affidavit of the intended grantee must be worded so as to clear off persons having a prior right to the grant, more particularly the affidavit must show on its face how those prior rights have been cleared off, whether by way of:

(a) the renunciation of the person(s) with a superior entitlement, or;
(b) citation to accept or refuse the grant of letters of administration; or
(c) the death of the person(s) with prior rights to the grant; or in Barbados
(d) obtaining the written consent of the person with the prior right to the grant. It is to be noted that in practice in Barbados written consents operate much in the same way as renunciations in that they are also used for the purposes of clearing off persons with a prior right to a grant of administration, although consents are applicable to cases of equal entitlement.

Jamaica

Position prior to January 1, 2003

Where the beneficiaries of the intestate's estate (the next-of-kin) were entitled to take out letters of administration, pursuant to s.12 of the Intestates' Estates and Property Charges Act, this statutory entitlement to the grant followed the beneficial entitlement to the intestate's estate as provided for by s.5 of the Intestates' Estates and Property Charges Act and the practice that developed. Accordingly the persons who were beneficially entitled to the intestate's estate (usually the spouse and children) were also deemed to be *equally* entitled to a grant of the intestate's estate. As such there was no order of priority among the beneficiaries with respect to entitlement to a grant of administration. This was unlike the position in England and the other territories, where there was an order of priority to the grant, which was separate and apart from beneficial entitlement to the intestate's estate. And in instances where the beneficiaries were required to obtain an order of the court so as to permit them, instead of the Administrator General, to apply for letters of administration, (usually in cases where one or some of the beneficiaries was/were minor(s), the court granted leave to the applicants, not based on any order of priority but rather where it was of the opinion that it would be for the benefit of the estate to make the grant to some other person other than the Administrator General. Accordingly it is submitted that clearing off of persons with a prior entitlement to a grant of letters of administration was not applicable to Jamaica, prior to the passage of the Supreme Court of Jamaica CPR 2002.

Position on or after January 1, 2003

Although entitlement to letters of administration is still governed by the substantive provisions of s.5 of the Intestates' Estates and Property Charges Act, the passage of Rule 68 CPR 2002, in particular Rule 68.18 has introduced for the first time, as was stated above, an express order of priority to grants of letters of administration. Accordingly, clearing off of persons with a prior entitlement to grants of administration is now applicable to Jamaica.

In addition, it is submitted that where an order of the court is being sought in instances where one or some of the beneficiaries are minors, the court is required to take into account, though not follow, the order of priority to the grant as is now provided for by Rule 68.18 CPR 2002.

Consents of Notices to Persons Equally Entitled
All jurisdictions

Where applicable, a recital to the effect that the persons with equal entitlement to the grant of administration have consented to the intended grantee applying for the grant on his and their behalf should be included in the oath and the written consents exhibited thereto.

Where the persons entitled will not consent, a recital to the effect that notice of the intended application was given to them should be included (a copy of the letter/notice should be exhibited to the oath).

Barbados

It is to be noted that in Barbados consents are also used, in the appropriate case and subject to the registrar's discretion, so as to permit a beneficiary with an inferior right, to make the necessary application for the grant. Accordingly the oath should recite, where applicable, that the beneficiary with the prior entitlement to the grant (usually the surviving spouse), has consented in writing to the beneficiary with the inferior right with respect thereto, (usually the child(ren) of the intestate), applying for the grant of administration. Alternatively, where the beneficiary with the prior right will not give his written consent, the oath should recite that notice of the intended application was served on him and that he has failed or refused to give his written consent within the time stated in the notice.

C. Written Consents of/Notices to Persons Equally Entitled

Written Consent

All jurisdictions (save Jamaica)

Although, as is the case with respect to letters of administration with will annexed, the written consent of the persons equally entitled to take out letters of administration is not required, it is nonetheless a good practice to obtain the consents of the other beneficiaries equally entitled thereto who have no objections to the application for grant being made by the intended grantee.

Jamaica

Previously, the application for the grant was made by one or some of the beneficiaries of the intestate's estate, the written consent of the adult beneficiaries equally entitled thereto, had to be obtained. Alternatively notice of the intended application had to be given to them. The former practice has now essentially been codified as provided for by Rule 68.21 CPR 2002.

Contents of Written Consent

The contents of the consent are similar to that which is applicable to letters of administration with will annexed,[37] save that the grant specified therein is a grant of letters of administration and the entitlement thereto is based on the rules of priority governing entitlement to a grant on an intestacy.

Barbados

As stated above in so far as Barbados is concerned written consents are also used for the same purpose as are renunciations and in fact are a common means of 'clearing off' beneficiaries with a prior right to the grant, without the beneficiary actually having to renounce or give up his or her right to administer the intestate's estate. By way of illustration the surviving spouse who is deemed to have a prior right to a grant of administration may give her written consent to the child of the intestate applying for the grant and this consent subject to the registrar's discretion is sufficient to permit the child(ren) to apply for the grant without the need to formally clear off the surviving spouse by obtaining his/her renunciation. In practice written consents are used more frequently than renunciations in Barbados because:

(a) although both acts are voluntary, renunciation is a far more final act. Once a renunciation is filed, it operates to completely clear off the renunciant's right to administer the deceased's estate, and it may not be retracted without leave of the court and then only for very cogent reasons; and

(b) there is no indigenous probate rule which requires that a particular order of priority with respect to entitlement of grants be observed. Although r.19 N.C.P.R 1954, England, is followed, the registrar nonetheless has the ultimate discretion conferred upon him/her under s.19(3) of the Succession Act Cap. 249 which section provides that the court has a discretion as to whom administration may be granted.

However it should be pointed out that if the beneficiary with the prior entitlement to the grant will not give his/her written consent, and the registrar in the exercise of his/her discretion will not waive this requirement, the beneficiary with the prior entitlement will have to be cleared off by citation or 'passing over' proceedings as the case may be.

D. Notice to Persons Equally Entitled

Barbados, Jamaica, St Lucia and Trinidad & Tobago [36]

Where administration is applied for by one or some of the next-of-kin, there being another or other next of kin equally entitled thereto, the registrar may require proof by affidavit of the giving of such notice to be filed with the papers to lead the grant.

This practice may have arisen in Barbados because although r.19 N.C.P.R. 1954, England, is generally followed for the purposes of determining priorities with respect to entitlement to letters of administration, s.19(3) of the Succession Act Cap. 249 effectively gives the Registrar discretion as to whom a grant of administration may be made.

Guyana, The Bahamas, Eastern Caribbean (save St Lucia) [37]

With respect to the above territories, the relevant non-contentious probate rules provides that a grant of administration may be made to any person entitled thereto in the same degree without notice to the other persons equally entitled thereto.

All jurisdictions

Although, as indicated above, in some of the jurisdictions there is no requirement for notice of intended application for letters of administration to be given to those persons equally entitled thereto, it is nevertheless good practice to do so. With respect to the form and content of the notice, it is similar to that which is applicable to letters of administration with will annexed save that the grant specified therein is a grant of letters of administration.

Barbados

It is to be noted that in Barbados, notice of the application for the grant is also given to those persons who are deemed to have an inferior right to the grant. By way of illustration a surviving spouse who has a prior right to administration, usually serves notice of her/his intention to apply for the grant on the children of the intestate.

Other documents required- By Jurisdiction

1. Jamaica

Order of the court

Where the beneficiaries are required to obtain an order of the court so as to apply for a grant of letters of administration (in practice, in instances where one or some of the beneficiaries is/are minors) an application granting leave to them to apply is made *ex parte* to a judge in chambers. The affidavit, as is the case with respect to letters of administration with will annexed, should set out all the relevant facts in order to satisfy the court that it would be for the benefit of the estate to make the grant to some other person other than the Administrator General. The basis of the Administrator General's entitlement to the grant, the death of the deceased intestate and the relationship of the applicant to the deceased should also be recited in the affidavit.

The affidavit should also include a recital similar to that contained in the affidavit in support of the application for leave to apply for letters of administration with will annexed, that is; the belief of the applicants that by permitting them to apply instead of the Administrator General there would be a substantial saving to the estate. The practice and procedure are also the same as that which are applicable to application for an order of the court with respect to letters of administration with will annexed.

Pursuant to Rule 68, CPR 2002, with respect to applications of grants made in the Supreme Court, on or after January 1, 2003, the following documents are no longer required:

- Letters of Administration and Kalamazoo Copy[38]
- Declaration of Counting of Letters of Administration[39]
- Kalamazoo Copy of Inventory[40]

2. The Bahamas

Prior to February 1, 2002

Affidavit of Heirship

As was stated previously, beneficial entitlement was regulated by the common law doctrine of descent, dower and curtesy. Accordingly, where the applicant for the grant of letters of administration was the heir-at-law, he was required to prove his title by an affidavit of heirship deposed to by some person who could swear positively to the relationship of kin between the heir-at-law and the intestate. This affidavit contained the following recitals:

(i) the name, address and description of the deponent;
(ii) the age of the deponent;
(iii) the blood relationship of the intended administrator to the intestate so as to establish that the intended administrator is the heir-at-law of the intestate in accordance with the rules prescribed by the former Inheritance Act chapter 9.

It should be noted that an affidavit of heirship was also required should the heir-at-law renounce his right to apply for letters of administration.

On or after February 1, 2002

As previously stated, the position with respect to beneficial entitlement to an intestate's estate is now governed by the Inheritance Act 2002, which abolished heirship and *inter alia* assimilated real and personal estate of an intestate for purposes of distribution. In addition, the Equal Status of Children's Act 2002, provides that a child born out of wedlock shall have the same rights of inheritance to his or her father's estate as a child born in wedlock to the intestate.

Accordingly, the persons entitled to an intestate's estate, both real and personal, include *inter alia*, in order of priority, the surviving spouse, the child/children (including children born out of wedlock), grandchildren and parents.

As such, in applications for grants of administration, the affidavit of heirship is no longer applicable, with respect to the estates of persons dying on or after February 1, 2002. Instead, the marriage certificate, birth certificate, and paternity orders, as the case may be, are now applicable for purposes of providing proof of entitlement to a grant of administration.

3. *Anguilla and in The Bahamas with respect to the estates of persons dying prior to February 1, 2002*

Affidavit of Kin

In Anguilla, and with respect to The Bahamas, prior to February 1, 2002, an affidavit of kin is sworn to by some person who can positively swear to the relationship of kinship between the intended administrator and the intestate. The affidavit should set out:

(i) the name, address and description of the deponent;
(ii) the names of the issue of the intestate;
(iii) the relationship of kinship and the entitlement of the intended administrator to the grant of letters of administration.

In The Bahamas this affidavit was required where the applicant for the grant of letters of administration was the next-of-kin and not heir-at-law. In Anguilla an affidavit of kin is required in all cases of application for grants of letters of administration, other than application made by the Crown *bona vacantia*.

However with respect to The Bahamas, the affidavit of kin was applicable only to issue and children of the deceased born in wedlock. However, as stated above, in respect of an affidavit of heirship, the affidavit of kin is no longer applicable as a result of the changes introduced to beneficial entitlement to an intestate's estate by virtue of the Inheritance Act 2002 and also by the Equal Status of Children's Act 2002. Instead, paternity orders or the father's name on the birth certificate is sufficient proof of paternity.

4. Anguilla. Antigua & Barbuda, Barbados, Guyana, St Christopher & Nevis and St Vincent & the Grenadines

Affidavit of kin

An affidavit of kin may be filed in the above territories in cases where the applicant for the grant is a child born out of wedlock to the deceased and there is no formal proof of paternity such as father's name appearing on the child's birth certificate.

Although strictly speaking, a declaration of paternity or some other legally recognised proof of paternity should be filed, the practice in these territories is to permit some person who knew the deceased and the child's mother (such as a relative of the deceased) to depose an affidavit as to the relationship of paternity between the deceased and applicant. It is to be noted that in Antigua & Barbuda until recently, it was also the practice to accept an affidavit of kin as proof of paternity.

5. Barbados and Jamaica

Affidavit of Statutory Spouse

In respect of Barbados, where the applicant for the grant is a statutory spouse[41] separate affidavits from two persons respectively, who knew the deceased and the statutory spouse, and who can depose to the duration of their union must be lodged with the papers to lead the grant.

With respect to Jamaica, the marriage certificate of the surviving spouse and the birth certificates of the intestates' children are not generally required to be filed with the papers to lead a grant of letters of administration. However proof of beneficial entitlement to the intestates estate, is required to be filed where the applicant for the grant of administration is:

- a child born out of wedlock. In such instances, to an affidavit of kin or alternatively a paternity older is required in cases where the fathers name does not appear on the child's birth certificate. The affidavit of kin or alternatively the declaration of paternity order must be exhibited to the oath to lead the grant;
- the statutory spouse of the intestate. An order recognising the spouse as a spouse within the meaning of s.2 of the Intestates' Estates and Property Charges Act must be exhibited to the oath to lead the grant.

Other documents Depending on the facts

Depending on the fact circumstances, the following documents should also be included:

All jurisdictions

A. An Affidavit of Alias;[42]

Barbados, Guyana. Jamaica and Trinidad & Tobago

B. An Affidavit of Delay[43]

Eastern Caribbean territories (save St Lucia) and The Bahamas

C. Nomination/Order of Appointment of Grantee

Wherever a minority or life interest arises on the intestacy of the deceased and there is only one administrator, not being a trust corporation, a second administrator must be nominated or appointed subject to the registrar's discretion to waive this requirement. Accordingly the nomination or order of appointment of the second administrator must be filed with the papers to lead the grant.

Grants to Administrator General

Jamaica

Due to the frequency with which applications for grants of letters of administration are made by the Administrator General in Jamaica, the relevant practice and procedure will be considered. This procedure is also relevant to applications made by the Administrator General for other type of grants including grants of letters of administration.

Practice and Procedure

The documents necessary for a grant to the Administrator General are to date still prepared in most instances by an attorney-at-law in private practice on the instructions of the Administrator General. However as of 1st June, 1996 with the establishment of a professional legal section, applications for grants are increasingly being prepared by the Department's 'in-house' attorneys.

As was mentioned, where applicable, particulars with respect to the deceased must be supplied to the Administrator General in a Form/ Declaration of Particulars, obtainable from the Administrator General's Department, Kingston Mall, Kingston.[44] The details supplied in the Form enable the Administrator General to make investigations regarding the beneficiaries and assets of the estate, call for further information and write to financial institutions regarding any money held by them for the estate of the deceased. Upon completion of investigations which may literally take years, the Administrator General instructs an attorney-at-law in private practice to prepare the usual papers to lead a grant of letters of administration with will annexed. The papers to lead the grant are thereafter submitted to the Administrator General.

Once the inquiries are completed and the Administrator General is satisfied that the papers are in order, he signs the oath before a Justice of the Peace and the papers to lead the grant are filed in the Supreme Court Register on behalf of the Administrator General.

On obtaining the relevant grant, the Administrator General collects in the personal assets and takes formal possession of the real assets of the deceased with a view to disposing of them.

Notes

1 See r.21 N.C.P.R. 1954, England
  See r.22 N.C.P.R. 1987, England.

2   See Arts, 549-583 Civil Code Ch. 242 with respect thereto; see also Art. 5790) Civil Code Ch. 242 as amended by Civil Code (Amendment (No. 3)) Act No. 12, 1991.
3   Section 17 Administration of Estates Ordinance Ch. 8 No. 1.
4   *Ibid.*
5   Section 32 Administration of Estates Ordinance Ch. 8 No. 1.
6   Section 18 Administration of Estates Ordinance Ch. 8 No. 1.
7   Section 76 Eastern Caribbean Supreme Court (St Lucia) Act 17/1969.
8   Section 78 Eastern Caribbean Supreme Court (St Lucia) Act 17/1969.
9   Section 79(1) Eastern Caribbean Supreme Court (St Lucia) Act 17/1969. Section 79(2) provides that a person is considered to be absent and unrepresented if after having been summoned by advertisements in three successive issues of the Gazette and of a newspaper (if any) circulating in the State, to appear before the Administrator General, he fails within one week after the last advertisement so to appear or unless it is within such period proved to the satisfaction of the Administrator General that such person is present in the State or is duly represented by some other person remaining in the State.
10 Section 80 Eastern Caribbean Supreme Court (St Lucia) Act 17/1969.
11
Anguilla, Montserrat, St Christopher & Nevis	- s.4(1)(f) and s.4(2) Intestates' Estates Act Cap. 36
Antigua & Barbuda	- s.4(6) Intestates Estate Act Cap. 225
Barbados	- s.55 Succession Act Cap. 249
Dominica	- s.4(1)f and 4(2) Intestate Estates Act Ch. 9:03
Grenada	- Intestates Estates Act Cap. 154 s.(4)(f)
Guyana	- s.5(6) Civil Law of Guyana Act Cap. 6:01
Jamaica	- s.4(1) Item 5 Bona Vacantia Intestates Estates & Property Charges Act
St Vincent & the Grenadines	- s.62 Administration of Estates Act Ch. 377
Trinidad & Tobago	- Part III Administration of Estates Ordinance Ch. 8 No. 1 - s.30(a) Wills & Probate Ord. Ch. 8 No. 2.

12 See chapter 9, p. 240.
13 See ss.3 and 4 of the repealed Escheat Act Ch. 141. See also chapter 9, p. 249-250.
14 Rules 5, 6, 30, 31 Supreme Court (Non-Contentious) Probate Rules 1959.
15 See Estate Duty (Repeal) Act 41/1981.
16 *Ibid.*
17 See rr. 1-11 Deceased Persons Estates' Administration Rules Cap. 12:01.
18 Rules 18-22, 27 of the repealed General Rules and Orders of the Supreme Court Part III Probate and Administration.
19 Rules 4, 16, 20 The Probate Rules, Ch. 35.
20 Rules 3,4, 32-35 First Schedule N.C.B.R. Ch. 8 No.2.
21 Eastern Caribbean - rr. 4, 5, 8, 9 N.C.P.R. 1987, England territories (save Dominica and St Lucia) Dominica - rr. 4, 5, 6, 7 N.C.P.R. 1954, England St Lucia - Arts 1015, Code of Civil Procedure Ch. 243.
22 See Stamp Duty (Amendment) Act 21/1969.
23 *Ibid.*
24 See Estate Duty (Amendment) Act 18/1985.
25 In practice, marriage/birth certificate are not usually lodged unless the Registrar so requests.

26 See Estate Duty (Repeal) (Ordinance) Act 21/1984.
27 *Ibid.*
28 See the Stamp Act (Amendment) Ordinance 13/1966.
29 See Art 1015 Code of Civil Procedure Ch. 243.
30 See chapter 5 pp. 104-105.
31 See Form 1 The Probate Rules Ch. 35.
32 Art 608 Civil Code Ch. 242.
33

Rules

Barbados	- r.6 Supreme Court (Non-Contentious) Probate Rules 1959
Dominica	- r.6 N.C.P.R. 1954, England
Eastern Caribbean (save Dominica and St Lucia)	- r.8 N.C.P.R. 1987, England
Guyana	- r.3 Deceased Persons Estates' Administration Rules Cap. 12:01
Jamaica	- Rule 68.9 CPR 2002, repealing and replacing r.27 General Rules and Orders of the Supreme Court Part III Probate and Administration
St Lucia	- Art 1015(1)(c) Code of Civil Procedure Ch. 243
The Bahamas	- r.4 The Probate Rules Ch. 35
Trinidad & Tobago	- rr.4. 32 First Schedule N.C.B.R. Ch. 8 No. 2.

Forms

Barbados	- Form No. 4 Appendix (Forms & Fees) Supreme Court (Non-Contentious) Probate Rules 1959
Guyana	- Schedule 2 The Deceased Persons Estates Administration Rules Cap. 12:01
Jamaica	- Form P.5 CPR 2002 repealing and replacing Form No. 4 General Rules and Orders of the Supreme Court Part III Schedule of Forms
The Bahamas	- Form No. V The Probate Rules Ch. 35
Trinidad & Tobago	- Form No. 2 First Schedule N.C.B.R. Ch. 8 No. 2.

NB. The Forms prescribed above are to be used with such modifications as are necessary so as to reflect the existing probate practices of the various territories

34 See chapter 5, p. 107.
35 See chapter 5, p. 108.
36

Barbados	- r.26 Supreme Court (Non-Contentious) Probate Rules 1959
Jamaica	- r.18 General Rules and Orders of the Supreme Court Part Part 68.21 which was repelled and replaced III Probate and Administration
St Lucia	- Art. 1016(2) Code of Civil Procedure Ch. 243
Trinidad & Tobago	- r.24 First Schedule N.C.B.R. Ch. 8 No. 2.

37

Dominica, Guyana	- r.25(1) N.C.P.R. 1954, England
The Bahamas, Eastern Caribbean (save Dominica and St Lucia)	- r.27(4) N.C.P.R. 1987, England.

38 See Form No. of the former General Rules and Orders of the Supreme Court Part III Schedule of Forms; see also Practice noted of the Supreme Court Jamaica dated 18th April, 1953 which provides for a copy of the grant 'type-written on special paper' to be filed with the application for letters of administration.
39 See Practice Notice of the Supreme Court, Jamaica dated 3rd March, 1955 with respect thereto; see also ch. 5 p. for contents and purpose of the Declaration.
40 See Practice Note of the Supreme Court, Jamaica dated 18th April, 1953 which required that a copy of the Inventory, 'type-written on special paper'be lodged with the application for the grant of letters of administration.
41 See chapter 7 p. 181 ante for definition of statutory spouse.
42 See chapter 5 p. 119.
43 Ibid.
44 See chapter 3, p. 82.

9

Small Estates, Nil Estates Unrepresented Estates

INTRODUCTION

Applications for small estate grants are made in cases where the value of the real and personal assets of a deceased person is below the statutory maximum as provided for by the respective small estates legislation of the various territories.[1]

As a general rule, applications for small estate grants are made with the assistance of the registrar who is under a statutory duty to 'fill up' the usual papers required by the court to lead the relevant grant of representation.

The intended applicant for the grant is interviewed by an authorised member of the Registry staff in order:

- to verify that the deceased's estate qualifies as a small estate; and
- if so, to obtain the information necessary to prepare the relevant papers to lead the grant.

The fees payable with respect to these applications are generally limited to a special fee of a nominal amount. The usual probate fees, or where applicable, stamp/estate and succession duties are either not chargeable or they are considerably reduced. This is so irrespective of whether or not the application was made prior to the abolition of such duties, if any.

Practice and Procedure

Trinidad & Tobago

Small estates: Estates valued at $4,800 and under [2]

Unlike large estate applications, which must be made through an attorney-at-law, an application for a small estate grant may be made either through an attorney-at-law or by the applicant in person.[3] When the application is made in person the requisite papers to lead the grant that is, the search certificate, the formal application for the grant, the oath of the executor or administrator may be obtained at the Probate Section of the Registry/Sub Registry. The applicant is interviewed by a member of the Registry staff and assisted in the preparation and completion of the papers.

Documents filed in the Probate Section of the Registry/Sub Registry

The usual documents necessary for a grant of probate/letters of administration (with or without will annexed) are required to be lodged save that the following documents are not required:[4]

- An estate duty certificate irrespective of whether the deceased died prior to or after the abolition of these duties;
- A filing fee receipt;
- An administration bond (with respect to applications for letters of administration (with or without will annexed).
- An inventory. The affidavit of the applicant should, however, contain particulars of the deceased's property and the gross value thereof.

The application for the grant is not advertised but it is screened in a conspicuous place in the Registry/Sub Registry for two consecutive weeks, at the end of which period the grant is signed by the registrar and issued to the applicant.[5]

Eastern Caribbean territories (save Anguilla)

Practice and Procedure in General

Applications for small estate grants are required to be made in accordance with the relevant Administration of Small Estates Acts of the respective Eastern Caribbean territories.

The applicant is interviewed by an authorised member of the Registry staff and the relevant papers to lead the grant are completed with the assistance of the registrar or an authorised member of staff.

With the exception of St Lucia and St Vincent & the Grenadines,[6] the registrar prepares and signs a report which is laid before a judge in chambers. The Registrar's Report along with the other papers to lead the relevant grant are read over by the judge who, if satisfied that the applicant is a person entitled to administer the estate of the deceased, directs the registrar to issue the relevant grant to the applicant.

The order for the grant to be issued is then drawn up and signed by the registrar. The grant is prepared in accordance with the order, signed by the registrar and issued to the applicant.

A duplicate copy of the grant is filed in the Registry in all the territories except in Antigua & Barbuda where the original grant is prepared and delivered to the applicant and the order for the issue of the grant kept on file.

Documents to lead Grant

The documents required vary somewhat from territory to territory but as a general rule the following documents are not required:

- Administration bond.
- Affidavit/Declaration and Account of the Estate of the deceased. (However an affidavit containing a valuation of the deceased's assets must be filed).
- Estate and Succession Duty Certificate or its equivalent irrespective of whether the deceased died prior to or after the abolition of these duties.

A special fee of a nominal value is the only fee or duty payable with respect to small estate applications.

As indicated by the practice and procedure outlined above, there are two documents peculiar to small estate applications. These are:

(a) the Registrar's Report; and
(b) the Direction for the issue of the grant to the applicant signed by a judge in chambers.

A. Registrar's Report [7]

The Registrar's Report is a document prepared and signed by the registrar and addressed to the judge in chambers. It states, amongst other matters:

(i) that the registrar has investigated the application;
(ii) that the statutory period (which varies between 3-6 months) has expired since the death of the deceased named therein;
(iii) the names of the persons entitled to the relevant grant and concludes with a request for the relevant grant of representation to be made to the proposed grantee named therein.

B. Direction for Issue of Grant [8]

A direction for the issue of the grant by the registrar is required to be prepared for signature by a judge. The direction states in effect that the judge, having read the Registrar's Report and the affidavit if any, of the applicant and being satisfied therewith, directs the registrar to issue the relevant grant to the applicant.

In most instances, the direction for the issue of the grant to the applicant is written by the judge on the face of the Report and his signature is affixed thereto.

C. Formal Application for Grant

The formal application for the grant addressed to the registrar is intituled In the Matter of the Estate of the Deceased named therein and In the Matter of the relevant Administration of Small Estates Act.

D. Affidavit of Identity of Applicant [9]

An affidavit of Identity of the applicant is lodged only when so requested by the registrar. The affidavit is deposed to by the applicant in order to establish the applicant's relationship to the deceased and his entitlement to the grant. In such instances, birth certificates and marriage certificates, where applicable, should be exhibited to the affidavit.

Antigua & Barbuda, Dominica, Grenada and Montserrat[10]

Estates not in excess of
Antigua & Barbuda	$2,500
Dominica	$5,000
Grenada	$ 250
Montserrat	$2,400

(1) The formal application for the grant
(2) Death certificate of the deceased named in the application
(3) Will, if any
(4) The Registrar's Report
(5) Direction for Issue of Grant
(6) Affidavit of due execution in cases where the deceased died testate
(7) Affidavit of Identity if requested by the registrar
(8) Judge's Direction

Antigua & Barbuda

(9) Oath of the applicant

Although s.5 of the Administration of Small Estates Act Cap. 8, Antigua & Barbuda specifically provides that an oath is not required, nevertheless in practice an oath containing the usual recitals, including the value of the estate of the deceased named therein is lodged with the other papers to lead the grant.

Montserrat and Dominica

(10) Affidavit of the value of the estate of the deceased at the date of death

The following documents are not required:

Antigua & Barbuda, Dominica, Grenada and Montserrat [11]

(1) Administration bond
(2) Estate/Stamp Duty Certificate irrespective of whether death occurred prior to or after the abolition of estate/stamp duty in these territories.
(3) Declaration and Account of the Estate

Antigua & Barbuda, Dominica and Montserrat [12]

(4) Oath of the executor or administrator (although as mentioned above in practive an oath is filed in Antigua & Barbuda).

St Christopher & Nevis [13] - *Estates not in excess of $5,000.00*

The practice and procedure with respect to small estate applications in St Christopher & Nevis are somewhat different mainly because a Certificate of Payment of Stamp Duty is required irrespective of whether the deceased died prior to or after the abolition of stamp duties. The formal application for the grant is a combination of the formal application for a grant, an oath of an executor or administrator and an affidavit of value of the deceased's estate. The application form which is available in the Registry is completed with the assistance of the registrar or an authorised member of his staff, and it is signed by the applicant before a Justice of the Peace.

The applicant is then required to submit the signed application together with the deceased's death certificate and will, if any, to the Stamp Duty

Section of the Inland Revenue Department for the purposes of obtaining a stamp duty certificate marked 'Exempt'.

Once the stamp duty certificate marked 'Exempt' is obtained, the following documents are required to be lodged in the registry:

(1) The application in the prescribed form
(2) Stamp Duty Certificate
(3) Death certificate
(4) Will, if any
(5) Affidavit of due execution (in cases where the deceased died testate)
(6) The Registrar's Report
(7) The Direction for signature by a judge in chambers. In practice the judge affixes his signature to the Registrar's Report and directs that the grant be issued.

The following documents are not required:[14]

(1) Administration bond
(2) Declaration on oath as to the value of the estate
(3) Administrator's or executor's oath.

Estates not in excess of $5,000

St Lucia [15]

Practice and Procedure

Although s.3(4) of the Administration of Small Succession Ordinance provides for the Registrar to prepare a report and lay it before a judge for the directions to be given to the registrar for the issue of the grant to the applicant, in practice this is not done. The relevant documents are prepared in the usual way and as in the case with non-contentious large estate applications, the registrar signs the order for issue of the grant to the applicant and the grant is accordingly prepared for signature by the registrar.

(1) Application in the form of a petition intituled in the matter of the Administration of Small Succession Ordinance and in the matter of Art 569 of the Civil Code Ch. 242. The petition sets out, *inter alia*, the place and date of death of the deceased named therein and whether he died testate or intestate as the case may be, and concludes with a prayer for the issue of the relevant grant to the petitioner.
(2) Affidavit of assets and liabilities of the deceased.

(3) Affidavit of the petitioner made pursuant to Art 1015(1)(d) of the Code of Civil Procedure Ch. 243, containing the following recitals, namely.
   (i) the names of person(s) entitled to the grant.
   (ii) that the deceased died testate or intestate as the case may be;
   (iii) the oath of the petitioner to faithfully administer the estate of the deceased and discharge the duties with respect thereto.
(4) The deceased's death or burial certificate;
(5) Will, if any;
(6) Affidavit of due execution (where the will, if any, is in the form of an English will);

The following documents are not required:[16]

- Administration bond
- Declaration and Account of the Estate
- any valuation other than that contained in the affidavit accompanying the application.

Estates not in excess of $240

St Vincent & the Grenadines[17]

Although the Administration of Small Estates Act Cap. 379 contains similar provisions to the Small Estates Act of Antigua & Barbuda, Dominica, Montserrat and Grenada respectively, the practice and procedure with respect to small estate applications in St Vincent is the same as that which is applicable to large estate applications. Accordingly, neither the Registrar's Report nor Judges' Direction is required in practice.[18] The usual documents for a grant of probate or administration are filed, except:[19]

- an administration bond
- any valuation of the estate, other than the affidavit accompanying the application;
- any affidavit or certificate as required by the Estate and Succession Duties Act (irrespective of the date of death).

Anguilla

By virtue of s.8 of the Death Duties (Abolition) Ordinance No. 6/1977 small estate applications have been formally abolished in Anguilla. As a consequence, the procedure and practice with respect to applying for grants of representation are the same irrespective of the value of the deceased's estate.

The reason for the legislative removal of the distinction between small and large estates in Anguilla has an historical basis. Prior to 1977 there were only two resident attorneys-at-Law - the Magistrate and the Registrar. The judge assigned to the Anguilla Circuit was not resident in Anguilla. As a result of this situation, the registrar and his staff assisted applicants in preparing papers to lead the relevant grant, irrespective of whether the grant applied for was with respect to a large or small estate. Indeed many estates in Anguilla as of that date remained unadministered partly because of the lack of private practitioners on the island. As a consequence, the passage in 1977 of the Death Duties (Abolition) Ordinance was mainly viewed as a regularisation and legal acknowledgment of an existing de facto situation.[20] However it should be noted that since 1977, there are attorneys-at-law engaged in private practice through whom an application for a grant of representation may be made.

However where the application is made through the registrar (as is invariably, if not always the case) a one percent estate fee based on the value of the estate at the time of death must be paid.[21] The estate fees are paid to the cashier at the Supreme Court and the applicant is issued a signed receipt and a notation to that effect is recorded on the application.

Eastern Caribbean territories

Observations

It seems anomalous that although non-contentious large estate application are granted by the registrar without the directions of a High Court judge, small estate grants may only be granted by the registrar pursuant to the written direction of a judge.

The explanation for this apparent incongruity lies in the fact that when the respective small estate acts were enacted, the registrar in these territories, had no power or jurisdiction to grant non-contentious large estate grants. However as was stated above, in St Lucia and St Vincent & the Grenadines the practice with respect to small estate applications is not in keeping with the law. In these two territories, small estate grants are made by the registrar without the requirement of a Registrar's Report or the Direction of a judge.

Estates valued at $15,000 and under

Barbados[22]

Applications for the administration of small estates in Barbados are made to the Public Trustee pursuant to s.44 of the Succession Act Cap. 249. Section 44(1) thereof provides that where the gross capital value of the estate of a person who dies without leaving a will does not exceed $15,000, the Public Trustee may on the application of the person or persons who have a prior entitlement to a grant of administration, and without a grant of administration, administer the estate of the deceased person and distribute that estate.

Practice and Procedure

The applicant attends the Attorney General's Chambers where he is interviewed. Based on the information furnished by the applicant at the interview an application in the form of a questionnaire is completed. Included on the form is information stating:

(i) the place and date of death of deceased;
(ii) whether the deceased died testate or intestate;
(iii) the relationship of the applicant to the deceased;
(iv) the marital status of the deceased;
(v) particulars of the liabilities, if any, of the deceased;
(vi) particulars of the assets of the deceased including monies held in bank accounts, insurance policies, share certificates, gratuities;
(vii) whether an application for a grant of probate or letters of administration, as the case may be, has been applied for.

After the form is completed the applicant reads it over or it is read over to him and then signed by him.

Other Documents required:

(1) Original death certificate (the applicant usually provides the original certificate which is photocopied and returned to him);
(2) Funeral/undertaker's receipts. The applicant usually brings in these receipts as in most cases it is he who has paid for the burial of the deceased.
(3) Certificate of Clearance from Inland Revenue to the effect that no property tax is owed by the deceased;
(4) Birth certificate, marriage certificate, etc.
(5) Proof of value of the estate including share certificates, pass book from bank and statement of account;
(6) Original will if any (this is photocopied and returned to applicant);
(7) Power of attorney, if any.

An authorised staff member from the Attorney General's department thereafter writes the deceased's bank, insurance companies, etc. to verify the information given by the applicant. Depending on the size and value of the deceased's estate the Public Trustee may cause to be published in a daily newspaper a notice to creditors, calling upon them to come in and prove their debts, within the time prescribed.

Once the period of the notice, if any, has expired and all relevant information has been verified, the following documents are prepared in duplicate:

(1) An affidavit to be sworn to by the applicant, intituled in the Matter of s.44 of the Succession Act Cap. 249 and in the Matter of the Estate of the Deceased named therein, It is sworn to by the applicant before a Justice of the Peace/Notary Public and contains the following information *inter alia*:
   (i) the place and date of death of the intestate;
   (ii) the relationship of the applicant to the intestate;
   (iii) the prior entitlement of the applicant to administer the estate of the deceased;
   (iv) whether the funeral expenses have been paid, and if not the sum which is due and owing;
   (v) particulars of the deceased's assets.
(2) A consent form for signature by the Solicitor General acting in his capacity as Public Trustee, which in effect provides that the Public Trustee consents to the payment of all relevant monies to the applicant;[23]
(3) A consent form for signature by the applicant with respect to receipt of the monies owing to the deceased.[24]
(4) A Deed of Indemnity made between the Public Trustee and the applicant which indemnifies the Public Trustee from all actions, proceedings, liability, claims, damages and expenses in relation to or arising out of the Public Trustee's consent to the said payment.

The Deed of Indemnity is signed by the Public Trustee and the applicant in the presence of a legal officer and sealed. The respective consent forms are thereafter signed by the Public Trustee and the applicant and both are stamped with the Public Trustee stamp. The original consents are then given to the applicant, who may then proceed to collect in the assets of the deceased based on the authority of the consents.

Estates valued not in excess of $1,000

Guyana [25]

The procedure and practice with respect to applications for small estate grants are the same as that which applies to large estate application subject to the following:

(a) The order for the grant to issue is made by the registrar not the Chief Justice. The grant itself is signed by the registrar as is the case with large estate applications.
(b) The documents required for the grant are the usual documents save that with letters of administration the requirement for an administration bond is usually waived.

Alternatively pursuant to s.19 of the Deceased Persons' Estates Administration Act Ch. 12:01, in cases of intestacy, the registrar may appoint an administrator where the value of the assets of the estate does not exceed $1,000. In practice the Public Trustee is usually appointed where the estate of the intestate is administered without a grant.[26]

Estates not in excess of $1.5 million

Jamaica [27]

Grant of Probate

Documents to be filed at Resident Magistrate's Court:
1. Covering letter addressed to the Clerk of the Court for the Parish.
2. Oath of executor.
3. Will bond.
4. Inventory in duplicate.
5. Affidavit in Proof of Death.
6. Probate (in triplicate).
7. Original will marked by the signatures of the executor, an attesting witness and the person before whom sworn (Commissioner for Oaths).
8. Three copies of will.
9. Declaration of Counting of Probate and copy will.
10. Declaration of Counting of Inventory.
11. Affidavit of attesting witness.

Grant of Letters of Administration with will annexed

Documents required:
1. Covering letter addressed to the Clerk of the Court for the Parish.
2. Oath of administrator.
3. Affidavit of due execution.

4. Original will marked by the signatures of the administrator, an attesting and the person before whom sworn (Commissioner for Oaths).
5. Three copies of will.
6. Administration bond with will annexed (not required when the applicant is the Administrator General).
7. Consent of beneficiaries (where applicable).
8. Formal Consent With The Will Annexed of the Administrator General.
9. Inventory in duplicate.
10. Declaration of Counting of Inventory.
11. Affidavit in Proof of Death.
12. Letters of Administration with will annexed (in triplicate).
13. Declaration of Counting of Letters of Administration with will annexed and copy will.
14. Justification of Sureties (only where required).

Grant of Letters of Administration

1. Covering letter addressed to the Clerk of the Court for the Parish.
2. Oath of administrator.
3. Affidavit in Proof of Death.
4. Administration bond (not required where the applicant is the Administrator General).
5. Justification of Sureties.
6. Inventory in duplicate.
7. Declaration of Counting of Inventory.
8. Consent of Beneficiaries (where applicable).
9. Letters of Administration (in triplicate).
10. Declaration of Counting of Letters of Administration.

Practice and Procedure

The application for estates valued at $1.5 million and under is made to the Resident Magistrate in accordance with the provision of the Judicature (Resident Magistrates) Act. The application is made within the parish in which the deceased had his fixed place of abode.[28] The rules, forms and procedure are essentially the same as those which were previously applicable to probate and administration in the Supreme Court,[29] save that the recording fees are paid in the form of judicial stamps.

Pursuant to the provisions of s.108 of the Judicature (Resident Magistrates) Act, the rules, forms and procedure relevant to applications for probate and administration in the Supreme Court were deemed to apply (subject to the payment of recording fees) to the practice and procedure for applications for grants made in the Resident Magistrates Court.

However, the new Supreme Court of Jamaica CPR 2002 and in particular Rule 68, is applicable only to the procedure and practice of the Supreme Court.

In this regard, the Judicature (Resident Magistrates) Act in particular s.129 regulates probate and administration matters which are applicable to the Resident Magistrates Court, including applications for grants of representation in cases where the value of the deceased's estate does not exceed $1.5 million The relevant sections (ss.108 to 129) set out in detail the documents required for applications for grants.

As at the date of writing, there is some uncertainty as to whether Rule 68, CPR 2002, applies to applications for grants made in the Resident Magistrates Court. It is submitted that the new probate rules do not apply for the following reasons:

- The Judicature (Resident Magistrates) Act constitutes substantive legislation and the relevant provisions of this legislation, to date, have not been repealed or amended to bring the forms, procedure and practice relevant to probate and administration matters in line with the new rules of procedure and practice relevant to the Supreme Court probate and administration applications.
- Although s.108 provides for the jurisdiction now vested in the Supreme Court over probate and the administration of estates to be conferred on the Resident Magistrates Court, s.108 also expressly provides that the rules, forms and practice in force in probate and administration in the Supreme Court is subject to the provisions of the Judicature (Resident Magistrates) Act. As such, up to the date of writing, the forms, procedure and practice relevant to applications for grants made to the Resident Magistrates Court is regulated by the provisions of the Judicature (Resident Magistrates) Act which provisions are in effect the same as the former procedure and practice, which regulated non-contentious probate matters prior to January 1, 2003, the date of passage of the Supreme Court Jamaica CPR 2002.

It is clear from the above that the failure to bring the non-contentious probate procedure and practice in the Resident Magistrates Court in line with that which is now applicable to the Supreme Court was as a result of legislative oversight, in particular the failure to amend the provisions of the Judicature (Resident Magistrates) Act in respect thereto.

Accordingly, in accordance with the current practice, after the relevant documents listed above are executed, they are filed with the Clerk of the Court for the parish. In the case of applications for letters of administration (with or without will annexed), the Clerk of the Court sends a Notice of Application for Administration (with or without will annexed) to the Government Printery for publication in the Gazette and to a newspaper of mass circulation. The application is advertised for two consecutive weeks[30] Additionally the Clerk of the Court is required to transmit to the registrar of the Supreme Court, a notice of application for probate or administration[31]

After publication in the Gazette[32] and a daily newspaper, in the case of letters of administration (with or without will annexed), and upon receipt of a certificate from the registrar of the Supreme Court to the effect that no previous application for probate or administration has been made with respect to the deceased's estate, the grant is placed before the Resident Magistrate. If all is in order, the Magistrate signs the grant and it is then issued to the applicant.

The Bahamas

Rule 6 of the Probate Rules Ch. 35 provides for the registrar to assist in filling up the paper to lead the grant. In practice the applicant may if he wishes apply in person by completing the required forms which are available in the Registry.

The only practical difference between small and large estate grants is that the minimum court fees and stamp duties are payable. Otherwise the documents required and the practice and procedure are the same as that which apply to applications for large estate grants.

NIL ESTATES[33]

A grant may be made notwithstanding the deceased left no estate. Such a grant may be required:

- for the purpose of making title eg. to land or personal property vested in the deceased wherein his interest ceased on his death.
- to constitute a personal representative for the purpose of bringing or defending legal proceedings.
- where there is a trust estate vested in the deceased.

In such instances the usual documents for a grant of representation are lodged.

The oath to lead the grant, however, must recite the reason why the grant is required and that the estate of the deceased named therein amounts to the sum of nil.

UNREPRESENTED ESTATES

When a person dies intestate leaving ownerless property within the relevant Caribbean territory, the residuary estate of the intestate vests in the Crown/State as *bona vacantia*.[34]

With the exception of Grenada and more recently, The Bahamas[35] the relevant statutory provisions of the various territories provide that the State/Crown may waive its rights to the whole or part of the estate of the intestate in favour of persons:

- who the deceased would have reasonably been expected to make provision for;[36]
- who have established to the satisfaction of the Administrator General a moral, legal or equitable claim to the estate of the deceased, or[37]
- who the Minister for Legal Affairs thinks fit.[38]

As a general rule the State/Crown is usually informed of the intestate's death by a person interested in the deceased's estate who falls within the aforementioned categories. Such persons usually go to the appropriate department informing the authorised officer of the deceased's death or alternatively their attorney-at-law writes a letter to that effect on their behalf.

They also supply relevant information with respect to the intestate including:

(i) his place and date of death;
(ii) proof the deceased's debts including funeral and burial receipts (in the vast majority of cases the person interested is usually the person who has paid for the deceased's funeral);
(iii) that the deceased died without leaving a spouse or next of kin surviving him. In this regard the wife, children or other next-of-kin, if any, must be accounted for in order to establish that the deceased's estate qualified as an estate of which the Crown/State can claim *bona vacantia*;
(iv) particulars of the deceased's assets.

Practice and Procedure and Documents Required

Eastern Caribbean [39]
(save St Lucia, St Vincent & the Grenadines and Grenada)

Based on the information supplied which is contained in an affidavit of an estate creditor or other person interested in the intestate's estate and which is supported by documentary evidence, such as funeral receipts, birth and marriage certificates, an application for an order to collect in the deceased's estate is made by the registrar in his/her capacity as *ex officio* Administrator of Estates pursuant to s.9 of the respective Unrepresented Estates Act of the Eastern Caribbean territories.[40] As at the date of writing, the application is made by petition, to a judge in chambers in accordance with s.9 of the respective Unrepresented Estates Acts of the above territories, and is supported by:

1. an affidavit of facts of the person interested in the deceased's estate;
2. an affidavit in verification and support thereof sworn to by some other person.

Contents of Petition

The registrar in his capacity as *ex officio* Administrator of Estates states that he has been informed and believes that the deceased died intestate:

- without widow/widower and without leaving next of kin; and
- possessed of property within the territory concerned. (The particulars of the property should also be included).

The petition ends with a prayer for the grant of an order to get in and collect the estate of the deceased named therein. The order is prepared in duplicate for signature by the judge in chambers. The petition and supporting affidavits are read over by the judge and once he is satisfied therewith he signs the order.

Pursuant to s.18 of the respective Unrepresented Estates Act of the various territories, a notice in the form of a report is sent to the Attorney General of the respective territories, nothing him of the possession of the estate.

Thereafter the registrar in his capacity as *ex officio* Administrator of Estates takes possession of the estate by writing to the deceased's bankers, former employer and others. He also causes an inventory of the estate mentioned in the order to be made and files the inventory in the Registry.[41]

Pursuant to s. 15 of the respective Unrepresented Estates Act of the various territories,[42] the registrar also causes to be published in the official Gazette and in one newspaper, a notice to creditors calling upon all creditors of the deceased's estate to come in on or before the date stated therein and prove their debts, The notice to creditors is also affixed to the door of the court house.

The estate creditors who come forward are paid off, provided that they can prove their debts. Such persons include the person who was responsible for paying the funeral expenses. After payment of the intestate's debts and the deduction of the Administrator's cost and charges for collecting and settling the debts of the deceased, the balance thereof is paid into the Treasury pursuant to s.18 of the respective Unrepresented Estate Act of the various territories.

Persons claiming balance of estate

Pursuant to s.30 of the respective Unrepresented Estates Act of the respective territories, if there is any person interested in the estate other than a creditor or lawful next of kin, such person may apply to the court by petition for an order that any balance which is in the hands of the Registrar as *ex officio* Administrator of Estates or in the hands of the Financial Secretary (in cases where the Registrar has already forwarded the balance remaining to the Treasury) be delivered over to the applicant. On the authority of the order the Administrator or Financial Secretary, as the case may be, delivers the balance to the applicant.

St Lucia

The person interested in the deceased's estate is required to write to the Cabinet Secretary petitioning him to invoke the powers conferred on the Crown pursuant to Art 608 of the Civil Code Ch. 242[43] which authorise him, the petitioner, to apply for a grant for letters of administration of the deceased's estate as nominee of the Crown. The petition should also set out the material facts in support thereof including:

(i)   the place and date of death of the deceased;
(ii) that the deceased died having no lawful next-of-kin;
(iii) particulars of the real and personal assets of the deceased;
(iv) particulars of the debts of the deceased including funeral expenses;
(v)   that the petitioner co-habited with the deceased, took care of him, as the case may be.

The application is then laid before Cabinet for its consideration and approval. Upon approval thereof, the petitioner is notified in writing that Cabinet has approved his application. Thereafter the petitioner applies for a grant of letters of administration in the capacity of nominee of the Crown. The petition and affidavit in support of the petition should include a recital that the petitioner is authorised to make the application as nominee of the Crown. The letter of approval should also be exhibited to the affidavit.

After the grant has been issued, the petitioner is required to write a letter to the Cabinet Secretary *inter alia* requesting that the property of which he is appointed administrator, be vested in him. A vesting deed with respect to the real property of the intestate is accordingly prepared. However, no such formal vesting is required with respect to the personal assets of the deceased.

St Vincent & the Grenadines

Applications under the Escheat Act Cap. 306 for the waiver of the Crown's right to the estate of an intestate, in favour of a person who has established a moral, legal or equitable claim to the satisfaction of the Governor General with respect thereto, have not been made within recent memory, if at all. As a consequence no procedural guidelines have been developed with respect to such applications.

However s.3 of the Escheat Act provides that all the personal estate of an intestate who dies without heirs or next of kin shall be appropriated and form part of the Consolidated Fund.

Section 4 of the Act makes provision for the Governor General to issue his warrant to the Accountant General for the payment out of the appropriated personal assets of the intestate to a person who has established to the Governor General's satisfaction a moral, legal or equitable claim with respect thereto.

Section 6 further provides that where real property becomes part of the Consolidated Fund that the Governor General may execute a deed of transfer with thereto to the Accountant General and such deed which takes the form prescribed in the Second Schedule to the Act shall be registered in the office of the Register of Deeds.

However pursuant to s.6(2) the Governor General may in effect waive the Crown's right to the real property of the intestate and direct a transfer thereof to any person who shall to the satisfaction of the Governor General establish a legal, equitable or moral claim thereto.

Grenada

Pursuant to s.4(f) of the Intestates' Estates Act Cap. 154, if there is no person entitled by law to the intestate's estate

> the same shall belong to the Crown as *bona vacantia* and in lieu of any right to escheat and shall form part of general revenue and be paid into the Consolidated Fund.

Unlike the other Eastern Caribbean territories, there is no provision for waiver of the Crown's right to an intestate's estate in favour of some person who may establish a moral or other claim to the deceased's estate and indeed such applications do not arise in practice.

Trinidad & Tobago[44]

The person applying for waiver of the State's rights to the deceased's estate is required to swear a petition,[45] supported by a statutory declaration verifying the facts contained in the petition and sworn to by some person who knew the deceased and the applicant.

The petition includes the following information:

(i) The fact that the deceased died intestate without a spouse or next of kin surviving him.
(ii) The facts which support the petitioner's claim, for example, in the case of a common law spouse that the intestate and the petitioner co-habited, that where applicable that the petitioner, took care of the intestate, and so on.
(iii) Particulars of the assets and liabilities of the intestate.
(iv) The fact that the petitioner (as in the vast majority of cases) paid for the deceased's funeral.

Pursuant *inter alia* to s.17 of the Administration of Estates Ordinance Ch. 8 No. 1, the Administrator General on behalf of the State is required to apply for the grant of letters of administration with respect to the estate of the deceased intestate named therein.

Once the grant is obtained, letters are written by an authorised officer of the Administrator General's department to the deceased's employer, insurance company, and other interested parties, so as to collect in the deceased's assets. In the meantime the matters set out in the petition and statutory declaration in support is investigated by a field officer attached to the Administrator General's department who at the completion of his investigation, submits a Field Officer's Report of his findings. A letter is also sent to the petitioner requesting him to attend the Revenue Office either in the district where the petitioner lives or in instances where the deceased left land, where the land taxes are paid.

Additionally, a memorandum is sent to the appropriate Revenue Office requesting that the petitioner's claim be investigated and that a report of the Revenue Officer's findings be submitted to the Administrator General. The petitioner is then interviewed by an authorised member of the District Revenue Office and the Revenue Officer's Report or the Warden's Report, as it is otherwise called, is thereafter submitted to the Administrator General. Thereafter the following documents with respect to waiver are prepared and sent to the Solicitor General:

(1) a Memorandum of Waiver setting out the material facts with respect to the estate mentioned therein, and recommending that the State waives its rights to the intestate's estate in favour of the petitioner;
(2) a copy of the grant of letters of administration;
(3) a copy of the petition, statutory declaration and other supporting documents such as funeral receipts;
(4) a Schedule of Particulars of the Estate of the deceased;
(5) the Warrant of Authority for signature by the Attorney General who is authorised by s.27 of the Administration of Estates Ordinance Ch. 8 No. 1 on behalf of the President of Trinidad & Tobago, to order the payment or transfer of the whole or any part of the deceased's residuary estate in favour of the petitioner. (A single warrant of authority is used where the deceased's estate comprises either real or personal assets and a double warrant where the estate comprises real and personal assets);
(6) District Revenue Officer's Report.

The documents submitted are checked by a member of the legal staff of the Solicitor General's department. Once all is found to be in order and the Solicitor General is satisfied, the Warrant of Authority is submitted to the Attorney General for his signature.

The Attorney General reviews the application for waiver and if he is satisfied, he signs the warrant authorising the distribution of the deceased's estate in favour of the petitioner. The petitioner is then notified in writing of the waiver in his favour of the State's right to the intestate's estate. When the estate comprises cash, it is paid out to the petitioner after the relevant administration fees have been deducted by the Administrator General. When any part of the residuary estate consists of land, a deed and memorandum of transfer in accordance with the terms of the warrant is executed by the Administrator General so as to vest the land in the petitioner.[46] Pursuant to s.29 of the Administration of Estates Ordinance Ch. 8 No.1, the deed of transfer is thereafter registered in the Real Property Register in the case of registered land, and in the case of land conveyed under the common law system, the transfer is entered in the Protocol of Deeds. It should be noted that only after the expiration of one year from such registration, that the legal estate in such land is deemed to pass to the petitioner.[47]

Jamaica [48]

Although the practice and procedure in Jamaica with respect to waiver of the Crown's right to the estate of an intestate is essentially the same as that which obtains in Trinidad & Tobago, it is a somewhat more involved and protracted process.

Pursuant *inter alia* to s.12 of the Administrator General's Act and s.12 of the Intestates' Estates Property Charges Act, the Administrator General is required to obtain a grant of letters of administration with respect to the intestate's estate on behalf of the Crown. The application for a grant of administration is applied for and obtained by the Administrator General in the usual way. In the mean while the person interested in the deceased's estate is required to submit a petition to the Governor General through the Permanent Secretary, Ministry of National Security and Justice for a waiver in his favour of the Crown's rights to the intestate's estate. The petition, which contains material facts in support of the application for waiver, is forwarded to the Administrator General's Department. The Administrator General carries out further investigations with respect to the deceased's estate in order to verify and confirm that there has been a 'failure of heirs' that is, that the deceased died without lawful next-of-kin.

Once the Administrator General is satisfied that the deceased died without lawful next-of-kin, the file is forwarded to the Permanent Secretary in the Ministry of National Security and Justice. The Police Commissioner is thereafter instructed to conduct investigations with respect to the petitioner's claim. Upon completion of the investigations, the Police Commissioner submits a report of his findings to the Permanent Secretary in the Ministry of National Security and Justice. The Ministry of National Security and Justice then forwards the Police Commissioner's report, the petition and other relevant documents to the Attorney General's Office for the Attorney General's consideration and approval. Once the Attorney General is satisfied that all is in order, he signifies his approval in writing. The Attorney General's written approval, together with the petitioner's file are forwarded to the Administrator General via the Ministry of National Security and Justice. A draft waiver is thereafter prepared by an attorney-at-law on the instructions of the Administrator General. The draft is then submitted to the Attorney General for his approval via the Ministry of National Security and Justice. Once the draft is approved by the Attorney General, it is resubmitted to the Administrator General's department with amendments, if any, noted thereon. A fair copy as amended is prepared in quadruplicate for signature by the Governor General. The Waiver is then sent to the Governor General via the Ministry of National Security and Justice. The Governor General signs the waiver which is then sent back to the Administrator General via the Ministry of National Security and Justice.

The Administrator General then informs the grantee that his petition for waiver has been approved. The petitioner attends the Administrator General's department and, if the residuary personal estate includes cash, a cheque in the sum payable is delivered to him after the deduction therefrom of the Administrator General's administration fees. With registered land, the memorandum of transfer is executed by the Administrator General. When the land is not registered land the waiver is considered the tide and the petitioner can then apply to bring the land under the registered system, if he so wishes.

Barbados

The person interested in the intestate's estate, either in person or through an attorney-at-law, writes to the Minister for Legal Affairs setting out the facts which support the application for waiver. The facts supplied should include information stating:

(i)   the place and date of death of the deceased;
(ii) the assets and debts of the deceased;
(iii) that the deceased died without spouse or next of kin surviving him and that the applicant believes that there is no person entitled by law to the deceased's estate; and
(iv) that the applicant cohabited with the intestate and/or took care of the deceased, as the case may be.

The deceased's death certificate, funeral receipts, if any, and other supporting documents should also be submitted. In accordance with the discretionary powers conferred on him under s.55 of the Succession Act Cap. 249 the Minister for Legal Affairs may exercise his power thereunder and waive in whole or in part the right of the Crown to the residuary estate of the intestate in favour of the applicant. The waiver may be effected by a simple letter signed by the Minister of Legal Affairs.

Guyana

The person interested in the deceased's estate attends the Office of the Public Trustee and applies by sworn declaration that the Public Trustee should administer the estate pursuant to s.6 of the Public Trustee Act Cap. 13:01.

The sworn declaration contains the following information:

(i)   particulars of the assets of the intestate;
(ii) the relationship, if any, of the declarant to the deceased eg. stepson, common law spouse;
(iii) that the funeral expenses have been paid by the declarant, if that is the case;
(iv) that the deceased had no lawful relatives and that to the best knowledge of the declarant, that the intestate had no lawful relatives; and

it concludes with a request for the Public Trustee to apply for administration of the intestate's estate.[49]

Pursuant to s.6(2) of the Public Trustee Act, the Public Trustee unless he has good reason for refusing, thereafter files in the Deeds Registry, an undertaking in writing signed by him to administer the intestate's estate.

After filing the undertaking, the Public Trustee applies for and obtains a grant of the intestate's estate on the basis that the estate belongs to the State as *bona vacantia*.[50]

In the meantime, the person interested in the waiver in his favour of the State's rights to the intestate's estate petitions the President for what is still referred to as Waiver of Escheat although escheat has been replaced by *bona vacantia* since 1917.[51] The petition which sets out all material facts in support of the application for waiver is addressed to the Office of the President. It is thereafter forwarded to the Attorney General's Chambers for the petition for waiver to be investigated and considered for the purposes of making the appropriate recommendation.

Upon receipt of the petition, the Attorney General sends the petition to the Public Trustee under cover of a letter requesting that the Public Trustee cause the petitioner's claim for waiver to be investigated by the Commissioner of Police. Alternatively, the petition and letter may be sent directly to the Commissioner of Police.

The petitioner's claim is investigated and the Commissioner's report forwarded to the Public Trustee for submission to the Attorney General's Chambers or directly to the Attorney General Chambers, as the case may be.

The report together with the petition and supporting documents are considered by an authorised legal officer of the Attorney General's chambers with a view to making the appropriate recommendation. The matters considered with respect thereto include:

(a) whether the petitioner performed substantial acts of kindness to the deceased; and
(b) whether there exists between the applicant and the deceased person any long period of association similar to a blood relationship.

If the Attorney General is satisfied that the petitioner falls within any of the guidelines, the recommendation for Waiver of Escheat is prepared and sent to the President for his approval. Upon approval, the President signs the recommendation and forwards it to the Attorney General's Chambers and a memorandum of Waiver of Escheat in favour of the petitioner is prepared.

In instances where the value of the estate of a deceased person does not exceed $2,500 the Attorney General is empowered to sign the Waiver of Escheat without having to lay the application for waiver before Cabinet.[52] In all other cases a Cabinet minute is prepared and laid before Cabinet for the approval of the Waiver of Escheat in favour of the petitioner. Once the Cabinet has approved the Waiver of Escheat, the Public Trustee is notified in writing of Cabinet's decision. The petitioner is then notified by the Public Trustee and the estate is accordingly distributed.

The Bahamas

Prior to the passage of the Inheritance Act 2002, the legal position with regard to ownerless property was governed by the repealed Escheat Act Ch. 141. The Escheat Act which was expressly repealed by the Inheritance Act 2002, provided that when a person died intestate without heirs or next-of-kin, the Crown:

(a) with respect to the personal property of the intestate may out of the whole or any part of suchproperty, provide for dependants of the intestate and other persons for whom the intestate might reasonably be expected to make provisions;[53]
(b) with respect to the intestate's real property may by deed, authorise the waiver of its rights to such property on such terms as may be specified in the deed.[54]

In practice the persons in whose favour the waiver was exercised were limited to illegitimate children of an intestate mother, the mother of an illegitimate child, and creditors of the deceased intestate, of whom an illegitimate child or common law spouse might be one.

It is submitted that with the passage of the Equal Status of Children's Act 2002 and the inclusion of specific provisions in the Administration of Estates Act, 2002, for creditors to apply for grants of representation, applications which were previously made to the Registrar for waiver of the Crown's Right to the intestate's estate both in law and in practice no longer arise.

Notes

1. Anguilla — See p. 232.
    Antigua & Barbuda — Administration of Small Estates Act Cap. 8
    Barbados — The Public Trustee Act Cap. 248
    Dominica — Administration of Small Estates Act Ch. 9:06
    Grenada — Probate Act Cap. 255
    Guyana — s.19 Deceased Persons Estates' Administration Act Cap. 12:01
    Jamaica — Judicature (Resident Magistrates) Act
    Judicature (Resident Magistrates) (Amendment) Act: 32/1995
    Montserrat — Administration of Small Estates Act Cap. 4
    St Christopher & Nevis — Administration of Small Estates Act Cap. 4
    St Lucia — Administration of Small Successions Ord. Cap. 20
    See also: Administration of Small Successions (Amendment) Act 5/1981
    St Vincent & the Grenadines — Administration of Small Estates Act Cap. 379
    The Bahamas — See p. 239.
    Trinidad & Tobago — rr. 5-15 First Schedule N.C.B.R. Ch. 8 No. 2.
2. The value of small estates was increased from $480 to $4,800 by LN 16/1984 Wills and Probate Non-Contentious Business (Amendment) Rules.
3. See r.5 First Schedule N.C.B.R. Ch. 8 No. 2.
4. *Ibid.*
5. *Ibid.*
6. See pp. 231-232.
7. Antigua & Barbuda — s.6 Administration of Small Estates Act Cap. 8
    Dominica — s.6 Administration of Small Estates Act Ch. 9:06
    Grenada — s.15(3) Probate Act Cap. 255
    Montserrat — s.6 Administration of Small Estates Act Cap. 80
    St Christopher & Nevis — s.6 Administration of Small Estates Act Cap. 4
    St Lucia — s.3(3) Administration of Small Successions Ordinance but see pp. 165-166 post.
    St Vincent & the Grenadines — s.6 Administration of Small Estates Act Cap. 379 but see p. 232.
8. See note 4 above.
9. Antigua & Barbuda, — s.5 Administration of Small Estates Act Cap. 8
    Dominica — s.5 Administration of Small Estates Act Ch. 9:06
    Grenada — Unlike the other Eastern Caribbean territories s.15(3) of

the Probate Act Cap. 255 does not expressly provide that an affidavit of identity be furnished when requested by the Registrar. However it is submitted that the effect of s.15(3) is the same as that of the other Eastern Caribbean territories

	Montserrat	- s.5 Administration of Small Estates Act Cap. 80
	St Christopher & Nevis	- s.5 Administration of Small Estates Act Cap. 4
	St Lucia	- s.3(3) Administration of Small Succession Ordinance Cap. 20
	St Vincent & the Grenadines	- s.5 Administration of Small Estates Act Cap. 379.
10	Antigua & Barbuda	- s.2 Administration of Small Estates Act Cap. 8
	Dominica	- s.2 Administration of Small Estates Act Ch. 9:06
	Grenada	- s.15(1) Probate Act Cap. 255 See also Small Estate Fees Rules 9/1990
	Montserrat	- Administration of Small Estates Act (Amendment) Act 12 of 1972.
11	Antigua & Barbuda	- s.5 Administration of Small Estates Act Cap. 8
	Dominica	- s.5 Administration of Small Estates Act Ch, 9:06
	Grenada	- s.15(4) Probate Act Cap. 255
	Montserrat	- s.5 Administration of Small Estates Act. Cap. 4.
12	Antigua & Barbuda	- s.5 Administration of Small Estates Act Cap. 8
	Dominica	- s.5 Administration of Small Estates Act Ch. 9:06
	Montserrat	- s.5 Administration of Small Estates Act. Cap. 4.

13 See s.2 Administration of Small Estates Act. Amendment 14/1985.
14 See s.5 Administration of Small Estates Act. Cap. 4.
15 Administration of Small Successions Ordinance (Amendment) Act 5/1981.
16 See s.3(4) Administration of Small Estates Ch. 20.
17 Administration of Small Estates Act Cap. 379.
18 See s.3 Administration of Small Estates Act Cap. 379.
19 See s.5 of the Administration of Small Estates Act Cap. 379.
20 Pursuant to s.7(4) Death Duties (Abolition) Ordinance 6/1977.
21 See s.7(3) of the Death Duties Abolition Ordinance 6/1977 which provides that it shall be the duty of the Registrar to whom application is made in any non-contentious matter and at the request of the applicant to fill up such papers as may be necessary to lead to the grant of letters of administration or probate as the case may be.
22 See s.5 Public Trustee Act Cap. 248.
23 See s.44(2), 44(3), 44(4) Succession Act Cap. 249.
24 See s.44(4) Succession Act Cap. 249.
25 See s.19 Deceased Persons Estates' Administration Act Cap. 12:01.
26 See s.25(b) Deceased Persons Estates' Administration Act Cap. 12:01.
27 The value of estates increased from $500,000 to $1.5 Million with respect to the estates of persons dying on or after February 26, 2000, 1995 pursuant to s.2 of the The Judicature (Resident Magistrates) (Amendment) Act 2000. See also ss.108-129 Judicature (Resident Magistrates) Act.
28 See s.108 Judicature (Resident Magistrates) Act.
29 *Ibid.*
30 See s.110 Judicature (Resident Magistrates) Act.
31 See s.112 Judicature (Resident Magistrates) Act.

32 In practice the Notice of Publication is not published in the Gazette. See chapter 4, p. 87.

33 Barbados — s.21 Succession Act Cap. 249
    Eastern Caribbean — s.2(1) of the repealed Administration of Justice Act 1932, territories (save St Lucia) England. This section is deemed to have been saved by the savings provisions of s.25 of the Supreme Court Act 1981, England
    The Bahamas — See s.31 of the Supreme Court Act 15/1996 which provides that the court may make a grant of probate or letters of administration in respect of a deceased person notwithstanding that the deceased person left no estate.

34 See chapter 8 p. 203.
35 See p. 246, 251.
36 Anguilla — s.4(1)(f), 4(2) Intestates Estates Act Cap. 36
    Antigua & Barbuda — s.4(6) Intestates Estates Act Cap. 225
    Dominica — s.4 Intestates Estates Act Ch. 9:03
    Guyana — s(6)(b)(ii) Civil Law of Guyana Act Cap. 6:01
    Jamaica — s.4(2) Intestates Estates and Property Charges Act
    Montserrat — ss.4(1) and 4(2) Intestates Estates Act Cap. 36
    St Christopher & Nevis — s.4(1)(f) and 4(2) Intestates Estates Act Cap. 36
    St Vincent & the Grenadines — s.62 Administration of Estates Act Cap. 377 Escheat Act Cap. 106.
    The Bahamas — ss.3, 4 Escheat Act Ch. 141.
37 Trinidad & Tobago — s.27 Administration of Estates Ch. 8 No. 1.
38 Barbados — s.55(2) Succession Act Cap. 249.
39 Anguilla — Unrepresented Estates Act Cap. 82
    Antigua & Barbuda — Unrepresented Estates Act Cap. 459
    Dominica — Unrepresented Estates Act Chap. 9:04
    Montseratt — Unrepresented Estates Act Cap. 82
    St. Christopher & Nevis — Unrepresented Estates Act Cap. 82
40 Pursuant to s.10(1) of the respective Unrepresented Estates Acts, an unrepresented estate is defined as:
    (a) the estate of every person who dies intestate, where the widow or next of kin of such person is unknown, or has refused to take out letters of administration, or is absent from the State without having an agent therein;
    (b) the estate of every person who dies leaving a will, and, owing to any cause, it is necessary to appoint administrators *cum testamento annexo*, or *de bonis non*, of such estate, and the person entitled to letters of administration are unknown, or refuses to take out letters of administration, or is absent from the State without having an agent therein;
    (c) every estate whereof the executors or administrators are absent from the State without having an agent therein;
    (d) the estate of every person who dies intestate and without leaving next of kin surviving him.
41 *Ibid.*
42 *Ibid.*
43 See also s.78 of the Eastern Caribbean Supreme Court (St Lucia) Act 17/1969 which provides that:

Where the estate and effects of a deceased person who has died out of the State come into possession of the Government and three months have elapsed since the same came into the possession of the Government, and it is proved to the satisfaction of the Administrator General, that no will has been admitted to probate and no administration has been taken out to the estate of such deceased person, and no person lawfully entitled to such estate and effects by testamentary or intestate succession, or otherwise, has claimed the same, the Governor may order such estate and effects to be paid, transferred, or delivered to any person who the Governor considers is lawfully or equitably entitled to the same in the circumstances.

44 Section 27 Part III Administration of Estates Ordinance Ch. 8 No. 1.
45 Statutory Declarations Act Ch. 7:04.
46 See s.27 Administration of Estates Ordinance Ch. 8 No. 1.
47 See ss.29-31 of the Administration of Estates Ordinance Ch. 8 No. 1.
48 Section 12 Intestates Estates' and Property Charges Act.
49 Section 6(1) Public Trustee Act Cap. 13:01.
50 Section 5(&) Civil Law of Guyana Act Cap. 6:01.
51 *Ibid.*
52 Pursuant to notice dated 2nd October, 1965 and made under s.39 of the repealed Interpretation Ordinance Ch. 5.
53 Section 3(1) of the Escheat Act Ch. 141.
54 Section 4 of the Escheat Act Ch. 141.

10

Stamp and Estate Duty

INTRODUCTION

As a general rule, upon the death of a person, whether testate or intestate, a duty or tax is or, in the territories where such duties are no longer payable, was chargeable not only on the assets to be covered by the grant of representation but also on all the real and personal property of the deceased, wherever situated.

The payment of death duties (whether called probate, stamp, estate, death, or succession duties in the various territories) as evidenced by a certificate issued by the appropriate officer is or was a condition precedent to the issuance to the applicant of the relevant grant of representation.

To date in most of the Caribbean territories, death duties have either been abolished or as in the case of Guyana and Jamaica have been repealed and replaced by another form of tax.

Death Duties in General

The procedure and practice to be followed with respect to the issuance of the certificate are essentially the same in the various territories.

The applicant or the applicant's agent (usually the applicant's attorney-at-law) is required to lodge in the Estate/Stamp Duty Section of the Inland Revenue Department, Ministry of Finance, the following documents:

1. An Affidavit/Declaration and Accounts for the Commissioner.
2. Death certificate of the deceased.
3. Will, if any.
4. Proof of value of the estate including:
    (a) valuation certificate of real property, if any
    (b) copies of land deeds;
    (c) Bank statements and share certificates.;
5. Funeral receipts and any other documentary evidence of the deceased's indebtedness.

The duties payable are calculated in accordance with the relevant schedule of the respective estate/stamp duty acts of the various territories. The applicant/agent is notified of the duties payable. He then pays the duties calculated together with any accrued interest thereon, to the cashier, Collection, Inland Revenue or its equivalent. The applicant/agent is then issued with a receipt which is submitted to the Estate/Stamp Duty section for the issuance of the appropriate certificate.

Affidavit/Declaration and Accounts of the Estate

The Affidavit/Declaration and Account of the Estate or its equivalent takes a prescribed form and may be collected from the relevant Estate/Stamp Duty Section, Inland Revenue of the respective territories. The form is completed by the applicant for the grant and executed before a person authorised to administer oaths in the respective territories.

The Affidavit/Declaration includes:

- (i) the name and address of the deceased;
- (ii) a description of the deponent;
- (iii) the place of domicil of the deceased;
- (iv) the date and place of death of the deceased;
- (v) the names of the beneficiaries and their relationship if any, to the deceased;
- (vi) a statement as to whether or not the deceased left a will;
- (vii) a statement that the various accounts annexed to the affidavit/declaration contain a true account of the particulars and gross value as at the date of death.

The various Accounts of the Estate set out the particulars of the deceased estate and its gross value including accounts of:

- (i) the real property situate within and outside the relevant territory;
- (ii) the personal property within and outside the relevant territory;
- (iii) the debts and encumbrances affecting the deceased's property within the relevant territory;
- (iv) Funeral expenses.

Succession Duties

Barbados, Jamaica, St Lucia and Trinidad & Tobago

Succession duties are an additional duty levied[1] and payable in respect of every interest or absolute power of appointment acquired or possessed by any person as the successor of the deceased with respect to property deemed to pass on the death of the deceased and chargeable with estate duty. It is payable as a general rule at the same time as the estate duty.

The persons entitled in succession to the benefit of the property are charged with the duties at the rate prescribed in the relevant schedule to the estate and or succession duty acts of the above territories.

Rates of Payment

The value of the succession and the relationship of the successor to the predecessor are factors taken into account in determining the rate at which such duties are payable.

Documents and Procedure by Jurisdiction

A. Trinidad & Tobago

Succession Duties abolished — 1st January, 1972[2]
Estate Duties abolished — 1st January, 1981[3]

Pursuant to s.9(1) of the Finance(Miscellaneous Provisions) Act 39/2000, the Estate and Successions Duties Act Ch. 76:02 is repealed. Section 9(2) further provides that estate duties payable in respect of the estate of persons who died before January 1, 1981, and which duties are outstanding on the commencement date of the Act (January 1, 1998) shall be waived. However, s.9(3) expressly provides that estate duties payable prior to the commencement date are non-refundable.

Accordingly, any application for a grant made on or after January 1 1998, in respect of an estate where the deceased died prior to the cut off date for the payment of estate duties, (January 1, 1981), such duties are no longer payable.

The effect of s.9(2) is that the procedure and practice relevant to the payment of estate duties is no longer applicable, save and except, with respect to applications for grants made prior to January 1, 1998 in respect of the estates of persons dying prior to January 1, 1981.

Although estate and succession duties are no longer payable, s.39 of the 'Wills and Probate Ord. Ch. 8 No. 2 provides in effect that no probate or letter of administration may be granted until the applicant has filed with the registrar an Estate and Succession Duties Certificate.[4] However in practice, prior to January 1, 1998, this certificate was lodged only in cases where the deceased died prior to January 1, 1981. The following documents were required to be filed in the Estate Duty Section, Inland Revenue prior to 1st January, 1998 with respect to the estates of person dying before January 1, 1981:

1. Estate and Succession Duty Affidavit;
2. Certified copy of death certificate;
3. Copy of will, if any;
4. Copy of land deeds (where the deceased left land);
5. Certificate of valuation of real estate (the original and copy);
6. Any other proof of value of estate including bank statements, share certificates, etc.;
7. Funeral receipts, and other proof of indebtedness of the deceased; and in cases where the deceased was the joint owner of real and personal property
8. An Account for the Commissioner.[5]

Regulations

In accordance with the repealed Estate and Succession Duties Regulations[6] the Affidavit and Accounts and other supporting documents are required to be delivered to the Board of Inland Revenue at its office in Port of Spain or to the District Revenue Office at San Fernando or Tobago within six months of the death of the deceased.

The duties payable are computed by an authorised officer of the Estate Duty Department.[7] When the amount is ascertained the said sum is certified in writing on the Affidavit and Account. The applicant/agent pays to a cashier, Treasury, Inland Revenue, the duty payable and a receipt is issued to him. The applicant/agent thereafter submits the receipt to the Estate Duty Division and the Estate and Succession Duties Certificate is prepared, signed by the Comptroller of Account and issued to the applicant/agent.[8] If no duty is payable the certificate is accordingly marked to reflect this.

B. *Barbados*

Estate and Succession Duties Act Cap. 70

Succession duties abolished with respect to the estate of persons dying on or after 31st August, 1977.[9]

Estate duties abolished with respect to the estate of persons dying on or after 31st March, 1981.[10]

The following documents are lodged in Estate Duty Section of Inland Revenue, Ministry of Finance:

1. Affidavit and Accounts for the Commissioner sworn by the applicant before a Justice of the Peace;[11]
2. Original death certificate (this is photocopied and the original is returned);
3. Copy of will, if any;
4. Proof of value of estate e.g. bank statements or statements from insurance companies;
5. Copies of land deeds (where the deceased left land);
6. Land Tax Bill which is in effect a statement of valuation of land as verified by the Commissioner of Land Valuation;
7. Funeral receipts and other proof of the deceased's indebtedness.

The Affidavit and Accounts are submitted to the Estate Duty section, Inland Revenue Department in Bridgetown. The duties and any interest payable are computed in accordance with the scale of rates set out in the First and Second Schedule to the Estate and Succession Duties Act, Cap. 70.

The applicant or his agent then pays the relevant duty together with interest, if any, to the Cashier Inland Revenue and a receipt is accordingly issued to him. The receipt is then submitted to the Estate Duty department where the Estate Duty Certificate is prepared, signed by the Commissioner of Inland Revenue and stamped accordingly. The applicant/attorney-at-law is thereafter notified in writing of the issuance of the certificate.

C. *Guyana*

Estate Duty Act Ch. 81:23

Estate Duty Act repealed by The Taxation laws (Relief) Act 6/1991 which replaced estate duty with process fees with respect to the estates of persons dying on or after 1st January, 1991.[12]

Although estate duty has been replaced by process fees the practice and procedure and the documents required to obtain the Certificate of Proper Officer remain the same.[13]

Documents lodged in Estate Duty Section, Inland Revenue:

1. Unsworn oath of the executor or administrator;
2. Certified copy of the death certificate of the deceased;
3. Copy of will, if any;
4. Copy of transport, deed of conveyance (where the deceased left land)
5. Certificate of Valuation of Real Property;
6. Any other proof of value of the estate including bank statements and share certificates;
7. Funeral receipts and other proof of indebtedness of the deceased;
8. Declaration and Inventory for the Commissioner of Inland Revenue.

Estate duty/process fees (depending on the date of death of the deceased) are calculated in accordance with s.4 of the Tax Act Cap. 88:01.

Upon assessment of the duty or process fees payable, a memorandum of the assessed amount is endorsed on the Declaration.[14]

The duties chargeable together with interest, if any, are then paid to the Cashier, Accountant General's Department and a receipt is issued to the applicant.[15] The applicant or his agent thereafter submits the receipt to the proper officer, for the issuance to the applicant of the Certificate of the Proper Officer, signed by the Commissioner, Inland Revenue.[16]

D. Jamaica

Estate Duty Law 60/1954 — Succession duty and legacy duty abolished with respect to the estates of persons dying on or after the 1st April, 1954.

Estate Duty (Amendment) Law 23/1963 — Estate duty abolished with respect to the estates of persons dying on or after 21st July, 1963.

Transfer Tax Act 1974 — A transfer tax is payable with respect to estate of persons dying on or after 1st June, 1974.

- **Estate Duty**

The following are the documents to be lodged at the Stamp Duty and Transfer Tax Department, Inland Revenue:

1. Revenue Affidavit deposed and sworn to by the grantee before the Commissioner of Oaths. This affidavit sets out:
    (i) the name, residence and a description of the applicant(s);
    (ii) the place and date of death of the deceased;
    (iii) the domicil of the deceased;
    (iv) Particulars of the estate including the assets and the funeral expenses and other debts of the deceased set out in the appropriate accounts;

2. Inventory — setting out details of all property owned by the deceased including furniture and clothes;[17]
3. Copy certificates of title (where the deceased left land);
4. Valuation Report of a reputable valuator with respect to real property, (if any);
5. Copy of will, if any;
6. Proof of the value of the estate such as statements from the deceased's bankers, insurance companies;
7. Proof of the deceased's debts such as funeral receipts, etc;
8. Copy of death certificate of the deceased;
9. Addendum — a form which provides addition information for the Department's Valuators when valuing deceased's estate;
10. Any additional information as required.

- **Transfer Tax**[18]

The following are the documents to be lodged at the Stamp Duty and Transfer Tax Department:

1. Revenue Affidavit which takes a prescribed form to be completed by the personal representative listing:
   (i) all assets owned by the deceased of which he was competent to dispose at his death and the value thereof, including property owned jointly by the deceased; and
   (ii) liabilities of the estate including funeral expenses, mortgage loans;
2. Copy of death certificate;
3. Copy of Certificate(s) of title (where the deceased left land);
4. Valuation report of a reputable valuator with respect to real property (if any);
5. Addendum — a form which provides additional information for the Department's Valuators when valuing deceased's estate;
6. Copy of inventory listing the deceased real and personal assets;
7. Copy of probated will, where the deceased left a will;
8. Copy of relevant grant of representation. This requirement is usually waived so as to facilitate expeditious payment of transfer tax. However once the grant is obtained, a copy of the grant must be submitted.
9. Declaration of surviving spouse;[19]
10. Copies of share certificates, debentures and other securities excluding government securities;
11. Copy of Affidavit of Value (This is lodged in practice and used to calculate the transfer tax payable).

The documents, practice and procedure relevant to the payment of estate duty/transfer tax are essentially the same. However with respect to the payment of estate duty, such duty is payable prior to the issue of the grant.[20] Accordingly the Stamp Commissioner's Certificate should be lodged with the papers to lead the relevant grant of representation. With respect to transfer tax, although it is payable after the issue of the relevant grant, in practice it may be paid prior to the grant being issued.

Estate Duty

Practice and Procedure

The estate duty documents are lodged in the Commissioner of Stamp and Estate Duty Office otherwise referred to as the 'Stamp Office'. Enquiries are then made by an authorised member of staff so as to verify the information contained in the Revenue Affidavit. A valuator is dispatched to inspect the deceased's real property to determine its value at the date of death; unless the valuation certificate is accepted.

The appropriate duty is assessed in accordance with the scale of rates set out in the First and Second Schedule to the Estate Duty Law 60/1954. The applicant/agent is then notified of the duty payable. He attends the 'Stamp Office' and pays the assessed duty to the cashier. A receipt of payment is generated by the computer and thereafter the Stamp Commissioner's Certificate, signed by the Stamp Commissioner is issued to the applicant.

Transfer Tax

Practice and Procedure

The Registrar of the Supreme Court is required to advise the Stamp Commissioner whenever an application is made for a grant of representation, where upon a notice is required to be sent to the applicant by the Stamp Commissioner, requesting the submission of the Revenue Affidavit and supporting documents. However in practice, because of the delays which may result, the applicant submits the Revenue Affidavit and other relevant documents without awaiting notification from the Stamp Commissioner. After the Revenue Affidavit and other supporting documents are submitted, the usual inquiries are conducted and the real property if any, inspected by valuators attached to the department, to determine its market value at the date of death. The tax chargeable is thereafter calculated and a notice of the sum payable is sent to the applicant. Upon receipt thereof, the applicant attends the 'Stamp Office' and pays the assessed tax to the cashier. A computerised receipt is issued to the applicant as proof of payment whereupon the Stamp Commissioner's certificate is issued. In cases where the tax is paid prior to the issue of the grant of representation, the applicant is required to bring into the 'Stamp Office', the grant, when issued, and Transfer Tax's Certificate. The back of the grant is endorsed to the effect that the transfer tax was paid on the date stated therein. The Transfer Tax's certificate number and the actual amount of tax paid are also endorsed on the back of the grant. It is to be noted that no transfer of any property subject to transfer tax can be registered unless the relevant Registrar is satisfied by the production of the Stamp Commissioner's Certificate that the tax has been duly paid, or that none is payable, as the case may be.

E. *Antigua & Barbuda, Montserrat and St Christopher & Nevis*

- *Antigua & Barbuda*
  Stamp Act Cap. 270
  Stamp Duty Abolished with respect to the estate of persons dying on or after 16th December, 1969.
- *Montserrat*
  Stamp Act Cap. 238
  Stamp Duty Abolished with respect to the estate of persons dying on or after 19th November, 1966.[22]
- *St Christopher & Nevis*
  Stamp Act Cap. 257
  Stamp Duty Abolished with respect to the estate of persons dying on or after 1st January, 1986.[23]

It is to be noted that with respect to St Christopher & Nevis that although Stamp Duty Probate has been abolished since 1986, an intended grantee is still required to lodge a Stamp Duty Certificate with the papers to lead the application for the relevant grant. When the deceased died on or after 1st January, 1986 the Stamp Duty Certificate is marked 'Exempt'.

The following are documents are to be lodged in the Stamp Duty Section, Inland Revenue of the above territories:

1. Declaration and Accounts of the Estate;
2. Copy of will, if any;
3. Death certificate;
4. Proof of the value of the deceased estate;
5. Funeral receipts and other proof of the deceased's indebtedness.

St. Christopher & Nevis

6. Affidavit of Kin (with respect to grants of letters of administration with or without will annexed); In practice the deceased's death certificate is not lodged;

> Proof of the value of the deceased's estate is not generally required. And in so far as real property is concerned, a valuation of the deceased's real estate is not lodged. In practice an Officer in the Stamp Duty department ascertains the value of deceased's real estate by checking the property tax records or visiting the site where the deceased's land is situate.

The Declaration and Account is submitted together with supporting documents to the Stamp Duty section and the duty payable is calculated in accordance with the rate set out in the Schedule to the respective Stamp Acts of the above territories.

On payment of the stamp duty, the applicant is issued with a receipt and the stamps to the value of the duty payable are impressed on the Declaration. The stamped declaration is then submitted to the Stamp Duty Section and the Stamp Duty Certificate is accordingly prepared and delivered to the applicant. In addition with respect to St. Christopher & Nevis (where death occurred on or after January 1, 1986) the Declaration and Account is submitted to the Stamp Duty Section. Upon verification that the estate is exempt from payment of stamp duty. The Declaration is duly notated and signed by an officer, attached to the Stamp Duty section and thereafter presented to the cashier. The Declaration is accordingly stamped 'Exempt' by the cashier. The applicant then submits the declaration duly stamped for the preparation and issuance of a Stamp Duty 'Exempt' Certificate.

F. *Grenada*

Estate Duty Ordinance Cap. 108
Estate duty abolished with respect to the estates of persons dying on or after 1st October, 1983.[24]

Documents to be filed in the Estate Duty Section:

1. Estate Duty Affidavit and Accounts signed by applicant;[25]
2. Certificate of valuation;
3. Original death certificate (photocopy made);
4. Proof of value of estate including bank statements;

5. Certified copy of will, if any;
6. Funeral receipts and other proof of the deceased's indebtedness.

Estate duty is calculated in accordance with the rates set out in the First Schedule to the Estate Duty Ordinance Cap. 108.

After the duty and interest, if any, are calculated, a Notice of Assessment is sent to the applicant if acting in person, or his solicitor as the case may be. The applicant pays to the cashier, Collection Section of Inland Revenue the amount due, as set out in the Notice. He is then issued a receipt, signed, dated and stamped. The receipt is then taken to the Estate Duty Section for the preparation and issuance of the Estate Duty Certificate.[26]

G. Dominica

Estate Duty Act Cap. 267
Estate Duty abolished with respect to estate of persons dying on or after 1st July, 1985.[27]

In cases where a person dies prior to 1st July, 1985 an Estate Duty certificate is required to be filed with the papers to lead the grant. In this regard, the following documents must be filed in the Estate Duty Section of Inland Revenue:
1. Declaration and Account of the Estate.
2. Proof of value of the deceased's estates including statements from banks, insurance companies, etc.
3. Certified valuation of land (in cases where deceased left real property).
4. Original death certificate. (This is discretionary and not required in practice.)
5. Copy of will, if any. (This is not required in practice);
6. Funeral receipts, bills and any other proof of the deceased's indebtedness.

When these documents are filed the amount of estate duty chargeable is usually computed at the same time and the applicant is verbally informed of the duty together with interest, if any, due and payable. The duties payable are computed in accordance with the scale of rates of the relevant schedule to the Estate Duty Act, Cap. 267.

The duty and interest, if any, is paid to the cashier in the Treasury and the applicant is issued a signed, stamped and dated receipt. The receipt is then taken to the Estate Duty Section and the Estate Duty Certificate is prepared and signed by the Commissioner, Inland Revenue.

H. St Lucia

Date of Abolition of Succession Duty — 1st October, 1988.
Although succession duties are no longer payable with respect to the estates of persons dying on or after 1st October, 1988 a Certificate of Non-objection is still required in cases of letters of administration irrespective of the date of death of the deceased.[28]

Practice and Procedure

The applicant or his attorney-at-law on his behalf is required to submit to the Audit Section Inland Revenue the documents necessary to lead the relevant grant of representation including:

1. A Declaration setting out *inter alia* the following particulars:
    (i) the name, surname and residence of the declarant and the deceased respectively;
    (ii) a description in detail of all property transmitted or passing on death together with the actual gross principal value thereof;
    (iii) the names, surnames, residence and classification of all creditors of the estate or succession. If the deceased died testate, the names, surnames, residence and category of the names and beneficiaries as well as executors and trustees, if any.[29]
2. Proof of the value of the deceased's estate including bank statements, and the Land Registry Form containing particulars of the real property owned by the deceased including the value thereof.
3. Death Certificate of the deceased.[30]
4. Will, if any.[31]
5. Funeral receipts and other proof of the deceased's indebtedness.

The documents are checked by an officer in the Audit Section for the purposes of updating the deceased's income tax assessment.

The succession number is recorded and the file containing all the papers to lead the grants are submitted to Collections, Inland Revenue, where the papers, are again checked to ascertain whether the deceased had any other source of income or owed property taxes at the date of death. If this is in fact the case either the certificate of non-objection will not be issued until the taxes in arrears are paid or alternatively the certificate will be issued and subsequently filed in the Registry against the real property owned by the deceased. This effectively prohibits the sale of the deceased's lands until the outstanding taxes are paid.

Additionally it is to be noted that the Collections Department may garnish the deceased monies deposited in his bank account. However, in practice the applicant or his attorney-at-law are called in with a view to affording the intended grantee an opportunity to settle the outstanding taxes.

Apart from ascertaining whether income or property taxes are outstanding, succession duties are calculated in accordance with the rate set out in the relevant Schedule to the Succession Duty Ordinance.[32]

The applicant is informed in writing of the amount claimed as duty and that the sum is payable within 30 days after the delivery of the notice.[33] The duty is payable to the Cashier, Collections, Treasury.[34] The applicant is thereafter issued with a receipt and the Certificate of Non-objection.

I. St Vincent & the Grenadines

Estate and Succession Duties Act Cap. 380
Estate and Succession Duties abolished in respect of the estates of persons dying on or after 5th August, 1993.[35]

In St Vincent & the Grenadines, when death occurred before 5th August, 1993, estate and succession duties[36] are paid when the papers to lead the relevant grant are filed.[37] The Declaration and Accounts[38] of the estate and the other papers to lead the relevant grant are submitted to the Estate Duty Office, Inland Revenue Department. When the estate includes land, a valuation certificate must also be included with the papers to lead the grant. The valuation certificate and Memorandum and Check of Valuation Form which is completed by an authorised clerk attached to the Estate Duty Office are submitted to the Land and House Tax Division, Valuation Department, Ministry of Finance so as to verify the information stated in the valuation certificate. Once the valuation is accepted a note is made on the Memorandum to that effect. It is then signed by the Chief Surveyor and a valuation officer. If the value stated in the valuation certificate is not accepted, the value is accordingly amended on the Memorandum. This may require a visit to and inspection of the land by one of the valuation officers attached to the Valuation Department.

The Memorandum duly signed and stamped is returned to the Estate Duty Office where the estate and succession duties are calculated. The estate duty is calculated in accordance with the graduated scale of rates as set out in the First Schedule to the Act[39] while the succession duty is calculated in accordance with the Scale of Rates as set out in the Second Schedule to the Act.[40] The value of the real estate as stated in the Memorandum and Check of Valuation and the value of the personal estate as stated in the Declaration and Accounts of the Estate are used for the purposes of calculating the estate and succession duties payable.

It is to be noted that although s.29 provides for the issue of a certificate by the Commissioner Inland Revenue, in practice this is not done.[41]

J. The Bahamas

There are no death duties payable in The Bahamas. When the application for the grant is lodged in the Registry, advertising fees, court fees and stamp duties payable on instruments and other documents in civil proceedings are the only duties and fees payable.[42]

K. Anguilla

Abolition of Stamp Duties — with respect to estates of persons dying on or after 29th September, 1977.[43]

The position in Anguilla is quite unique. Although the Death Duties Ordinance and other revenue collecting legislation including the Income Tax Act were not abolished until 29th September, 1977, the *de facto* position in Anguilla was that none of these ordinances was enforced. Anguillans in fact never paid, nor was any attempt ever made, to collect income tax death duties etc. by the local authorities. This was primarily because of the political situation which existed in Anguilla until 1967. Up to 1967 when the Kittitian government was 'evicted' in the so called Anguillan revolution, Anguilla was a member of the unitary state of St Christopher and Nevis. This was a source of great resentment for the Anguillans as all taxes, stamp duties, etc. were to be sent to St Christopher when collected. As a consequence no effort was even made to collect any taxes or duties.

This *de facto* situation continued until 29th September, 1977 when the decision was taken to regularise the situation. As a consequence the Death Duties Abolition Ordinance was passed thus bringing the *de jure* position in line with the de facto position.

It is to be noted that s.4 of the Death Duties Abolition Ordinance further provides that even where death occurred before the commencement date of the Ordinance, provided probate or letters of administration have not been granted, duties in respect of any property passing on the death of the deceased are to be remitted.

Estate Fees

In instances where the application for the grant is made with the assistance of the Registrar, as is invariably the case, a one percent estate fee is payable to the cashier, High Court Registry. The estate fees are calculated on the gross value of the deceased's estate at the date of his death. Accordingly, proof of the value of the estate as contained in the Declaration on Oath and additionally, in the case of real property, a Land Registry Valuation Certificate are required to be filed with the papers to lead the grant.

Land Registry Valuation Certificate[44]

The Land Registry Valuation Certificate is filed with the other papers to lead the grant in order to calculate:

(a) the estate fees payable; and
(b) the amount of the penalty for the bond.

In this regard the applicant is required to attend the Land Registry Department and complete a Land Registry Valuation form setting out the particulars of all land in which the deceased had an interest, including the value thereof:

(i) at the date of death; and
(ii) at the date of the application for the grant.

Upon verification of the value of the land, a Land Registry Valuation Certificate is issued to the intended grantee.

Declaration on Oath and Accounts

Although a Declaration on Oath and Accounts of the Estate is lodged with the papers to lead the grant, this is not required for the purpose of payment of any duties but rather to ascertain the amount of the penalty of the administration bond.

Notes

1. With respect to St Lucia it is the only form of death duties chargeable.
2. By virtue of s.43 Estate and Succession Duties Act Ch. 76:02 with respect to the estate of any person dying on or after 1st January, 1979.
3. See s.122 Succession Act No. 27/1981. Estate Duty is abolished with respect of the estate of any person dying on or after 1st January, 1981.
4. See also s.36 of the repealed Estate and Succession Duties Act Ch. 76:02 which also provides that no probate or administration shall be granted by the High Court until the Board of Inland Revenue has given a certificate that estate duty has been paid.
5. An Account for the Commissioner (Form 2) is used where all the real and personal estate

owned by the deceased is owned by him in the capacity of joint tenant and joint tenant only. This form is essentially the same as the Estate and Succession Duty Affidavit (Form 1), save that the property included therein is limited to joint property only.
6 Made under and by virtue of s.52 of the Estate and Succession Duties Act Ch. 76:02.
7 Section 36(3) of the repealed Estate and Succession Duties Act Ch. 76:02
8 Regulation 6 of the repealed Estate & Succession Duties Act. An Account for the Commissioner.
9 Estate and Succession Duties (Amendment) Act 36/1977.
10 Estate Duty (Repeal) Act 41/1981.
11 Section 25 Estate and Succession Duties Act Cap. 70.
12 This is by virtue of an s.3 Taxation Laws Relief Act 6/1991 which accordingly amended the Deceased Persons Estates' Administration of Estates Act Cap. 12:01. As a consequence s.15 of the Deceased Persons Estates' Administration Act now provides for the payment of process fees in accordance with s.14 of the Tax Act Cap. 80:01.
13 See s.13 Estate Duty Act Cap. 81:23; s.13 Deceased Persons Estates' Administration Act 12:01 as amended by the Schedule to the Taxation Laws (Relief) Act 6/1991.
14 Section 15(1) Estate Duty Act Cap. 81:23; s.15 Deceased Persons Estates' Administration Act Cap. 12:01 as amended by the Schedule to the Taxation Law (Relief) Act 6/1991.
15 Section 15(2) Estate Duty Act Cap. 81:23.
16 Section 15(3) Estate Duty Act Cap. 81:23.
Section 15D(3) Deceased Persons Estates' Administration Act Cap. 12:01.
17 A detailed inventory is required with respect to estates of persons dying prior to 1st April, 1954, the date of abolition of succession and legacy duty.
18 Transfer tax is payable with respect to land, a lease of land, stocks, shares and other securities or a beneficial interest in any of these (for example, as the result of a trust created in one's favour). However the matrimonial home, personal chattels, life insurance proceeds and cash are exempted from the payment of this tax. Although it is not so called, transfer tax payable on death effectively operates as a death duty.
19 A declaration containing the following information must be filed:
    (i) that the home in which the surviving spouse resides was the principal place of residence of the deceased,
    (ii) that it was occupied by the deceased and the surviving spouse immediately prior to his or her death; and
This declaration is required as the matrimonial home/principal place of the deceased is exempt from the payment of transfer tax.
20 Section 44(2) of the Estate Duty Law 60/1954.
21 Stamp (Amendment) Act 24/1969.
22 The Stamp Act (Amendment) Ordinance 13/1966.
23 By virtue of Fees (Miscellaneous Provisions) Act 14 1985.
24 Pursuant to Estate Duty (Repeal) Ordinance 2 1/1984.
25 See s.19 Estate Duty Ord. Cap. 108.
26 See also Forms, Second Schedule to Estate Duty Ordinance Cap. 108.
27 Pursuant to Estate Duty (Amendment) Act 18/1985.
28 Although the Succession Duty Ordinance Ch. 220 s.63 of which provided that no will or copy of any will is to be registered in the Registry of Deed until a certificate of non-objection has been obtained, has been repealed by virtue of the Succession Duty Ordinance (Repeal) Act 10/1988, Art 1015(b) Code of Civil Procedure Ch. 243 has not likewise been

repealed. Art 1015(b) requires that a certificate of non-objection must be obtained before the issue of letters of administration to the proposed grantee.

29 Section 15 Succession Duty Ordinance Ch. 220.
30 Ibid., s. 17.
31 Ibid.
32 Ibid., s. 18.
33 Ibid., s. 20.
34 Ibid., s. 27.
35 Estate and Succession Duties (Amendment) Act 25/1 993.
36 *Ibid.*
37 See chapter 4 pp. 94-95.
38 s.25 Estate and Succession Duties Act Cap. 380.
39 Ibid., s. 6.
40 Ibid., s. 36
41 See chapter 4 pp. 94-95.
42 See chapter 27 pp. 509, 512.
43 See ss. 3, 5, 6, Death Duties Abolition Ordinance No. 6/1977.
44 See chapter 5 p. 115.

11

Administration Bond/Surety Guarantee

ADMINISTRATION BOND[1]

Subject to certain exemptions, every person to whom a grant of administration with or without will annexed is made is required to give a bond,[2] for the due collecting, getting in and administering of the real and personal estate of the deceased.[3] With the exception of Barbados, the bond is lodged with the other papers to lead the relevant grant of representation.

Barbados

In practice, after the grant of letters of administration has been signed by the registrar, but prior to the issuance of the grant itself, the administrator and sureties are required to enter into a bond with the registrar. The bond is contained in a Bond Book kept in the Registry for that purpose. The applicant and sureties are required to attend the Registry for the purposes of executing the bond before a legal assistant.

Exemptions and Waivers

Persons who are exempted from giving a bond include:

(a) the Public Trustee by virtue *inter alia* of the Public Trustee Acts/Ordinances of the various territories;[4]
(b) the Administrator General in Jamaica and Trinidad & Tobago;[5] and in *all jurisdictions*
(c) applicants for small estate grants.

Jamaica

Although s.18 of the Administrator General's Act makes provision for the entering of a bond by an administrator, other than the Administrator General, the new CPR 2002, which takes effect from January 1, 2003, has with respect to probate applications made in the Supreme Court, expressly repealed and replaced the General Rules and Orders of the Supreme Court in particular rr.20, 21 and 22, Part III Administration and Probate. In this regard, although Rule 68 CPR 2002 does not expressly so provide, administration bonds as well as will bonds are no longer required in respect of applications for the respective grants of representation made in the Supreme Court.

However, with respect to applications for grants made in the Resident Magistrate's Court, (that is with respect to estates under $1.5 million) pursuant to the provisions of the Judicature (Resident Magistrates) Act, an administration bond is still required.

Accordingly, administration bonds sureties and justification of sureties are applicable only to applications for grants made in the Resident Magistrates Court

St Lucia [6]

Administration bonds are not usually required in St Lucia but may be ordered by the Court in the following circumstances:

(a) When any person takes letters of administration in default of the appearance of persons cited, but not personally served with the citation.
(b) If any person takes letters of administration for the use and benefit of a person of unsound mind, unless he is a curator appointed by the court.
(c) In practice, where the Registrar so requires, such as when the persons entitled to letters of administration are not in agreement or one or some of them is or are out of the jurisdiction of the court and cannot be located.

Guyana

According to s.30(2) of the Deceased Persons Estates' Administration Act Cap. 12:01,

> the court may require the administrator of any deceased person before the issue of letters of administration to give security in the amount and with sureties in the circumstances of each particular case, the Court deems reasonable for the due administration of and due accounting for, the estate.

Rule 5 of the Deceased Persons Estates' Administration Rules,[7] provides that the administrator or his attorney shall give a bond to cover the estate of the deceased within Guyana.

In practice the bond may be waived when the persons beneficially entitled to the deceased's estate give their written consent, with the approval of the Chief Justice, to the granting of letters of administration to the applicant(s) without the imposition of an administration bond.

Alternatively, a grant may be issued subject to a bond in instances where the attorney-at-law for the applicant undertakes, in writing, to ensure that the bond is given before any transaction or dealings with respect to the assets of the deceased are entered into or conducted. It is to be noted that the grant, though issued, is not released to the applicant until he either enters into the bond or he obtains an order of the court, waiving or dispensing with the required bond.

In practice a grant may be issued subject to a bond, in instances where the intended administrator is experiencing difficulty getting sureties for the bond, prior to the issue of the grant. In such circumstances the intended sureties may insist that the grant be issued before making the commitment to act as sureties.

Order for Waiver/Dispensing with Bonds

An order for waiver/dispensing with the requirements of a bond is made

(a) as a step subsequent to the issue of a grant subject to a bond, or
(b) at the same time as an application for the grant is lodged.

The application is made by summons supported by affidavit to the Chief Justice or to a judge assigned with the responsibility of granting probate for an order to dispense with/waive the requirement of a bond. The affidavit should set out *inter alia* the size, nature and value of the deceased's estate, the persons beneficially entitled thereto and the reasons for the application for waiver. In such instances the court will usually order the applicant to enter into a personal bond of a lesser sum.

It is to be noted that if the order is made and the grant was issued subject to a bond, a vide order is notated on the grant and the grant released to the applicant.

In practice an order dispensing with the requirement of a bond will not be made in circumstances where the estate comprises liquid assets only, proceeds of an insurance policy or where there are beneficiaries who are opposed to the waiver.

Waiver of Security

Trinidad & Tobago

Pursuant to s.81(2) of the Wills and Probate Ordinance Ch. 8 No. 2 unless the court otherwise orders, when the person applying is the widow or husband or only child or sole next of kin of the deceased or the Administrator General[8] or the Public Trustee, no security is required for the due administration of the estate. In practice these classes of persons are also exempted from giving a bond.

Penalty For Bond

The penalty for the bond depends on the jurisdiction concerned.

Trinidad & Tobago[9]

Unless the registrar otherwise directs, the penalty given for the bond is a minimum of the same amount as the value of the estate to be dealt with under the grant. The maximum by which this amount may be increased by the registrar may not exceed double the amount of the value of the real and personal estate.

Barbados, Grenada and Jamaica[10]

Unless otherwise directed by the registrar, the penalty of the bond is twice the value of the personal estate and twice the annual rateable value of the real estate placed in the possession of the administrator.

The Bahamas

According to r. 18 of The Probate Rules, Ch. 35 the penalty of the bond given is double the gross value of the personal estate. However pursuant to s.39(4) of the Supreme Court Act 15/1996 which became law on January 1, 1997 the penalty of the bond is now required to be double the amount at which the estate and effects of the deceased are sworn subject to the judge's discretion to reduce the amount thereof.[11]

Guyana

The amount of the penalty is the value of the estate to be covered by the estate in Guyana.[12]

Anguilla, Antigua &Barbuda, Dominica, Montserrat and St Christopher & Nevis

The penalty for the bond is the same as in England, that is, twice the gross value of the estate covered by the grant,[13] subject to the registrar's discretion to reduce the amount of the penalty or direct that more than one bond be given in the appropriate case.[14]

Form of Bond

The bond takes a prescribed form and should set out, *inter alia*, the following:

(i) the full name(s) and address(es) of the administrator(s) and sureties;
(ii) the amount of the penalty;
(iii) the title in which the administrator is applying; and
(iv) the name and address of the deceased.

Limitations on Estate to be administered

If there are any limitations imposed on the administrator with respect to the estate this must be stated after the words referring to the vesting of the estate in the personal representatives.

In the case of -

(a) second or subsequent grants, the words 'the estate left unadministered by A.B.';
(b) an infant/minor—the words 'for the use and benefit of the said infant/minor until he/she shall attain the age of 18/2 1 years as the case may be';
(c) incapacity—the words 'for the use and benefit of the said AB and during his incapacity';
(d) an attorney grant—the words 'for the use and benefit of the said AR until he shall apply for and obtain probate of the said will or letters of administration (with will annexed) of the said deceased, or for the use and benefit of the said AB and until further representation be granted as the case may be.'
(e) a *de bonis non* grant—the words 'the estate left unadministered by AB'; *(the former grantee)*

(For the appropriate words of limitations for the other types of limited grants see chapters 17 and 18.)

Execution

The signature of the administrator and any surety, not being a corporation, is required to be attested by an officer in the Registry authorised to administer oaths, or any other person duly authorised by law to administer oaths such as a Justice of the Peace, Notary Public or Commissioner for Oaths.

In the case of a corporation, the bond is executed by sealing in the manner prescribed by the corporation's constitution.

Assignment of Bond

When a condition of the administration bond has been broken, the court may on an application by some person interested in the deceased's estate, order the assignment of the bond to such person.[15] The application for assignment is made to a judge in chambers. An affidavit in support of the applications, setting out the details of the breach complained of, must also be filed, and copies served on the administrator and the sureties, if any.

Once the court is satisfied that a condition of the bond has been broken, an order assigning the grant to the applicant will be made. The assignee may then sue the administrator and sureties in his own name, as if the bond had originally been given to him instead of the registrar/judge, and to recover thereon as trustee to all persons interested, the full amount recoverable in respect of the breach of the condition(s) complained of.

Sureties

With the exception of Barbados and Jamaica,[16] where sureties are required, there must be a minimum of two sureties for every bond unless otherwise directed by the court. The sureties are the guarantors for the bond and they are liable both jointly and severally for any breach of the bond by the administrator. The registrar is required to ensure so far as possible that sureties are responsible persons. Additionally the sureties must be persons of full age and resident within the jurisdiction and because of the nature and extent of their liability they should be persons of some means.[17]

Non-Trust Corporation

When the proposed surety is a company or corporation (other than a trust corporation) an affidavit must be filed by the proper officer of the corporation to the effect that the officer is duly empowered to act as a surety and has executed the bond in accordance with the manner prescribed by its constitution. The affidavit should also contain sufficient information as to the sufficiency of assets of the company in the event of a breach of the bond by the administrator.[18]

No Surety Required

With the exception of Guyana, St Lucia and Trinidad & Tobago, sureties to the bond are required in practice, except where the grant is made to a trust corporation, a consular officer or otherwise where the registrar or Court directs. In Guyana, St Lucia and Trinidad & Tobago sureties to the bond are not required except where otherwise ordered by the registrar or Court, as the case may be.

Affidavit of Justification of Sureties

When sureties are required to justify they do so by filing an affidavit setting out the net worth in real and personal assets.[19]

All jurisdictions (save Barbados, Jamaica and Trinidad & Tobago)

In practice, where sureties are required, the sureties to an administration bond are not required to justify except where so directed by the registrar.[20] As stated previously, with respect to Jamaica, administration bonds are applicable only to applications for grants made in the Resident Magistrates court.

Barbados and Trinidad & Tobago

According to the relevant probate rule of Barbados and Trinidad & Tobago respectively,[21] the sureties to an administration bond are required to justify except where the registrar otherwise directs. But in practice sureties are not required in Trinidad & Tobago and consequently justification of sureties does not arise in practice. In Barbados sureties are required to justify in all cases unless otherwise directed by the registrar.

SURETY'S GUARANTEE - ST VINCENT & THE GRENADINES

Preliminary

By virtue of s.20 of the Administration of Estates Act Ch. 377, which is a verbatim reproduction of the equivalent English provision, the administration bond should have been replaced by the surety's guarantee as of December 27, 1989.[22]

Section 20(1) of the Administration of Estates Act Cap. 377, St Vincent & the Grenadines provides *inter alia*:

> As a condition of granting administration to any person the Court may, subject to the following provisions of this section. . . require one or more sureties to guarantee that they will make good, within any limit imposed by the court on the total liability of the surety or sureties, any loss which any person interested in the administration of the estate of the deceased may suffer in consequence of a breach by the administrator of his duties as such.

Further, by virtue of s.11(1) of the Supreme Court of Judicature Act of St Vincent, the so-called reception provision which receives the N.C.P.R., 1987 England, the surety's guarantee should no longer be mandatory. This is because the N.C.P.R 1987, contain no provision relating to guarantees. As such pursuant to s.20 of the Administration of Estates Act Cap. 377 and the N.C.P.R 1987, England a guarantee should be required only with respect to grants pending on December 27, 1989.

At the time of writing administration bonds are given in letters of administration.

Effect of Surety's Guarantee

Once the guarantee is given it endures to the benefit of every person interested in the administration of the deceased estate as if it were contained in a contract under seal made by the sureties. Further, as is the case with administration bonds, the sureties are both jointly and severally liable for any breach of duties by the administrator.

The requirements as to sureties, exemptions, justification and execution of the guarantee are the same as those which apply to the administration bond.

Form of Guarantee

The guarantee is in a prescribed form. The sureties are required to state that they are jointly and severally liable and that they will, when lawfully required to do so, make good any loss that any person interested in the administration of the estate of the deceased may suffer in consequence of the breach by the administrator of his duty with respect thereto.

The guarantee also sets out the maximum aggregate total liability of the sureties.

Enforcement of Guarantee

Any person interested in the deceased's estate may apply by summons for an order granting leave to bring an action against the surety/sureties for breach of a condition of the administration.

WILL BOND-JAMAICA[23]

In Jamaica, in any application for a grant of probate made in the Resident Magistrates Court, every executor is required to give or enter into a bond which is in a prescribed form. When the executor is resident abroad, a surety is required for the bond.[24]

In respect of applications made to the Supreme Court, the administration bond and will bond are no longer applicable pursuant to Rule 68 CPR 2002.

The Bahamas

Bond for Making Return into Registry and Paying Dues
In The Bahamas the executor or administrator is required to enter into a bond in the fixed sum of $400.[25]

Notes

1

		Legislation
	Barbados	- s.27 Succession Act Cap. 249
	Dominica, Antigua & Barbuda, Anguilla, Montserrat, St Christopher & Nevis	- s.167 Judicature Act 1925, England
	Grenada	- s.12 Probate Act Cap. 255
	Guyana	- s.30 Deceased Persons Estates' Administration Act Cap. 12:01
	Jamaica	- s.18 Administrator General Act
	St Lucia	- Art 602 Civil Code Ch. 242/Art 1023 Code of Civil Procedure Ch. 243
	St Vincent & the Grenadines	- s.20 Administration of Estates Act Cap. 377
	The Bahamas	- s.1 Probate Act Ch. 35
	Trinidad & Tobago	- s.81 Wills and Probate Ordinance Ch. 8 No. 2
		Rules
	All Jurisdictions	- With the passage in England of the Administration

		of Estates Act 1971, administration bonds were replaced with surety guarantees. As a consequence the original rr.38 and 39 N.C.P.R. 1954 were repealed and replaced by new rr.38 and 39. However the original rules, not the repealed rules are applicable to the Caribbean territories.
	Barbados	- r.30 Supreme Court (Non-Contentious) Probate Rules 1959
	Guyana	- r.5 Deceased Persons Estates' Administration Rules made under s.32 Deceased Persons Estates' Administration Act Cap. 12:01
	The Bahamas	- rr. 16, 17, 18, 19 The Probate Rules, Ch. 35
	Trinidad & Tobago	- rr. 33, 34, 35 First Schedule N.C.B.R. Ch. 8 No. 2. Forms
	Guyana	- See Schedule 2 of Deceased Persons Estates' Administration Rules Cap. 12:02
	Jamaica	- Forms Nos. 10 and 11 General Rules and Orders of the Supreme Court Part III Schedule of Forms (with respect to applications made in Resident Magistrates' Court only)
	The Bahamas	- Form X, XI, XII The Probate Rules Ch. 35.
2	Antigua & Barbuda, Montserrat, Dominica and The Bahamas	- To the Chief Justice or Judge of the Supreme Court
	Anguilla, Barbados, Grenada, St Vincent & the Grenadines, St Christopher & Nevis, Trinidad & Tobago	- To the Registrar of the Supreme Court
3	Barbados	- 5.27(1) Succession Act Cap. 249
	Grenada	- s.12(1) Probate Act Cap. 255
	Guyana	- s.30(1) Deceased Persons Estates' Administration Act Cap. 12:01
	The Bahamas	- r.18 The Probate Rules, Ch. 35
	Trinidad & Tobago	- s.81(1) Wills & Probate Ordinance Ch. 8 No.2.
4	Antigua & Barbuda	- s.20(2) Public Trustee Act 1993
	Barbados	- ss.27(5) and 27(6) Succession Act Cap. 249 s.12(5) Public Trustee Act Cap. 248
	Grenada	- s.12(4) Probate Act Cap. 255
	Guyana	- s.17(3) Public Trustee Act Cap. 13:01 s.13(4) Public Trustee Act Cap. 269
	St Vincent & the Grenadines	- s.13(5) Public Trustee Act Cap. 382
	The Bahamas	- s.15(3) Public Trustee Act Cap. 165; see also s.39 and 40 of the Supreme Court Act 15/1996.
	Trinidad & Tobago	- s.81(2) Wills & Probate Ordinance Ch. 8 No.2 s.13(4) Public Trustee Ordinance Ch. 8 No.4.
5	Trinidad & Tobago	- s.81 (2) Wills & Probate Ordinance Ch. 8 No. 2.
6	St Lucia	- Art 602 Civil Code Ch. 242; See also Art 1023

		Code of Civil Procedure Ch. 243.
7	Deceased Persons Estates' Administration Act Cap. 12:01.	
8	See also s.5 of the Administration of Estates Ordinance Ch. 8 No. 1.	
9	Trinidad & Tobago	- r.34 First Schedule N.C.B.R. Ch. 8 No. 2.
10	Barbados	- r.30 Supreme Court (Non-Contentious) Probate Rules 1959
	Grenada	- s.12(2) Probate Act Cap. 255
11	See s.52 which defines estate to include real and personal estate.	
12	r.5 Deceased Persons Estates' Administration Act Rules Cap 12:01.	
13	See s.82 Court of Probate Act 1857. England.	
14	*Ibid.* as amended by Grant of Administration (Bonds) Act 1919 (U.K.).	
15	Barbados	- s.27(4) Succession Act Cap. 249
	Eastern Caribbean,	- With respect to the assignment of bonds there are no indigenous procedural rules nor is there any substantive law setting out the practice and procedure relevant thereto. However the practice and procedure relevant hereto. However the practice with respect to assignment of bonds in these territories it is submitted is the same as that which obtains in the other territories.
	The Bahamas	- s.39(5) and s.39(6) Supreme Court Act 15/1996
	Trinidad & Tobago	- s.81(4) Wills and Probate Ordinance Ch. 8 No. 2
16	Barbados	- Pursuant to r.30 Supreme Court (Non-Contentious) Probate Rules 1959, unless otherwise expressly ordered by the court, only one surety is required to an administration bond,
	Jamaica	- Pursuant to r.20 General Orders and Rules of the Supreme Court Part III Probate and Administration, the administrator is required to give bond with one or more surety or sureties; in practice only one surety is required. (applicable only to applications for grants made in the Resident Magistrates' Court)
17	Barbados	- s.27 Succession Act Cap. 249 - r.31 Supreme Court (Non-Contentious) Probate Rules 1959
	Grenada	- s.12(1) Probate Act Cap. 255
	Guyana, Eastern Caribbean territories (save St Lucia)	- r.38 (2) & (4) N.C.P.R. 1954, England -
	St Lucia	- Art 1023 code of Civil Procedure Ch. 243; Art 602 Civil code ch. 242
	The Bahamas	- r.17 the Probate Rules Ch. 35
	Trinidad & Tobago	- r.35 First Schedule N.C.B.R. Ch. 8 No. 2.
18	The Original r.38(7) N.C.P.R. 1954, England Barbados, Guyana, Eastern Caribbean territories, The Bahamas	
19	Barbados	- Form No. 6 appendix (Forms and Fees) Supreme Court (Non-Contentious) Probate Rules, 1959
20	The Bahamas,	- The original r.39 N.C.P.R. 1954, England.

	Guyana, Eastern Caribbean (save St Lucia)	
21	Barbados	- r.31 Supreme Court (Non-Contentious) Probate Rules 1959
	Trinidad & Tobago	- r.35 First Schedule N.C.B.R. Ch. 8 No. 2.
22	The commencement date of the Administration of Estates Act Cap. 377.	
23	Jamaica	- See the repealed r.5 General Rules and Orders of the Supreme Court part III Probate and Administration
24	See chapter 5 p. 117.	
25	The Bahamas (Corporation)	- s.2 Probate Act Ch. 35; r.17 The Probate Rules Ch. 35.

12

Minority and Life Interest and Second Administrators

INTRODUCTION

Eastern Caribbean territories (save St Lucia) The Bahamas and Jamaica

The law and practice with respect to minority, life interest and second administrators are applicable to the Eastern Caribbean territories (save St Lucia),[1] and more recently the Bahamas with the passage of the Supreme Court Act 15 1996,[2] and to a qualified extent, to Jamaica, as a consequence of the passage of the CPR 2002.

MINORITY AND LIFE INTEREST

Pursuant to:

(a)   (i)   s.14(2) and (3) of the Administration of Estates Act Cap. 377, St Vincent & the Grenadines,
        (ii)   s.114(2) and (3) of the Supreme Court Act 1981, England—Eastern Caribbean territories (save St Vincent & the Grenadines),[3] and

(b)   r.6(2) of the N.C.P.R. 1954, England in the case of Dominica and r.8(4) N.C.P.R. 1987, England with respect to the other Eastern Caribbean territories,

on an application for a grant of administration the oath must state whether or not any minority or life interest arises under a will or intestacy.

Accordingly, the oath to lead a grant of administration (with or without will annexed) must include a statement as to whether or not a minority or life interest arises under the deceased's will or intestacy.

The Bahamas

Although s.42(2) and (3) of the Supreme Court Act 15/1996 are essentially the same as s.114(2) and (3) of the Supreme Court Act, 1981, England, s.42 specifically provides that the requirements with respect to minority and life interests, are applicable not only to grants of administration but are also applicable to grants of probate. The oath to lead a grant of probate as well as administration (with or without will annexed) should, with respect to applications for grants made on or after June 1, 1997, include a recital as to whether or not a minority or life interest arises under the deceased's will or intestacy.

Jamaica

The Forms prescribed for the respective oaths to lead grants of probate, letters of administration with or without will annexed, (Forms P1, P3 and P5 Appendix 2 CPR 2002), all include a recital as to whether or not a minority or life interest arises under the will or intestacy of the deceased. However, there is no requirement either in the substantive law or in the provisions of Rule 68 CPR 2002, for the appointment of a co-administrator where such minority or life interest arises. Accordingly, other than including this recital in the respective oaths to lead the relevant grants of representation, the requirement that a co-administrator be appointed in such instances, does not apply to Jamaica, in the absence of express rules or statutory provision(s) to the contrary.

SECOND ADMINISTRATOR

In accordance with s.14(2) of the Administration of Estates Act Cap. 377, St Vincent & the Grenadines, and s.114(2) of the Supreme Court Act, 1981, England, the provisions of which are incorporated into and form part of the probate law of the Eastern Caribbean territories, a second administrator is required wherever a minority or life interest arises under a will or intestacy, subject to certain exceptions.

In the case of The Bahamas, subject to the exceptions outlined below, s.42(2) of the Supreme Court Act 15/1996 provides that where a minority or life interest arises under the deceased's will or intestacy, a second administrator is required both in cases of administration as well as probate.

EXCEPTIONS

A grant of letters of administration, and in the case of The Bahamas, a grant of probate where applicable, may be issued to one individual in the following instances:

- where the applicant for the grant of administration is a trust corporation.[4]
- where the application is for a grant *pendente lite*.[5]
- where the application is for a grant to a Consular official under the relevant Administration of Consular Convention Acts of the respective Eastern Caribbean territories and The Bahamas;
- in any circumstances where it appears expedient to the court to appoint one individual.

Such circumstances include, in practice, those when the proposed administrator is a solicitor or an accountant; and those when the minority interest is with respect to a minor shortly to attain the age of majority.

No Order Required [6]

Where there are two or more persons equally entitled in priority to take out the relevant grant of administration, two or more of them, up to a maximum of four, may apply for the relevant grant of administration with or without will annexed.

If, there is only one person with a prior right to the grant, such person may in certain circumstances, without leave of the court, nominate a second administrator to act as co-grantee. Accordingly, nomination by a co-administrator may be made in the following circumstances:

(a) When, on a testacy or intestacy, the proposed second administrator is one of the class of persons next entitled to be joined as co-grantee with the applicant for the grant.

(b) When, on a testacy or intestacy, the proposed second administrator, not being one of the class of persons next entitled, is on the renunciation of all those persons in the intermediate class, next entitled to be joined as co-grantee.

(c) When the proposed second grantee is any kin of the deceased having no beneficial interest in the estate; provided all persons with a prior right to be joined as second administrator have renounced.

(d) When the proposed second grantee is nominated by the guardian (testamentary, statutory or court-appointed) of a minor for whose use and benefit the application for the grant is being made; provided that there is no other person competent and willing to join with the guardian in the application for the grant.

(e) When the only other person entitled to act as second grantee is a minor, the guardian (testamentary, statutory or court-appointed) of the minor may be joined as co-grantee.

(f) When the second administrator is nominated by the first applicant being the only person willing and competent to take out a grant of administration for the use and benefit of an incapable person and during his incapacity; provided that all those entitled to act as second administrator have renounced.
(g) When the second administrator is a trust corporation; in such instances the consents of all those entitled to act as second administrator should be lodged in the Registry.
(h) When the co-applicant for the grant is the duly appointed attorney of the person first entitled to the grant.
(i) When the proposed second administrator is the attorney of the person next or equally entitled. In such cases the grant of letters of administration with or without will annexed, will be 'limited until further representation be granted'.[7]

Form of Nomination

The nomination by the first applicant of the proposed second grantee should be lodged in the Registry with the papers to lead the grant. The nomination should set out:

(i) the place and date of death of the deceased;
(ii) the minority or life interest arising under the estate of the deceased;
(iii) the entitlement of the first applicant to take out the relevant grant of administration, and with respect to The Bahamas, the grant of probate;
(iv) the clearing off by renunciation or otherwise of any persons having a prior right to act as second administrator;
(v) any facts relevant to the circumstances of each case.

ORDER REQUIRED

In all other instances the second administrator must be appointed by order of the court. In making the application, in the Eastern Caribbean territories, whether made pursuant to Rule 23 NCPR 1954 England or rule 26 NCPR 1987 England, the application, in practice, is not made in accordance with the general practice and procedure set out in Part 11 CPR 2000.[8]

Applications under r.23 Non-contentious Probate Rules 1954,

England, Dominica

The application for an order for joinder is made to the registrar or a judge in chambers in accordance with the procedure and practice set out in Part 11 of the CPR 2000. The affidavit in support should set out details of the first grant and the subsistence of a life and/or minority interest. The written consent of the proposed second administrator should be lodged with the affidavit together with any such evidence that the court may require. The Part 11 application is served on the persons who are equally entitled to take out the grant and on all persons in a lower degree but in priority to the proposed second administrator. The appointment of the second administrator is recorded on the original grant.

Application under r. 26 of Non-contentious Probate Rules 1987.

England, Eastern Caribbean territories (save Dominica) and The Bahamas

An application for the appointment of an additional administrator under s. 114(4) of the Supreme Court Act 1981, England, and s.14(4) of the Administration of Estates Act Cap. 377, St Vincent & the Grenadines, is made in accordance with the Part 11 application, CPR 2000. With respect to The Bahamas, pursuant to s.42(4) of the Supreme Court Act 15/1996, the application should be made *ex parte* on affidavit to the registrar.

Affidavit/Oath to Lead Grant of Administration

Whether or not an order of joinder of a co-grantee is necessary, the affidavit/oath to lead the relevant grant of administration must in all instances specify whether there is a minority interest and a life interest arising under the will or intestacy of the deceased. In addition, where applicable, the clearing off of all persons, with prior rights to act as second administrator must also be recited.

APPOINTMENT OF ADDITIONAL GRANTEE
(After Grant has been issued)

According to s.14(4) of the Administration of Estates Act Cap. 377, St Vincent & the Grenadines and s.114(4) of The Supreme Court Act, 1981, England, with respect to the other Eastern Caribbean territories and s.42(4) of the Supreme Court Act 15/1996, with respect to The Bahamas:

if at anytime during the minority of a beneficiary or the subsistence of a life interest under a will or intestacy, there is only one personal representative (not being a trust corporation), any person interested or the guardian or receivers of such person may in accordance with the relevant probate rules apply to the Court for the appointment of an additional personal representative to act during the subsistence of the minority or life interest until the estate is fully administered. The application for the appointment of an additional representative after the issue of a grant usually arises where one of two grantees has died or if it is subsequently discovered that a previously unknown minority or life interest arises.

By virtue of the above provisions, the appointment of an additional personal representative to act with an executor does not have the effect of including him in any chain of representation.

Procedure and Practice

Dominica

In accordance with r.24 of the N.C.P.R. 1954, England, the application for an order appointing an additional administrator was previously made by summons. However, in accordance with the new CPR 2000, the application is made in practice by a Part 11 application supported by affidavit setting out all relevant facts. In addition, the written consent of the proposed co-administrator must also be lodged together with any other evidence as the registrar may require.

Eastern Caribbean territories (save Dominica) and the Bahamas

Although not expressly provided for an application for the appointment of an administrator should be made in accordance with Part 11 applications as set out in CPR 2000 instead of *ex parte* on affidavit as prescribed by r.26 NCPR 1987, England. Additionally, the written consent to act of the proposed co-grantee is required to be lodged as well as any other evidence that the Registrar may require. With respect to The Bahamas, the application is made by summons to a judge in chambers.

Practice Note

According to r.26 N.C.P.R., 1987/r.24 N.C.P.R, 1954 respectively, on any such application, the registrar may direct that a note be made on the original grant of the addition of a further representative or he may impound or revoke the grant or make such other order as the circumstances may require.

Post-Script

Grenada

There is some contention as to whether the affidavit to lead a grant of administration should include a recital with respect to minority and life interests. Some attorneys-at-law are of the view, not without some justification, that the English law and procedure with respect to minority and life interests and second administrators are not received in Grenada because the procedural requirements came into existence in England as a consequence of the land laws which were enacted in England in 1925. These land laws provided *inter alia* that a minor could not hold a legal interest in land as was previously the position under the common law. Accordingly because of the change in the English land laws, provisions were enacted as a means of accounting for and protecting the interest of minors and persons whose interest in land was limited to a life interest. In Grenada, a minor can still hold a legal interest in land as the common law is still applicable. As such it is argued by some attorneys-at-law that in the absence of indigenous legislation the requirement with respect to minority and life interests and second administrators is not applicable to Grenada.

Notes

1. St Lucia — English probate law is not received in St Lucia. As a result the English law with respect to minority and life interests and second administrators is not applicable to St Lucia. See Introduction, p. 9-10. Accordingly, St Lucia is hereafter excluded from the term Eastern Caribbean, as it appears in this chapter.
2. See also Introduction, p.10 with respect to the reception of probate law in The Bahamas.
3. St Vincent & the Grenadines — The provisions of s.14(2) and (3) of the Administration of Estates Act Cap. 377 St Vincent and the Grenadines are identical to those of s. 114(2) and (3) of the Supreme Court Act, 1981.

    s.114(2) provides:

    'Where under a will or intestacy any beneficiary is a minor or a life interest arises, any grant of administration by the High Court shall be made either to a trust corporation (with or without an individual) or to not less than two individuals, unless it appears to the court to be expedient in all the circumstances to appoint an individual as sole administrator.'

    s.114(3) further provides:

'For the purpose of determining whether a minority or life interest arises in any particular case the court may act on such evidence as may be prescribed'.

4   Pursuant to s.14(2) of the Administration of Estates Act Cap. 377; with respect to St Vincent and the Grenadines, and s.114(2) of the Supreme Court Act 1981. England, with respect to the Eastern Caribbean and s.42 Supreme Court Act 15/1996 with respect to The Bahamas.
5   See *Re Haslip* [1958] 2 All E.R. 275; [1958] 1 W.L.R. 583.
6   Dominica   - rr.21, 23. 31(4) N.C.P.R. 1954, England
    Eastern Caribbean   - rr.25(1), 25(3), 32(3), 35(3) N.C.P.R. 1987, England.
    territories (save Dominica)
7   By virtue of a Practice Direction of the High Court of England dated 22 February, 1949, the written consent of the first grantee to this special form of limitation must be obtained. If the first grantee will not consent to this limitation, an application for joinder of the attorney of the person equally or next entitled to be joined as second administrator must be made to the Registrar/Judge in Chambers supported by affidavit. Upon the making of the order, a general grant will be made to the first applicant and the donor's attorney. The donor of the power will have lost all rights to subsequently displace his attorney and apply for a grant to himself. As such the donors written consent to such a grant being made, must first be obtained.

13

Deceased Dying Domiciled Outside Jurisdiction

INTRODUCTION

Where a person dies domiciled outside of the respective Caribbean jurisdictions considered in this text, and leaves property located therein, the original grant obtained in the country of domicile may be resealed, provided that the deceased's country of domicile is one to which resealing applies. Where resealing is not applicable, an ancillary grant, depending on the jurisdiction concerned, will have to be obtained in the respective Caribbean territory, to lawfully administer the deceased's property located there.

In this regard, the following should be noted:

St. Lucia, Barbados and Antigua & Barbuda[1]

In the case of St. Lucia and Barbados, grants may be resealed from any part of the world. Ancillary grants, therefore, would not arise in practice. In Antigua, quite apart from the fact that grants issued out of a British Commonwealth territory and the U.S.A. can be resealed, the practice and procedure which is adopted in respect of grants issued in these territories, is not the procedure and practice relevant to an ancillary grant application.

Trinidad & Tobago and Anguilla[2]

In Trinidad & Tobago and Anguilla, as in the case with all the other jurisdictions considered in this text (other than St. Lucia, Barbados and to a limited extent, Antigua & Barbuda), resealing applications are restricted to grants issuing out of British Commonwealth territories. However, it is not the practice to apply for ancillary grants where resealing is not an alternative. Instead, the application for the grant in these jurisdictions is made in the same manner as a general grant of representation subject to the special requirements in respect thereto.

All jurisdictions (save St. Lucia, Antigua & Barbuda, Anguilla, Barbados and Trinidad & Tobago).

In these jurisdictions, as in the case in Trinidad & Tobago and Anguilla, resealing is limited to grants obtained in a British Commonwealth territory, pursuant to the relevant statutory provision of these territories.

Accordingly, an ancillary grant must be obtained in Guyana, Jamaica, and the Eastern Caribbean territories (save St. Lucia, Antigua & Barbuda and Anguilla) in the absence of local practice, statutory provision or subsidiary legislation to the contrary.

ADMISSIBILITY AND REVOCABILITY OF WILL AND ENTITLEMENT TO GRANT

Where resealing is not an alternative, irrespective of whether an ancillary grant is or is not applied for, the admissibility of a will to proof and its revocability must be determined in accordance with the law and practice relevant to the respective jurisdiction.

With respect to entitlement to the grant, in cases where resealing is not an alternative, and the jurisdiction is one to which ancillary grants apply, the entitlement of the applicant to the ancillary grant must be determined in accordance with the relevant probate rules of the respective jurisdiction whether, indigenous or received.

ADMISSIBILITY OF WILL TO PROOF

Admissibility to proof of the testamentary dispositions made under the will of a deceased person who has died domiciled outside the jurisdiction, in which an application for a grant with respect to his estate is made, is generally dependent on whether the common law or the statutory position applies to the respective Caribbean territory.

A. Common Law Position

Anguilla,[3] *Guyana, and Jamaica*

Movable Estate

According to the common law, a will is valid to pass movable estate if it is executed in accordance with the law of the testator's last place of domicile, a factor which may sometimes cause hardship if the testator subsequently changed his domicile since executing his will.

Anguilla, Jamaica, Guyana, and Trinidad & Tobago

Immovable Estate

In so far as immovable estate is concerned, a will is deemed to be valid if it is executed in accordance with the law of the country where the estate is situated (the *lex situs*). Accordingly, in the above-mentioned territories a will is valid to pass immovable estate only if it is executed in accordance with the statutory provisions relevant to the execution of wills in these territories.[4]

B. Statutory Position[5]

Trinidad & Tobago — Movable Estate only

According to s.41 of the Wills and Probate Ordinance Ch. 8 No. 2, a will made outside of Trinidad & Tobago by a Commonwealth citizen[6] is deemed to be properly executed in so far as the validity of testamentary dispositions of personal estate (which includes leaseholds) is concerned, irrespective of the domicile of the deceased at the time of death, provided that:

(i) it was executed in accordance with the law of the place where it was made; or
(ii) it is valid by the law of the place where the testator was domiciled when it was made; or
(iii) it is valid by the law in force in a Commonwealth territory where the testator had his domicile of origin.

In every other case in which the testator is not a Commonwealth citizen, the common law position applies.

Eastern Caribbean territories (save Antigua & Barbuda and Anguilla) and The Bahamas

Pursuant to:

(a) s.4 of the Wills Act Cap. 384, St Vincent & the Grenadines; and
(b) the Wills (Formal Validity) Ordinance 37/1965, St Lucia;[7] and

(c) The Wills Act 1963, England, in so far as the other Eastern Caribbean territories (save Antigua & Barbuda and Anguilla) are concerned,[8] and
(d) ss.35 and 36 of the Wills Act 2002, with respect to the Bahamas,

A will is treated as properly executed with respect to real and personal property, irrespective of the date of the will, the domicile, residence or nationality of the testator. It must however, be executed in accordance with the internal law in force in the territory where it was executed, or in the territory where at the time of its execution or of the testator's death, he:

(a) was domiciled; or
(b) had his habitual residence; or
(c) was in a state of which, at either one of those times, he was a national.

Additionally, a will is deemed to be properly executed in these territories:

(d) if it is executed on board a vessel or aircraft of any description and the execution of the will conforms to the internal law in force in the territory with which, having regard to its registration (if any) and other relevant circumstances, the vessel or aircraft may be taken to have been most closely connected;
(e) where it disposes of immovable estate, provided its execution conforms to the internal law in force in the territory where the property is situate.

Antigua & Barbuda

For the purposes of giving validity to the will of a deceased person, there must be compliance with the statutory formalities for execution of wills provided for by the Wills Act Cap. 473. This is irrespective of the deceased's place of domicile.

Barbados

The statutory provision in Barbados is effectively the same as that in the Eastern Caribbean territories (save Antigua & Barbuda and Anguilla).

According to s.86 of the Succession Act Cap. 249 a testamentary disposition is valid if it complies with the internal law:

(a) of the place where the testator made it; or,
(b) of a nationality possessed by the testator either at the time when he

(c) of a place in which the testator had his domicile either at the time when he made the disposition or at the time of his death; or
(d) of the place in which the testator had his habitual residence either at the time when he made the disposition or at the time of his death; or
(e) in so far as immovables are concerned, of the place where they are situated. In this regard, s.87 provides that a testamentary disposition made on board a vessel or aircraft shall also be valid if its form complies with the internal law of the place with which, having regard to its registration (if any) and any other relevant circumstances, the vessel or aircraft may be taken to have had the most real connection.

AFFIDAVIT AS TO FOREIGN LAW

Where a deceased dies testate and domiciled outside the jurisdiction in which a grant with respect to his estate is being sought, an affidavit as to foreign law may have to be filed with the papers to lead the grant in order *inter alia* to admit the will to proof and consequently give validity to the testamentary dispositions made thereunder.

- Will proved by the court of domicile

All jurisdictions (save Anguilla, Antigua & Barbuda, Guyana, Jamaica, The Bahamas and Trinidad & Tobago)

As a general rule where the will of a deceased person has been proved by a court of competent jurisdiction in the deceased's place of domicile, it will be accepted as properly executed, without the need to file an affidavit as to foreign law.

Anguilla, Guyana, Jamaica, The Bahamas and Trinidad & Tobago

Where the will of a deceased person has been proved by a competent court of jurisdiction in the deceased's place of domicile, it should be accepted as properly executed only insofar as testamentary dispositions of personal estate are concerned. With respect to testamentary dispositions of real estate situate in the above territories, such disposition should be invalid unless the will was executed in accordance with the formalities for execution of wills within these territories.

Accordingly, with respect to the admissibility to proof of testamentary dispositions of real estate, the equivalent of an affidavit of due execution should be filed irrespective of whether the will has or has not been proved by a competent court of jurisdiction in the deceased's place of domicile. However in practice, where a grant has been previously obtained from a court in the deceased's place of domicile, it is deemed to be valid to pass testamentary dispositions of real and personal property. Additionally, in practice an affidavit as to foreign law, which is required in instances where a grant was not previously obtained, is deemed to cover testamentary dispositions of the deceased's real and personal estate.

Antigua & Barbuda

In Antigua & Barbuda, a will is valid, both with respect to real and personal estate, only if it complies with the statutory formalities set out in the Wills Act Cap. 473, Antigua. Accordingly, an affidavit of due execution, not an affidavit as to foreign law, is necessary to give validity to testamentary dispositions of real and personal property.

Contents of Affidavit as to Foreign Law

Where an affidavit of foreign law is required, it is deposed to by an attorney-at-law or some other person suitably qualified to give expert evidence to the effect that the will was executed in accordance with the formalities applicable *inter alia* to the deceased's domicile or residence as may be relevant to the respective territories. The affidavit insofar as it purports to give effect to the validity of the will and in particular the testamentary dispositions made thereunder, should be dependent on whether the common law or statutory position is applicable to the Caribbean territory in which court the will is sought to be admitted.[9]

The affidavit as to foreign law should recite the following:

(i) that the deponent is an attorney-at-law/notary public/advocate and is conversant with the laws of the foreign territory and that he is an attorney-at-law/notary public/advocate in that country for 'X' years as the case may be;

(ii) that a certified copy of the will was produced to the deponent and marked by him;

(iii) that the will was made in conformity with and is valid by the law of the foreign country concerned;

(iv) where the will is a certified copy of a notarial will, the affidavit should set out that the original will is in the permanent custody of the notary public; that it cannot be extracted; and that a notarial copy is accepted in evidence in the country where the deceased died domiciled.

(v) where applicable, the affidavit should also deal with the applicant's entitlement to administer the testator's estate;
(vi) *The Bahamas, Barbados and Eastern Caribbean territories (save Antigua & Barbuda and Anguilla)*
where there is more than one system of law in the territory concerned, the affidavit must recite which system of law is relied upon and in particular it should state if the system of law is applicable by virtue of a rule of law in force throughout the territory. If that is the case, the affidavit should recite the system of law to which the deceased was most connected at the time of execution of the will.

AFFIDAVIT OF FACTS

Where the will of a person dying domiciled abroad is required to be proved, affidavit evidence of the facts relied upon must be filed. The affidavit should include, where applicable:

(i) the place of execution of the will;
(ii) the domicile of the testator at the time of execution of the will or at his death as the case may be; and
(iii) the habitual residence of the testator at the date of his death.

INTERNATIONAL WILLS

Barbados

By virtue of s.86 of the Succession Act Cap. 249 international wills, that is, wills made in accordance with the provisions of the Annex to the Convention on International Wills entered into force on 9th February, 1978, are admissible to probate in Barbados irrespective of the place of execution.

The Bahamas

Section 6 of the Wills Act 2002, makes provision for the Minister to make regulations governing the validity and recognition to wills and other testamentary dispositions with a foreign element executed on board an aircraft or vessel or which for any other reason may not comply with the law of The Bahamas.

ENTITLEMENT TO ANCILLARY GRANT

All jurisdictions (save Antigua & Barbuda, Anguilla, Barbados, St. Lucia and Trinidad& Tobago)

With respect to those jurisdictions to which ancillary grants are applicable, either by practice or in accordance with the relevant non-contentious probate rule, whether indigenous or received, the entitlement of the applicant to the ancillary grant must first be determined before an application for an ancillary grant may be made.

1. Grants to Executor, Executor According to The Tenor[10]

An executor including an executor according to the tenor or his attorney on his behalf may be granted probate of the will of a testator who has died domiciled abroad without an order of the registrar/judge in chambers, provided it is admissible to proof in the territory concerned.

The executor and the person, if any, entrusted with the administration of the deceased's estate by the court of domicil are equally entitled to apply for the relevant grant of the deceased's estate. However if the person entrusted and the executor are the same person, he may elect to apply in either capacity. If he elects to apply as the person entrusted he must first obtain an order of the court.

The usual documents for a probate grant are required to be filed subject to the following:

1. An affidavit as to foreign law/certificate of a Notary Public, where applicable, should be lodged with the papers to lead the grant. The will should be marked as an exhibit in the usual way.
2. The oath should recite the place of domicil of the deceased and should describe the applicant as the person appointed by the will of the testator who died domiciled outside the jurisdiction.

2. Grants with respect to Immovable Estate only[11]

Where the whole of the estate of the deceased within the Caribbean territory concerned, consists of immovable property, or in the case of Jamaica, wholly or substantially all of the immovable property, a grant may be made without an order of the court in accordance with the law which would have been applicable if the deceased had died within that territory.

In addition, the rules with respect to entitlement to grants of representation within the relevant territory are applicable irrespective of whether the deceased died testate or intestate.

Oath to lead Grant

The oath should recite that the deceased died possessed of immovable property within the territory concerned and the grant will accordingly be limited to such property.

3. Person Entrusted by Court of Domicile[12]

Where the grant of representation or similar authority has been issued by a court of competent jurisdiction in the country where the deceased died domiciled, an application for the relevant grant of representation may be made by the person entrusted with the administration of the estate of the deceased or alternatively by the attorney of such person.

The grant issued to the applicant in such circumstances will only be made where a grant or similar order of the court of domicil of the deceased has been issued. Cases of doubt should be referred to the registrar/judge in chambers.

Except where the person entrusted is the executor or attorney of the executor or where the estate of the deceased situate in the relevant Caribbean jurisdiction, consists solely of, or in the case of Jamaica, wholly or substantially of immovable property, an application for an order for the grant to be made to the person entrusted by the court of domicil is required to be made *ex parte* by lodging the following documents:

1. an affidavit of facts sworn to by the applicant deposing to the relevant facts to lead the order including the place of domicil of the deceased, whether he died testate or intestate and the issue of the grant or similar authority by the deceased's country of domicile;
2. the grant, decree, order or authority or official copy thereof under the seal of the court of issue, empowering the applicant to collect and administer the deceased's estate, including an official copy of the will, if any, of the deceased.
3. the certified copy of the power of attorney - where the applicant for the grant is the attorney of the person entrusted;
4. where the grant or authority is in a foreign language, a notarised translation thereof;
5. *Guyana, Jamaica and The Bahamas*
   An affidavit of due execution should be lodged with respect to immovables as the affidavit as to foreign law is applicable to testamentary dispositions of personal estate only.

However, it is to be noted that once the will, if any, has been accepted as a valid testamentary document, an affidavit as to foreign law is not required.

PROCEDURE AFTER GRANTING OF ORDER

Once the order is made, the above documents (2 to 5) or office copies, should then be lodged in the Registry, together with the following:

1. covering letter/application for the grant;
2. a copy of the order granting leave to the person entrusted, where the application for the grant is made pursuant to an order of the court;
3. The oath should include the following:
   (i) in cases where the applicant is the executor, that he is the person entrusted with the administration of the deceased's estate by the court having jurisdiction at the place where the deceased died domiciled;[12] or alternatively
   (ii) in cases where the person entrusted has been appointed by an order of the Registrar/Judge in Chambers, that by Order of Mr Registrar/Mr Justice dated the .... day of .... 20xx, it was ordered that letters of administration (with will annexed) of the estate of the said deceased be granted to AB/BC, the applicant(s) named therein;
   (iii) the place of domicile of the deceased;
   (iv) where the application is made by an attorney, the following words of limitation; 'for the use and benefit of the said AB/CD and until further representation be granted';
   (v) the gross value of the estate to be covered by the grant.

Eastern Caribbean territories (save Anguilla, Antigua & Barbuda and St. Lucia) and Jamaica

   (vi) The usual recitals with respect to minority and life interests.

4. The bond, where applicable should recite that the applicant is a person authorised to draw the grant by order of Mr Justice/Mr Registrar dated 20XX. The gross value of the estate should also be recited and in cases where the application is made by an attorney, the words of limitation as stated in the oath.
5. Justification of sureties, where required.
6. Inventory, Statement of Assets and Liabilities, Affidavit of Value, or its equivalent—limited to particulars of the value of the estate to be covered by the grant.

7. Estate/Stamp Duty Certificate, or its equivalent in the various territories, where applicable.
8. *Eastern Caribbean territories (save Anguilla, Antigua & Barbuda and St. Lucia) and The Bahamas*
   Nomination of a co-administrator, if according to the terms of the will or the law of the deceased's domicil, a minority or life interest arises.

Filing documents for both applications

The documents necessary for the preliminary order of appointment and the papers to lead the grant may also be filed at the same time. However where this alternative is adopted the date of the granting of the order will be left blank in the oath and the bond to be inserted therein, by the registrar, upon the making of the order.

4. Person Beneficially Entitled by Law of Domicile[13]

An application for a grant to a person entitled by the law of domicil is made in circumstances where grants of representation or similar authorities are not issued by the court in the country of domicil of the deceased (as is the case in most European and Latin American countries).

In such instances an *ex parte* application is required to be made to the registrar/judge in chambers for an order for a grant to be issued to the person beneficially entitled to the deceased's estate by the law of the place where the deceased died domiciled. In addition the admissibility of the deceased's will, if any, should be dealt with in this application.

The *ex parte* application is made prior to the application for the grant by lodging the following documents:

1. The will or official sealed copy; where the will is a notarial will, a certified copy should be lodged (in cases where the deceased died testate);
2. A Notary Public's certificate or an affidavit sworn by an attorney-at-law or other person who can give expert evidence on the law of the territory with respect to:

   (a) entitlement to grant; and
   (b) admissibility to proof of the will, if any.

In this regard, the certificate or affidavit should set out:

(i) the facts relevant to the case including the place of domicil of the deceased;
(ii) whether he died testate or intestate;
(iii) that the will, if any, was made in conformity with and is valid by the law of the deceased's domicile or of the foreign country concerned as the case may be
(iv) by reference to the facts, the law with respect to beneficial entitlement (including the priorities with respect thereto) to the estate of the deceased person in the country of domicile. The will, if any, should be marked as an exhibit.

3. Where the will is in a foreign language, a translation thereof certified by a Notary Public or other qualified person.
4. The certified copy of the power of attorney where the application is made by an attorney of the person beneficially entitled.
5. *Guyana, Jamaica and The Bahamas*
An affidavit of due execution should be lodged with respect to immovables as the affidavit as to foreign law is applicable to testamentary dispositions of personal estate only.

No order

The order granting leave to apply for the relevant grant as a person beneficially entitled, will not be made where the deceased died domiciled in a place where to the court's knowledge, grants of representation are normally required, such as the U.S.A. In such instances, the usual practice is first to extract a grant in the country of the deceased's domicile.

Once the order is granted, the applicant may proceed to apply for the relevant grant of representation.

Documents to lead the Grant

The above documents (2 to 5), together with those which are filed with respect to grants made to a person entrusted by the court of domicile should be lodged in the Registry save that;

1. The oath/affidavit of the applicant should include the following recitals:
    i. a description of the applicant as the person authorised by order of Mr Registrar AB/Mr Justice CD dated 20XX as the person beneficially entitled to the estate of the deceased where he died domiciled. (A copy of the order granting leave to the applicant should be filed with the application)

ii. the place of domicile of the deceased.
iii. where the application is made by the attorney(s) of the applicant, the words of limitation 'for his/her use and benefit until further representation be granted'.
2. The bond should also describe the applicant as the person authorised to obtain a grant by order of Mr Registrar/Mr Justice dated 20XX Additionally where the application is made by an attorney, the bond should recite the words of limitation included in the oath of an attorney.

Procedural Alternative

The documents necessary for the preliminary order of appointment and the papers to lead the grant may also be filed at the same time.

5. Discretionary Powers of the Court[14]

The court has the discretion to issue a grant to such person as it thinks fit in cases:

(a) where no person has been entrusted to administer the deceased's estate by the court having jurisdiction at the place where the deceased died domiciled;
(b) where there is no person beneficially entitled to the estate by the law of the place of domicile; and,
(c) where in the opinion of the court, the circumstances so require, even though there is some person so entrusted or beneficially entitled who is willing and able to act.

In such instances, an application for an order of appointment is made *ex parte* to the registrar/judge in chambers before the oath and bond are drawn up. The application is made by lodging the following documents:

1. An affidavit of facts reciting *inter alia*:
   (i)   the death of the deceased;
   (ii) whether he died testate or intestate;
   (iii) the domicile of the deceased at the date of death
   (iv) the circumstances in which the order is being sought;
   (v)   and, where applicable, the reason why no grant has been applied for in the court where the deceased died domiciled.
2. The will or official sealed copy thereof; where the will is a notarial will, a certified copy should be lodged (in cases where the deceased died testate);

3. A Notary Public's certificate or an affidavit as to foreign law setting out *inter alia*, by reference to the facts of the case, the person(s) beneficially entitled to the deceased's estate in accordance with the law of the deceased's and where applicable entitlement thereto in order of priority. The validity of any will should also be dealt with.
4. *Guyana and The Bahamas*
An affidavit of due execution should be filed to give effect to testamentary dispositions of immovables.
5. Certified copy of power of attorney, where applicable.

Documents to lead the Grant

Once the order is granted, the above documents (2 to 5), together with the equivalent of the documents which are filed with respect to grants made to a person entrusted by the law of domicil, should be lodged save that:

(1) The oath should:
 (i) describe the applicant as the person authorised to obtain a grant by order of Mr Registrar AB/Mr Justice CD dated 20XX;
 (ii) state the domicile of the deceased;
 (iii) give details of the order;
 (iv) describe the estate covered by the grant within the jurisdiction, and with the exception of Barbados and St Lucia, the value of the estate to be covered by the grant; and
(2) The bond should describe the applicant as the person authorised (as in the oath);

Procedural Alternative

Alternatively the documents necessary for the preliminary order of appointment and the papers to lead the grant may be filed at the same time.

APPLICATION FOR GRANTS OF REPRESENTATION

Where Deceased Died Domiciled Outside of Jurisdiction

Anguilla, Antigua & Barbuda, Barbados, St Lucia and Trinidad & Tobago

In cases where resealing is not an available alternative, an application for the relevant grant of representation in the estate of the deceased person who dies domiciled outside the jurisdiction of any of the above territories, is made in the same manner as general grants of representations are made in these territories.

Documents to lead the Grant

The usual papers to lead the relevant grant of representation in the respective territories are lodged in the Registry subject to the following:

1. A certified or sealed copy of the grant decree order or authority of the court, including an official copy of the will of the deceased, if any;
2. Certified copy of the power of attorney, where the application is made by a duly appointed attorney of the applicant.
3. Inventory/Affidavit of Value setting out particulars of the assets of the estate of the deceased within the respective territory.
4. The oath/affidavit to lead the grant. The oath/affidavit should include the following recitals:
   (i) the date and place of death of the deceased.
   (ii) with the exception of Antigua & Barbuda and St Lucia,[15] the place of domicile of the deceased,
   (iii) where applicable, the granting of probate/letters of administration of the deceased named therein. Particulars of the date and place of issue of the grant and the person to whom the grant was issued should be recited.
   (iv) the entitlement of the applicant to the grant.
   (v) with the exception of Barbados[16] the gross value of the deceased's estate within the relevant territory.

5. *Anguilla, Barbados, Jamaica, St Lucia and Trinidad & Tobago*

Affidavit as to foreign law.

This affidavit is only required in practice where a grant with respect to the deceased's estate has not previously been obtained in the deceased's place of domicil.

Anguilla, Antigua &Barbuda, Guyana, Jamaica and Trinidad & Tobago

6. **Affidavit of Due Execution**

In Anguilla, Guyana, Jamaica and Trinidad & Tobago with respect to testamentary dispositions of real property situtate in these countries and in Antigua & Barbuda, with respect to real and personal property, an affidavit of due execution should be lodged irrespective of whether or not a grant was previously obtained.[17]

Trinidad & Tobago

Exemplification

The proceedings relevant to the issuance of a grant by a court in Trinidad & Tobago in circumstances where the deceased has died domiciled abroad but leaving property within Trinidad & Tobago, is referred to as exemplification of probate/letters of administration, as the case may be.

However, exemplification is not the appropriate procedure as according to *Tristram and Cootes Probate Practice* 27th ed. (London: Butterworths), 497:

> An exemplification, which is a document sometimes required by foreign courts, contains an exact copy of the will (if any), and a virtual, though not an exact, copy of the grant.

Accordingly, applications for exemplification of grants are applicable only in circumstances where a foreign court requests an exact copy of the grant and/or will of the deceased.

REVOCATION OF WILLS

Anguilla, Guyana, Jamaica, The Bahamas and Trinidad & Tobago

Movable Estate

The revocation of a will or other testamentary document may only be effected by a later will or other properly executed document which must be executed in accordance with the law of the deceased's last place of domicil; or alternatively in Trinidad & Tobago[18] with respect to the will of Commonwealth citizens, in accordance with:

(a) the law of the place when it was made regardless of the testator's domicile at the time of death; or,
(b) the law of the place where the testator was domiciled when it was made; or
(c) the law where the testator had his domicil of origin within the British Commonwealth.

Anguilla, Guyana, Jamaica, The Bahamas and Trinidad & Tobago

Immovable Estate

The revocation of a will or other testamentary documents is effective in so far as dispositions of immovable estate are concerned only if effected by a later will or other duly executed document(s).

The later will or document must be executed in accordance with the *lexus situs*—with the statutory formalities relevant to the execution of wills in the above territories.

Barbados, Eastern Caribbean territories (save Anguilla and Antigua & Barbuda)and The Bahamas

A revocation, whether total or partial, of a will may be effected either by a later will or document or a testamentary act and is deemed to be valid irrespective of the deceased's domicile habitual residence or nationality at the date of death or the date of the will, provided that it is executed in accordance with the forms required by:

(a) the internal law of the place of execution; or,
(b) the place of the testator's domicil or habitual residence or nationality at the time of execution or at the time of death; or,
(c) any system of law which could be applied to establish that the will or any provision thereof was itself duly executed.

Antigua & Barbuda

With respect to real and personal property, revocation of a will or other testamentary documents is effective only if the revocation is effected by a later will or other duly executed document, which document must be executed in the same manner as wills are executed in Antigua & Barbuda.

Notes

1. See chapter 20, p. 398-399.
2. *Ibid.*
3. Although s.11 of the respective Supreme Court Acts of the various Eastern Caribbean territories (save St Lucia) allows for the reception of English probate law, the common law position with respect to the validity of wills of persons domiciled abroad is applicable to Anguilla.

4   See chapter 2 pp. ante. See also *Pepin v. Bruyere* [1902] 1 Ch. 24 and *Freke v. Lord Carbery* (1873) L.R. Eq. 461.
5   See s.3 Wills and Probate Ordinance Ch. 8 No. 2 which provides in effect that the court *inter alia* shall have jurisdiction to determine the validity and admissibility to probate of the will or the granting of administration of the estate of any person wherever domiciled dying seised and possessed of property within Trinidad & Tobago.
6   Although s.41 uses the term British subject not Commonwealth citizen, Commonwealth citizen has been substituted with respect thereto.
7   See also Art 798A Ch. 242 which provides that where any person who has had and has ceased to have his domicil in St Lucia dies outside St Lucia, having made outside St Lucia, a will which is valid under the law of St Lucia, and such person leaves property in St Lucia, such will may be proved therein as if it had been made and such person had his domicil therein.
8   The Wills Act 1963. England is received in the other Eastern Caribbean territories (save St Vincent & the Grenadines) by virtue of s.11 of the respective Supreme Court Acts of these territories.
9   With respect to the territories which have the common law position, although an affidavit of foreign law should be applicable only to dispositions of personal property, in practice the affidavit is deemed valid to covet testamentary dispositions of real and personal property.
10 Guyana, Dominica   - r.29(a) N.C.P.R 1954, England
    The Bahamas, Eastern   - r.30(a) N.C.P.R 1987, England.
    Jamaica   - Rule 68.25(2) and (3) CPR 2002
11 The Bahamas, Eastern   - r.30(b) N.C.P.R 1987, England
    Caribbean (save Anguilla,
    Antigua & Barbuda,
    St Lucia)
    Dominica   - r.29 N.C.P.R 1954 England
    Jamaica   - Rule 68.25(4) CPR 2002
12 Guyana, Dominica,   - r.29(c) N.C.P.R 1954, England
    The Bahamas, Eastern   - r.30(1)(c) N.C.P.R. 1987, England.
    Caribbean territories(save
    Anguilla, Antigua & Barbuda,
    St. Lucia and Dominica)
    Jamaica   - Rule 68.25(c) CPR 2002
13 Guyana and Dominica   - r.29(a)(ii) N.C.P.R. 1954, England
    The Bahamas, Eastern   - r.30(3) N.C.P.R. 1987, England.
    Caribbean territories
    (save Anguilla, Antigua &
    Barbuda and Dominica)
14 The Bahamas, Eastern   - r.30 3(b) N.C.P.R. 1987, England
    Caribbean (save Anguilla,
    Antigua & Barbuda
    and Dominica)
    Dominica and Guyana   - r.29(b) N.C.P.R. 1954. England.
15 With respect to these two territories, the place of domicile of the deceased is not recited in the affidavit of the applicant.
16 The gross value of the deceased estate is stated in the Affidavit of Value.

17 It is to be noted that in Antigua & Barbuda a will is valid with respect to real and personal estate only if it is executed in accordance with the statutory formalities set out in the Wills Act Cap. 473, Antigua. Accordingly, an affidavit of due execution, not an affidavit as to foreign law is necessary to give validity to testamentary dispositions of real and personal property in Antigua. This is irrespective of the deceased's place of domicil.
18 See s.41 of the Wills & Probate Ordinance Ch. 8 No. 2.

14

Grants to Trust Corporations, Non-Trust Corporations and the Public Trustee

TRUST CORPORATIONS

All jurisdictions (save Jamaica)

A trust corporation includes the Public Trustee, a corporation appointed by the Court in any particular case to be a trustee or a person authorised to act as custodian/ trustee under the rules of the public trustee legislation of the relevant Caribbean territories.[1]

Jamaica and The Bahamas[2]

A trust corporation is any corporation authorised to act as an executor of the will of any deceased person or as administrator of the estate of any deceased person or as a trustee of any settlement whether constituted by being any instrument or otherwise.

GRANT TO TRUST CORPORATIONS[3]

All jurisdictions (save Jamaica)

A grant of representation may be made to a trust corporation acting alone or jointly with another person.
    In this regard a trust corporation may be:

> (a) named as executor of a will, in which event a grant of probate is issued to the trust corporation either solely or jointly with any other person(s) named as executor(s);
> (b) nominated to take a grant of letters of administration (with or without will annexed) on behalf of the person(s) entitled thereto;
> (c) authorised by a duly registered power of attorney to act as attorney of the persons entitled thereto.

Jamaica

Where a trust corporation is appointed executor, a grant of probate may be issued to the trust corporation either solely or jointly with any other person named executor. However where an application for a grant of letters of administration (with or without will annexed) is made by a trust corporation on behalf of the person entitled to the relevant grant, the application may be made by the trust corporation either by power of attorney or otherwise by an order of the court, granting leave to the trust corporation to make the application for the relevant grant.

In the latter instance, the adult beneficiaries who have a prior entitlement to the grant are required to make the application for the order of appointment. The consent to act of the trust corporation, and the written consent(s) of the concerned beneficiaries to the application being made by the trust corporation, must be filed with the application for the order of appointment. In filing the documents for the grant, the order of appointment, is filed with the application.

Who May apply

Any officer of a trust corporation (so authorised by the corporation or directors or governing body of such corporation) may apply for the relevant grant. The officer is authorised to swear affidavits, give security and do any act or thing necessary with a view to taking a grant.[4] However a trust corporation is not permitted by law to appoint any nominee or syndicate to apply for a grant on its behalf.[5]

Consents/ Notices[6]

All jurisdictions (save Jamaica)

Where a trust corporation applies for a grant of administration (with or without will annexed) otherwise than as a beneficiary or attorney of some person, the consent by or notice to all persons of full age who are entitled to the grant and all persons interested in the residuary estate of the deceased must be lodged with the papers to lead the grant. This is subject to the power of the court to dispense with any such consents as it may think fit.

Jamaica

As stated above it is the order of the court granting leave to the trust corporation to apply for the grant of administration and where applicable, the power of attorney in cases of letters of administration with will annexed which is required to be filed with the application for the grant. However, it is to be noted that with effect from January 1, 2003, there is now an order of priority in respect to grants of letters of administration (with or without will annexed). Accordingly, where applicable, the consent of/ notice to those persons equally entitled to the relevant grant must be obtained whether an order of the court or power of attorney is sought. This is unless the court otherwise disposes with this requirement.

Renunciation and Consent of Executors

All jurisdictions (save Jamaica)

Where an executor wishes a grant to be made to a trust corporation, his renunciation must be lodged in the Registry either prior to or together with the other papers to lead the grant. Additionally where the renouncing executor is entitled to take a grant in another capacity for example as a residuary beneficiary, his consent together with the consent of all other persons having an interest in the residuary estate should be obtained, subject to the registrar's power to dispense with such consent(s).

Jamaica

Where an executor renounces his right to probate, a power an order of the court must first be obtained before a trust corporation will be permitted to apply for a grant of letters of administration with will annexed on behalf of the persons entitled to the general grant of administration with will annexed.

Minors

    (i)   Executor(s)
All jurisdictions (save Jamaica)
Where the executor or all the executors are minors, a grant limited until the executor or one of them (if more than one of them) shall attain the age of majority may be made to a trust corporation on the consent of the persons beneficially entitled to the residuary estate of the deceased.

    (ii) Administrator(s)
All jurisdictions (save Jamaica)
Where all the persons entitled to apply for the grant of administration are minors, a grant for the use and benefit of

the minors may be issued to a trust corporation on the consent of the statutory testamentary or otherwise lawfully appointed guardian of the minor. If there are no persons so qualified, the issue of the grant to a trust corporation is subject to the discretion of the Registrar.

Jamaica

An order of the Court is required before a trust corporation will be admitted to apply for the grant for the use and benefit of a minor executor pursuant to Rule 68.28(2) CPR 2002, unless, pursuant to Rule 68.19 CPR 2002, the Administrator General gives his written consent.

However, where the minor is the sole person entitled to the grant of probate, and that minor has an interest in the residuary estate, the persons entitled to apply for a grant for use and benefit of a minor, as provided for by Rule 68.28, can where the Administrator General gives his consent, give a power of attorney to a trust corporation to apply for the grant. Where the Administrator General's consent is not forthcoming, an order of the Court will have to be obtained by the person(s) entitled to apply for a grant of letters of administration with will annexed, granting leave to the trust corporation to apply for the grant.

In cases of administration, where a minor is entitled to a share of an intestate's estate, pursuant to Rule 68.18(4) CPR 2002, the Administrator General, in such instances, is required to apply for the grant unless an order of the Court is otherwise obtained. Where the minor is the only beneficiary entitled to a share of the estate of the intestate, and is also the sole person entitled to the grant of administration, in accordance with the rules of priority set out in Rule 68.18 CPR 2002, the applicant for the order of the court, grant having to the trust corporation to apply for the grant in such circumstances, should be made in accordance with the order of priority for grants of the use and benefit of a minor as provided for by Rule 68.28, CPR 2002.

In cases of letters of administration with will annexed, where the minor is the sole person entitled to apply for letters of administration with will annexed, as provided for by Rule 68.11, the person(s) entitled to apply for a grant for the use and benefit of a minor as prescribed by Rule 68.28, may subject to the consent of the Administrator General (such consent to be given by the issuance of the Administrator General Certificate) give a power of attorney to the trust corporation to apply for the grant. Where the consent of the Administrator General is not forthcoming, the persons first entitled to apply for the grant for the use and benefit of a minor can apply for an order of the court for the grant to be made to a trust corporation

Renunciation by Trust Corporation

The renunciation by a trust corporation is made under the seal of the corporation and by the person authorised by resolution to renounce on behalf of the trust corporation. A sealed or certified copy of the resolution should be filed with the renunciation.

DOCUMENTS TO BE LODGED FOR GRANT

The usual documents required for an application for grant of probate or letters of administration (with or without will annexed) must be lodged subject to the following:

1. Covering letter/Formal Application for Grant
   The application for the grant is made in the name of the trust corporation and not in the name of the officer applying on its behalf. Where the application is being made jointly with an individual, the name of the individual should appear first.
2. *All jurisdictions*
   Consent(s) of all those persons who are *sui juris* and entitled to the grant whether of probate or administration.
3. *Jamaica*
   The order of the court granting leave to the trust corporation to make the necessary application on behalf of the beneficiaries must also be lodged, where applicable.
4. Renunciation(s) of the executor(s)/administrator(s) where applicable.
5. A certified copy of the resolution properly sealed with the seal of the corporation authorising the officer so appointed to apply for the grant on behalf of the trust corporation must be lodged.[7]
6. The oath should contain the usual recitals with respect to grants of probate or administration as the case may be. In addition, the oath should recite:
   (i) that the trust corporation is a trust corporation within the meaning of the relevant act of the respective territories;
   (ii) that the charter or memorandum of association of the trust corporation named therein empowers such corporation to make such an application[8], and
   (iii) the circumstances in which the applicant was appointed executor/administrator.
   (iv) *Jamaica*
   Where applicable, the oath should recite the order of the court granting leave to the trust corporation to make the application for the relevant grant on behalf of the beneficiaries.

7. Power of attorney where the application is made as attorney, the recitals in the oath should include the recitals contained in an application for a grant by an individual appointed as attorney.

NON-TRUST CORPORATION

All Jurisdictions (save St Lucia)[9]

A non-trust corporation may be named as an executor in a will or may be nominated by the persons entitled to the relevant grant of administration (with will annexed). This is provided the corporation is empowered by its constitution to undertake the duties of an executor or administrator.

The application for the grant is made by a nominee of the corporation appointed specially to act in each case. Unlike the case of a trust corporation, a non-trust corporation may appoint an attorney for the purposes of applying for and obtaining a grant on its behalf. In such instances the renunciation of persons with a superior entitlement to the grant must first be filed and the oath to lead the grant must recite that the grant is limited for the use and benefit of the corporation and until further representation is granted.[10]

Jamaica

With respect to Jamaica the same restrictions which are relevant to applications for grants by a trust corporation not appointed executor, are also applicable to non-trust corporations.

Renunciation of a Non-Trust Corporation

A non-trust corporation may appoint a nominee for the express purpose of renouncing its right to a grant. In this regard a sealed or certified copy of the resolution, appointing the nominee to renounce must be filed with the renunciation.

Documents Required For Grant to Non-Trust Corporation

The usual documents necessary for a grant of probate or letters of administration (with or without will annexed) must be lodged subject to the following:

1. A certified copy of the resolution appointing the nominee must be lodged with the papers to lead the grant.

2. A copy of the constitution of the corporation must be lodged along with the other papers to lead the grant so as to establish that the corporation is empowered by its constitution to take a grant through a nominee.
3. Power of attorney (where applicable).
4. The oath must set out
   (i) that the corporation is not a trust corporation within the meaning of the relevant Trust Corporation Acts of the respective territories;[11]
   (ii) that by resolution of the corporation's board of directors, the applicant named therein was appointed nominee for the purpose of applying for and obtaining the relevant grant; and
   (iii) that the constitution of the corporation empowers the corporation to act as executor/administrator as the case may be; and

   Jamaica
   (iv) where applicable, the oath should recite the order of the court granting leave to the trust corporation to make the application for the relevant grant on behalf of the beneficiaries.
5. *Jamaica*
   Order of the court, where applicable.

PUBLIC TRUSTEE

Antigua & Barbuda, Barbados, Grenada, Guyana, St Vincent & the Grenadines, The Bahamas and Trinidad & Tobago

The Public Trustee is a body corporate with perpetual succession and a common seal and may be sued and may sue in his corporate name. He is empowered by statute to act in the administration of the estates of deceased persons, and as an executor or administrator.[12]

GRANTS OF REPRESENTATION

As administrator, the Public Trustee is as equally entitled to a grant as any other person(s) first entitled to letters of administration with or without will annexed, save that:

   (i) the consent or citation of the Public Trustee is not required for a grant of letters of administration to be made to any other person; and
   (ii) as between the Public Trustee and the surviving spouse or

next of kin of the deceased, such persons are preferred to the Public Trustee unless good cause to the contrary is shown.[13]

Where the Public Trustee is named as one of the executors in a will, a grant of probate will not be made to other executors until the Public Trustee is notified of the application and inquiries made as to his desire to act as executor.

Practice and Procedure — Preliminary Steps

Antigua & Barbuda and Guyana

As a preliminary step to the Public Trustee applying for the relevant grant of representation and in accordance with the relevant statutory provisions of the respective Public Trustee Acts of Guyana and Antigua & Barbuda, any person in the Public Trustee's opinion who would be entitled to apply to the High Court for an order for the administration of a deceased's estate, is required to apply to the Public Trustee to file an undertaking to administer the estate.[14]

The application, which is made by sworn declaration[15] should set out:

(i) particulars of the real and personal property of the deceased including the value thereof;
(ii) the marital status of the deceased;
(iii) the names of the persons interested in the deceased's estate and their relationship to the deceased;
(iv) whether the deceased died testate or intestate;
(v) funeral expenses and other debts and expenses of the deceased;

The sworn declaration should end with a request for the Public Trustee to apply for a grant of letters of administration of the deceased's estate.

The applicant should also bring in:

(1) a certified copy of the death certificate of the deceased;
(2) all receipts and other proof of the deceased's indebtedness including funeral receipts, water and electricity bills; and
(3) proof of the value of the deceased's estate including any bank statements, land deeds.

Unless he has good reasons to refuse, the Public Trustee is required to file an undertaking in writing signed by him to administer the deceased's estate. This undertaking is filed in the Deed Registry in the case of Guyana and in the Supreme Court Registry in the case of Antigua & Barbuda.[16]

The Public Trustee may then proceed to apply for the relevant grant of administration in the usual way, by filing the requisite documents in the Supreme Court Registry.

All jurisdictions

The usual documents required for a grant of probate, letters of administration (with or without will annexed) must be lodged subject to the following:

1. An administration bond and consequently justification of sureties are not required in cases of administration.[17]
2. The oath, which should include the usual recitals and clearing off, if applicable. It should be noted that the oath may be sworn on behalf of the Public Trustee by some other person appointed for that purpose.

ADMINISTRATION OF ESTATES — NO GRANT REQUIRED

Barbados, Grenada, St Vincent & the Grenadines, The Bahamas and Trinidad & Tobago

In the above-mentioned territories, the Public Trustee may without a grant, administer the estate of a deceased person on behalf of any person who:

(1) in the Public Trustee's opinion would be entitled to apply to the High Court for an order for administering such estate; and
(2) where the value of the estate to be administered does not exceed:
    (a) $15,000, in the case of Barbados;[18]
    (b) $14,400, in the case of Trinidad & Tobago;[19]
    (c) $3,000, in the case of St Vincent & the Grenadines;[20]
    (d) $15,000, in the case of Grenada.[21]
    (e) $10,000, in the case of The Bahamas.[22]

Practice and Procedure

The Public Trustee upon application in writing is required by law to file an undertaking in the Supreme Court Registry to administer the estate of the deceased named therein.[23]

The filing of the undertaking by the Public Trustee has the effect of vesting the deceased's estate in the Public Trustee 'in like manner as a vesting orders had been made by the High Court'.[24] Accordingly as from the vesting of the estate in the Public Trustee, he is entitled to administer the estate without the need for a grant and exercise all such powers relevant thereto including distribution of the said estate in favour of the applicant.[25]

Antigua & Barbuda and Guyana[26]

The filing of the undertaking merely confers on the Public Trustee the same power as if he had been appointed by a last will of the deceased to be executor. Accordingly, after filing the undertaking to administer the estate of the deceased named therein, the Public Trustee is required to apply for and obtain the relevant grant of representation with respect to the deceased's estate subject to the following exception[27] where:

(a) the court makes an order for an estate to be administered by the Public Trustee;

(b) proceedings have been instituted in any court for the administration of an estate and by reason of the small value of the estate, it appears to the court that the estate can be mote economically administered by the Public Trustee than by any other person or that for any other reason it is expedient that the estate should be administered by him instead of any other person.

Guyana

Pursuant to the provisions of s.25 of the Deceased Persons Estates' Administration Act Cap. 12:01 and s.6 of the Public Trustee Act Cap. 13:01, the Public Trustee may administer the estate of a deceased person without a grant when:

(a) according to s.25(1)(b) of the Deceased Persons Estates' Administration Act, the Public Trustee pursuant to s.6 of the Public Trustee Act Cap. 13:01 undertakes to administer the estate of a deceased person which in his opinion does not exceed in value the sum of G$ 1,000.

(b) the Registrar, pursuant to s.19[28] of the Deceased Persons Estates' Administration Act Cap. 12:01 has appointed the Public Trustee to administer an estate and has delivered a certificate to the Public Trustee to that effect.

Notes

1	Anguilla	- s.2 Trust Corporations (Probate & Administration) Act Cap. 80
	Antigua & Barbuda	- s.2 Trust Corporations (Probate & Administration) Act Cap. 445
	Barbados	- s.22(4) Succession Act Cap. 249
	Dominica & Grenada	- s.128 Supreme Court Act 1981, England
	Montserrat	- s.2 Trust Corporation (Probate & Administration) Act Cap. 80
	St Christopher & Nevis	- s.2 Trust Corporation (Probate & Administration) Act Cap. 80
	The Bahamas	- s.52 Supreme Court Act 15/1996
	St Lucia	- Art 2141 Civil Code Ch. 242 See also ss. 2, 3 Trust Corporation (Probate & Administration) Ordinance Cap. 21
	St Vincent & the Grenadines	- s.2 Administration of Estates Act Cap. 377
	Trinidad & Tobago	- s.3(6) Wills & Probate Ordinance Ch. 8 No. 2 See also s.2 Trustee Ordinance Ch. 8 No. 3.
2	Jamaica	- s.3, The Judicature (Trust Corporations) Act Cap 182
	The Bahamas	- s.7, Probate Act Ch. 35.
3	Anguilla	- s.2 Trust Corporations (Probate and Administration) Act Cap. 80
	Antigua & Barbuda	- s.2 Trust Corporations (Probate and Administration) Act Cap. 445
	Barbados	- s.22(1) Trust Corporation (Probate and Administration) Cap. 249
	Dominica & Grenada	- s.115(1) Trust Corporation (Probate and Administration) Supreme Court Act 1981, England
	Jamaica	- s.4 Judicature (Trust Corporation) Act Cap. 182
	St Christopher & Nevis, Montserrat	- s.2 Trust Corporation (Probate and Administration) Act Cap. 80
	St Lucia	- s.4 Trust Corporation (Probate and Administration) Ordinance Cap. 21
	St Vincent & the Grenadines	- s.15(1) Trust Corporation (Probate and Administration) Ch. 8 Ch. 377
	The Bahamas	- s.31 Administration of Estates Act 2002; See also s.43(1) Supreme Court Act 15/1996
	Trinidad & Tobago	- s.36(1) Trustee Ordinance Ch. 8 No. 3.
4	Anguilla, Antigua, Montserrat, Barbados	- s.22(3) Succession Act Cap. 249
	Dominica & Grenada	- s.115(3) Supreme Court Act 1981 England (by virtue of The respective Supreme Court Acts of these territories)
	Jamaica	- s.5 Judicature (Trust Corporation) Act Cap. 182
	St Christopher & Nevis	- s.3(3) Trust Corporations (Probate and Administration Act) Cap. 80

	St Lucia	- s.5 Trust Corporation (Probate and Administration) Ordinance Cap. 21
	St Vincent & the Grenadines	- s.15(3) Administration of Estates Act Cap. 377
	The Bahamas	- r.2 The Probate (Corporation) Rules Ch. 35
	Trinidad & Tobago	- s.36(3) Wills & Probate Ordinance Ch. 8 No. 2.
5	Anguilla, St Christopher & Nevis, Montserrat	- s.3(2) Trust Corporations (Probate & Administration) Cap. 80
	Antigua & Barbuda	- s.2 Trust Corporations (Probate & Administration) Act Cap. 445
	Barbados	- s.22(1) Succession Act Cap. 249
	Dominica & Grenada	- s.115(2) Supreme Court Act 1981 England
	Jamaica	- s.6 Judicature (Trust Corporation) Act Cap. 182
	St Lucia	- s.6 Trust Corporation (Probate & Administration) Cap. 21
	St Vincent & the Grenadines	- s.15(2) Administration of Estates Act Cap. 377
	The Bahamas	- s.7 Probate Act Ch. 35; See also s.42(2) Supreme Court Act 15/1996
	Trinidad & Tobago	- s.36(2) Wills & Probate Ordinance Ch. 8 No. 2.
6	Barbados, Trinidad & Tobago, Guyana, Dominica	- r. 34(2) N.C.P.R 1954, England
	Eastern Caribbean territories (save Dominica), The Bahamas	- r. 36(3) N.C.P.R 1987, England.
7	Barbados	- r.10 Supreme Court (Non-Contentious) Probate Rules 1959
	Dominica	- r.34(1) N.C.P.R. 1954. England
	The Bahamas	- r.3 The Probate (Corporation) Rules Ch. 35
	Trinidad & Tobago	- r.8 First Schedule N.C.B.R. Ch. 8 No. 2
	The Bahamas, Eastern Caribbean territories (save Dominica),	- r.36(2) N.C.P.R. 1987, England.
8	Barbados	- r.10 Supreme Court (Non-Contentious) Probate Rules 1959
	Dominica	- r.34(1) N.C.P.R. 1954, England
	The Bahamas, Eastern Caribbean territories (save Dominica)	- r.36(1) N.C.P.R. 1987, England
	Trinidad & Tobago	- r.8 First Schedule N.C.B.R Ch. 8 No. 2.
9	St Lucia is excluded by virtue of Art 325 Civil Code Ch. 242 which provides that corporations cannot be curators, tutors, or undertake any administration which necessitates taking an oath or imposes responsibilities.	
10	The Bahamas, Eastern Caribbean	- r.36 4(a) N.C.P.R. 1987, England

	(save Dominica and St. Lucia) Trinidad & Tobago, Guyana, Dominica	- r.34(3) N.C.P.R. 1954, England.
11	Eastern Caribbean (save Dominica)	- r.36(4)(c) N.C.P.R. 1987, England
	Guyana, Dominica, The Bahamas,	- r.34(3) N.C.P.R. 1954, England.
12	Antigua & Barbuda	- s.3 Public Trustee Act 16/1995. Although s.20 of the Public Trustee Act 16/1995 makes provisions for the Minister responsible for Legal Affairs to make rules with respect to the Public Trustee, no rules have to date been made. However it is submitted that by virtue of s.11 of the Eastern Caribbean Supreme Court Act, the Public Trustee Rules 1912 of England may be applied in prac-tice.
	Barbados	- s.3 Public Trustee Act Cap. 248
	Grenada	- s.3 Public Trustee Act Cap. 269. Although s.15 of the Public Trustee Act Cap. 248 make provisions for the Governor General to make rules with respect to the Public Trustee, no such rules have to date been made. Again it is submitted that by virtue of s.11 of the Eastern Caribbean Supreme Court Act of Grenada, that the Public Trustee Rules 1912 of England may be applied
	Guyana	- s.3 Public Trustee Act Cap. 13:01; Public Trustee Rules made under s. 18 of the Public Trustee Act Cap. 13:01
	The Bahamas	- s.3 Public Trustee Ord. Ch. 165; Public Trustee Rules made under s.16 of the Public Trustee Act Ch. 165
	St Vincent & the Grenadines	- s.3 Public Trustee Act Cap. 382; the Public Trustee Rules of England are applicable by virtue of s.15(3) of the Public Trustee Act Cap. 382 which provides that 'unless and until rules are made under sub-section (1), rules in force in England shall be rules made for the purpose of this Act'.
	Trinidad and Tobago	- s.3 Public Trustee Ord. Ch. 8 No, 4; Public Trustee Rules made under s.15 of the Public Trustee Ord. Ch. 8 No. 4.
13	Antigua & Barbuda	- s.10 Public Trustee Act 16/1995
	Barbados	- s.8 Public Trustee Act Cap. 248
	Grenada	- s.8 Public Trustee Act Cap. 269
	St Vincent & the Grenadines	- s.8 Public Trustee Act Cap. 382
	The Bahamas	- s.9 Public Trustee Ordinance Ch. 165
	Trinidad & Tobago	- s.8 Public Trustee Ordinance Ch. 8 No. 4.
14	Antigua & Barbuda	- s.5(1) Public Trustee Act 16/1995
	Guyana	- s.6(1) Public Trustee Act Cap. 13:01.

15 Antigua & Barbuda — s.5(2) Public Trustee Act 16/1995
   Guyana — s.6(2) Public Trustee Act Cap. 13:01.
16 Antigua & Barbuda — s.5(2) Public Trustee Act 16/1995
   Guyana — s.6(2) Public Trustee Act Cap. 13:01.
17 Antigua & Barbuda — s.18(2) Public Trustee Act 16/1995
   Barbados — s.12(5) Public Trustee Act Cap. 248
   Grenada — s.13(4) Public Trustee Act Cap. 269
   Guyana — s.12(5) Public Trustee Act Cap. 13:01
   St Vincent & the Grenadines — s.13(5) Public Trustee Act Cap. 382
   The Bahamas — s.6 Probate Act Ch. 35; See also s.15(3) of the Public Trustee Act Ch. 165. See also s.40 of the Supreme Court Act 15/1996
18 Section 5(1) Public Trustee Act Cap. 248.
19 Section 5(1) Public Trustee Ordinance Ch. 8 No. 4.
20 Section 5(1) Public Trustee Act Cap. 382.
21 Section 5(1) Public Trustee Act Cap. 269.
22 Section 6(1) Public Trustee Act Ch. 165.
23 Barbados — s.5(2) Public Trustee Act Cap. 248 Grenada
   Grenada — s.5(2) Public Trustee Act Cap. 269
   St Vincent & the Grenadines — s.5(2) Public Trustee Act Cap. 382
   The Bahamas — s.6(2) Public Trustee Act Ch. 165
   Trinidad & Tobago — s.5(2) Public Trustee Ordinance Ch. 8:04.
24 *Ibid.*
25 *Ibid.*
26 Antigua & Barbuda — s.5(2) Public Trustee Act 16/1995
   Guyana — s.6(2) Public Trustee Act Cap. 13:01.
27 Antigua & Barbuda — s.5 Public Trustee Act 16/1995
   Guyana — s.6 Public Trustee Act Cap. 13:01.
28 Section 19 provides *inter alia* that the Registrar may summarily appoint an administrator where value of the assets of the intestate does not exceed $1,000.

15

Commorientes

COMMON LAW POSITION

Anguilla and Grenada,[1] Barbados,[2] Guyana,[3] The Bahamas[4] and Trinidad & Tobago

At common law where persons who are in immediate succession to each other die whether on a testacy or an intestacy, in circumstances in which it is uncertain which of them died first, it is a matter of proof which of them, if either, survived the other. Although there is no presumption that they died simultaneously, nonetheless if the evidence fails to establish the survivorship of either of them, each would be presumed to have predeceased the other and the grant of the estate of each of them is made on that footing.

However it should be noted that in cases of testacy, a testator may by his will make express provisions for the disposition of his estate which can effectively exclude the operation of this doctrine.[4]

The most common instance in which the doctrine of commorientes arises is where spouses perish in the same accident either dying intestate or leaving mutual wills. In such instances in the absence of proof to the contrary, the husband will be deemed to have died a widower and the wife a widow. In both cases neither spouse takes an interest under the intestacy or under the will of the other.

STATUTORY POSITION

A. Eastern Caribbean territories (save Anguilla, Grenada and St Lucia) and Jamaica[5]

In the above territories there is a presumption in cases of simultaneous death of persons in immediate succession to each other that the parties have died in order of seniority, that is the younger is presumed to have survived the elder.[6]

B. Eastern Caribbean territories (save Anguilla, Grenada and St Lucia)

This statutory presumption is however subject to a major qualification contained in the Intestate Estates Act 1952, England which added the following provision as subsection 3 to s.46 of the Administration of Estates Act 1925:[7]

> Where the intestate and the intestate's husband or wife have died in circumstances rendering it uncertain which of them survived the other and the intestate's husband or wife is by virtue of section 184 of the Law of Property Act 1925, deemed to have survived the intestate, this section shall, nevertheless, have effect as respects the intestate as if the husband or wife had not survived the intestate.

According to the above provisions, with respect to deaths occurring on or after January 1st, 1953, the statutory presumption that the younger is presumed to have survived the elder in cases of simultaneous death is excluded in the case of the intestacy, partial or total, of the elder spouse irrespective of whether the younger spouse has died testate or intestate. It is to be noted that where the deceased died partially intestate the statutory presumption contained in s.184 of the Law of Property Act, is applicable only to that part of the deceased's estate which devolves on an intestacy.

A testator may however by contrary provisions contained in his will expressly or impliedly exclude the statutory presumption or the statutory qualification of this presumption as the case may be.[8]

C. The Bahamas

Pursuant to s.28 of the Inheritance Act 2002, where two or more parties die at the same time, or in circumstances rendering it uncertain which of them survived the other, the estate of each person shall be disposed of distributed or divided as if each person had survived the other.

However, with respect to a husband and wife situation on an intestacy, s.4(2) of the Act in effect provides that where an intestate and the intestate's husband or wife have died in circumstances rendering it uncertain which of them has survived the other, they each will be presumed to have predeceased the other.

D. St Vincent & the Grenadines

It is unsettled whether the common law position is applicable to St Vincent & the Grenadines or whether the English statutory provisions are received in this territory:

(i) in light of the judicial interpretation of s.11 of the Eastern Caribbean Supreme Court (St Vincent & the Grenadines) Act Cap. 18 (the so-called reception provision). According to Sir Vincent Floissac, Chief Justice of the Eastern Supreme Court in the case of *Panacom Int. v. Sunset Investments*,[9] 'In enacting s.11, the legislature of St Vincent & the Grenadines could not have intended to import English substantive law.' However as this author noted[10] with respect to the reception of English substantive probate law, the enactment in 1989 of the current succession legislation merely reduced the extent of reception of English probate law as prior to the passage of the succession legislation, most notably the Administration of Estate Act Cap. 377, the English substantive probate law in so far as it impacted on probate practice and procedure, was effectively received in the territory; and

(ii) in the light of the non-inclusion of a statutory provision with respect to commorientes in the succession legislation which was enacted in 1989, when the laws of St Vincent & the Grenadines were revised. However it is the opinion of this author, that this apparent lacuna may have arisen as a result of a legislative oversight as the main English provision with respect to commorientes is not contained in the English succession legislation, but in the Law of Property Act 1925. Although the succession legislation was repealed and replaced by new legislation in St Vincent & the Grenadines, the land and land related laws were not similarly revised.

In the absence of any express statutory provision to the contrary, and the lack of legislative certainty with respect to the scope and intent of s.11 of the Supreme Court Act of St Vincent & the Grenadines, the English statutory provisions in so far as they relate to commorientes, are applicable to St Vincent & the Grenadines.

E. St Lucia

According to Arts 546-548 of the Civil Code Ch. 242 in cases where it is impossible to ascertain the order of survivorship, the presumption of survivorship is determined by the circumstances and in the absence thereof by the following rules:

(a) where those who perished together were under 15 years, the eldest is presumed to have survived;
(b) if they were all above the age of 60 years, the youngest is presumed to have survived;
(c) if some were under the age of 15 years and others over 60 years, the former are presumed to have survived;
(d) if some were under 15 years or over 60 years, and the others in the intermediate age, the presumption of survivorship is in favour of the latter;
(e) if those who perished together were all between the full ages of 15 years and 60 years, and of the same sex, the order of nature is followed, according to which the youngest is presumed to survive;
(f) where they were of different sexes, the male is always presumed to have survived;

PROCEDURE AND DOCUMENTS

The applicant for the grant must submit to the registrar, as early as possible, affidavit(s) setting out full details of the circumstances of death. An affidavit of the persons who found the bodies as well as an affidavit of the doctor who examined the bodies should be submitted. The death certificates of the deceased, coroner's report, if any, and where applicable birth and marriage certificates of the deceased persons should also be lodged with the registrar.

If the registrar is satisfied that it is not possible to determine the order of survivorship, the applicant may proceed to file the affidavits together with the usual documents to lead a grant of representation on the basis of uncertainty as to the order of survivorship. The grant in such instances will be issued to the applicant in accordance with the common law or statutory position, whichever is applicable to the relevant territory.

The Oath

The oath must set out *inter alia*:

i. that all possible inquiries as to survivorship have been made but that it appears that the deceased persons named therein have died in circumstances rendering it uncertain which of them survived the other.
ii. a description and the entitlement of the applicant to the grant of the estate of the said deceased person. This will be based amongst other things on whether the deceased died testate or intestate and whether the statutory or common law position applies.

Petition

St Lucia

The petition should, in so far as applicable, include the usual recitals contained in a petition for a grant of probate or letters of administration (with or without will annexed), as the case may be. Accordingly, the recitals outlined above, which are peculiar to this type of grant, should be included. However it is to be noted that the actual oath to administer, collect in, etc. the estate of the deceased, is not included in the petition, but in the oath to lead the grant.

Will of the Commoriens

The will of the commoriens, if any, must also be proved even if it has been rendered effectively inoperative.

Notes

1. Although s.11 of the respective Supreme Court Acts of the various Eastern Caribbean territories (save St Lucia) allows for the reception of English probate law, in practice in Anguilla and Grenada the English common law, not the English statutory position with respect to commorientes is applied.
2. Section 105 of the Succession Act Cap. 249, Barbados codifies the common law position.
3. Section 2 of the Civil Law Act Ch. 601 provides that the English common law in force in England as of 1st June 1917, is applicable to and received in Guyana. Accordingly the common law position on commorientes is applicable to Guyana.
4. *Underwood v Wing* (1855) 4De GM&G 633.
5. The statutory position applies to Jamaica by virtue of s.2 of the Law Reform (Commorientes) Act 50/1968, Jamaica.
6. See *Hickman v. Peacy* [1945] AC 304; [1945] 2 All E.R. 215, for an extensive discussion on the effect of this provision where it was held *inter alia* that it was not possible to establish that death occurred so simultaneously so as to rebut the statutory presumption that death occurred in order of seniority.
7. By virtue of s.11(1) of the Supreme Court Acts of the above Eastern Caribbean states, s.46(3) of the Administration of Estates Act 1925, England is received in these territories. See also Megarry and Wade (5th Ed.) *The Law of Real Property*, 551-552 for a more detailed discussion of the effect of the various statutory provisions on the doctrine of commorientes.
8. See *Re Pringle, Baker v. Matheson* [1946] Ch. 124; [1946] 1 All E.R. 88.
9. (1994)47 W.I.R. 139 at 149. See *Re Guggenheim's Estate* (1941) Times, 20 June.
10. See Introduction, p. 7-16.

16

Limited Grants

INTRODUCTION

A grant of representation may be limited in regard to time, certain property or to a particular object. When a person is entitled to a general grant he will not be allowed to obtain a limited grant except by special permission of the court and then only for very cogent reasons.[1] Furthermore, limited administration is not to be granted unless every person entitled to a general grant is either dead or has consented/renounced or, where applicable, has been cited and failed to apply or otherwise under the direction of the Court.[2]

RULES OF PRACTICE AND PROCEDURE

As was stated in chapter 1, none of the territories considered in this book, except Jamaica, with effect from January 1, 2003, has detailed non-contentious probate rules which prescribe the procedure to be adopted with respect to applications for limited grants of representation. Accordingly, the relevant English non-contentious probate rules 1954/1987 are received and applied in these territories, subject to necessary modifications to local probate practice and procedure.

POWERS OF REGISTRAR TO GRANT PRELIMINARY ORDERS

Trinidad & Tobago and Barbados

In accordance with the jurisdiction and powers conferred by law and the relevant rules of court, the registrars in these territories may grant all such preliminary orders with respect to the issue of grants of representation which may be made by a judge in chambers. Accordingly, preliminary orders other than those which are required by law or the rules of court to be heard in open court, are granted by the registrar subject to the registrar's discretion to direct that any such applications be made to a judge in chambers or open court.

Eastern Caribbean territories

As was mentioned in the Introduction,[3] the Eastern Caribbean Rules of the Supreme Court, 1970, have been repealed and replaced by the Eastern Caribbean Supreme Court CPR 2000. In this regard, RSC O.47r.5 of the repealed Supreme Court Rules 1970 conferred on the registrars of these territories the power to grant applications for probate or administration, other than those applications in which there is contention, until such contention is disposed of. In practice, the powers thereby conferred on the registrar were not exercised in a uniform manner. Although the new CPR 2000, in particular Part 2 Rule 2.5 contains a provision with respect to the exercise of the powers of the court, *inter alia,* by the registrar, this provision does not address the ambit of the powers and duties of the registrar in respect of non-contentions probate proceedings, nor is there any rule which so provides in the new CPR 2000. Accordingly, the ambit of the powers, duty and authority of the registrar in respect of non-contentious probate matters is deemed to be governed, in the absence of specific rules or statutory provisions to the contrary, by the general provisions of Rule 2.5, CPR 2000.

To date, attorneys-at-law continue to make applications for preliminary orders in the first instance to a judge in chambers even in those Eastern Caribbean territories where the registrar is prepared to make preliminary orders.

This practice stems partly from the fact that until the passage on April 17, 1971, of the now repealed Eastern Caribbean Rules of the Supreme Court, the registrars in these territories, save St Lucia,[4] had no statutory power to grant probate or administration.

Indeed, all non-contentious probate applications were required to be made to a judge and all preliminary order applications were made either by summons to a judge in chambers or by motion to a judge in open court, as the case may be.

This was essentially the position in England until the passage of the N.C.P.R. 1954. These rules conferred on the registrar the powers to deal with matters which were previously the reserve of judges.

In this regard, the non-inclusion of specific non-contentious probate rules in the CPR Rules 2000 has not assisted in clarifying the position.

The Bahamas and Guyana[5]

The relevant legislation and rules of court of The Bahamas and Guyana still reflect the pre-1954 position in England. Accordingly, the respective registrars of these territories have no power to grant preliminary orders. All preliminary applications are required to be made to a judge in chambers or open court.[6]

Jamaica

In practice, preliminary applications with respect to the issue of grants were made to a judge in chambers. However, with the passage of CPR 2002 in particular Rule 68.48(1), all applications in respect of non-contentious probate matters are to be made in the first instance to the registrar in Form P.21 Appendix 2 CPR 2002. Rule 68.48(4) further provides that when an application is opposed, the registrar may give directions and adjourn the application to a judge, or pursuant to Rule 68.48(5), the registrar may at any time refer any non-contentious probate application to a judge.

GRANTS TO CONSULAR OFFICERS[7]

All jurisdictions[8] (save Barbados, Guyana and Jamaica)

Grants to consular officers are made in all jurisdictions where a person who is a citizen or subject of a foreign country to which the Consular Convention Act provision of the respective territories applies:

a) either dies outside that foreign country or within a Caribbean territory to which the Consular Convention Act/ provision applies, leaving property within the relevant Caribbean territory; and
b) there is no person present within the Caribbean territory at the time of his death who is entitled to administer his estate.[8]

In such circumstances, provided the consular officer or no other person is authorised by power of attorney to apply for a grant on behalf of the person entitled to administer the deceased's estate, the consular officer may apply forthwith and obtain from the court, letters of administration for the property of the deceased limited in such manner and for such time as the court shall deem fit. The application is submitted by the consular officer and the grant is made to him in his official capacity.

In addition the consular officer may take possession and have custody of the property of such deceased person, apply the same in payment of his debts and funeral expenses and retain the surplus for the benefit of the persons entitled thereto.

The Bahamas, Eastern Caribbean (save St Lucia)

Minority and Life Interest

A grant may be made to a consular officer alone, irrespective of whether a life or minority interest arises.

Practice, Procedure and Documents

The usual documents for a general grant of letters of administration (with or without will annexed) must be lodged subject to the following:

1. The administration bond, where applicable, must include the following words of limitation 'for the use and benefit of the national and until further representation be granted'. There are no surities to the bond, and consequently no affidavit of justification is required.[10]
2. The oath must recite, amongst other things:
    (i) that the applicant is a national of a territory to which the relevant Consular Convention Act applies;
    (ii) that the person entitled to administer the deceased national's estate is outside the jurisdiction;
    (iii) that neither the consular officer nor any other person has been appointed attorney by the person entitled to take out the grant;
    (iv) the relevant words of limitation (as set out in the administration bond above).

In all other respects the wording of the oath is similar to the oath to lead the grant to an attorney.

Petition

St Lucia

The petition should, in so far as applicable, include the usual recitals contained in a petition for a grant of letters of administration (with or without will annexed), as the case may be. Accordingly, the recitals outlined above, which are peculiar to this type of grant, should be included. However the recital to administer and collect in the estate of the deceased is not included in the petition but rather in the oath to lead the grant.

St Vincent & the Grenadines

The Petition, if filed, includes the recitals set out in the oath.

GRANTS TO ATTORNEYS

These are grants made for the use and benefit of some person who is entitled to a grant but at the material time, in most instances, is resident outside the territory in which the relevant grant is being sought.[10] It should be noted that in such instances it is not compulsory for a grant to be issued to an attorney; the person entitled to the grant may, if he wishes, apply in person.

If, however, the application for the grant is made by power of attorney, the grant is limited in respect of time and remains in force until the person entitled to the relevant grant applies for and obtains a grant in his or her name or until the registrar so directs.

A duly appointed attorney has the same powers as the donor. In England however, until October 11, 1974, a chain of representation could not be constituted through him.

Accordingly, a person appointed attorney of the estate of a deceased person could not subsequently take a grant in the estate of another deceased in the capacity of personal representative of the first deceased unless the power of attorney was worded so as to authorise him.

Guyana and Trinidad & Tobago

The pre-October 1974 English position still obtains in these territories by virtue of the relevant cut off dates for the reception of English probate practice and procedure and the lack of indigenous practice directions on this matter.

Eastern Caribbean territories, Jamaica and The Bahamas

In England a practice direction was issued on October 11, 1974 which makes it possible for an attorney to obtain a grant in another's estate, to which the donor of the power is entitled in his capacity as personal representative. Accordingly, by virtue of:

- s.11 of the respective Supreme Court Acts of the various Eastern Caribbean territories; and
- s.41 of the Supreme Court Act 15/1996 with respect to The Bahamas,

this practice direction, it is submitted, may be applicable to these territories.

Jamaica

With the passage of CPR 2002, and in particular Rule 68.23 which specifically provides for the procedure and practice relevant to grants to attorneys, the common law pre-1974 position applies to Jamaica in the absence of express provisions to the contrary.

Donor Resident within Jurisdiction

Barbados, Jamaica, St Lucia and Trinidad & Tobago

Although a grant to an attorney may be made when the intended donor resides within the jurisdiction, leave under the discretionary powers of the court[11] must first be obtained before a grant may be issued to the attorney of such persons. Leave is required in these territories as the relevant indigenous probate rule of these territories is referable only to cases which the person entitled to the relevant grant is resident outside the jurisdiction. The application for leave is made *ex parte* on affidavit to the registrar/judge in chambers. The grant so issued is made for the use and benefit of such person, limited until such person obtains a grant or limited in such other way as the registrar/Judge may direct.

Guyana

Rules 2 and 3 of the Deceased Persons Estates' Administration Rules Cap. 12:01 do not specify the circumstances in which an attorney may apply for a grant of representation on behalf of the persons entitled thereto. It is submitted however, that the position in Guyana is governed by the practice and procedure as provided for by r.30(2) N.C.P.R. 1954 England. According to r.30(2) leave must first be obtained before a grant to an attorney will be made where the donor of the power is resident within the jurisdiction.

Dominica

The practice in Dominica is governed by r.30 N.C.P.R. 1954, England as discussed above.

Eastern Caribbean territories (save Dominica) and The Bahamas

By virtue of r.31 of the N.C.P.R. 1987, England, leave is no longer required where the donor is resident within the jurisdiction.

As a result it is now the practice in England, and by extension in the above territories, for a physically incapacitated person who is first entitled to a grant of representation to appoint an attorney to apply for a grant on his behalf.

Words of limitation

1.   Attorney of Executor(s)
     (a)   *Sole Executor*
           When an attorney is appointed by the testator's sole executor the grant of letters of administration with will annexed is issued 'for the use and benefit of the executor and until he shall apply for and obtain probate'.
     (b)   *Two or more executors*
           When there are two or more executors a grant to the attorney of one or more of them, but not all, (as the case may be) is limited until one or more of them shall apply for and obtain probate. In such instances, notice of the intended application must be given to the other executors, unless this requirement is dispensed with by the Registrar.[13]

           A grant to the attorney of all the executors is made 'for the use and benefit of the executors until they shall apply for and obtain probate'.
     (c)   *Sole surviving executor*
           A grant to the attorney of the sole surviving executor is made for the use and benefit of the executor until he shall apply for and obtain probate or further representation be granted.

2.   Attorney of Administrator (with or without will annexed)

When one or more but not all persons who are entitled to a grant of administration (with or without will annexed) appoint an attorney to obtain the relevant grant on their behalf, the written consent of the other persons equally entitled must be obtained or alternatively a notice of such application must be given to those persons, if any, who are equally entitled to the grant unless the Registrar otherwise directs.

The grant in such instances is made for the use and benefit of AB/CD (as the case may be) until he or they shall apply for and obtain letters of administration (with or without will annexed).

Similarly, in instances where there is only one person first entitled to take out letters of administration (with or without will annexed) the grant is made for the use and benefit of AB until he shall apply for and obtain letters of administration (with or without will annexed).

3.   Attorney of Guardian

A grant to the attorney of the guardian of a minor(s) is made for the use and benefit of the minor(s) and until he or one of them, if more than one, shall attain the age of majority, or until further representation be granted.

A person entitled to a grant may renounce his rights and title thereto through an attorney, but the power of attorney must expressly authorise the attorney to renounce.

Cessate Grants to Attorney

When an attorney dies without completing the administration of the estate of which he was appointed attorney, the grant to the attorney ceases to have effect and, the donor of the power, may apply for a cessate grant in his own name. Alternatively he may appoint another attorney to complete the administration on his behalf, in which case a cessate grant will be made to the attorney so appointed. When there are two or more attorneys appointed by the power of attorney, the other attorney(s) may take this grant under the original power of attorney, provided it is not revoked by the donor.

***De Bonis Non Administratus* Grant**

In instances where the donor of the power of attorney dies before the estate is fully administered, a grant *de bonis non administratus* will be required in order to complete the administration of the estate.

***Power of Attorney*[13]**

The power of attorney is required to be under seal, witnessed by a disinterested person and filed in the Supreme Court Registry/Land Registry in St Lucia/Deeds Registry in Guyana prior to the application for the grant.

Authentication of Power of Attorney Executed Abroad

In cases where the donor of the power resides abroad, the power of attorney executed abroad is required to be authenticated by:

(a) a diplomatic agent, a consular officer of the jurisdiction concerned; or
(b) a judge of a superior court, justice of the peace, notary public, mayor of any city or corporations or other person legally authorised to administer oaths.

The power of attorney is also required to be executed in the presence of at least one witness, not being a party thereto. The signing and delivery must be attested to by one such witness who is required to subscribe his name with the addition of his address, home or business, and his profession and occupation. The power must include the name and address of the deceased, the name and address of the donor and his entitlement to the grant. It must also specify the precise authority conferred on the attorney thereunder. When it is intended, as in most instances, that the attorney administers the estate of the deceased named therein, this must be expressly stated.

Practice Procedure and Documents

The usual documents for a grant of letters of administration (with or without will annexed) must be lodged subject to the following:

1. A copy of the registered power of attorney should be exhibited.
2. The administration bond, where applicable, should include the relevant words of limitation.
3. The oath/affidavit of the applicant should recite:
   i) the entitlement of the donor to the grant whether as executor, or as administrator (with or without will annexed);
   ii) the appointment of the applicant as attorney of the said donor; and
   iii) the oath of the applicant to collect, get in and administer according to law the real and personal estate of the deceased ending with the relevant words of limitation.
4. Petition

St Lucia

The petition should, in so far as applicable, include the usual recitals contained in a petition for a grant of letters of administration (with or without will annexed), as the case may be. Accordingly, the recitals outlined above, which are peculiar to this type of grant, should be included. However it is to be noted that the actual oath to administer and collect in the estate of the deceased, is not included in the petition, but in the oath to lead the grant.

St Vincent & the Grenadines

The petition, if filed, includes the recitals set out in the oath.

GRANTS FOR THE USE AND BENEFIT OF A MINOR

Grants for the use and benefit of a minor limited until the minor attains the age of majority are made in circumstances where the person entitled by law to apply for the general grant of representation of the deceased's estate is a minor.[14] (It should be noted that in all the jurisdictions except Grenada and Anguilla, the age of majority has been reduced from 21 to 18 years.)[15]

When there is a person of full age who is as equally entitled as the minor, to apply for the relevant grant, the grant will be made to such person or persons in preference to the parent or guardian/tutor (in St Lucia) of the minor. However, the following should be noted:

(a) **Minor Co-Executor**
When a minor is appointed a co-executor, the co-executor(s) of full age may obtain probate with power reserved to the minor upon attaining the age of majority to apply for a double probate grant. In such instances the original grant is not limited; it merely reserves the right of the co-executor to apply for a full grant on reaching 18/ 21 years as the case may be.

(b) **Minor—Sole Executor**
When a minor is appointed sole executor but has no interest in the residuary estate of the deceased, administration for the use and benefit of the minor until he attains 18/21 years will, unless the registrar otherwise directs, be granted to the person(s) entitled to the residuary estate.[17]

When, however, the minor has an interest in the residuary estate, administration for his use and benefit, limited until he attains 18/21 years will be granted in order of priority *inter alia*, to the parents of the minor jointly or to the statutory, testamentary or court appointed guardian/tutor (in St Lucia) of the minor.

In both instances the minor upon attaining the age of majority may either renounce his right to probate, or apply for a cessate grant of probate.

Jamaica

Pursuant to Rule 68.33(5) CPR 2002, a minor executor's right to probate may be renounced on his behalf by a guardian appointed for that purpose.

(c)   **Minor Administrator**

All jurisdictions (save Jamaica)

When a minor is the sole person entitled to administration, a grant for his use and benefit will be made limited until he attains the age of majority at which time he may apply for a cessate grant.

As mentioned above, however, if there are other persons entitled in the same degree to administration who are not under a disability, a general grant of letters of administration will be made to those persons in preference to the parents or guardians of the minor.

Jamaica

Pursuant to the passage of the new CPR 2002 and in particular Rule 68.25, grants for the use and benefit of a minor are equally applicable to grants of probate and letters of administration (with or without will annexed). However, this entitlement, pursuant to Rule 68.28 is subject to the provisions of s.12 of the Intestates' Estates and Property Charges Act. Section 12 in effect provides that where a minor is entitled to a share in the estate of an intestate, the Administrator General is under a duty to apply for the grant unless the court orders otherwise. What this means is that where a minor is a beneficiary under the estate of the intestate, applications for grants for the use and benefit of a minor would not arise unless an order of the court is first obtained. In such instances, the order of priority for grants of administration as provided for by Rule 68.18 CPR 2002 would be relevant where the person applying for the order is applying on behalf of a minor, who in accordance with Rule 68.18 CPR 2002 would otherwise be entitled to the grant if he or she were not a minor.

However, with respect to grants of letters of administration with will annexed, a grant for the use and benefit of a minor who is next entitled in order of priority to the grant can be obtained, provided the Administrator General gives his consent by the issuance to the proposed applicant of the Administrator General's Certificate to the proposed applicant.

Indeed, Rule 68.29(2) CPR 2002 expressly provides that where the executor or executors who are not minors renounce, or on being cited to accept or refuse a grant, fail to make an effective application for a grant, an appointment may be made under the terms of Rule 68.28. Rule 68.28 provides *inter alia* for applications for letters of administration (with or without will annexed) to be made for the use and benefit of a minor.

To Whom Grant Made — Order of Prioroty[17]

(a) Parents jointly.[18]
(b) Statutory guardian/tutor in St Lucia, that is, the surviving parent.[19]
(c) Testamentary guardian that is the guardian appointed by a deceased parent, by his will or deed to act as guardian/tutor.[20]

With respect to (a),(b),and (c) above, no order of appointment is required. However the oath should clearly establish the capacity of the applicant i.e. whether he is applying as parent or guardian/tutor of the minor as the case may be. All relevant exhibits should be annexed, for example, the birth certificate of the minor.

(d) **Court Appointed Guardian/Tutor (in St Lucia)**[21]
The application for a court appointed guardian may be made by notice of motion to a judge in open court or as is the usual practice by originating summons to a registrar/judge in chambers, in the case of Trinidad and Tobago, Barbados and The Bahamas. In the case of the Eastern Caribbean territories, the application in practice, is made by Fixed Date Claim Form as provided for by CPR 2000, and in the case of Jamaica, in accordance with Rule 68.48(1) to the registrar in the form prescribed (Form P21, Appendix 2).

Contents of Affidavit in support of Application

The affidavit should set out:

(i) the age of the minor and his relationship, if any, to the proposed guardian/tutor;
(ii) the minor's entitlement to the relevant grant of representation;
(iii) whether there is any statutory testamentary or other lawfully appointed guardian/tutor and, if so, the reasons why it is desired that such guardian/tutor should not act; and
(iv) the gross value of the estate to be administered.

Affidavit of fitness

An affidavit of fitness to act of the proposed guardian/tutor must also be lodged except in Jamaica where the guardian is the Administrator General. This affidavit which is sworn to either by the next-of-kin of the minor or otherwise by some responsible person should set out that the proposed guardian/tutor is ready and willing to undertake guardianship/tutorship and that he had no interest adverse to the minor with respect to the succession of the deceased.

Consent

The signed consent to act of the proposed guardian/tutor should also be lodged with the application.

(e)   Elected/ Nominated Guardian

Trinidad & Tobago

Pursuant to rr.29 and 30 First Schedule N.C.B.R. Ch. 8 No. 2, persons 14 years and over may elect a guardian for the purposes of applying for grants of administration. When there are persons 14 years and over and persons under the age of 14 years, the guardian elected may act for both without being specially assigned by the Court.

Barbados, Dominica and Guyana

Pursuant to r.32(1) (b) N.C.P.R. 1954, England, a minor who has attained the age of 16 years may nominate any of his next-of-kin to act as guardian for the purpose of applying for a grant on behalf of such infant. However although the N.C.P.R. 1954, England are received in these territories, where no indigenous rules or provisions exist, it is not the practice to elect a guardian in these territories.

The Bahamas and Eastern Caribbean territories (save Dominica and St Lucia)

It should be noted that the N.C.P.R 1987, England, contain no provision for the nomination/election of a guardian by an infant who has attained the age of 16 years and it is not to be the practice to nominate a guardian in any of these jurisdictions.

St Lucia and Jamaica

There is no provision for the election or nomination of a tutor.

Form of Election/Nomination

The election, which is signed by the minor and witnessed sets out:

(i) details of the death of the deceased;
(ii) the entitlement of the minor to the relevant grant of the deceased's estate;
(iii) the age of the minor;
(iv) that there is no statutory, testamentary or other lawfully appointed guardian;
(v) the election or nomination of the minor's next of kin as his guardian for the purpose of obtaining letters of administration of the estate of the deceased named therein for the use and benefit of the minor, until he attains 18/21 years;

(f) **Assigned Guardian/Tutor in St Lucia**
In default of or jointly with or to the exclusion of a statutory, testamentary or other lawfully appointed guardian/tutor, a guardian/tutor may be assigned by the Registrar/judge in chambers.

A guardian/tutor may also be assigned:

a) if it is desired for just cause to pass over the statutory testamentary or other lawfully appointed guardian, or
b) for the purpose of renouncing a minor's right to a grant of administration, (with or without will annexed),[22] but with the exception of Jamaica, not his right to probate.[23]

Jamaica

Rule 68.33(5) CPR 2002, provides that a guardian may be appointed to renounce a minor's right to probate. This rule, although it does not expressly so provide, is also applicable to instances where the minor is the sole person entitled to s grant of letters of administration with will annexed.

The application for assignment is made in:

(a) *Eastern Caribbean territories, Barbados and Trinidad & Tobago ex parte* supported by affidavit to the Registrar/judge in chambers; and
(b) *Guyana and the Bahamas ex parte* summons supported by affidavit to a judge in chambers.

The contents of the affidavit are similar to the contents of the affidavit with respect to an application for a court appointed guardian. An affidavit of fitness and the consent of the proposed guardian/tutor should also be filed with the application.

Jamaica

Rule 68.28 makes express provision for a court appointed guardian but makes no provision for an assigned guardian for any purpose other than renouncing a minor's right to a grant. As such, assigned guardians do not apply to Jamaica, save and except for the purposes of such renunciation.

Nomination of Co-administrator

Eastern Caribbean (save St Lucia) and The Bahamas

When a minority or life interest arises and there is only one guardian willing and able to take a grant, the registrar may require that such guardian nominate some other person to act as co-administrator.[24]

Other Jurisdictions

Pursuant to the relevant statutory provision(s) contained in the Guardianship of Minor Act or its equivalent in the various territories, two guardians may be required to apply for the grant where the court so directs.

Documents required for Grant

The usual documents required for a grant of letters of administration (with or without will annexed) should be lodged subject to the following:

1. Administration bond, where applicable
   The Administration bond must include the words of limitation for the use and benefit of the said minor(s) until he or one of them attains the age of majority.
2. Where relevant, an office copy of the order of appointment or assignment as the case may be, must also be included in the papers to lead the grant. In Trinidad & Tobago where the minor elects a guardian, the election must be lodged.
3. A certified copy of the birth certificate of the minor must also be lodged in order to establish the minority of the minor for whose use and benefit the grant is being applied for.
4. The oath/affidavit of the applicant should include the following information:
    i. The fact that the person entitled to the grant of representation is a minor. The age of the minor should be stated.
    ii. The capacity in which the applicant is applying, that is,

whether as the parents jointly or as the statutory, testamentary, elected or other lawfully appointed guardian/tutor of the minor. When applicable, details of the order of appointment/assignment or election should also be included in the oath/affidavit.

  iii. The fact that the applicant will administer according to the law all the estate that by law devolves to and vests in him for the use and benefit of the said minor named therein and during his minority.

  iv. The usual recitals with respect to the getting in and collecting of the estate of the deceased named therein.

5. Petition

St Lucia

The petition should, in so far as applicable, include the usual recitals contained in a petition for a grant of letters of administration (with or without will annexed). Accordingly, the recitals outlined above, which are peculiar to this type of grant, should be included. However it is to be noted that the actual oath to administer, collect in, etc. the estate of the deceased, is not included in the petition, but in the oath to lead the grant.

St Vincent & the Grenadines

The petition, if filed, includes the recitals set out in the oath.

6. Nomination of Co-Administrator

Eastern Caribbean (save St Lucia) and The Bahamas

When the grant is required to be made to not less than two administrators and there is only one person competent and willing to take the grant, the nomination of a co-administrator or order of appointment must also be lodged with the papers to lead the grant.

GRANTS FOR THE USE AND BENEFIT OF A MENTALLY INCAPABLE PERSON[25]

A grant for the use and benefit of a mentally incapable person is made in circumstances where the person entitled to a grant is incapable of managing his affairs due to mental incapacity. In such circumstances a grant may be made to some other person for the use and benefit of such disabled person until the cesser of his/her disability. As with other limited grants, however, when there are persons who are entitled in the same degree as the incapable person, the grant will not be made to such persons unless they have been cleared off or unless the registrar otherwise directs.

Clearing off a Mentally Incapable Executor/Administrator

A mentally incapable person's right to probate or administration may be renounced by some person specially authorised to do so under the relevant Mental Health/Supreme Court legislation of the various territories.[26]

Alternatively where no person is so authorised, a mentally incapable person's right to probate or administration may be cleared off by citation or alternatively may be passed over under the relevant passing over provision of the various territories.

Given the alternatives available and the court's preference to granting general rather than limited grants, grants for the use and benefit of a mentally incapable person rarely arise in practice.

Proof of Mental Incapacity

All jurisdictions

Proof of the mental incapacity of the person entitled to the grant of representation may be proved:

a. by an order of the court where some person has been authorised by the court to act as administrator under the relevant Mental Health/Supreme Court legislation of the respective jurisdictions; [27]
b. by a medical certificate issued by the appropriate medical officer of the institution where the incapable person is resident; or,
c. by a medical certificate of the incapable person's doctor in cases where he is not resident in an institution.

The certificate in either case should contain the following information:

   i) The nature and extent and the likely duration of the mental incapacity of the incapable person.
   ii) The belief and opinion of the medical doctor that the person named therein is incapable of managing his affairs and property.

To Whom Grant Made- Order of Prioroty

Barbados, Dominica, Guyana and Trinidad & Tobago[28]

(a) Person(s) appointed by order of the High Court under the relevant Mental Health/Supreme Court Act of the above territories.
(b) When no person has been authorised by the court:
  i) If the incapable person is an executor with no beneficial interest in the estate, the grant is made to the person entitled to the residuary estate.
  ii) In any other case, the grant is made to the person who would be entitled to the grant in the estate of the incapable person if the latter had himself died intestate.
  iii) To such person as the Registrar may by order direct.

Eastern Caribbean territories (save Dominica) and The Bahamas[29]

  i) a person authorised by the court;
  ii) where there is no person so authorised, to the lawful attorney of the incapable person acting under a registered enduring power of attorney;
  iii) where there is no such attorney or the attorney renounces, to the person entitled to the residuary estate of the deceased;
  iv) to such person(s) as the Registrar/Judge may by order direct.

Jamaica [30]

Pursuant to Rule 68.30(3) CPR 2002:

(a) to any person authorised under the Mental Health act or any other relevant statutory authority;
(b) to the person entitled to the residuary estate of the deceased ;or
(c) to such person or persons as the registrar may by order direct.

Documents Required for Grant

The usual documents for a grant of letters of administration (with or without will annexed) must be lodged subject to the following:

1. The administration bond, where applicable, must include the words of limitations 'for the use and benefit of AB and during his incapacity'.

2. Depending on the jurisdiction, a certified copy of the court order where the person is authorised by the High Court/Mental Health/Supreme Court legislation or failing such order, a certificate from the mental institution where the patient is resident or a certificate from incapable person's doctor if not resident in an institution or order of the Registrar as the case may be.
3. The oath/affidavit should include information giving:
    i. details of the death of the deceased;
    ii. the entitlement of the incapable person to the grant whether as executor, as residuary beneficiary, next of kin or surviving spouse, as the case may be;
    iii. that the person so entitled is by reason of his or her mental incapacity incapable of managing his affairs and property;
    iv. the right and entitlement of the applicant to the grant
    v. that the applicant will administer according to law all the estate which by law devolves to and vests in the personal representative of the deceased for the use and benefit of the said incapable person and during his incapacity.
4. Nomination of Co-Administrator
    Eastern Caribbean (save St Lucia) and The Bahamas
    When the grant is required to be made to not less than two administrators, and there is only one person competent and willing to take the grant, the nomination of a co-administrator or order of appointment as the case may be, must also be lodged with the papers to lead the grant.
5. Petition
    St Lucia
    The petition should, in so far as applicable, include the usual recitals contained in a petition for a grant of letters of administration (with or without will annexed), as the case may be. Accordingly, the recitals outlined above, which are peculiar to this type of grant, should be included. However it is to be noted that the actual oath to administer, collect in, etc. the estate of the deceased, is not included in the petition, but in the oath to lead the grant.

    St Vincent & the Grenadines
    The petition, if filed, contains the recitals set out in the oath/affidavit of the applicant.

GRANTS FOR THE USE AND BENEFIT OF A PHYSICALLY INCAPABLE PERSON

Introduction

1. Barbados, Dominica, and Guyana

In accordance with r.33 N.C.P.R. 1954, England, where a person is incapable of managing his affairs by reason of physical incapacity, a grant of administration may be made for his use and benefit limited during his incapacity to the person(s) so authorised.

Persons authorised in Order of Priority[31]

A.   No Interest Residuary Estate

When the person incapable is entitled as executor and has no interest in the residuary estate of the deceased, administration (with or without will annexed) will be granted to the person(s) entitled to the residuary estate of the deceased. Unless otherwise directed by the registrar/judge in chambers.

B.   Interest in Residuary Estate

Where the incapable person is an executor who has an interest in the residuary estate of the deceased or is entitled in order of priority to letters of administration (with or without will annexed), letters of administration be granted for the incapable person's use and benefit:

> (i) to the person who would be entitled to a grant in respect of the deceased's estate if he had died intestate; or,
> (ii) to such other person as the Registrar/Judge may by order direct.

Notice of Intended application

Unless otherwise directed by the court/registrar, notice of intended application for such a grant is required to be given to the physically incapable person.

Proof of Incapacity

Physical incapacity must be proved to the satisfaction of the court; in such instances an affidavit of the incapable person's doctor should be filed with the papers to lead the relevant grant of representation.

Documents required for Grant

The usual documents for a grant of letters of administration (with will annexed) must be lodged subject to the following:

1. The oath should include the following:
   (i) The fact that the person entitled to the grant of the deceased estate is now by reason of his physical incapacity incapable of managing his affairs.
   (ii) The entitlement of the applicant to the residuary estate of the deceased, or otherwise that the applicant is entitled to apply for a grant of letters of administration for the use and benefit of the incapable person, as the case may be.
   (iii) The usual clearings off where there are persons with a prior entitlement to the grant for the use and benefit of the incapable person.
   (iv) The oath of the administrator to collect, get in and administer the deceased's estate ending with the words of limitation 'for the use and benefit of the incapable person and during his incapacity'.
2. Affidavit of the patient's doctor (as proof of physical incapacity).
3. The administration bond, where applicable, should include the words of limitation as recited in the oath.

2. The Bahamas and Eastern Caribbean (save Dominica)

The N.C.P.R. 1987, England which apply to the above territories, contain no provisions for grants to be issued for the use and benefit of a physically disabled person. The current practice in England and it is submitted by extension the above-mentioned territories, is for the person incapable of managing his affairs, by reason of physical as opposed to mental incapacity, to appoint a suitable person as his attorney for the purpose of applying for the relevant grant. Indeed in the N.C.P.R. 1987, England, the physically disabled person has been excluded by r.35 as a category of applicants for whom this type of special grant is necessary.[32] This practice is to be recommended in the other territories.

Jamaica

The new CPR 2002, in particular Rule 68, makes no provision for grants to be made for the use and benefit of a physically incapable person. However, as is the case in England, a grant to the attorney of a physically incapable person should in such circumstances be applicable.

Trinidad & Tobago

In practice, where the person enabled to a grant of representation is physically incapable, he may appoint an attorney for the purpose of applying for the relevant grant on his behalf.

LOST OR ORAL WILL GRANTS [33]

An application for a lost will grant is necessary when the original will/codicil of the testator has been lost, misplaced or accidentally destroyed so that the original testamentary papers cannot be admitted to probate. With respect to those jurisdictions to which privileged wills apply, an application must be made to admit to proof an oral will in cases where the deceased left such a will.

Practice and Procedure for Preliminary Order

In the above instances, an application for an order admitting to proof an oral will or a will contained in a copy completed draft or reconstruction may be made in:

(a) *Eastern Caribbean territories (save St. Lucia), Barbados, Grenada, Jamaica and Trinidad & Tobago* in the first instance to the registrar *ex parte* on affidavit unless the registrar otherwise directs that the application should be made in the first instance to a judge; and in

(b) *Guyana, St Lucia and The Bahamas* in the first instance, by summons supported by affidavit(s) to a judge in chambers; or,

(c) *All jurisdictions*
to a judge in open court where the registrar/judge in chambers so directs, or alternatively when it is apparent from the facts that the application should be made to a judge in open court as for example where although there is no active opposition to the application, the person who may be prejudiced by the application, refuses to or cannot, because of his minority, give his consent thereto.

A. Original Will Not Produced

In cases where the original will cannot be produced, the affidavits[34] filed in support of the application should seek to establish the following:

(i) The existence of the will after the testator's death; if no such evidence is available, the facts on which the applicant relies to rebut the presumption that the will was destroyed by the testator *animo revocandi*.

(ii) The efforts made to find the will; that is, if any advertisements have been published the page clipping from the newspapers (showing the date thereof) should be exhibited and annexed thereto.
(iii) Due execution of the original will by an affidavit of one of the attesting witnesses if possible.
(iv) The fact where applicable that the draft copy of the will was examined with the original and found to be complete and accurate. In such instances an affidavit of some person who can verifr its contents such as the attorney-at-law who was responsible for its preparation should also be filed.
(v) in the case of a reconstruction of a will, the accuracy of the reconstruction; and
(vi) with respect to jurisdictions to which privileged wills apply, the contents of that will.

The respective affidavits should be made by the applicant for the grant and supported by affidavits of one of the attesting witnesses if available, the person who examined the original with the draft/copy thereof and the person who can swear to the circumstances of its loss or destruction and the efforts made to find it.

Consent in Writing

The consent in writing of all those who are *sui juris* and who would be prejudiced by admission of the will to probate should also be lodged. Such persons include those persons who would be entitled to a share or greater share of the deceased's estate on an intestacy.

Limitation

When it is known that the will is lost or destroyed the order of the court should include a direction that the grant be limited until a more authentic copy of the will be proved. Should the original will be found after the issue of the lost will grant, the grantee must apply for a cessate grant.

B. Oral Will

Where the will to be proved is an oral will, affidavit evidence must be adduced as to the contents of the will.

Documents Required for Grant

The usual documents for a grant of probate/letters of administration with will annexed subject to the following:

1. A copy of the order of the registrar/judge should be lodged with the papers to lead the grant;
2. The oath to lead the grant should recite:
    (i) the granting of the order by the registrar/judge, including its date and effect, and in the case of a lost or destroyed will, the relevant words of limitation;
    (ii) a description of the applicant and his relationship, if any, to the testator.
    (iii) the belief of the applicant that the paper writings now produced to and marked by him contain the said copy, draft, reconstruction or contents of the oral will as the case may be.
    (iv) the oath of the executor/administrator, to collect, get in and administer the deceased's estate including in the case of a lost or destroyed will, the words of limitation as set out in the order.
3. The administration bond, where applicable, should include the words of limitation recited in the oath.

3. Petition

St Lucia

The petition should, in so far as applicable, include the usual recitals contained in a petition for a grant of probate or letters of administration (with or without will annexed), as the case may be. Accordingly, the recitals outlined above, which are peculiar to this type of grant, should be included. However it is to be noted that the actual oath to administer and collect in the estate of the deceased, is not included in the petition, but in the oath to lead the grant.

St Vincent & the Grenadines

The petition, if filed, contains the recitals set out in the oath/affidavit of the applicant.

Original Will in the Custody of a Foreign Court or Official

When the original will is in the custody of a foreign court no order of the court is required for the admission of a copy to proof. In such instances a duly authenticated copy issued by the court or official is accepted as the equivalent to the original.

Proof in Solemn Form

The will may have to be proved in solemn form:
(a) where there is serious opposition to the application being made; or
(b) if the missing or lost will was last known to be in the possession of the testator, in order to rebut the presumption of destruction *animo revocandi*.[35]

Damaged Will

When a will has been damaged or mutilated it may be necessary to first obtain an order of the court to admit to proof the damaged will as contained in a copy.

Procedure

The first step is to submit the damaged will together with an examined copy for inspection by the registrar. If the will is badly damaged, an application to admit a draft/copy will be ordered by the registrar. If not, the damaged will may be admitted to probate with the usual documents for a grant of probate/letters of administration with will annexed together with an affidavit of plight and condition.[36]

Notes

1	Barbados	- r.28 Supreme Court (Non-Contentious) Probate Rules 1959
	Guyana	- s.17 Deceased Persons Estates' Administration Act Cap. 12:01
	St Lucia	- Ant 1018 Code of Civil Procedure Ch. 243
	Trinidad & Tobago	- r.27 N.C.B.R. First Schedule Ch. 8 No. 2.
2	Barbados	- r.27 Supreme Court (Non-Contentious) Probate Rules 1959
	St Lucia	- Art 1017(1) Civil Code Ch. 243
	Trinidad & Tobago	- r.25 N.C.B.R. First Schedule Ch. 8 No, 2.
3	See Introduction pp. 11-12.	

4   Pursuant to Art. 1013 Code of Civil Procedure Ch. 243 the registrar in St Lucia was empowered since 1957 to make common form grants of probate and letters of administration.
5   See Introduction p. 13.
6   *Ibid.*
7
Legislation

Antigua & Barbuda	- Administration of Estates by Consular Officer Act Cap. 6 Consular Conventions Act Cap. 95
Barbados	- Succession Act Cap. 249 Consular Conventions Act Cap. 17
Dominica	- Administration of Estates by Consular Officers Act Ch. 9:08 Consular Conventions Act Ch. 17:51
Grenada	- Consular Conventions Act Cap. 63 Deceased Americans Consular Representation Act Cap. 77
Guyana	- Consular Conventions Act Cap. 18:02
Jamaica	- Consular Convention Act 1973 Revised Laws
St Christopher & Nevis, Anguilla	- Administration of Estates by Consular Officers Act Cap. 136 Consular Conventions Act Cap. 138
St Lucia	- Administration of Estates by Consular Officers Act Cap. 22 Consular Conventions Act Cap. 23
St Vincent & the Grenadines	- Administration of Estates by Consular Officers Act Cap. 378 Consular Conventions Act
The Bahamas	- s.33 Administration of Estates Act 2002 100; See also s.51 Supreme Court Act 15/1996
Trinidad & Tobago	- s.35 Wills and Probate Ordinance Ch. 8 No. 2

8
Anguilla	- s.2 Administration of Estates by Consular Officers Act Ch. 136
Antigua & Barbuda	- s.2 Administration of Estates by Consular Officers Act Cap. 6
Dominica	- s.2 Administration of Estates by Consular Officers Act Ch. 9:08
Montserrat	- s.2 Administration of Estates by Consular Officers Act Cap. 127
St Lucia	- s.2 Administration of Estates by Consular Officers Ch. 22
St Christopher & Nevis	- s.2 Administration of Estates by Consular Officers Act Ch. 136
St Vincent & the Grenadines	- s.2 Wills Act Cap. 378
The Bahamas	- s.33 Administration of Estates Act 2002
Trinidad & Tobago	- s.35(2) Wills & Probate Ordinance Ch. 8 No. 2.

9
Anguilla, St. Christopher & Nevis	- s.2(4) Consular Conventions Act Cap. 138
Antigua & Barbuda	- 5.2(1) Consular Conventions Act Cap. 95
Barbados	- s.3(1) Consular Conventions Act Cap. 17
Dominica	- s.4(1) Consular Conventions Act Ch. 17:51
Grenada	- s.2(1) Consular Conventions Act Cap. 63

	Guyana	- 5.2(1) Consular Conventions Act Cap. 18:02
	Jamaica	- s.3(1) Consular Conventions Act 1973 Revised Laws Applicable only in respect of estates of persons Dying prior to January 1, 2002 pursuant to Rule 68, C.P.R. 2002
	Montserrat	- s.2 Consular Conventions Act Cap. 129
	St. Lucia	- Although an administration bond is not generally required in St. Lucia, s.2(3) of the Consular Convention Act expressly makes reference to administration bonds. However, there is No mention of whether sureties to bond are required. See chapter 13.
	St Vincent & the Grenadines	- s.7(1) Consular Conventions Act Cap. 134
	The Bahamas	- s.8(1) Probate Act (1. 35; See also s.51 of the Supreme Court Act 27/1996 (not yet law).
10	Barbados	- s.24 Succession Act Cap. 249; r.29 Supreme Court (Non-Contentious Probate) Rules, 1959
	Dominica, Eastern Caribbean (save Dominica and St Lucia),The Bahamas	- r.30 N.C.P.R. 1954, England - r.31 N.C.P.R, 1987, England
	Guyana	- rr. 2, 3 Deceased Persons Estates' Administration Rules
	Jamaica	- Rule 68.23 which repealed and replaced r.29 General Rules and Orders of the Supreme Court Part III Probate and Administration
	St Lucia	- Art 1019 Code of Civil Procedure Ch. 243
	Trinidad & Tobago	- r.28 First Schedule N.C.B.R. Ch. 8 No. 2.
11	See r.30(2) N.C.P.R. 1954, England.	
12	*Ibid.*	
13	Anguilla, Montserrat, St Christopher & Nevis	- Registration and Records Act Cap. 69
	Barbados	- s.149 Evidence Act 4/1994 - Property Act Cap. 236 Part X Powers of Attorney
	Dominica	- ss, 9-14 Registration and Records Act Ch. 19:04 (See also Evidence Ord. Cap. 64)
	Grenada	- Evidence (Amendment) Act 9/1995 - See also: Deeds and Land Registry Act Cap. 79
	Guyana	- Powers of Attorney Act Ch. 5:08 Deeds Registry Act Cap. 5:01 See also: ss. 22. 27-33 Evidence Act Cap. 5:03
	Jamaica	- The Probate of Deeds Act
	St Lucia	- Art 1152 Civil Code Ch. 242 as amended by s.5 Civil Code (Amendment) (No.3) Act 3/1991
	St Vincent & the Grenadines	- Powers of Attorney Act Cap. 91 s.32 Evidence Act Cap. 158

See also: Registration of Documents Act Cap. 93, Registra-tion of Documents (Amendment)

	Act 11/1993	
	The Bahamas	- Registration of Records Act Ch. 175
		Power of Attorney Act 1992
	Trinidad & Tobago	- Registration of Deeds Act Ch. 19:06.
14	Barbados	- s.25 Succession Act Cap. 249
	Eastern Caribbean	- s.118 Supreme Court Act 1981, England
	(save St Vincent &	
	the Grenadines and	
	St Lucia), The Bahamas	
	Guyana	- s.6 Infancy Act Cap. 46:0 1
	Jamaica	- Rule 68.28 CPR 2002 repealing and replacing r.19
		General Rules and Orders of the Supreme Court
		Part III Probate and Administration
	St Lucia	- Art 591 Civil Code Ch. 242
		Art 1020 Code of Civil Procedure Ch. 243
	St Vincent &	- s.18 Administration of Estates Act Cap. 377
	the Grenadines	
	The Bahamas	- See s.47 of the Supreme Court Act 15/1996
	Trinidad & Tobago	- s.19 Wills & Probate Ordinance Ch. 8 No. 2.

Rules

	Barbados, Guyana,	- rr. 31, 32, 33, N.C.P.R 1954, England
	Dominica	
	Eastern Caribbean,	- rr.32, 33, 34 N.C.P.R. 1987, England
	(save Dominica)	
	Jamaica	- Rule 68.28 CPR 2002 repealing and
		replacing r.19 General Rules and Orders of the
		Supreme Court Part III Probate and Administration
	St Lucia	- Art 1021 Code of Civil Procedure CE, 243
	Trinidad & Tobago	- rr. 29, 30, 31 First Schedule N.C.B.R. CE. 8 No. 2.
15	Antigua & Barbuda	- Age of Majority Act Ch. 11
	Barbados	- Law of Minors Act Cap. 215
	Dominica	- Age of Majority Act Ch. 37:01
	Grenada	- s.2(1)(b) and (2) Citizenship Act 12/1976
	Guyana	- Age of Majority Representation of the People
		(Adoption of Laws) Act 1973
	Jamaica	- Law Reform (Age of Majority) Act 1979
	Montserrat	- Constitution and Elections Ord. Cap. 153
	St Christopher &	- Age of Majority Act 1983
	Nevis	
	St Lucia	- Civil Code (Amendment) Act 4/1988
	St Vincent &	- Law of Minors Act Cap. 169
	the Grenadines	
	The Bahamas	- Minors Act Ch. 6
	Trinidad & Tobago	- Age of Majority Act Ch. 46:06.
16	Barbados, Dominica,	- r.32(l) N.C.P.R. 1954, England
	Guyana	
	Jamaica	- Rule 68.28(2) CPR 2002

	Trinidad & Tobago Eastern Caribbean (save Dominica) The Bahamas	- r.33(1) N.C.P.R. 1987, England.
17	Dominica, Barbados, Guyana	- r.31(1) N.C.P.R. 1954, England
	St Lucia	- Art 1021 Code of Civil Procedure Ch. 243, Arts 216-227 Civil Code Amendment Act 13/1989
	The Bahamas, Eastern Caribbean (save Dominica)	- r.32(1) N.C.P.R. 1987, England.
	Jamaica	- Rule 68.28 CPR 2002

18 Although the relevant non-contentious probate rule of St Lucia, and Trinidad & Tobago does not specifically provide for parents to apply for a grant for the use and benefit of a minor as is the case with respect to Barbados, Guyana, The Bahamas and the Eastern Caribbean territories, save St Lucia, which territories receive the English probate rules, (r.31(1) N.C.P.R. 1954, England/r.32(1) N.C.P.R. 1987, England) the practice nevertheless is to permit the parent to apply for the grant on behalf of the minor. However it is to be noted that unlike the Eastern Caribbean territories (save St Lucia), and the Bahamas where two administrators are required whenever minority or life interests arises, the application for the grant may be made by one parent in the other jurisdictions unless otherwise directed by the court. However it is to be noted that with respect to the Bahamas this requirement has not yet been implemented.

	Jamaica	- Rule 68.28 (1)(a) CPR 2002
19	Antigua & Barbuda	- s.6 Guardianship of Infants Act Cap. 197
	Barbados	- s.4 Law of Minors Act Cap. 215
	Dominica	- s.3 Guardianship of Infants Act Ch. 37:04
	Guyana	- s.12 Infancy Act Cap. 46:01
	Jamaica	- Rule 68.28 (1)(b) CPR 2002
	Montserrat	- s.6 Guardianship of Infants Act Cap. 297
	St Lucia	- Art 218 Civil Code Ch. 242
	St Vincent & the Grenadines	- s.6 Law of Minors Act Cap. 169 -
	The Bahamas	- s.3 Guardianship and Custody of Infants Act Ch. 118
	Trinidad & Tobago	- s.7 Family (Guardianship of Minors, Domicile and Maintenance) Act Ch. 46:08.
20	Antigua & Barbuda	- s. 7 Guardianship of Infants Act Cap. 197
	Barbados	- s.5 Minors Act Cap. 215 Part III
	Dominica	- s.4 Guardianship of Infants Act Ch. 37:04
	Guyana	- s.13 Infancy Act 46:01 Cap. 46:01
	Jamaica	- Rule 68.28 (1)(b) CPR 2002
	Montserrat	- s.8 Guardianship of Infants Act Cap. 297
	St Christopher & Nevis/Anguilla	- s.7 Guardianship of Infants Act Cap. 323
	St Lucia	- Art 219 Civil Code Ch. 242
	St Vincent & the Grenadines	- s.7 Law of Minors Act 49/1989

	Jurisdiction	Reference
	The Bahamas	- s.4 Guardianship and Custody of Infants Act Ch. 118
	Trinidad & Tobago	- s. 8 Family (Guardianship of Minors, Domicile and Maintenance) Act Ch. 46:08.
21	Antigua & Barbuda	- ss. 6, 7, 8, Guardianship of Infants Act Cap. 197
	Barbados	- ss. 4, 5 Law of Minors Act Cap. 215
	Dominica	- ss. 3, 4, Guardianship of Infants Act Ch. 37:04
	Guyana	- ss. 12, 13, Infancy Act Cap. 46:01
	Jamaica	- Rule 68.28 (1)(c) CPR 2002; It is to be noted that pursuant to the provisions of ss.24, 27 and 28 of the Administrator General Act, the Administrator General may be appointed guardian of an infant by the Supreme Court provided he consents to the appointment and is invested with the entire administration of such property
	Montserrat	- ss.7, 8, 9, Guardianship of Infants Act Cap. 297
	St Christopher & Nevis, Anguilla	- ss.6, 7, 8, Guardianship of Infants Act Cap. 323
	St Lucia	- Arts 2 17-222 Civil Code Ch. 242
	St Vincent & the Grenadines	- ss. 6, 7, 8, Law of Minors Act 49/1989
	The Bahamas	- ss. 2, 3, 4, 5, 6, Guardianship and Custody of Infants Act Ch. 118
	Trinidad & Tobago	- ss. 7, 8, 9, Family (Guardianship of Minors, Domicile and Maintenance) Act Ch. 46:08.
22	Barbados, Dominica, Guyana	- r. 31(6) N.C.P.R. 1954, England
	Eastern Caribbean, (save Dominica & St Lucia)	- r.34(2) N.C.P.R. 1987, England
	St Lucia	- Art 1021 Code of Civil Procedure Ch. 243
	Trinidad & Tobago	- r.31 N.C.B.R. First Schedule Ch. 8 No. 2.
	Jamaica	- Rule 68.33 CPR 2002
23	Barbados, Guyana, Dominica, Trinidad & Tobago	- r.32(2) N.C.P.R. 1954, England
	Jamaica	- Rule 68.33(5) CPR 2002
	The Bahamas, Eastern Caribbean (save Dominica)	- r.34(1) N.C.P.R. 1987, England.
24	Eastern Caribbean (save Dominica and St Lucia)	- r.32(3) N.C.P.R. 1987, England
	Dominica	- r.31(3) N.CPR. 1954, England.
25	The Bahamas, Eastern Caribbean (save Dominica)	- r.35 N.C.P.R. 1987, England
	Trinidad & Tobago, Guyana, Dominica,	- r.33 N.C.P.R. 1954, England.

	Barbados	
	Jamaica	- Rule 68.28 CPR 2002
26	See note 27 below.	
27	Barbados	- s.19 Mental Health Act Cap. 45
		See also: s.12 Supreme Court of Judicature Act Cap. 117A
	Dominica	- ss. 18, 19 Mental Health Act Ch. 40:62
	Eastern Caribbean territories (save St Lucia)	- s.7(2) of the respective Supreme Court Acts of these jurisdictions
	Guyana	- Section 17 High Court Act Cap. 3:02
	Jamaica	- Rule 68.30 CPR 2002. See also s.25 of the Administrator General Act which provides in effect that the Administrator General maybe appointed committee of the estate of 'an idiot or a lunatic'. However such appointments will not he made except with the consent of the Administrator-General
	St Lucia	- Arts 28 5-296 Civil Code Ch. 242
		See also: Arts 297-307 Civil Code Ch. 242
	St Vincent & the Grenadines	- s.19 Mental Health Act Cap. 228
	The Bahamas	- s.36 Mental Health Act Ch. 215
	Trinidad & Tobago	- ss.37-39 Mental Health Act Ch. 28:02
		See also s.11 Supreme Court of Judicature Act Ch. 4:01.
28	Barbados, Dominica Guyana, Trinidad & Tobago	- r.33(1) N.C.P.R. 1954, England.
29	The Bahamas, Eastern Caribbean (save Dominica)	- r.35(2) N.C.P.R. 1987, England.
30	See also ss. 25-30 Administrator General Act.	
31	Rule 33 (1) (b) N.C.P.R. 1954, England.	
32	For the relevant practice, procedure and documents with respect to grants to attorneys, see pp. 336-340.	
33	Barbados, Trinidad & Tobago, Guyana, Dominica	- r.53 N.C.P.R. 1954, England
	Jamaica, The Bahamas, Eastern Caribbean (save St Lucia and Dominica)	- r.54 N.C.P.R. 1987. England
	Jamaica	- Rule 68.17 CPR 2002
	St Lucia	- Arts 797,798, Civil Code Ch. 242. See also Art 1017 Code of Civil Procedure Ch. 243.
34	See chapter 2.	
35	Jamaica	- Rule 68.17 CPR 2002
36	See chapter 5, p. 119.	

17

Limited Grants cont'd

GRANTS *DURANTE ABSENTIA*[1]

As a general rule if after the expiration of six months (Trinidad & Tobago) or 12 months, (the other jurisdictions) from the date of death of any person, the personal representative to whom representation has been granted, is residing out of the jurisdiction of the court, the court may, on the application of the Administrator General (in the case of Trinidad & Tobago) or any creditor or person having a beneficial interest in the deceased's estate, grant a special administration of the estate of the deceased, such administration to be limited during the absence of such person.

Trinidad & Tobago

Pursuant to s.35(1) of the Wills and Probate Ordinance Ch. 8 No. 2, applications for grants *durante absentia* are limited to instances where the executor is residing out of the jurisdiction of the court and has been so resident for a period of six months or more from the date of the death of the deceased.

Eastern Caribbean territories (save St Lucia)

In contrast to the Judicature Act 1925, and the N.C.P.R. 1954, England, the Supreme Court Act 1981 and the N.C.P.R. 1987, England contain no provision with respect to grants *durante absentia*.

Grants *durante absentia* may no longer be applicable to the Eastern Caribbean territories mentioned above including Dominica, which is in a somewhat anomalous position as it receives the N.C.P.R. 1954, England but not the Judicature Act 1925 on which the procedural law contained in the N.C.P.R. 1954 is based.

Jamaica

The CPR 2002, in particular Rule 68, contains no provision with respect to grants *durante absentia*. Additionally the indigenous probate legislation contains no provision with respect to applications for such grants. This type of grant is therefore not applicable to Jamaica.

Discretionary Grants- Alternative

All jurisdictions (save Jamaica)

As an alternative to grants *durante absentia* an application may be made for a grant under the discretionary powers of the court as is now the practice in England.

Grants Durante Absentia

Practice and Procedure for Preliminary Order

The application for a grant *durante absentia* is made to the court on motion. A notice of the intended application is required to be sent to the postal address of the grantee and may also have to be given to any person with a prior right to the grant.

The application for the grant is made under the relevant statutory provision of the respective territories and is usually limited until the absentee personal representative returns to the jurisdiction of the court.

The application and the affidavit in support should be intituled *inter alia* In the Matter of the Estate of the Deceased named therein and In the Matter of the relevant statutory provision of the respective territories.

Contents of Affidavit in Support

The affidavit should recite *inter alia*:

(i) The date and place of death of the deceased;
(ii) that 6/12 months or whatever longer period have elapsed since the date of death of the deceased;
(iii) that the person to whom the grant has been made is to the knowledge and information of the applicant residing out of the jurisdiction and has to date failed or neglected to administer the deceased's estate within the time prescribed;
(iv) that a notice in writing of the intended application was posted

as the case may be to the postal address of the grantee and that such grantee has failed or neglected to reply. A copy of the notice should be exhibited;
(v) where applicable, that notice in writing of the application was sent to the person(s) having a prior entitlement to the grant. A copy of the notice should also be exhibited.
(vi) the entitlement of the applicant to apply for the grant whether as the Administrator General, as a creditor or as a person beneficially interested in the estate of the deceased, as the case may be; in the case of a creditor, particulars and evidence of the deceased's indebtedness must be included.

Documents Required

Once the order is granted the usual papers to lead a grant of letters of administration (with or without will annexed) must be lodged in the Registry, subject to the following:

1. The oath should
   (i) be intituled in the same manner as the application;
   (ii) recite the particular order of the court;
   (iii) include the relevant words of limitation.
2. The administration bond, where applicable, should also contain the words of limitation recited in the oath.
3. The former grant where possible should also be lodged.
4. A copy of the order and of the notices of the intended application should also be lodged.
5. Petition

St Lucia

The petition should, in so far as applicable, include the usual recitals contained in a petition for a grant of letters of administration (with or without will annexed), as the case may be. Accordingly, the recitals in the oath outlined above, which are peculiar to this type of grant, should be included. However the actual oath to administer and collect in the estate of the deceased, is not included in the petition, but in the oath to lead the grant.

GRANTS LIMITED TO PROPERTY[2]

A grant of probate or administration may be made either separately in respect of real estate or in respect of personal estate and limited in any way the court thinks fit. Grants may be so limited:

(a) where the applicant is entitled only to a limited grant in respect of part of the deceased's estate; or in all jurisdictions save Jamaica
(b) where the person entitled to the grant of the entire estate wishes to apply for a grant of part only of the estate.

However where the estate of the deceased is known to be insolvent it will not be so severed except with respect to trust estate in which the deceased had no beneficial interest.

Jamaica

The indigenous succession legislation contains no provision with respect to grants limited to property. Accordingly, this type of limited grant is not applicable to Jamaica. However where the applicant is entitled only to a limited grant in respect of part of the deceased's estate, the practice and procedure which obtains in the other territories is applicable to Jamaica.

Practice and Procedure

A.   Order Required

All jurisdictions (save Jamaica)

An order granting leave to apply for a grant limited to a part of an estate is made where the applicant is a person who is entitled to a general grant but who wishes to apply for a grant of part only of the deceased's estate. In such instances the application is made in:

a)   *Barbados, Eastern Caribbean Territories and Trinidad & Tobago*
     In the first instance *ex parte* on affidavit to the registrar unless the registrar directs that the application be made to a judge in chambers.
b)   *Guyana*
     To a judge in chambers in the first instance.
c)   *All jurisdictions*
     Alternatively to a judge in open court where the registrar/judge in chambers otherwise directs.

Contents of Affidavit in support of Application

The affidavit in support should:

a) state whether the estate of the deceased is known to be insolvent and, in cases where there are persons entitled to a general grant in priority to the applicant, should
b) show how such persons if any, have been cleared off. In such cases renunciation(s) if any should be filed with the application.

Post Script

It should be noted that:

(a) where the intended grantee is not entitled in priority to the grant (subject to any clearings off), an order under the discretionary powers of the court must be applied for, and
(b) where a grant limited to part of the deceased's estate is made pursuant to an order of the court, a grant of the remainder of the estate may be made without further order of the court.

B. No Order Required

All jurisdictions

Where the grantee is a person entitled to a limited grant, in respect of part only of the deceased's estate, no order of the court is necessary.

Documents Required for Grants

The usual documents for a grant of probate/letters of administration with will annexed subject to the following:

1. The oath/affidavit of the grantee should include:
   i) particulars of the order of the registrar/judge where the application for the grant is made pursuant to an order of the court. A copy of the order should be exhibited thereto;
   ii) where applicable, the terms of the will limiting the grant to the property to be covered by grant e.g. that "AB has named me executor of his will save and except the real property owned by him and situate at..."
   iii) recitals with respect to the clearing off of persons with a superior

right and more particularly the manner in which such persons have been cleared off. In such instances renunciations and the death certificate of the person with a prior right, as the case may be, should be exhibited;

iv) that the executor/administrator will administer the estate which by law devolves to vests in the personal representatives of the said deceased save and except the property not covered by the grant;

2. The Inventory, Declaration and Account, and Affidavit of Value, is limited to a description and the value of the property to be covered by the grant.
3. Administration bond (with or without will annexed) in cases of grants of administration, where applicable. The bond should include the words of limitation included in the oath.
4. The copy of the order of the Judge/Registrar, where applicable.
5. Petition

St Lucia

The petition should, in so far as applicable, include the usual recitals contained in a petition for a grant of letters of administration (with or without will annexed), as the case may be. Accordingly, the recitals outlined in the oath above, which are peculiar to this type of grant, should be included. However, the actual oath to administer and collect in the estate of the deceased, is not included in the petition, but in the oath to lead the grant.

GRANTS MADE UNDER THE DISCRETIONARY POWERS OF COURT[3]

All jurisdictions (save Jamaica)

A grant made under the discretionary powers conferred on the court by the relevant statutory provisions of the various Caribbean territories in effect permits the court by reason of the insolvency of the deceased's estate or of any other special circumstances to pass over the person(s) primarily entitled to administer the deceased's estate and appoint as administrator (with or without will annexed) such other person(s) as it thinks necessary or expedient, for the better realisation of the estate or for the benefit of any person interested therein. In such instances, the persons to whom administration is granted are usually those persons next entitled to take out the relevant grant of representation of the deceased's estate.

Instances of such special circumstances include where the person primarily entitled is of a bad or criminal character.[4] However applications for discretionary grants are not limited to circumstances in which it is sought to 'pass over' a person with a prior entitlement to the relevant grant. Indeed, because of the wording of the respective statutory provision of the various jurisdictions, discretionary grants are also applicable in the following circumstances:

(a) where, because of the wording of a will, it is unclear who is first entitled to the grant;[5]
(b) where the person first entitled to the grant is abroad and the grant is required urgently;[6]
(c) where a grant is required to constitute a party to an action.[7]
Although the relevant statutory provision of the various territories speaks only of passing over the person entitled by law to the grant of administration, this provision, nevertheless is deemed to apply to executors as well.

Barbados

Although discretionary grants are relevant to Barbados, they are of limited application given that the Registrar, pursuant to s.19(3) of the Succession Act Cap. 249 has a wide discretion with respect to determining to whom administration should be granted. This statutory discretion may in the appropriate circumstances be exercised in favour of beneficiaries with an inferior right to a grant of administration, even in instances where the beneficiary with the prior entitlement to the grant of administration will not consent or renounce. Accordingly, applications for discretionary grants are usually made in cases where it is sought to pass over an executor's right to probate.

Jamaica- Impact of Rule 68.11, Rule 68.18 CPR 2002

There is no statutory provision in Jamaica, as obtains in the other jurisdictions, nor any provision contained in Rule 68 of the CPR 2002, which specifically provides for the court to issue a discretionary grant and effectively pass over the person(s) primarily entitled to take out letters of administration (with or without will annexed). This may perhaps, in part, be because until January 1, 2003 (the date of the coming into operation of CPR 2002) there was no order of priority with respect to entitlement to grants of letters of administration (with or without will annexed).

The closest equivalent to a 'passing over provision' is s.12 of the Intestates' Estate and Property Charges Act.[8] In this regard, section 12 in effect provides that unless the court is satisfied that it would be for the benefit of the estate, that letters of administration ought to be granted to some other person, letters of administration to such estate shall be granted to the Administrator General.

However, with the introduction of an order of priority to grants of administration (with or without will annexed) that where the applicant for the grant is not the Administrator General, an order of the court must be obtained, in cases where the applicant for such grant is not first entitled in accordance with the order of priority as set out in Rule 68.11 and Rule 68.18 CPR 2002, respectively, and where such person(s) with the prior entitlement has/have not been otherwise cleared off. In such instances, a s.12 application in effect operates as a discretionary grant application. However, where the order of priority as provided for in Rule 68.11 and Rule 68.18 is observed, the Administrator General Certificate should be obtained in such circumstances in accordance with the procedure and practice relevant to general grants of administration.

With respect to an executor, there is no specific statutory provision which allows the Court to pass over the executor's right to probate. However, as is the case in the other jurisdictions, s.12 of the Intestates' Estates and Property Charges Act, which is the equivalent 'passing over' provision for Jamaica such provision is equally applicable to the executor.

Practice and Procedure for Preliminary Order[9]

The application for leave to apply for a discretionary grant is made in:

(a) Barbados, Eastern Caribbean Territories, Jamaica and Trinidad & Tobago to the registrar *ex parte* on affidavit unless the registrar directs that the application be made to a judge in chambers
(b) Guyana and The Bahamas *ex parte* supported by affidavit to a judge in chambers.

Contents of Affidavit

The supporting affidavit should recite *inter alia*:

(i) the reasons why it is being sought to pass over the person with the primary entitlement to the relevant grant of representation;
(ii) the fitness to act of the proposed administrator (not applicable where the proposed grantee is the Administrator General).

The consent in writing of the proposed grantee should also be lodged.

A draft order for initialling by the registrar/judge should also be prepared and lodged with the affidavit. The order should recite the powers which have been conferred by the court and the limitations, if any, which must also be repeated in the bond and the grant issued by the court.

The summons/affidavits should be intituled In the Matter of the relevant 'passing over' provision of the various territories and In the Matter of the Estate of the Deceased named therein.

Documents Required for Grant

The usual documents necessary to lead a grant of letters of administration (with or without will annexed) as the case may be, should be lodged subject to the following:

1. A copy of the order of the court granting leave to apply for the grant under the discretionary powers of the court.
2. An administration bond containing the words of limitation as set out in the order of the court, where applicable.
3. The oath to lead the grant should set out *inter alia* the date and effect of the order of the court including the relevant statutory provision and Act under which the order was made and the limitations, if any, imposed by the court.
4. The Petition

St Lucia

The petition should, in so far as applicable, include the usual recitals contained in a petition for a grant of letters of administration (with or without will annexed), as the case may be. Accordingly, the recitals outlined above, which are peculiar to this type of grant, should be included. However the actual oath to administer and collect in the estate of the deceased, is not included in the petition, but in the oath to lead the grant.

GRANTS *PENDENTE LITE*

Introduction

Where legal proceedings are pending concerning the validity of a will or the granting, recalling or revocation of probate or letters of administration, an application may be made to the High Court to grant administration limited to the continuance of the litigation to an administrator pending suit.[10] The purpose of such a grant is to ensure that during the pendency of the probate action, the estate of the deceased is managed and preserved for the benefit of those entitled.

An administrator so appointed has all the rights, duties and powers of a general administrator save and except distribution of the estate or any part thereof, unless leave of the court is granted. He is also entitled to receive remuneration, such remuneration to be paid out of the estate.

He is also subject to the immediate control of the court and acts under its direction and in accordance with many of the rules which apply to a receiver. In fact, most of the provisions of the relevant Orders and Rules of the Supreme Court which relate to receivers are applicable to administrators *pendente lite*.[11]

Jamaica

There is no indigenous legislation which specifically provides for applications to be made for a grant *pendente lite*. However s.23 of the Administrator General's Act makes provision for the Administrator General 'to take possession of, hold and deal with' the estate of a deceased person by order of the court until the relevant grant is obtained, in circumstances where it is doubtful who will apply for and obtain letters of administration or letters testamentary.

It is unclear from the wording of this section whether it is intended to govern and include the specific instance where there are legal proceedings pending concerning the validity of a will.

However given the general language of this provision, it is sufficiently wide to permit the Administrator General to administer without the necessity of a grant, a deceased person's estate pending the outcome of litigation with respect to the validity of a will. Where the Administrator General applies for an order of the court pursuant to s.23 of the Administrator General's Act the practice and procedure is similar to the preliminary application for an order of appointment of an administrator *pendente lite*.[11]

Where the applicant is some person other than the Administrator General, apart from an order of the court appointing such person administrator *pendente lite*, a grant *pendente lite* will also have to be obtained as the provisions of s.23 are applicable only to the Administrator General.

Practice and Procedure for Preliminary Order

The application for the appointment of an administrator *pendente lite* is made to the registrar on Form P21, Appendix 2, CPR 2002, in Jamaica; by summons to a judge/master in chambers in Guyana, Trinidad & Tobago,

Barbados and The Bahamas, and by Part 11 application in the case of the Eastern Caribbean territories if there are current proceedings. If there are no current proceedings, the application should be made by a Fixed Date Claim form in the case Jamaica and the Eastern Caribbean territories and by originating summons in the case of Barbados, Guyana, Trinidad & Tobago and The Bahamas. The application should name the proposed administrator and ask for the directions necessary.

The affidavit in support should set out all the facts relied upon including:

(i) the reasons why the appointment is required;
(ii) the value of the property which is likely to come into the hands of the applicant;
(iii) except where the applicant is the Administrator General, the fitness to act of the proposed applicant.

The consent in writing of the proposed grantee to act should also be filed. In compliance with the relevant Orders and Rules of the Supreme Court of the respective territories, the order of appointment will be subject to the applicant giving security by a given date with liberty to act at once, on an understanding that he will be liable for any sums received by him. The amount of the security is fixed at the hearing and may be subject to a guarantee. In Jamaica, where the Administrator General is the applicant, the requirement with respect to the giving of security is waived.

Once the order is made the appointee may apply *ex parte* for a grant of letters of administration *pendente lite*. It should be pointed out:

(a) that since the grant is one of administration, the will is neither proved nor annexed to the grant.
(b) for the same reason, an affidavit of due execution is not included in the application for the grant.
(c) upon the determination of the action the grant *pendente lite* comes to an end, although it revives for the period of an appeal if any.

Documents to be lodged

The usual documents for a grant of letters of administration must be lodged together with:

1. An office copy of the order of appointment;
2. The administration bond, where applicable. In the case of administration *pendente lite* the recitals in the bond are somewhat different and should include the following:

       i.   details of the pending action;
      ii.   the grant of an order of appointment of an administrator limited in accordance with the limitations set out in the order if any;
     iii.   that the estate which by law devolves and vests in the personal representative is limited (as aforesaid); and
     iv.   that the intended administrator shall pending the action well and truly administer the said estate under the direction and control of the court, save distributing the residue thereof.

3. The oath of the administrator *pendente lite* The oath should:
       i.   recite that there is a pending action (stating the title thereof) touching and concerning the validity of the will of the deceased or the estate of the deceased as the case may be;
      ii.   recite the granting of the order of appointment, specifying the date the order was made and that letters of administration of the estate of the said deceased were granted pending the outcome of the said action (adding any words of limitation imposed by the order)
     iii.   recite that the administrator shall faithfully administer the estate of the deceased, save distribution of the residue thereof, pending the said action, under the directions and control of the court;

4. The Petition

St Lucia

The petition should, in so far as applicable, include the usual recitals contained in a petition for a grant of letters of administration (with or without will annexed), as the case may be. Accordingly, the recitals outlined above, which are peculiar to this type of grant, should be included. The actual oath to administer and collect in the estate of the deceased, is not included in the petition, but in the oath to lead the grant.

Determination of Action

Upon the determination of the action a full grant, not a cessate grant, may be applied for in the usual way. An office copy of the final order of the court in respect of the action must also be included in the papers to lead the grant of probate/letters of administration with will annexed as the case may be. The oath must include details of the order and of the previous grant *pendente lite*.

ALTERNATIVE TO *GRANTS PENDENTE LITE*

Trinidad & Tobago

As an alternative to applying for a grant *pendente lite,* s.37 of the Wills and Probate Ordinance Ch. 8 No. 2 provides *inter alia* that pending the hearing of any action, petition, summons or other proceeding, whether in the nature of contentious or common form business, the Administrator General or any person interested in the estate of a deceased person can apply *ex parte* on affidavit to the court for:

a) the appointment of an interim receiver; or
b) the granting of an interim injunction; or
c) an order for the sale of any perishable property in the estate, it being shown that the estate is in danger of spoilation or for any other reason, steps are required to be taken for the custody or preservation of any property or any part of such estate and on such terms as to security and otherwise as the court shall seem fit.

Although the power to grant such orders is limited to cases *where there is a pending the hearing of an action, petition or summons or other proceeding whether contentious or common form,* this is nevertheless a useful alternative procedure to be considered in cases of real urgency, as upon the grant of an interim order thereunder, the receiver so appointed can begin to act without having to first apply for and obtain a grant *pendente lite.*

Guyana

With respect to Guyana, see page 376 for the relevant practice and procedure.

GRANTS *AD COLLIGENDA BONA*[14]

A grant *ad colligenda* or preservation grant as it is otherwise called, may be made even to perfect strangers where:

a) it is shown that the estate of any deceased person is in danger of spoilation or for any other reasons urgent steps are required to be taken for the custody or preservation of any property forming part of the estate of the deceased, and;
b) owing to the circumstances, it is not possible to constitute a general personal representative in sufficient time to meet the needs of the estate for example where the person entitled to the full grant may be abroad or cannot be found at the relevant time.

The grant is limited for the purposes only of collecting and getting in and receiving the estate and doing such acts as may be necessary for the preservation of the same and until further representation be made. If any other acts not covered by the above words of limitation are contemplated by the applicant, these must be specifically included in the order.

When the purpose for which it was granted has been fulfilled, the grant *ad colligenda* ceases, and thereafter a general grant of representation may be applied for in the usual way. Details of the former grant and the order granting leave to apply for the *ad colligenda bona* grant must be included in the oath to lead the application for the general grant of representation.

Jamaica

Pursuant to s.23 of the Administrator General's Act, the Administrator General may by order of the court 'take possession of, hold and deal with the property of a deceased person' until the relevant grant is obtained, in circumstances where the property of such estate is likely to be damaged for want of a proper person to take charge thereof.

This section in effect permits the Administrator General to administer the estate of a deceased person without a grant until a grant is obtained in situations of urgency in which the estate is in need of immediate attention, which cannot await the issuing of the relevant grant.

Where the Administrator General applies for an order of the court pursuant to s.23 of the Administrator General's Act the contents of the affidavit are similar to the contents of the affidavit in support of an application for leave to apply for a grant *ad colligenda bona*.

However, where the intended applicant in such circumstances is some person other than the Administrator General (such as a creditor), a grant *ad colligenda bona* would have to be obtained pursuant to Rule 68.46 CPR 2002, as the provisions of s.23 above are applicable only to the Administrator General.

Practice and Procedure for Preliminary Order

All jurisdictions

The order for a grant *ad colligenda bona* grant may be made in:

(a) *Trinidad & Tobago, Jamaica, Eastern Caribbean Territories*
 ex parte on affidavit to the registrar unless the registrar directs that the application be made to a judge in chambers

(b) *Guyana and The Bahamas*
   ex parte to a judge in chambers in the first instance; or
(c) *All jurisdictions*
   to a judge in chambers or open court.

The affidavit should set out *inter alia*:

(i) the reasons why the grant, (order in the case of the Administrator General in Jamaica) is urgently required, for example, that there are fruits and vegetables or other perishable items owned by the deceased in urgent need of harvesting or sale;

(ii) that the person entitled to the general grant of representation of the deceased named therein cannot be located, is abroad or is temporarily incapacitated;

(iii) that the applicant is a fit and proper person to act; and

(iv) the type of grant being applied for with the words of limitation as aforesaid. This recital is not applicable where the Administrator General is applying for an order pursuant to s.23 of the Administrator General's Act.

The application should also be supported by the consent in writing of the proposed grantee to act as administrator; and a draft order for initialling by the judge/registrar containing the relevant words of limitation should also be lodged. Once the order containing the relevant words of limitation is granted, the applicant for the grant may apply for the grant, by lodging the requisite documents in the Registry/Sub-Registry of the Supreme/High Court.

Documents Required for Grant

The usual documents required for a grant of letters of administration subject to the following:

1. The will, if any, is not proved as the grant applied for is a grant of administration. As such it is not lodged with the other papers to lead the grant.

2. For the same reason an affidavit of due execution is not lodged in instances where the deceased died testate.

3. The administration bond must contain the following information *inter alia*:

   i) the amount of the bond;

ii) the granting of the order (setting out the words of limitation included in the order);
iii) It should also specify that the estate which by law devolves on and vests in the personal representative is limited as aforesaid.
4. An office copy of the order granting leave to apply for the a*d colligenda bona* grant must also be lodged with the other papers to lead the grant.
5. The oath should include the following information:
   i) the usual details of the death of the deceased including his place of domicil at the time of death;
   ii) that an order was granted to the applicant named therein, by Mr Registrar/Mr Justice AB to apply for a grant ad colligenda bona limited as hereinafter mentioned;
   iii) that the administrator shall faithfully collect, get in and administer the estate of the deceased limited to collecting, getting in and receiving the estate and doing such acts as may be necessary for the preservation of the same and until further representation be granted.
   iv) the gross value of the estate covered by the grant, in the event that the entire estate has not been included in the application.

The oath need not include any statement as to whether a will exists or not, nor does it state whether the deceased died, testate or intestate. The usual 'clearings off' are also not included in the oath.

6. The Petition

St Lucia

The petition should, in so far as applicable, include the usual recitals contained in a petition for a grant of letters of administration. Accordingly, the recitals outlined above, which are peculiar to this type of grant, should be included. The actual oath to administer and collect in estate of the deceased, is not included in the petition, but in the oath to lead the grant.

7. The Inventory/Statement of Assets is limited to particulars of the estate covered by the grant. This is in the event that the entire estate has not been ascertained at the time the grant was applied for.

ALTERNATIVE TO GRANTS *PENDENTE LITE/AD COLLIGENDA BONA*

Guyana

Section 23 of the Deceased Persons Estates' Administration Act Cap. 12:01 also makes provision for alternative proceedings to be adopted. According to this section, the court may appoint an interim receiver until probate or letters of administration is granted in circumstances where it appears necessary or expedient to do so.

A receiver so appointed is empowered to take custody and charge of the estate of the deceased person including the collecting of debts and the sale or disposing of perishable property belonging to the estate. The appointment of a receiver is not limited to circumstances where litigation is pending but extends to any circumstances where the court deems it expedient and necessary to make such an appointment.

The affidavit in support of the application for the order, which is required to be made to a judge, should contain the same information as is contained in the affidavit for leave to apply for the grant *ad colligenda bona*.

GRANTS LIMITED TO AN ACTION

Introduction

All jurisdictions (save Jamaica)

A grant limited to an action is made for the purpose of constituting a party to an action, usually in circumstances where the person entitled to the general grant refuses or neglects to apply for the relevant grant constitute himself personal representative. A common fact situation in which this type of grant is applied for is where a person injures or kills another as a result of his negligent driving and then dies, leaving little or no property, save monies payable under his motor car insurance policy and the person entitled to the general grant of the estate will nor apply for a grant so that the proposed plaintiff or his personal representatives (if he too has died as a result of the accident) has no one to sue and more specifically, is unable to bring an action for damages for personal injuries against the deceased's estate. Although by virtue of the survival of causes of action legislation/provisions of the respective Caribbean territories, the cause of action does not abate,[13] there is a risk that the proposed action may become statute barred as a result of the neglect, default or delay in applying for the relevant grant of representation by the person so entitled.

In such instances, an application may be made to the court under the relevant 'passing over' provision of the respective territories for the appointment of a person (nominee) selected by the plaintiff or such other person as may be considered expedient, for the purpose of obtaining a grant of letters of administration limited to an action. Although the provision speaks only of the court's discretion to appoint as an administrator some person other than the person who would have otherwise been entitled by law to a grant of administration, this provision is interpreted to include persons appointed as executors as well.

Jamaica

Grants limited to an action would not arise in Jamaica as pursuant to the provisions of s.12 of the Intestates' Estates and Property Charges Act, applications for a general grant of letters of administration (with or without will annexed) in such fact situations as mentioned above, may be made by the Administrator General.

Practice and Procedure

All jurisdiction (save Jamaica)

Prior to the application being made, notices should be sent to the persons interested in the estate, for example the surviving spouse or executor, if any, the Administrator General or his equivalent in the various territories, the insurance company of the deceased (in the case of a running down action) informing them *inter alia* of the intended application and calling upon the insurance company the surviving spouse or other persons entitled to the grant to indicate in writing by a specified date whether they would be willing to act as administrator *ad litem* or otherwise whether they would wish to nominate someone to so act.

Once the time indicated in the respective letters has elapsed, the proposed plaintiff/ his personal representatives may proceed to apply for the order.

An order for a grant under the relevant 'passing over' provision is made:

(a) *Eastern Caribbean territories, Barbados and Trinidad & Tobago*
In the first instance, to the registrar *ex parte* on affidavit or where the registrar so directs by summons to a judge in chambers or on motion to a judge in open court.

(b) *Guyana and The Bahamas*
In the first instance by *ex parte* application to a judge in chambers. The affidavit in support should recite *inter alia*:

(i) the facts giving rise to the proposed legal proceedings against the estate of the deceased defendant;
(ii) the failure, default or refusal of the persons entitled to the grant of the estate of the deceased defendant to apply for and obtain the relevant grant of representation;
(iii) the efforts made by the proposed plaintiff to have the personal representatives constituted from some person interested in the estate of the deceased defendant. Copies of the notices sent to the relevant person should be exhibited and annexed; and
(iv) the willingness and fitness to act as administrator *ad litem* of the proposed nominee.

Affidavit of Fitness/Consent to Act

An affidavit of fitness to act of the proposed administrator deposed by some responsible person should also be lodged together with the written consent to act of the proposed administrator ad litem.

Draft Order

In practice a draft order may be drawn up for initialling by the registrar/judge stating *inter alia* that AB is authorised under the relevant passing over provision of the respective jurisdictions to apply for and obtain letters of administration of the estate of the said deceased limited for the purpose of bringing an action, for example, for damages arising out of the negligent driving by the said CD deceased but no further or otherwise.

Once the order is granted, the nominee appointed may apply for the grant limited to an action.

Documents required for Grant

The usual documents required for a grant of letters of administration must be lodged subject to the following:

1. A copy of the court order should be lodged with the papers to lead the grant;
2. The administration bond, where applicable, should include the relevant words of limitation of the grant;

3. The Estate Duty Certificate (or its equivalent) to the effect that no duty is payable (nil estate) where applicable;
4. The oath/affidavit of administrator
   Since the grant is one of administration limited to the bringing or defending of an action the following should be noted:
   (i) the oath need not recite whether the deceased died testate or intestate, nor is the will, if any, referred to in the oath; and
   (ii) As the grant is for a nil estate the value of the estate is sworn to as 'amounting to the sum of nil';
   (iii) The date and effect of the order including the relevant words of limitation with respect thereto should be recited;
5. The Petition
   St Lucia
   The petition should, in so far as applicable, include the usual recitals contained in a petition for a grant of letters of administration. Accordingly, the recitals outlined above, which are peculiar to this type of grant, should be included. The actual oath to administer and collect in the estate of the deceased, is not included in the petition, but in the oath to lead the grant.
6. The Inventory/Statement of Assets and Liabilities, etc. is for a 'nil estate' and as such the assets and liabilities of the deceased are not stated therein.

An affidavit of due execution is not required in cases where the deceased died testate.

Determination of Action

Once the proceedings have terminated a cessate grant of representation following a grant limited to an action may be applied for in the usual way by the person entitled thereto.

The oath to lead cessate grant in such instances should recite *inter alia* that:

(i) on the date stated therein that letters of administration were granted to AB, limited to prosecuting or defending an action in the High Court to be brought against the personal representative of the deceased, as the case may be; and

(ii) that the proceedings in the said action have since terminated whereby the said letters of administration have ceased and expired.

Barbados, Guyana and Trinidad & Tobago[14]

An application for a grant limited to an action may also be made in cases where dependants of a deceased person wish to bring a claim for financial provisions under the relevant Family Provision legislation of these territories and are prevented from so doing because there is no person entitled or the person entitled to the general grant is unwilling to make the necessary application, and as a consequence there is no personal representative for the purpose of commencing the action. In such cases the Public Trustee/ Administrator General or other appropriate legal officer of the above territories may be approached to make the application under the relevant 'passing over' provision.

Eastern Caribbean territories (save St Lucia)

Prior to the passage of the CPR 2000, it could be argued that the RSC O.15 r.6A England, applied to the Eastern Caribbean territories by virtue of s.11 of the respective Supreme Court Acts of the respective Eastern Caribbean territories. In this regard, RSC O.15 r.6A provides an alternative method of commencing proceedings against the estate of a deceased person where the cause of action survives him. According to the provisions of RSC O.15 r.6A .

According to the provisions of RSC O.15 r.6A the plaintiff may bring the action describing the defendant as 'The personal representative of AB deceased' although there is no such personal representative and without naming anyone as being such person. However once the action is so commenced the plaintiff must then obtain an order from the court to continue the proceedings.

One of the main reasons for permitting a plaintiff to commence the action against the estate without first having to constitute a party, is to prevent the cause of action from becoming statute barred.

However, the position with respect to the commencement of proceedings where a grant has not been obtained by the person entitled, is now governed by the indigenous provisions of Rule 21.4, CPR 2000. Rule 21.4 provides for the court to appoint a representative party with respect, *inter alia*, to proceedings about estates where, *inter alia*, it is expedient for the court to do so for any reason. Rule 21.4(4) expressly provides that such person may be either a claimant or a defendant.

Trinidad & Tobago

In Trinidad & Tobago applications are routinely made pursuant to O.15

r.15 of the Order and Rules of the Supreme Court of Judicature of Trinidad & Tobago 1975 for the appointment of an administrator *ad litem* in circumstances where proceedings with respect to the deceased's estate have not commenced. Upon the granting of the order by the court, the person appointed administrator *ad litem* is permitted to defend/prosecute the proceedings as the case may be without having to obtain a grant of administration *ad litem*.

However, it is submitted that this option is not supported by the law as RSC O.15 r.15 which confers upon the Court the discretionary power to appoint a person to represent a deceased person in circumstances where the deceased person:

(a)   has an interest in any matter in question in the proceedings and;
(b)   there is no personal representative to represent him,

applies only to the representation of a deceased person in proceedings already commenced.

Notes

1	Barbados	- s.23 Succession Act Cap. 249
	Guyana	- s.16(c) Deceased Persons Estates' Administration Act Cap. 12:01
	St Lucia	- Art 589 Civil Code Ch. 242
	The Bahamas	- s.46 Supreme Count Act 15/1996
	Trinidad & Tobago	- s.35(1) Wills & Probate Ordinance Ch. 8 No. 2
	Trinidad & Tobago, Dominica, Guyana,	
2	Barbados	- s.20 Succession Act Cap. 249
	Guyana	- s.17(a) Deceased Persons Estates' Administration Act Cap. 12:01
	St Lucia	- Art 586 Civil Code Ch. 242
	St Vincent & the Grenadines	- s.13 Administration of Estates Act Cap. 377
	Eastern Caribbean territories (save St Lucia and St Vincent and the Grenadines)	- s.113 Supreme Court Act 1981, England
	The Bahamas	- s.34 of the Supreme Court Act 15/1996
3	Anguilla, St Christopher & Nevis, Dominica, Antigua & Barbuda, Montserrat	- s.116 Supreme Court of Judicature Act 1981, England
	Barbados	- s.19, Succession Act Cap. 249
	Grenada	- s.7, Probate Act Cap. 255

Guyana	- ss.16, 17, 28, Deceased Persons Estates Administration Act Cap. 12:01
The Bahamas	-
St Lucia	- Art 586(6)(b) Civil Code Ch. 242
St Vincent & the Grenadines	- s.16 Administration of Estates Act Cap. 377
Trinidad & Tobago	- ss.17(1), 25(1) and 37, Wills & Probate Ordinance Ch. 8 No. 2.

4 *Re Potticary* [1927] P.202, *Re Galbraith* [1951] P.422; *Estate of Biggs* [1966] P.118. See also chapter 25 p. 450.
5 *Re Last* [1958] P. 137; 1958 1 All E.R. 316; *Re Drawmer's Estate* (1913) 108 L.T. 732.
6 In the *Goods of Escot* (1858) 4 Sw & Tr 186; *In the Goods of Cholwill* (1866) L.R. 1 P & D 192. See also Grants *Ad Colligenda Bona* p. 372-375.
7 *In the Goods of Knight* [1939] 3 All E.R. 928. See also Grants Limited to an Action p. 376-381.
8 See s.12 of the Intestates' Estates and Property Charges Act below which sets out the circumstances in which the Administration General is entitled to take out administration (with or without will annexed). In this regard, s. 12 of the Intestates' Estates Property and Charges Act provides that:

> 'Notwithstanding anything contained in the Administrator-General's Act, or any enactment amending or substituted for the same, where the residuary estate of the intestate does not exceed one thousand dollars, or where it exceeds than sum and a minor is entitled to a share thereof or where a testator does not appoint an executor or where the executor has died before the testator or renounces, it shall be the duty of the Administrator-General to apply for letters of administration to the estate and, unless the court is satisfied that it would be for the benefit of the estate that letters of administration ought to be granted to some other person, letters of administration to such estate shall be granted to the Administrator-General.'

9 | | |
|---|---|
| The Bahamas, Eastern Caribbean (save Dominica) | - r.52 N.C.P.R. 1987, England |
| Trinidad & Tobago, Barbados, Guyana, Dominica | - r.51 N.C.P.R. 1954, England. |

10 | | |
|---|---|
| Anguilla, Antigua & Barbuda | - s.117 Supreme Court Act 1981, England |
| Barbados | - ss.19(5), 19(6) Succession Act Cap. 249 |
| Grenada | - ss.5,6 Probate Act Cap. 255 |
| Guyana | - s.23 Deceased Person Estates' Administration Act Ch. 12:01 |
| St Christopher & Nevis, St Vincent & the Grenadines | - s.17 Administration of Estates Act Cap. 377 |
| The Bahamas | - s.45 of the Supreme Court Act 15/1996 |
| Trinidad & Tobago | - ss. 17, 18, 37 Wills and Probate Ordinance Ch, 8 No. 2. |

11	Barbados	- R.S.C. O.74 r.14 Rules of the Supreme Court 1982
	Eastern Caribbean territories	- Part 51, CPR 2000
	Guyana	- R.S.C. O.43 r.13 Rules of the High Court Cap 3:02
	Jamaica	- Part 51, CPR 2002
	The Bahamas	- R.S.C. O.68 r.14 The Rules of the Supreme Court 1978
	Trinidad & Tobago/ Barbados	- R.S.C. O.74 r.14 Orders and Rules of the Supreme Court of Judicature of Trinidad & Tobago 1975.
12	Eastern Caribbean (save Dominica), The Bahamas, Trinidad & Tobago, Barbados, Guyana, Dominica	- r.52 N.C.P.R. 1987, England - r.51 N.C.P.R. 1954, England.
	Jamaica	- Rule 68.46, CPR 2002
13	Anguilla	- Causes of Action (Survival) Act Cap. 11
	Antigua & Barbuda	- Causes of Action (Survival) Act Cap. 12
	Barbados	- Law Reform (Miscellaneous Provisions) Act Cap. 25
	Dominica	- Law Reform (Miscellaneous Provisions) Act 1991
	Grenada	- Law Reform (Miscellaneous Torts) Act Cap. 159
	Guyana	- Law Reform (Miscellaneous Provisions) Act Cap. 6:02 as amended by the Law Reform (Miscellaneous Amendments Act) No. 14 1988
	Jamaica	- Law Reform (Miscellaneous Provisions) Act
	Montserrat	- Causes of Action (Survival) Act Cap. 11
	The Bahamas	- Survival of Actions Act 1992
	St Christopher & Nevis	- Causes of Action (Survival) Act Cap. 11
	St Lucia	- Art. 609 Civil Code Ch. 242
	St Vincent & the Grenadines	- Tortfeasors Act Cap. 46
	Trinidad & Tobago	- s. 27 Supreme Court of Judicature Act Ch. 4:01 16
14	Barbados	- Part VII & Part X Succession Act Cap. 249
	Guyana	- Family and Dependant Provisions Act 1990
	Jamaica	- Inheritance (Provision for Family and Dependants) Act, 1993
	Trinidad & Tobago	- Part VIII Succession Act 27/1981 as amended by the Distribution of Estates Act 28/2000
	The Bahamas	- Part III, Inheritance Act 2002

18

Leave to Swear Death[1]

INTRODUCTION

Circumstances may arise in which an applicant for a grant of probate or administration is unable because of the lack of direct evidence, to swear positively to the death of the person with respect to whose estate the grant is required. This must be distinguished from cases where the actual date of death, as opposed to the fact of death, cannot be determined. In cases where the death is known to have occurred between two specified dates, an order for leave to presume dead is not required.[2] When, however, there is sufficient affidavit evidence available an order may be obtained from the court granting leave to swear that the person concerned has died 'on or since' a specified date. The court does not presume the person to be dead, so that should he later be discovered to be alive, that person may apply to the court for a rescission of the order and a revocation of the grant.

The main circumstances in which this type of grant is sought are:

(a) where the person concerned has disappeared for an extended period of time; or
(b) where the circumstances indicate that he has committed suicide or has perished at sea or in an aircraft crash.

A. DISAPPEARANCE OVER EXTENDED PERIOD

The general rule is that where a person has not been seen or heard of for a period of seven years or more, such person may be presumed dead. However, in order to satisfy the court that such person may be presumed dead, all due inquiries appropriate to the circumstances of the case are required to be made before leave to swear death will be granted.[3]
As Harman, J. pointed out in *Re Watkins:*[4]

In the absence of statute, there is no magic in the mere fact of a period of seven years elapsing without there being positive evidence of a person being alive. It is generally speaking a matter in each case of taking the facts as a whole and balancing, as a jury would, the respective probabilities of life continuing or having ceased.

However, in cases of disappearance, leave may be obtained in a shorter period where there is cogent evidence to raise such presumption.[5]

B. DISASTER-RELATED DISSAPPEARANCE

In cases of disaster-related disappearance, such as a plane crash, leave to swear death may be granted before any extended period has elapsed once the evidence is sufficiently cogent to raise the presumption of death.

APPLICATION FOR ORDER TO SWEAR DEATH

The application for the order may be made by or on behalf of the intended applicant:

(a) *Eastern Caribbean territories, Barbados and Trinidad & Tobago*
In the first instance to the registrar *ex parte* on affidavit unless the registrar directs that the application be made by summons to a judge in chambers, and in the case of the Eastern Caribbean territories where the application was previously made by summons, it is to be made in practice in accordance with a Part II application CPR 2000.

(b) *Guyana and The Bahamas*
In the first instance *ex parte* by summons supported by affidavit to a judge in chambers.

(c) *Jamaica*
In accordance with Rule 68.47 CPR 2002, the application for leave is made to the registrar, and must be supported by evidence on affidavit:
  (i) giving details of any policies of insurance effected on the life of the presumed dead; and
  (ii) the grounds for supposing the presumed dead to be dead.
  In addition, Rule 68.47(3) provides that the registrar may require further evidence to be given on affidavit.

(d) *All Jurisdictions*
Where the registrar/judge otherwise directs on motion to a judge in open court.

1. Contents of Affidavit in cases of Disappearance/Suicide

The affidavit(s) in support of the application should set out:
- (i) the date and circumstances in which the 'deceased' was last heard of;
- (ii) his age;
- (iii) the applicant's belief that he is dead;
- (iv) details of the efforts made to find him including any advertisements, if any, which have been inserted (the newspaper clippings being exhibited);
- (v) whether any letters or other written communications have been received from him since the date of his disappearance;
- (vi) particulars of any bank account, including the last date on which they were operated;
- (viii) particulars of any insurance policies owned by the 'deceased' and whether notices of the application have been given to the companies concerned. (Copies of the notices sent and any replies received should be exhibited and annexed);
- (ix) particulars of the value of the estate of the 'deceased';
- (x) whether the 'deceased' died testate in which case the will should be exhibited; and
- (xi) whether he died intestate, in which case the names of the persons entitled on intestacy should be given.

Affidavits sworn by family members or some other persons acquainted with the deceased who can corroborate the material particulars set out in the affidavit of the applicant should also be filed.

2. Contents of Affidavit in cases of Loss of a Ship or Aircraft

The affidavit should establish:

- (i) that the 'deceased' was on board the aircraft/ship at the time of its disappearance;
- (ii) the date and place where the aircraft/ship was last seen;
- (iii) the details of its loss including evidence of its non-arrival;
- (iv) what news has been received since the aircraft/ship was last seen;
- (v) particulars of insurance of the aircraft or ship, including whether the underwriters have paid for the total loss; and
- (vi) particulars of any policies of insurance effected on the life of the 'deceased'. Supporting affidavits deposed to by airline/Coast Guard officials, as the case may be should also be filed.

3. Order for leave to Swear Death
The order granting leave to swear death must state that on an application for the relevant grant of the deceased's estate the death may be sworn to have occurred on or since the date specified therein, being the date that the presumed deceased was last seen alive. The order is kept in the Registry. The applicant or his attorney-at-law, however, may attend the Registry and inspect the order and extract notes to enable the relevant recitals to be made in the oath.

DOCUMENTS TO LEAD GRANT

The usual documents for Grant of Probate/Letters of Administration (with will annexed) should be submitted subject to the following:

1. The oath must set out:
    (i) that the deceased died on or since the date set out in the order;
    (ii) that the applicant is unable to depose as to the place of death of the deceased, if that is the case; and
    (iii) that by directive of Mr Registrar/Mr Justice dated... it was ordered that on an application for a grant of letters of administration (with or without will annexed)/probate (as the case may be) that the death may be sworn to have occurred on or since the date shown in the order, being the date on which the deceased was last known to be alive.
2. The administration bond must include the relevant words of limitation as contained in the oath/affidavit.
3. The Petition.
   St Lucia
   The petition should, in so far as applicable, include the usual recitals contained in a petition for a grant of letters of administration. Accordingly, the recitals outlined above, which are peculiar to this type of grant, should be included. The actual oath to administer and collect in the estate of the deceased, is not included in the petition, but in the oath to lead the grant.

WHERE 'PRESUMED DEAD' DIED DOMICILED ABROAD

A. Declaration and Vesting Order

Where the person presumed dead died domiciled abroad and there has been a declaration of presumption of death by a competent court of the domicile of a presumed dead, followed by an order of a like court of that country vesting the estate of the presumed dead in the person or persons entitled thereto, although an order is required for leave to presume such person to be dead, the registrar has the discretion, in granting leave, to require no further evidence as to the circumstances from which death might be presumed.[6]

B.   Declaration Only

Where there is only a declaration of death by the court of domicile and no vesting order, the registrar in granting leave for such person to be presumed dead, will require further evidence as to the circumstances from which death might be presumed.[7]

C.   Issuance of Death Certificate by Court of Domicile

Where the court of domicile has issued a death certificate, (as opposed to a declaration of death) on the basis that a person believed to have died, has in fact died on a specified date, no preliminary order granting leave to presume dead is required.[8]

However, if the death certificate issued by the registrar states that the person is presumed dead in consequence of a land, sea or air disaster or for any other cause, an order granting leave to presume death will have to be obtained before the application for a grant can be made.

POSITION IN ST. VINCENT AND THE GRENADINES IN DISASTER RELATED DEATH

With respect to St. Vincent and The grenadines, grants for leave to swear death are of very limited application as a consequence of the provisions of s.32 of the Registration of Births and Deaths Act Cap.179
Section 32(1) provides:

> Where the death of any person occurs in circumstances of disaster on land, sea or in the air, wheresoever such disaster may occur, and the body of such person cannot be found, recognized or identified and no coroner's inquest has been held or is in progress, or is incapable of being held without inordinate delay for whatever good and sufficient reason, the registrar may, upon being
> satisfied beyond reasonable doubt that such death has in fact occurred, register the death of such person with such particulars as to the date and place of death as to him may seen appropriate.

Before the registration of any such death, the registrar is required to cause to be published for three consecutive weeks, a notice in the Form prescribed by s.32(2).

At the expiration of 14 clear days after the publication of the third notice, provided that the registrar receives no objection in writing to such registration, the registration of the death shall be effected by the registrar in the form and manner prescribed that is:

> Presumed dead in consequence of land/sea/air disaster (inapplicable words to be omitted).

Pursuant to s.32(4), any individual or juridical person having a legally relevant interest in the registration or non registration of any disaster-related death:

(a) may in writing, request the registrar to register such death in accordance with the procedure set out in this section, giving the registrar such particulars, or such further particulars, as the registrar may require concerning the person presumed dead or the circumstances of the disaster or the nature of the legally relevant interest of the person making the request; or

(b) may in writing object to the proposed registration of death or to any material particular thereof, giving the registrar such particulars, or such further particulars, as the registrar may require concerning the nature and grounds of the objection and the nature of the legally relevant interest of the person making the request.

Further, s.32(7) provides:

> An objector who is aggrieved by the ruling of the registrar, or any person having a legally relevant interest in the matter and whose interest is likely to be adversely affected by the ruling of the registrar, may appeal therefrom to a judge of the High Court within seven days of the publication by the registrar of his ruling.

Accordingly, in St. Vincent and The Grenadines, where the death certificate of the registrar is forthcoming under s.32 of the Act, an application for leave to swear death is not required, provided that the application for the grant is first made in St. Vincent and The Grenadines.

Where however, an ancillary grant or a grant is first applied for in any of the other jurisdictions considered in this text, leave to presume dead will have to be obtained as a death certificate issued by the registrar in St.

Vincent does not state that the deceased is dead, but rather that he is presumed to be dead.

Revocation of Grant

Where the person presumed to have died is subsequently discovered to be alive, application should be made to the registrar or the judge in chambers, depending on the jurisdiction, for rescission of the order and for revocation of the grant.

The affidavit in support of the application should set out *inter alia*:

(i) that the grant was issued pursuant to an order for leave to swear death. The date of the order must be stated in the affidavit, and a certified copy thereof exhibited to the affidavit.
(ii) the circumstances which have since arisen, that is that the person presumed to have died is alive and the facts relevant to his or her reappearance.
(iii) An order seeking revocation of the grant and a declaration that the grant is null and void.

Notes

1. Barbados, Dominica, Guyana, Trinidad & Tobago Eastern Caribbean (save Dominican), The Bahamas — r.52 N.C.P.R 1954, England
— n.53 N.C.P.R. 1987, England
Jamaica — Rule 68.47 CPR 2002
2. *In the Estate of Long-Sutton* [1912] P.97.
3. *In the Goods of Winstone* [1898] P.143.
4. [1953] 1 WLR 1323 at p.1330. See also *Bradshaw vs Bradshaw* [1956] P.274, where the order was not granted for leaves to swear death although the husband had not been heard from for 19 years.
5. *Hogton vs Hogton* (1933) 50 TLR 18 where death within six years was presumed.
6. *In the Goods of Spenceley* [1892]P.255. See also *In the Goods of Dowds*, Presumed Deceased [1948] P.256.
7. *In the Goods of Frantiska Schulhof* [1948] P.66.
8. *In the Goods of Schlesinger* (1950) CLY 1549.

19

Second or Subsequent Grants of Representation

A. GRANTS *DE BONIS NON-ADMINISTRATUS*

A grant *de bonis non administratus* is made following a general grant of representation where the person entitled to it has for some reason failed to complete the administration of the deceased's estate. Unless there is a chain of representation (not applicable to Barbados, after November 13, 1975)[1] a grant in respect of the unadministered portion of the estate will be made to a new personal representative to complete the administration of the deceased's estate.

A grant *de bonis non* is necessary in the following circumstances:

- on the death of a previous grantee.
- on the mental incapacity of a previous grantee.
- on the death of the donor of a power of attorney.
- on the death of a minor or person suffering from a mental illness for whose use and benefit the previous grant was issued.

Entitlement to the Grant

The rules governing priority to a grant *de bonis non* are the same as those which are applicable to a grant of letters of administration (with or without will annexed) in the various territories.

Jamaica

Where the Administrator General is the original grantee, an application for a grant *de bonis non* would not arise.

Procedure and Documents Required

The procedure with respect to the application for and issuance of grants *de bonis non* is the same as that which is applicable to general grants of representation discussed in chapter 4.

Documents to be lodged Ex Parte in the Registry/Sub Registry

Depending on whether the deceased died testate or intestate the documents which are lodged in the Registry/Sub Registry are generally those which are required for a general grant of letters of administration (with or without will annexed) in the respective territories. However because of the nature and operation of this type of grant there are differences in the documents and their contents. These are as follows:

1. The covering letter/application for the grant, whether made by petition or otherwise, must specify the nature of the grant being applied for, that is, whether the application is for a grant *de bonis non administratus* or a grant *de bonis non administratus* with will annexed.
2. The original grant or an office copy thereof must be lodged with the papers to lead the grant.
3. The Inventory/Statement of Assets and Liabilities (or its equivalent), is limited to a description of the property to be administered by the second grantee together with the value thereof. Additionally a copy of the original inventory, statements of assets and liabilities etc. is lodged with the application.
4. An administration bond where applicable containing the recitals relevant to this type of grant must also be lodged with the other papers to lead the grant. It is, however, noted that in Barbados, although required, the bond is not one of the documents lodged by the applicant for the grant.
5. In cases where the application is for a *grant de bonis non administratus* with will annexed:
   (a) An office copy of the original will must be marked by the proposed second grantee and by the person authorised to administer oaths. Alternatively the applicant may attend the Registry and mark either the original will or the previous grant with his signature before the proper officer in the Registry.
   (b) An affidavit of due execution is not lodged with the papers to lead the grant.
6. A Search Certificate/Affidavit must be filed.
   Trinidad & Tobago
   A certificate of search certified by the Registrar to the effect that no caveat has been lodged and no other application for a grant *de bonis non administratus* has been made must also be lodged.
   Barbados
   The affidavit of search basically contains the same recitals as those in

the usual affidavit of search save that it specifies that no other application for probate or administration has been made previous to the present application other than the first application in which a grant was issued to the original applicant. The number and year of the original grant is specified therein.

7. Anguilla and St Vincent & the Grenadines
With respect to St Vincent & the Grenadines, a valuation certificate is not filed with the papers to lead the *grant de bonis non* nor is a Land Registry Valuation Certificate filed in Anguilla.

8. The oath/affidavit should contain certain information, *inter alia:*
    (i) The date of death and domicil of the deceased.
    (ii) 'Whether the deceased died testate or intestate. In the event that he died testate, the affidavit should recite the appointment of the executor(s) and the producing and marking of an official copy of the testator's will by the second grantee, and person before whom sworn, and the belief of the second grantee that it is a true copy of the original will of the deceased testator.
    (iii) A description of the applicant and his entitlement to the grant. If there are other persons with a prior right to the grant, including an executor by representation, the appropriate clearing off must also be recited.
    (iv) The reasons for the failure of the original grantee to complete the administration of the deceased estate. Where there is no estate left to be administered but a grant is nevertheless required for the purposes of constituting a personal representative the reason for the application must be recited in the oath.
    (v) The usual recitals with respect to the collecting, getting in and administering by the applicant of the unadministered estate of the deceased.
    (vi) *All jurisdictions save St Lucia and Barbados*

A recital with respect to the gross value of the unadministered estate to be covered by the grant.

Where there are no assets left to be administered, the oath must include a recital to the effect that the original grantee failed to complete the administration of the estate.

All relevant exhibits should be annexed to the affidavit or oath, for example, when the original grantee died before completing the administration of the deceased's estate, a certified copy of the grantee's death certificate should be exhibited.

9. Petition
   St Lucia
   The petition sets out all the matters included in the affidavit in support of the petition save that it is not necessary to include recitals relevant to the collecting and getting in of the deceased's estate to be administered.
   St Vincent & the Grenadines
   The recitals contained in the oath and in the petition, if included, are the same.
   The Bahamas
   It takes the form of a simple petition for a grant *de bonis non administratus*.
10. Estate/Stamp Duty Certificate
    Where applicable, a copy of the original estate duty certificate must also be lodged with the documents to lead the grant *de bonis non*.

B. CESSATE GRANT

Definition

A cessate grant is one which issues as the result of a previous grant having ceased to be effective either:

- by reason of the fulfillment of a condition or limitation contained in it, for example the attainment of majority by a minor, the recovery of mental capacity, the finding and proving of a will after a copy has been admitted to proof, the determination of proceedings arising out of a grant limited to an action; or
- because the original grantee has died leaving the condition or limitation in the original grant unfulfilled, for example the death of a sole or sole surviving attorney or guardian.

Unlike a *de bonis non* grant, a cessate grant is a renewal of the whole of the deceased estate. As such, the applicant must swear in his oath to administer the whole of the estate as contained in the inventory exhibited, but the value shown in the oath will be that of the estate remaining to be administered.

Entitlement to Grant

The entitlement to a cessate grant follows the order of priority applicable to grants of letters of administration (with or without will annexed).

Procedure and Documents Required

The procedure with respect to the issuing and applying for a cessate grant is the same as that which is applicable to general grants of representation.

Because the nature and purpose of a cessate grant are similar to that of grants *de bonis non administratus*, the documents that are lodged are identical to those which are required for such grants as discussed above. With respect to applications for cessate grants however, the following should be noted in so far as the contents of the documents are concerned:

1. The Inventory and Statement of Assets and Liabilities
   Because a cessate grant is a regrant of the entire estate, the inventory and statement of assets and liabilities should contain a description of all the assets comprising the deceased's estate: those which already have been administered by the original grantee and those which are still to be administered by the applicant. In practice a copy of the original inventory/statement of assets and liabilities is lodged with the other documents to lead the grant.

2. Certificate/Affidavit of Search
   Trinidad & Tobago
   The certificate of search must specify that no caveat has been lodged and that no other application for a cessate grant has been made.
   Barbados
   Apart from the usual recitals, the affidavit of search deposed to by the attorney-at-law should set out that no other application for a grant other than the previous grant issued to the first applicant has been made. The number and year of the first grant must be specified therein.

3. Oath
   The recitals in the oath are similar to those which are set out in the oath/affidavit with respect to grants *de bonis non administratus*. In particular, the affidavit should include:
   (i) A description of the applicant and his entitlement to the grant.
   (ii) Details of the former grant, that is, to whom it was made and its place and date of issue.
   (iii) A recital with respect to the producing and marking by the applicant, of an official copy of the last will and testament of the deceased, where applicable.
   (iv) The circumstances or facts relevant to the ceasing to operate of the former grant: for instance, the attainment of majority

of the minor for whose use and benefit the original grant was obtained. All relevant exhibits should be annexed to the oath/affidavit, for example, the birth certificate of the former minor, the medical certificate as evidence of mental recovery of the applicant or the death certificate of the attorney or guardian as the case may be.

(v) *All the jurisdictions (save Barbados and St Lucia)*

The gross value of the unadministered estate to be covered by the grant.

4. Petition

St Lucia

The petition should set out all the matters included in the oath save that it is not necessary to include the recitals relevant to the collecting and getting in of the estate to be administered.

C. DOUBLE PROBATE GRANTS

An application for a grant of double probate is made when more than one executor has been appointed by a testator and probate has been granted to some or one but not all of them. In such circumstances power is reserved to such executor who has or executors who have not renounced their executorship to apply for a grant of double probate at a later date. Both the first grant and double grant run concurrently and confer the same rights and duties on their respective grantees.

Procedure and Documents Required

The procedure is the same as that which is applicable to general grants of representation which is discussed in detail in chapter 4.

The documents required for a double probate grant are basically the same as those which are necessary for a general grant of probate. However the following differences should be noted:

1. The testator's death certificate is not lodged, neither is an affidavit of due execution required.
2. An office copy of the original grant should be lodged with the other papers to lead the double probate grant.
3. An office copy of the original will must be marked by the executor to whom power was reserved and the person before whom sworn. Alternatively the executor may attend the Registry/Sub-Registry and mark the original will with his signature before the proper officer in the Registry.

4. A photocopy of the original inventory or affidavit of assets and liabilities or its equivalent in the respective territories, should also be lodged.
5. The oath/affidavit of the executor should set out:
    (i) details of the grant of probate to one or some of the executors, with power being reserved to the applicant executor to apply;
    (ii) the belief of the executor that the will or office copy thereof which is now produced to and marked by him is either an official copy of the true and original or is the true and original as the case may be; and
    (iii) the usual oath of the executor to collect, get in, and administer the estate of the deceased testator, and where called upon by law to exhibit a true and perfect inventory of the estate.
6. Where applicable a copy of the Inland Revenue Affidavit and Certificate of Non-Objection with respect to the former grant should also be lodged.
7. Petition

    St Lucia

    The petition should, in so far as applicable, include the usual recitals contained in a petition for a grant of letters of administration (with or without will annexed), as the case may be. Accordingly, the recitals outlined above, which are peculiar to this type of grant, should be included. The actual oath to administer and collect in the estate of the deceased, is not included in the petition, but in the oath to lead the grant.

Notes

1. See s.11 of the Succession Act Cap. 249 which provides that 'where the sole or last surviving executor of a testator dies after 13th November, 1975, the executor of such executor shall not be the executor of that testator.' Section 11(2) further provides that s.11(1) applies whether the testator died before or after the commencement of the Act.

20

Resealing of Grants

INTRODUCTION

Resealing is the procedure by which a grant of representation obtained in one probate jurisdiction is sealed with the seal of the court of another probate jurisdiction, rendering it of equal force and effect as a grant sealed within the jurisdiction in which the application for resealing is made.[1]

Applications to reseal are usually made in circumstances where a deceased person has either left assets to be administered within more than one probate jurisdiction or, in other cases, in order that legal proceedings with respect to the estate of a deceased person may be brought or defended within another probate jurisdiction. It is a convenient and relatively expedient procedure as it obviates the necessity of applying for an ancillary grant which would otherwise be necessary, depending on the jurisdiction concerned.[2] However, most of the Caribbean territories limit the probate jurisdiction from which resealing applications can be made.

APPLICATION FOR RESEALING

Anguilla, Dominica, Grenada, Guyana, Jamaica, Montserrat, St Christopher & Nevis, St Vincent & the Grenadines and Trinidad & Tobago[3]

These territories restrict resealing applications to grants of representations issuing out of Britain, a British court in a foreign country or a colonial or Commonwealth territory.

Antigua & Barbuda[4]

Grants issuing out of a Commonwealth country or such other country as Cabinet may approve may be resealed in Antigua. Further, by virtue of Statutory Instrument 31 of 1993 Cabinet by a decision dated February 10, 1993, approved the United States as a country from which resealing applications may be made.

The Bahamas[5]

Apart from British, Commonwealth and colonial grants, grants of representation issuing out of the United States of America may be resealed in The Bahamas.

Barbados and St Lucia[6]

Grants of representation issuing from any country may be resealed in these territories save that in the case of St Lucia, Arts 1152A and 1152B of the Civil Code Ch. 242 expressly provides that:

(a) the proper and due authentication of the relevant grant must in addition be proved by a certificate under seal of a British Diplomatic or Consular Officer exercising his functions in such place.
(b) want of a seal does not of itself invalidate a grant or other equivalent instrument provided that the authenticating person or authority certifies that such person has no seal or if the Judge or Registrar is satisfied as to its authentication otherwise.

All jurisdictions

It is to be noted that with respect to England the Colonial Probates Act 1892 (U.K.) and other Acts passed thereafter regulate the resealing of grants in Britain. These Acts together with the Colonial Probates Act, Application Order 1965, make provision for the resealing in England of grants issuing out of a number of territories including the countries listed above.[7]

PROCEDURE AND DOCUMENTS REQUIRED IN GENERAL[8]

An application to reseal is made *ex parte* by lodging the requisite documents in the Probate Section of the High/Supreme Court Registry. The application may be made by the personal representative(s), the grantee(s), or, as is often the case, by a person so authorised by the personal representative(s).[9] In Barbados the application may also be made by an attorney-at-law registered in Barbados acting on behalf of any personal representative or grantee.[10]

However as with other non-contentious probate applications, certain preliminary steps may need to be taken prior to the substantive application.

PRELIMINARY STEPS

When the application to reseal is made by power of attorney, the power must be registered prior to the substantive application.

Barbados

The person authorised by the power of attorney given by a personal representative or grantee is also required to produce to the Registrar an affidavit stating that the power has not been revoked.[11]

Eastern Caribbean territories, Guyana, Jamaica and The Bahamas

In the case of all the above-mentioned territories, save Jamaica though the relevant N.C.P.R., England[12] provides that the application for resealing may be made to any person/ agent authorised in writing to apply on behalf of the original grantee, the practice is to require that the authority for resealing be given to the proposed applicant by power of attorney, duly registered. In the case of Jamaica, Rule 68.26(1) CPR 2002 expressly provides that the application may be made in writing by an agent of the person to whom the grant was made. The Rule does not specify that the written authority be given by a Deed Power of Attorney although it is still the practice to do so.

Notice of Intention to Apply for Resealing

Barbados, Guyana, Jamaica, The Bahamas and Trinidad & Tobago

A Notice of Intention must be published in the above territories in accordance with the manner and form prescribed for each territory. However, irrespective of the jurisdiction the notice must specify the name, place, and date of death of the deceased.

Barbados

The applicant is required to place an advertisement approved by the Registrar in two issues of a daily or bi-weekly newspaper circulating in Barbados. This must be done not less than 21 days before the application for resealing is made. The advertisement should state that the applicant intends to make an application to reseal and it calls upon any person wishing to oppose the application to lodge a caveat with the Registrar by a date specified therein (being not more than 21 days after the date of publication of the advertisement).[13]

Guyana

Pursuant to r.2 of the Deceased Persons Estates' Administration Rules, a notice of intention to apply for resealing is required to be published in the Gazette.[14]

Jamaica

A certified or sealed copy of the original grant together with an original and one copy of the advertisement for resealing are submitted to the registrar for approval.[15] The advertisement which takes a prescribed form,[16] provides that after the expiration of eight days an application will be made for the sealing of the grant of representation of the deceased. Once all is in order, directions signed by the registrar to the effect that the notice of application be advertised once in a daily newspaper are endorsed on the notice. The original notice together with the registrar's directions endorsed thereon, is then delivered to the applicant who advertises the notice in the newspaper in accordance with the directions of the registrar.

The Bahamas

Upon payment of the requisite fees, the registrar, not the applicant, causes to be published a Notice of Intention to Apply for Resealing in three successive issues of the Gazette.[17] In practice, the notice is also published in a daily newspaper.

Trinidad & Tobago

The notice is in a prescribed form[18] and simply states that after the expiration of 14 days from the date published, an application to reseal will be made in the Registry. The Notice must be advertised by the applicant once a week for two successive weeks in one of the local daily newspapers.[19]

Eastern Caribbean territories

Publication of the Notice of Intention to Apply for Resealing is not compulsory; firstly, because r.41(2)(c) of the repealed N.C.P.R. 1954, England, provided for the Notice to be published only if the Registrar so required, and secondly because this discretionary requirement was omitted from the 1987 N.C.P.R., England. Indeed in Montserrat, St Lucia, St Vincent & the Grenadines and Grenada, a Notice of Intention to Apply is not published as a general rule.

However in practice a notice is published in Anguilla, Antigua & Barbuda, Dominica and St Christopher & Nevis.

Antigua & Barbuda and Dominica

A notice to the effect that after eight days an application to reseal the grant of representation specified therein is advertised by the applicant in one issue of a daily newspaper for two successive weeks.

Dominica

In addition, a notice of intention to apply for resealing addressed to the Registrar and signed by the solicitor's applicant or the applicant if acting in person, is also lodged with the other papers for the application for resealing.

Anguilla

In practice, when the documents for resealing are filed, the notice of intention to apply for resealing is advertised by the registrar. It is published in the Gazette in three successive publications. The Gazette is published once a month or bi-monthly. However, the registrar may upon written request by the applicant waive the requirement for the application to be advertised.

St Christopher & Nevis

Although advertising is discretionary in St Christopher & Nevis, in practice the notice of intention to apply for resealing is published once a week in one of the local newspapers for two successive weeks.

Limited Grants

All jurisdictions (save Barbados and Jamaica)

When the grant to be resealed is a special, limited or temporary grant, an application must first be made for an order granting the applicant leave to apply for resealing.[20] The application is made to the registrar/judge in chambers.

Barbados

Although there is no provision expressly requiring that leave be first obtained to reseal a limited grant, s.5(5) of the Probate and Letters of Administration (Resealing) Act Cap. 247 provides in effect that the Registrar may refer any application for resealing to the High Court and where an application is so referred, the grant may not be resealed except in accordance with an order of the High Court.

Jamaica

Rule 68.26 C.P.R. 2002 prescribes the procedure and practice to be followed in respect of applications for re-sealing, made pursuant to the Probate (Re-sealing) Act . These new rules contain no provision requiring that leave be first obtained in cases where the grant to be re-sealed is a special limited or temporary grant. Accordingly, in the absence of express provisions, it is submitted that there is no such requirement in Jamaica.

SUBSTANTIVE APPLICATION - DOCUMENTS REQUIRED

Petition

A.   Covering Application

All jurisdictions (save The Bahamas)

Once these preliminary matters have been addressed, a covering application signed by the applicant or his attorney-at-law on his behalf should be lodged.

The covering application for resealing contains, *inter alia*, the following:

(i) the name and a description of the applicant including the capacity in which he is applying; whether as executor, attorney, etc.
(ii) a description of the grant including the date of issue thereof, and,
(iii) the court out of which the grant was issued.

The Bahamas

The application for resealing takes the form of a simple petition.

Petition

St Lucia

Apart from the covering application, a petition is also lodged. Unlike The Bahamas, this petition is quite comprehensive and includes the following information:

   (i)   the name and a description of the applicant;
   (ii) the place of domicile of the deceased, although this is not required;
   (iii) the place and date of death of the deceased;
   (iv) a description of the grant of representation;
   (v)   the date and place of issue thereof; and,
   (vi) a recital to the effect that the Attorney General has no objection to the application being made.
         The petition is dated and signed by the petitioner or by his solicitor on his behalf.

St Vincent & the Grenadines

The petition contains essentially the same recitals as those set out in the oath of the applicant.

B. Affidavit/Oath in Support of the Application for Resealing

Jamaica, Guyana, The Bahamas and Trinidad & Tobago

An affidavit/oath in support of the application for resealing is required to be filed.[21]

Barbados

The applicant has the option either of swearing one affidavit or separate affidavits containing the required information.

Eastern Caribbean territories

Although there is no longer any requirement in England for an affidavit to be lodged with the application for resealing, the practice in the Eastern Caribbean territories (which have received the 1987 N.C.P.R., England) is to file an affidavit as required by r.41(2) of the repealed 1954 N.C.P.R., England.

Contents of affidavit

All jurisdictions

The affidavit should contain the following recitals:

  (i) the name, address and description of the applicant;
  (ii) the entitlement of the applicant whether as original grantee or attorney thereof;
  (iii) the domicile of the deceased, with the exceptions of Antigua & Barbuda and St Lucia;
  (iv) the type of grant, to whom it was issued, the court of issue and the date of issue thereof;
  (v) where applicable, that the notice of application for resealing was duly advertised/published; and
  (vi) the value of the personal and real assets of the deceased within the jurisdiction.

Barbados[22]

When the applicant opts for separate affidavits, the following affidavits must be filed:

  (i) an affidavit of value containing a description and the value of the deceased's estate in Barbados;
  (ii) an affidavit of advertisement reciting the date, the number of occasions that the notice of application was advertised and the newspaper in which the notice was advertised;
  (iii) an affidavit of domicile stating the place of domicile of the deceased at the date of death;
  (iv) an affidavit of the attorney. Where the application is made by power of attorney, the affidavit should recite that power was granted and that the power has not been revoked.

C.   Affidavit of Domicile[23]

All jurisdictions (save Antigua &Barbuda and St Lucia)

The domicile of the deceased at the time of death must be sworn to in the affidavit in support of the application for resealing. However in any case where it appears that the domicile of the deceased at the time of death differs from that stated in the grant, the registrar may require the applicant to file a separate affidavit as to the deceased's domicile. If it appears that the deceased was not at the time of death domiciled within the jurisdiction of the Court in which the grant was issued, the grant will not be resealed unless the grant is such that it would have been made by the court within which the application for resealing is made.

D. The Original Grant or a Duplicate Certified or Sealed Copy Thereof.[24] An Exemplified/Official Copy of the Will, if any.[25]

E. The Newspaper Clippings of the Advertisements/Publications in the Gazette, where applicable.

F. A Certified Copy of the Power of Attorney, where applicable.

When the application is made by an attorney, a certified copy of the power of attorney expressly authorising the resealing of the grant within the local jurisdiction should be lodged with the documents for resealing.

G. Administration Bond[26]

Subject to the exceptions below, an administration bond must be entered into where the grant to be resealed is a grant of letters of administration (with or without will annexed) irrespective of whether the applicant is the original grantee or attorney thereof.

Jamaica

Pursuant to the passage of CPR 2002 and in particular Rule 68.26(3), an administration bond is no longer required with respect to probate and administration applications made in the Supreme Court.

Guyana

In practice the bond may be dispensed with where the persons beneficially entitled to the deceased's estate give their written consent to the resealing of the grant without the imposition of the bond.

St Lucia

An administration bond (with or without will annexed) is usually not required in practice.[27]

The Bahamas

An administration bond is not required in practice where the grant to be resealed is a grant of letters of administration with will annexed.

H. **Affidavit of Justification of Sureties,**[28] **where required.**

I. **Estate Duty Certificate/Stamp Duty Certificate, etc or its equivalent.**

When required, the appropriate estate/stamp duty certificate (or its equivalent in each jurisdiction) must be lodged with the other papers for resealing.

J. **Affidavit of Value, Inventory, Declaration and Account, Statement of Assets and Liabilities**

An Affidavit of Value, Declaration and Account of the estate or its equivalent, setting out particulars of the estate to be covered by the grant and the value, must be lodged except in the following territories:

(i) Grenada and Trinidad & Tobago – an inventory is not filed;
(ii) The Bahamas — the Schedule of the Real Property and the Schedule of the Personal Estate are also not filed; and
(iii) Antigua & Barbuda — a Declaration and Account is not filed as is also the case with respect to applications for grants.
(iv) Jamaica – with effect from January 1, 2003, pursuant to Rule 68.26 CPR 2002 an inventory is no longer required.

ADDITIONAL DOCUMENTS- BY JURISDCTION

1. *Guyana, Jamaica and Trinidad & Tobago*

Certificate/Affidavit of Delay[29]

When the application to reseal is made after a lapse of three years from the death of the deceased, the reason for the delay is required to be certified to the registrar. In practice the reason is recited in the oath/affidavit of the applicant.

2. Barbados, Eastern Caribbean territories and Guyana

Order of the Court

The order for signature by the Registrar/Chief Justice in Guyana, directing that the Record of the Grant be sealed with the seal of the Court is filed with papers for resealing. In the Eastern Caribbean territories this is invariably prepared by the applicant's solicitor.

3. St Vincent & the Grenadines

Warrant of Authority

The Warrant of Authority must also be filed with the application for resealing.

4. The Bahamas

(a) Bond for Making a Return into the Registry and Paying Dues;
(b) Return of the Value of the Personal Estate and Effects of the deceased; and
(c) Certified copy of Death Certificate.

5. Jamaica

In accordance with CPR 2002 and in particular Rule 68.26(3), the following documents are no longer required in respect of resealing applications made in the Supreme Court on or after January 1, 2003:

(a) Inventory;
(b) Kalamazoo copy of inventory;
(c) Declaration of Counting of Inventory
(d) Declaration of Counting of Probate/Letters of Administration (with will annexed) and of copy will, if any;
(e) Bond of Executor — in cases where the grant to be resealed is a probate grant;
(f) Administration Bond; and
(g) Affidavit of justification of sureties.

Procedure after Resealing of Grants[30]

Once the certified copy of the grant is signed and sealed with the seal of the court and delivered to the applicant, the registrar is required to send a notice of the sealing to the court from which the original grant was issued.

Notes

1.
Anguilla	- s.3 Probates (Resealing) Act Cap. 62
Antigua & Barbuda	- s.3 Probates (Resealing) Act Cap. 344
Barbados	- s.3 Probate and Letters of Administration (Resealing) Act Cap. 247
Dominica	- s.3 Probate (Resealing) Act Ch. 9:02
Grenada	- s.19 Probate Act Cap. 255
Guyana	- s.32(2) Deceased Persons Estates' Administration Act Cap. 12:01
Jamaica	- s.3 Probates (Re-Sealing) Act Cap. 309
Montserrat	- s.3 Probates (Resealing) Act Cap. 63
St Vincent & the Grenadines	- s.3 Probates (Resealing) Act Cap. 381
St Christopher & Nevis	- s.3 Probates (Resealing) Act Cap. 62
St Lucia	- Art 1152A Civil Code Ch. 242
The Bahamas	- s.49(1) and 49(2) of the Supreme Court Act 15/1996
Trinidad & Tobago	- s.85 Wills & Probate Ordinance Ch. 8 No. 2.

2. See chapter 13.
3.
Anguilla, St Christopher & Nevis	- s.3 Probates (Resealing) Act Cap. 62
Guyana	- s.32 Deceased Persons Estates' Administration Act Cap. 12:01
Antigua & Barbuda	- s.3 Probates (Resealing) Act Cap. 344
Dominica	- Probates (Resealing) Act ch 9:02
Grenada	- s.19 Probate Act Cap. 255
Jamaica	- s.3 Probates (Re-Sealing) Act
Montserrat	- s.3 Probates (Resealing) Act Cap. 63
St Vincent & the Grenadines	- s.3 Probates (Resealing) Act Cap. 381
Trinidad & Tobago	- s.85 Wills & Probate Ordinance Ch. 8 No. 2.

4. Section 3 Probates (Resealing) Act Cap. 344; Probates (Resealing) (Amendment) Act 15/1989.
5. Section 49(1) Supreme Court Act 15/1996
6. Section 3(1) Probate and Letters of Administration (Resealing) Act Cap. 247
   St Lucia - Arts 1152A, 1152B Civil Code Ch. 242
7. S.I. 1965 No. 1530.
8. The Probate and Letters of Administration (Resealing) Act Ch. 247 The Probate and Letters of Administration Resealing Rules 92/1981
   | Dominica, Guyana | - r.41 N.C.P.R. 1954, England |
   | Eastern Caribbean | - r.39, N.C.P.R. 1987, England |

	(save Dominica)	
	Jamaica	- Rule 68.26 CPR 2002 repealing and replacing theGeneral Rules and Order of the Supreme Court Part III -Rules under the Probates (Re-Sealing) Act
	The Bahamas	- rr. 11, 25-29 The Probate Rules Ch. 35
	Trinidad & Tobago	- rr. 56-68 First Schedule N.C.B.R. Ch. 8 No. 2.
9	Barbados	- s.3 The Probate and Letters of Administration (Resealing Act) Cap. 247
	Guyana, Dominica,	- r.41(1) N.C.P.R. 1954, England
	The Bahamas, Eastern Caribbean (save Dominica)	- r.39(1) N.C.P.R. 1987, England
	Trinidad & Tobago	- r.56 First Schedule NC.B.R. Ch. 8 No. 2.
	Jamaica	- Rule 68.26 (1) CPR 2002
10	Section 3(2)(c) Probate and Letters of Administration (Resealing) Act Cap. 247.	
11	Barbados	- s.3(4)(d) Probate and Letters of Administration (Resealing) Act Cap. 247. It is to be noted that an attorney-at-law registered in Barbados may act on behalf of a personal representative or grantee without a power of attorney.
12	Guyana, Dominica	- r.41 (1) N.C.P.R .1954, England
	The Bahamas, Eastern Caribbean (save Dominica),	- r.39 (1) N.C.P.R. 1987, England.
13	Barbados	- s.3(3) Probate and Letters of Administration (Resealing) Act Cap. 247.
14	Rule 2 is deemed to apply to resealing of grants by virtue of s.32(6) of the Deceased Persons Estates Administration Act Cap. 12:01 which provides in effect that the rules of court regulating the procedure and practice for sealing of probate or letters of administration shall apply to applications with respect to resealing of grants.	
15	Rule 68.26(3) CPR 2002 repealing and replacing r.3 General Rules and Orders of the Supreme Court Part III — Rules under the Probates (Re-Sealing) Act.	
16	Form P12, Appendix 21 CPR. 2002, repealing and replacing General Rules and Orders of the Supreme Court Part III — Probate (Re-Sealing) Act Schedule of Forms.	
17	Rule 26 The Probate Rules Ch. 35.	
18	See Form 23 First Schedule N.C.B.R. Ch. 8 No.2.	
19	Rule 57(d) First Schedule N.C.B.R. Ch.8 No.2,	
20	Eastern Caribbean (save Dominica)	- r.39(4) N.C.P.R 1987, England
	The Bahamas Guyana, Dominica	- r.41(4) N.C.P.R 1954, England
	Trinidad & Tobago	- r.65 First Schedule N.C.B.R. Ch. 8 No. 2.
21		**Rules**
	Guyana	- r.3 Deceased Persons Estates' Administration Rules Cap. 12:01 which is deemed to apply to resealing applications by virtue of s.32(6) of the Deceased Persons Estates' Administration Act Cap. 12:01

	Jamaica	- Rule 68.26(3)(a) CPR 2002 repealing and replacing r.2 General Rules and Orders of the Supreme Court Part III - Rules under the Probates (Re-Sealing) Act
	The Bahamas	- r.25 The Probate Rules Ch. 35
	Trinidad & Tobago	- r.57(c) First Schedule N.C.B.R. Ch. 8 No. 2.

Forms

	Jamaica	- Form P 13 Appendix 2, CPR 2002
	Trinidad & Tobago	- Form No. 24 First Schedule N.C.B.R. Ch. 8 No. 2.
22	Section 3(4) The Probate and Letters of Administration (Resealing) Act Cap. 247.	
23	Anguilla, St Christopher & Nevis,	- s.4 Probates (Resealing) Ace Cap. 62
	Antigua & Barbuda	- s.4 Probates (Resealing) Act Cap. 344. In practice the domicile of the deceased is not recited in the affidavit
	Barbados	- ss.(4)(e) and 5(1)(3) Probate and Letters of Administration (Resealing) Act Cap. 247
	Dominica	- s.4 Probates (Resealing) Act Ch. 9:02
	Guyana	- s.32(3) Deceased Persons Estates' Administration Act Cap. 12:01
	Jamaica	- Rule 68.26(b) CPR 2002 repealing and replacing s.7 Probates (Re-Sealing) Act: rr.7, 8 General Rules and Orders of the Supreme Court Part III - Rules under the Probates (Re-Sealing) Act
	Montserrat	- s.4 Probates (Resealing) Act Cap. 63
	The Bahamas	- s.49(1)(a) of the Supreme Court Act 15/1996
	St Lucia and Grenada	- Although there is no specific provision which requires that proof of the deceased's domicile be furnished, it is the practice to do so.
	St Vincent & the Grenadines	- Although there is no statutory provision requesting that the domicile of the deceased be stated, it is the practice to do so.
	Trinidad & Tobago	- s.86 Wills & Probate Ordinance Ch. 8 No.2; rr.61, 62 First Schedule N.C.B.R. Ch. 8 No. 2.
24	Anguilla, St Christopher & Nevis,	- s.6 Probates (Resealing) Act Cap. 62
	Antigua & Barbuda	- s.6 Probates (Resealing) Act Cap. 344
	Barbados	- s.3(4)(a) Probate and Letters of Administration (Resealing) Act Cap. 247
	Dominica	- s.6 Probates (Resealing) Act Ch. 9:02
	Grenada	- Probate Act Cap. 255
	Guyana	- s.32(5) Deceased Persons Estates' Administration Act Cap. 12:01

	Jamaica	- s.6 Probates (Re-Sealing) Act; Rule 68.26(3)(a) CPR 2002 repealing and repalcing r.9 General Rules and Orders of the Supreme Court Part III - Rules under the Probates (Re-Sealing) Act
	Montserrat	- s.6 Probates (Resealing) Act Cap. 63
	The Bahamas	- s.49 Supreme Court Act 15/1996
	St Lucia	- Arts 1152(1), 1 l52A Civil Code Ch. 242
	St Vincent & the Grenadines	- s.5 Probate Resealing Act Cap. 381
	Trinidad & Tobago	- s.88 Wills & Probate Ordinance Ch. 8 No. 2; r.57(a) First Schedule N.C.B.R. Ch. 8 No. 2.
25	Anguilla St Christopher & Nevis, Antigua & Barbuda	- s.4(b) Probates (Resealing) Act Cap. 62 - s.4(a) Probates (Resealing) Ace Cap. 344
	Barbados	- s.5(1)(a) Probate and Letters of Administration (Resealing) Act Cap. 247
	Dominica	- s.4(b) Probates (Resealing) Act Ch. 9:02
	Guyana	- s.3(b) Deceased Persons Estates' Administration Act Cap. 12:01
	Jamaica	- Rule 68.26(3)(b) repealing and replacing r.9 General Rules and Orders of the Supreme Court Part III - Rules and Probates (Re-Sealing) Act
	Montserrat	- s.4(b) Probates (Resealing) Act Cap. 63
	St Lucia	- Arts 1152(1), 1152A Civil Code Ch. 242
	St Vincent & the Grenadines	- s.4 Probate Resealing Act Cap. 381
	The Bahamas	- s.49 Supreme Court Act 15/1996
	Trinidad & Tobago	- r.57(b) First Schedule N.C.B.R Ch 8. No. 2.
26	Barbados	- s.5(1)(b), (2) Probates and Letters of Administration (Resealing) Act Cap. 247. (It is to be noted that the bond, though required, is not lodged by the applicant for the grant.)
	Guyana	- r.5 Deceased Persons Estates' Administration Rules Cap. 12:01 which is deemed to apply to resealing applications by virtue of s.32(6) Deceased Persons Estates' Administration Act Cap. 12:01
	Jamaica	- Pursuant to the provision of Rule 68 CPR 2002 an administration bond is no longer required with respect to probate and administration applications made to the Supreme Court.
	The Bahamas	- r.27 The Probate Rules Ch. 35
	Trinidad & Tobago	- r.59 First Schedule N.C.B.R. Ch. 8 No. 2
27	See chapter 11 p. 272.	
28	Ibid., p. 277.	
29	Guyana	- r.9 Deceased Persons Estates' Administration Rules Cap. 12:01 which is deemed to apply to resealing

Jamaica	applications by virtue of s.32(6) of the Deceased Persons Estates' Administration Act Cap. 12:01. - Rule 68.26(3)(d) CPR 2002 repealing and replacing r.10 General Rules and Orders of the Supreme Court Part III - Rules under the Probates (Re-Sealing) Act
Trinidad & Tobago	- r.57(g) First Schedule N.C.B.R. Ch. 8 No. 2.
30 Anguilla, St Christopher & Nevis	- s.4(a) Probates (Resealing) Act Cap- 62
Montserrat	- s.4(a) Probates (Resealing) Act Cap. 63
Antigua & Barbuda	- ss.4(a) Probates (Resealing) Act Cap. 344
Barbados	- s.5(1)(b) Probate and Letters of Administration (Resealing) Act Cap. 247
Dominica	- s.4(a) Probates (Resealing) Act Ch. 9:02
Guyana	- s.3(a) Deceased Persons Estates' Administration Act Cap. 12:01; r.10 Deceased Persons Estates' Administration Rules Cap. 12:01
Jamaica	- Part 68.26(8) CPR 2002 repealing and replacing r.11 General Rules and Orders of the Supreme Court Part III - Rules under the Probates (Re-Sealing) Act
The Bahamas	- r.28 The Probate Rules Ch. 35
Trinidad & Tobago	- r.66 First Schedule N.C.B.R, Ch. 8 No. 2.

21

Renunciation and Retraction[1]

RENUNCIATION

A person who has a right to probate or administration may renounce all rights and title with respect thereto by filing the appropriate form of renunciation in the Probate Section of the High/Supreme Court Registry. Once the renunciation is filed it takes immediate effect and cannot be retracted except with leave of the court.[2]

EFFECT OF RENUNCIATION

A. *Renunciation by executor*[3]

With respect to Trinidad & Tobago and Barbados, when an executor renounces probate of a will not only do his rights in respect to the executorship wholly cease but the representation of the testator and the administration of his real and personal estate devolves as if he had not been appointed executor. However in the case of the Eastern Caribbean territories (save St. Lucia), Jamaica and The Bahamas, an executor who renounces probate does not thereby renounce any right to a grant of administration unless he expressly renounces that right.

B. *Renunciation by person(s) entitled to administration*[4]

Barbados, Trinidad and Tobago and St. Lucia

A person who renounces administration of the estate of a deceased person in one character will not be allowed to take representation in another character.

Jamaica, Guyana, Eastern Caribbean territories (save St. Lucia) and The Bahamas

A person who has renounced administration (with or without will annexed) may obtain administration in another capacity with the permission of the registrar.

PURPOSE OF RENUNCIATION

A renunciation is a simple and inexpensive means of clearing off persons with superior rights and title to probate or, in all the jurisdictions save Jamaica, right and title to administration as the case may be, thereby permitting those persons with inferior rights to make the necessary application for the appropriate grant of representation in respect of the estate of a deceased person. Renunciations are filed in the following circumstances:

A. In Cases of Testacy

All jurisdictions (save Jamaica)

(a) Sole executor —where the renunciant is the sole or sole surviving executor of the testator. Additionally it is to be noted that, in the case of all the jurisdictions, save Trinidad and Tobago, Barbados and St. Lucia, the sole executor may also be the person first entitled to take out letters of administration (with or without will annexed);

(b) No executor — where there is no executor or alternatively no surviving executor and the renunciant is the person first entitled to take out letters of administration (with or without will annexed);

(c) When the renunciant is a non-proving executor. An executor with power reserved may, if he wishes, take out a double probate grant at any time. As such, should the proving executor die or become incapacitated, the executor with power reserved, would but for his renunciation, be first entitled to take out a grant of representation.

(d) Executor by representation[5]— where the renunciant is an executor by representation of any will of which his testator is executor. With the exception of a non-proving executor who decides to take out a double probate grant and prove the will of his testator, an executor by representation has a prior right to administer any estate of which his testator is executor. This is provided he has proved his testator's will.

In cases of Intestacy

All jurisdictions (save Jamaica)

When the renunciant is the sole person first entitled to take out letters of administration—if there are others equally entitled to administration their consent rather than renunciation should be sought, by those person(s) wishing to take out letters of administration.

POSITION IN JAMAICA

Prior to January 1, 2003

Although renunciation is a means of clearing off a person with a superior title, in the context of Jamaica it was applicable only to cases where the renunciant was an executor. This was so because:

(a) the Administrator General was and still is the sole person entitled by law to take out letters of administration with will annexed or to take out letters of administration *simpliciter* where the value of the residuary estate exceeds one thousand dollars and a minor/minors is/are the beneficiaries thereof; and

(b) in all cases where the beneficiaries of the estate,
    (i) were either entitled by law to apply for the grant;
    (ii) had obtained the Formal Consent of the Administrator General; or
    (iii) had obtained an order of the court,
    clearing off persons with a prior entitlement to the relevant grant, if any, did not arise in practice in Jamaica.

As such the only circumstances in which renunciation might have previously arisen in practice in Jamaica were in cases of testacy and then only where the renunciant was the sole executor, a non-proving executor or executor by representation. However unlike the position in the other jurisdictions, when an executor renounced and was thereby cleared off, the sole person next entitled by law to take out a grant was, and still is, the Administrator General, not a beneficiary, unless there were other executors who had nor renounced their right to the executorship; or in the appropriate case where the Administrator General had given his Formal Consent to the beneficiaries applying, or otherwise where the court so ordered.

The General Rules and Orders of the Supreme Court Part III Schedule of Forms contained a precedent (Form No. 14) with respect to renunciation of administration with will annexed and a precedent (Form No. 15) with respect to renunciation of administration. However in light of the *de facto* and *de jure* position in Jamaica, prior to January 1, 2003, these forms were of no practical effect.

Alternative to Renunciation

B. On or After January 1, 2003

As a result of the passage of the CPR 2002, in particular Rules 68.11 and 68.18, an order of priority has now been expressly provided in respect of applications for letters of administration (with or without will annexed) made in the Supreme Court.

Although the substantive statutory position provided by s.12 of the Administrator General Act and ss.12 and 5 of the Intestates' Estates and Property Charges Act remains unchanged, the entitlement of the Administrator General, in so far as grants of administration (with or without will annexed) and in addition, the circumstances in which beneficiaries of the estate will be allowed to apply, has been significantly changed as there is now an order of priority among the various classes of beneficiaries for such grants.

In this regard, Rule 68.33 CPR 2002 provides for renunciation of probate and administration, and has essentially codified the position. In particular, the following obtains in respect of applications for probate and administration, in particular, the following should be noted:

(i) an executor may renounce probate in accordance, using the form prescribed (P.14 Appendix 2) and in accordance with the Executors (Renunciation) Act;
(ii) a person entitled to a grant of administration, with or without will annexed, may do so using Form P.15/P.16, Appendix 2, respectively.
(iii) A person entitled to probate does not renounce any right to a grant of administration unless he or she expressly renounces that right;
(iv) A person who renounces administration (with or without will annexed) in one capacity may not obtain administration another capacity without the permission of the registrar.

All Jurisdictions

Renunciation is a voluntary act. As such, it may become necessary to resort to citation or passing over proceedings as a means of clearing off those persons with superior rights and title to probate and/or administration who are not only unwilling to take out probate or letters of administration but are also refusing to renounce their rights and title.

RENUNCIATION ON BEHALF OF A MINOR/INFANT

With the exception of Jamaica, a minor's right to probate may not be renounced by anyone on his behalf.[6] However upon reaching the age of majority, he is free either to renounce or alternatively to apply for the appropriate grant of representation in his own right. In the case of Jamaica, Rule 68.33(5) CPR 2002, expressly provides that a guardian may be appointed by the registrar, for the purposes of renouncing on behalf of the minor, his right to probate

All jurisdictions

A minor's right to administration (with or without will annexed) may be renounced by a person assigned by the Court for that purpose. This will be done only if it is necessary to clear off the minor's right to administration so as permit a person with a lower title, to make the necessary application for a grant of representation.[7]

RENUNCIATION ON BEHALF OF A MENTALLY INCAPABLE PERSON

A person appointed by the Court under the relevant Mental Health Act/ Supreme Court Act of the various territories, and specifically authorised may renounce a mentally incapable executor's right to probate. Additionally, in all the other jurisdictions including Jamaica, with effect from January 1, 2003 such person may also renounce a mentally incapable person's right to administration.

Eastern Caribbean (save Dominica) and The Bahamas

An attorney appointed under an enduring power of attorney in the above-mentioned may also renounce administration for the use and benefit of an incapable person by virtue of r.35(2)(c) N.C.P.R. 1987, England.

ALTERNATIVE TO RENUNCIATION

All jurisdictions

In cases where no person has been appointed by the court to renounce probate or administration on behalf of the mentally incapable person, such person will have to be cleared off by citation proceedings. Alternatively, in special circumstances an application may be made for an order passing over the incapable person under the relevant 'passing over' provision of the various territories.

RENUNCIATION BY ATTORNEY

A person expressly authorised by power of attorney may renounce an executor's right to administration.

FORM OF RENUNCIATION

In order to be accepted for registration, a renunciation must contain the name and a brief description of the deceased and the renunciant and the place and date of death of the deceased. The renunciation must also be dated and signed by the renunciant and should be witnessed by a disinterested person whose address and occupation should be included.

Trust Corporations

If the renunciant is a trust corporation the renunciation must either be under seal or signed by an official appointed for the express purpose of executing the renunciation.

Non-Trust Corporation

In the case of a non-trust corporation, a sealed or properly authenticated copy of a resolution appointing a nominee to renounce its rights to the grant on its behalf must be lodged with the renunciation.

FORM OF RENUNCIATION

Apart from the above, a renunciation takes a variety of forms which depends largely on the fact circumstances.

1. RENUNCIATION OF PROBATE[8]

   This form is used when the renunciant is either one of the executors or the sole or sole surviving executor of the testator.
   In all jurisdictions save Trinidad & Tobago, Barbados and St. Lucia, where the renunciant is the sole executor and is also first entitled to take out letters of administration (with or without will annexed), the renunciation must also include a recital by the sole executor renouncing all rights and title. This is necessary because in all jurisdictions save Trinidad & Tobago, Barbados and St. Lucia, a renunciation of probate by an executor does not operate as a renunciation of any right which he may have to a grant of administration (with or without will annexed), in some other capacity, unless he expressly renounces such right. Indeed if this recital is nor included in the renunciation the registrar will refuse to accept it for filing.

2. RENUNCIATION OF ADMINISTRATION WITH WILL ANNEXED[9]

   This form is used where the testator has either failed to appoint an executor or the executor so appointed has predeceased the testator and the person first entitled to take out letters of administration with will annexed wishes to renounce his rights and title thereto. Apart from the usual recitals, the renunciation must include a recital by the renunciant renouncing all rights and title to letters of administration with will annexed, and in the case of Trinidad and Tobago, Barbados and St. Lucia, right and title letters of administration also, if relevant.

3. RENUNCIATION OF LETTERS OF ADMINISTRATION

   This form is used where the deceased has died intestate and the person first entitled to take out letters of administration, wishes to renounce all rights with respect thereto. In such cases the renunciation must include a recital by the renunciant expressly renouncing all rights and title to administration of the estate of the deceased.

The Bahamas

Prior to the passage of the Inheritance Act 2002, which came into operation on February 1, 2002, and abolished the common law doctrine of descent, where the heir-at-law renounced his right to a grant of administration, he is required to file the requisite renunciation and an affidavit of heirship, setting out his entitlement to the grant.

PRACTICE AND PROCEDURE

The renunciation is effected by filing the appropriate form of renunciation in the Probate Section of the High/Supreme Court Registry. This may be done either before or upon application for a grant by another.

If it is filed before the application for the grant, the will and other testamentary papers not deposited in the Depository of Wills of Living Persons (or its equivalent in the various territories) where applicable, must be lodged with the renunciation. In that case the applicant for the grant will be required to attend the Registry to swear the oath/affidavit and to mark the will before the proper officer.

However the more usual practice is to lodge the renunciation along with the other papers to lead the grant of representation by the applicant.

1. INVALID RENUNCIATION

A. *By Executor*

The general rule of law is that an executor who prior to probate performs any executorial acts with respect to the estate of his testator, is barred from renouncing his right to probate and may accordingly be cited to prove the will of the testator, usually by the person next entitled to administration (with or without will annexed).[10] If he still refuses to take probate after having been cited, the recalcitrant executor may be liable to a fine and attachment.[11]

However, in the case of Trinidad and Tobago, pursuant to s.21 of the Wills and Probate Ordinance Ch.8 no. 2 and s.10(4) of the Administration of Estates Ordinance Ch.8 no.1, the legal title to the estate of a testator does not devolve on the executor until the grant of probate is obtained. Accordingly, an executor in Trinidad and Tobago, although personally liable pursuant to s.11of the Wills and Probate Ordinance, as an executor *de son tort* for his acts of intermediary prior to the grant, cannot be cited to take probate, as he may, until the grant is obtained, renounce his right to probate.

B. *By Administrator*

All jurisdictions

The person first entitled to take out letters of administration (with or without will annexed) who has intermeddled cannot and will not be compelled to take out a grant since his appointment as administrator is made by the court and only becomes operative upon a grant of representation being made.[12] In such circumstances if the person first entitled to administration refuses to renounce he can be cited to accept or refuse to take out the appropriate grant. If he refuses, the citer or other person interested in the deceased's estate will, upon application, be given leave to apply for the appropriate grant of representation. The defaulting administrator will however be personally liable as an executor *de son tort* for any loss which may have accrued to the deceased's estate as a result of his intermeddling.

RENOUNCING PROBATE OR ADMINISTRATION IN ANOTHER CAPACITY

Eastern Caribbean territories, Jamaica and The Bahamas[13]

Pursuant to the relevant N.C.P.R. England and Rule 68.33(2) and (4) CPR 2002, in the case of Jamaica, renunciation of probate does not operate as a renunciation of any right and title the renunciant may have to take a grant of administration in some other capacity unless he expressly renounces such right.

However, unless the registrar otherwise directs, no person who has renounced administration in one capacity may obtain a grant thereof in some other capacity.

Trinidad & Tobago, Barbados, St. Lucia[14]

No person who renounces probate or administration of the estate of a deceased person in one character is to be allowed to take representation to the same deceased in another character.

RETRACTION[15]

An administrator or executor who has renounced his rights to probate and/or administration will not be permitted to retract his renunciation merely because he has had a change of heart.

A. By Executor

The law is quite clear that an executor will be permitted to retract a renunciation of probate only in exceptional cases after a grant has been made to some other person in a lower capacity.[16] Such exceptional circumstances include cases in which he can establish to the satisfaction of the court that the retraction is for the benefit of the estate. In St Lucia, Art 847 of the Civil Code Ch. 242 provides that an executor who has accepted office may renounce it with leave of the Court for sufficient cause. And according to Art 847 a difference of opinion between an executor and the majority of co-executors may constitute sufficient cause.

B. *By Administrator*

Except in Jamaica, by virtue of Rule 68.33(6) and (7) CPR 2002, there is no rule of law prohibiting an administrator from retracting his renunciation. However in practice he will be permitted to retract only when it is deemed necessary.[17] In either case leave must first be obtained to retract.

PRACTICE

The application for an order granting leave to retract may be made in

- (i) *Eastern Caribbean territories and Jamaica*
  by Part 11 CPR 2000/Part 11 CPR 2002 application supported by affidavit to the registrar;
- (ii) *Trinidad & Tobago and Barbados*
  Exparte on affidavit to the registrar
- (iii) *The Bahamas and Guyana*
  ex parte summons supported by affidavit to a judge in chambers

The affidavit must clearly state the reasons why the retraction is being sought. The grant or a copy thereof, must also be lodged with the application.

Once leave is granted, a memorandum of the subsequent grant to the renunciant, is endorsed on the original grant of probate or administration, and retained in the Registry.[18]

EFFECT OF RETRACTION

Once the order of retraction is granted, the renunciant may take out probate or administration, which then takes effect and is deemed to have taken effect without prejudice to previous acts and dealing of and notices to any other representative who has previously proved the will or taken out letters of administration.[19]

Notes

1	Barbados	- ss.9, 10 Succession Act Cap. 249
	Jamaica	- The Executor's Renunciation Act;
	Eastern Caribbean, Grenada, St Vincent & the Grenadines	- s.5 Administration of Estates Act, 1925 England
	St Lucia	- Art 847 Civil Code Ch. 242
	St Vincent & the Grenadines	- ss. 27, 28 Administration of Estates Act Cap. 377
	The Bahamas	- ss. 6 and 7 Administration of Estates Act 2002
	Trinidad & Tobago	- ss. 12, 13 Wills and Probate Ord. Ch. 8 No. 2

Rules

	Barbados	- rr. 32, 33 Supreme Court (Non-Contentious) Probate Rules, 1959
	Dominica, Guyana	- r. 35 N.C.P.R. 1954. England
	Jamaica	- Rule 68.33 CPR 2002
	The Bahamas, Eastern Caribbean (save St Lucia and Dominica)	- r. 37N.C.P.R. 1987, England
	St Lucia	- Arts 1017, 1025 Code of Civil Procedure Ch. 243
	Trinidad & Tobago	- rr. 36, 37 First Schedule N.C.B.R. Ch. 8 No. 2. See also all jurisdictions pp. post

2 With respect to Jamaica pursuant to s.3 of the Executor's Renunciation Act, a renunciation cannot be retracted. However Rule 68.33(6) and (7) CPR 2002 provides otherwise see p. 422-423.

3	Barbados	- s.9 Succession Act Cap. 249
	Grenada	- s.11 Probate Act Cap. 255
	Jamaica	- s.3 The Executors' Renunciation Act
	Eastern Caribbean (save St Lucia & St Vincent & the Grenadines)	- s.5 Administration of Estates Act 1925, England
	St Lucia	- Art 847 Civil Code Ch. 242
	St Vincent & the Grenadines	- s.27 Administration of Estates Act Cap. 377
	The Bahamas	- s.7 of the Administration of Estates Act 2002
	Trinidad & Tobago	- s.12 Wills & Probate Ordinance Ch. 8 No.2.
4	Barbados	- r. 33 Supreme Court (Non-contentious) Probate Rules, 1959
	Trinidad & Tobago	- r. 37 First Schedule N.C.B.R. 8 no.2
	St. Lucia	- Art 1025 Code of Civil Procedure 243
	Eastern Caribbean territories	- r. 37 NCPR 1987, England
	Dominica, Guyana	- r.35 NCPR 1954, England
	Jamaica (save St. Lucia and Dominica)	- Rule 68.33(3) CPR 2002

5 Not applicable to Barbados with respect to the estates of people dying on or before November 13, 1975 pursuant to s.11 Succession Act Cap. 249.

6 Barbados, Trinidad & Tobago, Guyana, Dominica — r.32(2), N.C.P.R 1954, England

   Jamaica — Rule 68.33(5) CPR 2002

   The Bahamas, Jamaica, Eastern Caribbean (save Dominica) — r.34(1), N.C.P.R. 1987, England.

   Jamaica — Rule 68.33(5) CPR 2002, by implication

7 Eastern Caribbean territories (save Dominica), The Bahamas — r.34(2) N.C.P.R 1987, England

   Trinidad & Tobago, Guyana, Barbados, Dominica — r.31(6) N.C.P.R 1954, England.

8 Barbados — Forms No. 7 and 8 Appendix (Forms & Fees) Supreme Court (Non-Contentious) Probate Rules 1959

   Jamaica — Form P14 Appendix 2, CPR 2002, repealing and replacing Form No. 14 General Rules and Orders of the Supreme Court Part III Schedule of Forms

   Trinidad & Tobago — Form No. 19 First Schedule N.C.B.R. Ch. 8 No. 2.

9 Barbados — Form No. 9 Appendix (Forms and Fees) Supreme Court (Non-Contentious) Probate Rules 1959

   Jamaica — P.16 Appendix 2 CPR 2002

   Trinidad & Tobago — Form No. 21 First Schedule N.C.B.R. Ch. 8 No. 2.

10 *In the Goods of Davis* (1860) 4 Sw & Tr 213; *In the Goods of Fell* (1861) 2 Sw & Tr 126. See also chapter 26.

11 *Ibid.*

12 *In the Goods of Davis* (1860) 4 Sw & Tr 213.

13 The Bahamas, Eastern Caribbean (save Dominica) — r.37(2) N.C.P.R. 1987, England

   Dominica, Guyana — r.35(2) N.C.P.R. 1954, England

14 Barbados — r.33 Supreme Court (Non-Contentious) Probate Rule 1959

   St Lucia — Art 1025 Code of Civil Procedure Ch. 243

   Trinidad & Tobago — r.37 First Schedule N.C.B.R. Ch. 8 No. 2.

15 Barbados — s.10 Succession Act Cap. 249

   Eastern Caribbean territories (save St Vincent & the Grenadines and St Lucia) — s.6 Administration of Estates Act 1925

   St Lucia — Art 847 Civil Code Ch. 242

   St Vincent & the Grenadines — s.28 Administration of Estates Act Cap. 377

	The Bahamas	- s.7 Administration of Estates Act 2002
	Jamaica	- Rule 68.33(6) and (7) CPR 2002
	Trinidad & Tobago	- s.13(1) Wills & Probate Ordinance Ch. 8 No.2.
16	Guyana. Dominica, Barbados, Trinidad & Tobago	- r.35(3) N.C.P.R. 1954, England
	The Bahamas, Eastern Caribbean, (save Dominica)	- r.37(3) N.C.P.R. 1987, England.
	Jamaica	- Rule 68.33(7) CPR 2002
17	*In the Goods of Gill* [1873] 3 P & D 113.	
18	Barbados	- s.10 Succession Act Cap. 249
	Eastern Caribbean (save St Lucia)	- s.6 Administration of Estates Act 1925, England
	St Lucia	- Although the English substantive probate law is not received in St Lucia, it is submitted that the position with respect to the effect of retraction is applicable to the other territories
	St Vincent & the Grenadines	- s.28 Administration of Estates Act Cap. 377
	The Bahamas	- s.7 Administration of Estates Act 2002
	Trinidad & Tobago	- s.13(1) Wills & Probate Ordinance Ch. 8 No.2.

22

Amendment and Notation of Grants

AMENDMENT OF GRANTS

A. Errors discovered

Subsequent to the issue of a grant of representation an error may be discovered in the grant itself. If the error is relatively minor, such as a mistake in the spelling of the forename of the deceased named therein, or an error in the deceased's place or date of death, an order for amendment of the grant will be made. If however, it is an error of substance for example, where the deceased's actual surname is wrong as opposed to a mistake in its spelling, the grant will not be amended but will have to be revoked.

Procedure and Documents Required

Pursuant to r.42 of the N.C.P.R. 1954 England/r.41 of N.C.P.R. 1987, England,[1] depending on the territory concerned, and in the case of Jamaica, pursuant to Rule 68.37 CPR 2002, where the registrar is satisfied that a grant should be amended he may so order but such power is to be exercised:

(a) on the application or consent of the person to whom the grant was made; and
(b) otherwise only in exceptional circumstances.

An application for an order for the amendment of a grant of representation is made *ex parte* to the registrar.

The documents to be lodged are:

1. Covering notice/letter addressed to the Registrar (discretionary);
2. Affidavit of the grantee — containing the following recitals, *inter alia*:

	i)	the date and issue of the grant;
	ii)	the nature of the error subsequently discovered;
	iii)	the necessity for the alteration(s);
	iv)	the nature of the amendment required;
3.		the birth/death certificate of the deceased to which the grant relates. This is lodged if the nature of the amendment sought is with respect to an error in the name or date of death of the deceased named therein.
4.		The grant.

B. *Alteration in Value of Estate*

In the vast majority of cases amendments are sought because the grantee omitted to include property owned by the deceased in the application for the grant. This omission may have arisen because at the time of making the application for the grant, the grantee was unaware of the existence of property to which the deceased's estate was entitled. In such circumstances, an *ex parte* application on affidavit should be made by the grantee to amend the grant so as to reflect the increased value of the deceased's estate.

PROCEDURE AND DOCUMENTS REQUIRED

1. Covering notice/letter addressed to the registrar (discretionary);
2. An affidavit of increase containing the following recitals, *inter alia*:
    i) the gross value of the estate as stated in the original application;
    ii) the discovery of an error in the gross value of the estate after issue of the grant;
    iii) the revised gross value of the estate.
3. The grant.
4. An amended Affidavit/Statements of Assets and Liabilities, Declaration and Account (or its equivalent in the various jurisdictions) setting out the gross value of the estate already returned, the gross value now returned with a brief description of the property.
5. Amended/Further Bond where a bond is required. This may be necessary if the penalty in the original bond is not sufficient to cover the increased value of the estate.

    However where the revised value is relatively insubstantial a further bond may not be required.
6. Where applicable, an amended/corrective Estate Duty/Stamp Duty Certificate or its equivalent in the respective jurisdictions reflecting the increased value of the estate.

PROCEDURE AFTER LODGING OF DOCUMENTS- IN GENERAL

After the above-mentioned documents have been lodged in the Registry, either in cases of amendment to errors in the grant or the gross value of the deceased's estate, the registrar signs an order granting the amendment sought. A copy of the order is sent to or may be collected by the grantee's attorney-at-law. Upon the payment of the relevant fees the grant is amended by drawing a red line through the error and typing above, in red, the amendment sought.

Notation of Grants of Representation

Circumstances may arise where it becomes necessary to make a notation on a grant of representation.
These include:

(a) where a renouncing executor has been granted leave to retract his renunciation (not applicable to Jamaica);[2]

(b) where power was reserved to an executor and the proving executor becomes incapable and the grant is impounded. In such instances the double probate grant issued to the executor with power reserved will bear a marginal note as to the impounding of the original grant.

(c) where an incapable grantee whose grant was impounded has recovered from his incapacity and has applied for the release of the original grant to him. In such cases a note will be made on the temporary grant that it has ceased and expired.

(d) *Guyana, Jamaica, Trinidad & Tobago and The Bahamas*[3]
In accordance with the relevant family provisions legislation of Jamaica and Guyana, Trinidad & Tobago and The Bahamas, a copy of every order made thereunder is required to be sent to the registrar for filing and a memorandum of the order endorsed on or permanently annexed to the probate or letters of administration under which the estate is being administered.

Notes

1 Eastern Caribbean (save Dominica) and The Bahamas — r.41 N.C.P.R. 1987, England

   Trinidad & Tobago, Barbados, Guyana, Dominica — r.42 N.C.P.R. 1954, England.

   Jamaica — Rule 68.36, CPR 2002

2   See chapter 21, p. 422-423.
3   Guyana   - s.16(3) Family & Dependants Provision Act 1990
    Jamaica   - s.20 The Inheritance (Provision for Family and
                         Dependants) Act 1993.
    The Bahamas   - s.21(4) Inheritance Act 2002
    Trinidad & Tobago - s.113(3) Succession Act 27/1981

23

Revocation and Impounding of Grants

REVOCATION OF GRANTS[1]

A grant of probate and administration (with or without will annexed) may be revoked by the court:

a) by an order made by a judge in open court;
b) in an action for revocation of a grant;
and with respect to non-contentious probate business,
c) on the application or with the consent of the grantee[2] unless the grant is clearly one to which the grantee is not entitled.

With respect to (c) a grant may be revoked for a variety of reasons which may be conveniently classified as follows:

(i) When the original grant contains a substantial error such as an incorrect statement (as opposed to a misspelling) of the deceased's surname.
(ii) When the grant has been made to a person who had no rights and title thereto. This may arise as a result of a false statement made by such person either fraudulently, by mistake or through ignorance of the real facts. Examples of this include the discovery of a will after administration has been granted, discovery of a later will after probate of an earlier will has been granted, or the issuing of a grant of probate where the testator is in fact still alive.
(iii) When the grant has ceased to be operative because of a material change in circumstances after its issue such as the disappearance, infirmity or incapacity of the original grantee.

Death of Grantee(s)

Where the death of the grantee occurs prior to the sealing of the grant, the grant is a nullity; where it occurs after the grant has been sealed, but before the estate has been administered, the grant may be revoked.[3]

Incapacity of one of Several Grantees

Where one of several executors becomes incapable of managing his affairs, the grant of probate issued to them will be revoked by the court, and a new grant issued to the capable executors, with a power reserved to the incapable executor to apply for a double probate grant on the cesser of his incapacity. Where one of several administrators (with or without will annexed) becomes incapable the grant is similarly revoked and a fresh grant of administration issued to the capable administrator(s).

Incapacity of Sole Grantee

When the sole grantee becomes incapable the grant is impounded not revoked.

Practice and Documents Required

The practice and procedure with respect to the revocation of grants in the various territories are regulated, depending on the jurisdiction concerned[4] by the English practice and procedure codified by r.42 N.C.P.R., 1954/ r.41 of N.C.P.R., 1987, England, and in the case of Jamaica, by Rule 68.37 CPR 2002. The application for revocation is made *ex parte* on affidavit to the registrar.

The following documents are filed in the Probate Section of the Supreme/ High Court Registry:

1. Covering notice/letter addressed to the registrar (discretionary)
2. The affidavit of the applicant setting out *inter alia*:
    (i) details of the first grant;
    (ii) the grounds on which the revocation is sought;
    (iii) the right of the applicant to a new grant.
    The affidavit should be made either by the existing grantee or new proposed grantee, if not the same person.
3. Where the applicant for the new grant is not the original grantee, the signed consent of the original grantee to the revocation of the grant, should be annexed to the affidavit. Where this cannot be obtained a good reason for dispensing with it must be given.
4. A medical certificate or other evidence of incapacity or the death

certificate of the original grantee in circumstances where the original grantee has died/become incapacitated as the case may be.
5. The original grant

Once the application is in order, the registrar signs the order revoking the original grant. The original grant is then cancelled by striking through with a pen and writing the word 'Revoked' thereon. The revoked grant is then filed away. A copy of the order together with a covering letter informing the applicant of the revocation of the grant is sent to him or his attorney-at-law as the case may be. The applicant may then apply for a fresh grant of representation of the deceased's estate.

Application for Fresh Grant of Representation

The usual documents for a grant of probate letters of administration (with or without will annexed) should be lodged. However the following should be noted:

(a) *Oath/Affidavit of Applicant*
The oath should recite the making of the first grant and its revocation (A copy of the order of revocation should also be annexed thereto);
(b) *Marking of will*
Where the applicant for the new grant is the original grantee the will, if any, is not marked again.

Combined Application for Revocation and Issue of Fresh Grant

Where one of the proving executors becomes incapable, a combined application for revocation of the grant of probate and issue of new grant may be made by lodging one affidavit serving both to lead the order for revocation and as the oath/affidavit for the fresh grant.

IMPOUNDING OF GRANTS

A grant may be impounded[5] and a new grant issued both in cases of testacy and intestacy in the following instances:

(a) *Incapacity of the Sole Executor* — where the sole or sole surviving executor becomes incapable. In such cases the grant is impounded (that is, lodged in the Registry pending the recovery of the grantee) and a grant *de bonis non administratus,* limited for the use and benefit of the incapable executor during his incapacity, made to the person who would have been next entitled to take out the grant had the executor been incapable at the time when the first grant was issued.

(b) *Sole Proving Executor* — where the proving executor becomes incapacitated, and power is reserved to a non-proving executor. In such cases the grant is impounded and a grant of double probate made to the executor with power reserved. The double probate grant will bear a notation with respect to the impounding of the first grant.

(c) *Incapacity of Sole Administrator* — where the sole administrator becomes incapable. In such cases the grant is impounded and a grant *de bonis non administratus* for the use and benefit of the incapable administrator and during his incapacity is made, to a person who either was equally entitled to the original grant or where the original grantee was the only person first entitled, to the person who would have been next entitled had the original grantee been incapable at the time when the first grant was issued.

PRACTICE AND DOCUMENTS REQUIRED

Preliminary Observations

Eastern Caribbean territories (save Dominica), Jamaica and The Bahamas

The practice and procedure with respect to the impounding of grants are not regulated by any rule whether indigenous or received and it is to be noted that in England this practice has been discontinued by Registrar's Directions dated July 9, 1985. As such the practice of impounding grants in the above territories should also have been discontinued by virtue of the relevant reception provisions of these territories.

Barbados, Dominica, Guyana and Trinidad & Tobago

In accordance with the pre-1985 practice in England, an application for an order for impounding of a grant may be made *ex parte* on affidavit to the registrar.

The following documents should be lodged in the Registry:
1. Covering letter/notice addressed to the registrar (discretionary);
2. An affidavit by the intended grantee setting out:
    (i) the issue of the grant to the original grantee;

(ii) the incapacity of the original grantee with evidence of such incapacity. This evidence may be provided by an affidavit or certificate of a medical practitioner who has attended to the incapable grantee;
3. The grant.

Upon lodging the above documents, an order impounding the grant is made. The impounded grant is then filed. A copy of the order is sent to the applicant who is then free to apply for a new grant limited, where applicable, to the recovery of the original grantee.

Application for Fresh Grant

The fresh grant issued to the applicant may either be a double probate grant if it is issued to an executor with power reserved, or otherwise, a grant *de bonis non administratus* limited for the use and benefit of the original grantee and during his incapacity.

In either case the usual documents necessary for either of the two grants must be lodged. The oath/affidavit of the applicant should recite *inter alia* the incapacity and subsequent impounding of the first grant. A copy of the order impounding the grant should be annexed to the oath/affidavit.

Combined Application

The intended grantee may make a combined application for an order impounding the grant and the issue of a fresh temporary grant to him by lodging one affidavit reciting all the relevant facts to lead both the order for impounding and to serve as the oath/affidavit for the fresh grant. All the relevant documents for the order for impounding and the new grant should be lodged in the Registry at the same time.

Grantee's Recovery

Should the original grantee recover, he may apply for a release of the original grant to him by lodging the following documents in the Registry:

1. the temporary grant;
2. an affidavit of a medical practitioner as to the recovery of the grantee; and
3. the written consent of the temporary grantee.

Once the application is successful the registrar will order that the temporary grant be noted that it has ceased and is of no effect.

Death of Incapable Grantee

In the event that the original grantee dies without recovering from his incapacity, the original grant may be released to his personal representative(s) by order of the registrar in certain circumstances, for example, in order to establish a chain of executorship through him/them.[6]

Notes

1. Barbados — ss.18(2), 19(2) Succession Act Cap. 249
    Eastern Caribbean — s.121 Supreme Court Act 1981, England
    (save Grenada, St Lucia, St Vincent & the Grenadines)
    Grenada — ss.9, 10 Probate Act Cap. 255
    Guyana — s.29 Deceased Persons Estates' Administration Act Cap. 12:01
    St Lucia — Art 586(4) Civil Code Ch. 242
    St Vincent & the Grenadines — ss.21, 52 Administration of Estates Act Cap. 377
    Jamaica — Rule 68.37, CPR 2002
    Trinidad & Tobago — s.3 Wills & Probate Ordinance Ch. 8 No. 2.
2. In all other instances revocation by way of action is required.
3. Where the administration of the estate has commenced, but is incomplete, a grant *de bonis non administratus* should be obtained.
4. Trinidad & Tobago, Guyana, Dominica, Barbados — r.42 N.C.P.R. 1954, England
    The Bahamas, Eastern Caribbean (save Dominica) — r.41 N.C.P.R. 1987, England.
5. Where the new grantee is authorised to apply for the grant by the Supreme Court pursuant to the relevant mental health legislation of the various territories, the old grant remains at large.
6. A chain of representation is not applicable to Barbados with respect to the estates of persons dying after 13th November, 1975 pursuant to s.11 of the Succession Act Cap. 249.

24

Caveats[1]/ Cautions[2]

INTRODUCTION

Any person intending to oppose a grant of probate or administration may do so by entering a caveat and in the case of Jamaica, with effect from January 1, 2003, a caution in the Office of the Registry at any time subsequent to the application for the grant of representation and prior to the issue of the grant.[3]

WHY ENTER A CAVEAT/CAUTION

Among the usual purposes for entering a caveat/caution are:

- to give the caveator or cautioner, as he is referred to in Jamaica, time to determine whether he has grounds for objecting to the issue of a grant to some other person,
- as a preliminary step to commencing a probate action or the issuing of citation proceedings, to give the caveator an opportunity to apply to the court for an order that the surety/sureties to an administration bond do justify (This is not applicable to Jamaica as bonds are no longer required in respect of applications made in the Supreme Court, pursuant to the provision of Rule 68 CPR 2002).
- to permit a person with an equal right to letters of administration as that of the applicant, to obtain the necessary order from the court as to whom the grant should be made; and in

Barbados, Eastern Caribbean territories (save St Lucia) Jamaica and The Bahamas

- to afford any person interested in the estate of the deceased named therein, the opportunity to bring before the court any question in respect of the application for the grant.[4]

EFFECT OF CAVEAT/CAUTION

No grant of probate or administration (with or without will annexed) shall be sealed at any time if the registrar has knowledge of an effective caveat/caution. Although the relevant probate rules of Barbados, Dominica, St Lucia, Trinidad & Tobago and Guyana[5] do not specifically so provide, it is submitted that a *grant pendente lite* and a grant *ad colligenda bona* may be sealed in cases where a caveat is entered, in accordance with the provisions of r.44(1) N.C.P.R. 1987, England.[6] With respect to Jamaica, Rule 68.38(5) CPR 2002, expressly provides that the registrar may not allow any grant to be sealed (other than a grant *ad colligenda bona*) if he or she has knowledge of an effective caution.

DURATION OF CAVEAT/CAUTION

A caveat remains in force for a period of six months commencing from the date of its entry and then ceases to have effect. However, it may be renewed from time to time to keep it in force by either the caveator, if acting in person, or his attorney-at-law on his behalf:[7]

- making a written request to the registrar to that effect; or
- endorsing on the caveat/caution lodged in the Registry, the request for an extension of time.

The request should be made within the last month of the six month period.[8]

REMOVAL OF CAVEAT/CAUTION

A caveat/caution may be removed in the following ways:

- by the expiration of six months, or any period of renewal in respect thereof since the entry of the caveat/caution;
- by the non-appearance/default of acknowledgement of service of the caveator/cautioner to the warning to the caveat, as the case maybe;
- by withdrawal of the caveat/caution; or
- by a discontinuance order of the court.

Once removed the caveat/caution ceases to have effect. As such, provided that no other caveat/caution is entered, the grant in respect of the estate of the deceased named therein may be sealed.

ENTRY OF CAVEAT/CAUTION

The person objecting to the issue of a grant of representation to the applicant must first lodge at the Office of the Registrar a caveat together with copies. The caveat/caution is then entered in the Caveat Book and in the case of Jamaica pursuant to Rule 68.36(4) CPR 2002, by the registrar in the Register of Cautions.

The Caveat Book may be inspected by attorneys-at-law or members of the public who wish to know whether there is an effective caveat/caution lodged against the issue of the grant to the estate of a specified person.

FORM OF CAVEAT/CAUTION

A caveat/caution is a notice in writing addressed to the registrar to the effect that no grant is to be sealed without notice to the caveator/cautioner. By reason of the wording a caveat/caution does not prevent a grant from being issued to the caveator/cautioner himself.

The caveat/caution which takes a prescribed form,[9] contains the following particulars:

- the name and address of the deceased;
- the date of death of the deceased;
- the name of the caveator/cautioner;
- if acting through an attorney-at-law, the name of the attorney-at-law; and
- the address for service within the jurisdiction of the caveator/cautioner or his attorney-at-law, as the case may be.

Additionally the caveat/caution must bear the date of its entry and must be signed either by the caveator/cautioner if acting in person or his attorney-at-law on his behalf.

SEPARATE CAVEATS/CAUTIONS

Separate caveats/cautions must be lodged by each person wishing to oppose the issue of the grant as the name of no more than one caveator/cautioner may appear on each caveat/caution.

Practice and Procedure After Entry of Caveat/ Caution

Once the caveat/caution is lodged and duly entered the next step varies, depending on the jurisdiction.

Guyana, Jamaica, Montserrat, St Vincent & the Grenadines and Trinidad & Tobago

In practice, a letter signed by or on behalf of the registrar is sent to the applicant for the grant, notifying him/her of the entry of the caveat/caution.[10]

Other jurisdictions (including Guyana)

In the other jurisdictions, including Guyana, it is the practice for the caveator to serve a certified copy of the caveat on the applicant for the grant. In Barbados the caveator is required after entry of the caveat to serve within seven days, a certified copy of the caveat on the applicant for the grant.[11]

Warning to the Caveat/Caution[12]

The proceedings subsequent to the entry of the caveat/caution and the notice/service thereof, are called the Warning to the Caveat, and in the case of Jamaica, the Warning to the Caution. The warning is a notice in a prescribed form calling upon the caveator/cautioner within six (6) days exclusive of Sunday in the case of Trinidad & Tobago and St Lucia, within fourteen(14) days inclusive of the day of service in the case of Jamaica, and within eight (8) days inclusive of the day of service, in the other jurisdictions:

(a) in the case of *Trinidad & Tobago, St. Lucia and Guyana* to enter an appearance;
(b) and in keeping with the respective civil procedure rules of *Barbados, Eastern Caribbean territories (save St Lucia) and The Bahamas* to acknowledge service thereof; or
alternatively in *Barbados, Eastern Caribbean territories (save St. Lucia) and the Bahamas and Jamaica*
(c) to cause to be issued a summons/notice of applciation for directions returnable before the registrar/judge in Chambers, as the case may be.

In St. Lucia, the practice and procedure relevant to caveat proceedings is prescribed by the indigenous provisions of Arts. 1026 – 1030 Code of Civil Procedure Ch. 243. Accordingly, in the absence of specific rules in respect of the procedure to be adopted, the law and the procedure (including entry of appearance to warnings,) as prescribed by the above-mentioned Articles are still applicable to St. Lucia.

The warning further provides that in default, the court will proceed to do all things necessary with respect thereto.

In addition, the warning calls upon the caveator/cautioner to state:

(i) his interest in the estate of the deceased which is contrary to that of the party warning the caveat/cautioner and if he claims under a will to state the date of the will and his interest thereunder whether as executor or legatee, or alternatively in

Barbados, Eastern Caribbean territories (save St Lucia) Jamaica and The Bahamas

(ii) his objections to the sealing of the grant where he has no such contrary interest.

The name of the person at whose instance the warning is issued together with his address for service must also be given.

The warning together with copies are prepared by the person at whose instance the warning was issued or his attorney-at-law on his behalf. The warning is then lodged in the Registry, signed by the registrar and accordingly issued.

The Bahamas

In The Bahamas it is the practice for the person warning the caveat or his attorney-at-law on his behalf, to sign the warning.

Service of Warning[13]

A filed copy of the warning is served on the caveator/cautioner by leaving a copy or sending a copy by registered post to the address for service of the caveator/cautioner or by serving it personally on the caveator/cautioner which is the more usual practice.

Entry of Appearance/Acknowledgement of Services/Summons for Directions[14]

Once the warning is served on the caveator/cautioner, the caveator/cautioner in compliance with the directions given in the warning either:

(a) enters an appearance/ acknowledges service thereto; or alternatively in

Barbados, Eastern Caribbean territories (save St Lucia) Jamaica and The Bahamas

(b)   where he has no such contrary interest, he takes out a summons for directions in the case of Barbados, a Part 11 application in the case of the Eastern Caribbean territories (save St. Lucia) and a notice of application for directions in the case of Jamaica.

Effect of Entry of Appearance/ Acknowledgement of Service

All jurisdictions (save Trinidad & Tobago and Jamaica)

Once an appearance is entered, acknowledgement of service is filed. No grant can be issued and the caveat remains in force until contentious probate proceedings are commenced unless otherwise directed by order of the court.[15]

Trinidad & Tobago

Unlike the other Caribbean jurisdictions, the entry of an appearance to a caveat in Trinidad & Tobago does not keep the caveat in force until a probate action is commenced. What this means is that in the event of the expiry and the non-renewal of a caveat prior to the commencement of a probate action, the caveat ceases to have any effect whatsoever. However, once a probate action is commenced by the issuing of a writ of summons, no grant will be issued even though the caveat has expired in the meantime.[16]

Effect of Summons for Directions

Barbados, Eastern Caribbean territories (save St Lucia) and The Bahamas

A caveat remains in force beyond the six-month period by the issue of the summons for directions until the summons is either disposed of or the registrar gives directions that the caveat cease to have effect.[17]

Position in Jamaica

There appears to be an inconsistency with respect to the requirements of Rule 68.40(1) CPR 2002 and the Form prescribed (Form 18 Appendix 2) in respect of the warning to the cautioner, and in particular the procedure to be adopted, subsequent to the service of the warning on the cautioner.

Based on Rule 68.40(1), where a person wishes to oppose a grant, he is required to file in the registry and serve on the cautioner an acknowledgement of service (Form P19 Appendix 2) *and* to issue and serve on the cautioner, an application for directions and to do so pursuant to Rule 68.40(2) not later than 14 days after service of the warning on him.

However, the warning to the cautioner which takes the form prescribed (Form P18) directs that the cautioner either file an acknowledgement of service setting out his interest which is contrary to that of the person on whose behalf the warning was issued *or* if he has no such contrary interest, but wishes to show cause against the sealing of the grant to such party, to serve a notice of application for directions by the registrar, on the party issuing the warning.

Form P18 which outlines alternative procedures to be adopted by the cautioner is consistent not only with the English Non-Contentious Probate Rules, but is also consistent with the other provisions of Rule 68.40.

In this regard, Rule 68.40 provides for two circumstances in which a caution shall cease to have effect:

(i) where in the case, a notice of application for direction is issued, Rule 68.40(4) provides that any directions so issued, shall remain in force until the commencement of a probate action, unless, upon giving direction, the registrar orders the caution to cease to have effect; or

(ii) pursuant to rule 68.40(5) and (6); that upon the application for a grant being made, a person shown to be entitled by the decision of the court in the probate claim, the caution shall cease to have effect, unless the registrar by order, made on application otherwise directs.

Based on the above, the position in Jamaica is the same as that in the Eastern Caribbean territories (save St. Lucia) where the issuing of a notice for an application for directions is separate and distinct from the procedure to be adopted where the cautioner has a contrary interest and is required to file an acknowledgement of service.

REMOVAL OF CAVEAT/CAUTION

A. *Clearing Off of Caveat/Caution —No Appearance Entered/ Acknowledgement of Service Filed* [18]

All jurisdictions (save St Lucia)

A person whose application for a grant has been blocked may have the caveat/caution cleared off by filing a request for a search for the entry of an appearance or the issue of a summons/ applications for directions. A search is then conducted by the search clerk in the Registry and once no appearance/ acknowledgement has been entered/ filed or summons/ application for directions issued, a note to that effect, dated and signed by the clerk on behalf of the registrar is endorsed on the request or alternatively a certificate of non-appearance default of acknowledgement may be issued by or on the behalf of the registrar. The applicant for the grant or his attorney-at-law may then proceed to file:

Trinidad & Tobago
(1) a formal request for the caveat to be cleared off, signed by the attorney-at-law/applicant for the grant and addressed to the registrar.

All jurisdictions
(2) An affidavit of the attorney-at-law/applicant setting out that the warning was duly served on the caveator/ cautioner, that a request for a search was made and that no appearance/ acknowledgement of service was entered/summons/ application for directions issued to the warning and in all the jurisdictions save Trinidad & Tobago, a request that the registrar clear off the caveat/ caution entered;
(3) An affidavit of service deposed to by the process server to the effect that the warning to the caveat/ caution was duly served by the process server on the caveator/ cautioner at the place and on the date deposed to therein; and
(4) The request for the search duly endorsed to the effect that no appearance was entered/ acknowledgement of service or alternatively a certificate of non-appearance/ default of acknowledgement of service must also be lodged.

Once all is in order the caveat/ caution ceases to have effect and the registrar/ judge issues the grant.

St Lucia

In St Lucia an order clearing off the caveat must be obtained before the caveat can be removed and the grant in respect thereof issued.

The attorney-at-law for the applicant is required to file a written request addressed to the registrar for a search to be made for the entry of an appearance to the warning. Once no appearance has been entered thereto, a certificate of non-appearance signed by the registrar or the search clerk on his behalf, is delivered to the applicant for filing with the application for removal of the caveat.[19]

The next step is for the attorney-at-law to apply by summons to a judge in chambers for an order clearing off the caveat and granting leave to the applicant to proceed with his application for the grant. The summons is supported by an affidavit containing the relevant particulars. An affidavit of search for appearance and non-appearance and an affidavit of service of the warning, together with the certificate of non-appearance are also required to be filed with the application.[20] Once the order is granted, the caveat is removed and the applicant may then proceed with his application for the grant.

B. Withdrawal of Caveat/ Caution

A caveator/ cautioner may withdraw his caveat/ caution at any time before he has entered an appearance/ acknowledgement service to the warning, by serving forthwith a notice of withdrawal on the person who warned the caveat/ caution. Thereupon the caveat/ caution ceases to have effect.[21]

However if the caveat/ caution is withdrawn before the warning stage, the registrar is required to serve a notice to that effect on the person whose grant is being opposed. The notice should also include a request as to whether or not the applicant wishes to proceed with the application for the grant.

Discontinuance Order

Once an appearance to the warning has been entered/the summons/ application for directions issued, the party objecting to the issuing of the grant to the applicant may decide to abandon his opposition thereto. In such cases the caveator/ cautioner may apply to the court by summons supported by affidavit(s) for discontinuance proceedings and for the issue of the grant to the applicant notwithstanding the caveat/ cautioner, warning and appearance thereto. Once the order is granted removing the caveat/ cautioner, the grant may be issued to the applicant.

Notes

1	Eastern Caribbean (save St Vincent & the Grenadines, St Lucia)	- s.5 Administration of Estates Act 1925, England
	St Lucia	- Arts 1026-1030 Code of Civil Procedure Ch. 243
	St Vincent & the Grenadines	- s.8 Administration of Estates Act Cap. 377
	The Bahamas	- s.32 Supreme Court Act 15/1996

	Trinidad & Tobago	- s.39 Wills & Probate Ordinance Ch. 8 No. 2

Rules

	Barbados	- rr. 35-42 Supreme Court (Non-Contentious) Probate Rules, 1959
	Eastern Caribbean (save St Lucia), The Bahamas	- 44 N.C.P.R. 1987, England
	Guyana, Dominica	- r.45 N.C.P.R. 1954, England
	St Lucia	- Atts 1026-1030 Code of Civil Procedure Ch. 243
	Trinidad & Tobago	- rr. 42-52 First Schedule N.C.B.R. Ch. 8 No. 2.
2	Jamaica	- Rules 68.38, 68.39 and 68.40 CPR 2002, repealing and replacing rr. 30-37 General Rules & Order of the Supreme Court Part III Probate and Administration
3	Barbados	- r.35 Supreme Court (Non-Contentious) Probate Rules 1959
	Dominica, Guyana	- r. 44(1) N.C.P.R. 1954, England
	Jamaica	- Rule 68.39(1) CPR 2002 repleaing and replacing r. 30 General Rules and Orders of the Supreme Court Part III Probate and Administration
	St Lucia	- Art 1026(2) Code of Civil Procedure Ch. 243
	The Bahamas, Eastern Caribbean (save Dominica)	- r.44(1) N.C.P.R. 1987, England
	Trinidad & Tobago	- r.42 First Schedule N.C.B.R. Ch. 8 No.2.
4	Barbados	- r.42 The Supreme Court (Non-Contentious) Probate Rules 1959
	Dominica	- r.44(10) N.C.P.R. 1954, England
	The Bahamas, Eastern Caribbean (save Dominica & St Lucia)	- r.44(6) N.C.P.R. 1987, England.
	Jamaica	- Rule 68.39 (2) CPR 2002
5	Barbados Rules, 1959	- r.39 Supreme Court (Non-Contentious) Probate Rules 1959
	Dominica	- r.44(1) N.C.P.R. 1954, England
	St Lucia	- Art 1028 Code of Civil Procedure Ch. 243
	Trinidad & Tobago	- r.47 First Schedule N.C.B.R. Ch. 8 No. 2.
6	The Bahamas, Eastern Caribbean (save Dominica & St Lucia)	- See r.44(1) N.C.P.R. 1987 England, which rule has codified Eastern Caribbean the practice with respect to *pendente lite* and *ad colligenda* grants.
7	Barbados	- r.37 Supreme Court (Non-Contentious) Probate Rules 1959
	Dominica, Guyana	- r.44 (4) N.C.P.R. 1954 England
	St Lucia	- Art. 1027 Code of Civil Procedure Ch. 243

Caveats/Cautions / 447

	The Bahamas, Eastern Caribbean (save St Lucia and Dominica)	- r.44 (3)(a) N.C.P.R, 1987, England
	Jamaica	- Rule 68.38(3) CPR 2002
	Trinidad & Tobago	- r.45 First Schedule N.C.B.R. Ch. 8 No. 2.
8	The Bahamas, Eastern Caribbean (save Dominica)	- r.44(3)(a), N.C.P.R. 1987, England
	Trinidad & Tobago, Barbados, St Lucia, Guyana. Dominica	- r.44(4), N.C.P.R. 1954, England.
	Jamaica	- Rule 68.38(2) CPR 2002
9	Barbados	- r.36, Supreme Court (Non-Contentious) Probate Rules, 1959
	Trinidad & Tobago	- rr.44 & 45 First Schedule N.C.B.R. Ch. 8 No. 2

Form

	Barbados	- Form No. 10 Appendix (Forms and Fees) Supreme Court (Non-Contentious) Probate Rules
	Dominica, Guyana	- Form 4 First Schedule N.C.P.R. 1954, England
	Jamaica	- Form P.17 Appendix 2, CPR 2002 repealing and replacing Form No. 22 General Rules and Orders of the Supreme Court Part III Schedule of Forms
	The Bahamas, Eastern Caribbean (save Dominica)	- Form 3 First Schedule N.C.P.R. 1987, England
	Trinidad & Tobago	- Form No. 10 First Schedule N.C.B.R. Ch. 8 No. 2.
10	Guyana, Monsteratt, Jamaica St Vincent & the Grenadines	- This is in accordance with the practice
	Trinidad & Tobago	- r.43 First Schedule N.C.B.R. Ch. 8 No. 2.
11	Barbados	- r.38 Supreme Court (Non-Contentious) Probate Rules 1959.
12	Barbados	- r.40 Supreme Court (Non-Contentious) Probate Rules, 1959
	Guyana, Dominica	- r.44(7) N.C.P.R. 1954. England
	St Lucia	- Art 1029 Code of Civil Procedure Ch. 243
	Jamaica, The Bahamas, Eastern Caribbean (save Dominica and St Lucia)	- r.44(5) N.C.P.R. 1987, England
	Jamaica	- Rule 68.39 CPR 2002
	Trinidad & Tobago	- r.49 First Schedule N.C.B.R. Ch, 8 No. 2.

Forms

	Barbados	- Form No. 11 Appendix (Forms and Fees) Supreme

	Dominica, Guyana Jamaica	Court (Non-Contentious) Probate Rules 1959 - Form 5 First Schedule N.C.P.R. 1954, England - Form P.18 Appendix 2, CPR 2002 replacing Form No. 23 General Rules and Orders of the Supreme Court Part III Schedule of Forms
	Trinidad & Tobago	- Form No. 11 First Schedule N.C.B.R. Ch. 8 No. 2
	The Bahamas, Eastern Caribbean (save Dominica)	- Form 4 First Schedule N.C.P.R. 1987, England
13	Barbados	- r.40 Supreme Court (Non-Contentious) Probate Rules 1959
	Guyana, Dominica	- r.44(7) N.C.P.R. 1954, England
	Jamaica	- Rule 68.39(3) CPR 2002 repealing and replacing r.34 General Rules and Orders of the Supreme Court Part III Probate and Administration
	The Bahamas, Eastern Caribbean (save Dominica & St Lucia)	- r.44(5) N.C.P.R. 1987, England
	St Lucia	- Art 1020(4) Code of Civil Procedure Ch. 243
	Trinidad & Tobago	- r.48 First Schedule N.C.B.R. Ch. 8 No. 2
14	Barbados	- r.42 (1) Supreme Court (Non-Contentious) Probate Rules
	Eastern Caribbean (save Dominica)	- r.44 (6) & (10) N.C.P.R. 1987 England
	Guyana, Dominica, Trinidad & Tobago	- r.44(9) and (10) N.C.P.R. 1954, England
	Jamaica	- Rule 68.40(1) CPR. 2002 repealing and replacing r.37 General Rules and Orders of the Supreme Court Part III Probate and Administration.

Forms

	Barbados	- See Form No. 12 Appendix (Forms and Fees) Supreme Court (Non-Contentious) Probate Rules 1959
	The Bahamas, Eastern Caribbean (save Dominica)	- Form 5 First Schedule, N.C.P.R. 1987, England
	Jamaica	- Form P19 Appendix 2 C.P.R. 2002 repealing and replacing Form 6 First Schedule, NC.P.R. 1954, England.
15	Barbados	- r.42(4) Supreme Court (Non-Contentious) Probate Rules 1959
	Guyana, Dominica, The Bahamas, Eastern Caribbean (save Dominica)	- r.44(12)(b), N.C.P.R. 1954, England r.44 r.13, N.C.P.R. 1987, England.
16	Trinidad & Tobago	- r.52 First Schedule N.C.B.R. Ch. 8 No. 2

See *Re Schuler's Estate* (1985) 37 W.I.R 371 at p. 395 where Warner JA noted in effect that by virtue of the conjunctive effect of ss. 4 and 24 of the Wills and Probate Ordinance Ch. 8 No. 2, that English probate practice and procedure are applicable to Trinidad & Tobago only in so far as any indigenous ordinance, rules and order of court 'do not extend'. However as Warner JA further observed 'Our own rules of court fully extend to the question of when caveats lapse. In the circumstances, recourse cannot be had to different provisions under the English 1954 rules,' Accordingly, Justice Warner JA concluded that a caveat entered without renewal lapses at the expiration of six months pursuant to r.52 First Schedule N.C.B.R. Ch. 8 No. 2.

17 Barbados — r.42(3) Supreme Court (Non-Contentious) Probate Rules 1959

Eastern Caribbean (save Dominica & St Lucia) The Bahamas — r.44(12) N.C.P.R. 1987, England

Dominica — r.44(11) N.C.P.R. 1954, England.

18 With respect to the position in St Lucia see p. 444.

Barbados — r.42(3) Supreme Court (Non-Contentious) Probate Rules 1959

Dominica, Guyana, The Bahamas, — r.44(11) N.C.P.R. 1954, England

Eastern Caribbean (save Dominica & St Lucia) — r.44(11) N.C.P.R. 1987, England

Jamaica — Rule 68.40(3) CPR 2002

Trinidad & Tobago — r.51 First Schedule NC.B.R. Ch 8 No.2

19 See Art 1030(1)(b) Code of Civil Procedure Ch. 243.
20 Pursuant to Art 1030(1)(a) Code of Civil Procedure Ch. 243.
21 Barbados — r.41 Supreme Court (Non-Contentious) Probate Rules 1959

Dominica, Guyana, Trinidad & Tobago, — r.44(8) N.C.P.R. 1954, England

The Bahamas, Eastern Caribbean (save Dominica) — r.44(11) N.C.P.R. 1987, England.

Jamaica — Rule 68.36(6) CPR 2002

25

Citation Proceedings

INTRODUCTION

A citation is an instrument issuing out of the Supreme/High Court Registry under the seal of the court and signed by the registrar, setting out the reason for its issue and the interest of the person at whose instance it was issued, and calling upon the person cited (the citee) to enter an appearance/ acknowledge service of the citation within the time prescribed and to take the steps indicated. It also sets out the nature of the order that the court is asked to make unless good cause is shown.

In non-contentious probate business, citations are issued-:

(a)   to accept or refuse a grant;
(b)   to take probate; or
(c)   to propound testamentary papers.

CLEARING OFF

With respect to (a) and (b) above, citation proceedings are a means of clearing off a person with superior rights to a grant of representation who not only refuses or neglects to take out the relevant grant, but also refuses to renounce his rights. In the event of such person being cited and failing to enter an appearance or acknowledge service of the citation, the court is free to make an order for a grant to issue to the citor instead.[1]

Where the person with a superior title cannot be traced, a citation served by advertisement may be ordered by the court.

Jamaica

Prior to the passage of the CPR 2002, it was unclear whether citations to accept or refuse a grant of letters of administration (with or without will annexed) were applicable to Jamaica. This was primarily because of the absence of specific probate rules or statutory provisions so providing and also because, until the coming into effect of Rule 68.11 and 68.18 CPR 2002, there was no order of priority in respect of entitlement to grants of letters of administration (with or without will annexed).

However, citations to take probate and citations to accept or refuse probate were and still are applicable to Jamaica although there was no specific rule to that effect until the passage of Rule 68.42, CPR 2002. However, the Executor's Renunciation Act, which provides for an executor to renounce his right to probate, clearly indicated, although not expressly, that an executor's right to probate could be cleared off in Jamaica, not only by renunciation, but also by citation to accept or refuse a grant of probate or otherwise by citation to take probate, depending on the circumstances given that the purpose of such citation, was essentially the same as that of the executor's renunciation.

The position with respect to citation and the ambit and scope of its application have now been expressly clarified by Rule 68.41, 68.42 and 68.44 CPR 2002, the provisions of which provide for the various types of citations.

Clearing off Executor with Power Reserved

All jurisdictions

With respect to an executor with power reserved, although he is equally entitled as the proving executor(s) to take out a probate grant, he may nonetheless be cited by the proving executor(s) or, in all the jurisdictions save Barbados, in which jurisdiction the chain of representation has been abolished since November 13, 1975, by the executor of the last surviving proving executor (executor by representation) to accept or refuse a grant. However, apart from this exception, persons with equal rights to a grant are not cleared off, whether by citation or otherwise. Where the non-proving executor is cited by the executor by representation, to accept or refuse a grant of probate and he appears to the citation/ acknowledges service thereof, and takes out the probate grant, the rights of the executor by representation to administer the testator's estate are thereby extinguished.[2]

Waiver of Citation Proceedings

Trinidad & Tobago

Where the person having a prior right to administration is either not resident or not living within Trinidad & Tobago, the court in such circumstances may grant administration to any person resident therein who would otherwise be entitled to the same without the previous citation to or consent of the party with the superior rights and title. Such administration is granted with reservation of the right of the person having the prior right.[3]

TYPES OF CITATION

1. Citation to Accept or Refuse a Grant[4]

At any time after the expiration of six months from the date of death of the deceased, a citation to accept or refuse a grant of probate or alternatively, a citation to accept or refuse a grant of administration (with or without will annexed) may be issued at the instance of any person interested in the deceased's estate. This is usually a person who would himself be next entitled to the grant, in the event of the person cited renouncing his rights thereto. In this regard, citations to accept or refuse a grant are issued in the following circumstances:

In cases of Testacy

    (i) Executor - an executor who has not intermeddled may be cited to accept or refuse a grant of probate by the person next entitled to take out a grant;

    (ii) Executor with Power Reserved - a non-proving executor to whom power was reserved at the time of issue of the grant, may be cited to accept or refuse a grant either by the proving executor(s) or the executor of the last surviving proving executor so as to clear off his rights to take out a double probate grant and thus establish a chain of executorship through another executor.[6] However once the executor with power reserved takes out a double probate grants after being cited to do so, any chain of executorship constituted through another executor will thereby be broken. As stated above, with respect to the estates of persons dying on or after November 13, 1975, the chain of representation is no longer applicable to Barbados, pursuant to s.11 Succession Act Cap. 249.

    (iii) No executor — where the deceased has died leaving a valid will but has either failed to appoint an executor or the executor appointed has predeceased him, the person next entitled to take out letters of administration with will annexed (usually the residuary devisee/legatee) may be cited to accept or refuse a grant by the person next entitled (usually the devisee/legatee).

    (iv) Intermeddling Executor - Trinidad & Tobago

In instances where an executor has intermeddled prior to obtaining a grant of probate, the appropriate form of citation, is the citation to accept or refuse a grant of probate, and not as in the other jurisdictions, a citation to take probate.

This is because of the unique position of the executor in Trinidad and Tobago. According to the conjunctive effect of s.10(4) of the Administration of Estates Ordinance ch.8 no.1 and s.21 of the Wills and Probate Ordinance ch.8 no.2, the legal title to the testator's estate is vested in the Administrator General until the same is vested by the grant of probate in some other person or persons. As such, until the grant of probate, the executor in Trinidad and Tobago is in the same position as the administrator, in that the legal title is vested in the Administrator General until the grant is obtained so as to prevent the estate from lapsing.

And although as Wooding C.J. observed, in *Arthur v Gomes*,[5] that the Administrator General is merely a depository so to speak holding things, *in medio* until such time as a grant is obtained, the legal title is nonetheless not vested in the executor in Trinidad and Tobago, unlike the position in the other jurisdictions, including England.

However, the doctrine of relation back as it pertains to executors in the other jurisdictions, is equally applicable to the executor in Trinidad and Tobago. As was observed by Wooding C.J. in *Arthur v Gomes*, the beneficial title vests in the executor upon death, and vesting of the bare legal title in the Administrator General does not alter this fact

In this regard, according to the doctrine of relation back, probate is deemed to bear relation to the time of the testator's death in that the acts of the executor after the death of the testator, but before the granting of probate, are regarded in light of the grant as if they followed and did not precede the grant. Accordingly, unlike the administrator who obtains his title from the court, the executor can, before obtaining the grant take control of the testator's estate, receive and release debts due to the testator and even assign and give valid title to land. However, once it becomes necessary to prove his title, the grant must be obtained. In short, an executor can do any acts in relation to the testator's estate in so far as it is not necessary for him to prove title.[6]

(b) In cases of Intestacy

Where a person has died wholly intestate, the person first entitled to take out letters of administration (usually the surviving spouse) may be cited to accept or refuse a grant of letters of administration by the person(s) next entitled (usually the child/children of the deceased).

Contents of Citation

The citation to accept or refuse a grant is in a prescribed form. It calls upon the citee to enter an appearance/ acknowledge service within eight/ fourteen days—depending on the jurisdiction—inclusive of the day of service and to accept or refuse the grant, or to show cause why the grant should not be made to the citor. It also notifies the citee that in the event of his non-appearance to/ default of acknowledgement of service of/ to the citation, his rights and title to take out the grant indicated will wholly cease and that the court may proceed to grant letters of administration (with or without will annexed), as the case may be, to the citor or other person interested in the deceased's estate.

2. Citation to take Probate[7]

All Jurisdictions save Trinidad & Tobago

A citation to take probate is issued where an executor intermeddles in the estate of the deceased but neglects or fails to apply for a probate grant within six months of the testator's death. In such cases he may be cited to take probate (not accept or refuse a grant) usually by the person next entitled for strictly speaking an intermeddling executor has no choice but to take probate as it is too late for him to renounce. If he fails to take out probate after being cited, and ordered by the court to do so, such refusal may amount to a contempt of court and thereby render the recalcitrant citee liable to a fine and attachment.

The citation to take probate sets out *inter alia*:

(i) the execution and the date of the deceased's will;
(ii) the appointment of the citee as executor; and,
(iii) the intermeddling of the citee in the estate of the deceased.

The citation further calls upon the citee to enter an appearance/ acknowledge service and to show cause why he, the citee, should not be ordered to take probate of the deceased's will.

Trinidad & Tobago

As stated above, because of the unique statutory position of the executor in Trinidad & Tobago, although the doctrine of relation back essentially applies to the executor in Trinidad & Tobago, to the same extent as is applicable to the other jurisdictions, citation to take probate is not applicable to the executor in Trinidad & Tobago as the legal title is not vested in the executor until the grant is obtained.

3. Citation to Propound Testamentary Papers[8]

A citation to propound testamentary papers is issued where a person interested in the estate of a deceased person, either on an intestacy or under a will, becomes aware of the existence of an alleged will/later will which would prejudice his rights with respect thereto. In such instances, he may cite the executor and the beneficiaries under the deceased's will.

The citation calls upon the citee to enter an appearance/ acknowledge service within the prescribed time and to propound the alleged testamentary paper or in default thereof it notifies the citee that the court may proceed to issue a grant of representation to the citor as if the said purported will were invalid.

The citation sets out *inter alia*:

(i) the alleged existence of a will appointing the citee as executor; and
(ii) a description of the citor and his entitlement to the estate of the deceased whether on an intestacy or under an earlier will.

CITATION PROCEEDINGS IN GENERAL[9]

The draft citation in the appropriate form must be lodged for settling by the registrar.[10] Additionally the following documents are required to be lodged:

(1) An unsworn affidavit deposed by the person issuing the citation verifying the facts set out in the citation. The affidavit in support should set out the date of death of the deceased, the date and execution of the will if any, the prior entitlement of the citee to the relevant grant and his failure or neglect to apply for the grant. Where the citation is taken out against an executor who has intermeddled, the affidavit should set out the instances of intermeddling.

(2) The will, if any — if a will is referred to in the citation it must be lodged before the issue of the citation unless it is not in the citor's possession and the registrar is satisfied that it is impracticable to require it to be lodged.[11]

Affidavit in support of citation

After the draft citation is settled, the affidavit in support is sworn to by the citor or in special circumstances, his attorney-at-law. It should never be sworn *before* the citation is settled.

Praecipe for Citation

Guyana and Trinidad & Tobago

In practice in Guyana and in Trinidad & Tobago,[12] a praecipe for citation is also prepared by the citor's attorney-at-law for filing in the Registry.

Lodging of Caveat/Caution

A caveat /caution, in the case of Jamaica, must be entered before the issuing of the citation to prevent a grant from being sealed while citation proceedings are being taken.[13] In this regard, it is the caveat/caution which prevents a grant from being sealed and not the citation. Further, unless withdrawn by the citor, the caveat remains in force until an application is made for the relevant grant by the person entitled thereto pursuant to an order of the court made in such proceedings.

The settled draft citation together with fair copies for signing and sealing, a praecipe for citation (Trinidad & Tobago and Guyana) and the sworn affidavit with copies, are lodged at the Registry. The citation together with copies thereof is signed by the registrar and copies collected by the citor for service on the citee.

Service of Citation

A filed copy of the citation is served personally on the citee. Where personal service is impracticable an *ex parte* application for an order for substituted service (usually by advertisement) may be obtained.[14]

Appearance to/ Acknowledgement of Service of Citation[15]

The appearance to/ acknowledgement of service of the citation should be entered/ filed by the citee within the time prescribed, but may be entered/ filed at any time thereafter provided no step in default has been taken by the citor. The appearance/ acknowledgement of service must be entered/ filed in the Registry and a sealed copy thereof served on the citor.

PROCEDURE SUBSEQUENT TO APPEARANCE/NON-APPEARANCE ACKNOWLEGEMENT/DEFAULT OF ACKNOWLEDGEMENT

The procedure subsequent to appearance/non-appearance/acknowledgment/ default of acknowledgment of service to a citation, is dependent on the type of citation issued, and with respect to citation to take probate, the jurisdiction concerned.

1. CITATION TO ACCEPT OR REFUSE A GRANT

(a) Acknowledgement of Service/Appearance and Acceptance[15]

After entering an appearance/ acknowledging service and serving a sealed copy thereof on the citor, the citee should apply for an order for a grant to be issued to him. The application is made *ex parte* on affidavit to the registrar.

The affidavit should recite:

 (i) the date of issue of the citation;
 (ii) the service of the citation on the citee;
 (iii) the date of entry of appearance/ acknowledgment of service thereto;
 (iv) the service of a certified copy of the appearance/ acknowledgement of service on the citor;
 (v) that the citee has not been served by the citor with notice of any application for a grant to himself; and
 (vi) the willingness of the citee to take out the relevant grant, notwithstanding the caveat and citation.

Upon obtaining the order, the citor may apply for the grant in the usual way. The order of the court is lodged with the papers to lead the grant.

(b) Appearance/Acknowledgement of Service then Default[17]

If the citee enters an appearance/ acknowledges service but takes no further step, the citor may apply by summons/ Part 11 application, depending on the jurisdiction, for an order for to strike out the citee's appearance/ acknowledgement and for an order for the issue of a grant to himself, notwithstanding the caveat, citation and appearance/ acknowledgment of service. An affidavit in support of the application should also be filed. The affidavit should recite:

    (i)   the material facts establishing that the citor is the person next entitled to the grant;

    (ii) the entry of appearance/ acknowledgment of service of the citee; and

    (iii) his failure to apply for the grant.

Where there is more than one citee, one or some of whom has/have not entered an appearance/ acknowledged service, a certificate of non-appearance/ default of acknowledgement of service and an affidavit of service with respect to such citee, must be lodged with the application for the order.

Executor with Power Reserved[18]

The citor in such cases may apply by summons/ Part 11 application, depending on the jurisdiction, for an order striking out the appearance/ acknowledgment of service, and an endorsement on the grant of a note to the effect that all the citee's rights in respect of the executorship have wholly ceased.

(c)   **No Appearance/ Acknowledgement of Service**[19]

If no appearance is entered or acknowledgement of service filed to the citation, the citor may apply *ex parte* for an order for a grant to be made to himself setting out *inter alia* the non-appearance/ default of acknowledgment of the citee to the citation. The affidavit in support of the application should recite the non-appearance/ default of acknowledgment of the citee to the citation. In addition the following documents should be filed with the application:

(1)   An affidavit of service deposed to by the process server, which should state *inter alia* the means by which the citee was identified. The citation duly endorsed by the process server should be exhibited to the affidavit.

(2)   The certificate of non-appearance/default of acknowledgment/in practice the search for appearance/ acknowledgment of service may be filed instead provided that the non-appearance/ default of

acknowledgment of service of the citee is duly noted thereon by the search clerk.

Executor with Power Reserved

In the case of the non-appearance/ default of acknowledgment of an executor with power reserved, the citor may apply *ex parte* supported by affidavit[20] for an order that a note be made on the grant that the executor in respect of whom power was reserved has been duly cited and has not appeared/ acknowledged service and that all his rights in respect of the executorship have wholly ceased.

2. CITATION TO TAKE PROBATE

All jurisdiction save Trinidad & Tobago

(a)   Appearance/ Acknowledgment of Service and Acceptance[21]

If the citee is cited to take probate he may enter an appearance/ acknowledge service of the citation and subsequently apply *ex parte* for an order for a grant to issue to him notwithstanding the caveat and citation.

(b)   No Appearance/ Acknowledgement of Service[22]

If the citee does not appear to/ acknowledge service of the citation, the citor should apply by summons/ Part 11 application, depending on the jurisdiction, for an order either:

(i) requiring the citee to take a grant within a specified time; or
(ii) for an order that a grant be made to the citor or other person interested in the estate of the deceased, notwithstanding the intermeddling of the executor.

Order for Grant to Citor

With respect to option (ii) above, Jamaica pursuant to Rule 68.44(1)(c), CPR 2002, is the only jurisdiction which has expressly provided for this alternative application to be made by the citor.

With respect to the Eastern Caribbean territories and The Bahamas, in the absence of indigenous provisions, the position with regard to citation to take probate is regulated by the English N.C.P.R. 1954/N.C.P.R. 1987, depending on the cut off date for reception in the respective jurisdictions.

In this regard, option (ii) is expressly provided for in the N.C.P.R. 1987 England. With respect to Dominica, the only Eastern Caribbean territory which does not receive the English N.C.P.R. 1987, because of the cut off date of June 1, 1984, option (ii) is nevertheless applicable as rr46(5) and (7) were added in 1967 to the N.C.P.R. 1954 England. In this regard, rr.46(5) and (7) make provision for option (ii) to be adopted in instances of citation to take probate.

The English N.C.P.R. 1954 are received in Guyana. However the cut off date for reception of these rules, including any amendments thereto, is May 25, 1966. In this regard, the amendment to the N.C.P.R. 1954 which introduced option (ii) was made in 1967 by S.I. 1967 no. 748. As such, strictly speaking, option (ii) should not apply to Guyana. However, since this rule was added in part as a result of the decision In *the Estate of Biggs*[23] where it was held that an executor in special circumstances, notwithstanding his intermeddling, could be passed over under the relevant statutory *passing-over* provision, and secondly because the decision reached by the court *in the Estate of Biggs* adopted the decision of the much earlier case of *Re Potticary's Estate*,[24] that although, not expressly provided for, option (ii) is nevertheless applicable.

Barbados

With respect to Barbados, r.48(7) of the Supreme Court N.C.P.R. 1959 expressly provides for the practice and procedure to be adopted with respect to citations to take probate. The rule is essentially identical to the N.C.P.R. 1954 prior to its amendment in 1967. As such, strictly speaking, particularly in light of the specific indigenous provisions of rule 48(7), it may be properly argued that option (ii) is not applicable to Barbados. However for the reasons stated above, in respect of Guyana and more significantly from a clearly practical perspective, which perspective clearly informed the decision to amend this rule in 1967, it is submitted that in practice, option (ii) should be applicable to Barbados.

In any event, whether option (i) or (ii) is exercised, the application in both cases must be supported by an affidavit showing *inter alia* that the citation was duly served on the citee, and the failure of the citee to appear to/acknowledge service of the citation and to take probate with reasonable diligence. An affidavit of service of the citation and certificate of non-appearance/default of acknowledgment should also be filed with the application.

With respect to (i) above, the order, if granted, should be endorsed with a penal notice. The order must be personally served on the citee. Disobedience to the order to take probate within a specified time amounts to a contempt of court and renders the citee liable to a fine or committal proceedings.

(c) **Appearance/Acknowledgment Then Default**

If the citee appears to/acknowledges service of the citation then defaults, the procedure to be adopted is similar to that for non-appearance or default of acknowledgment of service of the citation, save and except that an affidavit of service and certificate of non-appearance/default of acknowledgment are not necessary unless one of the citees where more than one, has not entered an appearance to/acknowledged service of the citation.[25]

Alternative to Citation Proceedings

Rather than pursue citation proceedings, a person with an inferior title may apply instead in all the jurisdictions save Jamaica, for an order to pass over the executor under the relevant passing over provision of the respective territory and for a grant of letters of administration with will annexed to be made to him, notwithstanding the intermeddling of the executor.

CITATION TO PROPOUND A WILL[26]

(a) Appearance/ Acknowledgment of Service and Acceptance

If the citee wishes to propound the will or other testamentary paper of the deceased, he should enter an appearance to/ acknowledge service of the citation and then cause to be issued, a writ of summons/ claim form, as the case may be, to prove the will in solemn form.

(b) No Appearance/ Acknowledgment of Service[27]

If the citee fails to enter an appearance to/ acknowledge service of the citation, the citor should apply *ex parte* for an order for a grant as if the will were invalid, reciting therein the non-appearance/ default of acknowledgment of service of the citee to the citation. An affidavit of service and certificate of non-appearance/ default of acknowledgment of service should also be filed with the application.

(c) Appearance/ Acknowledgement of Service Then Default [28]

Where the citee enters an appearance/acknowledges service but then fails to proceed with reasonable diligence to propound the will or other testamentary document, the citor should apply by summons/ Part 11 application, depending on the jurisdiction, for an order for a grant as if the will were invalid. An affidavit of service and certificate of non-appearance/default of acknowledgment of service are not necessary unless there is more than one citee, one or some of whom has/have not entered an appearance to/ acknowledge service of the citation.

Notes

1.
Barbados	- s.9 Succession Act Cap. 249
Grenada	- s.13 Probate Act Cap. 255
Eastern Caribbean territories (save St Lucia, Grenada and St Vincent & the Grenadines)	- s.5 Administration of Estates Act 1925, England
St Lucia	- Art 1023 Code of Civil Procedure Ch. 243
St Vincent & the Grenadines	- s.27 Administration of Estates Act Cap. 377
Jamaica	- Rule 68.44 CPR 2002
Trinidad & Tobago	- ss. 12, 32 Wills & Probate Ordinance Ch. 8 No. 2.

2. The rights of a non-proving executor maybe sought to be cleared off by citation in order to break any chain of executorship which may subsequently be constituted through him, had he not been cleared off; or alternatively so that a grant *de bonis non* may be issued to the persons beneficially entitled to the deceased's estate. It is to be noted that where the non-proving executor is also one of the residuary beneficiaries, his entitlement to take the grant in such capacity, will not be cleared off unless he is cited both in the capacity of executor and beneficiary.

3. Section 33 Wills & Probate Ordinance Ch. 8 No. 2.

4.
Barbados	- r.48 Supreme Court (Non-Contentious) Probate Rules 1959
The Bahamas, Eastern Caribbean (save Dominica), Jamaica	- r.47 N.C.P.R 1987, England
Trinidad & Tobago, Guyana, Dominica	- r.46 N.C.P.R 1954, England.
Jamaica	- Rule 68.42 C.P.R. 2002

Forms

Trinidad & Tobago	- Forms Nos. 13 and 14 First Schedule NC.B.R, Ch. 8 No. 2.

5. (1967) 11 W.I.R. 25. See also *Walcott v Alleyne* HCA no. 192/1985 Unreported, Trinidad & Tobago.

6. *Hewson v Shelley* [1914] 2 Ch. 13.

7. Barbados — r. 48(3) Supreme Court (Non-Contentious) Probate

	The Bahamas, Eastern Caribbean (save Dominica), Guyana, Dominica	Rules 1959 - r.47(3) N.C.P.R. 1987, England - r.46(3) N.C.P.R. 1954, England.
	Jamaica	- Rule 68.42(3) and (4) C.P.R. 2002
8	Barbados	- r.49 Supreme Court (Non-Contentious) Probate Rules 1959
	The Bahamas, Eastern Caribbean (save Dominica)	- r. 48 N.C.P.R. 1987, England
	Dominica, Guyana, Trinidad & Tobago	- r.47 N.C.P.R. 1954, England.
	Jamaica	- Rule 68.43 CPR 2002
9	Barbados	- r.43 Supreme Court (Non-Contentious) Probate Rules 1959
	Eastern Caribbean (save Dominica)	- r.46(2) N.C.P.R. 1987, England.
	The Bahamas, Jamaica Guyana, Dominica, Trinidad & Tobago	- r.45(2) N.C.P.R. 1954, England - r.53 First Schedule N.C.B.R. Ch. 8 No. 2,
	Jamaica	- Rule 68.41 CPR 2002

Forms

	Barbados	- See Forms No, 13 and 14 Appendix (Forms & Fees) Supreme Court (Non-Contentious) Probate Rules 1959 with respect to affidavits to lead citations to accept or refuse administration and citations to propound a will, respectively.
	Trinidad & Tobago	- See Forms No. 6 and 7 First Schedule N.C.B.R. Ch. 8 No. 2 with respect to affidavits to lead citations to accept or refuse administration and citations to propound a will, respectively.
10	Jamaica	- Rule 68.41(3) CPR 2002
	Eastern Caribbean territories (save Dominica) The Bahamas Dominica, Guyana	- r.46(1) NCPR 1987 England
	Barbados Trinidad & Tobago	- r.45(1)NCPR. 1954, England
11	Barbados	- r.46 Supreme Court (Non-Contentious) Probate Rules 1959
	Jamaica, The Bahamas, Eastern Caribbean (save Dominica)	- r.46(5) N.C.P.R. 1987, England
	Trinidad & Tobago,	- r.45(5) N.C.P.R. 1954. England.

	Guyana, Dominica	
	Jamaica	- Rule 68.41(7) CPR 2002
12	Trinidad & Tobago	- See Form No. 15 First Schedule N.C.B.R. Ch. 8 No, 2.
13	Barbados	- r.44 Supreme Court (Non-Contentious) Probate Rules 1959
	Guyana, Dominica	- r.45(3) N.C.P.R. 1954, England
	Jamaica	- Rule 68.41(1) C.P.R. 2002 repealing and replacing r.39 General Rules and Orders of the Supreme Court Part III Probate & Administration
	The Bahamas, Eastern Caribbean (save Dominica)	- r.46(3) N.C.P.R. 1987, England
	Trinidad & Tobago	- r.50 First Schedule N.C.B.R. Ch. 8 No. 2.
14	Barbados	- r.45 Supreme Court (Non-Contentious) Probate Rules 1959
	Guyana, Dominica	- r.45(4) N.C.P.R. 1954, England
	The Bahamas, Eastern Caribbean (save Dominica).	- r.46(4) N.C.P.R. 1987, England
	Jamaica	- Rule 68.41(4) C.P.R. 2002
	Trinidad & Tobago	- rr.54, 55 First Schedule N.C.B.R. Ch. 8 No. 2.
15	Barbados	- r.47 Supreme (Non-Contentious) Probate Rules 1959
	The Bahamas, Eastern Caribbean (save Dominica)	- r. 46(6) N.C.P.R. 1987, England
	Trinidad & Tobago, Guyana, Dominica	- r.45(6) N.C.P.R. 1954, England.
	Jamaica	- Rule 68.41 (8) CPR 2002
		Forms
	Barbados	- See Form No. 12 Appendix (Forms & Fees) Supreme Court (Non-Contentious) Probate Rules 1959
	The Bahamas, Eastern Caribbean (save Dominica),	- See Form 5 First Schedule N.C.P.R. 1987, England
	Trinidad & Tobago	- See Form 6 First Schedule N.C.P.R. 1954, England
	Jamaica	- Form P 19 Appendix 2 CPR 2002
16	Guyana, Dominica	
	Barbados	- r.48 (4), Supreme Court (Non-Contentious) Probate Rules 1959
	The Bahamas, Eastern Caribbean (save Dominica), Jamaica	- r.47(4), N.C.P.R. 1987, England
	Trinidad & Tobago, Guyana, Dominica	- rr.46(4), N.C.P.R. 1954, England.

17	Jamaica	- Rule 68.42(6) AND (7) CPR 2002
	Trinidad & Tobago, Guyana, Dominica	- r.46(7)(a) N.C.P.R. 1954, England
	The Bahamas, Eastern Caribbean (save Dominica),	- r.47(7)(a) N.C.P.R. 1987, England
	Jamaica	- Rule 68.44(2)(a) CPR 2002
	Barbados	- r.48(7)(a) Supreme Court (Non-Contentious) Probate Rules 1959
18	Barbados	- r.48(5)(b) Supreme Court (Non-Contentious) Probate Rules 1959
	The Bahamas, Eastern Caribbean (save Dominica)	- r.47(5)(b) N.C.P.R. 1987, England
	Trinidad & Tobago, Guyana, Dominica	- r.46(5)(b) N.C.P.R. 1954. England.
	Jamaica	- Rule 68.44(2)(b) CPR 2002
19	Barbados	- r.48(5)(a) Supreme Court (Non-Contentious) Probate Rules 1959
	Eastern Caribbean (save Dominica), Jamaica, The Bahamas	- r.47(5)(a) N.C.P.R. 1987, England
	Trinidad & Tobago, Guyana. Dominica	- r.46(5)(a) N.C.P.R. 1954, England.
	Jamaica	- Rule 68.44(1)(a) CPR 2002
20	Barbados	- r.48(5)(b) Supreme Court (Non-Contentious) Probate Rules 1959
	The Bahamas, Jamaica Eastern Caribbean territories (save Dominica)	- r.47(5)(b) N.C.P.R. 1987, England
	Trinidad & Tobago, Guyana, Dominica	- r.46(5)(b) N.C.P.R. 1954, England.
	Jamaica	- Rule 68.44(2)(b) CPR 2002
21	Barbados	- r.48(4) Supreme Court (Non-Contentious) Probate Rules 1959
	Eastern Caribbean territories (save Dominica)	
	The Bahamas	- r.47(4) NCPR, 1987, England
	Trinidad & Tobago, Guyana, Dominica	- r.46(4) NCPR 1954, England.
	Jamaica	- Rule 68.42(5) and (7) CPR 2002
22	The Bahamas, Eastern Caribbean (save Dominica)	- r.47(7)(c) N.C.P.R. 1987, England
	Trinidad & Tobago, Guyana, Dominica	- r.46(7)(c) N.C.P.R, 1954, England.
	Jamaica	- Rule 68.44(1)(c) CPR 2002
23	[1966] P.118	

24	[1927]P.202	
25	Barbados	- r.48(7)(c) Supreme Court (Non-Contentious) Probate Rules 1959
	The Bahamas	- r.47(7)(c) N.C.P.R. 1987, England
	Dominica, Guyana, Trinidad & Tobago	- r.46(7)(c) N.C.P.R. 1954, England.
26	Barbados	- r.49(2) Supreme Court (Non-Contentious) Probate Rules 1959
	Guyana, Trinidad & Tobago	- r.47 N.C.P.R. 1954, England
	The Bahamas, Eastern Caribbean (save Dominica)	- r.48 N.C.P.R. 1987, England.
	Jamaica	- Rule 68.43 C.P.R. 2002
27	Eastern Caribbean (save Dominica) The Bahamas Guyana, Trinidad & Tobago	- r.48 (2)(a) N.C.P.R. 1987, England
	Dominica	- r.47 (2)(a) N.C.P.R. 1954, England
	Jamaica	- Rule 68.44(3)(i) CPR 2002
	Barbados	- r.49(2) Supreme Court (Non-Contentious) Probate Rules 1959
28	Eastern Caribbean (save Dominica) The Bahamas Guyana, Trinidad & Tobago	- r.48 (2)(b) N.C.P.R. 1987, England
	Dominica	- r.47 (2) N.C.P.R. 1954, England
	Jamaica	- Rule 68.44(3)(ii) CPR 2002

26

Family Provision

INTRODUCTION

One of the fundamental principles governing the law of testate succession is that of testamentary freedom—the right of a testator to dispose of his property as he wishes. Indeed in most of the Caribbean territories a testator still enjoys this unrestricted testamentary freedom.

However in Barbados, Guyana, Jamaica, Trinidad & Tobago, and most recently, The Bahamas[1] this freedom is not an unfettered one. In these jurisdictions, qualifying members of the deceased's family circle have been given the statutory right to apply to the court for financial provision out of the deceased's net estate in the following circumstances:

(a) in cases of testacy — where the deceased's will has failed to make any or any adequate provision for them;
(b) with the exception of The Bahamas, in cases of intestacy — where the statutory provisions governing distribution of an intestate's estate fail to do so; and
(c) with the exception of The Bahamas, in cases of partial intestacy/testacy — where the combined effect of the deceased's will and the laws relating to intestacy fail to do so.

This statutory entitlement is a powerful weapon in the hands of an applicant for it effectively allows the court, in cases of intestacy, to vary the statutory rules of distribution and in cases of testacy, to virtually rewrite the deceased's will.

But the court's jurisdiction to do so is as a general rule exercised 'with great circumspection and to a limited extent.'[2] As Wooding CJ observed in his judgment in *Lewis v Baker*:[3]

> The jurisdiction of the Court is limited to intervention, when but only when . . . it can express the affirmative opinion that he (the deceased) did not make reasonable provision for the applicant.

PERSONS WHO MAY APPLY FOR FINANCIAL PROVISION

1. SPOUSES

A.   Lawful Spouse[4]

Guyana, Jamaica, The Bahamas and Trinidad & Tobago

In the above-mentioned territories, the applicant who has gone through a ceremony of marriage with the deceased is *prima facie* a lawful spouse and entitled to apply for financial provision in that capacity. However, the following should be noted:

(a) Valid Marriage — the party claiming relief must have been a party to a valid marriage in which case a marriage certificate is accepted as *prima facie* proof thereof;
(b) Voidable Marriage – a party to a voidable marriage may apply provided the marriage was not annulled during the deceased's lifetime.
(c) Void Marriage — a party to a void marriage may be entitled to family provision if he/she can prove that:
    (i) the marriage was entered into in good faith;
    (ii) the marriage was not annulled or dissolved during the lifetime of the deceased;
    (iii) the deceased died domiciled within the jurisdiction in which the application is made;
    (iv) the applicant had not remarried during the lifetime of the deceased.

Living Apart Twelve Months or More

The Bahamas

Pursuant to s.12(2) of The Inheritance Act 2002, where a husband and wife have been living apart for a period of 12 months or more, the court may refuse to make an order for financial provision if it considers that in all the circumstances of the case it is just and reasonable to refuse such an order.

B. Former Spouse[5]

Trinidad & Tobago

A former spouse may apply to the court for reasonable provision out of the deceased's net estate on the ground that the deceased did not make reasonable provision for his or her maintenance. This is provided that:

(a) he/she had not remarried during the deceased's lifetime or;
(b) the marriage had not been annulled or dissolved.

Jamaica

A former spouse who has not remarried may also apply for financial provision out of the deceased's net estate. But this entitlement is of more restrictive application in Jamaica, compared to Trinidad & Tobago. According to s.4(2)(d) of the Inheritance (Provision for Family and Dependants) Act, 1993, a former spouse qualifies if he or she:

> was being maintained wholly or partly or was entitled under an existing order of a court of competent jurisdiction or under an agreement between the parties to be maintained wholly or partly by the deceased immediately before his death

C. Statutory Spouse/ Cohabitant

Statutory Spouse

- *Guyana*

In Guyana, for the purposes of the Family and Dependants Provision Act, 22/1990 a reference to a spouse includes a common law spouse within the defined statutory limits of the Act.[6]

This statutory recognition of the common law spouse in Guyana, is especially significant in cases of intestacy because in Guyana as is the case in all the Caribbean jurisdictions, save Barbados and Jamaica and more recently Trinidad & Tobago, a common law spouse has absolutely no rights of inheritance on the intestacy of his/her common law spouse.

Prior to the passage of this ground-breaking legislation a survivor's sole recourse in cases of common law unions was to apply to the court for a declaration of a resulting trust. Even so, this relief would be granted only if the court was satisfied that there was sufficient evidence of a common intention—an intention at the time of acquisition of the property, (the subject matter of the proceedings) that the applicant/survivor was to have a beneficial interest in that property.[7]

In England it is only as of January 1, 1996, that the common law spouse qualified as a member of the deceased's family circle for the purposes of entitlement to financial provision.[8]

Persons Co-habiting as Husband and Wife

- *Jamaica*

According to s.4(2)(e) of the Inheritance (Provision for Family and Dependants) Act, 1993 a person who was a single man or woman who was living with the deceased who was also a single woman or man as the case may be, qualifies as a person who may apply to the court for reasonable financial provision out of the deceased's net estate.

Unlike Guyana such persons are not referred to as spouses; and the term 'single man', 'single woman' has not been further defined in this Act so as to include a widow, widower or divorcee. This is particularly significant as The Intestates Estates and Property Charges Act as amended, by Act 3 of 1988 — single man, single woman as used with the reference to the definition of spouse is so defined so as to include widow or widower, as the case may be, or a divorcée.

Co-habitant

- *Trinidad & Tobago*

Pursuant to s.95(1) of the Succession Act 27/1981 as amended by the Distribution of Estates Act 28/2000, which brought into operation Part VIII of the Succession Act 27/1981, a new class of applicant, the cohabitant, was created.

In this regard, co-habitant is defined as:

> in relation to a man, a woman who has been living with or who has lived together with a man in a *bona fide* domestic relationship for a period of not less than five years immediately preceding the date of his death; and
> in relation to woman, a man who has been living with or has lived together with a woman in a *bone fide* domestic relationship for a period of not less than five years immediately preceding the date of her death.

Unfortunately, as is the case with respect to intestate succession, the statutory definition of co-habitant as it applies to family provision applications, is equally vague and imprecise. In particular, no guidance or assistance is given in the Interpretation section of Part VIII of the Succession Act as amended by s.2 of the Distribution of Estates Act 28/2000, as to what constitutes a *bona fide* domestic relationship. The Act only specifies that only one such relationship shall be taken into account for the purposes of Part VIII.

What is clear however, is that neither co-habitant need be single. Accordingly, as is the case with respect to intestacy, married persons who have lived together in a co-habitational relationship for the minimum period of five years preceeding the deceased co-habitant's death, now qualify as distinct and separate applicants for financial provision.

Further, the co-habitant's entitlement once he or she satisfies this rather vague statutory test, is the same as that of a lawful spouse in that once the deceased cohabitant dies without leaving a surviving lawful spouse, the surviving co-habitant's entitlement on an application for financial provision is not limited to maintenance, but extends in accordance with s.95(1) as amended by s.2 of the Distribution of Estates Act 28/2000:

> to such financial provision as would be reasonable in all the circumstances for a spouse or co-habitant to receive whether or not that provision is required for his or her maintenance.

However, the difficulty which arises is with regard to the definition of a co-habitant, in which the only requirement (which is vague at the very least) is that the surviving co-habitant and the deceased co-habitant should be living in a *bona fide* domestic relationship.

The reality is that a married person living with another married person can qualify as a co-habitant and period of co-habitation can commence during the lifetime of the lawful spouse. As a consequence, a married man could, during the pendancy of his marriage leave the matrimonial home to live with a woman who may herself be married.

The period of co-habitation, in such instances commences from the date of such co-habitation, As such, were the lawful wife to die two years after such co-habitation commenced and should the deceased himself die three years later from such date, the surviving co-habitant would be entitled quite apart from her rights on intestacy, to apply for financial provision on the same footing as a surviving spouse.

In such circumstances, the deceased co-habitant's estate, if his lawful wife were to die intestate, would also be comprised of his intestate spouse's estate, to which the co-habitant would indirectly be entitled both on an intestacy and also under a family provision application.

The statutory definition of co-habitant both in respect of entitlement on intestacy, and with respect to financial provision applications should be revisited, not only for purposes of clarifying the meaning of *bona fide* domestic relationships, but further, on the grounds of public policy. In this regard the definition of co-habitant should be restricted, as is the case in Jamaica, Guyana and England, to single persons—persons who are widowed, divorced or never married.

Persons Co-habiting as Husband and Wife but not Qualifying as Such

Barbados[9]

In cases where the deceased dies wholly intestate:

    (i) any woman living together with a man other than her spouse; or
    (ii) any man living together with a woman other than his spouse

who was immediately preceding the date of death of the deceased wholly or mainly maintained by him or her, may apply to the court for provision for maintenance. Such applicants may include persons co-habiting as husband and wife for a period less than the statutory minimum of five years, or persons living with a married man or woman as the case may be, irrespective of the number of years.

Judically Separated Spouse

Guyana, Trinidad & Tobago, The Bahamas

    Pursuant to:

- ss.3(2) and 5(3) of the Family and Dependant Provision Act 22/1990, Guyana;
- s.14(3) of the Inheritance Act 2002, The Bahamas; and
- s.97(2) of the Succession Act 27/1981 and s.94 as amended by the Distribution of Estates Act 28/2000, Trinidad and Tobago.

a judicially separated spouse, is not entitled to financial provision on the same basis as a spouse or statutory spouse.

Spouse Not a Qualifying Member

Barbados

In Barbados, a spouse (and this includes a common law/statutory spouse)[10] is not a qualifying member of the deceased's family circle. This is so because in cases of:

(a) *Testacy* — where the deceased dies wholly testate and there is a devise or bequest to the surviving spouse under the will, he or she may elect within six months of the probate of the will, to take either that bequest or devise or his or her legal right on an intestacy. This legal right is a minimum of one quarter to a maximum of one half of the net estate of the deceased and it takes priority over devises, bequests and shares on intestacy.[11]
(b) *Intestacy* — where the deceased has died wholly intestate the surviving spouse is entitled to a minimum of one third to a maximum of two thirds of the deceased's net estate.[12]
(c) *Partial Intestacy* — where the deceased has died partly testate and partly intestate, the spouse has the right of election between;
   (i) his or her legal right; or
   (ii) his or her share under the intestacy, together with any devise or bequest under the will of the deceased.[13]

This statutory entitlement of a surviving spouse in cases of testacy, intestacy or partial intestacy is clearly regarded as making more than adequate financial provision for a surviving spouse.

However, a lawful spouse against whom the deceased obtained a judicial separation, a lawful spouse who failed to comply with a decree of restitution of conjugal rights obtained by the deceased or a lawful spouse guilty of desertion which has continued up to the deceased's death for three years or more is precluded from taking any share in the estate of the deceased as a legal right or on intestacy.[14]

2. CHILDREN OF THE DECEASED

In General

Barbados, Jamaica, Trinidad & Tobago and The Bahamas

A son or daughter of the deceased includes one who is legally adopted by the deceased,[15] born out of wedlock to the deceased,[16] and a child who is *en ventre sa mere*.[17]

By Jurisdiction

A. Trinidad & Tobago

- Estates of Persons Dying Prior to September 25, 2000

Prior to the passage on September 25, 2000, of Part VIII of the Succession Act 27/1981, the class of persons who qualified as a child of the deceased for the purpose of family provisions application were the following:

(a) a daughter who has not married irrespective of her age (until her marriage);[18]
(b) an infant son (that is a son under the age of twenty-one years);[19]
(c) a son or daughter who is by reason of some mental or physical disability incapable of maintaining himself or herself (until the cesser of his/her disability).[20]

However a child of the deceased did not include:

(a) a child of the family; or
(b) a daughter of the deceased who was under the age of twenty-one years and married.

- Estates of Persons Dying on or after September 25, 2000

With the passage of Part VIII of the Succession Act 27/1981, as amended by the Distribution of Estates Act 28/2000, ss.95(a) and 95(c), respectively, provide that the following persons qualify as a child of the deceased:

(a) a child (this is irrespective of age or mental or physical capacity or incapacity)
(b) a child of the family—a person not being a child of the deceased who in the case of any marriage to which the deceased was at the time a party, was treated by the deceased as a child of the family in relation to the marriage.

B. Guyana

A child of the deceased in Guyana,[21] for the purposes of family provision applications, includes:

(a) a child of the deceased irrespective of age, mental or physical capacity; and

(b) a child of the family—a person not being a child of the deceased who in the case of any marriage to which the deceased was at any time a party, was treated as a child of the family in relation to that marriage.

C. Jamaica and The Bahamas[22]

A child of the deceased means a child, under the age of 18 years and includes a child of the family—any person not being a child of the deceased's husband and who, as the case may be had been accepted as one of the family.

However, a child over the age of 18 years as defined above, may be regarded as a child for the purpose of a family provision application:

(a) if such child is under the age of 23 years and pursuing academic studies or receiving trade or professional instructions; or
(b) if there are special circumstances (including physical and mental disability) which justify the disregard of the age limit.

D. Barbados[23]

Testacy

In cases where the testator has failed to make proper provision whether by will or otherwise, the following classes of children may apply to the court for family provisions:

(a) a minor child (that is a child under the age of 18 years)
(b) a child who because of some mental or physical disability is incapable of maintaining himself/herself (until the cesser of his/her disability).

Intestacy

In instances where the deceased dies intestate, s.57, Part VII of the Succession Act Cap. 249, which is intituled *Provision for dependants*,[24] provides that a child who is presumed to be a child of the deceased and who is:

(a) under the age of eighteen years; or
(b) who suffers from a mental or physical disability and is thereby incapable of maintaining himself/herself,

qualifies as a statutory dependent provided that, in either case, he/she was wholly or partly maintained by or was living with the deceased person at the date of his death.

A child is presumed to be a child of a deceased person, whether he was born in or out of wedlock, if that child is one in whose favour a presumption of paternity is established in accordance with s.7 of the Status of Children Reform Act Cap. 220.[25]

In this regard, for purposes of inheritance on an intestacy, Part VI of the Succession Act which is intituled *Distribution on Intestacy* provides *inter alia* that a child of the deceased has an automatic legal entitlement, in the case of the intestacy of his or her father or mother, to a minimum of one third share of the intestate parent's estate.

However, s.58 of the Succession Act Cap. 249 expressly provides that an application for maintenance under Part VII of the Act may be made by a child presumed to be a child of the deceased but limits the ground of the application to one ground only, that is:

> on the ground that the law relating to intestacy does not make provision for the maintenance of such dependant.

As such, given that there is no definition in the Succession Act Cap. 249 of child or, of child presumed to be a child of the deceased, it is submitted that the expression child presumed to be a child of the deceased as used in Part VII *Provisions For Dependants,* is limited to a child who pursuant to s.10 of the Status of Children Reform Act, although unable to establish any of the presumptions under s.7 of the Act, is nevertheless able to satisfy the court on a balance of probabilities of the existence of the relationship of father and child between himself and the intestate.

In such instances, pursuant to s.10(3), a declaration from the high court is necessary to prove paternity. However s.10(2) clearly provides that where paternity is sought to be established under this section (where there is no person recognised under s.7 as being the father of the child) the application for a declaratory order may not be made:

> unless both persons with respect of whom the relationship is sought to be established, are living.

3. PARENTS

Jamaica

According to s.4(2)(c) of the Inheritance (Provision for Family and

Dependants) Act, a parent, including a person who stands in *loco parentis* to the deceased and who was being maintained wholly or partly or was legally entitled to be maintained wholly or partly by the deceased immediately before his death, is entitled to apply for financial provision out of the deceased's net estate.

It is clear from the above statutory definition that the parental relationship whether based on consanguinity or not is not a sufficient statutory qualification. Financial dependency, total or partial, immediately preceding the deceased's death must be established for the purposes of entitling this class of applicant to apply for financial provision.

4. OTHER CLASSES OF APPLICANTS

Guyana and Trinidad and Tobago[26]

Any person who immediately before the death of the deceased was either wholly or partly maintained by him is entitled to apply for an order for financial provision. Although this class of applicants is potentially extensive and may embrace such diverse applicants as aunts, grandparents, nieces, nephews or even persons not related by blood to the deceased, including former spouses, and persons who neither qualify as lawful or statutory spouses, the financial dependency of the intended applicant is a prerequisite to qualifying as an applicant.

Meaning of Maintenance

For the purposes of applications made by persons who do not fall under any specific category of applicant, but whose claim for financial provision is based on maintenance, s.95(3) of the Succession Act 27/1981 Trinidad & Tobago, and s.3(3) of the Family and Dependants Provision Act 22/1990, Guyana, expressly provide for the purposes of such class of applicant, that a person shall be treated as maintained by the deceased, either wholly or partly as the case may be, if the deceased, otherwise than for full valuable consideration was making a substantial contribution in money or money's worth towards the reasonable needs of that person.

FAMILY PROVISION ORDERS

Test Applied

Testacy — In determining whether the testator has made reasonable provision for the applicant in his will, the court applies an objective, not subjective, test.[27]

As was stated by Megarry J in *Re Goodwin deceased*[28] and quoted with approval in the Trinidad & Tobago High Court judgement of *Taylor, Taylor, Taylor v. Philbert:*[29]

> The question is simply whether the will or the disposition has made reasonable provision, and not whether it was unreasonable on the part of the deceased to have made no provision or no larger provision for the defendant.

Intestacy

In cases of intestacy, the Courts have the power to vary the statutory rules of distribution of a deceased's estate. But clearly in such instances, the subjectivity or objectivity of the deceased is not in issue.

Practice and Procedure

An application for a family provision order is made to a judge in chambers under the relevant rules of the Supreme Court of the respective territories.[30]

The application is made by originating summons/ fixed Date Claim Form, in the case of Jamaica and is intituled In the Matter of the relevant Family Provision Act and In the Matter of the Estate of the deceased to whom the summons relates.

- Parties to the Application

The plaintiff is the claimant and the executor or other personal representative of the deceased's estate is the defendant. In the event that the plaintiff is the sole executor or sole personal representative, the defendant shall be some person having a substantial interest in opposing the application.[31]

- Office Copy of Probate

On the hearing of the application the executor or personal representative is required to produce in court, an office copy of the probate or letters of administration.[32]

- Time for making Application

The application for an order for reasonable financial provision shall not be made, except with permission of the court, in:

(a) *Trinidad & Tobago*[33] *The Bahamas and Jamaica*[34] — after the end of the period of six months from the date on which representation with respect to the estate of the deceased is first taken out;
(b) *Guyana*[35] — after the end of one year from the date on which representation with respect to the estate of the deceased is first taken out.
(c) *Barbados*[36] — after 12 months from the first taking out of representation of the deceased's estate

- Extension of Time

In exceptional circumstances the court may extend the time for making an application for financial provision, when the time for so doing has expired.

In this regard, the following three cases are instructive to the factors which the court take into account in the exercise of its discretion:

- In *Re C*,[37] the application for financial provision on behalf of the eight year old illegitimate child of the deceased was made three and one half years after the death of the deceased. Probate was granted one year after the deceased's death and for the next two and one half years, the mother of the child did nothing in respect of making an application for provision on behalf of the child.
  The court however granted leave for the following reasons:

  (a) that the claimant was the child, not the mother, and if permission were to be refused, the child claimant, would suffer as a result of another's fault;
  (b) that the beneficiaries and other claimants of the estate would suffer no prejudice as the estate, up to the date of the application for extension of time, had not been administered.

- In *Stock v Brown*,[38] an application for family provisions was made by the childless widow of the deceased six (6) years out of time. The deceased, who had no children, had left a will conferring a life interest on his widow, with the remainder to his nieces and nephews.

  In granting leave to apply for financial provision, the court took into account that:
  (a) there was no objections by the beneficiaries to the application being made;
  (b) the widow was aged 85 years at the time of the application and had received no independent advice as to the implication of not challenging her husband's will;
  (c) the dramatic fall in interest rates in 1993, the date of

the application, and the increasing cost of living, meant that the widow no longer had enough on which to live; and

(d) no one was prejudiced by the application as the estate, as at the date of application, had not been administered.

- On the other hand, in the case of *Re Salmon*,[39] although the applicant made the application for financial provision only five and one half months out of time, the application was not allowed. In turning down the application, the court took into account that:

    (a) the applicant had married the deceased in 1932, then left him in 1944, and they never saw each other again until 1978, the year of his death;
    (b) the delay in making the application was deemed to be substantial and more significantly was entirely the fault of the widow;
    (c) the widow probably had a remedy against her attorneys for failing to advise her of the statutory period of limitation for applying for financial provision and in the court's view it would be unjust to extend the statutory period, when the widow had such a remedy; and
    (d) almost the entire estate had been distributed at the date when the application was made.

Although the cases cited above are English cases, the factors considered by the court are equally relevant to the respective Caribbean jurisdictions. What is clear from these three cases is that the court is influenced, *inter alia*, by the conduct of the applicant to the deceased, and whether or not the estate has already been administered by the date of the application.

Affidavit of Applicant

Although a qualified member of the deceased's family circle is entitled by law to apply to the court for an order for financial provision out of the deceased's net estate, it cannot be over-emphasized that this is no guarantee that he will be successful.

As was stated by Bennett, J., in *Re Brownbridge*,[40] and quoted with approval by Edoo, J., in *Piggott v. Royal Bank Trust Co. (T'dad)*[41] the family provision legislation:

does not throw upon a testator to provide for his dependants; it merely entitles the court to intervene if it finds its dispositions unwarranted.

Accordingly, whether, and in what manner, the court will exercise its discretion, will depend on whether the applicant can satisfy the court that the dispositions of the deceased's estate effected by his will or by the law relating to intestacy or a combination of both, have failed to make reasonable financial provision for him.

As Wooding, CJ., remarked in *Lewis v Baker*[42]

> What is reasonable is of course relative and must depend on the circumstances. I must be satisfied that taking all relevant factors into account that the testator acted reasonably.

Thus the affidavit(s) of the applicant(s) and that of the party opposing the application are of critical importance. This is so because the evidence upon which the court will makes its determination is required to be by affidavit verifying a statement of the facts and matters relied upon.[43]

Factors taken into account

The court in the exercise of its extensive powers is entitled to take any matter which in the circumstances of the case, it considers relevant or material. In this regard, Guyana, Jamaica and The Bahamas have codified many of the factors taken into account by the court while Trinidad & Tobago still relies largely on case law authority to provide the necessary judicial guidelines. However whether the material factors have been codified or whether they are still governed by case law authority, the courts in these jurisdiction take similar matters into account, some of these being general in scope while others relevant only to a particular class of applicant.

The general factors include:

- the financial resources and financial needs which the applicant including any other applicant has or is likely to have in the foreseeable future;[44]
- the financial resources and needs which any beneficiary of the estate of the deceased has or is likely to have in the foreseeable future;
- any obligations and responsibilities which the deceased had towards any applicant or towards any beneficiary of the deceased's estate. This includes any moral obligation which the deceased may have to the applicant;[45]

- the conduct of the applicant towards the deceased;[46]
- the size, nature and value of the net estate of the deceased;[47]
- the deceased's reasons so far as ascertainable, including any statement in writing signed by the deceased and dated;[48]
- the relationship of the applicant to the deceased and the nature of any provision for the applicant which was made by the deceased during his lifetime;
- any physical or mental disability of any applicant or any beneficiary of the estate of the deceased.

Specific Statutory Factors

A. Spouse[49]

All Jurisdictions

Where the applicant is a spouse, the court in making an order for reasonable provision also takes into account:

(a) the age of the applicant and the duration of the marriage;
(b) the contribution made by the applicant to the welfare of the family of the deceased, including any contribution made by looking after the home or caring for the family; and
(c) the provision which the applicant might have reasonably have expected to receive if on the day the deceased died the marriage instead of being terminated by death had been terminated by a decree of divorce, subject to any decree of judicial separation in force and continuing at the date of death of the deceased.

With respect to a lawful spouse, the Trinidad & Tobago cases of *Thompson v Roach and Roach*[50] and *Chamroo v Rookmin and Satnarine*[51] and *Lewis v Baker*[52] are instructive. In all three cases, the applicant's spouse and the deceased were separated for a significant period preceding the deceased spouse's death.

The court was persuaded to turn down the respective applications for financial provision, not only because of the lengthy period of separation, but also because of the alleged conduct of the applicant to the deceased. This is epitomised in the rather emotive remarks of Wooding, C.J. in *Lewis v Baker*, when in describing the applicant spouse, he observed:

> She impressed me as being a vengeful vixenish person where he was as I believe, the quiet sort who looked upon long suffering as one of life's trials to be patiently endured.[53]

The court also noted in *Chamroo v Rookmin and Satnarine*[54] and *Thompson v Roach and Roach*,[55] that the applicant spouse since the date of separation, supported herself and in the case of *Lewis v Baker* it was the deceased, who during and after the couple's separation, had given financial support to the applicant spouse.

In all these cases, the court was also influenced by the size of the estate, which in the case of *Chamroo v Rookmin* was small, and also by the claims of other persons to the deceased's estate

B. Former Spouse

Trinidad & Tobago[56] and Jamaica

With respect to applications for financial provisions made by the former spouse, such applications are not usually successful. This is mainly because, as was explained in *Re Fullard*,[57] in light of the powers of the court to make capital adjustments between spouses on a divorce (by property adjustment orders and orders for lump sum payments), there would in practice be few cases where it would be possible for a former spouse to satisfy the conditions precedent for the award of financial provision out of a deceased's estate, namely that the court had to be satisfied that the deceased's will, or the intestacy did not make reasonable financial provision for the former spouse.

Further, where the deceased's estate is small, the former spouse had a heavy onus of satisfying that condition because the application for financial provision would diminish the estate and cause great hardship to the deceased's beneficiaries if they were ultimately successful.

However, as was observed in *Re Fullard supra*, a former spouse's application for financial provision may prove successful where:

(a) a long period of time has elapsed since the dissolution of the marriage in which there has been a continuing obligation by the deceased to make periodical payments to the former spouse;
(b) the deceased is found to have a reasonable amount of capital in his estate; or
(c) the death unlocks a substantial capital sum from which the deceased, ought to have made provision for the surviving spouse.

However, according to Purchas J in *Re Fullard*,[58] it is doubtful whether the mere accumulation of wealth, after the dissolution of the marriage, would, of itself, justify an application by a former spouse for financial provision.

C. Statutory Spouse/Co-habitant

Trinidad & Tobago

Pursuant to the provisions of s.97(2) of the Succession Act 27/1981 as amended by the Distribution of Estates Act 28/2000, the statutory guidelines prescribed by s.97(a) are also applicable to a cohabitant. Accordingly, where the word marriage appears, the words or 'co-habitational relationship' are to be inserted thereafter.

Guyana

The statutory guidelines which are prescribed for the lawful spouse do not apply to the statutory spouse because of the restrictive wording of s.5(2) of the Family and Dependants Provision Act 1990 which provision is limited to marriage. The absence of express provisions, including the statutory spouse, may have been as a result of legislative oversight as there is no specific statutory guidelines in respect of the statutory spouse as the case with respect to Trinidad & Tobago.

D. Man and Woman Co-habiting as Husband and Wife but not Qualifying as Such

Barbados

Where an application for maintenance is made by a person who co-habited with the deceased intestate as a spouse, but who does not qualify as such, s.58 of the Succession Act prescribes that the following factors be taken into account *inter alia:*

- the income of the person by or on whose behalf the application is made;
- the mental state or physical condition of the dependant; or
- any other matter (including the conduct of the person by or on whose behalf the application is made, or of any other person) which in the circumstances of the case the Court considers relevant.

E. Persons not Qualifying as Co-habitant/Statutory Spouse

Trinidad & Tobago and Guyana

There is no specific classification for applicants who do not quality as cohabitants or statutory spouses as defined by the relevant provisions of these territories. However, where a person has lived with a deceased in a spousal relationship but does not satisfy the statutory requirements in respect of the definition of spouse (Guyana) and co-habitant (Trinidad & Tobago), such person may make an application for financial provision under the classification of persons who were wholly or partly dependent on the deceased immediately preceding his death.

Quite apart from the general statutory guidelines in respect of the meaning of maintenance for persons falling under this generic class, there are a number of English cases which specifically deal with applications for financial provision by persons falling into this category, under the equivalent English statutory provision contained in the Inheritance (Provision for Family and Dependants) Act 1975, England.

The following are some of the issues which are particularly relevant to this class of applicant:

(a)   Meaning of Maintenance

According, *inter alia*, to the authority of the Court of Appeal decision in *Bishop v Plumley and another*,[59] the test of whether the applicant was being maintained is whether he or she had received a substantial contribution in money or money's worth towards his needs otherwise than for valuable consideration.

As a general principle, in determining whether the deceased had made a substantial contribution to the applicant's needs otherwise than for full valuable consideration, the court takes a common sense view of the relationship between the parties and as such strikes a balance between the benefits received by the applicant from the deceased against those provided by the applicant to the deceased. If there is doubt whether the balance is tipped in favour of the deceased's contributions being the greater, the matter should be adjudicated upon. If the contributions were equal and therefore there was no dependency of the applicant on the deceased, because either the deceased depended upon the applicant or there was a mutual dependency, the application should not be made, as being bound to fail.[60]

With respect to determining what would constitute valuable consideration, the care and support given by an applicant is not to be considered in isolation from the mutuality of what is essentially a domestic relationship and consequently as a matter which balances out the financial support provided by the deceased, thereby disentitling an applicant to financial provision on the ground that the care and support was provided for valuable consideration.

The existence at the deceased's death of a subsisting agreement providing for the maintenance of the applicant by the deceased is generally difficult to raise the presumption that the deceased assumed responsibility for the applicant's maintenance.

However, it is not necessary for an applicant to prove, by any overt act, that the deceased had intended to maintain the applicant after his or her death. In this regard, it is sufficient if the deceased's conduct was such that the applicant had been wholly or partially dependent on the deceased for his or her maintenance during the deceased's lifetime.

As Stephenson L.J. observed in *Jelley v Illife* when commenting on the legislative intent of the provision, which provision is identical to that of Trinidad & Tobago and Guyana:

> Its object is surely to remedy where reasonably possible, the injustice of one who has been put in a position of dependency on him being deprived of any financial support, either by accident or by the design of the deceased, after his death.[61]

(b) Meaning of Immediately Preceding the Deceased's Death

In determining what constitutes immediately before the death of the deceased as was stated by Sir. Robert Megarry V.C in *Re: Beaumont*[62] and adopted in *Jelley v Illife*:[63]

> it is the settled basis or general arrangement between the parties as regards maintenance during the lifetime of the deceased which has to be looked at, not the actual, perhaps fluctuating variation of which exists immediately before his death.

F. Child of the Deceased

Barbados

- *Testacy*

Where the applicant is a qualifying child of the deceased the sole statutory factor which the court is required to take into account is whether it is of the opinion that the testator failed in his moral duty to make provision for the child in accordance with his means.[64] Section 100(4) of the Succession Act Cap. 249 specifically provides that an order for reasonable provision with respect to a child of the deceased shall not affect the legal right of a surviving spouse or if the surviving spouse is the mother or father of the child, any devise or bequest to the spouse or any share to which the spouse is entitled on intestacy.

- *Intestacy*

With respect to applications for maintenance made by a child presumed to be a child of the intestate, the statutory factors relevant to persons cohabiting as husband and wife, but who do not qualify as such, are also applicable to the child presumed to be a child of the intestate.

Jamaica, Guyana, The Bahamas and Trinidad & Tobago[65]

With respect to a child of the deceased, the relevant statutory provisions of Jamaica, The Bahamas and Trinidad and Tobago provide that the court shall in the exercise of its powers (to make an order for reasonable provision) also have regard to the manner which the child was, or is expected to be educated or trained.

There is no age resctriction in the case of The Bahamas, Trinidad & Tobago and Guyana. Accordingly, in Trinidad and Tobago and Guyana an application for financial provision can be made for or by a child irrespective of age, marital status or physical or mental capacity or incapacity.

Even so, as a general rule, where the applicant is an able-bodied adult based, *inter alia*, on the general principles enunciated in *Re Coventry (deceased)*,[66] an adult child, who is able to earn and earns his own living must establish some special circumstances to support an application for financial provision.

As a general rule, the moral obligation of the deceased to the applicant child is deemed to qualify as such exceptional circumstances. In this regard, the case of *Re Goodchild (deceased)*[67] is instructive on the issue of moral obligation to an adult child. In that case, the adult successfully applied for financial provision out of his father's estate. In arriving at its decision, the court took into account the following that:

(a) there was only one other beneficiary under the deceased's will and she was able to cater for herself; further, she was only married to the deceased for a short time prior to his death, and appeared not to have any particular expectations arising from his will.
(b) that the assets comprising the deceased father's estate (as was the case in *Re Sivyer*)[68] consisted principally of assets derived from the first wife, the mother of the applicant; and
(c) that given the applicant's need at the time of the deceased death, it was not in the court's view reasonable for him not to have made provision for his son.

In determining whether a moral obligation arises, based, *inter alia*, on the authority of *Re Jennings (deceased)*[69] the existence of a mere blood relationship is not a sufficient basis for making an order for financial provision.

The moral obligation and responsibility of a deceased to an applicant adult child does not as a general rule apply to the past but rather to obligations and responsibilities which the deceased had immediately preceding his death.[70]

G. *Child of the Family*

Guyana, Trinidad and Tobago, The Bahamas and Jamaica

With respect to a child of the family, the court takes into account the following:

(a) the extent (if any) to which the deceased had on or after acceptance of the child as one of the family, assumed responsibility for the child's maintenance;
(b) the liability of any person other than the deceased to maintain the child; and
(c) *with respect to The Bahamas and Trinidad & Tobago*, whether in assuming and discharging that responsibility, the deceased did so knowing that the applicant was not his own child.

The considerations which apply to a child of the deceased, in respect of each jurisdiction, are also applicable to the child, of the family. As such, in the case of Trinidad and Tobago and Guyana, in order for an able-bodied adult child of the family to succeed on an application for financial provision, he or she must establish exceptional or special circumstances.[71]

TYPES OF FAMILY PROVISION ORDERS

1. *Preliminary*

In giving effect to the family provision legislation of the respective territories, the court has been empowered to make financial provision orders in favour of the applicant out of the net estate of the deceased

2. *Meaning of Net Estate*

For the purposes of family provision orders, net estate means in the case of:

A. Guyana

(a) any property received by any person as a *donatio mortis causa*;[72]
(b) any property held on joint tenancy for the deceased. However, for joint property to qualify as net estate, the application for an order for financial provision must be made before the end of one year from the date on which representation was first taken out[73]
(c) dispositions of property for with full valuable consideration was not given (either by the person to whom the benefit of the disposition was given or by any other person) and which disposition was made not less than five years preceding the date of death of the deceased; and with the intention of defeating an application for financial provision. In this regard, disposition includes:
 - any payment of money including payment of a premium under a policy of insurance;
 - any conveyance, assurance or appointment or gift of property of any description whether made by instrument or otherwise, but does not include any disposition in a will or any *donatio mortis causa* or any appointment of property otherwise than by will in the exercise of a special power of appointment.[74]
(d) property or any sum of money in respect of which the deceased made a contract to leaves such property or sum of money to a person with the intention of defeating an application for financial provision.[75]

B. Jamaica

(a) a disposition of property for which full valuable consideration was not given (identical to that which is applicable to Guyana at (c) above), save and except the statutory period specified, is not less than one year before the date of death of the deceased;[76] and
(b) property or sum of money in respect of which the deceased made a contract to leave such property or sum of money to a person with the intention of defeating an application for financial provision.[77]

C. The Bahamas

(a) any sum of money or other property received by any person as a *donatio mortis causa* by a deceased person[78]
(b) contracts to leave property by will.[79]

However, pursuant to s.20 Inheritance Act 2002, joint property is not treated as part of the deceased's estate for the purpose of a financial provision application.

D. Trinidad & Tobago

(a) any sum of money or other property received by any person as a *donatio mortis causa*;[80]
(b) in accordance with the provisions of any enactment, the nomination of any sum of money or other property to which the deceased would have been entitled to receive on his death;[81]
(c) property held on joint tenancy by the deceased, save and except that an application for an order for financial provision, would not include such joint property if such application is not made before the end of the period of six months from the date on which representation with respect to the estate of the deceased was first taken out; [82]
(d) dispositions of property for which full valuable consideration was not given (identical to that which is applicable to Guyana at (c) above save and except the statutory period specified is less than six years before the date of death of the deceased; [83] and
(e) contracts to leave a sum of money or property by will (the provisions of which are identical to Guyana at (d) above). [84]

E. Barbados

There is no statutory definition of net estate *per se*. However, s.2(6) of the Succession Act Cap. 249 provides that it includes:

(a) real estate includes chattels, real, and land in possession, remainder or reversion, and every estate or interest in or over land (including real estate held by way of mortgage or security, but not including money to arise under a trust for sale of land, or money secured or charged on land);
(b) the estates of a deceased person in an estate tail shall be deemed to be an estate or interest ceasing on his death, but any further or other estate or interest of the deceased person in remainder or reversion which is capable of being disposed of by his will shall not be deemed to be an estate or interest so ceasing; or
(c) the estate of a deceased person under a joint tenancy where any tenant survives the deceased person shall be deemed to be an estate or interest ceasing on his death.[85]

3. Nature of the Orders Made

Preliminary Point

Apart from the exception of the spouse which includes in Guyana, the statutory spouse and in Trinidad & Tobago a co-habitant,[86] a financial provision order is limited to that which would reasonable in all the circumstances of the case for maintenance of the applicant.

The following are the orders which the court may make in respect of an application for financial provision:

Barbados, Guyana, Jamaica, The Bahamas and Trinidad & Tobago

(1) Periodical Payment Orders[87] —This is an order for the making to the applicant out of the net estate of the deceased such periodical payments and for such items as may be specified.
(2) Lump Sum Payment Orders[88]—again this is made out of net estate of the deceased. Lump sum payments may also be made by installments as specified in the order

Guyana, Jamaica, The Bahamas and Trinidad &Tobago[89]

(3) Variation Orders — this is an order:
   (a) varying a previous order whether by way of a lump sum or periodical payment order, on the ground that there has been a substantial change in circumstances of the applicant or a person beneficially interested in the property in the deceased estate; or
   (b) for making provision for the maintenance of another applicant; or

Jamaica, Trinidad & Tobago and Guyana only

   (c) varying any ante-nuptial or post-nuptial settlement made by the parties to a marriage to which the deceased was one of the parties.

Guyana, Jamaica, The Bahamas and Trinidad & Tobago

(4) Interim Orders:[90]
An application for an interim order for maintenance is made in circumstances when it appears to the court that:
   (a) the applicant is in immediate need financial assistance, but it is not yet possible to determine what order, if any, should be made; and
   (b) that the property forming part of the net estate of the deceased is or can be made available to meet the need of the applicant.

(5) Transfer of Property Order[91]

An order for the transfer to the applicant of such property comprised in the net estate of the deceased as may be so specified.

PROTECTION FROM EVICTION FROM MATRIMONIAL HOME

The Bahamas

Pursuant to the provisions of Part V of the Inheritance Act 2002, s.24 in particular, a surviving spouse who is not entitled by virtue of a beneficial estate or trust or by virtue of any other written law giving him or her the right to remain in occupation, shall have, as regards the matrimonial home, on the death of the other spouse who was entitled, a right to continue to reside in the matrimonial home, and not to be evicted or excluded from the house or any part thereof in which the surviving spouse was residing at the time of the death of the deceased spouse.

The right of occupation of the surviving spouse however ceases upon the death or remarriage of the surviving spouse according to s.24(2) Inheritance Act 2002.

Further, an application may be made by originating summons supported by affidavit(s) by anyone adversely affected, for an order regulating the exercise by the surviving spouse of the right of occupation of the matrimonial home. In this regard, s.24(4) of the Act sets out the factors which the court is required to take into account in making such order. These are the needs of the surviving spouse or any children of the deceased spouse and all circumstances of the case.

With respect to such applications, the court may make the following orders:

(i) except part of the matrimonial home from the surviving spouse's right of occupation (and in particular) a part used wholly or partly for or in connection with the trade, business or profession of the other spouse;

(ii) order the surviving spouse to make periodical payments to the applicant in compensation for any damage or loss occasioned to the applicant by means of the exercise of the surviving spouse of the right of the occupation; and

(iii) impose on the surviving spouse the obligation to discharges any liabilities in respect of the matrimonial home having regard to the existing legal rights including any obligation under a mortgage of other persons in the home.

Protection Against Eviction of Child

Section 25 of the Inheritance Act expressly provides that in the event of the spouse who has a right of occupation predeceasing his or her spouse, and such right of occupation of the matrimonial home is existing at the time of death, any child of the predeceasing spouse shall also have right of occupation and this right shall continue to be of full effect against the surviving spouse to and for the benefit of any such child.

Notes

1. Barbados — Part VII and Part X Succession Act Cap. 249
    Guyana — Family and Dependants Provision Act 22/1990
    Jamaica — Inheritance (Provision for Family and Dependants) Act 14/1993
    The Bahamas — Part III Inheritance Act 2002
    Trinidad & Tobago — ss 94(4) and 95(1)(a) Succession Act 27/1981
2. *Franklyn v. Biddy* (1960) 2 W.I.R. 348 at 351 per Hyatali J.
3. (1966) 10 W.I.R. 122 at p. 123, See also *Chamroo v. Rookmin and Satnarine* (1968) 13 W.I.R. 470 at 471.
4. Jamaica — s.2 The Inheritance (Provision for Family and Dependants) Act, 14/1993
    Guyana — s.3(2) Family and Dependants Provision Act 22/1990
    Trinidad & Tobago — ss.90(1)(a), 92 Wills & Probate Ordinance Ch. 8. No. 2.
5. Section 95(1)(b) Succession Act 27/1981.
6. According to s.2 (6)(a) of the Family and Dependants Provision Act 22/1990:
    (i) a wife shall include a reference to a single woman living together with a single man in a common law union for seven years immediately preceding the date of his death;
    (ii) a husband shall include a reference to a single man living together with a single woman in a common law union for seven years immediately preceding the date of her death:
    Further, according to s.2 (6)(b). the term single man, single woman includes a widow or widower or a man or a woman who is divorced.
7. See Article on 'Trinidad & Tobago A Case for Reform in the Law of Succession' by Karen Tesheira, *The International and Comparative Law Quarterly,* Vol. 45, 1996.
8. According to s.2 (3)(1A) of The Law Reform (Succession) Act 1995, (which became law on November 8, 1995), an application for financial provision may be made by a person who lived with the deceased as husband or wife if:
    the deceased died on or after 1st January, 1996 and, during the whole of the period of two years ending immediately before the date when the deceased died, the person was living-
    (a) in the same household as the deceased, and
    (b) as the husband or wife of the deceased.
9. Section 57 Succession Act Cap. 249.
10. See s. 93 Succession Act Cap. 249.

11 Section 93, 94 Succession Act Cap. 249, See *Griffith v. Coward* H.C.A. 478/1985; H.C.A. 845/1985 Barbados (Unreported) *Hinds v. Smith* H.C.A. 969/1984 Barbados (Unreported).
12 Section 49 Succession Act Cap. 249.
13 Section 97 Succession Act Cap. 249.
14 Section 102 Succession Act Cap. 249.
15 Barbados — ss.48(2) 100(6) Succession Act Cap. 249
    Guyana — s.2(6) Family and Dependants Provision Act 22/1990
    Jamaica — s.2 The Inheritance (Provision for Family and Dependants) Act, 14/1993
    Trinidad & Tobago — Adoption of Children Act Chap. 46:03.
    The Bahamas — s.2(2) Inheritance Act 2002. See also s.94(8) Wills and Probate Ordinance Ch. 8 no. 2 as amended by s.2 Distribution of Estates Act 28/2000
16 Barbados — Status of Children Reform Act Cap. 220
    Guyana — s.2(6) Family and Dependants Provision Act 22/1990
    Jamaica — Status of Children Act 36/1976
    Trinidad & Tobago — Status of Children Act Chap. 46:07.
    The Bahamas — Equal Status of Children Act 2002
17 Barbados — s.2(2)(a) Succession Act Cap. 249
    Jamaica — s.2 The Inheritance (Provision for Family and Dependants) Act, 14/1993
    Trinidad & Tobago — s.94(8) Wills and Probate Ordinance Ch. 8 no.2 as amended by s.2 Distribution of Estates Act 28/2000
    Guyana — s.2(5) Family and Dependants Provision Act, 2002
    The Bahamas — s.2(2) Inheritance Act 2002
18 Trinidad & Tobago — s.90(1)(b) Wills and Probate Ordinance Ch. 8 No. 2.
19 Section 90(1)(c) Wills & Probate Ordinance Ord. Ch. 8 No.2; s.4 Age of Majority Act Ch. 46:06.
20 Section 90(1)(c) Wills & Probate Ordinance Ch. 8 No. 2.
21 Section 3(1)(c) Family & Dependants Provision Act 22/1990.
22 The Bahamas -s.12(1)(b) and (c) Inheritance Act;
    Jamaica- s. 2 Inheritance (Provision for Family and Dependants) Act, 14/1993.
23 Section 100 Succession Act Cap. 249.
24 Part VII of the Succession Act Cap. 249 which became law on January 1, 1980 is an amendment to the Succession Act which was originally enacted on November 13, 1975. Part VII of the Succession Act Cap. 249 and the Status of Children Reform Act Cap. 220 both became law on the same date pursuant to Act No. 41/1979.
25 According to s.7 of the Status of Children Reform Act, unless the contrary is proven beyond a reasonable doubt there is a presumption that a male person is the father of a child, *inter alia*, in the following circumstances:
    (a) the person marries the mother of the child after the birth of the child and acknowledges that he is the natural father;
    (b) the person has been adjudged or recognised in his lifetime by a court of competent jurisdiction to be the father of the child;

(c) the person has acknowledged in proceedings for registration of the child, in accordance with the law relating to the registration of births, that he is the father of the child;

(d) a person who is alleged to be the father of the child has given written consent to that child adopting his name in accordance with the law relating to the change of name.

When the Succession Act 1975 originally came into operation on November 13, 1975, the interpretation section of the Act defined child to include an illegitimate child. This was provided that the illegitimate child fell within the ambit of the restricted test therein laid down. According to s.2 of the Succession Act 1975, a child included an illegitimate child of a deceased person if:

(a) that person has been adjudged by the court or a Magistrate's Court to be the father or putative father, or

(b) that person has acknowledged himself to be the father under Section 8(6) of the Registration Act, or

(c) that person has by an affidavit sworn before a Justice of the Peace or a Notary Public, or by other document duly attested and sealed, together with a declaration by the mother of the child contained in the same instrument confirming that that person is the father of the child, admitted paternity, but such affidavit or other document shall be of no effect unless it has been recorded in the Registration Office.

26 Guyana — s.3(1)(d) Family and Dependants Provision Act 22/1990.
Trinidad & Tobago — s.95(1)(a) Succession Act 27/ 1981.

27 *Taylor, Taylor, Taylor v. Philbert* HCA 1345/1977 Trinidad & Tobago (Unreported).

28 [1969] 1 Ch. 283 at 288.

29 HCA 1345/1977 Trinidad & Tobago (Unreported). See also *Ramdaram v. Seusahai and Or.* 284/Reports of Judgments of the High Court of Justice and of the Court of Appeal of Trinidad & Tobago Vol. XIX 1966-69 Part II where Rees, J., observed at p.286 'it is now beyond question that a Judge should not vary a testator's will merely because if he were in the shoes of the testator he might have made a larger provision.'

30 Barbados — R.S.C. O.88 Rules of the Supreme Court 1982, Barbados

Trinidad & Tobago — R.S.C O.90 Orders & Rules of the Supreme Court of Judicature of Trinidad & Tobago 1975

Guyana — According to R.S.C. O.1 r.3 of Guyana, R.S.C. O.99, The Supreme Court Practice 1967 England, may be applied to Guyana. O.1 r.3 provides that: Wherever touching any matter of practice or procedure these Rules are silent, the Rules of the Supreme Court in force immediately before 23rd February, 1970, made in England under and by virtue of the Supreme Court of Judicature Act, 1925, of the United Kingdom or any law amending the same shall apply mutatis mutandis.

However because the Family and Provision Dependants Act of Guyana is modelled on the English Inheritance (Provision for Family and Dependants) Act, 1975, R.S.C.O 99 The Supreme

	Jamaica	Court Practice 1976 England is applied in Guyana in practice. However the substantive application for family provision does not include in its title, any reference to the English Rules. - Part 8 and Part 21 CPR 2002
	The Bahamas	- In the absence of specific rules providing for the procedure to be adopted, RSCO 99 The Supreme Court Practice 2002 is deemed to apply in practice.
31	Barbados	- R.S.C. O.88 r.2
	The Bahamas	
	Guyana	- R.S.C. O.99 r.2, England
32	Barbados	- R.S.C. O.88 r.3
	The Bahamas	-
	Guyana, Jamaica	- R.S.C. O.99 r.3, England
	Trinidad & Tobago	- R.S.C. O.90 r.12.
	Jamaica	- Part 21.4 CPR 2002
33	Trinidad & Tobago	- s. 98 Succession Act 27/1981
	The Bahamas	- s.5 Inheritance Act 2002

34 Section 5 The Inheritance (Provision for Family and Dependants) Act 14/1993.
35 Section 6 Family and Dependants Provision Act 22/1990.
36 Section 58(2), s.100(5) Succession Act Cap. 249.
37 [1995] 2 FLR 24.
38 [1984] 1 FLR 840.
39 [1980] 2 All E.R. 532.
40 (1942) LT Jo 185.
41 H.C,A, 1375/1983 Trinidad & Tobago (Unreported).
42 (1966) 10 W.I.R. 122 at 124.

43	Barbados	- R.S.C. O.88 r.8
	Guyana, Jamaica	- R.S.C. O.99 r.3, England
	Trinidad & Tobago	- R.S.C. O.90 r.8
44	Guyana	- s.5(1) Family and Dependants Provision Act 22/1990
	Jamaica	- s.7(l) The Inheritance (Provisions for Family and Dependants) Act, 14/1993
	Trinidad & Tobago	- s.97, Succession Act 27/1981
	The Bahamas	- s.14, Inheritance Act 2002

45 *Lewis v. Baker* (1966) 10 W.I.R. 122; *Re Clarke,* [1968] 1 All E.R. 451.
46 *Thompson v. Roach and Roach* (1968) 13 W.I.R. 297.
47 *Taylor, Taylor v, Philbert l*-ICA 134 5/1977 Trinidad & Tobago (Unreported).
48 *Franklyn v. Biddy* (1960) 2 W.I.R. 346.

	Jamaica	- s.7(1)(g) The Inheritance (Provision for Family and Dependants) Act 14/1993
49	Guyana	- s.5(2)(a) Family and Dependant Provision Act 22/190.
	Trinidad & Tobago	- s.97(2) Succession Act 27/1981

50 (1968) 13 W.I.R. 297.
51 (1968) 13 W.I.R. 470.
52 (1966) 10 W.I.R. 122.

53 *Ibid.*
54 (1968) 13 W.I.R. 470.
55 (1968) 13 W.I.R. 297.
56 See on this s,41(5) Matrimonial Proceedings and Property Act Ch. 45:51 No. 2 of 1972.
57 [1981] 2 All E.R. 796.
58 *Ibid.*
59 [1991]1 All E.R. 236.
60 See *Jelley v Iliffe* [1981]2 All ER 29 and *Bishop v Pumley* supra at n. 59.
61 [1981] 2 All E.R. 29 at p.36.
62 [1980] 1 All E.R. 266 at pp. 270-276.
63 [1981] 2 All E.R. 29 at p 34.
64 s. 1000) Succession Act Cap. 249
65 Jamaica — s.7(2) The Inheritance (Provision for Family and Dependants) Act 14/1993

   The Bahamas — s.14(3) Inheritance Act 2002

   Trinidad & Tobago — s.97(3) Succession Act 27/1981
66 [1980] 1 Ch.461. See also *Re Jennings* (dec'd) [1994] 3 All ER 670, *Re Dennis* (dec'd) [1981] 2 All E.R. 140.
67 [1996] 1 All E.R. 670.
68 [1967] 3 All E.R. 429 [1967] 1 WLR 1482.
69 [1994] 3 All E.R. 27.
70 *Ibid.*
71 *Re: Leach (dec'd)* [1985] 2 All ER 754, *Re Callaghan (dec'd)* [1984] 3 All E.R. 790.
72 Section 10 Family and Dependants Provision Act 22/1990.
73 Section 11 Family and Dependants Provision Act 22/1990.
74 Section 12(3)(4)(5) Family and Dependant Provision Act 22/1990.
75 Section 13 Family and Dependants Provision Act 22/1990.
76 Section 13 The Inheritance (Provision for Family and Dependants Act 14/1993.
77 Section 14 The Inheritance (Provision for Family and Dependants Act 14/1993.
78 Section 19 Inheritance Act 2002.
79 Section 22(3) Inheritance Act 2002.
80 Section 102(2) Succession Act 27/1981.
81 Section 102(1) Succession Act 27/1981.
82 Section 103 Succession Act 27/1981.
83 Section 104 Succession Act 27/1981.
84 Section 105 Succession Act 27/1981.
85 See also s.103 of the Succession Act Cap. 249 which provides that with respect to dispositions made for the purpose of *inter alia*, disinheriting children of the deceased, the term disposition includes a *donatio morris causa* and consideration given by a purchaser with respect to property disposed of by a donee.
86 Guyana — s.3(2) Family and Dependants Provision Act 22/1990

   Jamaica — s.4 Inheritance (Family and Dependants Provision) Act 14/1993

   The Bahamas — s.12(1) Inheritance Act 2002

   Trinidad & Tobago — s.95 Succession Act 37/1981 as amended by the Distribution of Estates Act 28/2000
87 Barbados — s.58(4)-(5), s.100(2) Succession Act Cap, 249

	Guyana	- s,4(1)(a) and s.4(2) Family and Dependants Provision Act 22/1990
	Jamaica	- s.6 The Inheritance (Provision for Family and Dependants) Act, 14/1993
	Trinidad & Tobago	- s.96(1)(a) Succession Act 27/1981 as amended by the Distribution of Estates Act 28/2000
	The Bahamas	- s.13 Inheritance Act 2002
88	Barbados	- s.58(4)-(5), s.100(3) Succession Act Cap, 249
	Guyana	- s.4(1)(b) Family and Dependants Provision Act 22/1990
	Jamaica	- s.6(1)(b) Inheritance (Family and Dependants Provision) Act 14/1993
	The Bahamas	- s.13(1)(b) Inheritance Act 2002
	Trinidad & Tobago	- s.6(1)(a) Succession Act 27/1981 as amended by the Distribution of Estates Act 28/2000
89	Guyana	- s.8 Family and Dependants Provision Act 22/1990
	Jamaica	- ss.10, 11 Inheritance (Family and Dependants Provision) Act 11/1993
	The Bahamas	- s17 Inheritance Act 2002
	Trinidad & Tobago	- s.100 Succession Act as amended by the Distribution of Estates Act 27/1981
90	Guyana	- s.7 Family and Dependants Provision Act 22/1990
	Jamaica	- s.8 Inheritance (Family and Dependants Provision) Act 14/1993
	The Bahamas	- s.8 Inheritance Act 2002
	Trinidad & Tobago	- s.99 Succession Act 27/1981 as amended by the Distribution of EstatesAct 28/2000
91	Guyana	- s.4(1)(c) Family and Dependants Provision Act 22/1990
	Trinidad & Tobago	- s.96(1)(c) Succession Act 27/1981 as amended by the Distribution of Estates Act 28/2000

27

Costs and Fees

COSTS

In the absence of an agreement for remuneration, the quantum of an attorney-at-law's fees with respect to non-contentious probate matters is regulated in Barbados, Guyana and Trinidad & Tobago by legislation and in the Eastern Caribbean territories, Jamaica and The Bahamas by practice, custom and convention.

Barbados, Guyana and Trinidad & Tobago

With respect to the above jurisdictions, statutory powers have been conferred on the relevant rule-making bodies[1] to formulate rules for regulating and prescribing the quantum of remuneration an attorney may change with respect to non-contentious business matters.

GUIDELINES IN GENERAL

In determining the appropriate fees to be charged by an attorney-at-law with respect to non-contentious probate matters, statutory and other regulatory guidelines are required to be taken into account by the respective rule making bodies of these territories.

Code of Ethics[2]

Trinidad & Tobago and Barbados

The relevant rule of the Code of Ethics made under and pursuant to the respective Legal Profession Acts of the above territories prescribes that in charging fees an attorney at law shall not charge fees that are unfair and unreasonable.

In determining the fairness and reasonableness of fees the following is required to be taken into account:

(a) the time and labour required, the novelty and difficulty of the questions involved and the skill required to perform the legal service properly;
(b) the likelihood that the acceptance of the particular employment will preclude other employment by the attorney-at-law;
(c) the fee customarily charged in the locality for similar legal services;
(d) the amount, if any involved;
(e) the time limitations imposed by the client or by the circumstances;
(f) the nature and length of the professional relationship with the client;
(g) the experience, reputation and ability of the attorney-at-law concerned; and
(h) any scale of fees or recommended guide as to charges prescribed by law or by the Judicial Advisory Council/Law Association.

STATUTORY GUIDELINES

Apart from the general guidelines set out in the Code of Ethics, s.35 of the Legal Profession Act Cap. 370A Barbados and s.52 of the Legal Profession Act 21/1986 Trinidad & Tobago, provide that in prescribing any scale of fees the Judicial Advisory Council/Law Association should take into account *inter alia* the following:

(a) the position of the person for whom the attorney is concerned in the business, that is, whether as vendor/purchaser;
(b) the amount of capital, money or rent to which the business relates;
(c) number and importance of the documents prepared and perused without regard to length; and
(d) the skill and labour and responsibility involved in the business on the part of the attorney.

OTHER GUIDELINES

Trinidad & Tobago

The Solicitors Remuneration Professional Charges Order made under s.55 of the repealed Solicitors Act Ch. 6:50 but deemed to have been saved by s.52(4) of the Legal Profession Act also sets out regulatory guidelines. The Solicitors' Remuneration Professional Charges Order contains essentially the same guidelines as provided for by Part B r.10 of the Code of Ethics.

Guyana

Order 60 Part V Appendix V of the Rules of the High Court Cap. 3:02

sets out the matters to be taken into account by an attorney-at-law in charging fees with respect to non-contentious matters. These guidelines are essentially the same as those set out in the Code of Ethics of Barbados and Trinidad & Tobago and include *inter alia*:

(a) the complexity of the matter or the difficulty or novelty of the questions raised;
(b) the skill, labour, specialised knowledge and responsibility involved on the part of the attorney-at-law; and
(c) the number and importance of the documents prepared or perused, without regard to length.

COSTS CHARGEABLE BY AN ATTORNEY-AT-LAW

Trinidad & Tobago[3]

With effect from May 1, 1997, the maximum fees chargeable by attorneys for the preparation of applications for probate or administration in common form is regulated by the Attorneys-at-Law (Remuneration) (Non-contentious Business) Rules 1997 made under s.52 of the Legal Profession Act 1986. Schedule 4 of the rules provides as follows:

1. The following scale of charges shall be applicable for preparing applications for Probate or Letters of Administration in common form and for all preliminary work done in connection therewith, including searches at the Depository of Wills of living persons and the Probate Registry, the taking of instructions and preparation of an inventory of estate and attendance to obtain or reseal a Grant:

	Value of Estate	Scale of Charges
(a)	Not exceeding $10,000.00	Five percent of such value with a minimum fee of $500.00
(b)	Exceeding $10,000.00 and not exceeding $250,000.00	Five percent on the first $100,000.00 of such value and three percent on the excess beyond $10,000.00
(c)	Exceeding $250,000.00	The same fee chargeable if the value of the Estate were $250,000.00 plus one percent on the excess beyond $250,000.00

2. The above scale of charges shall also apply in the case of:

   (a) applications for Double or cessate Probate and *de bonis non*; and
   (b) applications for the sealing or resealing of Probates

3. Fees for the administration of an estate including the calling in and distribution of same in accordance with the directions and provisions in a will or in accordance with the laws upon intestacy shall be fair and reasonable and shall be determined in accordance with the matters set out in Schedule 3.

Barbados[4]

   (a) Original Grant in Barbados -
Up to $10,000	$350.00
On the next $40,000	2%
On the next $500,000	$1\frac{1}{2}$%
Thereafter	¾%

   (b) Preparing bond for postponement of payment of death duties — $100.00

   (c) Resealing Grant outside of Island - 1 1/2% of estate in overseas country - minimum fee of — $350.00

   (d) Resealing Foreign Grant in Barbados - the fee as prescribed for an original grant in Barbados calculated on the gross value of the estate in Barbados

   (e) On a *grant de bonis non* on the above scale but calculated on the unadministered portion of the estate

   (f) On a second Grant — $250.00

Guyana[5]

   Estate Duty and Inventory
On the first $750.00 of the net value of the estate declared to in Guyana	30.00
On the next $49,250.00	two per cent

On the next $50,000.00	five per cent

Probate and Administration in common form or resealing grant of probate or administration.

On the first $750.00 of the gross value of the estate grant of probate or administration.

On the first $750.00 of the gross value of the estate declared to in Guyana	40.00
On the next $750.00	40.00
On the next $1,000.00	30.00
On the next $2,500.00	75.00
On the gross value of the estate in excess of $5,000.00 for each succeeding $5,000.00 or part thereof	30.00

Administration Bond —

Where the amount of the Bond does not exceed $1,000.00	20.00
Where the amount of the Bond does not exceed $5,000.00	35.00
Where the amount of the Bond exceeds $5,000.00	50.00
Preparing and filing accounts and affidavits in support thereof from	30.00

Eastern Caribbean territories (save St Lucia)

In the Eastern Caribbean territories there are no local statutory rule making bodies. However by practice, custom and convention the local Bar Associations of the respective Eastern Caribbean territories publish and prescribe a recommended scale of fees with respect to contentious and non-contentious matters.

In determining the recommended scale of fees with respect to non-contentious probate matters the various bar associations are guided by the Rules of the Supreme Court (Non-Contentious Probate Costs) 1956, England, the provisions of which are received in these territories. This is by virtue of the relevant reception provision of the Eastern Caribbean Supreme Court Acts of these territories[6] which provides that:

> Subject to rules of court, the law and practice relating to solicitors and the taxation and receiving of cost in force in England shall extend to and be in force

in the relevant territory and shall apply to all persons lawfully practising thereon as solicitors of the Court.

Pursuant to the provision of these Rules, a solicitor in effect takes into account the equivalent of the matters set out in the respective Code of Ethics of Trinidad & Tobago and Barbados.

In addition, the Organisation of the Eastern Caribbean States Bar Association (O.E.C.S) Code of Ethics which came into effect from January 15, 1991; is followed and applied in principle although it is of no legally binding effect.

In this regard Part B r.10 of the O.E.C.S Code of Ethics the provision of which are identical to the Code of Ethics of Barbados and Trinidad & Tobago, sets out the matters to be taken into account in determining the fees to be charged by attorney-at-law in non-contentious and contentious matters.

St Lucia

As is the case with the other Eastern Caribbean territories, fees charged by legal practitioners with respect to contentious as well as non-contentious matters are determined by the Bar Association of St Lucia. Although the Bar Association is an incorporated society with no statutory powers, nevertheless by convention and custom the Association determines and prescribes the scale of fees chargeable by barristers and solicitors.

Unlike the other Eastern Caribbean territories however, the Supreme Court Act of St Lucia contains no equivalent reception provision. As such the Solicitor Remuneration Order does not extend to and form part of the law of St Lucia.

In practice the factors outlined in the Rules of the Supreme Court (Non-Contentious Probate Costs) 1956 and more recently Part B r.10 of O.E.C.S. Code of Ethics are taken into account in determining the legal fees chargeable by solicitors with respect to non-contentious probate matters.

Jamaica

Prior to March 1993, an attorney-at-law's fees with respect to non-contentious probate matters were charged in accordance with the recommended scale of fees published by the General Legal Council of the Jamaica Bar Association. In arriving at this recommended scale of fees the Bar Association took into account the provisions of the Legal Profession (Canons of Profession Ethics) Rules made under the Legal Profession Act, the equivalent of the Code of Ethics of Barbados and Trinidad & Tobago.

However with the passage of the Fair Competition Act in March 1993, the Fair Trading Commission which was established under the Act, contended that the Legal Profession Act (Canons of Professional Ethics) Rules, including the canons made thereunder were governed by this legislation. As a consequence attorneys began charging fees in accordance with their own fee structure. However in 1995, the General Legal Council, eventually brought proceedings against the Fair Trading Commission,[7] seeking and obtaining a declaration that the Legal Profession Act was not governed by the Fair Competition Act.

As a result of this judgment, the position with respect to attorneys-at-law's cost is unsettled and it is the practice at present for attorneys-at-law to charge in accordance with their own fee structure.

The Bahamas

Although s.28 of the Legal Profession Act 20/1992 provides that:

> Nothing in the Act shall be construed or have the effect to authorising the imposition or sanction by the Bar Association or the Bar Council of a minimum scale of fees for services rendered by a counsel,

In practice, The Bahamian Bar Association publishes a recommended scale of professional fees with respect to contentious and non-contentious matters. The recommended scale of fees, although of no legal force, is followed by practitioners to the extent that in taxing Bills of Costs, the taxing master applies the recommended scale of fees as a guideline for purposes of determining the appropriate fees to be charged in a matter.

COURT FEES

Court Fees payable on filing of documents

Filing fees are payable in the form of postage stamps except in Guyana and The Bahamas where the fees are payable in cash or by cheque.

Antigua & Barbuda[8]

	$
Filing of documents	10.00
On taking a recognizance or bond	50.00

Barbados[9]

Fees to be taken by the Registrar on application for Probate or Administration, and to seal Commonwealth Probates.

		$
1.	Where the estate does nor exceed $1,500	25.00
2.	Where the estate exceeds $1,500 but does not exceed $10,000	50.00
3.	Where the estate exceeds $10,000	
	(a) fee on application	30.00
	(b) fee on issue of or on resealing grant on gross value of estate	
	(i) exceeding $10,000 but not exceeding $50,000	150.00
	(ii) exceeding $50,000 but not exceeding $100,000	250.00
	(iii) exceeding $100,000	500.00

Dominica[10]

		$
115.	On the lodging of a will	1.50
116.	On an application for a grant of probate or letters of administration	4.00
117.	On sealing a grant of probate or letters of administration	4.00
118.	On a citation	4.00
119.	On entry of a caveat	15.00

Grenada[11]

	$	
On petition	10.00	Petition
On citation	10.00	Citation

Guyana[12]

		$
1.	Drawing act of deposit of will of living person lodged for safe custody, registering same, sealing of document, making copy of act of deposit, and keeping will	10.00
2.	On deposit of will of deceased person, drawing act of deposit, affidavit in proof of due execution, and registering where the gross value of the	

	estate does not exceed $5,000.00	25.00
	exceeds $5,000.00	35.00
3.	On application for probate or letters of administration by Registrar	7.00
4.	On any other application for probate or letters of administration	
	Where the gross value of the estate does not exceed $5,000.00	25.00
	exceeds $5,000.00	35.00
5.	On the issue of probate or letters of administration —	
	On the first $500.00 of the gross value of the estate in Guyana	8.00
	On the next $1,000.00	8.00
	On the next $3,500.00	12.00
	On the next $10,000.00	12.00
	On the next $35,000.00 to $50,000.00	40.00
	On the gross value of the estate in excess of $50,000.00	50.00
6.	On the issue of grant of probate or letters of administration de bonis non or of probate or grant of administration pursuant to leave reserved, where full fees have not already been paid on prior issue of probate or administration in respect of the same estate, the balance to complete the fees shall be paid and in every case in addition to the full fees paid —	
	Where the gross value of the estate in Guyana does not exceed $5,000.00	15.00
	exceeds $5,000.00	30.00
7.	For drawing, swearing and registering second or subsequent affidavit in proof of due execution of will	7.00
8.	For filing application for summons to witness to prove due execution of will	5.00
9.	For each entry of caveat or filing any objections to the validity of a will	7.00
10.	On citation to accept or refuse a grant	7.00
11.	Sealing and certifying copies thereof for service, each	5.00
12.	Settling and signing abstract of citation for advertisement	5.00

13. For filing of consent of creditors to executor
or administrator administering estate of a
deceased person which is found to be solvent   5.00

Montserrat[13]

	$
Application for grant	8.50
Oath to lead the grant	5.50
Order for grant to issue	8.50
Administration bond (with will annexed)	8.50
Affidavit of due execution	5.50
Publication of Advertisement (2)	2.50
Reason for Delay in Applying	2.50
Renunciation	2.50
Declaration and Account of the Estate	5.50
Death certificate	2.50
Sealing of grant of probate/letters of administration with will annexed	12.00
Sealing of letters of administration	6.00
Entry of caveat	25.00
Citation	6.00

St Christopher & Nevis and Anguilla [14]

	$
On the lodging of a will	0.48
On an application for a grant of probate or letters of administration	1.20
On sealing a grant of probate or letters of Administration	1.20
On a citation	1.20
On entry of a caveat	4.80

St Lucia[15]

Probate and Letters of Administration	Fees
	$

39. On filing a petition or application for probate,
including order and probate, if non-contentious
or uncontested and for Letters of Administration   20.00
56. For sealing and document in any case not otherwise
provided for   5.00

St Vincent & the Grenadines[16]

Estate Documents

	Stamps
	$
Warrant to Act	2.00
Application for Grant	5.00
Petition	20.00
Oath of Administrator/Executor	10.00
Affidavit of Accounts	10.00
Certificates: Death, birth, marriage	2.00
Exhibit (each)	2.00
Will (probate)	5.00
Wills (letters of administration with will annexed)	5.00
Caveat	5.00
Citation	20.00
Grant	20.00

The Bahamas

Grants of Probate

Estates

	Under $142.00	$3.29
Between	$143-$286	$4.79
Between	$287-$1,428.	$5.50
Over	$1,428.00	$6.92

Letters of Administration

Estates

	0-$142.00	$2.07+10¢
Between	$143-$286	$3.93
Between	$286.00-$1,428.00	$4.83
Over	$1,428.00	$6.61
Caveats		$0.42¢

Trinidad & Tobago[17]

	$	c.
1. Where the estate does not exceed $480[18] for all fees and charges	4	80
2. Where the estate exceeds $480 but does not exceed		

	$1,440 for all fees and charges	12	00
3.	In all other cases:		
	(a) Fee on application	7	20
	(b) Fee on issue of or on resealing grant on gross value of estate:		
	Exceeding $1,440 and not exceeding $4,800	4	80
	Exceeding $4,800 and not exceeding $14,400	7	20
	Exceeding $14,400 and not exceeding $48,000	12	00
	Exceeding $48,000 and not exceeding	24	00
4.	Second or subsequent grants: When the application is for a grant of administration *de bonis non* or of probate or grant of administration pursuant to leave reserved, when full duty has already been paid on prior issue of probate or administration in respect of the same estate	2	40
5.	On each entry of caveat	1	20
6.	On renewal of caveat	0	60
7.	On issue of warning to caveator	0	60
8.	On issue of citation	2	40
9.	On other documents to be filed	0	24
10.	On any application for an order to convey or transfer land under subsection (2) of section 12 of the Administration of Estates Ordinance, or for directions under section 14 of the said Ordinance	1	20
11.	For searching probate file	0	60

Note. On applications to reseal British or Colonial Probates the above fees will be taken on the gross value of the estate situate in the Colony.

Jamaica

Stamp Duty on Probate Documents

There is no court or filing fee payable per se. However, prior to the coming into operation on January 1, 2003, of the Judicature (Rules of Court) Rules of the Supreme Court (Fees) 2002, stamp duty was payable on certain probate documents pursuant to the provisions of the repealed fees (Supreme Court) Rules 1941 as amended by the Fees (Supreme Court) (Amendment) Rules 1974. The Fees that were payable were as follows:

1.	Stamp on Oath of Executor or Administrator	$2.00
2.	Stamp on Affidavit of Attesting Witness	$2.00
3.	Stamp on Inventory	$0.40

4. Stamp on Declaration of Counting Inventory
— per folio of 72 words ... $0.02
5. Stamp on Declaration of Counting of Probate
& Will or Letters of Administration — per folio
of 72 words ... $0.02
6. Probate or Letters of Administration Grant

However, in accordance with the Rules of the Supreme Court (Fees) 2002, on an application for a grant, a flat fee of $2,000 is payable on one document only, the oath.

(b) Stamp Duty on Grant

By virtue of the Judicature (Rules of Court) Rules of the Supreme Court (Fees) 2000, the following is the stamp duty payable on the grants:

	Duty Payable
Where the net value of the estate does not exceed $500,000.00	$2,000.00
For every dollar over the next $2,000,000.00	$0.25
For every dollar of the remainder	$0.30
Resealing Applications	$2,000.00
Grants Limited to Settled Lands	$2,000.00

MISCELLANEOUS

Trinidad & Tobago[19]

Filing/Registration Fees

These are fees which are paid for the registration of a will with probate and letters of administration (including resealing), where the estate within the State and exclusive of what the deceased shall have possessed of or entitled to as a trustee for any other person and nor beneficially,
does not exceed the value of $50,000 ... $ 25.00
exceeds the value of $50,000 and

does not exceed the value of $100,000	$ 50.00
exceeds the value of $100,000 and does not exceed the value of $250,000	$ 75.00
exceeds the value of $250,000 and does not exceed the value of $400,000	$100.00
exceeds the value of $400,000 and does not exceed the value of $500,000	$200.00
exceeds the value of $500,000 and does not exceed the value of $750,000	$300.00
exceeds the value of $750,000 and does not exceed the value of $1,000,000	$400.00
exceeds the value of $1,000,000	$500.00

The Bahamas

Recording Fees
Recording of Will and Grant of $1.50 Per Page.
Advertising fees

Advertising Fees	$0.14

Stamp Duty

Stamp Duty on application for the grant	$3.00

Notes

1. Rule Making Bodies

Barbados	- Pursuant to s.35 Legal Profession Act Cap. 370A, the Bar Association with the approval of the Judicial Advisory Council
Guyana	- Pursuant to s.67 of the High Court Act Cap. 3:02; the Rules Committee consisting of the Chancellor, the Chief Justice, a puisne judge, four practising Attorneys-at-Law.
Trinidad & Tobago	- Pursuant to s.52 Legal Profession Act 21/1986, the Law Association with the approval of the Chief Justice and Minister of Legal Affairs.

2. | | |
   |---|---|
   | Barbados | - Part VIII r.66 The Legal Profession Code of Ethics, 198 |
   | Trinidad & Tobago | - Part B r. 10 Third Schedule Code of Ethics, Legal Profession Act 21/1986. |

3. Attorneys-At-Law(Remuneration)(Non-Contentious Business) Rules 1997 made under s.52 of the Legal Profession Act 27/1986

4. See The Attorneys-at-Law (Remuneration for Non-Contentious Business) Rules, 1983 made by the Bar Association in exercise of the powers conferred by Section 35 of the Legal

Profession Act Cap. 370A.
5 Appendix R Scale of Costs etc. of the Rules of the High Court made under s.67 of the High Court Act Cap. 3:02.

6	Anguilla	- s.78 Eastern Caribbean Supreme Court (Anguilla) Ord. 1982
	Antigua & Barbuda	- s.77 Eastern Caribbean Supreme Court (Antigua & Barbuda) Act Cap. 143
	Dominica	- s.78 Eastern Caribbean Supreme Court (Dominica) Act Ch. 4:02
	Grenada	- s.78 West Indies Supreme Court (Grenada) Act 17 1967 renamed Eastern Caribbean Supreme Court (Grenada) Act by Act 19 of 1991
	Montserrat	- s.78 Eastern Caribbean Supreme Court (Montserrat) Act (cited under S.I. 1983 1108) as the Anguilla, Montserrat and the Virgin Islands (Supreme Court) Order 1983.
	St Christopher & Nevis	- s.78 West Indies Supreme Court (St Christopher & Nevis) Act 17/1975 renamed Eastern Caribbean Supreme Court (St Christopher & Nevis) Act
	St Vincent & the Grenadines	- s.78 Eastern Caribbean Supreme Court (St Vincent & the Grenadines) Act Cap. 18.

7 The Judicature (Rules of Court) Act 59/1991 which provides for the costs payable to an attorney-at-law in the Supreme Court does not contain any provisions with respect to non-contentious probate matters.
8 See Supreme Court (Fees in Civil Proceedings) (Replacement of Schedule) 1991 S.I. 36/1991 for Item 31 and 109 respectively)
9 See Schedule to Supreme Court (Non-Contentious) Probate Rules, 1959 made under s.46 of the Supreme Court of Judicature Act Cap. 117.
10 Pursuant to the High Court (Civil Proceedings) Fees Order made under s.2 of the Courts of Justice Fees Act Chap. 4:31.
11 See Supreme Court Fees made under s.2(1) of the Stamp Act Cap. 315.
12 Appendix V Fees in Non-Contentious Business repealed and replaced by r.5 of 1986 of the Rules of the High Court made under s.67 of the High Court Act Cap. 3:02.
13 See Supreme Court Fees Civil Proceedings Order 36/1973 made under Courts of Justice Fees Act Cap. 230.
14 Pursuant to s.2 of the Courts of Justices Fees Act.
15 Cited as the Eastern Caribbean Supreme Court (St Lucia) (Tariff of Fees) Rules made under the Eastern Caribbean Supreme Court (St Lucia) Act 1969.
16 See Statutory Rules and Orders 1996 No. 1 (Gazetted 16th January, 1996) pursuant to s.5 of the Registrar's Act Cap. 212 Registrars (Fees) Notice, 1995.
17 See Third Schedule Part I of the Wills and Probate Ordinance Ch. 8 No, 2.
18 See the N.C.B.R. (Amendment) Rules made by the Rules Committee under s.24 of the Wills & Probate Ordinance Ch. 8 No. 2 and s.78 of the Supreme Court of Judicature Act Chap. 4:01 (published in L.N. 16/1984).
19 See Part II of the Wills & Probate Ordinance Ch. 8 No. 2 as amended by the Provisional Collection of Taxes Order made under s.3 of the Provisional Collection of Taxes Act Chap. 74:01.

Appendix I

Non-Contentious Probate/Business Rules

BAHAMAS

(Section 41)
(Commencement 6th October 1917)

1. (1) These Rules may be cited as The Probate Rules.
   (2) The expressions used in these Rules, unless the context otherwise requires, shall have the same meanings as an assigned to similar expressions by The Supreme Court Act or by The Interpretation Act.
   "The applicant" means the person seeking from the Court a grant of Probate or Letters of Administration, or the sealing of Probate or Letters of Administration, or other testamentary paper granted out of the jurisdiction of the Court.
2. An application for Probate or Letters of Administration, or for sealing a Probate or Letters of Administration or other testamentary paper granted out of the jurisdiction, must be made either in person or by counsel, except where the applicant is out of the jurisdiction in which case the may authorise someone by a Power of Attorney to make the application on his behalf, and the person so authorised may appear in person or by counsel.
3. An application must be made by filing a Petition in the Registry of the Court, after payment of the stamp duties and Court fees specified in Rule 30(2).
4. The following documents necessary to lead the grant must also be filed in the Registry:
   -In the case of Probate—

   (a) the original will or a photostatic copy thereof;
   (b) an affidavit of an attesting witness in proof of the due execution of the will, and if both attesting witnesses are dead or if from any

other circumstances no affidavit can be obtained from either of them, resort must be had to other persons (if any) who may have been present at the execution of the will or codicil. If no affidavit of any such other person can be obtained evidence on affidavit must be procured of that fact and of the handwriting of the deceased and the subscribing witnesses and also of any circumstances which may raise a presumption in favour of the rule execution;
(c) an affidavit of an executor showing the date and place of death, giving in the Schedule thereto a description of all the property of the deceased to be affected by the grant applied for and stating the estimated value of the personal estate.

In the case of Letters of Administration—

(a) an affidavit of the applicant proving and stating the same facts as those required in an executor's affidavit, and stating the grounds on which the applicant bases his claim; and
(b) if for Letters of Administration with the will annexed an affidavit of proof of the due execution of the will, to which affidavit the original will or a photostatic copy thereof must be made an exhibit. Where a will is filed, the Registrar may accept a fair copy thereof to be annexed to the Letters.

5. Where the application is for Letters of Administration of the estate of a bastard dying a bachelor, or a spinster, or a widower, or widow, without issue, notice of the application must be given by the Registrar to the Attorney General, and no grant shall issue until the Attorney General has signified the course he intends to take.

6. (1) Where an application is made in person and the goods and chattels of the deceased are under the value of ten pounds and the real estate is of very small value, the papers, where the applicant resides in New Providence, must be prepared by the Registrar, and where the applicant resides on an Out Island by the commissioner who, on completion thereof, shall forward the same without delay to the Registrar, together with the stamp duties and fees specified in Rule 30(2).

(2) Where counsel appears, he must prepare the papers and submit them for approval.

7. An affidavit may be sworn in an Out Island before the commissioner or other justice of the peace in such Out Island and in New Providence

before the Registrar or a notary public practising within the Colony.
8. Every testamentary paper referred to in the affidavit to which any deponent is sworn must be marked by the deponent and by the person before whom the affidavit is sworn in accordance with Rule 7.
9. An affidavit intended to be used before a Judge must first be filed in the Registry.
10. No Probate will be issued until after the lapse of fourteen days from the death of the testator except in a case of urgency when the facts of such case shall be laid before a Judge on motion in open Court.
11. (1) Where Letters of Administration are applied for, the Registrar shall, on the filing of the necessary papers, insert a notice of the application in three successive issues of the *Gazette* stating that the application will be set down to be heard by a Judge at the expiration of the time to be specified in such notice.
    (2) The time to be so specified for the setting down for hearing of an application, in relation to the estate of a deceased person whose place of residence had been at New Providence, shall not be earlier than fourteen days from the date of the notice. In relation to the estate of a deceased person whose place of residence had been on an Out Island, the Registrar when fixing the time to be specified in the notice shall allow such period, not less than fourteen days, as will afford the Court an opportunity for ascertaining whether notice of the application for Letters had been published at the Out Island in manner hereafter required.
    (3) Letters of Administration, in respect of the estate of a deceased person whose place of residence had been on an Out Island, shall not be issued unless and until the Court is satisfied that notice of the application therefore had been duly advertised at such Out Island. For this purpose (except in the case hereinafter expressly provided for) the Registrar shall by the earlier opportunity have a copy of the *Gazette* notice of the application sent to the commissioner of the Out Island with a request that he will cause the same to be affixed for publication in a conspicuous place near to the principal door of the police court or magistrate's office thereat for a period of at least six days, and that he will forward by the next return post thereafter a notification of the receipt of such notice and of its publication.

    Provided that it shall not be requisite for the Registrar to send a copy of the *Gazette* notice to the Out Island if it is proved to his satisfaction that the commissioner had already, and before the filing of the necessary papers in the Registrar's Office, caused a clear and sufficient notice to be affixed near to the door of his police court or magistrate's office to the effect that the applicant therein named had expressed his intention of applying at the earliest possible opportunity, to the Supreme Court for Letters of Administration of the estate of the deceased person therein named.

12. When all the papers deemed by the Registrar to be necessary in the case of an application for Probate have been filed or in the case of an application for Letters of Administration when the time mentioned in the *Gazette* notice has expired, and no caveat has been entered, the Registrar, by direction of a Judge, shall fix a day for the hearing of the application and on the day so fixed shall attend before the Judge with the papers.
13. Evidence of the identity of the applicant maybe required in cases where the application is made in person.
14. A Judge may require such evidence as he may think necessary for proof of identity, or for further proof of any fact stated in an affidavit, or for any other purpose. He shall direct whether the evidence shall be given on affidavit or *viva voce*.
15. If the Judge decided not to grant the application, the Registrar shall notify the applicant of such decision together with the grounds therefore, and shall certify a claim for the refund to the applicant of the stamps and fees mentioned in the proviso to Rule 30(3).
16. If the Judge decides to grant the application, the Registrar shall notify the applicant that upon the execution and filing of the necessary bond or bonds, the grant will issue.
17. Where the Judge decides to grant Probate or Letters of Administration, the applicant shall be required, in accordance with the provisions of The Probate Act, to enter into a bond with two or more sureties in the sum of one hundred pounds, with the conditions specified in the first section of the said Act.
18. Where the Judge decides to grant Letters of Administration, the applicant shall also be required to enter into another bond, to be called the "Administration Bond", for the due administration of the estate. The Administration Bond must be given in double the amount of the estate. If the estate is under fifty pounds, one surety will be required, if it is over that amount, two sureties will be required; unless, in any particular case, the Judge may approve of only one surety.
19. The Administration Bond shall be in such prescribed form as is specially applicable to the circumstances of the particular case; that is to say, Form X for administration of an estate under Letters with a will annexed; Form XI for administration of an intestate's estate; Form XII where the applicant had sought the grant as a creditor of the estate.

20. Where a grant is to be made to an applicant residing or being in the Island of New Providence, the bonds must be attested by the Registrar. Where a grant is to be made to an applicant residing and being at an Out Island the bonds must be attested by the commissioner.
21. (1) Upon the necessary bonds having been duly executed and all Court fees and stamp duties having been paid, the Judge will direct the Registrar to prepare the grant. The Judge will then sign it and the Registrar will issue it.
    (2) The Registrar is to take care that the copy of the will to be annexed to Letters of Probate, or Letters of Administration *cum testamento annexo*, is fairly and properly written and he is to reject that which is otherwise. The Registrar shall carefully examine the said copy and write "Correct copy" with his initials at the foot thereof and apply the seal of the Court thereon. When the copy is made in the Registry, and exceeds six folios (of seventy-two words) in length, the Registrar shall charge an extra fee of sixpence for each folio in excess of the said six folios.
22. In the case of a grant of Letters of Probate or Letters of Administration *cum testamento annexo,* the Judge will sign a duplicate (or office) copy of such grant, which copy shall be attached to the will and transmitted therewith by the Registrar to the Registrar of Records, who after recording shall return the same to the Registrar for filing.
23. The Judge will, if necessary, at any time issue a warrant of appraisement directing certain persons to ascertain the value of the personal estate of the deceased, or any part thereof, and to make a return setting forth the nature and value of the same and such return must be filed in the Registry.
24. The persons making the return referred to in Rule 23 must at the time of making it also make a declaration as to its truth. This declaration in the Island of New Providence must be made before the Registrar, and in an out island must be made before the commissioner.
25. Where application is made for the resealing of a Probate or Letters of Administration or other testamentary paper granted out of the jurisdiction or any duplicate or certified copy thereof, the applicant shall lodge such document in the Registry and shall also file a copy thereof certified as a correct copy and an affidavit showing the domicile of the deceased, the place and date of his death and a description and the estimated value of the estate within the Colony. Upon the resealing, the document lodged in the Registry when duly resealed shall be returned to the applicant and the copy filed in the Registry shall also be resealed and transmitted to the Registrar of Records, who, after recording, shall return the same to the Registrar of the Court for filing.

26. Notice that the application has been made shall (unless otherwise ordered by a Judge) be published in the same way as in the case of an application for Letters of Administration. On the expiration of the time notified, if no caveat has been entered, the Registrar, by direction of the Judge, will fix a day for the hearing of the application.
27. The applicant must be prepared to give adequate security for the payment of debts due from the estate to creditors in the Colony, if the Judge so requires it. He must also give a bond as required by section 2 of The Probate Act and, where Letters of Administration are sought to be sealed, also a bond for the due administration of the estate found in the Colony.
28. The Registrar, upon sealing any such document, shall without delay give written notice of such sealing to the Court, Registry or office from which such document has issued.
29. All other matters in connection with the sealing of testamentary papers granted out of the jurisdiction shall be governed and regulated by these Rules with the necessary changes.
30. (1) All Court fees and stamp duties payable in respect of matters transacted under these Rules shall be paid to the Registrar, or on an out island to the commissioner, in the following manner.

    (2) At or before the filing of the Petition the applicant shall (unless, in any particular case, otherwise ordered by a Judge) deposit with the Registrar, or in a case where the applicant resides in an out island shall pay to the commissioner, to be deposited with the Registrar, the value in money of the stamp duties and fees, payable in probate matters according to the following scale.[1]
    Plus, in the case of an application for Letters of Administration, the amount of stamp duty chargeable upon the principal sum in the Administration Bond (which sum is, according to Rule 18, to be in double the declared value of the personal estate).

    (3) The Registrar shall give the applicant a receipt for the deposit which shall be paid into the Treasury; and such deposit shall be received as made in respect of fees and stamps payable upon the following documents: the "Petition", the "Affidavits" mentioned in Rule 4, and the "Order of the Court", and in addition (in contemplation of the application being granted) the "Bond, or Bonds", the "Grant" and the "Return of Personal Estate":

---

[1] N.B. rr. 50-56 are no longer applicable since the passage on 1 August 1982 of the Probates and Letters of Administration (Resealing) Act Cap 247, makes new provisions for resealing of grants in Barbados.

Provided that, in a case where a judge shall decide not to issue a grant, the Registrar shall certify a claim for the refund from the Treasury to the applicant of such portion of the applicant's deposit as represents the stamps and fees payable in respect of the bond or bonds, the grant and the return as aforesaid.

(4) In a case where fees other than those herein referred to become payable, such fees shall be paid by the applicant in advance.

(5) When the documents, in respect of which stamps and fees have been paid as aforesaid, are received at the Registry they shall, before being filed, be stamped by the Registrar in accordance with The Stamp Rules.

31. Where, after a grant of Letters of Probate or Administration has been made, it shall transpire that the applicant had, in the affidavit filed with the Petition, made an error in the estimated value of the personal estate of the deceased, the Registrar may require the grantee to return the Letters for rectification by the Judge, who may make such an order either for a refund of or for further payment of Court fees or stamp duties and, in the case of Administration, for more security by way of bond or otherwise as the circumstances of the case shall require.

*The scale of fees is no longer applicable. See Chapter 27.

BARBADOS

Supreme Court of Judicature
SUPREME COURT (NON-CONTENTIOUS) PROBATE RULES, 1959

Made by the Judicial Advisory Council under section 46 of the Supreme Court of Judicature Act.

1. These Rules may be cited as the Supreme Court (Non-Contentious) Probate Rules, 1959.
2. (1) The Interpretation Act shall apply to these Rules as if they were an Act.
   (2) In these Rules, unless the context otherwise requires:
   "Registry" means the Supreme Court Registry;
   "Registrar" means the Registrar of the Supreme Court and includes the Deputy Registrar;
   "Will" has the same meaning as that ascribed to it in the Wills Act.

Application

3. Application for a grant of probate or letters of administration shall be made at the Registry.
4. Application may be made through an attorney-at-law or by the propounder of a will or a proposed administrator in person. Application made through an attorney-at-law shall bear the signature of such attorney-at-law or the signature of his firm.
5. Applications for probate shall be in writing in the form set out in the Appendix hereto and there shall be filed therewith:-
    (a) an affidavit in support of the said application undertaking to get in and administer the said estate;
    (b) an affidavit or affidavits by the persons attesting or one of them as to the due execution of the will:
        (1) Provided that if the will is a holograph will there shall be filed therewith an affidavit by a person or persons who were well acquainted with the deceased and with the character of his handwriting;
    (c) a certificate of death or burial or a statement in writing to the satisfaction of the Registrar for the non-production thereof;
    (d) an affidavit by the person applying or by someone on his behalf that from search made in the Registry it appears that no other application for probate or administration to the same estate has been made, and that there is or is not any other will filed for probate in the Registry.
    (e) the certificate from the Commissioner in accordance with the provisions of section 31(3) of the Estate and Succession Duty Act.
        (2) The affidavits shall be in the respective forms appearing in the Appendix hereto with such variations as the case may require.
6. (1) Applications for letters of administration shall be in writing and there shall be filed therewith an affidavit by the applicant in support of his application in which he shall depose that the deceased left no will (or as the case may be exhibiting any will of the deceased which the applicant desires to be annexed to such administration) and showing the relationship or other circumstances entitling him to such administration.
    (2) The provisions of Rule 5(c) and (e) shall apply to applications for administration.

Advertisement

7. Public notice of an application for probate or for letters of administration shall be given by one notice in the *Official Gazette* and two notices in a daily newspaper of this Island. From the date of the notice in the *Official Gazette* and from the date of the second notice in a daily newspaper not less than fourteen days shall elapse before an application is submitted to the Court.
8. Every will to which an executor or administrator with the will annexed is sworn must be marked by such executor or administrator and by the person before whom he is sworn.
9. In every case where probate or administration is, for the first time, applied for after a lapse of three years from the death of the deceased, the reason for the delay is to be certified to the Registrar. Should the certificate be unsatisfactory, the Registrar is to require such proof of the alleged cause of delay as he may see fit.
10. Where application is made for probate or administration by a corporation other than the Public Trustee, the officer appointed by the corporation for such purpose shall in every case file in the Registry a sealed copy of the resolution appointing him, and shall depose, in the oath to the grant, that the charter or memorandum of association of such corporation empowers such corporation to make such application.
11. The Registrar is not to allow probate or administration to issue until all the enquiries which he may see fit to institute have been answered to his satisfaction. The Registrar is, notwithstanding, to afford as great facility for the obtaining of grants of probate or administration as is consistent with a due regard to the prevention of error or fraud.

Affidavit of Subscribing Witness

12. If on perusing the affidavit of the subscribing witness it appears that the requirements of the Wills Act have not been complied with, the Court or Judge shall refuse probate.
13. If the subscribing witnesses are dead, or refuse to swear to the affidavit of execution, or if from other circumstances no affidavit can be obtained from any of them, resort must be had to other persons (if any) who may have been present at the execution of the will; but if no affidavit of any such other person can be found, evidence on affidavit must be procured of the fact and of the handwriting of the deceased and the subscribing witnesses, and also of any circumstances which may raise a presumption in favour of the due execution, and thereupon it shall be lawful for the Court or Judge to grant probate without the filing of an affidavit or due execution.

14. If on perusing the affidavit setting forth the facts of the case it appears doubtful whether the will has been duly executed, the Registrar may require the parties to bring the matter before a Judge in chambers.
15. If the testator was blind or the will was executed by a testator subscribing his signature by means of a mark, then one of the subscribing witnesses or the person who has appended the name of the testator must by affidavit depose to the fact that the will was read over to the testator and approved by him before its execution.
16. Any applicant for a grant of probate or administration shall be at liberty to request the Registrar to issue a *subpoena ad testificandum* to an attesting witness or to any person who may be required to prove the handwriting or death of any person. The *subpoena* shall be issued under the *teste* of the Chief Justice and shall bear the seal of the Court.
17. Any person to whom a *subpoena* is issued under the preceding rule shall be entitled to the remuneration and travelling expenses to which a witness is entitled under the Rules of practice of the Supreme Court.

Interlineations and Alterations

18. Interlineations and alterations are invalid unless they existed in the will at the time of its execution, or, if made afterwards, unless they have been executed and attested in the mode required by the Wills Act, or unless they have been rendered valid by the re-execution of the will or by the subsequent execution of a codicil thereto.
19. When interlineations or alterations appear in the will (unless duly executed, or recited in, or otherwise identified by the attestation clause) an affidavit or affidavits in proof of their having existed in the will before its execution must be filed, except when the alterations are merely verbal or when they are of but small importance and are evidenced by the initials of the attesting witness.
20. Erasures and obliterations are not to prevail unless proved to have existed in the will at the time of its execution or unless alterations thereby effected in the will are duly executed and attested, or unless they have been rendered valid by the re-execution of the will or by the subsequent execution of a codicil thereto. If no satisfactory evidence can be adduced as to the time when such erasures and obliterations were made, and the words erased or obliterated be not entirely effaced, but can upon inspection of the paper be ascertained, they must form part of the probate.
21. In every case the words having been erased or obliterated which might have been of importance, an affidavit must be required.

Documents Referred to in Will

22. If a will contains a reference to any deed, paper, memorandum or other document, of such a nature as to raise a question whether it ought or ought not to form a constituent part of the will, the production of such deed, paper, memorandum or other document must be required, with a view to ascertaining whether it be entitled to probate; and, if not produced, its non-production must be accounted for.
23. No deed, paper, memorandum or other document can form part of a will unless it was in existence at the time when the will was executed.

Appearance of the Paper

24. If there are any vestiges of sealing wax or wafers or other marks upon the testamentary papers, leading to the inference that a paper, memorandum, or other document has been annexed or attached to the same, they must be accounted for, or the production of such paper, memorandum, or other document must be required; and, if not produced, its non-production must be accounted for.
25. Any appearance of an attempted cancellation of a paper by burning, tearing, obliteration, or otherwise, and every circumstance leading to a presumption of abandonment or revocation of a paper on the part of the testator must be accounted for.

Notice to Other Next-of-Kin

26. Where administration is applied for by one or some of the next-of-kin only, there being another next-of-kin equally entitled thereto, the Registrar may require proof by affidavit that notice of such application has been given to such other next-of-kin.

Limited and Special Administration

27. Limited administrations are not to be granted unless every person entitled to the general grant has consented or renounced, or has been cited and failed to appear, except under the direction of the Court.
28. No person entitled to a general grant in respect of the estate of a deceased person will be permitted to take a limited grant except under the direction of the Court.

Grants to an Attorney

29. Probate or administration may be granted to an attorney duly constituted in a case where an executor or administrator is out of the jurisdiction of the Court: the power of attorney is to be duly recorded in the Registry.
30. In all cases of administration, except where it is expressly ordered otherwise by the Court, only one surety shall be required to an administration bond, and the bond shall be given in twice the value of the personal estate and twice the annual value of the realty to be placed in the possession of the administrator.
31. The Registrar is to take care that the sureties to administration bonds are responsible persons, and except where the Registrar otherwise directs, the sureties must justify.
32. Renunciation shall be in such of the forms set out in the Appendix hereto as may be applicable to the case.
33. No person who renounces probate or administration of the estate of a deceased person in one character is allowed to take representation to the same deceased in another character.
34. (1) Affidavits to be used in probate or administration must be taken before the Registrar or Deputy Registrar or any officer of the Registry authorised to administer oaths in civil proceedings.
    (2) Affidavits to be sworn out of the jurisdiction may be sworn before a notary public in the British Commonwealth territory or before a British Consul or other accredited officer in a foreign territory: Provided that where an affidavit is sworn to before a notary public in a foreign territory, the seal of such officer shall be certified by a British Consular Officer.
35. Any person who wishes to ensure that no grant is issued without notice to himself may enter a *caveat* in the Registry.
36. A *caveat* may be in the form set out in the Appendix hereto, but any written document signed by the party objecting or an attorney-at-law on his behalf shall be sufficient.
37. Except as otherwise provided by these Rules, a *caveat* shall remain in force for six months from the date on which it is entered and shall then cease to have effect, without prejudice to the entry of a further *caveat* or *caveats*.
38. A person entering a *caveat* (in these rules called a caveator) shall within seven days serve on the applicant for a grant a certified copy thereof.
39. The Registrar shall not allow any grant to issue if he has knowledge of an effective *caveat* in respect thereof.
40. A *caveat* may be warned by issue from the Registry of a warning in the form in the Appendix hereto at the instance of any person interested

which shall state his interest, and, if he claims under a will, the date of the will. The warning shall be prepared by the person issuing the same or his attorney-at-law and signed by the Registrar. This warning is to be served on the caveator.

41. A caveator who has not entered an appearance to a warning may at any time withdraw his *caveat* by giving notice to the Registry and the *caveat* shall thereupon cease to have effect, and, if it has been warned, the caveator shall forthwith give notice of withdrawal of the *caveat* to the person warning.

42. (1) A caveator having an interest contrary to that of the person warning may, within eight days of the service of the warning by him, exclusive of the date of such service, or at any time thereafter if no affidavit has been filed under paragraph 3 of this rule, enter an appearance in the Registry in the form in the Appendix hereto and serve a sealed copy thereof on the person warning. Proceedings subsequent to the entry of appearance shall be deemed contentious business and the Rules of the Supreme Court shall apply.

(2) A caveator having no interest contrary to the person warning but wishing to show cause against the sealing of the grant to that person, may, within eight days of service of the warning upon him exclusive of the day of such service, or at any time thereafter if no affidavit has been filed under paragraph 3 of these rules, issue and serve a summons for directions which shall be returnable before a Judge.

(3) If the time limited for appearance has expired and the caveator has not entered an appearance, the person warning may file in the Registry an affidavit showing that the warning was duly served and that he has not received a summons for directions under the last foregoing paragraph, and thereupon the *caveat* shall cease to have effect.

(4) Unless a Judge by order made on summons otherwise directs—
   (a) a *caveat* in respect of which an appearance to a warning has been entered shall remain in force until the commencement of a probate action;
   (b) any *caveat* in force at the commencement of a probate action or of proceedings by way of citation or motion shall (subject to the provisions of rule 42) remain in force until an application for a grant is made by the person shown to be entitled thereto by the decision of the Court in such action or proceedings, and upon such application any *caveat* entered by a party who has notice of the action or proceedings shall cease to have effect.

Citations

43. No citation is to issue under the seal of the Court until an affidavit in verification of the averments it contains sworn by the person issuing the citation (hereinafter called the citor) has been filed in the Registry.
44. The citor shall enter a *caveat* before entering a citation.
45. (1) Citations are to be served in the same manner as writs of summons issued out of the Supreme Court when that can be done.
    (2) Where citations cannot be served as required in the proceeding Rule, substituted service may be effected by way of advertisement or in such manner as a Judge may direct. Application for substituted service may be made to a Judge by way of affidavit.
46. Every will referred to in a citation shall be lodged in the Registry before the citation is issued, except where the will is not in the citor's possession and the Registrar is satisfied that it is impracticable to require it to be lodged.
47. A person who has been cited to appear may, within eight days of service of the citation upon him inclusive of the day of such service, or at any time thereafter if no application has been made by the citor under paragraph (5) of rule 48 or paragraph (2) of rule 49, enter an appearance in the Registry and shall forthwith thereafter serve on the citor a certified copy of his entry of appearance.
48. (1) A citation to accept or refuse a grant may be issued at the instance of any person who would himself be entitled to a grant in the event of the person cited renouncing his right thereto.
    (2) Where power to make a grant to an executor has been reserved, a citation calling on him to accept or refuse a grant may be issued at the instance of the executors who have proved the will or of the executors of the last survivor of deceased executors who have proved.
    (3) A citation calling on an executor who has intermeddled in the estate of the deceased to show cause why he should not be ordered to take a grant may be issued at the instance of any person interested in the estate at any time after the expiration of six months from the death of the deceased:
    Provided that no citation to take a grant shall issue while proceedings as to the validity of the will are pending.
    (4) A person cited who is willing to accept or take a grant may apply *ex parte* to the Registrar for an order for a grant on filing an affidavit showing that he has entered an appearance and that he has not been served by the citor with notice of any application for a grant to himself.

(5) If the time limited for appearance has expired and the person cited has not entered an appearance, the citor may—
    (a) in the case of a citation under paragraph (1) of this rule apply to the Registrar for an order for a grant to himself;
    (b) in the case of a citation under paragraph (2) of this rule, apply to the Registrar for an order that a note be made on the grant that the executor in respect of whom power was reserved has been duly cited and has not appeared and that all his rights in respect of the executorship have wholly ceased;
    (c) in the case of a citation under paragraph (3) of this rule, apply to the Registrar by summons (which shall be served on the person cited) for an order requiring such person to take a grant within a specified time.

(6) An application under the last foregoing paragraph shall be supported by an affidavit showing that the citation was duly served and that the person has not entered an appearance.

(7) If the person cited has entered an appearance but has not applied for a grant under paragraph (4) of this rule, or has failed to prosecute his applications with reasonable diligence, the citor may—
    (a) in the case of a citation under paragraph (1) of this rule, apply by summons to the Registrar for an order for a grant to himself;
    (b) in the case of a citation under paragraph (2) of this rule, apply by summons to the Registrar for an order striking out the appearance and for the endorsement on the grant of such a note as is mentioned in subparagraph (b) of paragraph (5) of this rule;
    (c) in the case of a citation under paragraph (3) of this rule, apply by summons to the Registrar for an order requiring the person cited to take a grant within a specified time;
    and the summons shall be served on the person cited.

49. (1) A citation to propound a will shall be directed to the executors named in the will and to all persons interested thereunder, and may be issued at the instance of any citor having an interest contrary to that of the executors or such other persons.
    (2) If the time limited for appearance has expired and no person cited has entered an appearance, or if no person who has appeared proceeds with reasonable diligence to propound the will, the citor may apply on motion for an order for a grant as if the will were invalid.

Resealing of British, Commonwealth and Colonial Probate[1]

50. Application under section 39 of the Administration of Estates (Jurisdiction and Procedure) Act, to have a grant of probate, administration or confirmation resealed shall be made in the Registry.
51. On such application being made, the following documents shall be filed in the Registry—
    (a) the original grant or duplicate or certified or sealed copy thereof;
    (b) an exemplified copy of the will (if any);
    (c) an affidavit by the executor, administrator, attorney or attorney-at-law in the form set out in the Appendix hereto.
    (d) A copy of the advertisement in a local daily newspaper announcing the intention to reseal: this advertisement must have appeared at least 7 days prior to the lodging of the application for resealing.
    (e) The certificate required by Rule 5(1)(e).
        (1) If the application is made by an attorney, the power of attorney must be first recorded in the Registry, and it must expressly contain authority to make such application.
52. The Registrar is to be satisfied that the notice of such application has been duly advertised.
53. On application to seal letters of administration the administrator shall comply with the provisions of these rules in regard to the bond and the sureties.
54. Special or limited or temporary grants are not to be sealed without an order of the Court made on summons in chambers.
55. Notice of the sealing in the Island of a grant is to be sent to the Court from which the grant is issued.
56. When intimation has been received of the resealing of a grant issued by the Courts in this Island notice of the revocation of, or any alteration in such grant is to be sent to the Court by whose authority such grant was resealed.
57. All probates, letters of administration or confirmation when sealed with the seal of the Court shall be recorded in the Wills Book of the Registration Office and shall be indexed in the index books to such wills.
58. The Registrar, the Deputy Registrar and all officers of the Registration Office of and above the rank of Senior Clerk shall by virtue of their offices have authority —
    (1) to administer oaths and to take oaths and affidavits in probate matters;
    (2) to sign all documents requiring the seal of the Court except the following which shall be signed by the Registrar or the Deputy

Registrar:-
(a) grant of probate or administration;
(b) warning of *caveat*.

59. The fees set out in the Schedule hereto shall be received and taken by the Registrar in respect of proceedings mentioned therein and shall be paid by the party requiring any duty performed or any process to be executed by the Registrar.

ENGLAND

THE NON-CONTENTIOUS PROBATE RULES, 1954

Dated June 15, 1954

S.I. 1954 No. 796 (L.6)

Arrangement of Rules

1. Citation and commencement
2. Interpretation
2A. Probate sub-registries
3. Applications for grants through solicitors
4. Personal applications
5. Duty of registrar on receiving application for grant
6. Oath in support of grant
7. Grant in additional name
8. Marking of wills
9. Engrossments for purposes of record
10. Evidence as to due execution of will
11. Execution of will of blind or illiterate testator
12. Evidence as to terms, condition and date of execution of will
13. Attempted revocation of will
14. Affidavit as to due execution, terms, etc., of will
15. Wills not proved under section 9 of Wills Act, 1837
16. Wills of persons on military service and seamen
17. Wills of naval personnel
18. Evidence of foreign law
19. Order of priority for grant where deceased left a will
20. Grants to attesting witnesses, etc.
21. Order of priority for grant in case of intestacy
22. Right of assignee to a grant
23. Joinder of administrator

24. Additional personal representatives
25. Grants where two or more persons entitled in same degree
26. Exceptions to rules as to priority
27. Grants to persons having *spes successions*
28. Grants in respect of settled land
29. Grants where deceased died domiciled outside England
30. Grants to attorneys
31. Grants on behalf of infants
32. Grants where infant is a co-executor
33. Grants in case of mental or physical incapacity
34. Grants to trust corporations and other corporate bodies
35. Renunciation of probate and administration
36. Consent of Administrator of enemy property
37. Notice to Crown of intended application for grant
38. Guarantee
39. *[Revoked]*
40. *[Revoked]*
41. Resealing under Colonial Probates Acts, 1892 and 1927
41A. Application for leave to sue on guarantee
42. Amendment and revocation of grant
43. Certificate of delivery of Inland Revenue affidavit
44. Caveats
45. Citations
46. Citation to accept or refuse or to take a grant
47. Citation to propound a will
48. Address for service
49. Application for order to bring in a will or to attend for examination
50. Limited grants under section 155 of Act
51. Grants of administration under discretionary powers of court, and grants *ad colligenda bona*
52. Applications for leave to swear to death
53. Grants in respect of nuncupative wills and copies of wills
54. Grants *durante absentia*
55. *[Revoked]*
56. Notice of election by surviving spouse to redeem life interest
57. Information as to grants in district probate registries to be sent to principal registry
58. Issue of copies of original wills and other documents
59. Taxation of costs
60. Power to require applications to be made by summons or motion
61. Exercise of powers of judge during Long Vacation
62. Appeals from registrars

63. Service of notice of motion and summons
64. Notices, etc.
65. Affidavits
66. Time
67. Application to pending proceedings
68. Revocation of previous Rules

First Schedule — Forms
Second Schedule — Rules, Orders and Instructions revoked

1. These Rules may be cited as the Non-Contentious Probate Rules, 1954, and shall come into operation on the first day of October, 1954.[1]
2. (1) The Interpretation Act, 1889, shall apply to the interpretation of these Rules as it applies to the interpretation of an Act of Parliament.
   (2) In these Rules unless the context otherwise requires — "The Act" means the Supreme Court of judicature (Consolidation) Act, 1925;
   "Authorised officer" means any officer of a registry who is for the time being authorised by the President to administer any oath or to take any affidavit required for any purpose connected with his duties; "The Crown" includes the Crown in right of the Duchy of Lancaster and the Duke of Cornwall for the time being;
   "England" includes Wales;
   "Gross value" in relation to any estate means the value of the estate without deduction for debts, incumbrances, funeral expenses or estate duty;
   "Oath" means the oath required by rule 6 to be sworn by every applicant for a grant;
   "Personal applicant" means a person other than a trust corporation who seeks to obtain a grant without employing a solicitor, and "personal application" has a corresponding meaning;
   "The President" means the President of the [Family Division];[2]
   "The principal registry" means the [principal registry of the Family Division];[3]
   "Registrar" means a registrar of the principal registry and includes

   (a) (except in rules 45 and 46) in relation to an application for a grant made or proposed to be made at a district probate registry, and
   (b) in rules 24 and 42, in relation to a grant issued from a district probate registry,

the registrar of [a district probate registry][4]

"Registry" means the principal registry or a district probate registry; ["The Senior Registrar" means the principal registrar of the Family Division or, in his absence, the senior of the registrars in attendance];[5]

"Statutory guardian" means a surviving parent of an infant under the power conferred by [section 3 of the Guardianship of Minors Act, 1971];

"Testamentary guardian" means a person appointed by deed or will to be guardian of an infant under the power conferred by [section 4 of the Guardianship of Minors Act, 1971];[6] Ibid.

"The Treasury Solicitor" means the solicitor for the affairs of Her Majesty's Treasury and includes the solicitor for the affairs of the Duchy of Lancaster and the solicitor of the Duchy of Cornwall;

"Will" includes a nuncupative will and any testamentary document or copy or reconstruction thereof.

(3) A form referred to by number means the form so numbered in the First Schedule; and such forms shall be used wherever applicable, with such variations as a registrar may in any particular case direct or approve.

2A. Sub-registries may be established at such places and under the control of such registrars as the President may from time to time direct.[7]

3. (1) A person applying for a grant through a solicitor may apply otherwise than by post at any registry [or sub-registry] and may apply by post at such registries [or sub-registries] as the President may direct,[8]

(2) Every solicitor through whom an application for a grant is made shall give the address of his place of business within the jurisdiction.

4. (1) A personal applicant may apply for a grant otherwise than by post at any registry [or sub-registry][9] or to an officer attending at such place as the President may direct.

(2) A personal applicant may not apply through an agent, whether paid or unpaid, and may not be attended by any person acting or appearing to act as his adviser,

(3) No personal application shall be received or proceeded with if —
   (a) it becomes necessary to bring the matter before the court an motion or by action;
   (b) an application has already been made by a solicitor on behalf of the applicant and has not been withdrawn;
   (c) the registrar otherwise directs.

(4) After a will has been deposited in a registry by a person applicant, it may not be delivered to the applicant or to any other person unless in special circumstances the registrar so directs,

(5) A personal applicant shall produce a certificate of the death of the deceased or such other evidence of the as the registrar may approve.

(6) A personal applicant shall supply all information necessary to enable the papers leading to the grant to be prepared in the registry, or may himself prepare such papers and lodge them unsworn.

(7) Unless the registrar otherwise directs, every oath, affidavit or [guarantee] required on a personal application (other than a [guarantee] given by a corporation in accordance with rule 38) shall be sworn or executed by all the deponents or [sureties] before an authorised officer.[10]

(8) No legal advice shall be given to a personal applicant by any officer of a registry and every such officer shall be responsible only for embodying in proper form the applicant's instruction for the grant.

(9) [Revoked by N.C. Probate (Amendment) Rules, 1968.]

5. (1) A registrar shall not allow any grant to issue until all inquiries which he may see fit to make have been answered to his satisfaction.

(2) The registrar may require proof of the identity of the deceased or of the applicant for the grant beyond that contained in the oath.

(3) Except with the leave of two registrars, no grant of probate or of administration with the will annexed shall issue within seven days of the death of the deceased and no grant of administration shall issue within fourteen days thereof.

(4) The registrar shall not require a guarantee under section 167 of the Act as a condition of granting administration to any person without giving that person or, where the application for the grant is made through a solicitor, the solicitor an opportunity of being heard with respect to the requirement.[11]

6. (1) Every application for a grant shall be supported by an oath in the form applicable to the circumstances of the case, which shall be contained in an affidavit sworn by the applicant, and by such others papers as the registrar may require.

(2) On an application for a grant of administration the oath shall state whether, and if so, in what manner, all persons having a prior right to a grant have been cleared off, and whether any minority or life interest arises under the will or intestacy.

(3) Where the deceased died on or after the 1st January, 1926, the

oath shall state whether, to the best of the applicant's knowledge, information and belief, there was land vested in the deceased which was settled previously to his death and not by his will and which remained settled land notwithstanding his death.

(4) Unless otherwise directed by a registrar, the oath shall state where the deceased died domiciled.[12]

7. Where it is necessary to describe the deceased in a grant by some name in addition to his true name, the applicant shall state in the oath the true name of the deceased and shall depose that some part of the estate, specifying it, was held in the otherwise name, or as to any other reason that there may be for the inclusion of the other name in the grant.

8. Every will in respect of which an application for a grant is made shall be marked by the signatures of the applicant and the person before whom the oath is sworn, and shall be exhibited to any affidavit which may be required under these Rules as to the validity, terms, condition or date of execution of the will:

Provided that where the registrar is satisfied that compliance with this rule might result in the loss in the will, he may allow a photographic copy thereof to be marked or exhibited in lieu of the original document.

9. (1) Where the registrar considers that in any particular case a photographic copy of the original will would not be satisfactory for purposes of record, he may require an engrossment suitable for photographic reproduction to be lodged.

(2) Where a will contains alterations which are not admissible to proof, there shall be lodged an engrossment of the will in the form in which it is to be proved.

(3) Any engrossment lodged under this rule shall reproduce the punctuation, spacing and division into paragraphs of the will and, if it is one to which paragraph (2) of this rule applies, it shall be made bookwise on durable paper following continuously from page to page on both sides of the paper.

(4) Where any pencil writing appears on a will, there shall be lodged a copy of the will or of the pages or sheets containing the pencil writing, in which there shall be underlined in red ink those portions which appear in pencil in the original.[13]

10. (1) Where a will contains no attestation clause or the attestation clause is insufficient or where it appears to the registrar that there is some doubt about the due execution of the will, he shall, before admitting it to proof, require an affidavit as to due execution from one or more of the attesting witnesses or, if no attesting witness is conveniently available, from any other person who was present at the time the will was executed.

(2) If no affidavit can be obtained in accordance with the last foregoing paragraph, the registrar may, if he thinks fit having regard to the desirability of protecting the interests of any person who may be prejudiced by the will, accept evidence on affidavit from any person he may think fit to show that the signature on the will is in the handwriting of the deceased, or of any other matter which may raise a presumption in favour of the due execution of the will.

(3) If the registrar, after considering the evidence —
   (a) is satisfied that the will was not duly executed, he shall refuse probate and shall mark the will accordingly;
   (b) is doubtful whether the will was duly executed, he may refer the matter to the court on motion.[14]

11. Before admitting to proof a will which appears to have been signed by a blind or illiterate testator or by another person by direction of the testator, or which for any other reason gives rise to doubt as to the testator having had knowledge of the contents of the will at the time of its execution, the registrar shall satisfy himself that the testator had such knowledge.[15]

12. (1) Where there appears in a will any obliteration, interlineation, or other alteration which is not authenticated in the manner prescribed by section 21 of the Wills Act, 1837, or by the re-execution of the will or by the execution of a codicil, the registrar shall require evidence to show whether the alteration was present at the time the will was executed and shall give directions as to the form in which the will is to be proved:

Provided that this paragraph shall not apply to any alteration which appears to the registrar to be of no practical importance.

(2) If from any mark on a will it appears to the registrar that some other document has been attached to the will, or if a will contains any reference to another document in such terms as to suggest that it ought to be incorporated in the will, the registrar may require the document to be produced and may call for such evidence in regard to the attaching or incorporation of the document as he may think fit.

(3) "Where there is doubt as to the date on which a will was executed, the registrar may requite such evidence as he thinks necessary to establish the date.[16]

13. Any appearance of attempted revocation of a will by burning, tearing, or otherwise, and every other circumstance leading to a presumption of revocation by the testator, shall be accounted for to the registrar's satisfaction.[17]

14. A registrar may require an affidavit from any person he may think fit for the purpose of satisfying himself as to any of the matters referred to in rules 11, 12 and 13, and in any such affidavit sworn by an attesting witness or other person present at the time of the execution of a will the deponent shall depose to the manner in which the will was executed.
15. Nothing in rule 10, 11, 12 or 13 shall apply to any will which it is sought to establish otherwise than by reference to section 9 of the Wills Act, 1837, as explained by the Wills Act Amendment Act, 1852, but the terms and validity of any such will shall be established to the registrar's satisfaction.
16. If it appears to the registrar that there is *prima facie* evidence that a will is one to which section 11 of the Wills Act, 1837, as amended by any subsequent enactment, applies, the will maybe admitted to proof if the registrar is satisfied that it was signed by the testator or, if unsigned, that it is in the testator's handwriting.
17. Every application for a grant in respect of the estate of a person who has at any time served in a capacity to which the Navy and Marines (Wills) Act, 1865, applies shall be supported by a certificate of the Inspector of Seamen's Wills as to the existence of any will in his custody: Provided that no such certificate shall be required where—
    (a) the application relates to a will made after the deceased had ceased to serve in such capacity as aforesaid which revokes all previous wills made by him, or
    (b) the deceased was at the date of his death in receipt of a pension in respect of his service.
18. Where evidence of the law of a country outside England is required on any application for a grant, the affidavit of any person who practises, or has practised, as a barrister or advocate in that country and who is conversant with its law may be accepted by the registrar unless the deponent is a person claiming to be entitled to the grant or his attorney, or is the spouse of any such person or attorney:

    Provided that the registrar may accept the affidavit of a solicitor practising in Scotland, Northern Ireland, the Channel Islands, the Isle of Man or the Republic of Ireland as to the law of the country in which he practises, and may in special circumstances accept the affidavit of any other person who does not possess the qualifications required by this rule if the registrar is satisfied that by reason of such person's official position or otherwise he has knowledge of the law of the country in question.[18]
19. Where the deceased died on or after the 1st January, 1926, the person or persons entitled to a grant of probate or administration with the will annexed shall be determined in accordance with the following

order of priority, namely:-
(i) The executor;
(ii) Any residuary legatee or devisee holding in trust for any other person;
(iii) Any residuary legatee or devisee for life;
(iv) The ultimate residuary legatee or devisee or, where the residue is not wholly disposed of by the will, any person entitled to share in the residue not so disposed of (including the Treasury Solicitor when claiming *bona vacantia* on behalf of the Crown) or, subject to paragraph (3) of rule 25, the personal representative of any such person:

Provided that where the residue is not in terms wholly disposed of, the registrar may, if he is satisfied that the testator has nevertheless disposed of the whole or substantially the whole of the estate as ascertained at the time of the application for the grant, allow a grant to be made (subject however to rule 37) to any legatee or devisee entitled to, or to a share in, the estate so disposed of, without regard to the persons entitled to share in any residue not disposed of by the will;

(v) Any specific legatee or devisee or any creditor or, subject to paragraph (3) of rule 25, the personal representative of any such person or, where the estate is not wholly disposed of by the will, any person who, notwithstanding that the amount of the estate is such that he has no immediate beneficial interest therein, may have a beneficial interest in the event of an accretion thereto;
(vi) Any legatee or devisee, whether residuary or specific, entitled on the happening of any contingency, or any person having no interest under the will of the deceased who would have been entitled to a grant if the deceased had died wholly intestate.

20. Where a gift to any person fails by reason of section 15 of the Wills Act, 1837 (which provides that gifts to attesting witnesses or their spouses shall be void), such person shall not have any right to a grant as a beneficiary named in the will, without prejudice to his right to a grant in any other capacity.[19]

21. (1) Where the deceased died on or after the 1st January, 1926, wholly intestate, the persons having a beneficial interest in the estate shall be entitled to a grant of administration in the following order of priority, namely:-
(i) The surviving spouse;
(ii) The children of the deceased, or the issue of any such child who has died during the lifetime of the deceased;

(iii) The father or mother of the deceased;
(iv) Brothers and sisters of the whole blood, or the issue of any deceased brother or sister of the whole blood who has died.[20]

(2) If no person in any of the classes mentioned in sub-paragraphs (ii) to (iv) of the last foregoing paragraph has survived the deceased, then, in the case of—
(a) a person who died before the 1st January, 1853, wholly intestate, or
(b) a person dying on or after the 1st January, 1953, wholly intestate without leaving a surviving spouse, the persons hereinafter described shall, if they have a beneficial interest in the estate, be entitled to a grant in the following order of priority, namely:-
(i) Brothers and sisters of the half blood, or the issue of any deceased brother or sister of the half blood who has died;
(ii) Grandparents;
(iii) Uncles and aunts of the whole blood, or the issue of any deceased uncle or aunt of the half blood who has died [(q)].

(3) In default of any person having a beneficial interest in the estate, the Treasury Solicitor shall be entitled to a grant if he claims *bona vacantia* on behalf of the crown.

(4) If all persons entitled to a grant under the foregoing provisions of this rule have been cleared off a grant may be made to a creditor of the deceased or to any person who, notwithstanding that he has no immediate beneficial interest in the estate, may have a beneficial interest in the event of an accretion thereto.

(5) Subject to paragraph (3) of rule 25, the personal representative of a person in any of the classes mentioned in paragraphs (1) and (2) of this rule or the personal representative of a creditor shall have the same right to a grant as the person whom he represents: Provided that the persons mentioned in sub-paragraphs (ii) to (iv) of paragraph (1) and in paragraph (2) of this rule shall be preferred to the personal representative of a spouse who has died without taking a beneficial interest in the whole estate of the deceased as ascertained at the time of the application for a grant.

(5A) The provisions of the Adoption Act, 1958, shall apply in determining the entitlement to a grant as they apply to the devolution of property on intestacy].[21]

(6) In this rule references to children of the deceased include references to his illegitimate and legitimated children, and "father or other of the deceased" shall be construed accordingly].[22]

22. (1) Where all the persons entitled to the estate of the deceased

(whether under a will or on intestacy) have assigned their whole interest in the estate to one or more persons, the assignee or assignees shall replace, in the order of priority for a grant of administration, the assignor or, if there are two or more assignors, the assignor with the highest priority.

(2) Where there are two or more assignees, administration may be granted with the consent of the others to any one or more (not exceeding four) of them.

(3) In any case where administration is applied for by an assignee, a copy of the instrument of assignment shall be lodged in the registry].[23]

23. (1) An application to join with a person entitled to a grant of administration a person entitled in a lower degree shall, in default of renunciation by all persons entitled in priority to such last-mentioned person, be made to the registrar and shall be supported by an affidavit by the person entitled, the consent of the person proposed to be joined as personal representative and such other evidence as the registrar may require.

(2) An application to join with a person entitled to a grant of administration a person having no right thereto shall be made to a registrar and shall be supported by an affidavit by the person entitled, the consent of the person proposed to be joined as personal representative and such other evidence as the registrar may require:[24]

Provided that there may without any such application be jointed with a person entitled to administration —

(a) on the renunciation of all other persons entitled to join in the grant, any kin of the deceased having no beneficial interest in the estate, in the order of priority described in rule 21;

(b) unless a registrar otherwise directs, any person whom the guardian of an infant may nominate for the purpose under paragraph (4) of rule 31;

(c) a trust corporation.

(3) [*Revoked by N.C. Probate (Amendment) Rules, 1967.*]

24. (1) An application under subsection (2) of section 160 of the Act to add a personal representative shall be made to a registrar and shall be supported by an affidavit by the applicant, the consent of the person proposed to be added as personal representative and such other evidence as the registrar may require.[25]

(2) [*Revoked by N.C. Probate (Amendment) Rules, 1967.*]

(3) On any such application the registrar may direct that a note shall be made on the original grant of the addition of a further personal representative, or he may impound or revoke the grant or make such other order as the circumstances of the case may require.

25. (1) A grant may be made to any person entitled thereto without notice to other persons entitled in the same degree.

(2) A dispute between persons entitled to a grant in the same degree shall be brought by summons before a registrar of the principal registry.

(3) Unless a registrar otherwise directs, administration shall be granted to a living person in preference to the personal representative of a deceased person who would, if living, be entitled in the same degree and to a person not under disability in preference to an infant entitled in the same degree.

(4) If the issue of a summons under this rule is known to the registrar, he shall not allow any grant to be sealed until such summons is finally disposed of.[26]

26. (1) Nothing in rule 19, 21, 23 or 25 shall operate to prevent a grant being made to any person to whom a grant may or may require to be made under any enactment.

(2) The rules mentioned in the last foregoing paragraph shall not apply where the deceased died domiciled outside England, except in a case to which the proviso to rule 29 applies.

27. When the beneficial interest in the whole estate of the deceased is vested absolutely in a person who has renounced his right to a grant and has consented to administration being granted to the person or persons who would be entitled to his estate if he himself had died intestate, administration may be granted to such person or one or more (not exceeding four) of such persons;

Provided that a surviving spouse shall not be regarded as a person in whom the estate has vested absolutely unless he would be entitled to the whole of the estate, whatever its value may be.[27]

28. (1) In this rule "settled land" means land vested in the deceased which was settled previously to his death and not by his will and which remained settled land notwithstanding his death.

(2) The special executors in regard to settled land constituted by section 22 of the Administration of Estates Act, 1925, shall have a prior right to a grant of probate limited to the settled land.

(3) The person or persons entitled to a grant of administration limited to settled land shall be determined in accordance with the following order of priority, namely:-

(i) The trustees of the settlement at the time of the application for the grant;
(ii) [*Revoked by N.C. Probate (Amendment) Rules, 1967.*]
(iii) The personal representative of the deceased.

(4) Where the persons entitled to a grant in respect of the free estate are also entitled to a grant of the same nature in respect of settled land, a grant expressly including the settled land may issue to them.

(5) Where there is settled land and a grant is made in respect of the free estate only, the grant shall expressly exclude the settled land.

29. Where the deceased died domiciled outside England, [a registrar may order that a grant do issue—[28]

(a) to the person entrusted with the administration of the estate by the court having jurisdiction at the place where the deceased died domiciled,

(b) to the person entitled to administer the estate by the law of the place where the deceased died domiciled,

(c) if there is no such person as is mentioned in paragraph (a) or (b) of this rule or if in the opinion of the registrar the circumstances so require, to such person as the registrar may direct,

(d) if, by virtue of section 160 of the Act, a grant is required to be made to, or if the registrar in his discretion considers that a grant should be made to, not less than two administrators, to such person as the registrar may direct jointly with any such person as is mentioned in paragraph (a) or (b) of this rule or with any other person:

Provided that without any such order[29] as aforesaid —

(a) probate of any will which is admissible to proof may be granted

(i) if the will is in the English or Welsh language, to the executor named therein;

(ii) if the will describes the duties of a named person in terms sufficient to constitute him executor according to the tenor of the will, to that person;

(b) where the whole of the estate in England consists of immovable property, a grant limited thereto may be made in accordance with the law which would have been applicable if the deceased had died domiciled in England.

30. (1) Where a person entitled to a grant resides outside England, administration may be granted to his lawfully constituted attorney for his use and benefit, limited until such person shall obtain a grant or in such other way as the registrar may direct:

Provided that where the person so entitled is an executor, administration shall not be granted to his attorney without notice to the other executors, if any, unless such notice is dispensed with by the registrar.

(2) Where a registrar is satisfied by affidavit that it is desirable for a grant to be made to the lawfully constituted attorney of a person entitled to a grant of administration and resident in England, he may direct that administration be granted to such attorney for the use and benefit of such person, limited until such person shall obtain a grant or in such other ways as the registrar may direct

31. (1) Where the person to whom a grant would otherwise be made is an infant, administration for his use and benefit until he attains the age of [eighteen years]³⁰ shall, subject to paragraphs (3) and (5) of this rule, be granted
    (a) [to both parents of the infant jointly or] to the statutory or testamentary guardian of the infant or to any guardian appointed by a court of competent jurisdiction, or
    (b) if there is no such guardian able and willing to act and the infant has attained the age of sixteen years, to any next of kin nominated by the infant or, where the infant is a married woman, to any such next of kin or to her husband if nominated by her

(2) Any person nominated under sub-paragraph (b) of the last foregoing paragraph may represent any other infant whose next of kin he is, being an infant below the age of sixteen years entitled in the same degree as the infant who made the nomination.

(3) Notwithstanding anything in this rule, administration for the use and benefit of the infant until he attains the age of [eighteen years may be granted to any person assigned as guardian by order of a registrar in default of, or jointly with, or to the exclusion of, any such person as is mentioned in paragraph (1) of this rule; and such an order may be made on application by the intended guardian, who shall file an affidavit in support of the application and, if required by the registrar, an affidavit of fitness sworn by a responsible person.³¹

(4) Where, by virtue of section 160 of the Act, a grant is required to be made to not less than two administrators and there is only one person competent and willing to take a grant under the foregoing provisions of this rule, administration may, unless a registrar otherwise directs, be granted to such person jointly with any other person nominated by him as a fit and proper person to take the grant.

(5) Where an infant who is sole executor has no interest in the residuary estate of the deceased, administration for the use and benefit of the infant until he attains the age of [eighteen years][32] shall, unless a registrar otherwise directs, be granted to the person entitled to the residuary estate.[33]

(6) An infant's right to administration may be renounced only by a person assigned as guardian under paragraph (3) of this rule and authorised to renounce by a registrar.[34]

32. (1) Where one of two or more executors is an infant, probate may be granted to the other executor or executors not under disability, with power reserved of making the like grant to the infant on his attaining the age of [eighteen years][35] and administration for the use and benefit of the infant until he attains the age of [eighteen years] may be granted under rule 31 if and only if the executors who are not under disability renounce or, on being cited to accept or refuse a grant, fail to make an effective application therefor.

(2) An infant executor's right to probate on attaining the age of [eighteen years] may not be renounced by any person on his behalf

33. (1) Where a registrar is satisfied that a person entitled to a grant is by reason of mental or physical incapacity incapable of managing his affairs, administration for his use and benefit, limited during his incapacity or in such other way as the registrar may direct, may be granted —

(a) in the case of mental incapacity, to the person authorised by the Court of Protection to apply for the grant, or

(b) where there is no person so authorised, or in the case of physical incapacity —

(i) if the person incapable is entitled as executor, and has no interest in the residuary estate of the deceased, to the person entitled to such estate;

(ii) if the person incapable is entitled otherwise than as executor, or is an executor having an interest in the residuary estate of the deceased, to the person who would be entitled to a grant in respect of his estate if he had died intestate; or to such other person as a registrar may by order direct.[36]

(2) Unless a registrar otherwise directs, no grant of administration shall be made under this rule unless all persons entitled in the same degree as the person incapable have been cleared off.[37]

(3) In the case of mental incapacity, notice of intended application for a grant under this rule shall be given to the Court of Protection, except where the person incapable is an executor with no beneficial

interest in the estate.

(4) In the case of physical incapacity, notice of intended application for a grant under this rule shall, unless a registrar otherwise directs, be given to the person alleged to be so incapable.[38]

34. (1) Where a trust corporation applies for a grant through one of its officers, such officer shall lodge a certified copy of the resolution authorising him to make the application and shall depose in the oath that the corporation is a trust corporation within the meaning of section 175 of the Act as extended by section 3 of the Law of Property (Amendment) Act, 1926, and that it has power to accept a grant:

Provided that it tall not be necessary to lodge a certified copy of the resolution where the trust corporation is a person holding an official position if the person through whom the application is made is included in a list filed with the [Senior Registrar[39] of persons authorised to make such applications.

(2) Where a trust corporation applies for a grant of administration otherwise than as attorney for some person, there shall be lodged with the application the consents of all persons entitled to a grant and of all persons interested in the residuary estate of the deceased, unless the registrar directs that such consents be dispensed with on such terms, if any, as he may think fit.

(3) Where a corporation (not being a trust corporation) would, if an individual, be entitled to a grant, administration for its use and benefit, limited until further representation is grant, may be granted to its nominee or, if the corporation has its principal place of business outside England, its nominee or lawfully constituted attorney, and a copy of the resolution appointing the nominee or, as the case may be, the power of attorney, sealed by the corporation or otherwise authenticated to the registrar's satisfaction, shall be lodged with the application for a grant, and the oath shall state that the corporation is not a trust corporation.

35. (1) Renunciation of probate by an executor shall not operate as renunciation of any right which he may have to a grant of administration in some other capacity unless he expressly renounces such right.

(2) Unless a registrar otherwise directs, no person who has renounced administration in one capacity may obtain a grant thereof in some other capacity.

(3) A renunciation of probate or administration may be retracted at any time on the order of a registrar:

Provided that only in exceptional circumstances may leave be given to an executor to retract a renunciation of probate after a grant has been made to some other person entitled in a lower degree.

(4) A discretion or order under this rule may be made either by the registrar of a district probate registry where the renunciations filed or a registrar of the principal registry.[40]

36. On an application for a grant —
    (a) in respect of the estate of a deceased person who was at the date of his death resident in Bulgaria, Germany, Hungary, Japan or Romania, or
    (b) to any person resident in one of these countries or to the attorney of any such person, there shall, if the deceased died before the 6th October, 1952, be lodged the consent in writing of the appropriate authority, which shall be obtained through the Administration of Enemy Property Department of the Board of Trade.

37. In any case in which it appears that the Crown is or may be beneficially interested in the estate of a deceased person, notice of intended application for a grant shall be given by the applicant to the Treasury Solicitor, and the registrar may direct that no grant shall issue within a specified time after the notice has been given.

38. (1) The registrar shall not require a guarantee under section 167 of the Act as a condition of granting administration except where it is proposed to grant it —
    (a) by virtue of rule 19(v) or rule 21(4) to a creditor or to the personal representative of a creditor or to a person who has no immediate beneficial interest in the estate of the deceased but may have such an interest in the event of an accretion to the estate;
    (b) under rule 27 to a person or some of the persons who would, if the person, beneficially entitled to the whole of the estate died intestate, be entitled to his estate;
    (c) under rule 30 to the attorney of a person entitled to a grant;
    (d) under rule 31 for the use and benefit of a minor;
    (e) under rule 33 for the use and benefit of a person who is by reason of mental or physical incapacity incapable of managing his affairs;
    (f) to an application who appears to the registrar to be resident elsewhere than in the United Kingdom;
    or except where the registrar considers that there are special circumstances making it desirable to require a guarantee.

(2) Notwithstanding that it is proposed to grant administration as

aforesaid, a guarantee shall not be required, except in special circumstances, on an application for administration where the applicant or one of the applicants is —
(a) a trust corporation;
(b) a solicitor holding a current practising certificate under the Solicitors Acts, 1957 to 1965;
(c) a servant of the Crown acting in his official capacity
(d) a nominee of a public department or of a local authority within the meaning of the Local Government Act, 1933.
(3) Every guarantee entered into by a surety for the purposes of section 167 of the Act shall be in Form 1.
(4) Except where the surety is a corporation, the signature of the surety on every such guarantee shall be attested by an authorised officer, commissioner for oaths or other person authorised by law to administer an oath —
(5) Unless the registrar otherwise directs —
(a) if it is decided to require a guarantee, it shall be given by two sureties, except where the gross value of the estate does not exceed £500 or a corporation is a proposed surety, and in those cases one will suffice;
(b) no person shall be accepted as a surety unless he is resident in the United Kingdom;
(c) no officer of a registry or sub-registry shall become a surety;
(d) the limit of the liability of the surety or sureties under a guarantee given for the purposes of section 167 of the Act shall be the gross amount of the estate as sworn on the application for the grant;
(e) every surety, other than a corporation, shall justify.
(6) Where the proposed surety is a corporation there shall be filed an affidavit by the proper officer of the corporation to the effect that it has power to act as surety and has executed the guarantee in the manner prescribed by its constitution, and containing sufficient information as to the financial position of the corporation to satisfy the registrar that its assets are sufficient to satisfy all claims which may be made against it under any guarantee which it has given or is likely to give for the purposes of section 167 of the Act.
Provided that the Senior Registrar may, instead of requiring an affidavit in every case, accept an affidavit made not less often than once in every year together with an undertaking by the corporation to notify the Senior Registrar forthwith in the event of any alteration in its constitution affecting its powers to become

a surety under that section.[41]

39. [*Revoked by N.C. Probate (Amendment) Rules, 1971.*]
40. [*Revoked by N.C. Probate (Amendment) Rules, 1971.*]
41. (1) An application under the Colonial Probates Acts, 1892 and 1927, for the resealing of probate or administration granted by the court of a country to which those Acts apply shall be made in the principal registry by the person to whom the grant was made or by any person authorised in writing to apply on his behalf.
    (2) On any such application —
        (a) an Inland Revenue affidavit shall be lodged as if the application were one for a grant in England;
        (b) if a registrar of the principal registry so requires, the application shall be advertised in such manner as he may direct and shall be supported by an oath sworn by the person making the application;[42]
    (2A) On an application for the resealing of a grant of administration:-
        (a) the registrar shall not require sureties under section 11 of the Administration of Estates Act, 1971, as a condition of resealing the grant except where it appears to him that the grant is made to a person or for a purpose mentioned in paragraphs (a) to (f) of rule 38 (1) or except where he considers that there are special circumstances making it desirable to require sureties;
        (b) rules 5(4) and 38(2), (4), (5) and (6) shall apply with any necessary modifications; and
        (c) a guarantee entered into by a surety for the purposes of the said section 11 shall be in Form 2.[43]
    (3) Except by leave of a registrar of the principal registry, no grant shall be resealed unless it was made to such a person as is mentioned in paragraph (a) or (b) of rule 29 or to a person to whom a grant could be made under the proviso to that rule.
    (4) No limited or temporary grant shall be resealed except by leave of a registrar of the principal registry.
    (5) Every grant lodged for resealing shall include a copy of any will to which the grant relates or shall be accompanied by a copy thereof certified as correct by or under the authority of the court by which the grant was made, and where the copy of the grant required to be deposited under subsection (1) of section 2 of the Colonial Probates Act, 1892, does not include a copy of the will, a copy thereof shall be deposited in the principal registry at the same time as the copy of the grant.
    (6) The registrar shall send notice of the resealing to the court which

made the grant.

(7) Where notice is received in the principal registry of the resealing of an English grant, notice of any amendment for revocation of the grant shall be sent to the court by which it was resealed.

41A. An application for leave under section 167(3) of the Act or under section 11(5) of the Administration of Estates Act, 1971, to sue a surety on a guarantee given for the purposes of either of those sections shall, unless the registrar otherwise directs under rule 60, be made by summons to a registrar of the principal registry, and notice of the application shall in any event be served on the administrator, the surety and any cosurety

42. If a registrar is satisfied that a grant should be amended or revoked he may make an order accordingly.
Provided that except in special circumstances no grant shall be amended or revoked under this rule except on the application or with the consent of the person to whom the grant was made

43. The certificate of delivery of an Inland Revenue affidavit required by section 30 of the Customs and Inland Revenue Act, 1881, to be borne by every grant shall be in Form 3.

44. (1) Any person who wishes to ensure that no grant is sealed without notice to himself may enter a caveat in any registry.

(2) Any person who wishes to enter a caveat (in this rule called "the caveator") may do so by completing Form 4 in the appropriate book at the registry and obtaining an acknowledgement of entry from the proper officer, or by sending through the post at his own risk a notice in Form 4 to the registry in which he wishes the caveat to be entered.[44]

(3) Where the caveat is entered by a solicitor on the caveator's behalf, the name of the caveator shall be stated in Form 4.

(4) Except as otherwise provided by this rule, a caveat shall remain in force for six months from the date on which it is entered and shall then cease to have effect, without prejudice to the entry of a further caveat or caveats.

(5) The [Senior Registrar[45]] shall maintain an index of caveats entered in any registry and on receiving an application for a grant in the principal registry, or a notice of an application for a grant made in a district probate registry, he shall cause the index to be searched and shall notify the appropriate registrar in the event of a caveat having been entered against the sealing of a grant for which application had been made in a district probate registry.

(6) The registrar shall not allow any grant to be sealed if he has knowledge of an effective caveat in respect thereof:
Provided that no caveat shall operate to prevent the sealing of a

grant on the day on which the caveat is entered.

(7) A caveat may be warned by the issue from the principal registry of a warning in Form 5 at the instance of any person interested (in this rule called 'the person warning") which shall state his interest and, if he claims under a will, the date of the will, and shall require the caveator to give particulars of any contrary interest which he may have in the estate of the deceased; and every warning [or a copy thereof] shall be served on the caveator.[46]

(8) A caveator who has not entered an appearance to a warning may at any time withdraw his caveat by giving notice at the registry at which it was entered and the caveat shall thereupon cease to have effect and, if it has been warned, the caveator shall forthwith give notice of withdrawal of the caveat to the person warning.

(9) A caveator having an interest contrary to that of the person warning may, within eight days of service of the warning upon him inclusive of the day of such service, or at any time thereafter if no affidavit has been filed under paragraph (11) of this rule, enter an appearance in the principal registry by filing Form 6 and making an entry in the appropriate book and shall forthwith thereafter serve on the person warning a copy of Form 6 sealed with the seal of the registry.

(10) A caveator having no interest contrary to that of the person warning but wishing to show cause against the sealing of a grant to that person may, within eight days of service of the warning upon him inclusive of the day of such service, or at any time thereafter if no affidavit has been filed under paragraph (11) of this rule, issue and serve a summons for directions, which shall be returnable before a registrar of the principal registry.

(11) If the time limited for appearance has expired and the caveator has not entered an appearance, the person warning may file in the principal registry an affidavit showing that the warning was duly served and that he has not received a summons for directions under the last foregoing paragraph, and thereupon the caveat shall cease to have effect.

(11A) Upon the commencement of a probate action the principal probate registrar shall, in respect of each caveat then in force (other than a caveat entered by the plaintiff), give to the caveator notice of the commencement of the action and, upon the subsequent entry of a caveat at any time when the action is pending, shall likewise notify the caveator of the existence of the action.[47]

(12) Unless a registrar of the principal registry by order made on

summons otherwise directs —

(a) any caveat in force at the commencement of proceedings by way of citation or motion shall, unless withdrawn pursuant to paragraph (8) of this rule, remain in force until an application for a grant is made by the person shown to be entitled thereto by the decision of the court in such proceedings, and upon such application any caveat entered by a party who had notice of the proceedings shall cease to have effect;

(b) any caveat in respect of which an appearance to a warning has been entered shall remain in force until the commencement of a probate action;

(c) the commencement of a probate action shall, whether or not any caveat has been entered, operate to prevent the sealing of a grant (other than a grant under section 163 of the Act) until application for a grant is made by the person shown to be entitled thereto by the decision of the court in such action, and upon such application any caveat entered by a party who had notice of the action, or by a caveator who was given notice under paragraph 11A of this rule, shall cease to have effect.[48]

(13) Except with the leave of a registrar of the principal registry, no further caveat may be entered by or on behalf of any caveator whose caveat has ceased to have effect under paragraph (11) or (12) of this rule.

(14) In this rule "grant" includes a *Scottish confirmation and*[49] a grant made by any court outside England which is produced for resealing by the High Court.

45. (1) Every citation shall issue from the principal registry and shall be settled by a registrar before being issued.

(2) Every averment in a citation, and such other information as the registrar may require, shall be verified by an affidavit sworn by the person issuing the citation (in these Rules called "the citor") or, if there are two or more citors, by one of them:
Provided that the registrar may in special circumstances accept an affidavit sworn by the citor's solicitor.

(3) The citor shall enter a caveat before issuing a citation.

(4) Every citation shall be served personally on the person cited unless the registrar, on cause shown by affidavit, directs some other mode of service, which may include notice by advertisement.

(5) Every will referred to in a citation shall be lodged in a registry before the citation is issued, except where the will is not in the

citor's possession and the registrar is satisfied that it is impracticable to require it to be lodged.

(6) A person who has been cited to appear may, within eight days of service of the citation upon him inclusive of the day of such service, or at any time thereafter if no application has been made by the citor under paragraph (5) of rule 46 or paragraph (2) of rule 47, enter an appearance in the principal registry by filing Form 6 and making an entry in the appropriate book, and shall forthwith thereafter serve on the citor a copy of Form 6 sealed with the seal of the registry.

46. (1) A citation to accept or refine a grant may be issued at the instance of any person who would himself be entitled to a grant in the event of the person cited renouncing his right thereto.

(2) Where power to make a grant to an executor has been reserved, a citation calling on him to accept or refuse a grant may be issued at the instance of the executors who have proved the will or of the executors of the last survivor of deceased executors who have proved.

(3) A citation calling on an executor who has intermeddled in the estate of the deceased to show cause why he should not be ordered to make a grant may be issued at the instance of any person interested in the estate at any time after the expiration of six months from the death of the deceased:

Provided that no citation to take a grant shall issue while proceedings as to the validity of the will are pending.

(4) A person cited who is willing to accept or take a grant may apply *ex parte* to a registrar for an order for a grant on filing an affidavit showing that he has entered an appearance and that he has not been served by the citor with notice of any application for a grant to himself.

(5) If the time limited for appearance has expired and the person cited has not entered an appearance, the citor may —

(a) in the case of a citation under paragraph (1) of this rule, apply to a registrar for an order for a grant to himself;

(b) in the case of a citation under paragraph (2) of this rule, apply to a registrar for an order that a note be made on the grant that the executor in respect of whom power was reserved has been duly cited and has not appeared and that all his rights in respect of the executorship have wholly ceased;

(c) in the case of a citation under paragraph (3) of this rule, apply to a registrar by summons (which shall be served on the person cited) for an order requiring such person to take a grant within a specified time [or for a grant to himself or to some other person specified in the summons].

(6) An application under the last foregoing paragraph shall be supported by an affidavit showing that the citation was duly served and that the person cited has not entered an appearance.

(7) If the person cited has entered an appearance but has not applied for a grant under paragraph (4) of this rule, or has failed to prosecute his application with reasonable diligence, the citor may—

    (a) in the case of a citation under paragraph (1) of this rule, apply by summons to a registrar for an order for a grant to himself;

    (b) in the case of a citation under paragraph (2) of this rule, apply by summons to a registrar for an order striking out the appearance and for the endorsement on the grant of such an note as is mentioned in sub-paragraph (b) of paragraph (5) of this rule;

    (c) in the case of a citation under paragraph (3) of this rule, apply by summons to a registrar for an order requiring the person cited to take a grant within a specified time [or for a grant to himself or to some other person specified in the summons].

and the summons shall be served on the person cited.[50]

47. (1) A citation to propound a will shall be directed to the executors named in the will and to all persons interested thereunder, and may be issued at the instance of any citor having an interest contrary to that of the executors or such other persons.

(2) If the time limited for appearance has expired and no person cited has entered an appearance, or if no person who has appeared proceed with reasonable diligence to propound the will, the citor may apply [by summons to a registrar of the principal registry][51] for an order for a grant as if the will were invalid.

48. All caveats, citations, warnings and appearances shall contain an address for service within the jurisdiction.

49. (1) An application under section 26 of the Court of Probate Act, 1857, for an order requiring a person to bring in a will or to attend for examination may, unless a probate action has been commenced, be made to a registrar of the principal registry by summons[52] which shall be served on every such person as aforesaid.

(2) An application under section 23 of the Court of Probate Act, 1858, for the issue by a registrar of the principal registry of a

subpoena to bring in a will shall be supported by an affidavit setting out the grounds of the application, and if any person served with the subpoena denies that the will is in his possession or control he may file an affidavit to that effect.

50. An application for an order for a grant under section 155 of the Act limited to part of an estate may be made to a registrar and shall be supported by an affidavit stating —
    (a) whether the application is made in respect of the real estate only or any part thereof, or real estate together with personal estate, or in respect of a trust estate only;
    (b) whether the estate of the deceased is known to be insolvent;
    (c) that the persons entitled to a grant in respect of the whole estate in priority to the applicant have been cleared off.[53]

51. An application for an order for —
    (a) a grant of administration under section 73 of the Court of Probate Act, 1857, or section 162 of the Act, or
    (b) a grant of administration *ad colligenda bona,* may be made to a registrar and shall be supported by an affidavit setting out the grounds of the application.[54]

52. An application for leave to swear to the death of a person in whose estate a grant is sought may be made to a registrar, and shall be supported by an affidavit setting out the grounds of the application and containing particulars of any policies of insurance effected on the life of the presumed deceased.[55]

53. (1) An application for an order admitting to proof a nuncupative will, or a will contained in a copy, a completed draft, a reconstruction or other evidence of its contents where the original will is not available, may be made to a registrar:
    Provided that where a will is not available owing to its being retained in the custody of a foreign court or official, a duly authenticated copy of the will may be admitted to proof without any such order as aforesaid.
    (2) The application shall be supported by an affidavit setting out the grounds of the application and by such evidence on affidavit as the applicant can adduce as to —
        (a) the due execution of the will,
        (b) its existence after the death of the testator, and
        (c) the accuracy of the copy or other evidence of the contents of the will, together with any consents in writing to the application given by any persons not under disability who would be prejudiced by the grant.

54. An application for an order for a grant of special administration under

section 164 of the Act where a personal representative is residing outside England shall be made to the court on motion.

55. [*Revoked by N.C. Probate (Amendment) Rules, 1967.*]

56. (1) Where a surviving spouse who is the sole personal representative of the deceased is entitled to a life interest in part of the residuary estate and elects under section 47A of the Administration of Estates Act, 1925, to have the life interest redeemed, he may give written notice of the election to the Senior Registrar[56] in pursuance of subsection (7) of that section by filing a notice in Form 7 in the principal registry or in the district probate registry from which the grant issued.

(2) Where the grant issued from a district probate registry, the notice shall be filed in duplicate.

(3) A notice filed under this rule shall be noted on the grant and the record and shall be open to inspection.

57. (1) The notice of an application for a grant made in a district probate registry required by subsection (1) of section 152 of the Act to be sent to the principal registry shall be in the form of an index card, stating the full name and address of the deceased, his age, if known, and the date of his death.

(2) The list of grants made by a district probate registrar required by subsection (5) of the said section 152 to be sent to the principal registry shall be sent once in every week, and shall include the full name of every person in respect of whose estate a grant has been made and the name of the county or town in which he resided, and a copy of every grant mentioned in such list shall be sent by the district probate registrar to the principal registry for filing.

58. (1) Where copies are required of original wills or other documents deposited under section 170 of the Act, such copies may be photographic copies sealed with the seal of the registry and issued as office copies and, where such office copies are available, copies certified under the hand of a registrar to be true copies shall be issued only if it is required that the seal of the court be affixed thereto.

(2) Copies, not being photographic copies, of original wills or other documents deposited under the said section 170 shall be examined against the documents of which they purport to be copies only if so required by the person demanding the copy, and in such case the copy shall be certified under the hand of a registrar to be a true copy and may in addition be sealed with the seal of the court.

59. (1) Every bill of costs (other than a bill delivered by a solicitor to his client which falls to be taxed under the Solicitors Act, [957][57] shall be referred to a registrar of the principal registry for taxation and may be taxed by him or such other taxing officer as the President may appoint.
(2) The party applying for taxation shall file the bill and give to any other parties entitled to be heard on the taxation not less than three clear days' notice of the time appointed for taxation, and shall at the same time, if he has not already done so, supply them with a copy of the bill.
(3) If any party entitled to be heard on the taxation does not attend within a reasonable time after the time appointed, the taxing officer may proceed to tax the bill upon being satisfied that such party had due notice of the time appointed.
(4) The fees payable on taxation shall be paid by the party on whose application the bill is taxed and shall be allowed as part of the bill.
60. (1) A registrar may require any application to be made by summons to a registrar or a judge, or to the court on motion.
(2) A summons for hearing by a registrar shall be issued out of the principal registry and heard by a registrar of that registry.
(3) A summons to be heard by a judge shall be issued out of the principal registry.[58]
61. All powers exercisable under these Rules by a judge in chambers may be exercised during the Long Vacation by a registrar of the principal registry.
62. (1) [Deleted by N.C. Probate (Amendment) Rules, 1967.]
(2) Any person aggrieved by a decision or requirement of a registrar may appeal by summons to a judge.
(3) If, in the case of an appeal under the last foregoing paragraph, any person besides the appellant appeared or was represented before the registrar from whose decision or requirement the appeal is brought, the summons shall be issued within seven days thereof for hearing on the first available day and shall be served on every such person as aforesaid.[59]
63. (1) A judge or registrar of the principal registry may direct that a notice of motion or summons for the service of which no other provision is made by these Rules shall be served on such person or persons as the judge or registrar may direct.
(2) Where by these Rules or by any direction given under the last foregoing paragraph a notice of motion or summons is required to be served on any person, it shall be served —

(a) in the case of a notice of motion, not less than five clear days before the day named in the notice for hearing the motion;

(b) in the case of a summons, not less than two clear days before the day appointed for the hearing, unless a judge or registrar of the principal registry, at or before the hearing, dispenses with service on such terms, if any, as he may think fit.

64. Unless a registrar otherwise directs or these Rules otherwise provide, any notice or other document required to be given to or served on any person may be given or served by leaving it at, or by sending it by prepaid registered post to, that person's address for service or, if he has no address for service, his last known address.

65. Every affidavit used in non-contentious probate business shall be in the form required by the Rules of the Supreme Court in the case of affidavits to which those Rules apply.

66. The provisions of Order 3 and Order 65, rule 7 of the Rules of the Supreme Court shall apply to the computation, enlargement and abridgement of time under these Rules, except that nothing in the former Order shall prevent time from running in the Long Vacation [t].

67. Subject in any particular case to any direction given by a judge or registrar, these Rules shall apply to any proceeding which is pending on the date on which they come into operation as well as to any proceeding commenced on or after that date:

Provided that where the deceased died before the 1st January, 1926, the right to a grant shall, subject to the provisions of any enactment, be determined by the principles and rules in accordance with which the court would have acted at the date of the death.

68. (1) The Rules, Orders and Instructions set out in the Second Schedule are hereby revoked,

(2) The following amendments shall be made in the Rules, Orders and Tables of Fees for the Court of Probate in respect of Contentious Business, dated 30th July, 1862:-

(a) rule 7 to 12 shall be revoked;

(b) in rule 73 the words "and by motion upon affidavit when no suit is pending" shall be deleted;[60]

Notes

1. The Rules are here printed as amended by the N.C. Probate (Amendment) Rules of 1961, 1962, 1967, 1968, 1969 and 1971.
2. Words in square brackets substituted by N.C. Probate (Amendment) Rules, 1971.

3. Ibid.
4. Rule amended by N.C. Probate (Amendment) Rules, 1967. Words in square brackets substituted by N.C. Probate (Amendment) Rules, 1969.
5. See note 2 above.
6. Ibid.
7. Rule added by N.C. Probate (Amendment) Rules, 1968.
8. Words in square brackets inserted by *ibid.* Remainder of rule revoked by N.C. Probate (Amendment) Rules, 1969.
9. Words in square brackets inserted by N.C. Probate (Amendment) Rules, 1968.
10. Words in square brackets substituted by N.C. Probate (Amendment) Rules, 1971.
11. Para. (4) added by *ibid.*
12. Revised paragraph substituted for former paras. (4) and (5) by *ibid.*
13. Rule amended by N.C. Probate (Amendment) Rules, 1967.
14. Proviso to rule 10(3) deleted by N.C. Probate (Amendment) Rules, 1967. Rules 10 and 13 do not apply in a will which it is sought to establish otherwise than by reference to s. 9 of the Wills Act, 1837; see N.C. Probate Rule 15, *post* p. 1152).
15. Rules 10 to 13 do not apply to a will which it is sought to establish otherwise than by reference to s. 9 of the Wills Act, 1837: see N.C. Probate Rule 15, *post,* p. 1152.
16. Ibid.
17. Ibid.
18. See also Civil Evidence Act, 1972, s. 4(1), referred to on p. 400, *ante.*
19. The operation of s.15 of the Wills Act, 1837, is restricted by the Wills Act, 1968.
20. Paras. (1) and (2) amended by N.C. Probate (Amendment) Rules, 1969.
21. Paragraph inserted by N.C. Probate (Amendment) Rules, 1971.
22. Paragraph substituted by N.C. Probate (Amendment) Rules, 1969, and amended by Rules of 1971.
23. Rule substituted by N.C. Probate (Amendment) Rules, 1967.
24. See note 1 above.
25. See note 2 above.
26. See note 4 above.
27. See note 7 above.
28. See note 8 above.
29. Ibid.
30. See note 10 above.

31. See note 13 above.
32. See note 12 above.
33. See note 13 above.
34. Ibid.
35. See note 12 above.
36. See note 14 above.
37. Ibid.
38. See note 15 above.
39. See note 18 above.
40. See note 19 above.
41. See note 20 above.
42. See note 21 above.
43. See note 22 above.
44. See note 2 above.
45. See note 4 above.
46. See note 7 above.
47. See note 8 above.
48. See note 9 above.
49. See note 10 above.
50. See note 11 above.
51. See note 13 above.
52. See note 12 above.
53. See note 13 above.
54. See note 14 above.
55. See note 15 above.
56. See note 19 above.
57. See note 20 above.
58. See note 21 above.
59. See note 22 above.
60. See note 1 above.

ENGLAND

THE NON-CONTENTIOUS PROBATE RULES 1987
S.I. 1987 No. 2024 (L.10)
Dated 24 November 1987

ARRANGEMENT OF RULES

1. Citation and commencement
2. Interpretation

3. Application of other rules
4. Applications for grants through solicitors
5. Personal applications
6. Duty of registrar on receiving application for grant
7. Grants by district probate registrars
8. Oath in support of grant
9. Grant in additional name
10. Marking of wills
11. Engrossments for purposes of record
12. Evidence as to due execution of will
13. Execution of will of blind or illiterate testator
14. Evidence as to terms, condition and date of execution of will
15. Attempted revocation of will
16. Affidavit as to due execution, terms, etc., of will
17. Wills proved otherwise than under section 9 of the Wills Act 1837
18. Wills of persons on military service and seamen
19. Evidence of foreign law
20. Order of priority for grant where deceased left a will
21. Grants to arresting witnesses, etc.
22. Order of priority for grant in case of intestacy
23. Order of priority of grant in pre-1926 cases
24. Right of assignee to a grant
25. Joinder of administrator
26. Additional personal representatives
27. Grants where two or more persons entitled in same degree
28. Exceptions to rules as to priority
29. Grants in respect of settled land
30. Grants where deceased died domiciled outside England and Wales
31. Grants to attorneys
32. Grants on behalf of minors
33. Grants where a minor is a co-executor
34. Renunciation of the right of a minor to a grant
35. Grants in case of mental incapacity
36. Grants to trust corporations and other corporate bodies
37. Renunciation of probate and administration
38. Notice to Crown of intended application for grant
39. Resealing under Colonial Probates Acts 1892 and 1927
40. Application for leave to sue on guarantee
41. Amendment and revocation of grant
42. Certificate of delivery of Inland Revenue affidavit
43. Standing Searches
44. Caveats

45. Probate actions
46. Citations
47. Citation to accept or refuse or to take a grant
48. Citation to propound a will
49. Address for service
50. Application for order to attend for examination or subpoena to bring in a will
51. Grants to part of an estate under section 113 of the Act
52. Grants of administration under discretionary powers of court, and grants *ad colligenda bona*
53. Applications for leave to swear to death
54. Grants in respect of nuncupative wills and copies of wills
55. Application for rectification of a will
56. Notice of election by surviving spouse to redeem life interest
57. Index of grant applications
58. Inspection of copies of original wills and other documents
59. Issue of copies of original wills and other documents
60. Taxation of costs
61. Power to require applications to be made by summons
62. Transfer of applications
63. Power to make orders for costs
64. Exercise of powers of judge during Long Vacation
65. Appeals from registrars
66. Service of summons
67. Notices, etc.
68. Application to pending proceedings
69. Revocation of previous rules

SCHEDULES -

First Schedule — Forms

Second Schedule — Revocations

The President of the Family Division, in exercise of the powers conferred upon him by section 127 of the Supreme Court Act 1981, and section 2 (5) of the Colonial Probates Act 1892, and with the concurrence of the Lord Chancellor, hereby makes the following Rules:
1. **Citation and commencement.** —These Rules may be cited as the Non-Con-tentious Probate Rules 1987, and shall come into force on 1 January 1988.

2. **Interpretation.** —
   (1) In these Rules, unless the context otherwise requires — 'the Act' means the Supreme Court Act 1981;
   'authorised officer' means any officer of a registry who is for the time being authorised by the President to administer any oath or to take any affidavit required for any purpose connected with his duties;
   'the Crown' includes the Crown in right of the Duchy of Lancaster and the Duke of Cornwall for the time being;
   'grant' means a grant of probate or administration and includes, where the context so admits, the resealing of such a grant under the Colonial Probates Acts 1892 and 1927;
   'gross value' in relation to any estate means the value of the estate without deduction for debts, incumbrances, funeral expenses or inheritance tax (or other capital tax payable out of the estate);
   'oath' means the oath required by rule 8 to be sworn by every applicant for a grant;
   'personal applicant' means a person other than a trust corporation who seeks to obtain a grant without employing a solicitor, and 'personal application' has a corresponding meaning;
   'registrar' means a registrar of the Principal Registry and includes—
   (a) in relation to an application for a grant made or proposed to be made at a district probate registry, and
   (b) in rules 26, 41 and 61 (2) in relation to a grant issued from a district probate registry, and
   (c) in relation to rules 46, 47 and 48.
   the registrar of that district probate registry;
   'registry' means the Principal Registry or a district probate registry;
   'the Senior Registrar' means the Senior Registrar of the Family Division or, in his absence, the senior of the registrars in attendance at the Principal Registry;
   'statutory guardian' means a surviving parent of a minor who is the guardian of the minor by virtue of section 3 of the Guardianship of Minors Act 1971;
   'testamentary guardian' means a person appointed by deed or will to be guardian of a minor under the power conferred by section 4 of the Guardianship of Minors Act 1971;
   'the Treasury Solicitor' means the solicitor for the affairs of Her Majesty's Treasury and includes the solicitor for the affairs of the Duchy of Lancaster and the solicitor of the Duchy of Cornwall;
   'trust corporation' means a corporation within the meaning of section

128 of the Act as extended by section 3 of the Law of Property (Amendment) Act 1926.

    (2) A form referred to by number means the form so numbered in the First Schedule; and such forms shall be used wherever applicable, with such variations as a registrar may in any particular case direct or approve.

3. **Application of other rules.** — Subject to the provisions of these Rules and to any enactment, the Rules of the Supreme Court 1965 shall apply, with the necessary modifications, to non-contentious probate matters, save that nothing in Order 3 shall prevent time from running in the Long Vacation.

4. **Applications for grants through solicitors**
    (1) A person applying for a grant through a solicitor may apply at any registry or sub-registry.
    (2) Every solicitor through whom an application for a grant is made shall give the address of his place of business within England and Wales.

5. **Personal applications.**
    (1) A personal applicant may apply for a grant at any registry or sub-registry.
    (2) Save as provided for by rule 39 a personal applicant may not apply through an agent, whether paid or unpaid, and may not be attended by any person acting or appearing to act as his adviser.
    (3) No personal application shall be proceeded with if—
        (a) it becomes necessary to bring the matter before the court by action or summons;
        (b) an application has already been made by a solicitor on behalf of the applicant and has not been withdrawn; or
        (c) the registrar so directs.
    (4) After a will has been deposited in a registry by a personal applicant, it may not be delivered to the applicant or to any other person unless in special circumstances the registrar so directs.
    (5) A personal applicant shall produce a certificate of the death of the deceased or such other evidence of the death as the registrar may approve.
    (6) A personal applicant shall supply all information necessary to enable the papers leading to the grant to be prepared in the registry.
    (7) Unless the registrar otherwise directs, every oath or affidavit required on a personal application shall be sworn or executed by all the deponents before an authorised officer.
    (8) No legal advice shall be given to a personal applicant by any

officer of a registry and every such officer shall be responsible only for embodying in proper form the applicant's instructions for the grant.

6. **Duty of registrar on receiving application for grant.**
   (1) A registrar shall not allow any grant to issue until all inquiries which he may see fit to make have been answered to his satisfaction.
   (2) Except with the leave of a register, no grant of probate or of administration with the will annexed shall issue within seven days of the death of the deceased and no grant of administration shall issue within fourteen days thereof.

7. **Grants by district probate registrars.**
   (1) No grant shall be made by a district probate registrar —
      (a) in any case in which there is contention, until the contention is disposed of; or
      (b) in any case in which it appears to him that a grant ought not to be made without the directions of a judge or a registrar of the Principal Registry.
   (2) In any case in which paragraph (1)(b) applies, the district probate registrar shall send a statement of the matter in question to the Principal Registry for directions.
   (3) A registrar of the Principal Registry may either confirm that the matter be referred to a judge and give directions accordingly or may direct the district probate registrar to proceed with the matter in accordance with such instructions as are deemed necessary, which may include a direction to take no further action in relation to the matter.

8. **Oath in support of grant.**
   (1) Every application for a grant other than one to which rule 39 applies shall be supported by an oath by the applicant in the form applicable to the circumstances of the case, and by such other papers as the registrar may require.
   (2) Unless otherwise directed by a registrar, the oath shall state where the deceased died domiciled.
   (3) Where the deceased died on or after the 1 January 1926, the oath shall state whether or not, to the best of the applicant's knowledge, information and belief, there was land vested in the deceased which was settled previously to his death and not by his will and which remained settled land notwithstanding his death.
   (4) On an application for a grant of administration the oath shall state in what manner all persons having a prior right to a grant have been cleared off and whether any minority or life interest

arises under the will or intestacy.
9. **Grant in additional name.** — Where it is sought to describe the deceased in a grant by some name in addition to his true name, the applicant shall depose to the true name of the deceased and shall specify some part of the estate which was held in the other name, or give any other reason for the inclusion of the other name in the grant.
10. **Marking of wills.** — Subject to paragraph (2) below, every will in respect of which an application for a grant is made—
    (a) shall be marked by the signatures of the applicant and the person before whom the oath is sworn; and
    (b) shall be exhibited to any affidavit which may be required under these Rules as to the validity, terms, condition or date of execution of the will.
    (2) The registrar may allow a facsimile copy of a will to be marked or exhibited in lieu of the original document.
11. **Engrossments for purposes of record.**
    (1) Where the registrar considers that in any particular case a facsimile copy of the original will would not be satisfactory for purposes of record, he may require an engrossment suitable for facsimile reproduction to be lodged.
    (2) Where a will —
    (a) contains alterations which are not to be admitted to proof; or
    (b) has been ordered to be rectified by virtue of section 20(1) of the Administration of Justice Act 1982,
    there shall be lodged an engrossment of the will in the form in which it is to be proved.
    (3) Any engrossment lodged under this rule shall reproduce the punctuation, spacing and division into paragraphs of the will and shall follow continuously from page to page on both sides of the paper.
12. **Evidence as to due execution of will.**
    (1) Subject to paragraphs (2) and (3) below, where a will contains no attestation clause or the attestation clause is insufficient, or where it appears to the registrar that there is doubt about the due execution of the will, he shall before admitting it to proof require an affidavit as to due execution from one or more of the attesting witnesses or, if no attesting witness is conveniently available, from any other person who was present when the will was executed; and if the registrar, after considering the evidence, is satisfied that the will was not duly executed, he shall refuse probate and mark the will accordingly.

(2) If no affidavit can be obtained in accordance with paragraph (1) above, the registrar may accept evidence on affidavit from any person he may think fit to show that the signature on the will is in the handwriting of the deceased, or of any other matter which may raise a presumption in favour of due execution of the will, and may if he thinks fit require that notice of the application be given to any person who may be prejudiced by the will.

(3) A registrar may accept a will for proof without evidence as aforesaid if he is satisfied that the distribution of the estate is not thereby affected.

13. **Execution of will of blind or illiterate testator.** — Before admitting to proof a will which appears to have been signed by a blind or illiterate testator or by another person by direction of the testator, or which for any other reason raises doubt as to the testator having had knowledge of the contents of the will at the time of its execution, the registrar shall satisfy himself that the testator had such knowledge.

14. **Evidence as to terms, condition and date of execution of will.**

    (1) Subject to paragraph (2) below, where there appears in a will any obliteration, interlineation, or other alteration which is not authenticated in the manner prescribed by section 21 of the Wills Act 1837, or by the re-execution of the will or by the execution of a codicil, the registrar shall require evidence to show whether the alteration was present at the time the will was executed and shall give directions as to the form in which the will is to be proved.

    (2) The provisions of paragraph (1) above shall not apply to any alteration which appears to the registrar to be of no practical importance.

    (3) If a will contains any reference to another document in such terms as to suggest that it ought to be incorporated in the will, the registrar shall require the document to be produced and may call for such evidence in regard to the incorporation of the document as he may think fit.

    (4) Where there is a doubt as to the date on which a will was executed, the registrar may require such evidence as he thinks necessary to establish the date.

15. **Attempted revocation of will.** — Any appearance of attempted revocation of a will by burning, tearing, or otherwise destroying and every other circumstance leading to a presumption of revocation by the testator, shall be accounted for to the registrar's satisfaction.

16. **Affidavit as to due execution, terms, etc., of will.** —A registrar may require an affidavit from any person he may think fit for the purpose of

satisfying himself as to any of the matters referred to in rules 13, 14 and 15, and in any such affidavit sworn by an attesting witness or other person present at the time of the execution of a will the deponent shall depose to the manner in which the will was executed.

17. **Wills proved otherwise than under section 9 of the Wills Act 1837.**
    (1) Rules 12 to 15 shall apply only to a will that is to be established by reference to section 9 of the Wills Act 1837 (signing and attestation of wills).
    (2) A will that is to be established otherwise than as described in paragraph (1) of this rule may be so established upon the registrar being satisfied as to its terms and validity, and includes (without prejudice to the generality of the foregoing) —
    - (a) any will to which rule 18 applies; and
    - (b) any will which, by virtue of the Wills Act 1963, is to be treated as properly executed if executed according to the internal law of the territory or state referred to in section 1 of that Act.

18. **Wills of persons on military service and seamen.** — Where the deceased died domiciled in England Wales and it appears to the registrar that there is *prima facie* evidence that a will is one to which section 11 of the Wills Act 1837 applies, the will may be admitted to proof if the registrar is satisfied that it was signed by the testator or, if unsigned, that it is in the testator's handwriting.

19. **Evidence of foreign law.** — Where evidence as to the law of any country or territory outside England and Wales is required on any application for a grant, the registrar may accept —
    - (a) an affidavit from any person whom, having regard to the particulars of his knowledge or experience given in the affidavit, he regards as suitably qualified to give expert evidence of the law in question; or
    - (b) a certificate by, or an act before, a notary practising in the country or territory concerned.

20. **Order of priority for grant where deceased left a will.** — Where the deceased died on or after 1 January 1926 the person or persons entitled to a grant in respect of a will shall be determined in accordance with the following order of priority, namely —
    - (a) the executor (but subject to rule 36 (4) (d) below)
    - (b) any residuary legatee or devisee holding in trust for any other person;
    - (c) any other residuary legatee or devisee (including one for life) or where the residue is not wholly disposed of by the will, any person entitled to share in the undisposed of residue (including the

Treasury Solicitor when claiming *bona vacantia* on behalf of the Crown), provided that —
  (i) unless a registrar otherwise directs, a residuary legatee or devisee whose legacy or devise is vested in interest shall be preferred to one entitled on the happenings of a contingency, and
  (ii) where the residue is not in terms wholly disposed of, the registrar may, if he is satisfied that the testator has nevertheless disposed of the whole or substantially the whole of the known estate, allow a grant to be made to any legatee or devisee entitled to, or to share in, the estate so disposed of, without regard to the persons entitled to share in any residue not disposed of by the will;
 (d) the personal representative of any residuary legatee or devisee (but not one for life, or one holding in trust for any other person), or of any person entitled to share in any residue not disposed of by the will;
 (e) any other legatee or devisee (including one for life or one holding in trust for any other person) or any creditor of the deceased, provided that, unless a registrar otherwise directs, a legatee or devisee whose legacy or devise is vested in interest shall be preferred to one entitled on the happening of a contingency;
 (f) the personal representative of any other legatee or devisee (but not one for life or one holding in trust for any other person) or of any creditor of the deceased.
21. **Grants to attesting witnesses, etc.** —Where a gift to any person fails by reason of section 15 of the Wills Act 1837, such person shall not have any right to a grant as a beneficiary named in the will, without prejudice to his right to a grant in any other capacity.
22. **Order of priority for grant in case of intestacy.**
 (1) Where the deceased died on or after 1 January 1926, wholly intestate, the person or persons having a beneficial interest in the estate shall be entitled to a grant of administration in the following classes in order of priority, namely —
  (a) the surviving husband or wife;
  (b) the children of the deceased and the issue of any deceased child who died before the deceased;
  (c) the father and mother of the deceased;
  (d) brothers and sisters of the whole blood and the issue of any deceased brother or sister of the whole blood who died before the deceased;
  (e) brothers and sisters of the half blood and the issue of any

deceased brother or sister of the half blood who died before the deceased;
(f) grandparents;
(g) uncles and aunts of the whole blood and the issue of any deceased uncle or aunt of the whole blood who died before the deceased;
(h) uncles and aunts of the half blood and the issue of any deceased uncle or aunt of the half blood who died before the deceased.

(2) In default of any person having a beneficial interest in the estate, the Treasury Solicitor shall be entitled to a grant if he claims *bona vacantia* on behalf of the Crown.

(3) If all persons entitled to a grant under the foregoing provisions of this rule have been cleared off, a grant may be made to a creditor of the deceased or to any person who, notwithstanding that he has no immediate beneficial interest in the estate, may have a beneficial interest in the event of an accretion thereto.

(4) Subject to paragraph (5) of rule 27, the personal representative of a person in any of the classes mentioned in paragraph (1) of this rule or the personal representative of a creditor of the deceased shall have the same right to a grant as the person whom he represents provided that the persons mentioned in sub-paragraphs (b) to (h) of paragraph (1) above shall be preferred to the personal representative of a spouse who has died without taking a beneficial interest in the whole estate of the deceased as ascertained at the time of the application for the grant.

23. **Order of priority for grant in pre-1926 cases.** —Where the deceased died before 1 January 1926, the person or persons entitled to a grant shall, subject to the provisions of any enactment, be determined in accordance with the principles and rules under which the court would have acted at the date of death.

24. Right of assignee to a grant.
    (1) Where all the persons entitled to the estate of the deceased (whether under a will or on intestacy) have assigned their whole interest in the estate to one or more persons, the assignee or assignees shall replace, in the order of priority for a grant of administration, the assignor or, if there are two or more assignors, the assignor with the highest priority.
    (2) Where there are two or more assignees, administration may be granted with the consent of the others to any one or more (not exceeding four) of them.
    (3) In any case where administration is applied for by an assignee

the original instrument of assignment shall be produced and a copy of the same lodged in the registry.

25. **Joinder of administrator.**
    (1) A person entitled in priority to a grant of administration may, without leave, apply for a grant with a person entitled in a lower degree, provided that there is no other person entitled in a higher degree to the person to be joined, unless every other person has renounced.
    (2) Subject to paragraph (3) below, an application for leave to join with a person entitled in priority to a grant of administration a person having no right or no immediate right thereto shall be made to a registrar, and shall be supported by an affidavit by the person entitled in priority, the consent of the person proposed to be joined as administrator and such other evidence as the registrar may direct.
    (3) Unless a registrar otherwise directs, there may without any such application be joined with a person entitled in priority to administration —
        (a) any person who is nominated under paragraph (3) of rule 32 or paragraph (3) of rule 35;
        (b) a trust corporation.

26. **Additional personal representatives.**
    (1) An application under section 114 (4) of the Act to add a personal representative shall be made to a registrar and shall be supported by an affidavit by the applicant, the consent of the person proposed to be added as personal representative and such other evidence as the registrar may require.
    (2) On any such application the registrar may direct that a note shall be made on the original grant of the addition of a further personal representative, or he may impound or revoke the grant or make such other order as the circumstances of the case may require.

27. **Grants where two or more persons entitled in same degree.**
    (1) Subject to paragraphs (2) and (3) below, where, on an application for probate, power to apply for a like grant is to be reserved to such other of the executors as have not renounced probate, the oath shall state that notice of the application has been given to the executor or executors to whom power is to be reserved.
    (2) Where power is to be reserved to partners of a firm, notice for the purposes of paragraph (1) above may be given to the partners by sending it to the firm at its principal or last known place of business.

(3) A registrar may dispense with the giving of notice under paragraph (1) above if he is satisfied that the giving of such a notice is impracticable or would result in unreasonable delay or expense.

(4) A grant of administration may be made to any person entitled thereto without notice to other persons entitled in the same degree.

(5) Unless a registrar otherwise directs, administration shall be granted to a person of full age entitled thereto in preference to a guardian of a minor, and to a living person entitled thereto in preference to the personal representative of a deceased person.

(6) A dispute between persons entitled to a grant in the same degree shall be brought by summons before a registrar.

(7) The issue of a summons under this rule in a district probate registry shall be notified forthwith to the registry in which the index of pending grant applications is maintained.

(8) If the issue of a summons under this rule is known to the registrar, he shall not allow any grant to be sealed until such summons is finally disposed of.

28. **Exceptions to rules as to priority.**

(1) Any person to whom a grant may or is required to be made under any enactment shall not be prevented from obtaining such a grant notwithstanding the operation of rules 20, 22, 25 or 27.

(2) Where the deceased died domiciled outside England and Wales rules 20, 22, 25 or 27 shall not apply except in a case to which paragraph (3) of rule 30 applies.

29. **Grants in respect of settled land.**

(1) In this rule 'settled land' means land vested in the deceased which was settled previously to his death and not by his will and which remained settled land notwithstanding his death.

(2) The special executors in regard to settled land constituted by section 22 of the Administration of Estates Act 1925 shall have a prior right to a grant of probate limited to settled land.

(3) The person or persons entitled to a grant of administration limited to settled land shall be determined in accordance with the following order of priority, namely —

(i) the trustees of the settlement at the time of the application for the grant;

(ii) the personal representatives of the deceased.

(4) Where the persons entitled to a grant in respect of the free estate are also entitled to a grant of the same nature in respect of settled land, a grant expressly including the settled land may issue to them.

(5) Where there is settled land and a grant is made in respect of the free estate only, the grant shall expressly exclude the settled land.

30. **Grants where deceased died domiciled outside England and Wales.**
    (1) Subject to paragraph (3) below, where the deceased died domiciled outside England and Wales, a registrar may order that a grant do issue to any of the following persons —
        (a) to the person entrusted with the administration of the estate by the court having jurisdiction at the place where the deceased died domiciled; or
        (b) where there is no person so entrusted, to the person beneficially entitled to the estate by the law of the place where the deceased died domiciled or, if there is more than one person so entitled, to such of them as the registrar may direct; or
        (c) if in the opinion of the registrar the circumstances so require, to such person as the registrar may direct.
    (2) A grant made under paragraph (1)(a) or (b) above may be issued jointly with such person as the registrar may direct if the grant is required to be made to not less than two administrators.
    (3) Without any order made under paragraph (1) above —
        (a) probate of any will which is admissible to proof may be granted —
            (i) if the will is in the English or Welsh language, to the executor named therein; or
            (ii) if the will describes the duties of a named person in terms sufficient to constitute him executor according to the tenor of the will, to that person; and
        (b) where the whole or substantially the whole of the estate in England and Wales consists of immovable property, a grant in respect of the whole estate may be made in accordance with the law which would have been applicable if the deceased had died domiciled in England and Wales.

31. **Grants to attorneys.**
    (1) Subject to paragraphs (2) and (3) below, the lawfully constituted attorney of a person entitled to a grant may apply for administration for the use and benefit of the donor, and such grant shall be limited until further representation be granted, or in such other ways as the registrar may direct.
    (2) Where the donor referred to in paragraph (1) above is an executor, notice of the application shall be given to any other executor unless such notice is dispensed with by the registrar.
    (3) Where the donor referred to in paragraph (1) above is mentally

incapable and the attorney is acting under an enduring power of attorney, the application shall be made in accordance with rule 35.

32. Grants on behalf of minors.

(1) Where a person to whom a grant would otherwise be made is a minor, administration for his use and benefit, limited until he attains the age of eighteen years. shall, unless otherwise directed, and subject to paragraph (2) of this rule, be granted to the parents of the minor jointly, or to the statutory or testamentary guardian, or to any guardian appointed by a court of competent jurisdiction; provided that where the minor is sole executor and has no interest in the residuary estate of the deceased, administration for the use and benefit of the minor limited as aforesaid, shall, unless a registrar otherwise directs, be granted to the person entitled to the residuary estate.

(2) A registrar may by order assign any person as guardian of the minor, and such assigned guardian may obtain administration for the use and benefit of the minor, limited as aforesaid, in default of, or jointly with, or to the exclusion of, any person mentioned in paragraph (1) of this rule; and the intended guardian shall file an affidavit in support of his application to be assigned.

(3) Where there is only one person competent and willing to take a grant under the foregoing provisions of this rule, such person may, unless a registrar otherwise directs, nominate any fit and proper person to act jointly with him in taking the grant.

33. Grants where a minor is a co-executor.

(1) Where a minor is appointed executor jointly with one or more other executors, probate may be granted to the executor or executors not under disability with power reserved to the minor executor, and the minor executor shall be entitled to apply for probate on attaining the age of eighteen years.

(2) Administration for the use and benefit of a minor executor until he attains the age of eighteen years may be granted under rule 32 if, and only if, the executors who are not under disability renounce or, on being cited to accept or refuse a grant, fail to make an effective application therefor.

34. Renunciation of the right of a minor to a grant.

(1) The right of a minor executor to probate on attaining the age of eighteen years may not be renounced by any person on his behalf.

(2) The right of a minor to administration may be renounced only by a person assigned as guardian under paragraph (2) of rule 32, and authorised by the registrar to renounce on behalf of the minor.

35. **Grants in case of mental incapacity.**
   (1) Unless a registrar otherwise directs, no grant shall be made under this rule unless all persons entitled in the same degree as the incapable person referred to in paragraph (2) below have been cleared off.
   (2) Where a registrar is satisfied that a person entitled to a grant is by reason of mental incapacity of managing his affairs, administration for his use and benefit, limited until further representation be granted or in such other way as the registrar may direct, may be granted in the following order of priority —
      (a) to the person authorised by the Court of Protection to apply for a grant;
      (b) where there is no person so authorised, to the lawful attorney of the incapable person acting under a registered enduring power of attorney;
      (c) where there is no such attorney entitled to act, or if the attorney shall renounce administration for the use and benefit of the incapable person, to the person entitled to the residuary estate of the deceased.
   (3) Where a grant is required to be made not less than two administrators, and there is only one person competent and willing to take a grant under the foregoing provisions of this rule, administration may, unless a registrar otherwise directs, be granted to such person jointly with any other person nominated by him.
   (4) Notwithstanding the foregoing provisions of this rule, administration for the use and benefit of the incapable person may be granted to such two or more other persons as the registrar may by order direct.
   (5) Notice of an intended application under this rule shall be given to the Court of Protection.

36. **Grants to trust corporations and other corporate bodies.**
   (1) An application for a grant to a trust corporation shall be made through one of its officers, and such officer shall depose in the oath that the corporation is a trust corporation as defined by these Rules and that it has power to accept a grant.
   (2) (a) Where the trust corporation is the holder of an official position, any officer whose name is included on a list filed with the Senior Registrar of persons authorised to make affidavits and sign documents on behalf of the office holder may act as the officer through whom the holder of that official position applies for the grant.
       (b) In all other cases a certified copy of the resolution of the

trust corporation authorising the officer to make the application shall be lodged, or it shall be deposed in the oath that such certified copy has been filed with the Senior Registrar, that the officer is therein identified by the position he holds, and that such resolution is still in force.

(3) A trust corporation may apply for administration otherwise than as a beneficiary or the attorney of some person, and on any such application there shall be lodged the consents of all persons entitled to a grant and of all persons interested in the residuary estate of the deceased save that the registrar may dispense with any such consents as aforesaid on such terms, if any, as he may think fit.

(4)   (a) Subject to sub-paragraph (d) below, where a corporate body would, if an individual, be entitled to a grant but is not a trust corporation as defined by these Rules, administration for its use and benefit, limited until further representation be granted, may be made to its nominee or to its lawfully constituted attorney.

    (b) A copy of the resolution appointing the nominee or the power of attorney (whichever is appropriate) shall be lodged, and such resolution or power of attorney shall be sealed by the corporate body, or be otherwise authenticated to the registrar's satisfaction.

    (c) The nominee or attorney shall depose in the oath that the corporate body is not a trust corporation as defined by these Rules.

    (d) The provisions of paragraph (4)(a) above shall not apply where a corporate body is appointed executor jointly with an individual unless the right of the individual has been cleared off.

37. Renunciation of probate and administration.

(1) Renunciation of probate by an executor shall not operate as renunciation of any right which he may have to a grant of administration in some other capacity unless he expressly renounces such right.

(2) Unless a registrar otherwise directs, no person who has renounced administration in one capacity may obtain a grant thereof in some other capacity.

(3) A renunciation of probate or administration may be retracted at any time with the leave of a registrar; provided that only in exceptional circumstances may leave be given to an executor to retract a renunciation of probate after a grant has been made to

some other person entitled in a lower degree.
(4) A direction or order given leave under this rule may be made either by the registrar of a district probate registry where the renunciation is filed or a registrar of the Principal Registry.

38. **Notice to Crown of intended application for grant.** — In any case in which it appears that the Crown is or may be beneficially interested in the estate of a deceased person, notice of intended application for a grant shall be given by the applicant to the Treasury Solicitor, and the registrar may direct that no grant shall issue within 28 days after the notice has been given.

39. **Resealing under Colonial Probates Acts 1892 and 1927.**
    (1) An application under the Colonial Probates Acts 1892 and 1927 for the resealing of probate or administration granted by the court of a country to which those Acts apply may be made by the person to whom the grant was made or by any person authorised in writing to apply on his behalf.
    (2) On any such application an Inland Revenue affidavit or account shall be lodged.
    (3) Except by leave of a registrar, no grant shall be resealed unless it was made to such a person as is mentioned in sub-paragraph (a) or (b) of paragraph (1) of rule 30 or to a person to whom a grant could be made under sub-paragraph (a) of paragraph (3) of that rule.
    (4) No limited or temporary grant shall be resealed, except by leave of a registrar.
    (5) Every grant lodged for resealing shall include a copy of any will to which the grant relates or shall be accompanied by a copy thereof certified as correct by or under the authority of the court by which the grant was made, and where the copy of the grant required to be deposited under subsection (1) of section 2 of the Colonial Probates Act 1892 does not include a copy of the will, a copy thereof shall be deposited in the registry before the grant is resealed.
    (6) The registrar shall send notice of the resealing to the court which made the grant.
    (7) Where notice is received in the Principal Registry of the resealing of a grant issued in England and Wales, notice of any amendment or revocation of the grant shall be sent to the court by which it was resealed.

40. **Application for leave to sue on guarantee.** — An application for leave under section 120(3) of the Act or under section 11(5) of the Administration of Estates Act 1971 to sue a surety on a guarantee

given for the purposes of either of those sections shall, unless the registrar otherwise directs under rule 61, be made by summons to a registrar and notice of the application shall be served on the administrator, the surety and any co-surety.

41. **Amendment and revocation of grant**
    (1) Subject to paragraph (2) below, if a registrar is satisfied that a grant should be amended or revoked he may make an order accordingly.
    (2) Except on the application or with the consent of the person to whom the grant was made, the power conferred in paragraph (1) above shall be exercised only in exceptional circumstances.

42. **Certificate of delivery of Inland Revenue affidavit.** — Where the deceased died before 13 March 1975 the certificate of delivery of an Inland Revenue affidavit required by section 30 of the Customs and Inland Revenue Act 1881 to be borne by every grant shall be in Form 1.

43. **Standing searches**
    (1) Any person who wishes to be notified of the issue of a grant may enter a standing search for the grant by lodging with the Senior Registrar, or sending to him by post, a notice in Form 2.
    (2) A person who has entered a standing search will be sent an office copy of any grant which corresponds with the particulars given on the completed Form 2 and which —
        (a) issued not more than twelve months before the entry of the standing search; or
        (b) issues within a period of six months after the entry of the standing search.
    (3) (a) Where an applicant wishes to extend the said period of six months, he or his solicitor may lodge at, or send by post to, the Principal Registry written application for extension.
        (b) An application for extension as aforesaid must be lodged, or received by post, within the last month of the said period of six months, and the standing search shall thereupon be effective for an additional period of six months from the date on which it was due to expire.
        (c) A standing search which has been extended as above may be further extended by the filing of a further application for extension subject to the same conditions as set out in sub-paragraph (b) above.

44. **Caveats**
    (1) Any person who wishes to show cause against the sealing of a grant may enter a caveat in any registry or sub-registry, and the registrar shall not allow any grant to be sealed (other than a grant *ad colligenda bona* or a grant under section 117 of the Act) if he

has knowledge of an effective caveat; provided that no caveat shall prevent the sealing of a grant on the day on which the caveat is entered.

(2) Any person wishing to enter a caveat (in these Rules called 'the caveator'), or a solicitor on his behalf, may effect entry of a caveat—
   (a) by completing Form 3 in the appropriate book at any registry or sub-registry; or
   (b) by sending by post at his own risk a notice in Form 3 to any registry or sub-registry and the proper officer shall provide an acknowledgement of the entry of the caveat.

(3) (a) Except as otherwise provided by this rule or by rules 45 or 46, a caveat shall be effective for a period of six months from the date of entry thereof, and where a caveator wishes to extend the said period of six months, he or his solicitor may lodge at, or send by post to, the registry or sub-registry at which the caveat was entered a written application for extension.
   (b) An application for extension as aforesaid must be lodged, or received by post, within the last month of the said period of six months, and the caveat shall thereupon (save as otherwise provided by this rule) be effective for an additional period of six months from the date on which it was due to expire.
   (c) A caveat which has been extended as above may be further extended by the filing of a further application for extension subject to the same conditions as set out in sub-paragraph (b) above.

(4) An index of caveats entered in any registry or sub-registry shall be maintained at the same registry in which the index of pending grant applications is maintained, and a search of the caveat index shall be made
   (a) on receipt of an application for a grant at that registry; and
   (b) on receipt of a notice of an application for a grant made in any other registry.

(5) Any person claiming to have an interest in the estate may cause to be issued from the registry in which the caveat index is maintained a warning in Form 4 against the caveat, and the person warning shall state his interest in the estate of the deceased and shall require the caveator to give particulars of any contrary interest in the estate; and the warning or a copy thereof shall be served on the caveator forthwith.

(6) A caveator who has no interest contrary to that of the person warning, but who wishes to show cause against the sealing of a

grant to that person, may within eight days of service of the warning upon him (inclusive of the day of such service), or at any time thereafter if no affidavit has been filed under paragraph (12) below, issue and serve a summons for directions.
(7) On the hearing of any summons for directions under paragraph (6) above the registrar may give a direction for the caveat to cease to have effect.
(8) Any caveat in force when a summons for directions is issued shall remain in force until the summons has been disposed of unless a direction has been given under paragraph (7) above.
(9) The issue of a summons under this rule shall be notified forthwith to the registry in which the caveat index is maintained.
(10) A caveator having an interest contrary to that of the person warning may within eight days of service of the warning upon him (inclusive of the day of such service) or at any time thereafter if no affidavit has been filed under paragraph (12) below, enter an appearance in the registry in which the caveat index is maintained by filing Form 5 and making an entry in the appropriate book; and he shall serve forthwith on the person warning a copy of Form 5 sealed with the seal of the court.
(11) A caveator who has not entered an appearance to a warning may at any time withdraw his caveat by giving notice at the registry or sub-registry at which it was entered, and the caveat shall thereupon cease to have effect; and, where the caveat has been so withdrawn, the caveator shall forthwith give notice of withdrawal to the person warning.
(12) If no appearance has been entered by the caveator or no summons has been issued by him under paragraph (6) of this rule, the person warning may at any time after eight days of service of the warning upon the caveator (inclusive of the day of such service) file an affidavit in the registry in which the caveat index is maintained as to such service and the caveat shall thereupon cease to have effect provided that there is no pending summons under paragraph (6) of this rule.
(13) Unless a registrar of the Principal Registry by order made on summons otherwise directs, any caveat in respect of which an appearance to a warning has been entered shall remain in force until the commencement of a probate action.
(14) Except with the leave of a registrar of the Principal Registry, no further caveat may be entered by or on behalf of any caveator whose caveat is either in force or has ceased to have effect under paragraphs (7) or (12) of this rule or under rule 45(4) or rule 46(3).

45. **Probate actions**
   (1) Upon being advised by the court concerned of the commencement of a probate action the Senior Registrar shall give notice of the action to every caveator other than the plaintiff in the action in respect of each caveat that is in force.
   (2) In respect of any caveat entered subsequent to the commencement of a probate action the Senior Registrar shall give notice to that caveator of the existence of the action.
   (3) Unless a registrar of the Principal Registry by order made on summons otherwise directs, the commencement of a probate action shall operate to prevent the sealing of a grant (other than a grant under section 117 of the Act) until application for a grant is made by the person shown to be entitled thereto by the decision of the court in such action.
   (4) Upon such application for a grant, any caveat entered by the plaintiff in the action, and any caveat in respect of which notice of the action has been given, shall cease to have effect.

46. **Citations**
   (1) Any citation may issue from the Principal Registry or a district probate registry and shall be settled by a registrar before being issued.
   (2) Every averment in a citation, and such other information as the registrar may require, shall be verified by an affidavit sworn by the person issuing the citation (in these Rules called the 'citor'), provided that the registrar may in special circumstances accept an affidavit sworn by the citor's solicitor.
   (3) The citor shall enter a caveat before issuing a citation and, unless a registrar of the Principal Registry by order made on summons otherwise directs, any caveat in force at the commencement of the citation proceedings shall, unless withdrawn pursuant to paragraph (11) of rule 44, remain in force until application for a grant is made by the person shown to be entitled thereto by the decision of the court in such proceedings, and upon such application any caveat entered by a party who had notice of the proceedings shall cease to have effect.
   (4) Every citation shall be served personally on the person cited unless the registrar, on cause shown by affidavit, directs some other mode of service, which may include notice by advertisement.
   (5) Every will referred to in a citation shall be lodged in a registry before the citation is issued, except where the will is not in the citor's possession and the registrar is satisfied that it is impracticable to require it to be lodged.

(6) A person who has been cited to appear may, within eight days of service of the citation upon him (inclusive of the day of such service), or at any time thereafter if no application has been made by the citor under paragraph (5) of rule 47 or paragraph (2) of rule 48, enter an appearance in the registry from which the citation issued by filing Form 5 and shall forthwith thereafter serve on the citor a copy of Form 5 sealed with the seal of the registry.

47. **Citation to accept or refuse or to take a grant.**
    (1) A citation to accept or refuse a grant may be issued at the instance of any person who would himself be entitled to a grant in the event of the person cited renouncing his right thereto.
    (2) Where power to make a grant to an executor has been reserved, a citation calling on him to accept or refuse a grant may be issued at the instance of the executors who have proved the will or the survivor of them or of the executors of the last survivor of deceased executors who have proved.
    (3) A citation calling on an executor who has intermeddled in the estate of the deceased to show cause why he should not be ordered to take a grant may be issued at the instance of any person interested in the estate at any time after the expiration of six months from the death of the deceased, provided that no citation to take a grant shall issue while proceedings as to the validity of the will are pending.
    (4) A person cited who is willing to accept or take a grant may, after entering an appearance, apply *ex parte* by affidavit to a registrar for an order for a grant to himself.
    (5) If the time limited for appearance has expired and the person cited has not entered an appearance, the citor may —
        (a) in the case of a citation under paragraph (1) of this rule, apply to a registrar for an order for a grant to himself;
        (b) in the case of a citation under paragraph (2) of this rule, apply to a registrar for an order that a note be made on the grant that the executor in respect of whom power was reserved has been duly cited and has not appeared and that all his rights in respect of the executorship have wholly ceased; or
        (c) in the case of a citation under paragraph (3) of this rule, apply to a registrar by summons (which shall be served on the person cited) for an order requiring such person to take a grant within a specified time or for a grant to himself or to some other person specified in the summons.
    (6) An application under the last foregoing paragraph shall be

supported by an affidavit showing that the citation was duly served.

(7) If the person cited has entered an appearance but has not applied for a grant under paragraph (4) of this rule, or has failed to prosecute his application with reasonable diligence, the citor may —
  (a) in the case of a citation under paragraph (1) of this rule, apply by summons to a registrar for an order for a grant to himself;
  (b) in the case of a citation under paragraph (2) of this rule, apply by summons to a registrar for an order striking out the appearance and for the endorsement on the grant of such a note as is mentioned in sub-paragraph (b) of paragraph (5) of this rule; or
  (c) in the case of a citation under paragraph (3) of this rule, apply by summons to a registrar for an order requiring the person cited to take a grant within a specified time or for a grant to himself or to some other person specified in the summons;
and the summons shall be served on the person cited.

48. **Citation to propound a will.**
  (1) A citation to propound a will shall be directed to the executors named in the will and to all persons interested thereunder, and may be issued at the instance of any citor having an interest contrary to that of the executors or such other persons.
  (2) If the time limited for appearance has expired, the citor may —
    (a) in the case where no person has entered an appearance, apply to a registrar for an order for a grant as if the will were invalid and such application shall be supported by an affidavit showing that the citation was duly served; or
    (b) in the case where no person who has entered an appearance proceeds with reasonable diligence to propound the will, apply to a registrar by summons, which shall be served on every person cited who has entered an appearance, for such an order as is mentioned in para-graph (a) above.

49. **Address for service.** — All caveats, citations, warnings and appearances shall contain an address for service in England and Wales.

50. **Application for an order to attend for examination or for subpoena to bring in a will.**
  (1) An application under section 122 of the Act for an order requiring a person to attend for examination may, unless a probate action has been commenced, be made to a registrar by summons which

shall be served on every such person as aforesaid.
(2) An application under section 123 of the Act for the issue by the registrar of a subpoena to bring in a will shall be supported by an affidavit setting out the grounds of the application, and if any person served with the subpoena denies that the will is in his possession or control he may file an affidavit to that effect in the registry from which the subpoena issued.

51. **Grants to part of an estate under section 113 of the Act.** — An application for an order for a grant under section 113 of the Act to part of an estate may be made to a registrar, and shall be supported by an affidavit setting out the grounds of the application, and
    (a) stating whether the estate of the deceased is known to be insolvent; and
    (b) showing how any person entitled to a grant in respect of the whole estate in priority to the application has been cleared off.

52. **Grants of administration under discretionary powers of court, and grants** *ad colligenda bona.* —An application for an order for —
    (a) a grant of administration under section 116 of the Act, or (b) a grant of administration ad colligenda bona, may be made to a registrar and shall be supported by an affidavit setting out the grounds of the application.

53. **Applications for leave to swear to death.** — An application for leave to swear to the death of a person in whose estate a grant is sought may be made to a registrar, and shall be supported by an affidavit setting out the grounds of the application and containing particulars of any policies of insurance effected on the life of the presumed deceased together with such further evidence as the registrar may require.

54. **Grants in respect of nuncupative wills and copies of wills.**
    (1) Subject to paragraph (2) below, an application for an order admitting to proof a nuncupative will, or a will contained in a copy or reconstruction thereof where the original is not available, shall be made to a registrar.
    (2) In any case where a will is not available owing to its being retained in the custody of a foreign court or official, a duly authenticated copy of the will may be admitted to proof without the order referred to in paragraph (1) above.
    (3) An application under paragraph (1) above shall be supported by an affidavit setting out the grounds of the application, and by such evidence on affidavit as the applicant can adduce as to —
        (a) the will's existence after the death of the testator or, where there is no such evidence, the facts on which the applicant relies to rebut the presumption that the will has been

revoked by destruction;
(b) in respect of a nuncupative will, the contents of that will; and
(c) in respect of a reconstruction of a will, the accuracy of that reconstruction.
(4) The registrar may require additional evidence in the circumstances of a particular case as to due execution of the will or as to the accuracy of the copy will, and may direct that notice be given to persons who would be prejudiced by the application.

55. **Application for rectification of a will.**
    (1) An application for an order that a will be rectified by virtue of section 20(1) of the Administration of Justice Act 1982 may be made to a registrar, unless a probate action has been commenced.
    (2) The application shall be supported by an affidavit, setting out the grounds of the application, together with such evidence as can be adduced as to the testator's intentions and as to whichever of the following matters as are in issue:-
        (a) in what respects the testator's intentions were not understood; or
        (b) the nature of any alleged clerical error.
    (3) Unless otherwise directed, notice of the application shall be given to every person having an interest under the will whose interest might be prejudiced by the rectification applied for and any comments in writing by any such person shall be exhibited to the affidavit in support of the application.
    (4) If the registrar is satisfied that, subject to any direction to the contrary, notice has been given to every person mentioned in paragraph (3) above, and that the application is unopposed. he may order that the will be rectified accordingly.

56. **Notice of election by surviving spouse to redeem life interest.**
    (1) Where a surviving spouse who is the sole or sole surviving personal representative of the deceased is entitled to a life interest in part of the residuary estate and elects under section 47A of the Administration of Estates Act 1925 to have the life interest redeemed, he may give written notice of the election to the Senior Registrar in pursuance of subsection (7) of that section by filing a notice in Form 6 in the Principal Registry or in the district probate registry from which the grant issued.
    (2) Where the grant issued from a district probate registry, the notice shall be filed in duplicate.
    (3) A notice filed under this rule shall be noted on the grant and the record and shall be open to inspection.

57. **Index of grant applications.**
    (1) The Senior Registrar shall maintain an index of every pending application for a grant made in any registry.
    (2) Notice of every application for a grant shall be sent by the registry in which the application is made to the registry in which the index is maintained and shall be in the form of a document stating the full name of the deceased and the date of his death.
    (3) On receipt of the notice referred to in paragraph (2) above, the registry shall search its current index and shall give a certificate as to the result of that search to the registry which sent the notice.
    (4) The requirements of paragraph (2) above shall not apply in any case in which the application for a grant is made in the registry in which the index is maintained.
    (5) In this rule 'registry' includes a sub-registry.
58. **Inspection of copies of original wills and other documents.** — An original will or other document referred to in section 124 of the Act shall not be open to inspection if, in the opinion of a registrar, such inspection would be undesirable or otherwise inappropriate.
59. **Issue of copies of original wills and other documents.** — Where copies are required of original wills or other documents deposited under section 124 of the Act, such copies may be facsimile copies sealed with the seal of the court and issued either as office copies or certified under the hand of a registrar to be true copies.
60. **Taxation of costs.** — Every bill of costs, other than a bill delivered by a solicitor to his client which falls to be taxed under the Solicitors Act 1974, shall be referred to a registrar of the Principal Registry for taxation and may be taxed by him or such other taxing officer in the Principal Registry as the President may appoint.
61. **Power to require application to be made by summons.**
    (1) A registrar may require any application to be made by summons to a registrar in chambers or a judge in chambers or open court.
    (2) An application for an inventory and account shall be made by summons to a registrar.
    (3) A summons for hearing by a registrar shall be issued out of the registry in which it is to be heard.
    (4) A summons to be heard by a judge shall be issued out of the Principal Registry.
62. **Transfer of applications.** — A registrar to whom any application is made under these Rules may order the transfer of the application to another registrar having jurisdiction.
63. **Power to make orders for costs.** — On any application dealt with by him on summons, the district probate registrar shall have full power to

determine by whom and to what extent the costs are to be paid.

64. **Exercise of powers of judge during Long Vacation.** —All powers exercisable under these Rules by a judge in chambers may be executed during the Long Vacation by a registrar of the Principal Registry.

65. **Appeals from registrars.**
    (1) An appeal against a decision or requirement of a registrar shall be made by summons to a judge.
    (2) If, in the case of an appeal under the last foregoing paragraph, any person besides the appellant appeared or was represented before the registrar from whose decision or requirement the appeal is brought, the summons shall be issued within seven days thereof for hearing on the first available day and shall be served on every such person as aforesaid.

66. **Service of summons.**
    (1) A judge or registrar of the Principal Registry or, where the application is to be made to a district probate registrar, that registrar, may direct that a summons for the service of which no other provision is made by these Rules shall be served on such person or persons as the judge or registrar may direct.
    (2) Where by these Rules or by any direction given under the last foregoing paragraph a summons is required to be served on any person, it shall be served not less than two clear days before the day appointed for the hearing, unless a judge or registrar at or before the hearing dispenses with service on such terms, if any, as he may think fit.

67. **Notices, etc.** — Unless a registrar otherwise directs or these Rules otherwise provide, any notice or other document required to be given to or served on any person may be given or served in the manner prescribed by Order 65 Rule 5 of the Rules of the Supreme Court 1965.

68. **Application to pending proceedings.** — Subject in any particular case to any direction given by a judge or registrar, these Rules shall apply to any proceedings which are pending on the date on which they come into force as well as to any proceedings commenced on or after that date.

69. **Revocation of previous rules.**
    (1) Subject to paragraph (2) below, the rules set out in the Second Schedule are hereby revoked.
    (2) The rules set out in the Second Schedule shall continue to apply to such extent as may be necessary for giving effect to a direction under rule 68.

GUYANA
SUBSIDIARY LEGISLATION
DECEASED PERSONS ESTATES' ADMINISTRATION RULES
made under section 32

1. These Rules may be cited as the Deceased Persons Estates' Administration Rules.
2. Application to record a grant of probate or letters of administration in the Registrar's office may be made by the executor or administrator or the attorney (lawfully authorised for the purpose) of such executor or administrator, either in person or through a barrister, advocate or solicitor.
3. Such application must be accompanied by an oath of the executor, administrator or attorney in the form in the Schedule, or as nearly thereto as the circumstances of the case will allow.
4. The Registrar shall be satisfied that notice of such application has been advertised in the *Gazette*.
5. On application to record letters of administration the administrator or his attorney shall give a bond (in the form set out in the Schedule) to cover the estate of the deceased within Guyana.
6. In every case, and especially when the domicile of the deceased at the time of death as sworn to in the affidavit differs from that suggested by the description in the grant, the Registrar may require further evidence as to domicile.
7. If it should appear that the deceased was not at the time of death domiciled within the jurisdiction of the Court from which the grant of probate or letters of administration issued, the grant shall not be recorded unless the grant is such as might lawfully, by the law of Guyana, be recorded in the Registrar's office.
8. Together with the grant to be recorded, and the copy to be deposited in the registry, duly authenticated copies of all testamentary papers admitted to probate must be recorded or deposited in the registry.
9. When application to record a probate or letters of administration is made after the lapse of three years from the death of the deceased the reason of the delay is to be certified to the Registrar. Should the certificate be unsatisfactory, the Registrar shall require such proof of the alleged cause of delay as he may deem necessary.
10. Notice of the recording in Guyana of a grant is to be sent by the Registrar to the Court from which the grant is issued.
11. The affidavit for testamentary duty and other revenue purposes shall be in the form in the Schedule, or in such form as may be prescribed by the Chancellor.

JAMAICA
CIVIL PROCEDURE RULES 2002
PART 68
PROBATE

Section 1
NON-CONTENTIOUS PROBATE RULES

Contents of this Part

Scope of this Section	Rule 68.1
Interpretation	Rule 68.2
Effect of these Rules	Rule 68.3
Forms	Rule 68.4
Where applications to be made	Rule 68.5
Address for service	Rule 68.6
How to apply for probate	Rule 68.7
How to apply for administration with the will	Rule 68.8
How to apply for administration	Rule 68.9
Proof of death	Rule 68.10
Order of priority where deceased left a will	Rule 68.11
Grants to attesting witnesses	Rule 68.12
Evidence as to due execution of will	Rule 68.13
Wills of soldiers etc	Rule 68.14
Alterations	Rule 68.15
Marking and exhibiting of wills, facsimiles and engrossments	Rule 68.16
Oral wills and copies	Rule 68.17
Order of priority in case of intestacy	Rule 68.18
Certificate of Administrator-General	Rule 68.19
Joinder of administrator	Rule 68.20
Grants where two or more people entitled in same degree	Rule 68.21
Delay Rule 68.22	
Grants to attorneys	Rule 68.23
Grants in additional name	Rule 68.24
Grants where deceased died domiciled outside Jamaica	Rule 68.25
Resealing of grants under the Probate (Re-sealing) Act	Rule 68.26
Evidence of foreign law	Rule 68.27

Grant to minor — Rule 68.28
Grants where minor a co-executor — Rule 68.29
Grants where person entitled mentally incapable — Rule 68.30
Limited grants — Rule 68.31
Settled land — Rule 68.32
Renunciation of probate and administration — Rule 68.33
Notice to Crown of intended application for grant — Rule 68.34
Duty of registrar on receiving application for grant — Rule 68.35
Action after grant made — Rule 68.36
Amendment and revocation of grant — Rule 68.37
Cautions — Rule 68.38
Warning of cautions — Rule 68.39
Opposing a grant — Rule 68.40
Citations — Rule 68.41
Citation to accept or refuse a grant — Rule 68.42
Citation to propound a will — Rule 68.43
Default of acknowledgment of service of citation — Rule 68.44
Application for an order to attend for examination or for summons to bring in will — Rule 68.45
Emergency grants (Grants ad colligenda bona) — Rule 68.46
Applications for leave to swear to death — Rule 68.47
Hearing of applications — Rule 68.48

Section 2
CONTENTIOUS PROBATE PROCEEDINGS

Contents of this Section
Scope of this Section — Rule 68.49
How to commence probate proceedings — Rule 68.50
Parties — Rule 68.51
Testamentary documents — Rule 68.52
Lodgment of grant in applications for revocation or rectification — Rule 68.53
Application for order to bring in will etc., — Rule 68.54
Contents of statements of case — Rule 68.55
Substitution and removal of personal representatives — Rule 68.56
Failure to file acknowledgment of service or defence — Rule 68.57
Counterclaim — Rule 68.58

Case management - the first hearing	Rule 68.59
Administration pending determination of probate proceedings	Rule 68.60
Summary judgment	Rule 68.61
Discontinuance and dismissal	Rule 68.62
Compromise of claim: trial on affidavit evidence	Rule 68.63
Probate counterclaim in other claims	Rule 68.64

Section 1
NON-CONTENTIOUS PROBATE RULES

Scope of this Section
68.1 (1) This Section sets out the procedure for -
    (a) obtaining -
        (i) probate of the will; and
        (ii) letters of administration of the estate, of a deceased person where there is no dispute as to the right of the applicant to obtain such a grant;
    (b) lodging a caution against the grant of probate or administration and warning the cautioner; and
    (c) issuing citations.
  (2) Section 2 of this Part deals with contentious probate claims.

Interpretation
68.2 In this Section -
"**administration**" means a grant of letters of administration of the estate of the deceased;
"**citor**" means the person who issues a citation;
"**grant**" means a grant of probate or administration;
"**gross value**" means the value of the estate without deduction for debts, incumbrances and funeral expenses;
"**probate**" means a grant of probate of the will (and codicils, if any) of the deceased; and
"**will**" includes any codicil to the will unless the context otherwise requires.

Effect of these Rules
68.3 Subject to the provisions of this Section the other provisions of these Rules apply with any necessary modifications to non-

contentious probate matters save that the provisions of rule 3.5 (time - vacations) shall not prevent time from running in the long vacation.

Forms

68.4   A form referred to by number means the form so numbered in Appendix 2 to these Rules with such variations as in a particular case the registrar may direct or approve.

Where applications to be made

68.5   Applications for the grant of probate or administration must be made to the registrar of the court, King Street, Kingston where all cautions, warnings, citations, acknowledgments of service and notices of application under this section must be filed.

Address for service

68.6   All -
  (a)   applications for a grant; and
  (b)   notices of application,
made by an attorney-at-law must contain an address for service for that attorney-at-law.

How to apply for probate

68.7 (1) An executor who seeks probate of the will of a deceased person must file at the registry -
  (a)   an oath in form P.1;
  (b)   the will marked in accordance with rule 68.16;
  (c)   evidence of the death of the deceased in accordance with rule 68.10;
  (d)   draft grant in form P.2 with Kalamazoo copy;
  (e)   where appropriate, affidavit of delay under rule 68.22; and
  (f)   if required by the registrar, the appropriate affidavits under rule 68.13.

(2) Where, on an application for probate, power to apply for probate is to be reserved to such other of the executors as have not renounced probate, the oath must state that notice of the application has been given to the executor or executors to whom power is to be reserved.

(3) The registrar may dispense with giving notice under paragraph (2) if satisfied that giving the notice would -
  (a) be impracticable; or
  (b) cause unreasonable delay or expense.
(4) Where an application is made for probate by one or more, but not all, executors named in the will and power is not reserved to the other executors, the applicant must account for the absence of the other named executors by exhibiting to the oath -
  (a) evidence of the death of the executor; or
  (b) a certified copy of the Deed of Renunciation made by that executor.

How to apply for administration with the will
68.8 (1) A person who seeks administration with the will annexed of the estate of a deceased person must file at the registry -
  (a) an oath in form P.3;
  (b) the will marked in accordance with rule 68.16;
  (c) evidence of the death of the deceased in accordance with rule 68.10;
  (d) draft grant in form P.4 with Kalamazoo copy;
  (e) copy of the advertisements under rule 68.36(1);
  (f) where required, the certificate of the Administrator-General under rule 68.19;
  (g) where appropriate, affidavit of delay under rule 68.22; and
  (h) if required by the registrar, the appropriate affidavits under rule 68.13.
 (2) The applicant must account for any named executors by exhibiting to the oath -
  (a) evidence of the death of the executor; or
  (b) a certified copy of the Deed of Renunciation made by that executor.

How to apply for administration
68.9 A person who seeks administration of the estate of a deceased person must file at the registry -
  (a) an oath in form P.5;
  (b) evidence of the death of the deceased in accordance with rule 68.10;

(c) draft grant in form P.6 with Kalamazoo copy;
(d) copy of the advertisements under rule 68.36(1);
(e) where required, the certificate of the Administrator-General under rule 68.19; and
(f) where appropriate, affidavit of delay under rule 68.22.

Proof of death

68.10 The applicant for a grant must prove the death of the deceased by -
(a) filing a certified copy of the deceased's death certificate with the oath;
(b) (if a certified copy of the death certificate is not available) filing an affidavit from a person present at the funeral of the deceased stating that fact and that he or she saw the body interred; or
(c) if evidence under paragraph (a) or (b) is not available the applicant must apply to the registrar for directions as to the form which evidence of death should take.

Order of priority for grant where deceased left a will

68.11 The person or persons entitled to a grant is to be determined in accordance with the following order of priority -
(a) the executor;
(b) any residuary legatee or devisee holding in trust for any other person;
(c) any other residuary legatee or devisee; or
(d) where the residue is not wholly disposed of by will, any person entitled to share in the undisposed of residue (including the Administrator General when claiming bona vacantia on behalf of the Crown), provided that -
  (i) unless the registrar otherwise directs, a residuary legatee or devisee who has a vested interest is to be preferred to one entitled on the happening of a contingency;
  (ii) where the residue is not in terms wholly disposed of, the registrar may, if he is satisfied that the testator has nevertheless disposed of the whole or substantially the whole of the known estate, allow a grant to be made to any legatee or devisee entitled to, or to share in, the estate so disposed of, without regard to the persons

entitled to share in any residue not disposed of by the will;
- (e) the personal representative of any residuary legatee or devisee (but not one for life, or one holding in trust for any other person) entitled to share in any residue not disposed of by the will;
- (f) any other legatee or devisee (including one for life or one holding in trust for any other person) or any creditor of the deceased, provided that, unless the registrar otherwise directs, a legatee or devisee whose interest in a legacy or devise is vested is to be preferred to one entitled contingently;
- (g) the personal representatives of any other legatee or devisee (but not one for life or one holding in trust for any other person) or of any creditor of the deceased.

Grants to attesting witness

68.12 Where a gift to any person fails because he or she has attested the will, that person is not entitled to a grant as a beneficiary.

Evidence as to due execution of will

68.13 (1) Paragraph (2) of this rule applies where -
- (a) a will contains no attestation clause;
- (b) the attestation clause is insufficient; or
- (c) it appears to the registrar that there is doubt about the due execution of the will.

(2) The registrar may require -
- (a) an affidavit of due execution from-
    - (i) one or more of the attesting witnesses in form P.11; or
    - (ii) (if no attesting witness is conveniently available) from any other person who was present when the will was made; or
- (b) if no evidence under paragraph (a) can be obtained, the registrar may accept -
    - (i) evidence on affidavit in form P.8 showing that the will is in the handwriting of the deceased; or
    - (ii) evidence on affidavit of any matter which may raise a presumption in favour of due execution of the will,

and may require that notice of the application be given to any person who may be prejudiced by the will.

(3) Where a will is undated the registrar may require a search to be made for subsequent wills and evidence to be supplied in form P.9.

Wills of soldiers etc.

68.14 Where the deceased dies domiciled in Jamaica and it appears to the registrar that there is prima facie evidence that a will is one to which the Wills Act, section 7, applies, the will may be admitted to proof without an affidavit under rule 68.13 if-
- (a) the registrar is satisfied on evidence -
  - (i) that it was signed by the testator; or
  - (ii) if unsigned, it is in the testator's handwriting; or
- (b) if oral, the provisions of rule 68.17 are complied with.

Alterations

68.15 (1) Where the will or codicil contains obliterations, interlineations or other alterations, the applicant must file evidence in form P.10 showing that the alterations were present when the will or codicil was executed unless -
- (a) the alterations are trivial and of no practical importance;
- (b) the alterations are evidenced by the initials of the attesting witnesses; or
- (c) the alterations have been confirmed by the re-execution of the will or by the execution of a codicil.

(2) The registrar must give directions as to the form in which the will is to be proved.

Marking and exhibiting of wills, facsimiles and engrossments

68.16 (1) The general rule is that every will for which an application for grant is made must be marked by the signatures of the applicant and one of the attesting witnesses to the will in accordance with form P.11 .

(2) The will must be exhibited to any affidavit which may be required under this Section as to the validity, terms, condition or date of execution of the will.

(3) The registrar may allow a facsimile copy of a will to be marked or exhibited instead of the original will.

(4) Where the registrar considers that in any particular case a facsimile copy of the original will would not be satisfactory for purposes of record, he or she may require an engrossment suitable for facsimile reproduction to be lodged.

(5) Where a will contains alterations which are not to be admitted to proof, an engrossment of the will in the form in which it is to be proved must be filed.

(6) Any engrossment filed in accordance with this rule must reproduce the punctuation, spacing and division into paragraphs of the will and must follow continuously from page to page on both sides of the paper.

(7) Where a will is not available because it is retained in the custody of a foreign court or official, a duly authenticated copy of the will may be admitted to proof.

Oral wills and copies of wills

68.17 (1) An application for an order admitting to proof -
    (i) an oral will;
    (ii) a will contained in a copy; or
    (iii) a reconstruction of a will,
where the original is not available, must be supported by such evidence on affidavit as the applicant can adduce as to-
  (a) the will's existence after the date of the testator's death or, where there is no such evidence, the facts on which the applicant relies to rebut the presumption that the will has been revoked by destruction;
  (b) in the case of an oral will, the contents of that will; and
  (c) in respect of a reconstruction of a will, the accuracy of that reconstruction.

(2) The registrar may -
  (a) require additional affidavit evidence as to -
    (i) due execution of the will; or
    (ii) the accuracy of the copy; and
  (b) direct that notice of the application be given to any persons who might be prejudiced by the application.

Order of priority in case of intestacy

68.18 (1) Where the deceased died without leaving a will the right to a grant of administration is to be determined in accordance with the following order of priority -

(a) the surviving spouse of the deceased;
(b) the children of the deceased and the issue of any child who died before the deceased;
(c) the father and mother of the deceased;
(d) brothers and sisters of the whole blood and the issue of any deceased brother or sister of the whole blood who died before the deceased;
(e) brothers and sisters of the half blood and the issue of any deceased brother or sister of the half blood who died before the deceased;
(f) grandparents;
(g) uncles and aunts of the whole blood and the issue of any deceased uncle or aunt of the whole blood who died before the deceased;
(h) uncles and aunts of the half blood and the issue of any deceased uncle or aunt of the half blood who died before the deceased;

(2) A person applying for a grant of administration
 (a) must in his or her oath account for all persons entitled to a grant in priority to him or her, but
 (b) subject to rule 68.21(2), need not obtain the consent of any person in the same or any lower degree of priority.

(3) In default of any person having a beneficial interest in the estate the Administrator-General is entitled to a grant if he claims bona vacantia on behalf of the Crown.

(4) Where -
 (a) a minor is entitled to a share in the estate; and
 (b) under the terms of the Intestates' Estates and Property Charges Act, section 12, the Administrator General is under a duty to apply for a grant,
 any other person wishing to apply for a grant must apply to the court for an order permitting him or her to do so.

(5) If none of the persons entitled to a grant under paragraphs (1) and (3) are capable of or prepared to apply for the grant, a grant may be made to -
 (i) any creditor of the deceased; or
 (ii) any person who has no immediate beneficial interest in the estate but may have such an interest in the event of an addition to the estate.

(6) The personal representatives of -

(i) a person who would have been entitled to a grant in accordance with paragraph (1); or
(ii) a creditor,

have the same right to a grant as the person whom he or she represents provided that the persons mentioned in sub-paragraphs (b) to (h) of paragraph (1) are to be preferred to the personal representatives of a spouse who has survived the deceased but died without taking a grant.

Certificate of Administrator-General

68.19 (1) This rule applies where under the terms of the Administrator-General's Act, section 12 or the Intestates' Estates and Property Charges Act, section 12, the Administrator-General is under a duty to apply for letters of administration and where no minor is entitled to any share of the estate.
(Rule 68.18(4) deals with the situation where there is a minority interest.)

(2) Before applying for a grant of administration, the applicant must file with the Administrator-General -
   (a) a declaration setting out
      (i) details of the estate of the deceased;
      (ii) details of all persons who are or would have been, had they not died before the deceased, entitled to a grant; and
      (iii) in the case of those persons who would have been entitled to apply in priority to the applicant, the reasons why those persons cannot apply;
   (b) a copy of the oath.

(3) Where the Administrator-General is satisfied that the applicant is entitled to a grant he may, without prejudice to his right to apply for a grant himself, issue a certificate consenting to the making of a grant to him or her.

Joinder of administrator

68.20 (1) A person entitled in priority to a grant of administration may, without leave, apply for a grant with a person entitled in a lower degree, provided that there is no other person entitled in a higher degree to the person to be joined, unless every such person has renounced.

(2) Where paragraph (1) does not apply, an application to join

another person must be made to the registrar.
(3) Such an application may be made without notice but must be supported by evidence on affidavit and the consent of the person proposed to be joined as administrator.

Grants where two or more persons entitled in same degree

68.21 (1) A grant may be made to any person entitled to it without the consent of any other persons entitled in the same degree.
(2) The applicant must give not less than 14 days notice to each other person entitled in the same degree before applying for a grant unless the registrar dispenses with the need for such notice
(3) The registrar may require the applicant to file an affidavit of service of the notice or notices under paragraph (2).
(4) Any person challenging the right of a person in the same degree to a grant of administration may apply to the registrar for directions.
(5) No grant may be issued until the application is finally disposed of.

Delay

68.22 Where an application for a grant is made for the first time more than three years after the death of the deceased, the applicant must file an affidavit explaining the delay.

Grants to attorneys

68.23 (1) Where the person entitled to apply for a grant resides outside Jamaica, grants of administration for the use and benefit of that person may be made to his or her attorney acting under a duly recorded Power of Attorney.
(2) Where the donor of the power is an executor, notice of the application must be given to any other executor unless the registrar otherwise directs.
(3) A grant to an attorney may be limited until a further grant is made or in such other way as the registrar may direct.

Grant in additional name

68.24 Where a grant is sought in a name in addition to the true name of the deceased, the applicant must give evidence on affidavit -

(a) stating the true name of the deceased;
(b) defining any part of the estate which was held in a name other than the deceased's true name; and
(c) stating any other reason for the inclusion of the other name in the grant.

Grants where deceased died domiciled outside Jamaica

68.25 (1) This rule applies where the deceased died domiciled outside Jamaica.

(2) If the deceased left a will in the English language which is admissible to proof, probate may be granted to the person named as executor.

(3) If the will described the duties of a named person in terms sufficient to constitute him executor according to the tenor of the will, probate may be granted to that person.

(4) Where the whole or substantially the whole of the estate in Jamaica consists of real property, a grant may be made to the person who would have been entitled to a grant had the deceased died domiciled in Jamaica

(5) In any other case the registrar may order that the grant be issued to any of -
  (a) the persons entrusted with the administration of the estate by the court having jurisdiction at the place where the deceased died domiciled;
  (b) where there is no such person, to the person beneficially entitled to the estate by the law of the place where the deceased died domiciled and, if more than one, to such of them as the registrar may direct; or
  (c) such other person as the registrar may direct.

Resealing of grants under the Probate (Re-sealing) Act

68.26 (1) An application under the Probate (Re-sealing) Act ("**the Act**") for the resealing of a grant may be made by the person to whom the grant was made or by any agent of that person authorised in writing to apply.

(2) The applicant must advertise the application in form P.12 once in the Gazette or such other newspaper as the registrar may direct

(3) The application is made by filing -
  (a) an application on oath in form P.13 exhibiting a certified

copy of the original grant;
- (b) a copy of any will to which it relates;
- (c) a copy of the advertisement under paragraph (2);
- (d) where the application to reseal a grant is made more than three years after the death of the deceased, an affidavit explaining the delay.

(4) An application by a creditor under section 5 of the Act is to be made to the registrar.

(5) An application under paragraph (4) may be made without notice but must be supported by evidence on affidavit setting out details of the creditor's claim.

(6) In any case the registrar may require such further evidence as seems to him necessary, especially where the evidence of domicile in the affidavit differs from that in the grant.

(7) If it appears that the deceased was not at the time of his or her death domiciled within the jurisdiction of the court which issued the grant, the grant may not be resealed unless it is such as would have been made by the Jamaican court.

(8) The registrar must send notice of the resealing to the court which made the grant.

(9) Where the registrar receives notice of the resealing of a grant issued in Jamaica, notice of any amendment or revocation of the grant must be sent to the court by which it was resealed.

Evidence of foreign law

68.27 Where evidence of foreign law is required on any application for a grant the registrar may accept an affidavit from a lawyer in the country concerned whom, having regard to the particulars of the deponent's knowledge or experience given in the affidavit, the registrar regards as suitably qualified to give expert evidence of the law in question.

Grant to minor

68.28 (1) Subject to the Intestates' Estates and Property Charges Act, section 12, where the only person who would otherwise be entitled to a grant is a minor, a grant of administration for the use and benefit of the minor, limited until he attains the age of eighteen years, shall (subject to paragraph (2)) be granted in the following order of priority -
- (a) to the parents of the minor jointly;

(b) to the statutory or testamentary guardian; or
(c) to any guardian appointed by a court of competent jurisdiction.

(Rule 68.18(4) deals with the situation where, because a minor is entitled to a share in the estate, the Administrator-General is under a duty to apply for the grant unless the court orders otherwise.)

(2) However, where the minor is a sole executor and has no interest in the residuary estate of the deceased, administration for the use and benefit of the minor, limited until he or she attains the age of eighteen years, shall be granted to the person entitled to the residuary estate unless the registrar otherwise directs.

Grant where minor a co-executor

68.29 (1) Where one or more minors has been appointed as executor jointly with other executors, probate may be granted to the executors who are not minors with power reserved to the minor executor or executors who shall be entitled to apply for probate on attaining the age of eighteen years.

(2) Where the executor or executors who are not minors renounce or, on being cited to accept or refuse a grant, fail to make an effective application for a grant, an appointment may be made under the terms of rule 68.28.

Grant where person entitled mentally incapable

68.30 (1) This rule applies where the registrar is satisfied that a person who would otherwise have been entitled to apply for a grant is by reason of mental incapacity incapable of managing his or her own affairs

(2) A grant may only be made under this rule if -
   (a) the absence of all persons entitled to apply for a grant in the same degree as the patient have been accounted for; or
   (b) the registrar otherwise directs.

(3) A grant of administration for the use and benefit of the patient, limited until further grant is made or in such other way as the registrar may direct, may be granted in the following order of priority -
   (a) to any person authorised under the Mental Health Act or any other relevant statutory authority;
   (b) to the person entitled to the residuary estate of the deceased; or

        (c) to such person or persons as the registrar may by order direct.

Limited grants

68.31   Any limited grant must state clearly the limitation imposed on that grant.

Settled land

68.32 (1) In this rule "settled land" means land vested in the deceased which was settled prior to his or her death and not by his or her will and which remains settled land after his or her death.

   (2) The person or persons entitled to a grant limited to settled land are to be determined in accordance with the following order of priority, namely -
      (a) the trustees of the settlement at the time of the application for the grant;
      (b) the personal representatives of the deceased.

   (3) Where the same person or persons are entitled to a grant in respect of both free estate and also settled land, a grant expressly including the settled land may issue to them.

   (4) Where there is settled land and a grant is made in respect of the free estate only, the grant must expressly exclude the settled land.

Renunciation of probate and administration

68.33 (1) An executor who wishes to renounce probate of a will must do so using form P.14 and in accordance with the Executors (Renunciation) Act.

   (2) An executor who renounces probate does not thereby renounce any right to a grant of administration unless he or she expressly renounces that right.

   (3) A person entitled to a grant of administration who wishes to renounce administration must do so in form P. 15 or P.16 as appropriate.

   (4) A person who has renounced administration (with or without the will annexed) in one capacity may not obtain administration in another capacity without the permission of the registrar.

   (5) The right of a minor executor to probate on attaining the age of eighteen may not be renounced by any person on his behalf

except a guardian appointed under rule 68.28(1)(c) and authorised by the registrar to renounce on behalf of the minor.
(6) The general rule is that a renunciation may be retracted with the permission of the registrar.
(7) However the registrar may not give permission to retract a renunciation after a grant has been made to some other person unless exceptional circumstances are shown.
(8) Where probate has been renounced, any person who subsequently applies for a grant must exhibit to his or her oath a certified copy of the renunciation.

Notice to Crown of intended application for a grant
68.34 Where the Crown is, or may be, beneficially interested in the estate of a deceased, notice of an intended application for grant must be given to the Administrator-General and no grant may be made until 28 days after notice has been given.

Duty of the registrar on receiving application for grant
68.35 (1) No grant may issue until -
 (a) in the case of probate, 7 days after the death of the deceased; and
 (b) in the case of administration (including a grant of administration with the will annexed), the application has been published for two successive weeks in the Gazette, unless the registrar otherwise directs.
(2) The registrar must not allow any grant to issue until all inquiries which he or she may see fit to make have been satisfactorily answered.
(3) The registrar may require the person applying for a grant to issue a witness summons to any person who may be able to assist the registrar carrying out his or her duty under paragraph (2).
(4) Where an affidavit of due execution is not available from one of the attesting witnesses as required by rule 68.13(1), the registrar may require notice of the application to be given to any person who may be prejudiced by the will.
(5) Where the registrar after considering the evidence, is satisfied that a will was not duly executed, he or she must refuse probate and mark the will accordingly.
(6) Where -

(a) the will appears to have been executed -
  (i) by a blind or illiterate person; or
  (ii) by another person at the direction and in the presence of the testator ; or
(b) there is any other reason to raise doubt as to the testator having had knowledge of the contents of the will,
the registrar must satisfy him or herself that the testator had such knowledge.

(7) Where a will contains any reference to another document in such terms as suggest that the document ought to be incorporated into the will, the registrar must require such document to be produced and may call for such evidence with regard to the incorporation of the document as seems fit.

(8) Where the registrar considers that the appearance of the will suggests attempted revocation by burning, tearing or by other means, the registrar may require evidence to displace any presumption of revocation.

(9) Where there is a doubt as to the date on which a will was executed, the registrar may require such evidence as appears to him or her to be necessary to establish the true date of execution.

Action after grant made

68.36 (1) Immediately upon the grant of probate or administration with the will annexed the registrar must -
  (a) record the will and any codicil in the registry; and
  (b) transmit the original will and any codicil to the Record Office.

(2) The registrar must -
  (a) maintain a register of probate and administration in which all grants must be recorded;
  (b) allow public inspection of the register at all reasonable hours; and
  (c) permit the taking of copies on payment of the prescribed fee.

Amendment and revocation of grant

68.37 (1) Where satisfied that it is appropriate to do so, the registrar may make an order amending or revoking a grant.

(2) An application for an order under paragraph (1) may be made without notice but must be supported by evidence on affidavit.
(3) The registrar may require notice of the application to be given to any person.
(4) Unless the person to whom the grant was made -
  (a) applies for; or
  (b) consents to,
  the revocation or amendment, such an order may be made only in exceptional circumstances.

Cautions

68.38 (1) Any person who wishes to oppose a grant may enter a caution in form P.17 at the registry giving an address for service.
(2) A caution remains in force for six months only.
(3) A caution may be renewed for a further period of six months by filing a written request for extension.
(4) The registrar must maintain a register of cautions and a search of the index must be made whenever an application for a grant is received.
(5) The registrar may not allow any grant to be sealed (other than a grant ad colligenda bona) if he or she has knowledge of an effective caution.
(6) A cautioner may withdraw the caution by giving notice to the registry at any time before filing an acknowledgment of service under rule 68.39(2) and the caution ceases to have effect.
(7) A cautioner withdrawing a caution must give notice to the person warning the caution.

Warning of cautions

68.39 (1) Any person claiming an interest in the estate may cause a warning to be issued to the cautioner.
(2) He or she does this by filing a warning in Form P.18 at the registry-
  (a) stating his or her interest in the estate;
  (b) if claiming under a will or codicil, stating the date of that will or codicil; and
  (c) requiring the cautioner to -
    (i) file an acknowledgment of service; and
    (ii) give particulars of any contrary interest in the estate.

(3) The registrar must then sign the warning and the person warning the caution must serve it on the cautioner at the address given in accordance with rule 68.38(1).

Opposing a grant

68.40 (1) A person who wishes to oppose a grant must -
- (a) file an acknowledgment of service in form P.19 at the registry;
- (b) serve a copy of the acknowledgment of service on the cautioner; and
- (c) issue and serve on the cautioner an application for directions.

(2) He or she must do this not later than 14 days after the service of the warning.

(3) If no acknowledgment of service is filed within the period stated in paragraph (2), the person warning the caution may file an affidavit proving service of the warning and the caution ceases to have effect.

(4) Any caution in force when an application for directions is issued remains in force until the commencement of a probate claim unless, upon giving directions, the registrar orders that the caution cease to have effect.

(5) Where a probate claim is commenced -
- (a) the claimant must give notice of the claim -
  - (i) to every cautioner, other than the claimant in that claim whose caution remains in force; and
  - (ii) to any subsequent cautioner;
- (b) the costs of filing a caution and warning that caution are costs in the claim; and
- (c) no grant may be sealed until an application is made by the person

shown to be entitled by the decision of the court in that claim unless the registrar by order made application otherwise directs.

(6) Upon an application for a grant being made by the person shown to be entitled by the decision of the court in the claim any caution-
- (a) entered by the claimant; or
- (b) in respect of which notice of the claim has been given under paragraph (5)(a), ceases to have effect.

Citations

68.41 (1) Before issuing a citation the citor must enter a caution.
   (2) The citation must be verified by affidavit.
   (3) The citation must be settled by the registrar.
   (4) Every citation must be served personally on the person cited unless the registrar directs some other form of service.
   (5) An application under paragraph (4) need not be on notice but must be supported by evidence on affidavit.
   (6) However, a citation against all persons in general is served by the insertion of the citation in the Gazette.
   (7) The citor must lodge with the citation every will referred to in the citation unless -
      (a) it is not in the citor's possession; and
      (b) the registrar is satisfied that it is impractical for it to be lodged.
   (8) Any person upon whom a citation is served may file an acknowledgment of service in form P.19 at the registry and must serve a copy of the acknowledgment of service on the citor.
   (9) The time within which such acknowledgment of service must be filed and served is 14 days from the date of service or publication of the citation.
   (10) Any caution in force at the commencement of citation proceedings remains in force until an application for a grant is made by the person shown to be entitled by the decision of the court in such proceedings unless -
      (a) withdrawn in accordance with rule 68.38(6); or
      (b) the registrar otherwise orders following an application on notice.
   (11) Upon an application being made under paragraph (10) any caution entered by a person who had notice of the proceedings ceases to have effect.

Citation to accept or refuse a grant

68.42 (1) Any person who would be entitled to a grant in the event of the person cited renouncing his or her rights to a grant may issue a citation to accept or refuse a grant.
   (2) Where power to make a grant to an executor has been reserved, a citation calling on him or her to accept or refuse a grant may be issued by -

(a) the executors who have proved the will;
(b) the survivor of such executors; or
(c) the executors of the last surviving executor who has proved the will.

(3) Where an executor has started to administer the estate of the deceased prior to obtaining probate, a citation calling on him to show cause why he or she should not be ordered to take a grant may be issued by any person interested in the estate.

(4) A citation under paragraph (3) may not be issued -
(a) until 6 months have expired from the death of the deceased; or
(b) while any proceedings as to the validity of the will are pending.

(5) Any person served with a citation may file an acknowledgment of service in form P.19 and must serve a copy of such acknowledgment on the citor.

(6) The time for filing and serving an acknowledgment of service is 14 days from service of the citation.

(7) After filing an acknowledgment of service a person cited may apply to the registrar for an order for a grant to him or herself.

(8) An application under paragraph (7) may be made without notice but must be supported by affidavit evidence.

Citation to propound a will

68.43 (1) A citation to propound a will may be issued at the request of any person having an interest contrary to that will.

(2) The citation must be directed to and served on the executors named in the will and to all persons interested under the will.

(3) Any person served with a citation may file an acknowledgment of service and must serve a copy of such acknowledgment on the citor.

(4) The time for filing and serving an acknowledgment of service is 14 days from service of the citation.

Default of acknowledgment of service of citation

68.44 (1) Where no acknowledgment of service has been filed in accordance with rule 68.41(8) and (9), the citor may -
(a) in the case of a citation under rule 68.42(1), apply to the registrar for a grant to him or herself;

(b) in the case of a citation under rule 68.42(2), apply to the registrar for an order that a note be made on the grant that -
  (i) the executor in respect of whom power was reserved has been duly cited;
  (ii) that executor has not filed an acknowledgment of service; and
  (iii) his or her rights in respect of the executorship have wholly ceased.
(c) in the case of a citation under rule 68.42(3), apply to the registrar on notice for an order requiring the person cited to take a grant within a specified time or for a grant to the person cited or to some other person specified in the application.

(2) Where the person cited has filed an acknowledgment of service but -
  (i) has not applied for a grant under rule 68.42(7); or
  (ii) has failed to proceed with his or her application with reasonable diligence,

the citor may -
(a) in the case of a citation under rule 68.42(1), apply to the registrar on notice to the person cited for a grant to him or herself;
(b) in the case of a citation under rule 68.42(2), apply to the registrar on notice to the person cited for an order striking out the acknowledgment of service and that a note be made on the grant that -
  (i) the executor in respect of whom power was reserved has been duly cited;
  (ii) that executor has not filed an acknowledgment of service; and
  (iii) his or her rights in respect of the executorship have wholly ceased.
(c) in the case of a citation under rule 68.43(3), apply to the registrar on notice to the person cited for an order requiring the person cited to take a grant within a specified time or for a grant to the person cited or to some other person specified in the application.

(3) Where -

(a) no acknowledgment of service is filed in accordance with rule 68.43(2); and
(b) the time limited for service under rule 68.43(3) has expired,

the citor may -
  (i) where no person has acknowledged service, apply to the registrar for an order for a grant as if the will were invalid; or
  (ii) where no person who has acknowledged service proceeds with reasonable diligence to propound the will, apply to the registrar on notice to every person cited who has acknowledged service for an order for a grant as if the will were invalid.

(4) Any application under this rule must be supported by an affidavit showing due service of the citation on each person who has not acknowledged service.

Application for an order to attend for examination or for summons to bring in will

68.45 (1) An application requiring a person to attend for examination may be made to the registrar on notice to such person.

(2) An application for a witness summons to bring in the will may be made without notice but must be supported by evidence on affidavit setting out the grounds of the application.

(3) The witness summons shall be in form P.20.

(4) A person served with a witness summons who denies that the will is in his or her possession or control may file an affidavit to that effect.

Emergency grants (Grants ad colligenda bona)

68.46 An application for an emergency grant may be made to the registrar and must be supported by evidence on affidavit setting out the grounds of the application.

Application for leave to swear to death

68.47 (1) An application for leave to swear to the death of a person in whose estate a grant is sought may be made to the registrar.

(2) The application must be supported by evidence on affidavit -
  (a) giving details of any policies of insurance effected on the life of the presumed deceased; and

            (b) the grounds for supposing the presumed deceased to be dead.
    (3) The registrar may require further evidence to be given on affidavit.

Hearing of applications
68.48 (1) All applications must be made in the first instance to the registrar in form P.21.
    (2) The registrar may direct that any notice of application be served on such persons as he or she may direct.
    (3) The registrar may make any order where the application is unopposed.
    (4) Where an application is opposed the registrar must give directions and adjourn the application to the judge.
    (5) The registrar may at any time refer any application under this Section to a judge.

Section 2
CONTENTIOUS PROBATE PROCEEDINGS

Scope of this Section
68.49 (1) This Section contains rules about -
        (a) probate claims
        (b) claims and applications to
            (i) substitute another person for a personal representative; or
            (ii) remove a personal representative,
        which in this Part are referred to as "**probate proceedings**".
    (2) Non-contentious proceedings are dealt with in Section 1.
    (3) In this Section -
        "**grant**" means a grant of probate of the will of, letters of administration with the will annexed or letters of administration of the estate of, the deceased,
        "**probate claim**" means a claim for-
            (i) the grant of probate of the will in solemn form, or letters of administration of the estate of a deceased person;
            (ii) the revocation or amendment of such a grant;
            (iii) for a decree pronouncing for or against the validity

of an alleged will, not being a claim which is non-contentious or common form probate business;

"**personal representative**" means the executor of the will of, or administrator of the estate of a deceased person;

"**testamentary document**" means a will or draft will, written instructions for a will made by or at the request or under the instructions of the testator and any document purporting to be evidence of the contents, or to be a copy, of a will which is alleged to have been lost or destroyed; and

"**will**" includes a codicil.

How to commence probate proceedings

68.50 (1) Probate proceedings must be begun by issuing a fixed date claim form in form 2.

(2) The claim form must be marked at the top "In the estate of [xx] deceased (Probate)"

(3) The claim form must state the nature of the interest of the claimant and of the defendant in the estate of the deceased person to which the claim relates.

(4) The claimant must -
   (a) file a particulars of claim with the claim form; and
   (b) give notice of the claim to -
      (i) every cautioner, other than the claimant, whose caution remains in force; and
      (ii) to any subsequent cautioner.

(5) Unless the court otherwise directs no grant may be made until the probate proceedings have been disposed of.

(6) The defendant must file an acknowledgment of service in accordance with Part 9.

Parties

68.51 (1) In proceedings for revocation of a grant every person who is entitled or claims to be entitled to administer the estate of a deceased person under or by virtue of an unrevoked grant must be made a party.

(2) Any claim form issued by any person other than the executors, administrators or trustees must be served on the executors, administrators or trustees as the case may be.

(3) The claimant must give notice to every person who may be

affected by probate proceedings, either as a beneficiary under a will in issue or under an intestacy, who is not joined as a party.

(4) The court may direct -
 (a) that any person be joined as a party; or
 (b) that notice of the claim be given to any person.

Testamentary documents

68.52 (1) Any testamentary document of the deceased person in the possession or control of any party must be lodged with the court.

(2) Unless the court otherwise directs, the claimant and every defendant who has entered an acknowledgment of service must swear an affidavit-
 (a) describing any testamentary document of the deceased person, whose estate is the subject of the action, of which he or she has any knowledge or, if such be the case, stating that he or she knows of no such document, and
 (b) if either party has knowledge of any such document which is not in his or her possession or under his or her control-
  (i) giving the name and address of the person in whose possession or under whose control it is; or
  (ii) that he or she does not know the name or address of that person.

(3) The affidavit must be sworn by the party or, in the case of a minor or patient, by that party's next friend unless the court otherwise orders.

(4) Unless the court otherwise directs -
 (a) the claimant must lodge his or her affidavit and any testamentary documents in his or her possession when the claim form is issued; and
 (b) the defendant must lodge his or her affidavit and any testamentary documents in his or her possession when filing an acknowledgment of service.

(5) Where any testamentary document required by this rule to be lodged or any part of it is written in pencil, then, unless the court otherwise directs, a facsimile copy of that document,

or of the page or pages containing the part written in pencil, must also be lodged and the words which appear in pencil in the original must be underlined in red ink in the copy.
(6) Except with the leave of the court, no party to probate proceedings may be allowed to inspect an affidavit filed, or any testamentary document lodged, by any other party to the proceedings under this rule, until an affidavit sworn by the first party containing the information referred to in paragraph (1) has been filed.

Lodgment of grant in applications for revocation or rectification

68.53 (1) This rule applies to applications for revocation of a grant.
(2) If the claimant is an executor or administrator, the claimant must lodge the grant at the court when the claim form is filed.
(3) If the grant is in the possession or under the control of any defendant, that defendant must lodge it at the court when filing his or her acknowledgment of service.
(4) Any person who fails to comply with paragraph (2) or (3) may, on the application of any party to the proceedings, be ordered by the court to lodge the grant within a specified time.
(5) Where an order is made under paragraph (4), the person against whom such an order is made may not take any step in the proceedings without the permission of the court until that person has complied with the order.

Application for order to bring in will etc.

68.54 (1) The court may order that any person -
(a) attend court for examination and to answer questions; and
(b) bring in any testamentary document in the possession or control of that person,
if there are reasonable grounds for believing that that person has knowledge of any testamentary document.
(2) Where there are reasonable grounds for believing that a person has in his or her possession, custody or power any testamentary document, the court may direct that a witness summons be issued to that person ordering him or her to bring in that document.

(3) Any party to probate proceedings may apply for an order under paragraph (1) or (2).
(4) An application for an order under paragraph (1) or (2) -
   (a) may be made without notice; but
   (b) must be supported by evidence on affidavit setting out the grounds of the application.
(5) Any person against whom a witness summons is issued under paragraph (2) who denies that the testamentary document referred to in the witness summons is in his or her possession, power or control may file written evidence to that effect and apply for the witness summons to be set aside.
(6) A notice of application under paragraph (5) must be served on the party making the application under paragraph (3).

Contents of statements of case

68.55 (1) Where any party disputes the interest of another party in the estate that party must state this in his or her statement of case setting out reasons for the dispute.
(2) In probate proceedings in which the interest by virtue of which a party claims to be entitled to a grant of letters of administration is disputed, the party disputing that interest must show in that party's statement of case that if the allegations made therein are proved, he or she would be entitled to an interest in the estate.
(3) Any party who contends that -
   (a) a will was not duly executed;
   (b) at the time of the execution of a will the testator -
      (i) did not know and approve of its contents; or
      (ii) was not of sound mind, memory and understanding; or
   (c) the execution of a will was obtained by undue influence or fraud,
   must specify the nature of the case on which he or she intends to rely giving particulars of the facts and matters relied on.
(4) (a) A defendant may state in his or her defence that the defendant does not raise any positive case but requires the will to be proved in solemn form.
   (b) The court will not then make an order for costs against that defendant unless it considers that there was no reasonable ground for opposing the will.

Substitution and removal of personal representatives

68.56 (1) This rule applies to applications for substitution or removal of a
personal representative.
   (2) An application under paragraph (1) must be made -
      (a) if in existing proceedings, by an application under Part 11; or
      (b) in any other case, by a fixed date claim form.
   (3) The claim form (or application) must be accompanied by -
      (a) a sealed or certified copy of probate or letters of administration; and
      (b) an affidavit setting out the grounds of the application and the following information so far as is known to the claimant or applicant -
         (i) brief details of the property comprised in the estate, with an approximate estimate of the capital value and of any income derived from it;
         (ii) brief details of any liabilities of the estate;
         (iii) the names and addresses of the persons who are in possession of any documents relating to the estate;
         (iv) the names of the beneficiaries and their respective interests in the estate; and
         (v) the name, address and occupation of any proposed substituted personal representative.
   (4) An application for the appointment of a substituted personal representative must be accompanied by -
      (a) a signed consent; and
      (b) evidence on affidavit as to the fitness to act,
      of the proposed substituted personal representative.
   (5) The personal representative must produce to the court the grant of representation to the deceased's estate at the hearing of the application.

Failure to file acknowledgment of service or defence

68.57 (1) Part 12 does not apply to probate proceedings.
   (2) Where any of several defendants to probate proceedings fails to file an acknowledgment of service or to file and serve a defence, the claimant may -
      (a) after the time for entering an acknowledgment of service

or filing a defence has expired; and
  (b) upon filing an affidavit proving due service of the claim form and particulars of claim on that defendant, proceed with the claim as if that defendant had entered an acknowledgment of service.
(3) Where the defendant, or all the defendants, to probate proceedings, fails or fail to file an acknowledgment of service or file and serve a defence, then, unless on the application of the claimant the court orders the claim to be dismissed or discontinued, the claimant may apply to the court at the first hearing for-
  (a) the claim to be dealt with summarily at that hearing; or
  (b) a trial date to be fixed and any necessary directions to be given.
(4) Before applying for an order under paragraph (3) the claimant must file an affidavit proving due service of the claim form and particulars of claim on the defendant.
(5) Where the court grants an order under paragraph (3), it may direct the proceedings to be tried on affidavit evidence.

Counterclaim

68.58 A defendant to probate proceedings who alleges that he or she has any claim or is entitled to any relief or remedy in respect of any matter relating to the grant of probate of the will, or letters of administration of the estate, of the deceased person which is the subject of the proceedings must add to the defence a counterclaim for that relief or remedy.

Case management - the first hearing

68.59 At the first hearing of the claim the court will consider -
  (a) whether any person who is, or may be, affected by the claim should be -
    (i) joined as a party; or
    (ii) given notice of the claim; and
  (b) whether to make an order under rule 21.4 (representation of parties who cannot be ascertained).

Administration pending determination of probate proceedings

68.60 (1) Any party may apply for an order for the grant of administration

pending the determination of a probate proceedings.
- (2) If an order is made under paragraph (1) -
  - (a) Part 51 applies as if the administrator were a receiver appointed by the court; and
  - (b) where the court allows the administrator remuneration under rule 51.5, it may make an order that such remuneration be paid out of the estate.
- (3) An appointment as administrator under this rule ceases when a final order is made in the probate proceedings but may be continued by the court pending the hearing of any appeal.
- (4) Wherever practicable any application under this rule should be made at the first hearing of the claim.

Summary judgment

68.61 (1) Part 15 applies to an application for an order pronouncing a will in solemn form.
- (2) The affidavit in support of an application for summary judgment must prove due execution of the will.
- (3) Where rule 68.55(4) applies, the defendant may require the witnesses who attested the will to attend court for cross-examination.

Discontinuance and dismissal

68.62 (1) Part 37 does not apply to probate proceedings.
- (2) At any stage of the proceedings the court, on the application of the claimant or of any party to the proceedings who has entered an acknowledgment of service may order -
  - (a) the proceedings to be discontinued or dismissed on such terms as to costs or otherwise as it thinks just,
  - (b) that a grant of probate of the will, or letters of administration of the estate of the deceased person, as the case may be, be made to the person entitled.

Compromise of claim: trial on affidavit evidence

68.63 (1) Where, whether before or after the service of the defence in probate proceedings, the parties to the proceedings agree to a compromise, the court may -

(a) order the trial of the proceedings on affidavit evidence (which will lead to a grant in solemn form);
(b) order that the claim be discontinued or dismissed under rule 68.62 (which will lead to grant in common form); or
(c) pronounce for or against the validity of one or more wills.

(2) An application for an order under paragraph (1)(c) must be supported by evidence on affidavit identifying the relevant beneficiaries and exhibiting the written consent of each of them.

Probate counterclaim in other claims

68.64 (1) In this rule "**probate counterclaim**" means a counterclaim in any claim other than probate proceedings by which the defendant claims any such relief as is mentioned in rule 68.49(1).

(2) Subject to the following paragraph, this Part applies with the necessary modifications to a probate counterclaim as it applies to probate proceedings.

(3) A probate counterclaim must contain a statement of the nature of the interest of each party in the estate of the deceased person to which the probate counterclaim relates.

ST LUCIA
SECTION III
PROBATE AND PROOF OF WILLS

Civil Code Ch. 242

794. (Subst. 23-1916). All wills must be presented for probate to the Supreme Court, together with a certificate of the death of the testator. Where no certificate of death can be produced, the person presenting the will must adduce such other evidence of death as the Court may require.

In matters of probate "Court" includes Judge or Registrar of the Supreme Court.

795. (Subst. 23-1916). Probate is granted as of course in case of the original or a certified copy of a notarial will; in the case of other wills, the authenticity of the handwriting of the testator, or the attestation of his will, must be proved by affidavit, or otherwise as may be directed.

The Court has discretion as to what evidence is necessary to establish the validity of a will.

The will must remain deposited in the Court unless it is a notarial will, the original of which is in the custody of a notary in the Colony.

796. (Subst. 23-1916). When the Court is satisfied that the will is valid, and that all requirements, including the requirements of the Succession Duty Ordinance, have been complied with, probate is granted.

A certified office copy of any probate may be obtained with a copy of the will or other instrument annexed, which, if it is notarial, may be a certified notarial copy.

On the registration of the probate and will in the Registry of Deeds effect is given to the Will.

The probate of wills does not prevent their contestation by persons interested.

797. (Subst. 23-1916). Where a will has been lost or accidentally destroyed, probate may be granted of the contents thereof upon proof of such contents and of the formalities required for execution, and of the facts which render production of the will impossible.

If it appears that the testator knew of and acquiesced in the loss or destruction of the will, such will is deemed to have been revoked.

The person who propounds an alleged will and cannot adduce any written evidence of its contents must prove such contents beyond all reasonable doubt. Where such proof is forthcoming, and there is evidence of a definite intention on the part of the testator to do some formal act and the evidence is consistent with that intention having been carried into effect, the Court may infer the actual observance of all due formalities.

798. When a will admits of proof under the preceding article, a probate may be obtained upon petition after positive proof, not only of the contents but of the facts which render production impossible. Probate of the will is held to be establishing according to the proof deemed sufficient and to such modifications as are made in the judgment.

798A.(Ad. 34-1956). When any person who has had and has ceased to have his domicile in the Colony dies outside the and having made, outside the Colony, a will which is valid under the law of the Colony, and such person leaves property in the Colony, such will may be proved in the Colony as if it had been made and such person had his domicile therein.

BOOK SIXTH
PROCEEDINGS RELATING TO SUCCESSIONS
CODE OF CIVIL PROCEDURE CH 243
CHAPTER FIRST
(Subst. 3-1957.)

GENERAL PROVISIONS

1012. Provisions relating to the probate of wills are contained in the Civil Code.

1013. In common form business grants of probate and letters of administration may be made by the Registrar but the Registrar may refer to the Judge any matter which he thinks fit.

1014. The Registrar is not to allow probate or letters of administration to issue until all the inquiries which he may see fit to institute have been answered to his satisfaction, The Registrar is, notwithstanding, to afford as great facility for the obtaining grants of probate or administration as is consistent with due regard to the prevention of error or fraud.

CHAPTER SECOND
(Subst. 3-1957.)
LETTERS OF ADMINISTRATION

1015. (1) The application for letters of administration shall be made in the Registry by petition and shall be accompanied by the following documents: -
    (a) a certified copy of the will of the deceased, if it is a notarial will, or the original will, if it is not a notarial will, (where the grant is to be annexed to a will),
    (b) the affidavit or affidavits of proof of due execution in the case of a non-notarial will (where the grant is to be annexed to a will),
    (c) an affidavit setting out the names and addresses of the persons entitled to the grant in order of priority and containing the administrator's oath,
    (d) an affidavit of the assets and liabilities of the deceased, and
    (e) a certificate of the death of the intestate or any other proof in lieu thereof.

(2) The letters of administration shall not be handed out until there has been produced to the Registrar a certificate in writing

under the hand of the Accountant General showing that the Accountant General does not object to such grant.

1016. (1) Letters of administration shall be granted to the persons entitled in the following order of priority —
(a) to the persons within the heritable degree in order of their right to succeed the deceased, or
(b) failing such persons, to the surviving wife or husband of the deceased, as the case may be, or
(c) failing such surviving wife or husband to the person nominated by the Crown to apply for administration.

(2) Where administration is applied for by one or some of the heirs only, there being another or other heirs equally entitled thereto, the Registrar may require proof by affidavit or statutory declaration that notice of such application has been given to such other heirs.

1017. (1) Limited administrations shall not be granted unless every person entitled to the general grant has consented or renounced or has been cited and failed to appear, except under the direction of a Judge.

(2) For the purpose of giving effect to subsection (4) of article 586 of the Civil Code, the practice and procedure relating to limited grants in force in the principal registry of the Probate, Divorce and Admiralty Division of the High Court of Justice in England shall, so far as the same is not inconsistent with the law of the Colony and is applicable in local circumstances, apply and have effect in the Colony.

1018. Save as in the Fourth Chapter of Part Third of the Civil Code expressly provided, no person entitled to a general grant in respect of the succession of a deceased person shall be permitted to take a limited grant, except under the direction of a Judge.

1019. In the case of a person residing out of the Colony, administration or administration with the will annexed, may be granted to his attorney acting under a power of attorney.

1020. Grants of administration may be made to tutors of minors for their use and benefit.

1021. In case of a minor not having a testamentary tutor or a tutor appointed by the Court, a tutor shall be assigned by order of a Judge founded on an affidavit showing that the proposed tutor is a fit and proper person to be appointed for the purpose of taking the administration, that he is consenting to the assignment as such tutor and is ready to undertake the tutorship and that he has no interest adverse to the minor in the succession of the deceased.

1022. (1) The oath to lead to a grant of administration or of administration with the will annexed shall be so worded as to clear off all persons having a prior right to the grant, and the grant shall show on the face of it how the prior interests have been cleared off.

(2) In all administrations of a special character the recitals in the oath and in the letters of administration shall be framed in accordance with the facts of the case.

1023. When any person takes letters of administration in default of the appearance of persons cited, but not personally served with the citation, and when any person takes letters of administration for the use and benefit of a person of unsound mind, unless he be a curator appointed by the Court, a declaration of all the property of the deceased shall be filed in the Registry, and the sureties to the administration bond (if ordered by the Court) shall justify.

1024. No letters of administration shall issue until after the lapse of fourteen days from the death of the deceased, unless under the direction of a Judge.

1025. Except where otherwise provided in this Book, no person who renounces administration (with or without the will) of the succession of a deceased person in one character shall be allowed to take representation to the same deceased in another character.

CHAPTER THIRD
(Subst. 3-1957)

CAVEATS

1026. (1) The Registrar shall provide and keep at a convenient place in the Registry a Caveat Book in which all caveats filed under these provisions shall be entered.

(2) Any person intending to oppose the issuing of a grant of probate or letters of administration or to commence any proceedings under these provisions shall, either personally or by his solicitor or attorney, enter a caveat in the Caveat Book.

1027. (1) Every caveat shall bear the date of the day on which it is entered, the name and address of the person entering it and an address within one mile from the Registry at which any documents may be left for him.

(2) A caveat shall remain in force for the space of six months only and then expire and be of no effect; but it may be renewed from time to time before the issue of the probate or letters of administration.

1028. No grant of probate or letters of administration shall be sealed at any time if the Registrar has knowledge of an effective caveat.

1029. (1) The person whose application for a grant is stopped by a caveat shall, if he desires to contest the caveat, issue a warning giving notice to the person entering the caveat to enter an appearance at the Registrar within six days.

(2) A warning to a caveat may be issued whether papers to lead to a grant have been lodged or not.

(3) The warning to a caveat shall state:
  (a) the name and interest of the party on whose behalf the same is issued, (and if such person claims under a will or codicil, the date of the will or codicil,) and
  (b) an address within one mile of the Registry at which any notice requiring service may be left.

(4) It shall be sufficient for the warning of a caveat that the Registrar send by the public post a warning signed by himself and directed to the person who entered the caveat at the address mentioned in it.

1030. (1) In order to clear off a caveat when no appearance has been entered to a warning duly served, —
  (a) an affidavit of the service of the warning, stating the manner of service, and an affidavit of search for appearance and of non-appearance, shall be filed, and
  (b) the applicant for probate of a will or for letters of administration shall obtain from the Registrar a certificate of non-appearance and apply to a Judge for an order that he be at liberty to proceed with his application and that the person entering the caveat be debarred from entering any further caveat in respect of that application.

(2) Upon such order being granted the applicant for probate or letters of administration shall be at liberty to proceed with his application as if such caveat had not been entered.

(3) The Judge may, upon making such order, direct that the person entering such caveat pay to the applicant all reasonable costs incurred by him by reason of the caveat having been entered and such costs shall be recoverable by means of a writ of execution.

TRINIDAD & TOBAGO
SCHEDULES
FIRST SCHEDULE

Non-Contentious Business Rules.

NON-CONTENTIOUS BUSINESS SHALL INCLUDE ALL COMMON FORM BUSINESS AS DEFINED BY THE ORDINANCE.

In these Rules — "registry" means the principal registry of the Supreme Court and unless a contrary intention is expressed the term shall include a sub-registry; "Ordinance" means the Wills and Probate Ordinance; "will" has the same meaning as that ascribed to it in the Ordinance.

Applications

1. Application for probate or letters of administration may be made at the registry of the Supreme Court, Port-of-Spain, in all cases. Application may also be made at either of the sub-registries in cases where the deceased, at the time of his death, had a fixed place of abode within the district in which the application is made, and not otherwise.

2. Such applications shall be made through a solicitor and shall not be received by letter nor through the medium of an agent. Applications shall not be accepted at the registry unless they bear the signature of the solicitor who prepared the same: Provided that in applications coming within the provisions of rule 5, the Registrar or Sub-Registrar, to whom application is made, shall prepare the necessary papers to lead to a grant of probate or administration, without the payment of any fees other than those mentioned in the said rule.

3. (1) Applications for probate shall be in writing and there shall be filed together therewith —
    (a) an affidavit by the applicant in support of the said application;
    (b) an affidavit by the person attesting, or one of them, exhibiting the will and stating in effect that the requirements of the Ordinance as regards its execution have been complied with;
    (c) a certified of death or burial of the deceased, or a statement in writing to the satisfaction of the Registrar for the non-

production thereof;
- (d) an inventory of the particulars of the estate of the deceased, showing the several items of property, the nature and extent thereof and the estimated gross value set upon each and showing also the particulars of the estate, if any, of the deceased, situate abroad and in respect of which no grant is required;
- (e) a certificate by the Registrar or an affidavit by the party applying or someone on his behalf that from search made in the registry it appears that no other application for probate or administration in the same estate has been made, and that no will other than that for which probate is sought is deposited in the registry under section 83 of the Ordinance;
- (f) the certificate mentioned in subsection (3) of section 35 of the Estate and Succession Duties Ordinance, or the certificate mentioned in subsection (2) or subsection (4) of section 36 of that Ordinance.

(2) (a) The inventory shall be annexed to the affidavit of the applicant in support of his application and he shall depose that the same comprises all the real and personal estate of the deceased and that the value therein set out is correct to the best of his knowledge and belief or with such exception as shall be shown therein.

(b) There shall be excepted what the deceased shall have been possessed of or entitled to as a trustee for any other person but not beneficially, and also any property therein specified which is so situate or circumstanced as to appear incapable of immediate valuation.

(3) The application, affidavits and the inventory shall be in the respective forms appearing in the Appendix hereto with such variations as the case may require.

4. (1) Applications for administration shall be in writing and there shall be filed together therewith an affidavit by the applicant in support of the said application in which he shall depose that the deceased left no will (or, as the case may be, exhibiting any last will of the deceased which the applicant desires to have annexed to such administration) and showing the relationship or other circumstances alleged as entitling the applicant to such administration.

(2) The provisions of rule 3 shall apply to applications for

administration except paragraph (1) (a) and (b).

5. (1) When any person shall die possessed of or entitled to estate the value of which does not exceed the sum of four hundred and eighty dollars, (note that pursuant to the Non-Contentious Business (Amendment) Rules, 1983, the sum of four hundred and eighty dollars has been increased to four thousand and eighty dollars. See L.M/16/1981) and application has been made for a grant of administration thereto by any person being husband, wife, child, descendant, father, mother, brother or sister or issue of a brother or sister of the deceased or for a grant of probate by an executor, the following provisions shall apply:-

    (a) On receipt of the application the Registrar shall make such enquiries into the facts stated therein as he shall think fit and shall report the same in writing to the court.

    (b) The court may, if satisfied therewith, grant administration or probate as the case may be to the applicant.

    (c) The applicant shall not be required to give any security or pay any registration or other fee, and the entire fee payable in respect of the application and issue of administration or probate shall be the sum of three dollars.

    (d) No certificate under subsection (3) of section 35 of the Estate and Succession Duties Ordinance shall be required.

    (e) No inventory need be filed, but in lieu thereof the applicant shall in his affidavit set out the information required by rule 3 (1) (d) of these rules.

    (f) There shall unless the court otherwise directs, be no advertisement of the application as provided for in these rules but the Registrar shall cause notice of the application to be screened in a conspicuous place in the registry where the application is made for a period of two weeks before the grant issues.

(2) Notwithstanding anything contained in the Commissioners of Affidavits Ordinance there shall be no fees payable to Commissioners of Affidavits in respect of any affidavit required in respect of applications made under this rule.

(3) In the absence of an executor a grant may be made of the persons named and in the order of priority mentioned in section 30 of the Ordinance.

(4) In all other respects the provisions of rules 3 and 4 of these rules shall apply.

6. Every will to which an executor or administrator with the will annexed is sworn, must be marked by such executor or

administrator and by the person before whom he is sworn.

7. In every case where probate or administration is, for the first time, applied for after a lapse of three years from the death of the deceased, the reason of the delay is to be certified to the Registrar. Should the certificate be unsatisfactory, the Registrar is to require such proof of the alleged cause of delay as he may see fit.

8. Where application is made for probate or administration by a corporation other than the Public Trustee the officer appointed by the corporation for such purpose shall in every case file in the registry a sealed copy of the resolution appointing him, and shall depose, in the oath to lead to the grant, that the charter or memorandum of association of such corporation empowers such corporation to make such application.

9. The Registrar is not to allow probate or administration to issue until all the enquiries which he may see fit to institute have been answered to his satisfaction. The Registrar is, notwithstanding, to afford as great facility for the obtaining grants of probate or administration as is consistent with a due regard to the prevention of error or fraud.

10. If on perusing the affidavit of the subscribing witness it appears that the requirements of the Ordinance have not been complied with, the court shall refuse probate.

11. If the subscribing witness are dead, or refuse to swear to the affidavit of execution, or if from other circumstances no affidavit can be obtained from any of them, resort must be had to other persons (if any) who may have been present at the execution of the will; but if no affidavit of any such other person can be obtained, evidence on affidavit must be procured of that fact and of the handwriting of the deceased and the subscribing witnesses, and also of any circumstances which may raise a presumption in favour of the due execution, and thereupon it shall be lawful for the court to grant probate without the filing of an affidavit of due execution.

12. If on perusing the affidavit setting forth the facts of the case it appears doubtful whether the will has been duly executed, the court may require the parties to bring the matter before a Judge in Chambers.

13. If the testator was blind or obviously an illiterate or ignorant person, then one of the attesting witnesses or the person who has appended the name of the testator must by affidavit depose to the facts, and that the will was read over to the testator and approved by him before its execution.

14. In every case where an affidavit is made by a subscribing witness to a will, such subscribing witness shall depose as to the mode in which the said will was executed and attested.
15. The fee payable to a subscribing witness in respect of his affidavit of the execution shall be $2.00 and he shall also be entitled to the reasonable travelling expenses and subsistence (if any) incurred by him incidental to the swearing of such affidavit.

Interlineations and alterations

16. Interlineations and alterations are invalid unless they existed in the will at the time of its execution, or, if made afterwards, unless they have been executed and attested in the mode required by the Ordinance, or unless they have been rendered valid by the re-execution of the will or by the subsequent execution of a codicil thereto.
17. When interlineations or alterations appear in the will (unless duly executed, or recited in, or otherwise identified by, the attestation clause) an affidavit or affidavits in proof of their having existed in the will before its execution must be filed, except when the alterations are merely verbal or when they are of but small importance and are evidenced by the initials of the attesting witnesses.
18. Erasures and obliterations are not to prevail unless proved to have existed in the will at the time of its execution or unless the alterations thereby effected in the will are duly executed and attested, or unless they have been rendered valid by the re-execution of the will or by the subsequent execution of a codicil thereto. If no satisfactory evidence can be adduced as to the time when such erasures and obliterations were made, and the words erased or obliterated be not entirely effaced, but can upon inspection of the paper be ascertained, they must form part of the probate.
19. In every case of words having been erased or obliterated which might have been of importance an affidavit must be required.

Documents referred to in will

20. If a will contains a reference to any deed, paper, memorandum, or other document, of such a nature as to raise a question whether it ought or ought not to form a constituent part of the will, the production of such deed, paper, memorandum, or other document

must be required, with a view to ascertain whether it be entitled to probate; and, if not produced, its non-production must be accounted for.
21. No deed, paper, memorandum or other document can form part of a will unless it was in existence at the time when the will was executed.

Appearance of the paper

22. If there are any vestiges of sealing-wax or wafers or other marks upon the testamentary papers, leading to the inference that a paper, memorandum, or other document has been annexed or attached to the same, they must be satisfactorily accounted for, or the production of such paper, memorandum, or other document must be required; and, if not produced, its non-production must be accounted for.
23. Any appearance of an attempted cancellation of a paper by burning, tearing, obliteration, or otherwise, and every circumstance leading to a presumption of abandonment or revocation of a paper on the part of the testator must be accounted for.

Notice to other next-of-kin.

24. Where administration is applied for by one or some of the next-of-kin only, there being another or other next-of-kin equally entitled thereto, the Registrar may require proof by affidavit that notice of such application has been given to such other next-of-kin.

Limited and special administration.

25. Limited administrations are not to be granted unless every person entitled to the general grant has consented or renounced, or has been cited and failed to appear, except under the direction of the court.
26. Applications under subsection (1) of section 35 of the Ordinance shall be made upon motion to the court, and the court may require notice to be given to persons having prior right to a grant or to such other persons as it may think fit. A grant under this subsection may be limited as regards time or portion of the estate or otherwise as the court may think fit.

27. No person entitled to a general grant in respect of the estate of a deceased person will be permitted to take a limited grant except under the direction of the court.

Grants to an attorney.

28. In the case of a person residing out of the Colony, administration may be granted to his attorney, acting under a power of attorney, registered in the office of the Registrar General. A certified copy of such power of attorney shall be filed with the application.

Grants to guardian.

29. Grants of administration may be made to guardians of minors and infants for their use and benefit, and elections by minors of their next-of-kin or next friend, as the case may be, will be required.
30. In all cases of infants under the age of fourteen years not having a testamentary guardian, or guardian appointed by the court, the guardian shall be appointed by the order of the court. For the purpose of obtaining such appointment, an affidavit shall be filed showing that the proposed guardian is either *de facto* next-of-kin of the infants, or that their next-of-kin *de facto* has renounced his right to the guardianship, and is consenting to the assignment of the proposed guardian, and that such proposed guardian is ready to undertake the proposed guardianship.
31. Where there are both minors and infants, the guardian elected by the minors may act for the infants without being specially assigned to them by order of the court, provided that the object in view is to take a grant. If the object be to renounce a grant, the guardian shall be specially assigned to the infants by order of the court.

Administrator's oath.

32. The oath of an administrator is to be so worded as to clear on all persons having a prior right to the grant, and the grant is to show on the face of it how the prior interests have been cleared off, and the oath is to set forth, when the fact is so, that the party applying is the only next-of-kin or one of the next-of-kin of the deceased. In all administrations of a special character the recitals in the oath and in the letters of administration must be framed in accordance with the facts of the case.

Administration bonds.

33. Administration bonds are to be arrested by an officer in the registry authorised to administer oaths, or by a solicitor, justice of the peace, notary public, warden or commissioner of affidavits. The bond shall be prepared by a solicitor who shall certify the fact thereon. The bond shall be filed in the registry, Port-of-Spain.

34. In all cases of administration, except where the court otherwise directs, two sureties are to be required to the bond, and the bond shall be given in the same amount as the value of the estate to be placed in the possession of, or dealt with by, the administrator by means of the grant: Provided that the court may in its discretion order that the bond may be given in such increased amount, not exceeding double the amount of the value of the estate to be placed in the possession of, or dealt with by, the administrator by means of the grant, as it may think fit: The bond shall be in such form in use in the Probate Court in England with such variations as are appropriate to the case, or in such other form as in special circumstances of the case the Registrar may direct.

35. The Registrar is to take care (as far as possible) that the sureties to administration bonds are responsible persons, and except where the Registrar otherwise directs, the sureties to the administration bond must justify.

Renunciation.

36. Renunciation shall be in such of the forms set out in the Appendix hereto or as nearly thereto as may be applicable to the case.

37. No person who renounces probate or administration of the estate of a deceased person in one character is to be allowed to take representation to the same deceased in another character.

Affidavits.

38. Order XXXVIII, of the Rules of the Supreme Court, shall apply, with the necessary modifications, to affidavits in all matters under this Ordinance.

39. The Registrar is not to allow any affidavit or other document to be filed (unless by leave of the court) which is not fairly and legibly written or printed on good clean paper, or in which there is any interlineation of such a nature as to cause such affidavit or other document to present an untidy appearance.

Advertisement.

40. Application for probate or administration shall be advertised in the form in the Appendix hereto, and shall be inserted once a week for not less than two weeks in one of the local daily newspapers and once in the *Royal Gazette*. From the date of the first advertisement three weeks shall elapse before any application is submitted to the court, except where the Administrator General on behalf of His Majesty the King is the applicant in which case the grant may issue at such time as seems fit to the court.
41. If no caveat shall have been entered in the sub-registry at which application has been made, the Sub-Registrar shall forward the application and other documents and a report by him to the Registrar.

Caveats, Warnings and Citations.

42. Any person intending to oppose a grant of probate or administration shall, either personally or by his solicitor, enter a caveat in the registry: Provided, however, that if the application for a grant has been made in a sub-registry the caveat shall be entered there and all subsequent proceedings consequential upon such caveat shall be conducted in such sub-registry.
43. The Registrar or Sub-Registrar shall note the caveat in the Caveat Book, and notify the solicitor of the applicant of the fact that a caveat has been entered.
44. A caveat may be in the form set out in the Appendix hereto, but any written document signed by the party objection or by a solicitor on his behalf shall be sufficient.
45. A caveat shall bear date on the day it is entered, and shall remain in force for the space of six months only, and then expire and be of no effect; but caveats may be renewed from time to time.
46. A caveat may be entered at any time subsequent to the application for a grant of probate or administration and prior to the issue of the grant.
47. No grant shall be issued at any time if the Registrar has knowledge of an effective caveat.
48. The warning to a caveat is to be left at the place mentioned in the caveat as the address of the person who entered it and may be served by the person requiring such issue; but it shall be sufficient for the warning of a caveat that the Registrar or Sub-Registrar send by post a warning directed to the person who entered the

caveat at the address mentioned in it.

49. The warning to a caveat is to state the name and interest of the party on whose behalf the same is issued, and if such party claims under a will is also to state the date of such will, and is to contain an address, within three miles of the registry or sub-registry at which any notice requiring service may be left. The warning shall be in the form set out in the Appendix hereto and shall be prepared by the solicitor issuing the same and signed by the Registrar or Sub-Registrar.

50. Before any citation is signed a caveat shall be entered against any grant being made in respect of the estate and effects of the deceased to which such citation relates.

51. In order to clear off a caveat when no appearance has been entered to a warning duly served, an affidavit of the service of the warning, stating the manner of the service and an affidavit of search for appearance or non-appearance shall be filed.

52. After a caveat has been entered, the Registrar shall not proceed with the grant of probate or administration to which it relates until it has expired or been subducted, or until the caveat has been warned and no appearance entered, or until the contentious proceedings consequent on the caveat have terminated.

53. No citation is to issue under seal of the court until an affidavit, in verification of the averments it contains, has been filed in the registry.

54. Citations are to be served in the same manner as writs of summons issued out of the Supreme Court, when that can be done.

55. Citations and other instruments which cannot be so served shall be served by the insertion of the same, or an abstract thereof, settled and signed by the Registrar or Sub-Registrar as an advertisement in the *Royal Gazette* and in a newspaper or newspapers to be approved by the Registrar and at such intervals as the court may direct. The cost of such advertisement shall be borne by the person at whose instance the citation is issued.

Re-sealing of British and Colonial Probates.

56. Application to seal a grant of probate or administration or copy thereof under Part II of the Ordinance shall be made in the registry, Port-of-Spain, by the executor or administrator or the attorney of such executor or administrator either in person or through a solicitor. Where the application is made by an attorney the power of attorney shall be registered in the office of the Registrar General

and a certified copy thereof filed with the application.
57. On such application being made the following documents shall be filed in the registry, Port-of-Spain:-
   (a) The original grant, or a duplicate, or certified or sealed copy thereof.
   (b) An exemplified copy of the will (if any). This copy should be made on foolscap paper.
   (c) The affidavit of the executor, administrator, attorney or solicitor in the form set out in the Appendix hereto or as nearly thereto as circumstances of the case will allow.
   (d) A copy of the advertisement in a local daily newspaper announcing the intention to reseal. This advertisement must have appeared at least fourteen days previous to the lodging of the application for resealing. The advertisement shall be in the form set out in the Appendix hereto.
   (e) The certificate required by rule 3(1)(f).
   (f) If application is made by an attorney, a certified copy of the power of attorney expressly authorising the resealing of the grant in this Colony.
   (g) The certificate required by rule 64 if more than three years have elapsed since the death of the deceased.
58. The Registrar is to be satisfied that notice of such application has been duly advertised once a week for two weeks in one of the local daily newspapers.
59. On application to seal letters of administration the administrator or his attorney shall give bond in the form and manner set out in rules 33, 34 and 35, in an amount equal to the value of the estate within the jurisdiction of the court put in possession of the administrator or attorney. The same practice as to sureties and amount of penalty in bond is to be observed as on application for administration.
60. Application by a creditor under section 87 of the Ordinance shall be made by summons in chambers supported by an affidavit setting out particulars of the claim.
61. In every case, and especially when the domicil of the deceased at the time of death as sworn in the affidavit differs from that suggested by the description in the grant, the Registrar may require further evidence as to domicil.
62. If it should appear that the deceased was not at the time of death domiciled within the jurisdiction of the court from which the grant issued, the seal is not to be affixed unless the grant is such as would have been made by the court in this Colony.

63. The grant (or copy grant) to be sealed must include all testamentary papers admitted to probate.
64. When application to seal a probate or letters of administration is made after the lapse of three years from the death of the deceased the reason of the delay is to be certified to the Registrar. Should the certificate be unsatisfactory, the Registrar is to require such proof of the alleged cause of delay as he may think fit.
65. Special or limited or temporary grants are not to be sealed without an order of the court made on summons in chambers.
66. Notice of the sealing in the Colony of a grant is to be sent to the court from which the grant issued.
67. When intimation has been received of the resealing of a grant issued by the court in this Colony notice of the revocation of, or any alteration in such grant is to be sent to the court by whose authority such grant was resealed.
68. On a grant being resealed, the provisions of section 76 of the Ordinance shall apply.

Miscellaneous.

69. The Registrar shall not permit testamentary papers and other documents once deposited in the registry to be removed or taken out therefrom, unless under special circumstances pending probate.
70. Legal advice is not to be given to applicants by officials in the registry, either with respect to the property to be included in the particulars of the estate or upon any other matter connected with the application, and the clerks in the department are only to be held responsible for embodying in a proper form the instructions given to them under rule 2 but they will as far as practicable assist applicants by giving them information and directions as to the course they must pursue.

    The forms in the Appendix hereto or forms to the like effect shall be used with such modifications as circumstances shall require; no notice or application or other document shall be deemed void for want of conformity with any form, provided that such document is in substantial compliance with the requirements of the Ordinance and of these rules, and the Registrar may in default of such substantial compliance return such document to the person rendering the same for such further entries or amendments as he may deem necessary.

Appendix 2

Rules under the Probates (Re-Sealing) Law, 1936

[See Jamaican Gazette of 18.2.1987.]

1. Application to seal a grant of Probate of Letter of Administration or a copy thereof under the Probates (Re-Sealing Law 1986 may be made to a Judge in Chambers by the Executor or Administrator or the Attorney (lawfully authorised for the purpose) of such Executor or Administrator, either in person or through a Solicitor.
2. Such application shall be accompanied by an oath of executor, Administrator or Attorney in the form of the Schedule hereto or as nearly thereto as the circumstances of the case will allow.
3. The Judge is to be satisfied that notice of such application in the form in the Schedule hereto has been duly advertised.
4. On every application to seal a grant of Probate pursuant to 'The Probate (Re-Sealing)' Law 1936, the Executor or his Attorney shall give Bond (with one surety) in the form set out in the Schedule hereto. Such Bond shall be in a penalty of the same amount as the value of the estate and effects of the deceased in this Island in addition to double the gross annual value of the real estate of the deceased in the island.
5. On application to seal Letter of Administration the Administrator or his Attorney shall give Bond in the form set out in the Schedule hereto in a penalty of double the amount of the alleged value of the personal estate and effects of the deceased in this Island in addition to double the gross annual value of the real estate of the deceased in this Island.
6. Application by a creditor under Section 5 of The Probates (Re-Sealing) Law 1936, is to be made by Summons before the Judge, supported by an affidavit setting out particulars of the claim.
7. In every case and especially when the domicile of the deceased at the time of death as sworn in the affidavit differs from that suggested by the description in the grant, the Judge may require further evidence as to domicile.
8. If is should appear that the deceased was not at the time of death domiciled within the jurisdiction of the Court from which the grant issued, the seal is not to be affixed unless the grant is such as would have been made by the Supreme Court of Judicature of Jamaica.

9. The grant (or copy grant) to be sealed and the copy deposited in Court must include copies of all testamentary papers admitted in probate.
10. When application to seal a Probate or Letters of Administration is made after a lapse of three years from the death of the deceased the reason of the delay is to be certified to the Judge. Should the certificate be unsatisfactory, the Judge is to require such proof of the alleged cause of delay as he may think fit.
11. Notice of the sealing in Jamaica of a grant is to be sent to the Court from which the grant is issued.
12. When intimation has been received of the re-sealing of a Jamaica grant, notice of the revocation of, or any alteration in such grant is to be sent to the Court by whose authority such grant was re-sealed.
13. The Fees of Court and Fees of Solicitors shall be in accordance with the Schedule hereto.

N.B.—The rules made under the United Kingdom Probates Law, 1804 on 17th December, 1894, 10th April, 1902 and 9th March 1905 are revoked.

Index

Additional grantee: appointment of, 287-289
Ademption: doctrine of, 62
Administration bond: rules relating to, 271-279
Administration of Estates Act 2002 (Bahamas), 9, 133
Administration of Estates Act Cap. 377 (1989): and English probate rules, 7, 8
Administration of Estates Act (St Vincent and the Grenadines), 277, 278; and recitals related to settled land, 108
Administration of Estates Ordinance: and beneficial entitlement, 166, 167
Administration of Estates Ordinance (T&T): definition of 'of kin', 168
Administrator General: and the granting of letters of administration with will annexed, 128–132; role of the, 14
Administrator General's Act 1873 (Jamaica), provisions, 201-203
Administrator General's Certificate: and the application for letters of administration with will annexed, 154
Administrator's oath/affidavit, 212-213
Administrator's oath (St Lucia): letters of administration with will annexed and recitals for, 144
Adopted children: and inheritance on an intestacy, 188
Affidavit as to foreign law: validity of will of deceased national domiciled outside jurisdiction and, 295-297
Affidavit of the administrator general, 211
Affidavit of alias, 119, 221
Affidavit/certificate of delay, 119
Affidavit/Declaration and Accounts of Estate, 255
Affidavit of delay, 221; and the application for letters of administration with will annexed, 156
Affidavit of heirship (Bahamas): and the application for letters of administration with will annexed, 156, 219-220
Affidavit of kin, 220
Affidavit of plight, condition and appearance, etc., 119
Affidavit in proof of death, 116
Affidavit of search, 114
Affidavit of statutory spouse, 220
Affidavit of undated wills, 115

Affidavit of value, 116
Affidavits of due execution: and the application for grants of probate, 109-113
Alterations: definition of, 55-56
Amendment of grants, 427-428
Ancillary grant: entitlement to, 298-304
Anguilla: applications for grant of probate, 101; court fees in, 508; documents for application for grants of letters of administration, 207, 232; entitlement to grants of letters of administration, 198; establishing paternity in, 185; inheritance rights of adopted children in, 188; granting of letters of administration with will annexed, 134
Animus revocandi: definition of, 47
Animus testandi: definition of, 34
Annulment: revocation of will by, 53
Antigua and Barbuda: application for grants of probate, 102; documents for application for grants of letters of administration, 207-208, 229; court fees in, 505; establishing paternity in, 184; inheritance rights of adopted children in, 188; resealing in, 398, 401, 404
Applications for grants of probate, 99, 104
Apparent: definition of, 57
Assets: ascertaining deceased's, 78
Attorney-at-law: limited grants of representation to, 333-338
Attorney's fees: for non-contentious probate matters, 501-505

Bahamas: administration bond in the, 274; application for grants of letters of administration for unrepresented estates in the, 249-250; applications for grants of representations, 86, 88, 89; appointment of second administrator in the, 284; attorney's fees for non-contentious probate matters in the, 505; *bona vacantia* in the, 204; childrens' entitlement to financial provisions in the, 475; Commorientes in the, 325; court fees in, 509, 512; documents for application for grants of letters of administration in the, 206; entitlement to grants of letters of administration in the, 194-196; establishing paternity in the, 185-186; indigenous probate rules in the, 9; international wills in the, 27; intestates legislation in the, 163-164, 177-179; issue of grant of representation in the, 90; meaning of net estate in the, 489; minority and life interest rules in the, 286; powers of the registrar in the, 13; recognition of international wills in the, 297; resealing in the, 399, 400, 401, 403; granting of letters of administration with will annexed in the, 132-133, 138, 143; service of caveats in the, 440; spouses' entitlement to financial provision in the, 468

Bahamas Supreme Court Act Ch. 41: and reception provisions for English probate rules, 3–4, 9

Bahamas Supreme Court Act 15/1966: and powers of the registrar, 13

Bahamas Wills Act 2002, 33, 34

Barbados: administration bonds in, 271, 274; application for grants of letters of administration for unrepresented estates in, 247; application for grants of probate in, 99; application for grants of representation in, 85, 87; attorney's fees in, 499, 502; childrens' entitlement to financial provisions in, 475-476, 486–487; citation to take probate in, 460; court fees in, 506; deposit and extraction of wills of living persons in, 71; documents required for application for grants of letters of administration in, 204-205, 233-235; documents required for application for letters of administration with will annexed in, 136, 146, 147, 148, 150, 156; entitlement to grants of letters of administration in, 191; grants under discretionary powers of court in, 366-368; international wills in, 26-27; intestates legislation in, 163-164, 174-175, 181-182; issue of grant limited to an action in, 380; meaning of net estate in, 490; powers of the registrar in, 12; preliminary requirements in, 81; reception provisions and applicable probate rules in, 2–3; resealing in, 399, 400, 403, 404, 405; revocation of will by marriage in, 51-52; granting of letters of administration with will annexed in, 127; service of caveats in, 440; spouses' entitlement to financial provision in, 472, 473; succession duties in, 256, 257-258; surety guarantee in, 277; establishing validity of wills of deceased nationals domiciled outside of jurisdiction in, 294-295; service of warning to the caveat in, 440-441

Barsington, Goods of: and the intention to revoke, 49

Beneficial entitlement: under intestacy, 163-167

Beneficiaries: applications for letters of administration and the consent of equally entitled, 149, 150

Bona vacantia: provisions re, 203

Bond for making return into registry and paying duties, 118

Breach of trust: mutual wills and action for, 22-23

Caribbean: application of English probate law in the, 10-11

Certificate of non-objection (St Lucia): and application for letters of administration with will annexed, 153

Certificate of search, 113-114

Cessate grant of representation: application for, 394-396; application following grant limited to an action, 374–376; definition of, 394-396

Children: entitlement to financial provisions, 473-476, 486-488; entitlement to grants of letters of administration (T&T), 197; intestacy and beneficial entitlement of, 182-188. *See also* Illegitimate children and Minors

Children Born Out of Wedlock (Removal of Discrimination) Act (Guyana) 1983, 187

Citation: meaning of, 450; types of, 452-455

Citation proceedings, 450-461; alternative to, 461

Civil Law of Guyana Act: and intestate succession, 174

Civil Procedure Rules 2000(CPR): impact of the, 14-16; and powers of the registrar, 11-14

Civil Procedure Rules 2002: and administrators oath re letters of administration with will annexed, 144, 145; rule 68 and letters of administration with will annexed, 130-132

Clearing off: of caveat/caution, 443–444; citations for, 450; of mentally incapable executor, 348; of prior rights, 80; recitals related to, 144-145

Code of Civil Procedure (St Lucia): and granting of letters of administration with will annexed, 143

Code of ethics: relating to fees for non-contentious matters, 499-500

Coercion: and undue influence, 39

Co-habitant: entitlement to financial provisions of, 469-472, 484; intestacy and beneficial entitlement of a, 169-172, 181. *See also* Common law spouse

Colonial Probates Act, Application Order 1965: regulation of resealing grants under, 399

Common form probate business: meaning of, 1

Common law spouse: right of inheritance on an intestacy, 181

Commorientes: rules relating to, 324-328

Community property: intestacy provisions relating to, 180

Conditional wills: probate rules in, 20-21

Conditional revocation: of will, 54, 57-58

Consent: to application for letter of administration with will annexed, 147-148, 149, 150

Consents of to persons equally entitled, 215-217

Consular officers: limited grants of representation to, 331-333

Court fees: for non-contentious probate matters, 505-512

Damaged will: grant of representation for, 353
Death: application for leave to swear, 384-390; proof of, 75-76
Death Duties (Abolition) Ordinance 1977 (Anguilla): and entitlement to grants of letters of administration, 198-199; general provisions, 267; and grants for small estates, 232-233
Deceased domiciled outside jurisdiction: grant of administration re estate of, 291-307;
Deceased Persons Estates' Administration Act (Guyana): entitlement to grants of letters of administration, 191-192; and letters of administration with will annexed, 127; and powers of the registrar, 13; and public trustees, 319; and small estates grant, 235-236
Declaration/affidavit and account of estate, 79
Declaration of counting of inventory, 116
Declaration of counting of probate and copy will, 116
Declaration of particulars, 82
Discontinuance order: for caveat/caution, 445
Distribution of Estates Act 28/2000: and beneficial entitlement under an intestacy, 172, 174, 181
Distribution of Estates Act 2000 (T&T), 470-471, 472, 484
Divorce: revocation of will by, 53
Doctrine of dower: and intestate succession, 165
Domiciled out of jurisdiction: application for leave to swear death for persons, 385
Dominica: application for grants of probate in, 102; court fees in, 506; deposit and extraction of wills of living persons in, 71, 72; documents required application for grants of letters of administration in, 208, 230; entitlement to grants of letters of administration, 199; granting of letters of administration with will annexed, 134; reception provisions for English probate rules in, 7;
Donor: resident within jurisdiction and issue of grant to attorney, 334
Double probate grants: application for, 396-397
Dower. *See* Doctrine of dower
Draft grant, 117

Eastern Caribbean: affidavits of due execution in the, 109; application for grants of letters of administration for unrepresented estates in the, 241-242; application for grants of representation in the, 88, 90; attorney's fees in the, 503-504;

documents required for application for grants of letters of administration in the, 227-228; Commorientes in the, 324-325; granting of letters of administration with will annexed, 134, 139-142, 143; impact of new CPR in the, 15-16; intestate succession rules in the, 163-164, 175; issue of grant limited to an action in the, 377; issue of grants *durante absentia* in the, 360; power of the registrar in the, 11-12; recitals relating to settled land in the, 107-108; resealing of grants of administration in the, 291-292, 398, 400, 404; service of caveats in the, 437; service of warning to the caveat in the, 441, 442; transfer tax payments in the, 261-267; validity of wills of deceased nationals domiciled outside the, 294
Eastern Caribbean Rules of the Supreme Court (revision): provisions, 15
Eastern Caribbean Rules of the Supreme Court (1970): application of probate rules in, 11
Eastern Caribbean Supreme Court CPR: powers of registrar, 330
Eastern Caribbean Supreme Court of Judicature Act (St Lucia): and reception provisions for English probate rules, 5
Eastern Caribbean territories: and reception provisions for English probate rules, 6–7, 11–12
England: resealing in, 399
English probate rules: application of, 2–16
English will: revocation of an, 48
Envelope cases: and testator's signature, 30
Equal Status of Children's Act 2002, (Bahamas) 133: and the establishment of paternity, 185-186
Estate accounts, 83
Estate Duty (Amendment) Law 1963, (Jamaica) 259
Estate Duty Law (Jamaica) 1954, 259
Estate duty/stamp duty certificate, 114
Estate and Succession Duties Act (Barbados), 257
Evidence of intention: in the revival of a will, 63-64
Executor's Oath/affidavit, 106

Family and Dependants Act (Guyana), 469, 484
Family provision: entitlement to, 467-493
Family provision orders, 488-492
Fees: non-contentious probate and attorney's, 499-505
Filing fees: on probate documents, 80
Formal consent with wills annexed (Jamaica): and the granting of letters of administration with will annexed, 128-129
Grandchildren: intestacy and beneficial entitlements

of, 168-169, 173
Grantee: revocation of grant on death or incapacity of, 431-432
Grant *ad colligenda bona*: and caveat/caution, 438; issue of, 372-375
Grant *de bonis non-administratis*: issue of, 336, 391-394
Grant *durante absentia*: applications for, 360-362
Grant *pendente lite*: and caveat/caution, 438; issue of, 368-371
Grants to administrator general, 222
Grants of letters of administration, 77, 160-166, 204-222; issue of, 287; persons entitled to, 191
Grants of letter of administration with the will annexed, 76-77
Grants limited to an action: issue of, 376-381
Grants of probate, 76: applications for, 99
Grant of representation, 71-83; amendment of, 427-429; application for fresh, 435; application for resealing of, 398; entry of caveat/caution opposing, 437-445; impounding of, 433-436; notation of, 429; procedure for obtaining, 85-96; re estate of deceased domiciled outside jurisdiction, 304-306; revocation of, 431-433; to trust and non-trust corporation, 310-316
Grants under discretionary powers of court, 365-368
Grenada: application for grants of letters of administration for unrepresented estates in, 244; application for grants of probate in, 102-103; application for grants of representation in, 88; court fees in, 506; deposit and extraction of wills of living persons in, 71, 72; establishing paternity in, 184; documents for application for grants of letters of administration in, 208, 229; inheritance rights of adopted children in, 188; intestate succession in, 175
Guardian/tutor: appointment of, 340-344
Guyana: alternative to grant *ad colligenda bona* in, 372; alternative to grant *pendente lite* in, 372; application for grants of letters of administration for unrepresented estates in, 240, 248-249; applications for grant of probate in, 100; applications for grant of representation in, 85, 87-88, 89; attorney's fees in, 500-501, 502-503; childrens' entitlement to financial provisions in, 474-475; deposit and extraction of wills of living persons in, 73; court fees in, 506–507; documents for application for grants of letters of administration in, 205, 235-236; entitlement to grants of letters of administration in, 191-192; establishing paternity in, 187-188; estate duty in, 258-259; inheritance rights of adopted children in, 188; granting of letters of administration with will annexed, 127; intestate succession in, 136, 166, 174; issue of grant limited to an action in, 376-377; meaning of net estate in, 489; powers of the registrar in, 13; resealing in, 398, 400, 401; service of caveats in, 440; service of warning to the caveat, 441; spouses' entitlement to financial provision in, 467, 468, 469-470, 484
Guyana High Court Act: powers of the registrar under the, 13
Guyana High Court Act Cap 3:02: and reception provisions for English probate rules, 4
Guyana Wills Act Cap.12:01, 32, 33

Holograph wills, 25; revocation of, 48

Illegitimate children: rights of inheritance of, 182-183, 183-188
Immediate grants of representation, 95
Immovable estate: deceased domiciled outside jurisdiction and validity of will passing on, 293
'In the presence of': meaning of, 31
Indigenous probate law: Bahamas, 9
Indigenous probate rules: territories with, 2-5; territories without, 6
Informal declaration: revocation of will by, 53
Inheritance: rules relating to real estate, 163
Inheritance Act (Bahamas) 2002, 133; intestacy provisions, 178; and protection from eviction from the matrimonial home, 492; and spouse's entitlement to financial provision, 468
Inheritance (Provision for Family and Dependants) Act (Jamaica), 469, 470
Intended application: notice of, 149
Interim order, 491
International wills, 26-27: recognition of, 297
Intestate succession: history of, 160-162
Intestates Estates (Amendment) Act (Grenada) 1991: provisions, 175
Intestates' Estates and Property Charges Act (Jamaica): and entitlement to grants of letters of administration, 192-194; intestacy provisions, 176-177; and letters of administration with will annexed, 128, 132
Intestates' Estates and Property Charges Act (Jamaica) 1937: and powers of the administrator general, 201-202
Inventory, 116
Jamaica: administration bond in, 271-272, 274;

application for grant *de bonis non-administratis* in, 391; application for grants of letters of administration for unrepresented estates in, 246-247; applications of grants of probate in, 100, 105; applications for grants of representation in, 91-93; attorneys fees for non-contentious probate matters in, 504-505; childrens' entitlement to financial provisions in, 475, 487-488; citation proceedings in, 450-451; Commorientes in, 324; documents required for application for grants of letters of administration in, 205-206, 236-239; entitlement to grants of letters of administration in, 192-194; establishing paternity in, 184; estate duty applicable in, 259; filing for renunciation in, 416; grant *durante absentia* in, 361; granting of letters of administration with will annexed, 128-132, 137, 144-145, 146, 147, 151, 152-153, 153-156; grants limited to property in, 363; grants of representation to trust and non-trust corporations, 311-314; grants under discretionary powers of court in, 366; inheritance rights of adopted children in, 188; impact of the new CPR in, 14-15; intestate succession in, 163, 176, 181; issue of grants *ad colligenda bona* in, 373; issue of grant limited to an action in, 377; issue of grant *pendente lite* in, 369-371; issue of grant of representation in, 93; meaning of net estate in, 489; minority and life interest in, 284; powers of the administrator general in, 200-203; powers of the registrar in, 14; preliminary requirements in, 81-82; recitals relating to settled land in, 107-108; resealing in, 398, 400, 401, 403, 404, 406, 408; service of cautions in, 440, 442-443; spouses' entitlement to financial provision in, 468, 469; succession duties in, 256; transfer tax in, 260-261; use of affidavits of due execution in, 109-110; will-bond in, 279

Joint Wills: probate rules in, 21

Judicature (Civil Procedure Code) Law Cap 177 (Jamaica): and reception provisions for English probate rules, 4;

Judicature (Resident Magistrates) Act (Jamaica): provisions, 15; and small estate grants, 237-239

Judicature (Supreme Court) Additional Powers of Registrar Act: and powers of the registrar, 14

Jurisdiction: admissibility of will of deceased domiciled outside, 293-295

Kalamazoo copy, 117; of inventory, 116; of probate will, 117

Knowledge and approval: principle, 37-39

Land registry valuation certificate, 115
Lapse: doctrine of, 62
Law of Property Act (1925), 8
Law of Property Act (Eastern Caribbean) 1925: and recitals related to settled land, 107-108
Law Reform (Illegitimacy) Ord. (Anguilla) 1982: and the establishment of paternity, 185
Leave to swear death: application for, 385-387; revocation of grant of, 390
Letter of administration with all annexed: grants of, 126-159
Limited grants of representation: rules relating to, 329-353
Lost wills: grant of representation for, 350
Lump sum payment order, 491

Maintenance: meaning of, 477, 485
Mariners: and privileged wills, 25
Marriage: revocation of will by, 51-53
Marriage *in extremis*: and the revocation of a will, 53
Matrimonial home: protection from eviction from the, 492
Mental capacity: test of, 34-37; wills and, 34-37
Mentally incapable persons: limited grants of representation on behalf of, 348–350; renunciation on behalf of, 418
Mental incapacity: proof of, 348
Mental Health Acts: statutory wills and, 23
Minority and Life Interest: recitals relating to, 108, 147; rules relating to intestacy and, 283-284
Minors: grants to trust corporations on behalf of, 312-313; limited grants on behalf of, 339-347; renunciation on behalf of, 418
Montserrat: application for grants of probate in, 103; applications of grants of representation in, 85; court fees in, 508; deposit and extraction of wills of living persons in, 73-74; documents required for application for grants of letters of administration in, 209, 229, 230; preliminary requirements in, 82-83
Movable estate: deceased domiciled outside jurisdiction and validity of will passing on, 292
Mutual Wills: probate rules in, 21-23

Net estate: meaning of, 488–490
'Next of kin': definition of, 167-168, 196; entitlement to grants of letters of administration (T&T), 196
Nil estates: grant for representation for, 239-240

Nomination/order of appointment of co-executor, 118
Nomination/order of appointment of grantee, 221
Non-contentious business: meaning of, 1
Non-trust corporation: grants of representation to, 315; renunciation by a, 419
Notarial wills, 25-26
Notation of grants, 429
Notice of intended application, 115
Notice to persons equally entitled, 217
Notice of revocation: mutual wills and, 21

Oral will: grant of representation for an, 351
Order of appointment of co-administrator (EC, Bahamas): and the application for letters of administration with will annexed, 156
Order of Court (Jamaica): and application for letters of administration with will annexed, 153, 218

Parents: beneficial entitlement under an intestacy, 172
Paternity: establishing, 183-188
Periodical payment orders: 491
Petition: for grant of letter of application, 211
Petition (St Lucia): letters of administration with will annexed and recitals for, 143-144
Physically incapable persons: limited grants of representation on behalf of, 348-350
Physical incapacity: proof of, 348-350
Power of attorney: authentication of, 336-338
Privileged wills, 23-25
Probate: citation to take, 459-461
Probate business: common form, 1
Probate and copy will, 116
Proof of death, 75-76
Property: grants of representation limited to, 362-365
Public trustee: grants of representation to, 316-318

Real Estate Devolution Act (Bahamas): and entitlement to grants of letters of administration, 194
Reception provision: for English probate rules in Barbados, 2–3
Recitals in the petition, 105, 107, 108
Rectification: of wills, 58-60
Registrar: and the issue of limited grants of representation, 329-331; power of the, 11–14
Renunciation: filing of, 414-423;
Republication: of will, 60-62
Resealing of grants of administration, 398: application for the, meaning of, 398-403

Resident magistrates: CPR 200 and, 15–16
Retraction: application for, 418–419
Return, 119
Revival: of wills, 62-65
Revocation of grants, 431-433

Second administrator: appointment of, 284-289
Second or subsequent grants of representation, 77
Settled land: recitals relating to, 107, 147
Settled Land Act (1925), 8
Settled Land Act 1925 (Eastern Caribbean): and recitals related to settled land, 107
Small estates: grants for, 226-239
Soldiers: and privileged wills, 24
Spouse: application for financial provision, 482-485; entitlement to financial provision, 467-473; intestacy and succession rights of surviving, 163, 169-172, 179, 181-182
St Christopher and Nevis: application for grants of probate in, 103; application of English probate law in, 10-11; court fees in, 508; documents required for application for grants of letters of administration, in 209, 230-231; establishing paternity in, 185; inheritance rights of adopted children in, 188
St Kitts and Nevis. *See* St Christopher and Nevis
St Lucia: administration bonds in, 272; application for grants of letters of administration for unrepresented estates in, 242-243; application for grants of probate in, 104, 105; attorney's fees for non-contentious probate matters in, 504; clearing off of caveat/caution in, 444-445; Commorientes in, 326-327, 328; court fees in, 508; documents required for application for grants of letters of administration in, 209-210, 231-232; entitlement to grants of letters of administration in, 199; granting of letters of administration with will annexed in, 134-135; grants of representation limited to property in, 363-365; inheritance rights of adopted children in, 188; intestate succession in, 165, 179, 182; issue of grant *ad colligenda bona* in, 368; issue of grant *pendente lite* in, 371; notarial wills in, 25; powers of the administrator general in, 200; reception provisions for English probate rules in, 5, 9; resealing in, 399, 404; revocation of wills in, 46, 48, 50; succession duties in, 256
St Lucia Art 789 Civil Code Ch. 242: provisions re wills, 31, 32
St Lucia Supreme Court of Judicature Act 17/1969: probate rules in the, 9–10

St Vincent and the Grenadines: Commorientes in, 325-326; court fees in, 509; documents required for application for grants of letters of administration, 210, 232; establishing paternity in, 185; grants of letters of administration for unrepresented estates in, 243; grants of probate, 103, 104; grants of letters of representation in, 94-95; leave to swear death in, 384; inheritance rights of adopted children in, 188; intestate succession in, 164, 176, 182; reception clause re English probate rules in, 6, 7-9; revocation of will by divorce in, 53; service of caveats in, 439; service of warning to caveat, 440; will made in expectation of marriage in, 52

St Vincent and the Grenadines Wills Act (2002), 34

Stamp duty, 79

Statute of Distributions) 1670 (England), 160-161

Statutes of Children Reform Act (Barbados): provisions re rights of inheritance on an intestacy, 183-184

Statutory wills, 23

Succession. *See also* Intestate succession

Succession Act (Barbados): and childrens' entitlement to financial provisions, 476; entitlement to grants of letters of administration, 191; and letters of administration with will annexed, 127

Succession Act 1981(T&T), 470, 474, 484

Succession duties: payment of, 256-257

Supreme Court Act 1981(England), 9

Supreme Court Act of St Vincent and the Grenadines: reception of provisions re English probate laws in the, 6

Supreme Court of Judicature Act Cap.117A: reception provisions for English probate rules in the, 2–3

Surviving spouse: entitlement to grants of letters of administration (T&T), 197

Suspicious circumstances: wills executed under, 38-39

Testamentary capacity. *See* Mental capacity

Testamentary freedom: right to, 467

Testator's signature: placement of, 29-30

The Probate Rules, Ch. 35: provisions of, 13

Transfer Tax: payments, 261-268

Transfer Tax Act 1974 (Jamaica), 259

Trinidad and Tobago (T&T): administration bond in, 274; alternative to grant *pendente lite* in, 372; application for small estates grant in, 226; application for grants of letters of administration for unrepresented estates in, 244-246; applications for grants of probate in, 101; applications for grants of representation in, 85, 86-87, 90; attorney's fees for non-contentious probate matters in, 501-502; beneficial entitlement under an intestacy in, 166, 181, 182, 184; childrens' entitlement to financial provisions in, 474; citation to take probate in, 455; court fees in, 509-510; deposit and extraction of wills of living persons, 74-75; documents required for application for grants of letters of administration, 206-207; entitlement to grants of letters of administration in, 196-198; establishing paternity in, 184; grant *durante absentia* in, 360; granting of letters of administration with will annexed, 133-134, 138; inheritance rights of adopted children in, 188; intestate legislation in, 164-165; issue of grant limited to an action in, 377; issue of grant of representation, 91; meaning of net estate in, 490; powers of the administrator general in 199-200; powers of the registrar in, 12; preliminary requirements in, 81; reception provisions for English probate rules in, 5, 9; resealing of grants of administration in, 291; service of caveats in, 440; service of warning to the caveat in, 440; spouses' entitlement to financial provision in, 468, 469, 470-472, 483, 484; succession duties in, 256-257; surety guarantees in, 277; waiver of citation in, 455;

Trust corporations: grants of representation to, 310-315; renunciation by a, 419

Undue influence: meaning of, 39-40

Unrepresented estates: grants of representation for, 240-250

Variation Order: intestacy provisions, 176, 491

Warning to a caveat/caution: service of the, 441

Will-bond, 80, 117: in Jamaica, 279

Will Act 2002 (Bahamas), 9, 133

Wills: alterations of, 54-58; and the application for grants of probate, 108; citation to propound, 461-462; deceased domiciled outside of jurisdiction and validity of, 291-307; definition of, 20; rectification of, 58-60; republication of, 60-62; revival of, 62-65; revocation of, 46-54; validity, 27-40. *See also* Damaged will, International will, Lost will, Notarial will, Oral will, Privileged will, Probate and Copy will and Statutory will

Wills Act 1873 (England): and the definition of 'otherwise destroying', 51, 53;

Wills and Probate Ordinance (T&T): entitlement to grants of letters of administration under the, 196;

power of the administrator general under the, 200;
reception provisions for English probate rules under the, 5

Witness: rules relating to, 31-34

Printed in the United States
204634BV00003B/79-108/A